CREATE!

CREATE!

BY RONALD RAND

HOW EXTRAORDINARY PEOPLE
LIVE TO CREATE AND CREATE TO LIVE

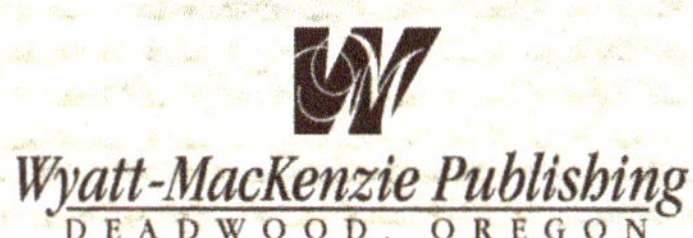

This book is dedicated to Martha Carpenter
for her love and faith,
her truth and dedication,
her inspiring life as an artist

CREATE!

How Extraordinary People Live To Create and Create To Live

Ronald Rand

Paperback ISBN: 978-1-942545-42-2
Hardcover ISBN: 978-1-942545-86-6
Library of Congress Control Number: 2016936887

Artwork and photo credits can be found on the inside edge of pages.

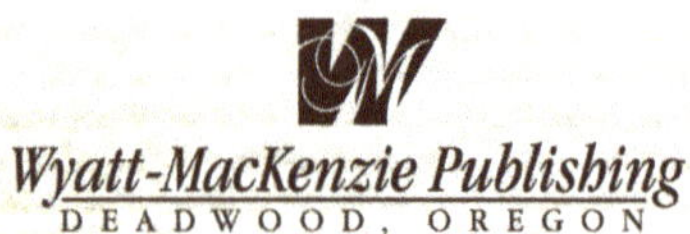

Wyatt-MacKenzie Publishing, Inc.
www.wyattmackenzie.com
Contact us: info@wyattmackenzie.com

ACKNOWLEDGEMENTS

CREATE! could have only been created with the help and enormous support of very caring individuals who believed in the journey of this book and the creative process.

First and foremost, is my enormous thanks to my publisher, Nancy Cleary, for her vision and foresight in believing in this book and its potential, for her creative gifts and fortitude. I'm deeply indebted to her extraordinary staff, especially Karen Kibler, who gave countless hours and deep care helping to make ***CREATE!*** as fine as it is.

I hold immense thanks to all those gifted artists and photographers who have contributed beautiful art and stunning photographs to this book, and to those who have supported my efforts in bringing ***CREATE!*** to its fruition, especially David Leopold and the Al Hirschfeld Foundation, Louise Kerz Hirschfeld, Alejandro Di Paz, Mary Jane Starke, Marilise Tronto, and Martha Carpenter—and to those whose generosity was indispensable: Trish Alley, Jane Carpenter, David Ellenstein, Ray Faiola, Jacoline Frank, Susan Hardie, Fred Jolly, Theodora Loukas, Thomas McKnight, Ninon Parker, Lester Shane, Helen Sheehy, Mayor Bill and Pat Shoemaker, Richard Skipper, Kimberly Vaughn, and Chad Winters.

With deep thanks to my mother, Maribee, a master watercolor artist and teacher, for her unwavering love and for putting a paintbrush in my hand before I could walk, always encouraging me to never let a day go by without creating something new; and my talented sister, Janice, for her immense dedication, support, and boundless talent.

And from deep in my soul—immense thanks to all the extraordinary artists within these pages who have been so kind to share through their passionate words about their lives and creativity. Their inspiring art is a beacon for all of humanity, reminding us how necessary it is to share in a meaningful and heart-filled way.

RONALD RAND

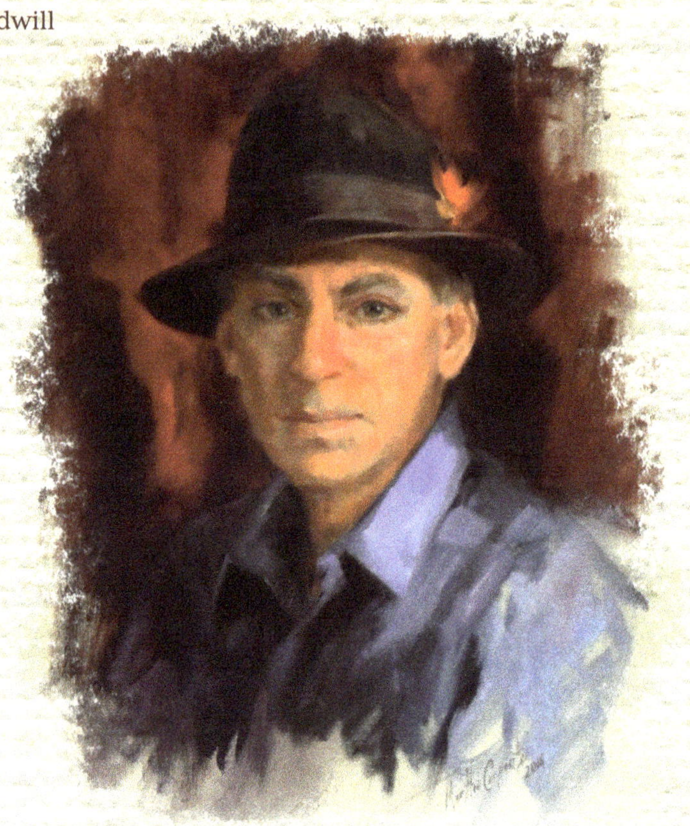

Ronald Rand art by Martha Carpenter, courtesy of the artist.

Ronald Rand is a celebrated U.S. Goodwill Cultural Ambassador, performing and teaching for over two decades on five continents, in twenty-three countries and twenty states, including two critically-acclaimed runs Off-Broadway, in his transformative performance in his solo play, *LET IT BE ART!* as Harold Clurman, the "elder statesman of the American Theatre."

Mr. Rand is the author of the best-selling book, *Acting Teachers of America*, and the Founder and Publisher of "The Soul of the American Actor," published in print and online for over fifteen years. A U.S. State Department Fulbright Specialist, he is the first Fulbright Specialist to teach at the University of Malaya in Kuala Lumpur, Malaysia, and at the University of Sarajevo's Academy of Dramatic Arts in Bosnia & Herzegovina.

Mr. Rand is the first American invited by the Malaysian Ministry of Culture to perform at their state theaters in Alor Setar, Ipoh and Kuala Terengganu, and the first American solo performer at Zimbabwe's BAFA Festival of Arts, India's Bareilly International Theatre Festival, Russia's "Voices of History" International Festival, and in the main courtyard of Tangier's Palace Dar el-Makhzen. His stage appearances include across Europe as the Fool in *King Lear*, Off-Broadway in *Julius Caesar* at Brooklyn Academy of Music, in *LUV* at New Hampshire's Barnstomers Theatre, the Stage Manager in *Our Town*, Polonius in *Hamlet*, and as Captain Keller in *The Miracle Worker* at Greensboro Arts Alliance Theatre in Vermont.

An internationally-acclaimed director, his award-winning production of the comedy, *LUV*, continues for several years running in repertory at Sarajevo's Chamber Theatre 55, and travels to several countries. Mr. Rand has appeared in over two hundred films and TV shows including opposite Christopher Plummer in *A Marriage: O'Keefe and Stieglitz* on American Playhouse, *Homeless* with Yoko Ono, and *Quiz Show* opposite Ralph Fiennes, directed by Robert Redford.

A prolific painter, poet, and renowned international director, his award-winning production of *LUV* is currently running at Sarajevo's Chamber Theatre 55. Mr. Rand's other works include a new opera, *IBSEN*, with German composer Harmut von Lieres, about Henrik Ibsen's last days, and the play *The Group Theatre!* soon to be a major motion picture. ■

TABLE OF CONTENTS

ACTORS AND ACTRESSES

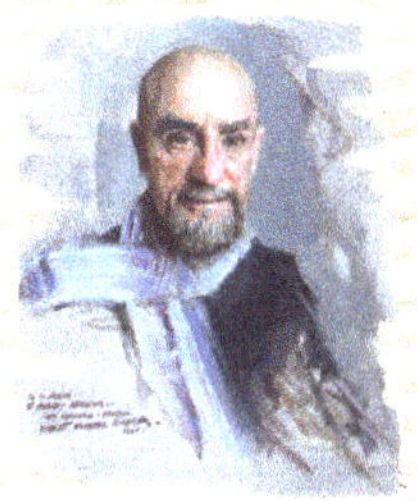
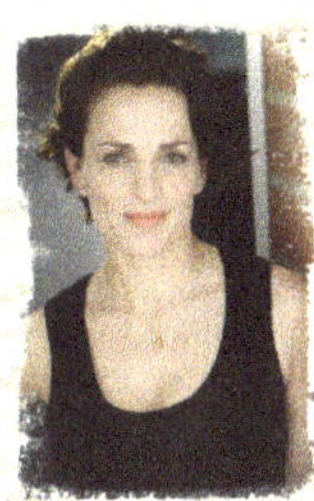
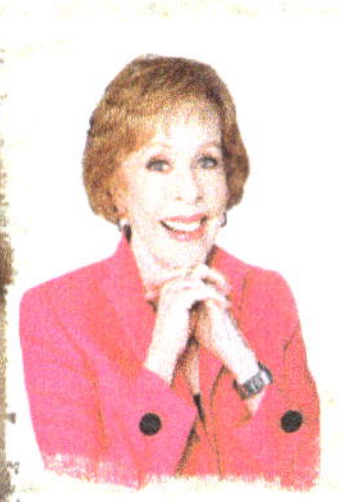
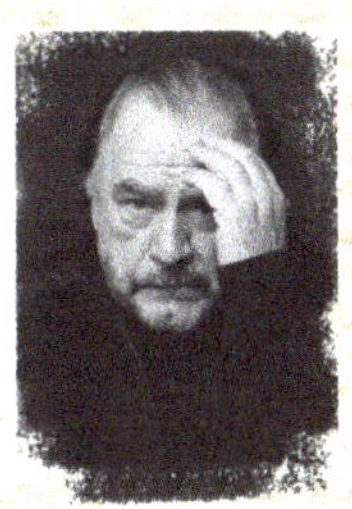
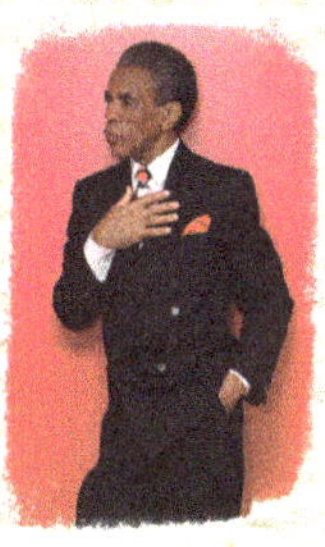
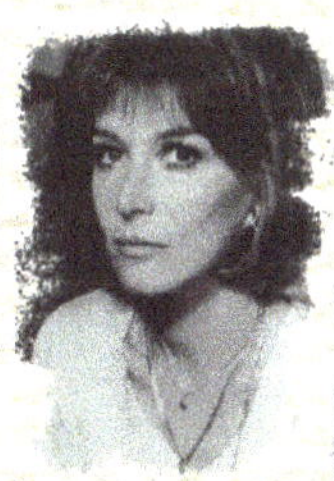
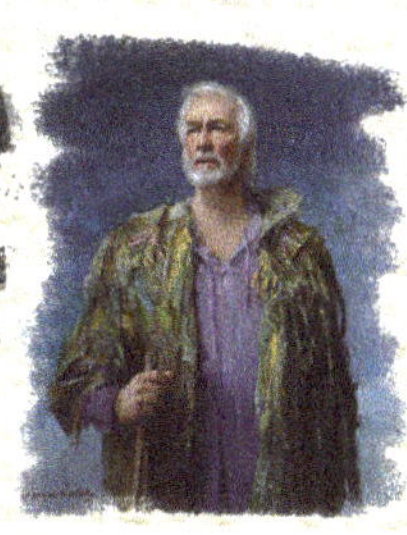

ARTISTS AND DESIGNERS

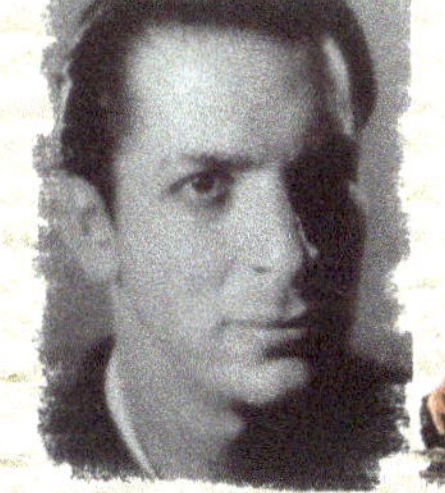
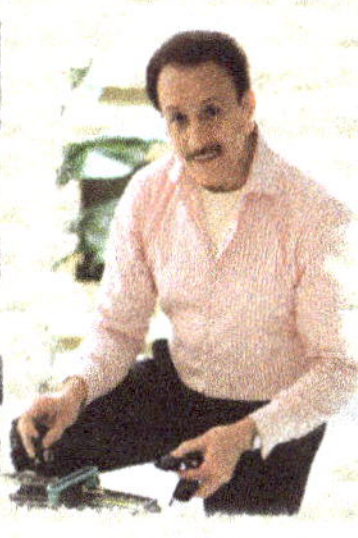
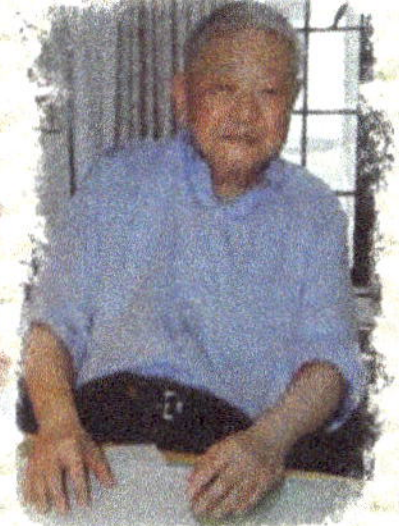
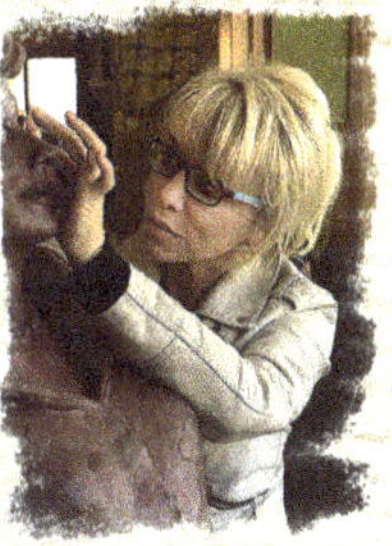
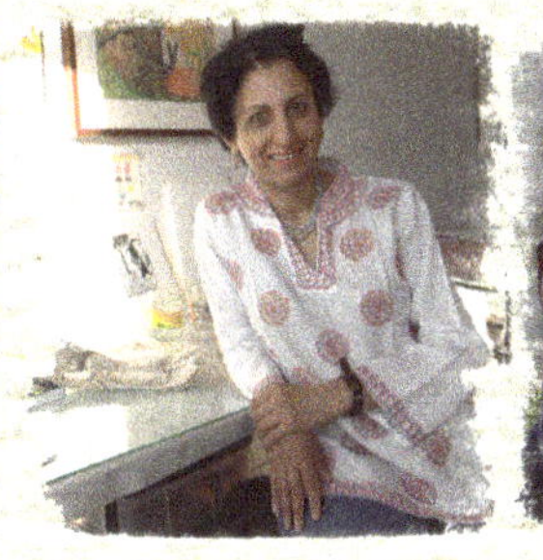
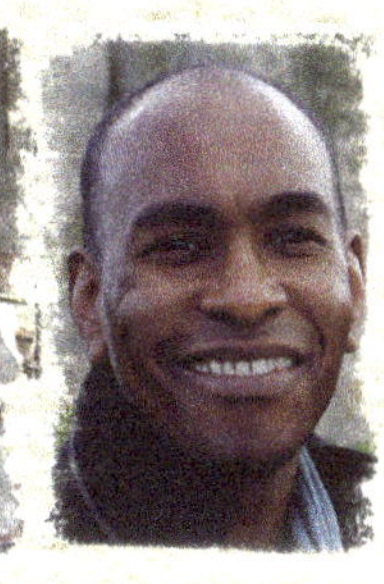

CHOREOGRAPHERS AND DANCERS

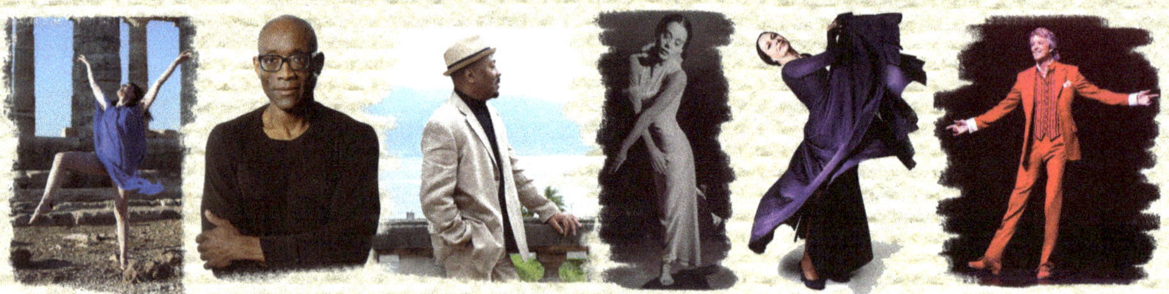

CLOWNS, MIME ARTISTS, AND PUPPETEERS

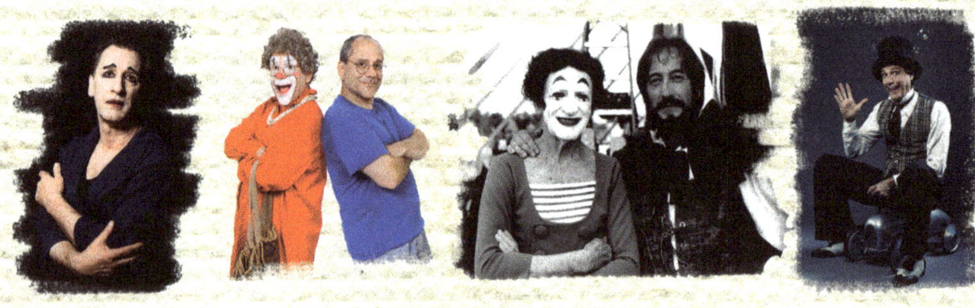

COMPOSERS AND LYRICISTS

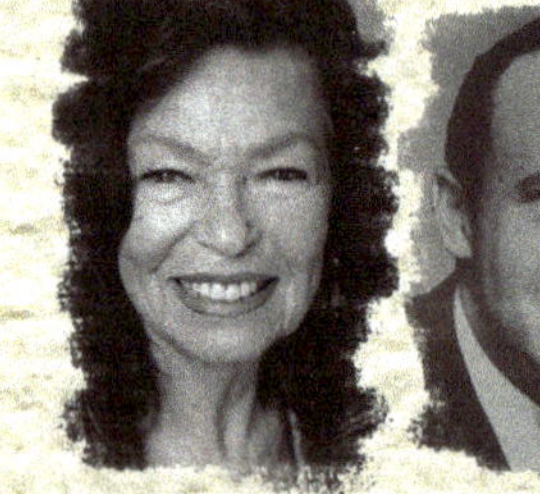

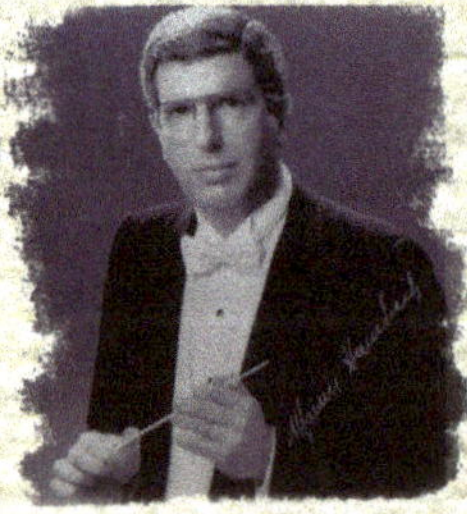

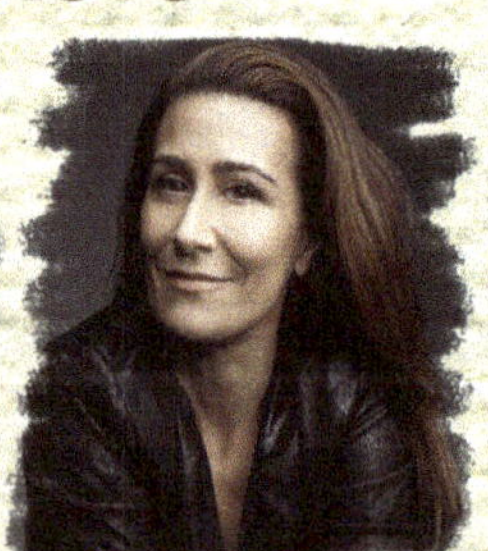

DIRECTORS

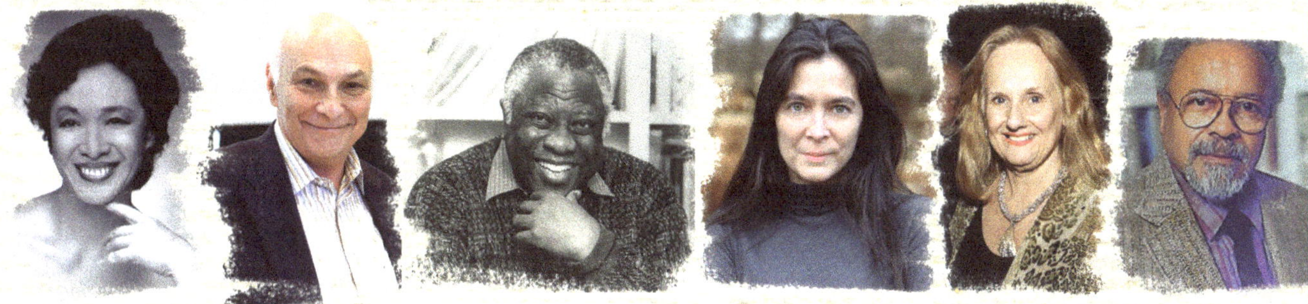

EDUCATORS

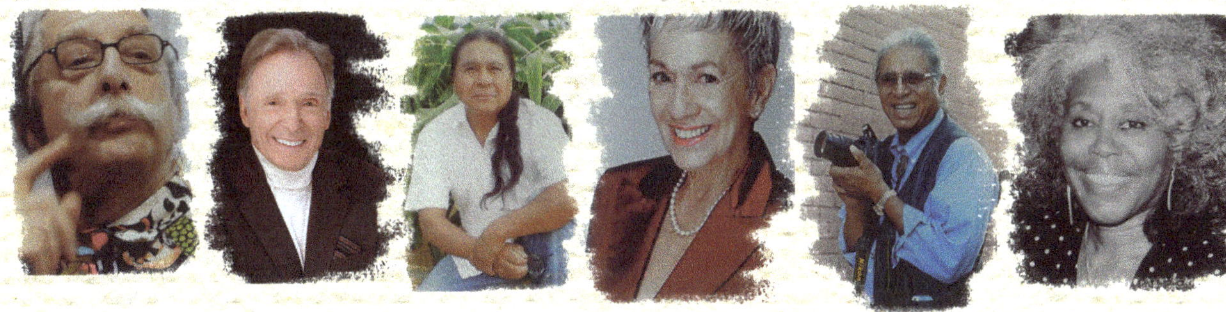

MUSICIANS AND SINGERS

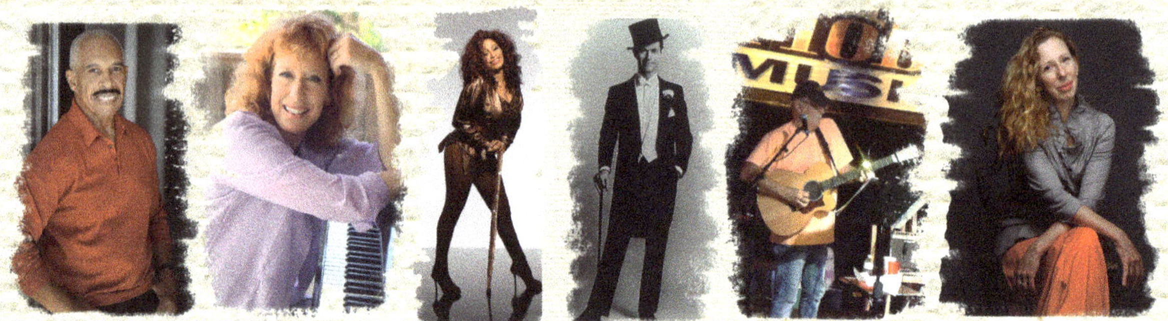

PLAYWRIGHTS, POETS, AND WRITERS

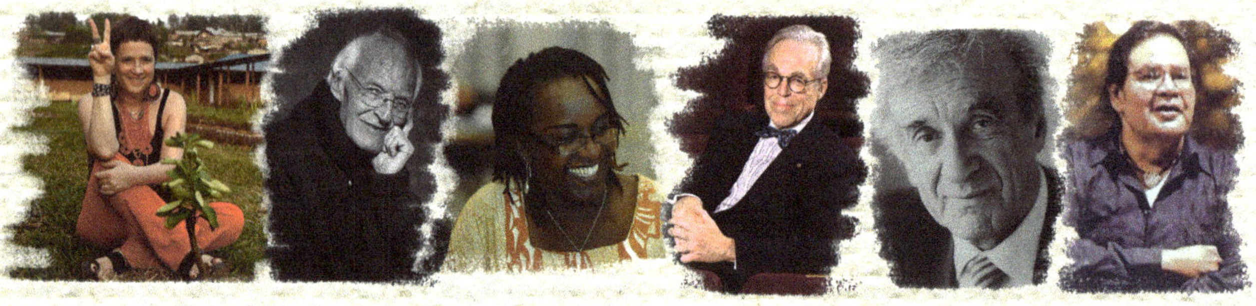

FOREWORD

The Creative State of Mind

by Mel Gordon

Like most newly-emeritized humanities professors from the baby-boomer generation, I spent the first year of my retirement sifting through the twists and turns of my protracted academic calling. This meant dredging up as many amusing recollections of classroom epiphanies and administrative reverses that I could remember. For four decades, I taught theatre history and acting at New York University and the University of California, Berkeley. Some of my students, like Alec Baldwin, Gina Gershon, Ronald Rand, Jackie Hoffman, Adam Sandler, Bridget Fonda, Jeremy Piven, Philip Seymour Hoffman, Donna Murphy, and John Leguizamo, found their way into Broadway or Hollywood eminence and even achieved national renown.

The vast majority of my undergraduate pupils, of course, did not make it into any IMDB actor lists. Their careers usually affixed themselves to positions in the performing arts or social media. But, meeting them in person in West Coast studios or cafes, I was startled by how unerringly many of them reminisced, almost by rote, about some lecture or obscure historical figure that I had conjured up. And one mantra-like phrase quickly tumbled into our back-in-the-day tête-à-têtes: "the Creative of State of Mind."

After a rickety performance during the Moscow Art Theatre's Central European tour in 1905, the Russian director/actor, Constantin Stanislavsky suffered a debilitating psychological break. Once, the handsome forty-two-year-old performer could mesmerize audiences with his dashing physical grace and sustained focus; his characters, even the grotesque and comic ones, captivated spectators with a charming aura and emotional complexity. Now he felt stiff and self-conscious. Something essential to theatre-making had disappeared in him.

During an enforced summer retreat in Finland, Stanislavsky was determined to overcome his inexorable artistic malaise. And, in doing so, the master would finally uncover "the ineffable secrets of great acting." That is, what did the legendary performers, like Tommaso Salvini and Eleonora Duse, innately possess onstage that vanished over the seasons from Stanislavsky's realistic portrayals? Watching amateur painters and children building sandcastles on the beach, Stanislavsky studied their peerless states of deep concentration and repose. The boundaries of normative time and space did not really exist for them; it seemed that an invisible mental bubble shielded them from all the distractions of the outside world. These laypeople were experiencing the ineffable "Creative State of Mind."

Excavating his diaries and notebooks, Stanislavsky traced the periods in his career when his acting most excelled. One productive interlude occurred during his courtship of his wife. The Moscow Art Theatre leader then bounded across the proscenium with gusto and unpretentious verve. His characters radiated a kind of magical presence and spontaneity. Maybe the outside-the-theater love impulse, devotion, or physical passion were the clandestine secrets of inspiration and inspired acting. For Stanislavsky, his "Creative State of Mind" correlated directly to the condition of being in love. But one could not easily will or feign that sentiment. It required intense psycho-physical training: exercises that stimulated muscular relaxation, alertness, sense memory, naivety, and emotional recall.

In my own acting classes at the Lee Strasberg Institute, the Michael Chekhov Studio, and University of California–Berkeley, I often referred to the "Creative State of Mind." This was Constantin Stanislavsky's idée fixe. I acknowledged that few pupils in the Introduction to Acting course would go on to perform professionally, but all of them could amplify their creative functions in their everyday lives and chosen fields of study.

For instance, I asked them to relate their weekend exploits and discuss how their erotic strategies frequently utilized spur-of-moment improvisation and fantastic ingenuity. Putting square pegs into square holes, the way that they got into elite universities, was not the most efficient means of conducting successful social interaction. They had to learn how to naturally augment their inventive and goal-driven sensibilities.

For group improvs, I added ridiculous imaginary rewards, such as $20,000 for the best classroom presentation. Since the adolescent brain hates to waste energy on an on-command pretense, this might persuade them to work at a higher level. Usually, it did. These classes, which appeared to be fast-draw nonsense for many of the students, were actually attempts to conflate fun with Stanislavsky's "Creative State of Mind." Reliving these manic sessions still rattles in my head as a blissful post-teaching memory.

I also admonished them never to anticipate their scenic results, plotting for expected laughs or applause. In this class, being "clever" was a major fault; instead they should endeavor to be "brilliant," relying on a part of the brain that functions best in momentous or extreme situations.

Learning to trust—and then to cajole—the subconscious mind is the first trick of every artist. It is the hidden conduit to the "Creative State of Mind."

Onward!

INTRODUCTION

by Ronald Rand

A bird sings
for many reasons
as do we.
The arc of a rainbow,
A morning's mist stillness,
A portrait upon a canvas,
The anticipation of an audience
in darkness waiting for something
to exist that has never existed before
and will never exist in the same way again.
A leap of faith through space defying gravity.
A note that's played or a song that haunts the heart.
A play, a poem, a story, a film that lives within the soul forever.
An idea that reminds us how much more life truly matters
when we love one another.

These are just a few of the life-lessons within these pages.

Each artist—a window revealing to us a way to see ourselves—into the richness of creativity. Their passion, their unique talent, their drive to keep creating while overcoming almost impossible odds. Their journey may have begun one way and then shifted, or remained as constant as the North Star—always finding a way to keep creating.

As a performing artist, it's how I choose to create. For over fifteen years, I've been traveling around the world to over twenty countries and across America, transforming myself into Harold Clurman through my solo play. During a two-hour process in my dressing room, Clurman comes, and then I'm able to share his passion for living life to its fullest. Once he arrives in his apartment on stage, he reveals to the audience how our very existence depends upon creating a more humane world.

We're all linked to one another on this planet. We may speak different languages but our humanity is what binds us—our creativity. We each have the potential to inspire one another. Creating is a way towards self-expression, a way to make a living, or to be in service to others or to a higher power. It can heal, soothe, entertain, reveal a world, or lift the soul.

Throughout *CREATE!* you'll discover these artists' words laid out in an interview format. You'll also find original art created by many of them—and accompanying each interview is either their photo, a painting or a drawing or an artistic creation they themselves have created, or by another artist. There may also be a photo that they've taken that's inspiring to them.

I hope you'll discover you can open to any page and have the opportunity to ask yourself, "Who's going to inspire me today?"

We're indeed blessed by these "worlds of creativity" that exist on our planet—filling each of us with wonder, beauty, illumination, and love.

ACTORS AND ACTRESSES

F. MURRAY ABRAHAM

Widely known for his Academy Award-winning portrayal as Antonio Salieri in *Amadeus*, he made his Broadway debut in *The Man in the Glass Booth*, directed by Harold Pinter. Mr. Abraham's other appearances on Broadway include *It's Only a Play*, receiving a Drama Desk Award nomination, Terrence McNally's *Bad Habits, Where Has Tommy Flowers Gone?, The Golden Age, Mauritius, Triumph of Love, A Month in the Country*, as Roy Cohn in *Angels in America*, as *Macbeth*, in *Teibele and Her Demon*, for which he received a Drama Desk Award, and *The Ritz*. He appeared in the 20th anniversary production of *The Caretaker, Waiting for Godot* directed by Mike Nichols, with Robin Williams, Steve Martin and Bill Irwin at Lincoln Center Theatre, *Uncle Vanya*, receiving an Obie award, *A Life in the Theatre*, receiving a Drama Desk Award, and has appeared in plays by many of the world's greatest playwrights including in the leading role as *Nathan the Wise*, as Shylock in *The Merchant of Venice* in New York City, on a National Tour with Theatre for a New Audience, and at The Swan Theatre as part of the Royal Shakespeare Company. He is the only American to perform in *The Jew of Malta* in repertory with *The Merchant of Venice*. His film appearances include *Scarface, All the President's Men, Star Trek: Insurrection, The Name of the Rose* with Sean Connery, *The Bridge of San Luis Rey*, Coen Brothers' *Inside Llewyn Davis, Perestroika, The Grand Budapest Hotel*, and many European films. Mr. Abraham's many television appearances include as a cast member of *Homeland*, receiving an Emmy and SAG award, *The Good Wife, A Season of Giants*, and as Blessed John Henry in *The Unseen World*. He was the primary narrator the PBS series, *Nature*. Mr. Abraham has received the "Premio per gli Italiani del Mondo" Prize, the John H. Finley Award, the Gielgud Award, the Moscow Art Theatre Morozov Award, and was inducted into the American Theatre Hall of Fame. Mr. Abraham taught theater at Brooklyn College.

Q You've given your heart and soul to creating. What does it give you?
It gives me my joy; it makes me happy, and miserable, too. I'm most alive when I'm working.

Q One of your wonderful talents is your gift of characterization. Laurence Olivier had his way of disguising himself with different noses. And yet, in this country, Harold Clurman once wrote: "American actors tend to shy away from overt physical characterization, thinking today's acting is geared towards realism, that the answer is being 'natural,' rather than expressively theatrical."
I'm a great admirer of Lord Olivier. His hard work and accomplishments are inspirational. I love that he did whatever he thought necessary to find the character, and always looked for a physical thing to catch his audience, like practicing for hours the toss of his derby across the room onto the hat rack or stepping off the dining room table in *Long Day's Journey* with a show-offy but 'perfectly in character' jump, or his spectacular deaths in so many roles. I agree with the philosophy, "use whatever works for you." There is no one technique, or method—take from everywhere.

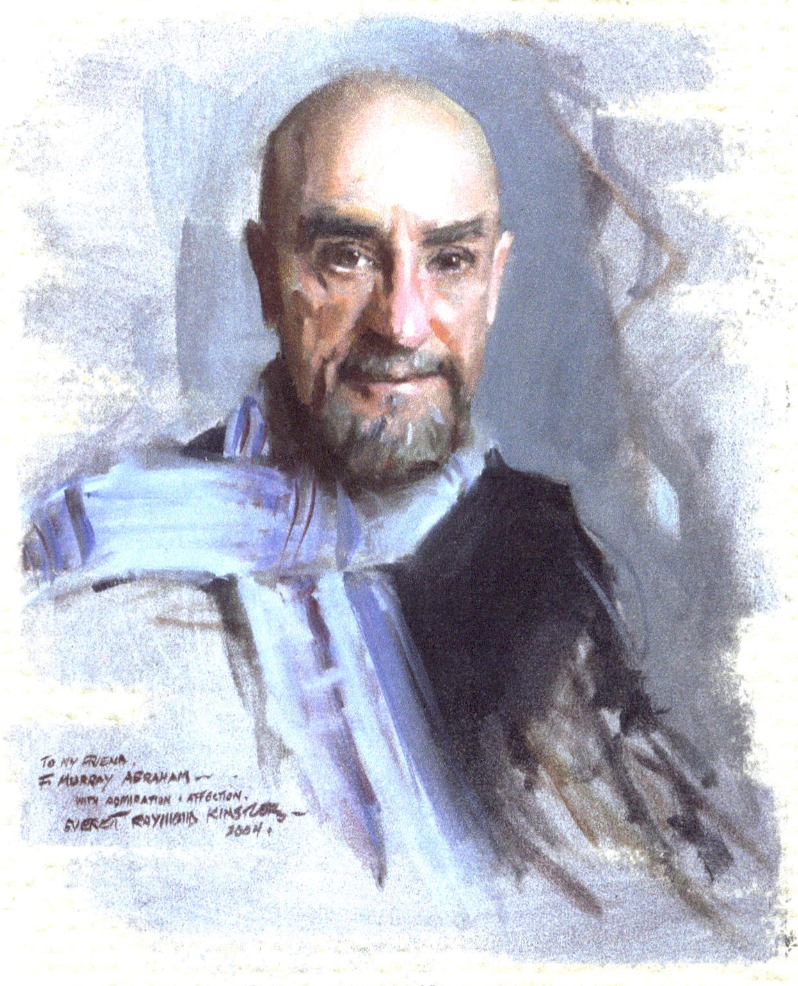

F. Murray Abraham by Everett Raymond Kinstler, courtesy of Mr. Kinstler

Q What do we owe the playwright when we approach a script?
We owe the playwright respect for every word they write. But not slavishly. Sometimes we are so careful of each individual word we lose the meaning, which is a mistake so many Americans make when doing Shakespeare, they hammer at each word. That's what I discovered when I played Cyrano; the words were so juicy I fell in love with them. The Players Club let me listen to a recording of the original Cyrano with Coquelin—he spoke like

lightning. I realized if the images are absolutely clear in your mind, the individual words come together as part of the whole musical score. On the page, the script belongs to the writer—in a performance, the language has to serve the actor—or it won't live.

Q How do you approach the emotional side of a role?

Instinct. I trust it completely. It's not always right, but it's thrilling to see where it takes me. And it's fun. After all, it's called a "play," right?

Q I have heard your eloquent and passionate speeches for art and theatre funding over the years. What more can we do?

We really have to codify clearly the reason that art is necessary, in terms everyone believes and understands. It's got to be clear: "Art is as important as food." In our society, there's tremendous random violence, which I believe coincides with the demise of art in the schools and the endless wars in the Middle East. Where politics and religion divides people, art cuts through all of them. We need it so much.

Q Joseph Chaikin wrote: "The most articulate performances are always those which have been pared away. What remains is a spare language which speaks of life and nature."

Joe was a friend of mine. He was a great man, and I agree with that statement completely, and so much else that he wrote. But don't misinterpret what he's saying and do nothing. Acting is doing. Take a chance. Don't be afraid.

Q What made it a special experience to play Dr. Newman in the film, *The Unseen World*, directed by Liana Marabini, with Nastassja Kinski?

I had so little time to prepare the normal way I have of putting it all together, and go very deeply. The director from Romania had planned on a specific script, but at the very last minute changed it so it would be after Dr. Newman's conversion.

I kept trying to locate God everywhere. I'd look here and there. Finally, I found a church nearby that practices what they teach. I discovered—any real manner of faith, any person who is truly a seeker, whatever faith they are studying or practice—have had terrible moments of doubt. I read the letters of Mother Theresa. She had that kind of open doubt; it's so reassuring. What it told me is we're allowed to doubt because you are tested. There are constant tests. When you look at the world today, you wonder how can God exist and let these things happen.

Q What surprised you about the depth of Shylock's journey in *The Merchant of Venice*?

Shylock is a universal role. I also played the rabbi who created the Golem in a NY Shakespeare Festival production in Central Park. He is not allowed to give life. How dare he! He believes it's necessary at the time. What Shylock has done is the same kind of thing. He has transgressed and stepped over the line. He doesn't want to admit it. But Shylock is aware of what he's doing.

Well, once he steps across the line, he's lost since he realizes he can't take someone's flesh and he knows it. Shylock realizes the logical conclusion is he has to give up his faith. That's the worst moment. I had some real problems when he is asked about it in the court. He says: "I am content." Is he content? I still don't how it can be said.

Q You starred in a production of *Nathan the Wise*. Why do you find it necessary to keep challenging yourself in the roles you play?

I have no choice. Once you stop, you're dead. I want to be as good as I possibly can—that means testing myself with the great roles. You throw yourself to the lions when you do the classics, because you're going to be compared with every great actor who's done it before you. Yes, it's scary, but what a great ride. ■

MARY ALICE

Miss Alice's wealth of experience includes her memorable performance on Broadway opposite James Earl Jones in August Wilson's *Fences*, for which she received a Tony Award, and a Drama Desk Award, and as the Oracle in *The Matrix Revolutions*. Her other appearances on Broadway and Off-Broadway include *No Place to be Somebody*, *The Shadow Box*, *Zooman and The Sign*, *Richard III*, and opposite Gloria Foster in *Having Our Say*, directed by Emily Mann, for which she received Tony Award and Drama Desk nominations. She performed as Cordelia in *King Lear* opposite Frank Silvera at Washington D.C.'s Arena Stage. Her film and television work includes *The Education of Sonny Carson*, *Just an Old Sweet Song*, *Malcolm X*, *Teachers*, *To Sleep with Anger*, *Awakenings*, *Down in the Delta*, *Sanford and Son*, *Cosby*, *Touched by an Angel*, and *I'll Fly Away*, for which she received an Emmy Award. Ms. Alice was inducted into the American Hall of Fame.

Q Did acting begin early for you?

This is my third career. I was a school teacher, I also worked for the Social Security Administration. I began in the theater in 1967 when I came to New York from Chicago. I didn't choose acting as a career, more as a hobby, but it became a career. It wasn't something I always wanted to do.

I was very fortunate to get into Lloyd Richards' class. He helped me develop a craft. And I became involved with the Negro Ensemble Company. If I hadn't been as fortunate as I was, I probably would have taught, or had gone back to Chicago to teach.

Q What did you learn when you played Dr. Bessie in *Having Our Say*?

That acting is very difficult. It was a two-character piece, not

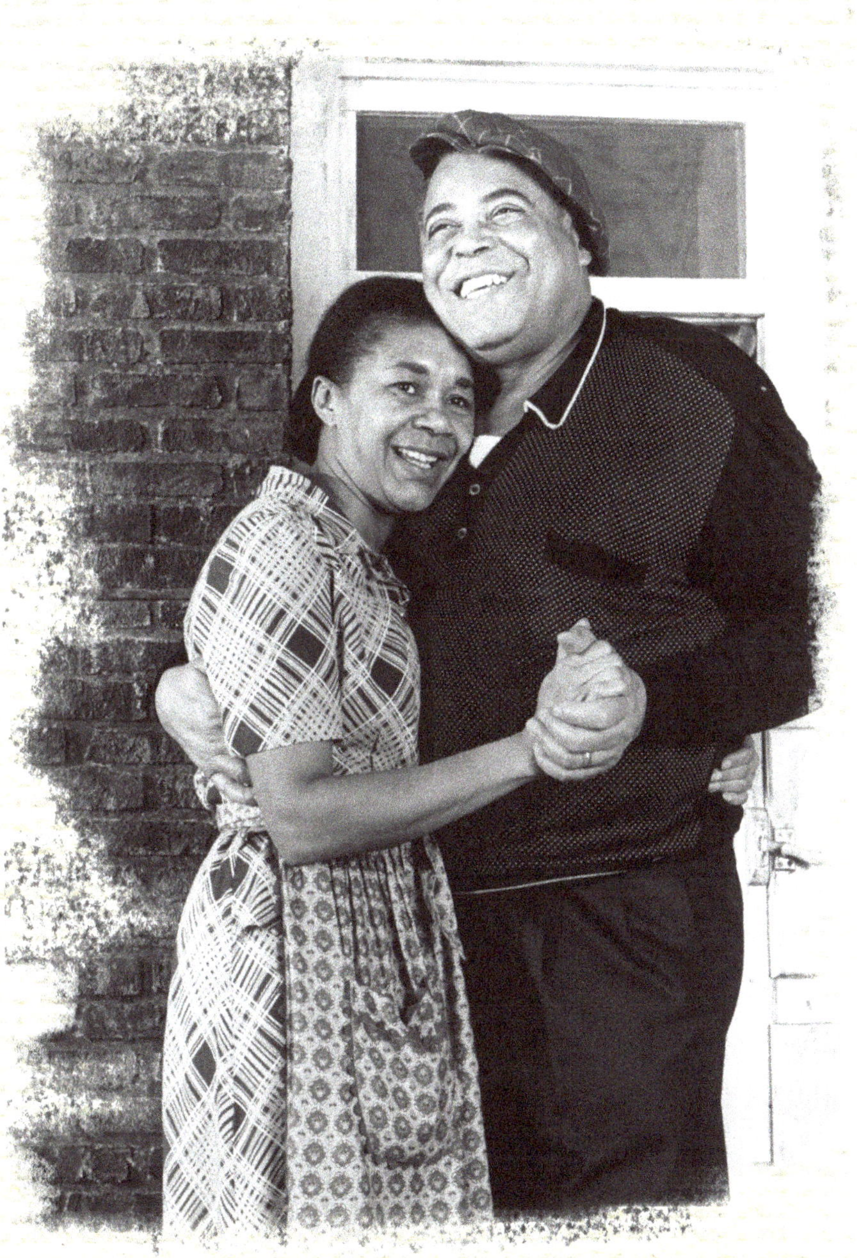

Mary Alice photo: Mary Alice and James Earl Jones in "Fences," courtesy of Yale Repertory Theatre

written in the traditional form, with no fourth wall. Some of the dialogue was between the sisters, but there were a lot of speeches. It was one of the most difficult projects I've worked on. It was rewarding playing a woman like Dr. Bessie, but very demanding because of what it took to do eight shows a week.

Q How do you begin to work on a character?

There's an initial attraction, a connection to the character, to the story. I've always felt that it's what Shakespeare wrote: "The play's the thing." I always try through my first impulse to find out who this woman is. I make a list of everything that's been said about her, whether it's important or not. All of it's useful. I try to give her what I've learned from the writer, to give her a history of life.

Q Then it widens?

Yes—another connection is made as one begins working with the other actors, with the director. Hopefully, the director has an understanding of the writer, and is able to bring all the people involved together to tell the story. Sometimes I make discoveries during rehearsals that even the writer might not have thought of. In a sense, it's the creativity extending what's already begun on the paper. I think of myself as a worker helping to tell the story the writer has written. I believe it is our responsibility to be true to that story. ■

SELMA ALISPAHIĆ

One of the foremost theater and film actresses in Eastern Europe, Ms. Alispahić is a permanent member of the Sarajevo War Theatre, known as SARTR, since 1998—her roles included Beatrice in *The Effect of Gamma Rays on Man-in-the-Moon Marigolds*, as *Anna Karenina*, Katarina Kosaca in *The Last Bosnian Queen*, Sylvia Plath in *Longing and Death of Sylvia Plath*, Natalia in *The Siege of Leningrad*, and the lead in *Caroline Neuber*. She performed in London with the Complicite Theatre in *Foe*, *Caucasian Chalk Circle*, and *Women of Troy* at the Royal National Theatre, *Blood Wedding* at the Young Vic Theatre, and as Andromache in *Trojan Women* in *Sarajevo Trilogy* at Royal Festival Hall. She has performed in many productions at the National Theatre in Sarajevo including *Hasanaginica*, *Woyzeck*, *Leons and Lena*, in several plays at the National Theatre of Tuzla including *Don Juan*, at Sarajevo's Chamber Theatre 55 in *The Sickness of Youth*, and as Carmela in *Ay, Carmela*, since 1999 with Dragan Jovičić Jovičić across Europe. Her film and television appearances include *Play to the End*, *Elgars Tenth Muse* opposite James Fox, *Bliss*, *Selam*, and *Broken Mussels*. She has received the "Woman of the Year in the Arts" Award and the International Center for Peace Sarajevo's "Freedom" Award. Ms. Alispahić has taught as a Professor of Acting at Tuzla's Academy of Dramatic Arts, and holds a Ph.D. in literary history sciences.

Selma Alispahić photo (headshot): courtesy of the artist

Q How young were you when you entered the theater?

Actually I began when I was about eight years old. My father is playwright and a dramaturg of a theater in Tuzla. I grew up backstage. It's where I learned respect for this profession. At sixteen years old, I became the youngest graduate student accepted into the Academy of Dramatic Arts in Sarajevo.

When the Bosnian war started, I was twenty-two years old. My mother was a doctor and a gynecologist, and she helped many of the raped women coming from eastern Bosnia to Tuzla; it was a terrible period. My parents saw what was happening and they sent me out of Bosnia. After I left, a friend of mine told me the only bridge into Bosnia had been destroyed so there was no going back.

For almost a year, I worked as a babysitter, a waitress, in a boutique, I cleaned houses, but I was grateful to be in London. I learned English, and through a friend of a casting director, met Tim Supple, a director at The Young Vic Theatre. I took several workshops there.

Later, Tim directed me in Lorca's *Blood Wedding* in a new translation by Ted Hughes. I had the opportunity to meet this great poet whose work, twenty years later, would become the theme of my Ph.D. thesis. I played Andromache in Euripides' *Trojan Women* which was part of a show called *Sarajevo Trilogy*. This led to my being cast in the National Theatre production of *Women of Troy*, directed by Annie Castledine, with Rosemary Harris in the company.

Q How did you cope?

It was a hard experience. I didn't really know anyone; I had only one friend. It was about survival. So I said to myself, "I will live my life with dignity. I won't be a victim of circumstances." I always say to my students: "Discipline your mind. It's a question of the moment. You should always believe in yourself no matter what." All the time I kept telling myself, "I will not give up."

Eventually I was able to work with the Complicite Company and became a friend with Simon McBurney. I feel what has happened to me as an actress was meant to be.

Q What was your experience working with Complicite Theatre?

Up to that point I had worked a lot from my head. Experiencing the work with Complicite, I learned how much we can do by listening to our emotional and physical memory of our bodies, without saying the lines. It was the most "incredibly-aware" experience I had acting in the theater.

When we did *Caucasian Chalk Circle*, I played five roles in the show and also understudied Juliet Stevenson playing the lead. It was wonderful that Simon felt I could do it all. We had one run-through with me in the lead role, and it was so exhilarating. Simon isn't afraid to listen to other people. He feels he has something to learn from everyone, which makes him a great director. He's very passionate about the work, and he's became a good friend.

Q How did returning to Bosnia after the war impact your feelings about acting?

Before the war I felt that it was nice to entertain, that the theater can help the audience relax. When I came back to Bosnia, I found a kind of greater purpose. I realized that every moment on stage is special. The people in the audience had gone through hell during the war, now they've chosen to buy a ticket and spend two hours of their time watching me. For me, that's a huge responsibility.

When I decide what roles to do now, I have to have at least one line which I believe might possibly change someone's day or their life. I insist in bringing a clear, clean honest emotion, to get to the core of the character's being. I think that is the only way that theater can survive today; the only reason that theater has survived for more than two thousand years. Story and emotions.

Q You have been performing in Jose Sanchis Sinisterra's *Ay, Carmela* for over fifteen years now with Dragan Jovičić, across Bosnia and many other countries.

Yes, we have performed it over two hundred times. It's like a celebration of life. A very unique atmosphere is created in the theater. When you do a show this long with an actor such as Dragan, it's a very special experience.

Q What was it like bringing this play across Bosnia right after the war?

One time we arrived in a town and there was no electricity, and we performed in the school's sports hall with candles. Every day in that town the school kids had to go around mine fields to get to their classes. We felt we had to bring some kind of dignity to their lives. They had lost so much during the bombardment in the war. They didn't have very much to eat. They came to the theater because they wanted to feel like human beings. A man came and brought his child with him. He was a doctor, and came in a black suit and a bow tie like he was going to La Scala. At the end, he kept saying "Thank you, thank you, thank you..."

Dragan and I also took the show to a small town in the northwest part of Bosnia. The auditorium windows were still broken and it began to rain during the show onto our stage. But we continued and acted in the rain. It felt as if we were stripped down to the basic way of communicating without necessities or power.

In that kind of situation, you give them a piece of your heart, and they feel you have come to celebrate life with them. To say, "Together let's bring our lives back to normality, to a place where our previous life was."

Q What does acting mean to you now?

I had stopped acting for a couple of months when I became a mother, twice. I feel having a child has brought something special to my acting, teaching me how precious life is, how we need to cherish every moment. We are not only responsible for ourselves; we have to take care of other human beings around us. Theater is a great opportunity to fulfill that task.

I really believe in what Stanislavsky said—that when you enter the theater you leave all your problems and negative thoughts on the doormat. We have the opportunity to bring all the love and joy and happiness we feel in life to our work. We're very lucky we can tell stories about life and love, even when we are talking about death and hatred, in order to renew life and give hope. ■

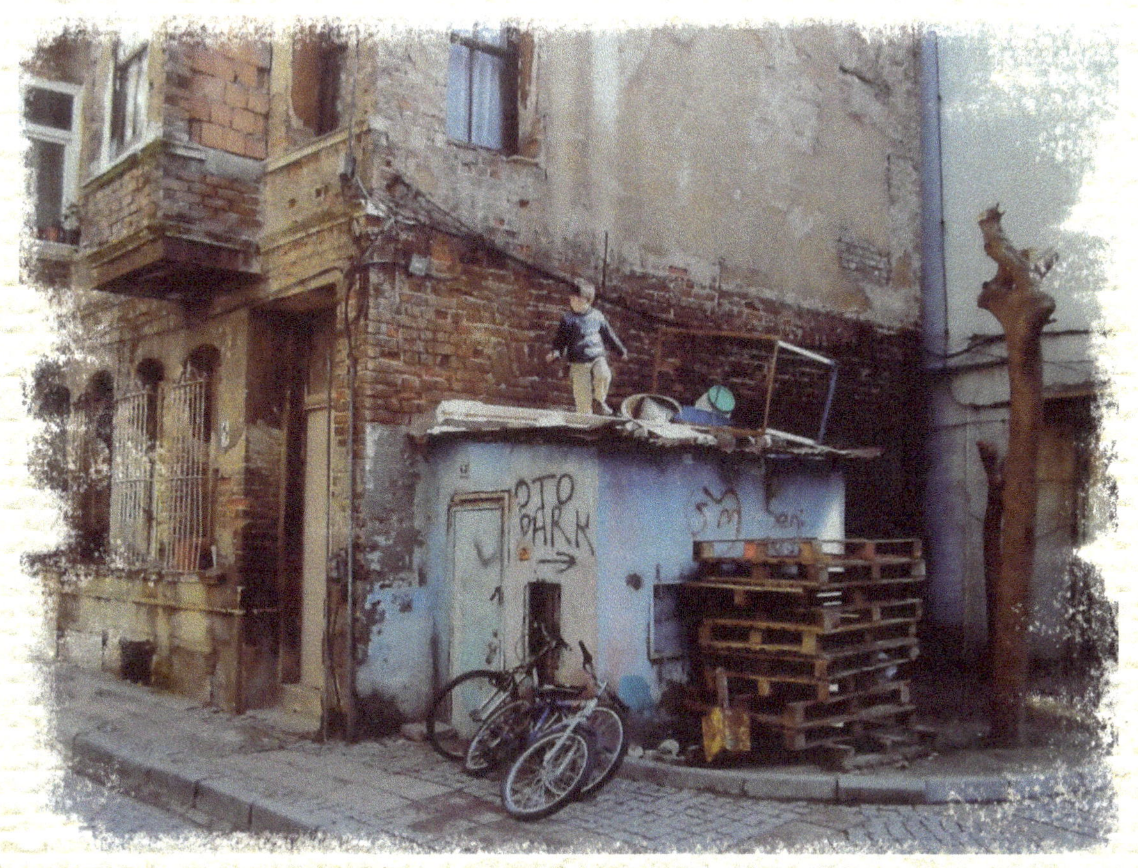

"Istanbul, Turkey" by Selma Alispahić, courtesy of the artist

NICOLE ANSARI

On Broadway and at London's Royal Court Theatre, Ms. Ansari originated the role of Lenka in Tom Stoppard's play, *Rock N' Roll*, directed by Trevor Nunn. She was a member of the internationally-acclaimed Theatre du Soleil, directed by Ariane Mnouchkine, in Paris, and on a tour throughout Europe. A founding member of the Shakespeare company, Berlin, Ms. Ansari also starred at the Public Theatre in Vienna as Roxanne in *Cyrano de Bergerac*, Irma in *Irma la Douce*, as *Berenice*, as *Romy, I* which she also co-wrote, and Alma Mahler in *Alma*. Off-Broadway, she appeared in *Shakespeare's Sister* at La Mama E.T.C. directed by Irina Brook, also touring across France. In regional theatre, Ms. Ansari appeared in *Island of Slaves* at Shakespeare and Company, as Queen Gertrude in *Hamlet*, and *Rosencrantz and Guildenstern are Dead* at the Greensboro Arts Alliance. On the Los Angeles stage, she performed in Valery Belyakovic's version of Gorky's *Lower Depth: The Shelter*, receiving an Ovation award nomination. Her film and television appearances include *Side Effects*, *Blumenthal* and *as Good as Dead*, both of which she also co-produced, *Mysteries of Laura*, HBO's *Deadwood*, *The Blacklist*, *Two Men, a Man, and a Baby*, *Herzog*, and the TV series, *Einstein*.

Q When did you know you wanted to act?

I am one of the lucky people who knew from a young age. One day they had a performance of *Rumpelstiltskin* in class. The teacher said, "Nicole, would you be so kind to portray the fire?" I said, "Sure," and got up on stage, waved my hands up and down, and when I got a lot of applause. I remember thinking, "This is what I want to do."

I was lucky my parents sent me to a Montessori school. My teacher was an actress, and in the evening she would perform in a small theater. So by the age of nine, I had seen a lot of plays by Sartre and other existentialist writers. I didn't understand them but it was exhilarating.

Q What led you to study with Uta Hagen?

Like everything in my life, it was a magical moment of serendipity. I really didn't know anything about Uta Hagen and Herbert Berghof's work. When I came to New York City, I signed up for Uta Hagen's Scene Study class. I created a monologue from Anaïs Nin's diaries. I had butterflies in my stomach when I auditioned for her. Uta came up to me and began speaking in German. Thankfully, I was accepted into her class, and began studying with her. I became very fond of her.

Q How would you describe her as a teacher?

Uta could detect a false note in anyone's performance. She gave you the way to build a role from "the ground up." She taught about intention—demanding that you put yourself in the situation of the character using your imagination—that you don't need to go back to your father's death for an emotion. She'd say: "By the time you're twenty-seven years old, you've got all these experiences, all the grief and pain you can suffer in this life."

When I saw her perform Off-Broadway in *Mrs. Klein* with Laila Robins—whom I later cast in the feature film, *Blumenthal*, which I produced—I will never forget the way Uta started the scene dunking her tea bag into a hot tea cup. She was so real; she made me feel the heat of the tea, the smell of the tea leaves. I felt like *I* was drinking the tea; that's how specific she was.

Q What did you discover when you performed as Roxanne in *Cyrano de Bergerac* at Vienna's Public Theatre?

Roxanne was my first ingénue. For some reason, I have always had a lot of maturity. I discovered an innocence, a purity within me that I had not allowed myself to feel. It was probably because I had grown up so fast. I had always been alone in big cities studying drama from an early age without my parents, so I had to parent myself. Now I was able, with the help of the writer, Rostand, to be an ingénue, and it felt wonderful.

Q How did it happen that you were chosen to be a Company member of the famed Theatre du Soleil in Paris?

I was in New York, and had just gotten into The Actors Studio as a working finalist and the Italian/French actress, Valeria Bruni Tedesci, who later became a star in French cinema, saw me doing *Agnes of God* in one of the sessions, moderated by Ellen Burstyn. Valeria told me that I had to go and audition for Ariane Mnouchkine in France. She said, "I think you're the actress for her."

I had known about the Theatre du Soleil from a book about their production of *Mephistopheles*, and was entranced by the pictures, and I thought to myself, "Wouldn't it be amazing to be part of a troupe like that?"

I was actually in a beautiful home in Saint-Germain-des-*Prés*, sitting at lunch when I suddenly jumped up, as if someone had stepped on my toe and I blurt out, "I have to call the Theatre du Soleil right now!" So I get through on the phone and they actually give me a date to come to be interviewed. I basically had no idea what to expect.

When I traveled out of Paris to the Cartoucherie—a community of theaters on the outskirts of Paris in the Bois de Boulogne—there were literally hundreds of people from all over the world: African, American, Lebanese, Israeli, German, French, actors from Brazil, Argentina and Russia, all there wanting to do a three-week workshop with Ariane Mnouchkine.

The interview was in French. During the interview, they asked me for a cooking recipe, which I was happy to give. It became clear to me that this theater group was more like an ashram— alternating between cooking, cleaning, building the stage, sewing costumes and of course, acting. I had spent time in an ashram doing

Seva—"selfless service"—and I knew I'd feel at home.

I was invited to audition, and found out the process is all improvisation with music. I joined a massive group of people doing one of the most excruciatingly bad improvs that was ever done. When we finally ended, Ariane said: "This is the worst day of my life. So little talent." She then asked, "Is there anyone who has anything to show—come and show me." Some do clown work, French Buffon type of acting, and circus stuff.

I think to myself, "This is your chance! You have to do something!" I had studied doing a "private moment" in acting classes with Susan Batson in New York, so I decided to "fall asleep, wake up from a nightmare, go into the kitchen and make an egg." That was the setup. So I did it, and as I'm cooking the egg, I looked out past the "fourth wall," and I see Ariane—her white hair like a halo around her distinctive face, this giant of the European Theatre—and I freeze.

She stopped me. "Nicole, what happened? You had me all the way until you looked out towards us, then it was all gone."

"I'm so sorry, Madame Mnouchkine. I really felt the music within the action but when I saw your face, I became self-conscious, and I thought to myself, 'Who are you fooling? This is the great Mnouchkine and you're cooking an egg in a stupid improv? You're wasting her time.'" I sat down and started to cry. "Okay," she said, "That a good ending to the day." I guess my honesty won. I was invited into the three-week workshop.

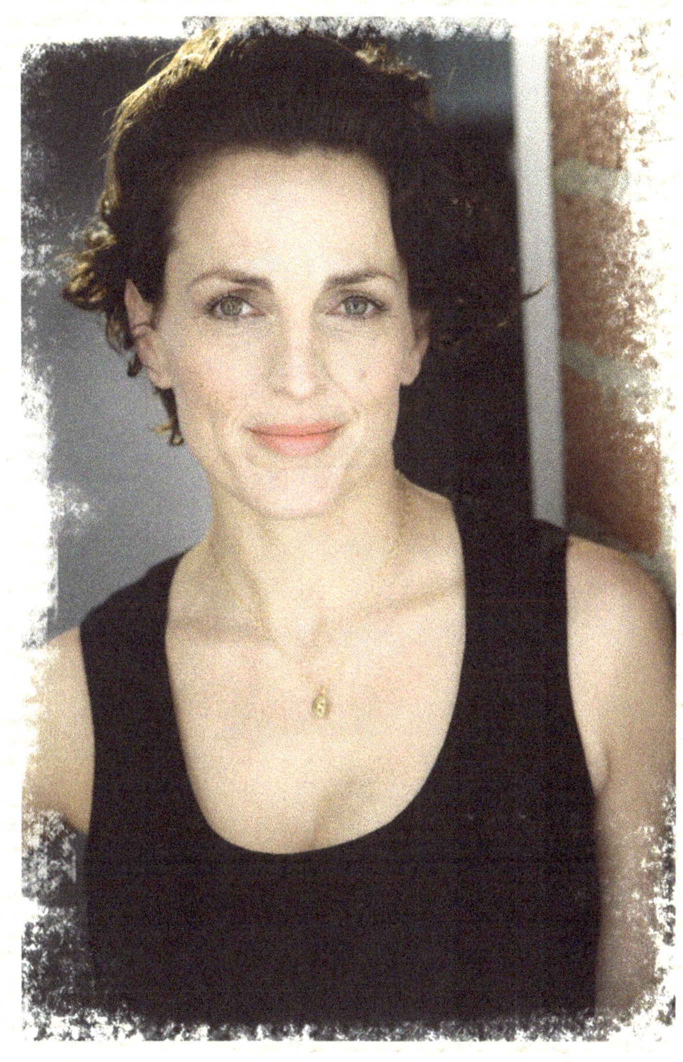

Nicole Ansari Photo: Tim Dobrovolny

Q What did you work on during the workshop?

Weeks of improvisations—working with Balinese masks and classical Commedia dell'Arte masks. I had a hard time. They kept telling me, "Feel the current within the mask." I tried a long improv as Casanova, and Ariane said to me, "You are blessed to know how to find the mask within a character without the mask, Nicole, but you lose it all when you put a mask on."

One day I'm so exhausted I decide to put on the mask of Dadu, the wise man of the Village from Bali, and just sit there. The Balinese are sitting stage left, the Commedia dell'Arte stage right. My eyes are closed; no one can see me behind the mask so I go into a deep mediation. That's all I was planning—to just sit and meditate.

On stage, an improv is going on. I hear them trying to decipher a long poem. Everyone's failing miserably. Ariane has an outburst and very loudly calls out: "Is there anyone who can explain this poem to me?"

From the corner of my eye, I see a shadow of a finger waving—to my great surprise, it is mine! Shaking it, all of a sudden I feel myself rising from the floor. I think to myself, "What are you doing? Sit down!" Ariane looks at me. "Dadu, do you have any suggestions?"

I get up slowly, as an old man would, and say in Dadu's voice, "I think I can explain the poem," and go into a long improvisation. I have no idea what I'm saying. I perform until tears are running down my cheeks under the mask. Ariane stops me. "Okay, Nicole, I think you're back. Welcome to mask work."

The workshop continued for almost three months, now we were down to twenty people. She takes me off to the side: "Nicole, at this point you must know that I want you to stay but the question is: Do you? If you do stay, I say, 'Welcome to hell.'" Of course I stay.

At the end of three months, I remember working on William Blake's famous poem: "Tiger, Tiger, burning bright..." as a girl who's reading it as a love letter as she gradually turns into a tiger. When I finish, Ariane speaks to me about Rimbaud, and to my searching look, she said, "Nicole, sometimes I ask myself if you understand me, if you actually speak French." I had to admit that I didn't speak it very well. I had been listening not to the words, but to the underlying intention. But within a year, my French was flawless. That type of listening revolutionized the way I approach the "music in the words." I began to understand that language is rhythm.

Q How would you describe Ariane Mnouchkine?
Ariane is one of the most fascinating artists and human beings I ever met and will meet. She surrenders to a higher power—the "Theater Gods." When something doesn't work, she's patient enough to trust that the Muse will come and touch us. With every play she re-invents the way she wants to tell the story in collaboration with the actors. It's a completely unique way of working as a theater artist, as a story teller.

Q How did that period of performing challenge you?
While I was there, I gave up the idea of having a life other than within the theater. There came a time when I had done a movie and wanted to attend the opening. So I asked Ariane if I could go. She said, "Nicole, you have to choose—is it film or theater? Are you in or are you out?" I didn't go. This absolute commitment of hers to the creation of theater was very humbling. But I loved film, too, and felt cut off.

The next show we did was the *Awakening of the Furies* coming back after thousand years of sleep because they smell blood that is rotten. Helene Cixous, a longtime collaborator of Ariane's wrote the original play, which became a prophecy. At that time in the 1990s, there was a huge scandal in France about contaminated blood; people were being infected with HIV, and the production was extremely controversial and we lost our subsidy. We had basically run out of money, so we had a big meeting. Everyone was asked what we should do. We could all go on unemployment, and the money would subsidize us. Then I said, "We should do a Moliere classic." Many disagreed, but in the end, we did.

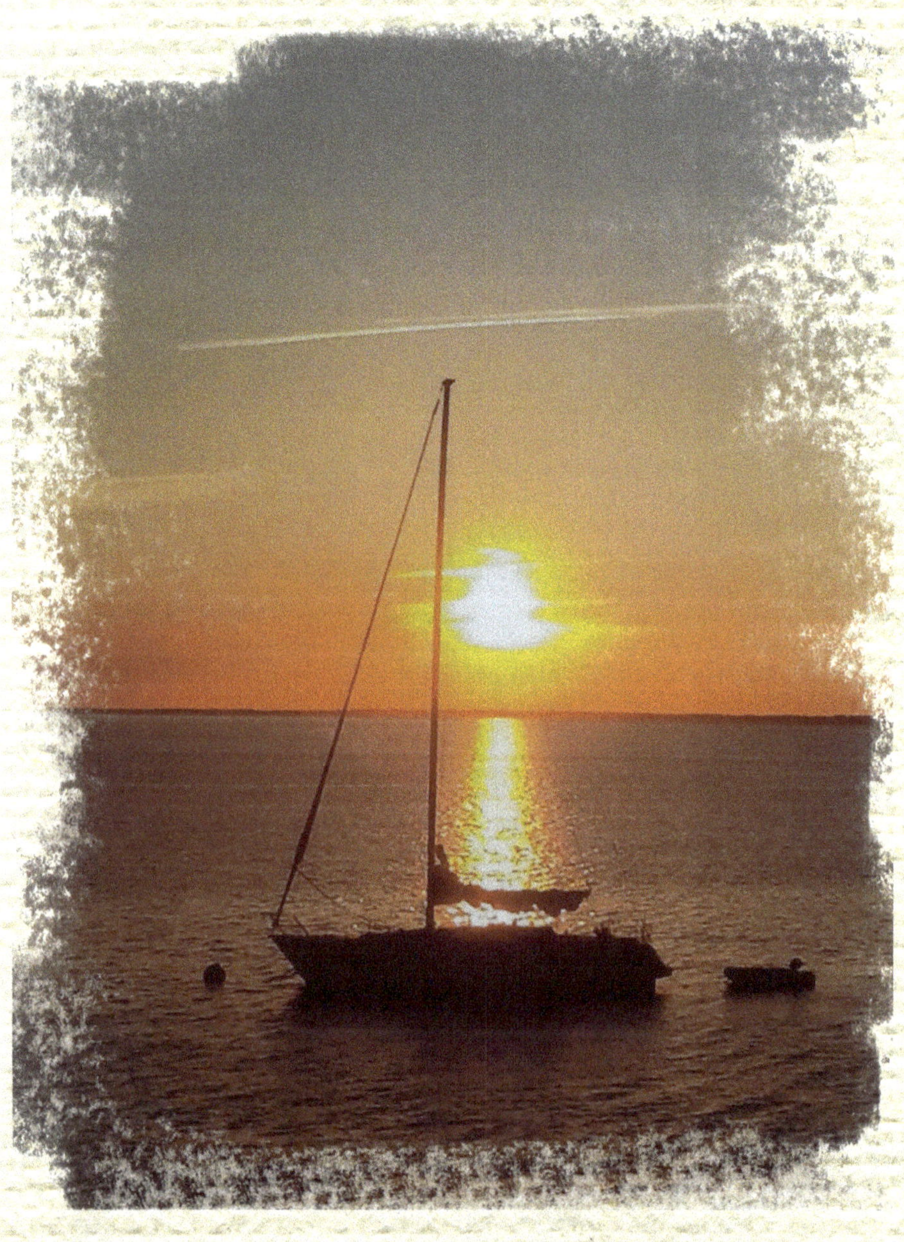

"Sunset" photo by Nicole Ansari, courtesy of the artist

I worked on the role of Marianne, the young ingénue in the play. I was thinking I had a good chance of playing her. But in the end, Ariane gave the role to someone else. We go out on tour with both plays, and I help with the lighting as the "super trouper" for *Tartuffe*. While we're performing in Avignon, it becomes clear to me what I need to do. At one performance I go backstage to Ariane. "Madame, it is with a very heavy heart but I will leave the company when we finish here in Avignon. I need to act." After a moment, she said, "Nicole, you are one of my dearest actresses. You can come back any time."

Q How did it happen that you were cast in Tom Stoppard's *Rock 'n' Roll*, directed by Trevor Nunn?

It was like a dream come true. Brian (Cox) had been offered a role in *Rock 'n' Roll* in London; Stoppard had written the part with Brian in mind. When I read the play and I got to the character of Lenka, I thought, "This is me!"

Lenka is a Czech student of Philology, a very spiritually hippie who philosophizes on the poetry of Sappho. I loved Sappho as a young acting student, so I told Brian, "I have to audition for this role." But being married to a famous actor doesn't make it any easier to be considered; it's actually the opposite. It's a complicated situation. Actually *Deadwood* and *Rock 'n" Roll* were the only times I dared to approach people about projects Brian was working on, concerning my own work.

Brian's agent got me an audition to read for Stoppard and Trevor Nunn. I worked on the role as if I was actually playing her with a Czech accent, read a ton of Sappho's poetry, and turned myself into Lenka.

When I finally auditioned, they saw on my resume that I had worked with Mnouchkine. Trevor told me before I began, "I just want you to know this requires a realistic approach of acting." I guess he wanted to make sure I don't pop out a mask and start dancing like I'm in *The Artrides*.

I was cast! On the first day of rehearsal, Trevor came up to me and said, "Nicole, before we start working I want you to know that the only reason you're playing this part is because you're right for it. Your chances were actually less at the audition, knowing you were the wife of Brian. But you proved us wrong." It was a very gracious approach, putting me completely at ease. And when the show moved to Broadway, I was lucky to be one of the people who moved with it.

Q What makes acting in the theater so meaningful for you?

For me, it's participating in a communal experience where the characters and spirits from the present and the past move me and the audience hopefully to a greater understanding, ultimately questioning what it means to be a human being. ■

LUCIE ARNAZ

Ms. Arnaz made her Broadway debut in *They're Playing Our Song*, receiving the World Theatre Award, and the Los Angeles Drama Critics Circle Award. On Broadway she also appeared in *Lost in Yonkers*, *Dirty Rotten Scoundrels* and *Pippin*. Her theater appearances include the international tour of *My One and Only* with Tommy Tune, receiving the Sarah Siddons Award, *Grace & Glorie*, *Pippin*, *Lost in Yonkers*, *They're Playing Our Song*, *Seesaw*, *Sonia Flew*, *The Witches of Eastwick*, *Vanities*, *Annie Get Your Gun*, *Cabaret*, and as Maria Callas in *Master Class*. She has co-starred with her husband, Laurence Luckinbill, in *Educating Rita*, *The Guardsman*, and *Whose Life is it, Anyway?* Her television appearances include *Here's Lucy* for seven years, *The Lucie Arnaz Show*, *Sons and Daughters* and *Who Is the Black Dalia?* Ms. Arnaz's film appearances include starring opposite Sir Laurence Olivier and Neil Diamond in *The Jazz Singer* receiving an Academy Award nomination and a Globe Award nomination, *Billy Jack Goes to Washington* and *Second Thoughts*. She debuted her nightclub act at Rainbow & Stars in New York City, and co-produced with her husband, *Lucy & Desi: A Home Movie* for NBC, receiving an Emmy Award. Ms. Arnaz is the daughter of Lucille Ball and Desi Arnaz.

Q There can be many ups and downs in this profession. How have you learned to protect your soul?

By ups and downs, it can mean different things. It could be getting bad reviews, although I don't put too much stock in them. If you're going to believe the good ones, then you have to believe the bad ones. But if you have a sense of yourself, you know when you've shortchanged the audience. Of course if you know you've done your best work and it's dismissed off-hand, then you have to go back to your soul to protect yourself. Sometimes critics may write something that makes you say inside, "I was trying not to see that," and you've got to deal with that, too. But much of it is like the old saying: "Like water off a duck's back."

Sometimes at the end of a night of a great show, at the bow, I'll take an extra deep breath and suck it all in, and "save it for the winter." I'm always working on something. I love writing, creating documentaries. I make speeches across the country; I do a night club act. I feel I'm always in the process of creating, even if it's just cooking a special dinner for friends I haven't seen in a while.

Q What role has challenged you the most?

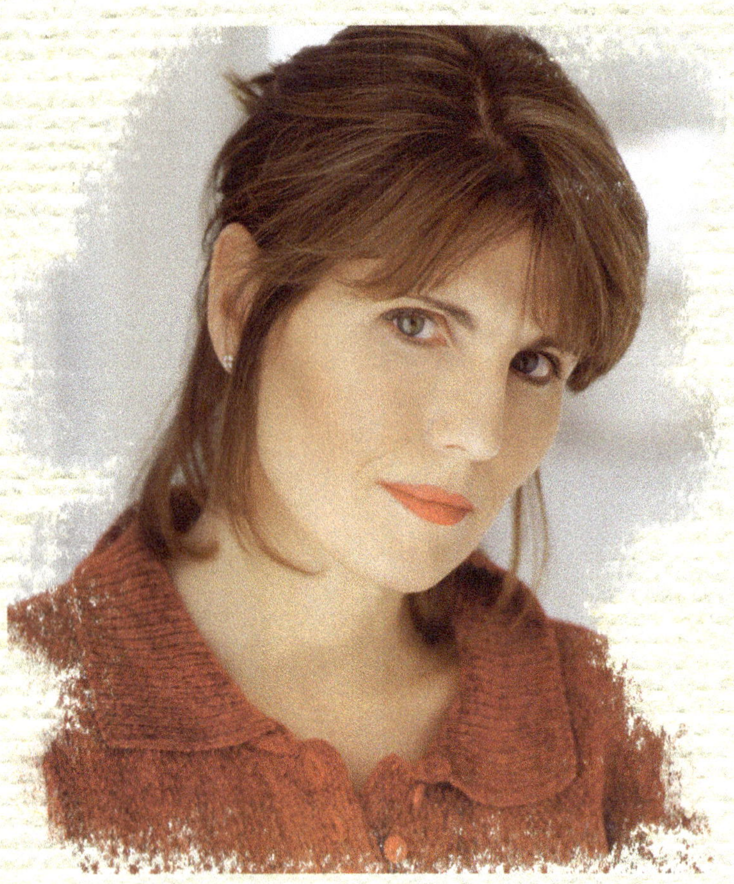

In some ways they all have, always teaching me something new. When I did *Master Class* at a theater in Portsmouth, New Hampshire, it was an amazing stretch, like doing a wilderness hike. I had worked with my director, Don Amendolia, in *Once Upon a Mattress* and on tour in *My One and Only*. He's a very good director and that was the main reason I decided to tackle the part.

Q How did you begin?
I made sure I had enough time to prepare for it properly. I had five months to work on the role. I first went to the Museum of Television and Radio and watched everything Maria Callas had done, taking copious notes. I read every book about her, got the entire master class she gave, which is on CD, listened to all the operas mentioned in the play, got an Italian coach. The hardest part was learning to speak Italian properly. There are so many different regions and hers was a blend of Italian, Greek and New York! I found out she wasn't nasty in her classes. That was difficult to deal with, because in the play she's quite sharp and sometimes cruel to her students. I had to find her vulnerability. To play any character you have to care about them.

For me, every role is like driving down a road. You learn to accelerate as you do it, learning all the curves. It was so much fun by the end but I was just beginning to be able to serve the audience. That only comes after many weeks of playing a role, when you don't have to think about what you're doing.

Q What gives you the greatest satisfaction performing in the theater?
So much of what we do is inbred—why we do what we do, why we've chosen to work in a particular profession. Why the theater? It's the satisfaction of knowing I'm doing it simply from beginning with a script, on a piece of paper. A tightrope is created between me and the audience, and it becomes my job to keep them interested for two hours.

Q Do you approach musicals differently than a straight play?
I came right out of television and began doing musicals. I never made any distinction between musicals and straight plays. I was doing shows like *Seesaw* and *Cabaret*, and they're full of dramatic moments. I feel I do comedy "straight" and try to find the humor in drama. I'd watch the best comediennes, like my mother, do their work, whatever the situation was, and everything they did was from truth.

And some of the things my mother did were pretty broad. For example, in a particular show of *I Love Lucy*, Ethel and Fred came in with chandeliers on their heads, and I could see my Mom and Dad drawing blood to their lips to keep a straight face—to stay in the reality. The situation only became funny by their staying in the truth of the moment.

Q How has your marriage for over twenty years to Larry Luckinbill spurred your creativity?
Larry's so smart and well educated. He's a history buff, an historian, and a voracious reader. He's given me insights on so many different levels on characters I've played I would never have thought of. I met him when I began working on *The Jazz Singer* in 1979, and the ideas he came up with made my character much more vulnerable, charming and funny—things I could play, something I could inhabit. He also helped fix a few of Neil Diamond's scenes. He has an honest, objective way of working with material, which also makes him an excellent director.

Q How have you learned to cope with everything that's occurring in the world?
I cope by counting my blessings. I'm not a very religious person but I thank God my family is safe—that I have a roof over my head. I can work and I can help as much as I can. I don't blame God

Lucie Arnaz photo: courtesy of the artist

either. Things don't happen because He let it. He created humans with free wills, and there are good people and bad people in the world. Some people are hurting inside, empty, and sometimes they think the only way to get attention is by violence. They're desperate, and so they do desperate things. You can imagine how bad God must feel for us all. But we have to learn to listen to the desperation in the world now, and really listening is one of the hardest things to do.

Q Who have you learned from how to listen?

My kids taught me a lot. I try and listen to what they're not saying. It's a great lesson that helps me listen on stage. If I'm really listening, then everything's fresh every night. I listen to the audience, trusting them to let me know if I'm connecting with them. Everything I do in my life, I've got to be passionate about, something I'm really in love with.

Q What are some of the lessons you learned from your mother and father—Lucille Ball and Desi Arnaz—that you continue to draw strength from?

The older I get I remember things they said and what they really meant by them. Really simple things that I've relied upon. My father was a good businessman. He never went to business school but he had a great instinct, a "common man" touch. He told me, "If you don't know what to do, don't do anything." And you'd think about it and you'd laugh. Now I'm a pretty well-organized person, a responsible person, a problem solver. But sometimes, something comes along when I truly don't know what to do. And I remember what he said.

Because for me, it means all the pieces haven't fallen into place, and you're better off listening and waiting. And that's what I do, whether they're little things or big things, I tell myself, "Just coast, open up your mind and be sensible." And I take a deep breath and inevitably something puts the last piece in the puzzle.

My mother told me—besides "Don't ever wear tennis shoes without socks"—"Be good to Lucie." Which meant to me, when a decision has to be made, and a voice is saying inside, "I don't know if this is good for me," trust it. In the big, big picture, it means: Take your vitamins, get your rest, don't neglect yourself. So many people aren't good to themselves. And without health, we have nothing. Oh, and another thing she said was, "Never leave your luggage." Words to live by. ■

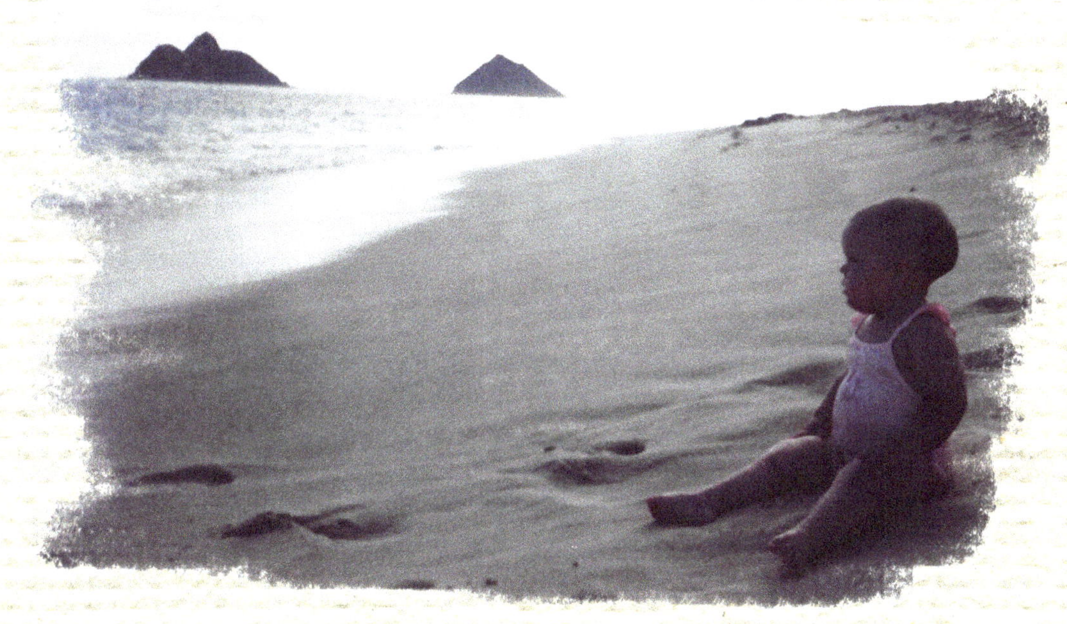

"Kate Alone on Beach," photo by Lucie Arnaz, courtesy of the artist

ELIZABETH ASHLEY

Ms. Ashley received the Tony Award and a Theatre World Award on Broadway in *Take Her, She's Mine*, directed by George Abbott. Her other notable Broadway appearances include opposite Robert Redford in the original production of Neil Simon's *Barefoot in the Park*, directed by Mike Nichols, receiving a Tony Award nomination, *Agnes of God* opposite Geraldine Page and Amanda Plummer, receiving the Albert Einstein Award, *Caesar and Cleopatra* with Rex Harrison, *August: Osage County*, Horton Foote's *Dividing the Estate*, *Enchanted April*, and Gore Vidal's *The Best Man* with James Earl Jones. She has starred in many Tennessee Williams' plays, including *Eight by Tenn*, the 1973 Broadway production of *Cat on a Hot Tin Roof*, receiving a Tony Award nomination, *Suddenly Last Summer*, *The Red Devil Battery Sign*, *The Milk Train Doesn't Stop Here Anymore*, *Out Cry*, *Sweet Bird of Youth* at Washington, D.C.'s Shakespeare Theatre receiving a Helen Hayes Award, *The Glass Menagerie* at Hartford Stage, Boston's A.R.T. The Alley Theatre receiving the Boston Globe Critic's Award, and *Night of the Iguana* on Broadway. Off-Broadway she played Isadora Duncan in *When She Danced*, and Edward Albee's *Me, Myself and I*. National tours and regional appearances include *The Enchanted* at the Kennedy Center, *Master Class* in Toronto, Regina in *The Little Foxes* at the Shakespeare Theatre, *Who's Afraid of Virginia Woolf*, *Eleemosynary* directed by Burt Reynolds, and *Mrs. Warren's Profession*. Her film appearances included *The Carpetbaggers*, *Ship of Fools* receiving a Golden Globe nomination, *Rancho Deluxe*, *Marriage of a Young Stockbroker*, *Cathouse Thursday* with Lee Marvin, *Coma*, *Dragnet*, *Vampire Kiss*, *A Man of Passion* with Anthony Quinn, *Happiness*, *Stagecoach* with Willie Nelson and Johnny Cash, *Severance*, *The Cake Eaters*, and as Aunt Mimi in HBO's *Treme*. On television Ms. Ashley's appearances include *The Rope* receiving a Cable ACE Award nomination, *Svengali* with Peter O'Toole and Jodie Foster, *Sandburg's Lincoln*, *Evening Shade* with Burt Reynolds receiving an Emmy nomination, and *The Tonight Show* with Johnny Carson. She authored "Actress: Postcards from the Road," and recorded the audio book of John Lahr's *Tennessee Williams: Mad Pilgrimage of the Flesh*.

Q What surprises you about a role?
It's usually something I never know until I'm deep into rehearsal, sometimes not even until during performances. I'm an obsessive "grease-monkey," it's the way I like to work. If I was a mechanic I'd have the "hood up" with the parts and the tools lying in rows in every direction. It's doing the "Nancy Drew detective work" that I like.

If you're really lucky, a role will come along your way that has your "name" on it. The great Lee Strasberg said, "When that happens, just leave that alone." Of course, on the other hand, it's thrilling when you discover that "something" that informs the character. Then everything becomes that much more specific. What I do is a deep examination to discover what lies underneath.

Q How would you describe what it was like when you began your career?
As a young woman who came of age in the 1960s, we knew we pissed off the establishment. It was like that in the theater ever since Brando, and others like Montgomery Clift, and the so-called 'Method' came onto the scene. In a way it was perceived as an assault on what had been done previously.

When I began, I worked with directors like George Abbott and Tyrone Guthrie; they were tyrants in ways, demanding certain things, but they understood that in rehearsal, an actor is "baring themselves." When Abbott preached, you felt the taste of his backhand.

I'm always shocked when a director during a rehearsal will say, "There'll be a laugh here." How can they say that! To tell you they want a "cheap" laugh on a certain line imposes something else on it and completely violates the whole process. Abbott told us, "A play, especially a comedy, has to be played without one laugh at all to work." The audience is a living organism. I have to allow them to react how they will.

Q How do you begin to work on a script?
I do a "close-reading" of a script, a word-by-word examination. I usually read at least twenty books having to do with the time of the play, the history of the writer, the class of my character. I have to know what influences informed that writer to write what he did. Where did it come from?

A play is a map, and there's twenty-five ways to go from "A to B." Of course, any performance you give has to be, in a way, in touch with the child-part of yourself. I always white-out all the stage directions because the publisher put them in there. What I also do, and some will consider it heresy, I also white-out punctuation. Some writers will go crazy when they hear me say this. But

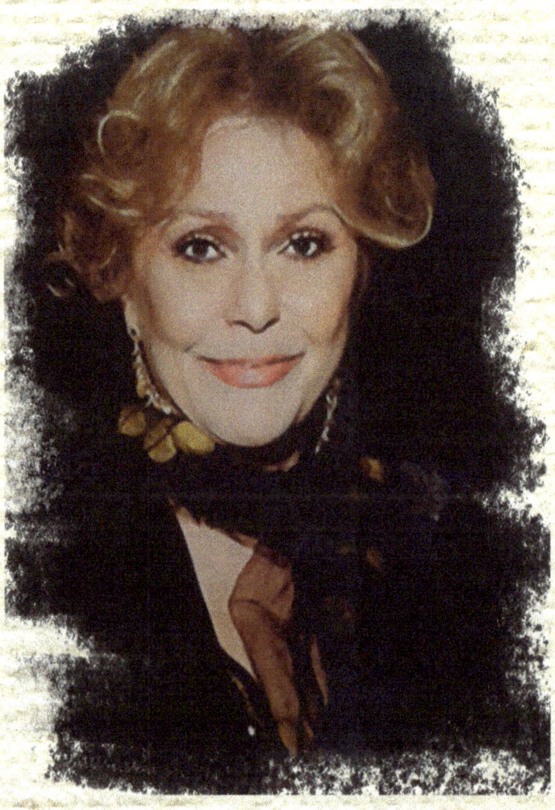

Elizabeth Ashley photo: courtesy of the artist

there's a reason: if you're working properly, you will naturally break up what you're saying according to how you as the character organically speaks and thinks.

Q What is your preparation during the day when you have an evening performance?

I'm nocturnal by nature; I like to sleep until noon, especially if I've had a performance the night before. I have to begin from the moment I wake up to arrive at my peak energies.

I like being at the theater at least two hours before "half hour." I run a "good" dressing room. Everyone stops by; I listen to everyone's stories. My dressing table is laid out like a mechanic's. My motors are revving up; I can still pay attention or not to, to what I hear around me. I'm always made-up by half-hour, I'm in costume, and I don't see anyone after that.

In the days when shows toured before they were brought into Broadway, there were constant rewrites between every performance. We'd ask, "What version are we doing tonight?!" I loved that aspect of it. Nowadays, there's just no time for out-of-town previews.

Q Do you ever go over the script before you go on?

I never go over my lines or I'm in trouble! If there's been a script change, I will work on that. If there was a problem during a performance, I always like to solve it immediately after the show. I consider acting a breathing, organic process, but with enormous discipline and objective thinking.

Fortunately, when I was young, I had a teacher who was extremely severe. It taught me how to be disciplined. And I believe that anything that happens on stage you deal with as the character. You have to be disciplined enough to play "in the light," which the lighting designer set for you. I'm shocked at how many young actors aren't that interested in knowing all the aspects of the theater, how everything works.

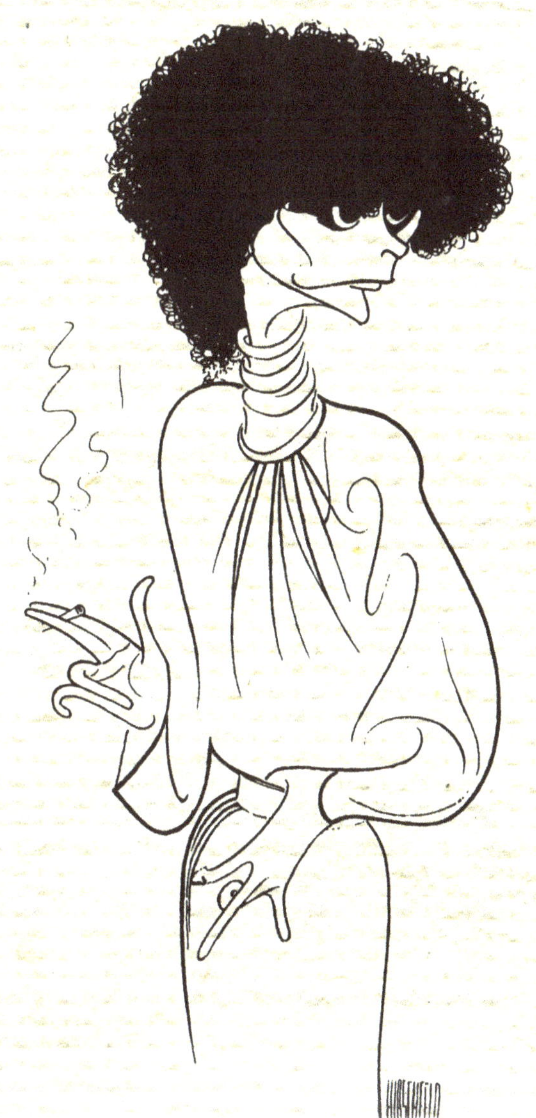

Elizabeth Ashley artwork: Al Hirschfeld © The Al Hirschfeld Foundation. www.AlHirschfeldFoundation.org

I'm a most consistent actor, but I never do anything exactly the same way I did it the night before; each performance gets a little deeper. In order to fly, you have to have built that "airplane"; it's the same in acting. It's thrilling to see an unforgettable performance and wonder how it came to be. I say go see Vanessa Redgrave anytime in anything! There's something so instinctive in her work, it's in her DNA; she got an "extra kiss by God." Her spirit has transcended her ego, such a generosity of spirit. I believe who you are as a human being determines who you are as an actor. You see actors today like Meryl Streep, Sean Penn, Johnny Depp, there is a largess, a "fat soul" in them.

Q Your performance as Maggie in *Cat on a Hot Tin Roof* on Broadway was an important landmark revival.

Michael Kahn had directed me up at Stratford in that famous 1973 revival of *Cat*. It got so much press they brought it into Broadway. It was a huge hit, and that "opened the gates" for more revivals.

Q You also performed opposite Geraldine Page in *Agnes of God*.

You couldn't work opposite the great Geraldine Page. You worked as her supplicant. Such a great actress! It was like getting into a boxing ring with Muhammad Ali. I was able to go places and be better than I ever dreamed was possible. It didn't get any more thrilling! But if I hadn't had my technique under my belt, I wouldn't have been able to do what I did.

I've been referred to as a "stream of consciousness" actor. But you dare not do that unless you have technique. I was a ship's captain, and I always retain an idea of that on stage. I'm always utterly focused.

When I was doing *Caesar and Cleopatra* with Rex Harrison, I was always falling to his feet, which was in character, as his sandals were always coming undone, and I was always fixing them.

I believe an actor has to act with "no net" on a trapeze, and the director should be there for the actor. Acting is one of the few jobs you have to really sweat to earn your pay; it's like sports. Because I'm dyslexic, I have my scripts blown up and write out my blocking with Xs and Os, beat by beat. I grew up on football; it's a lingo I understand.

Q The American theater has been gifted with an extraordinary tradition of unforgettable actresses such as Laurette Taylor, Rose McClendon, Kim Stanley, Julie Harris, Geraldine Page, Ethel Waters, Helen Hayes, Lynn Fontanne, Colleen Dewhurst to mention a very few—and your extraordinary performances are certainly part of this ongoing tradition. What does it mean being a part of it?
I'm more than flattered to be considered to be in that kind of company; you can't think of yourself that way. It is important to seek out other actors and watch their work, to be inspired by them, and to inspire your creative imagination. An actor has to always be willing to expand their creative imagination.

I'll tell you a great clue—if actors aren't able to learn from their fellow actors, then they can't see beyond themselves. We live in a culture that is so bent on "winning," but there's no number on my back! Even when I've received awards, there's no such thing as beating anyone else. Yes, you've got to deliver the goods, that's your job, but I also get to reveal truths that are universal, that are undeniable. I think I like this racket.

Q What are you ultimately hoping the audience will leave with?
Enlightenment. I want them to think about the play; to think about their lives, certainly not about me. The theatre used to be much more confrontational. The only reason you went to the theater, was that it was truly dangerous. First and foremost, you're telling a story and in so doing, you're seducing them with ideas so that they'll never think about things the same way ever again. ■

ALEC BALDWIN

Since 1980, Alec Baldwin has appeared in numerous productions on stage, in films, and on television. He has received a Tony Award nomination for *A Streetcar Named Desire* in 1992, and an Academy Award nomination for *The Cooler* in 2004, and has won two Emmy awards, three Golden Globes and seven consecutive Screen Actors Guild Awards as Best Actor in a Comedy Series for his role on NBC's *30 Rock*. His films include *The Hunt for Red October*, *Glengarry Glen Ross*, *Malice*, *The Edge*, *It's Complicated*, *Blue Jasmine*, *Still Alice*, and *Mission Impossible: Rogue Nation*, among many others. Mr. Baldwin is a 1994 BFA graduate of Tisch School of the Arts at New York University and received an honorary doctorate in 2010. He is Co-Chairman of the Board of the Hamptons International Film Festival. He is also the radio announcer for the New York Philharmonic. Mr. Baldwin has two daughters, Ireland Elliese Baldwin and Carmen Gabriela Baldwin.

Q You're one of our finest actors who keeps returning to the theater. Why is it so vital for you to create on stage?
Well, I decided plays are works that people tend to spend more time on, more thought goes into them. The ideas in the realm of theater are richer and much more interesting on an adult level. And they are important to who we are.

Q Is that why you had decided to play Stanley in Tennessee Williams' *A Streetcar Named Desire*?
I wanted to do it. Everyone was so tense about it, and I was saying to myself, "Why is everyone so uptight?" Perhaps it was that guilelessness that helped me. I didn't examine it; I just did it. Later on I began to realize it a bit more.

Gregory Mosher said to all of us, "We know the material works, so it's up to you to give it its life." See, you have to tackle the material, it's you and your limitations and you have to go beyond them. And when you do the work of a worthy writer, there're some nights, maybe two out of the week, where not only I, but everyone in the cast, you feel like you're doing it the best it could possibly be done—that's exciting.

Q What did you learn about yourself playing Macbeth at the New York Shakespeare Festival?
That I could tackle something very daunting, rather prohibitive. People looked at me and asked, "Are you sure?" They had doubts, I had some, but I said, "Let's do it." By sheer force of will I thought I could play this role, but the difference was this required a kind of acumen. With *Macbeth* you realize there are so many elements, the language demand, its rhythm.

Every great writer has a rhythm, all these playwrights are composers—Mamet, Shepard, O'Neill, and with Shakespeare you're confronted with an entirely different language, it's a whole "nother thing." I had this resistance for four weeks, this impulse to "change these lines." I mean, at one point I thought, "Play him as if he's Oliver North!"

I learned the quickest way was to "surrender," surrender to the world of Shakespeare on every level. That was my "virgin Shakespeare experience," and with a week to go I had to get into the "Shakespeare head" as quickly as possible!

Q Has there been someone who you'd say has been an important influence on your life as a creative artist?
Well, there have been people who not only taught me things on a technical level and gave me confidence, but also made me believe I could do things as an actor.

Elaine Aiken, who I had as an acting coach early on and was a dear friend of mine, was very important in my creative life. She was a very generous person, who I didn't feel was acting something out in class. It wasn't about her; it was about the work.

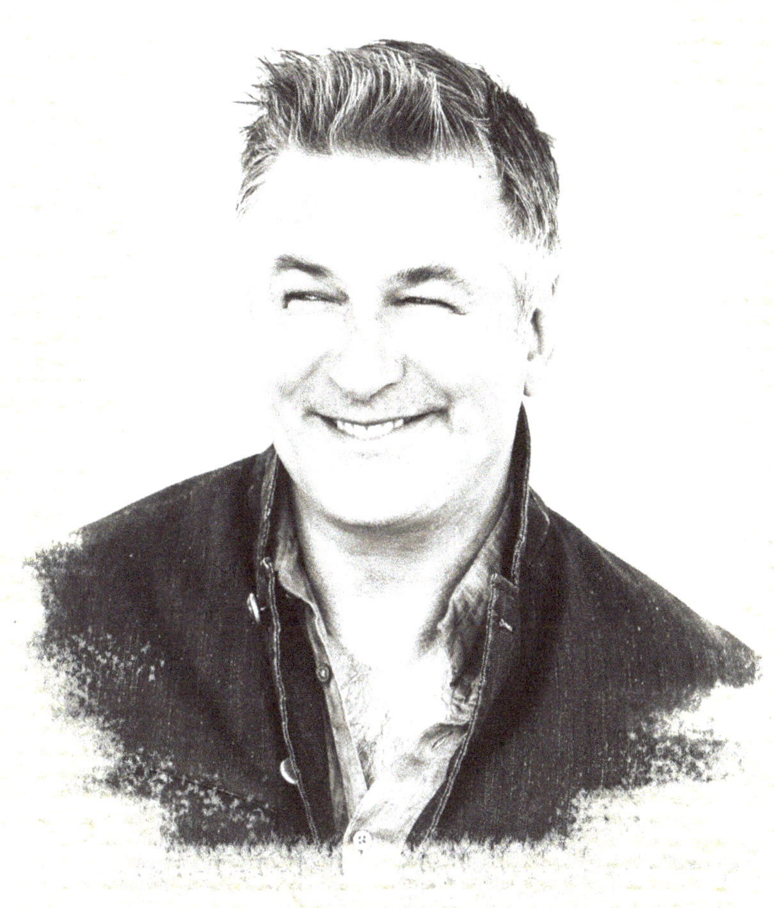

Alec Baldwin photo: Justin Jay

Q Harold Clurman said, "The artist must be a leader." You've spoken up at times and voiced your ideas. Does the artist have a moral responsibility to speak up about what needs to be addressed in society?
Actors don't always get to do what they set out to do in their quest for truth or beauty. A lot of the time we're unable to pursue it through our work, and you gain a certain level of articulation by becoming a "spokesperson for a cause."

What we have now are some actors who are probably no less experts than the government experts. I mean, Richard Masur knows as much as there is about health issues, Ted Danson knows about environmental issues, Jane Alexander knows about funding for the Arts, having run the NEA. I've spoken out for the National Endowment of the Arts, and for campaign finance reform; it's become a passion for me.

Q Do you think it will be possible to build a National Theatre Center in this country where artists like you would be able to work much more often?
I figure we could hatch it, that would be one thing. However, the fiscal health of the theater is always in question. When you look at theaters like the New York Shakespeare Festival, Manhattan Theatre Club, the Bay Street Theatre where I'm involved in fundraising events, they huff and puff every year to make it. It's like everyone's standing on the same street corner with "their hats in their hands." Still we're seeing a real evolution in some places.

One way to address it is to find a way of funding playwrights' organizations much more, perhaps through the film industry. After all, we're all in the same boat and it's what I said before—knowing our limitations and then going beyond. ■

PHOEBE BRAND

Ms. Brand was an original member of famed Group Theatre of the 1930s in America, which has been called "the bravest and single most significant experiment in the history of American theater." She first acted in several revivals of Gilbert and Sullivan operas and in the Theatre Guild production of Maxwell Anderson's verse play, *Elizabeth the Queen*. With The Group Theatre on Broadway, she originated the roles of Hennie Berger in Clifford Odets' *Awake and Sing*, Anna in *Golden Boy*, Minny Belle in Kurt Weill's *Johnny Johnson*, Florrie in the original production of *Waiting for Lefty*, and Barbara Dennin in *Men in White*. She appeared Off Broadway in *A Portrait of the Artist as a Young Man* and *The World of Sholem Aleichem*. Ms. Brand became an acting teacher and taught acting in California at The Actor's Lab. Included among her students were Marilyn Monroe, Ruby Dee, Ossie Davis, Shelley Winters, Tony Curtis, Janet Leigh, Lloyd Bridges, Patricia Neal, and Larry Parks. With her husband, the acclaimed Shakespearian actor, Morris Carnovsky, she taught acting in New York City. In the early 1960s, she co-founded Theater in the Street, presenting classic plays in both English and Spanish. In 1969, they toured across America in Tyrone Guthrie's production of *Lamp at Midnight*. At age 86, Ms. Brand appeared in Louis Malle's film, *Vanya on 42nd Street*. A week before her death in 2004, at age 96, she held her last acting class (this interview was conducted in 1998).

Q As a member of The Group Theatre, every actor was trained in the same way as you worked on new plays. Did that have an effect when you taught acting later in your career?

Essentially each actor has to arrive in their own way to what it means to act. When we studied the same way working on a play in The Group Theatre, we were able to become an ensemble. We may have been taught in the same way, but we still all arrived at different conclusions of what was most important. That's why I teach differently than Sandy Meisner, and he taught differently than Lee Strasberg or Stella Adler. Ideally, it's absolutely essential in a production for everyone to come together, no matter how they're taught—to achieve a unity of approach—of freely working together.

The Group had an ensemble which can only truly come from a permanent company. Andre Gregory did it for five years, and only because his actors agreed to do it; it was a marvelous accomplishment. I think you have to have a great leader, like Harold Clurman, to inspire this unity. He showed us it was possible and he showed us how. He said, "It can be done!"

Q What has been your greatest emphasis as a teacher?

For many years, I've been teaching the classics to students who become inspired and find themselves through this wonderful material. I see them grow and it raises their spirit and their soul. Unfortunately, too many writers today don't have a company to write for, like Clifford Odets did with The Group Theatre or Eugene O'Neill with The Theatre Guild.

Q What's necessary for the American artist to create vibrant and moving theater today?

Artists always find the ways and means to do what they must do. A lot of good work is being done across the country regionally. When I did Theatre in the Street in the 1960s with Billy Dee Williams and many other excellent actors, it was because it was so important to inspire people, to make them long for something, to experience the kind of theater that makes the spirit soar. There has to be so much more of that kind of imagination today to make the kind of theater possible we all long for. ■

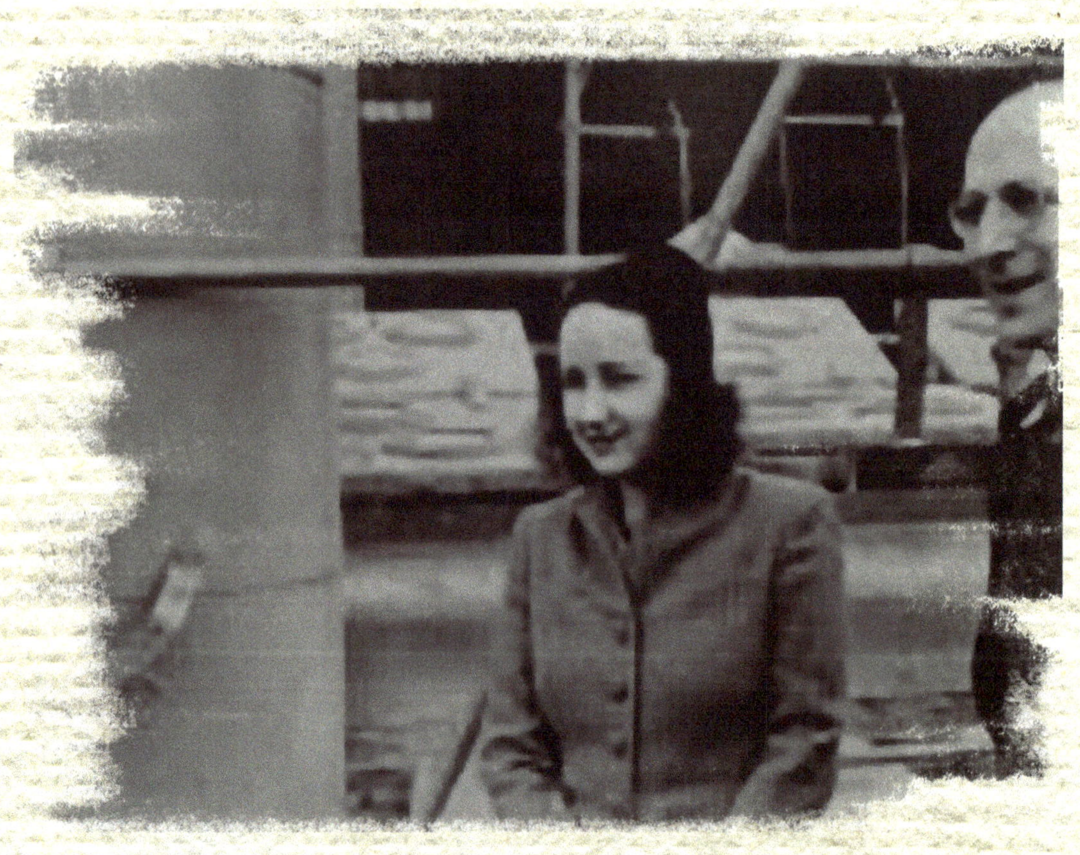

Phoebe Brand photo: Phoebe Brand with Morris Carnovsky, courtesy of Dennis Goodno

CAROL BURNETT

One of the most beloved performers in entertainment, known as the 'Queen of Comedy," her long-running TV variety show, *The Carol Burnett Show* on CBS ran for eleven years, was seen by thirty million viewers each week, and received twenty-five Emmy Awards. It is one of the most honored shows in television history. In 1957, she appeared on the New York circuit of cabarets and nightclubs, most notably for a hit parody number called "I Made a Fool of Myself over John Foster Dulles," which she performed on *The Tonight Show*. Achieving her first success on Broadway in 1959 in *Once Upon a Mattress*, receiving a Tony Award nomination, her other Broadway appearances include *Putting It Together*, *Love Letters*, and *Moon Over Buffalo*, receiving a Tony Award nomination. She appeared regularly on *The Garry Moore Show* for three seasons, receiving an Emmy Award. Ms. Burnett also appeared in specials with Beverly Sills, Dolly Parton, and in *Julie and Carol* at Carnegie Hall with Julie Andrews, receiving an Emmy Award. She was the first celebrity to appear on the children's series, *Sesame Street* in 1969. Ms. Burnett's films and television appearances included *Pete 'n' Tillie*, *The Four Seasons*, *Annie*, *Noises Off*, *Horton Hears a Who*, *6 Rms Riv Vu*, *Carol +2* with Lucille Ball as a special guest, *The Lucy Show*, *Friendly Fire*, *Mad About You*, receiving an Emmy Award, *Carol Burnett and Friends*, *Life of the Party: The Story of Beatrice*, *Desperate Housewives*, *Mama's Family*, *Hawaii Five-O*, *Glee*, and *Law & Order: Special Victims Unit*, receiving an Emmy Award nomination. Ms. Burnett and her daughter, Carrie Hamilton, co-wrote the play, *Hollywood Arms*, directed by Harold Prince on Broadway starring Michele Pawk and Linda Lavin. Her books include *One More Time*, *This Time Together*, *Laughter and Reflection*, *Carrie and Me: A Mother-Daughter Love Story*, and her newest book, *In Such Good Company*, published in 2016. Among Ms. Burnett's many awards include the Women in Film Crystal Award, induction in the Television Hall of Fame, Kennedy Center Honors, Mark Twain Prize for American Humor, Screen Actors Guild Lifetime Achievement Award, and the Presidential Medal of Freedom.

Q What gave you the greatest satisfaction in creating such memorable shows over eleven years of *The Carol Burnett Show*?

I think what I loved the most was hearing the laughter. You throw it out there and see if it works, and when the laughter comes, you get it back doubly. To make it work you also have to be in the "now," in the present moment. When you're doing it, you can't be thinking about yesterday.

I always felt when I did my show the audience was my "present moment'; we weren't a "live" show; we couldn't go "live" in the "covered wagon days." But we were, in a way, because they would fly the scenery out quickly and bring in another set for the next sketch. We didn't have a studio with a lot of "fly space" at TV City so we had to bring the scenery in from the hall as quickly as possible. I got to the point where I could shed my costumes and change faster than they could change the scenery. I tried to make it like a Broadway show as much as possible. The idea was if the audience "caught fire" laughing, it would carry the whole way through, and when you watch the shows now on YouTube, you can clearly hear it's not a laugh track. It's very telling; you can hear the jokes "land."

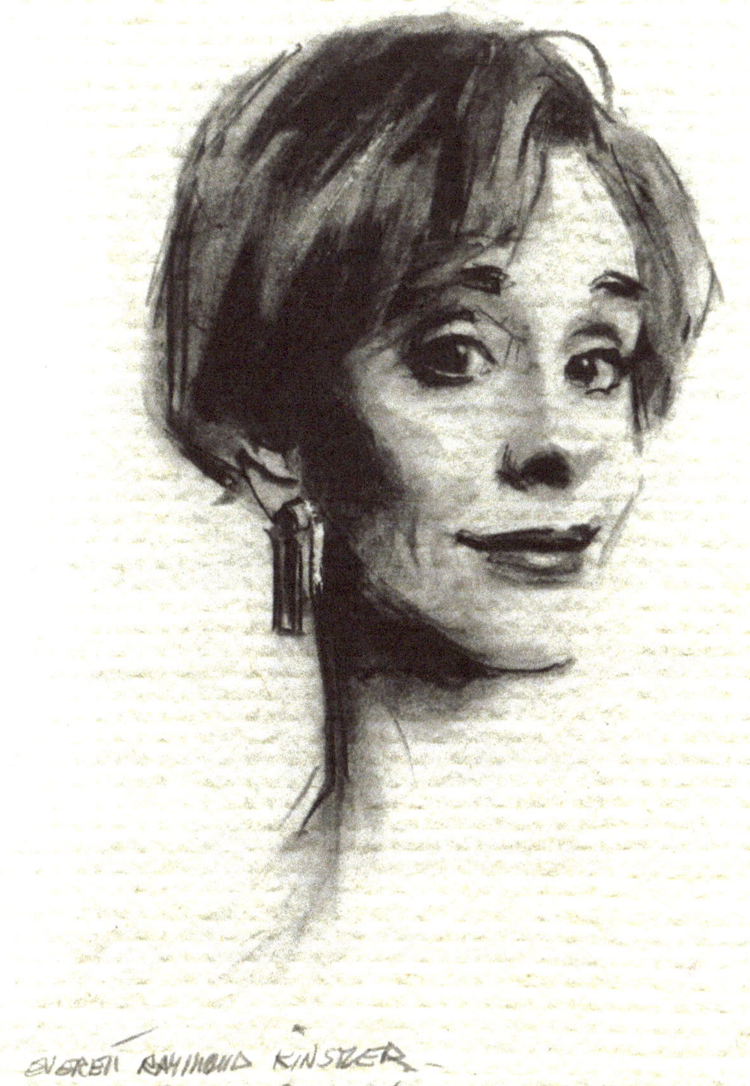

Carol Burnett by Everett Raymond Kinstler, courtesy of Mr. Kinstler

I remember every Saturday night watching the live Sid Caesar show called *Caesar's Hour*, not the *Show of Shows*. It had Carl Reiner and Nanette Fabray in the cast. I thought it was just wonderful and I'd never miss one of his shows. I had wanted my show to be like Sid Caesar's show, and the way it was on *The Garry Moore Show*, which were both true repertory shows. Many times we'd be sitting around reading the script for the week on *The Garry Moore Show*, and Garry would say: "For that joke, give it to Carol," because he knew Carol could say it funny.

Q How were you able to create such an amazing ensemble cast with Harvey Korman, Vicki Lawrence, Tim Conway, and Lyle Waggoner?

I wanted my show to be like it was on *The Garry Moore Show*; that I'd be supporting Tim or Harvey or Vicki to let them shine, and they would support me. I had seen Harvey on *The Danny Kaye Show*, and I thought, "That guy is like Carl Reiner and Art Carney." Harvey was such a great character comedic actor, so when *The Danny Kaye Show*, which Harvey was a part of, was going off the air, and we were going on the air in 1967, we thought, "Why not Harvey?" We called his agent, but as it turned out, I ran into him in the parking lot at CBS. I didn't know him but we recognized each other and I put it to him: "You just got to be on my show," and that's how it happened.

Vicki actually wrote me a fan letter. I was impressed by the letter and learned she would be in a contest for the title of Ms. Fireball of Englewood, California. Well, when I got the letter, the contest was actually happening the very next night. So I went with my husband to see her, thinking of having her in a recurring sketch. We hadn't gotten Harvey yet, but I thought they could be "a married couple." And she looked like me when I was seventeen. We went to the contest and she won. This was in December of '66; she turned eighteen in May the following year. We kept in touch and in the summer, we called her and she auditioned with another girl. She was very raw, "wet behind her ears," but we hired her. She came on my show at eighteen years of age, and she learned comedy in front of thirty million people. Harvey took her under his wing, teaching her how to listen to the other actors, and not to just listen for her cues.

Tim was a regular guest for the first eight years. We'd have him on once or twice every month. In the ninth year, finally we said, "Why don't you join us?"

Lyle was a great suggestion of Carl Reiner's. He said, "What you should hire is a good looking announcer who you could go after as a "man-hungry woman," and that's how we found Lyle. Yes, he was gorgeous, and he was also funny with a warped, crooked sense of humor, and it was very funny for the audiences seeing me swooning over Lyle. But then after two years, I decided, "I'm a married woman with a child," so we stopped doing those bits, and we became a very good rep company.

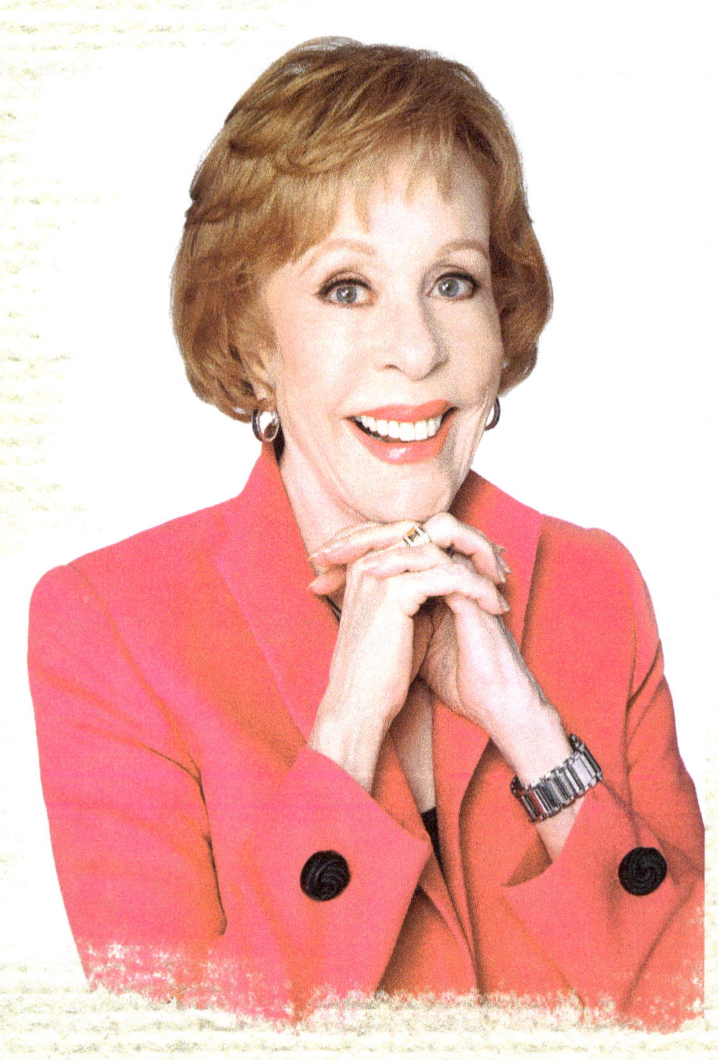

Carol Burnett photo: courtesy of the artist

Q Did your being offered your own show come from being in *Once Upon a Mattress* on Broadway?

No, I was offered my own show due to being on *The Gary Moore Show*.

Q When did you first meet Lucille Ball?

Lucy was a very good friend. She came to see me in *Once Upon a Mattress*, and came backstage. She always called me "kid." So after we talked together, she said, "Kid, if you need me for anything, let me know." Four years later I was lucky. CBS was interested to have me create a Special, an hour long show, but only if I could get a major guest star. My agent talked me into calling Lucy. I did and she said, "What is it, kid?" I told her about my new show but that I needed a guest star. She replied, "When do you want me?" And we became very good friends the rest of her life.

I did her show later, when she played Lucy Carmichael on *The Lucy Show*, and we did two or three shows together. She actually died on my birthday. I would always get flowers from her on my birthday. Well, this time, the flowers arrived before I heard the news, and they arrived with a note that said, "Happy birthday, kid." It was a double whammy!

Q How did the idea to create a play, *Hollywood Arms*, about your life come about?

Actually the idea came from my daughter, Carrie. I had written my book, *One More Time*, which is actually a love letter for my daughters about how I grew up. In the book I tell them what I went through growing up, what kind of a "hairpin" your mother is. I started with my earliest memories up until I was twenty-five and I stopped at that age. It was mostly about me being raised by my grandmother and my mother. So Carrie said to me, "We should do a play from what you wrote." So we set it up that the family lives a block north of Hollywood Boulevard.

We started writing it. She had a little cabin in Gunnison, Colorado where she would go away to write. And she'd write a scene and fax it to me in California, and I'd write a page or two and fax it to her. We never wrote together. When we had some of the early pages written, I knew a friend who worked at the Sundance Institute. So we sent what we had, and Carrie and I were invited to work on the play there in a ten-day workshop. We'd write scenes and a dramaturg would comment on them. We weren't exactly sure what we had.

But after we had about a hundred pages, I had a conversation with my good friend, Beverly Sills, who said to me, "Let me read what you have." After she did, she said, "I'm going to show it to Hal." My first thought was, "Harold Prince is going to read our play!!" Well, I thought at least he might recommend a director. So when we meet with him, I asked him, "Do you have any suggestions for a director?" He said after a hesitation, "Well, yes... me."

Well, Carrie and I were over the moon; we never dreamed he'd do it, and that's how it happened. In the age of fax machines, here I was writing from California, Carrie was writing from Colorado, and we'd put the scenes together and fax what we did to Hal in New York. He'd come back with his suggestions, and notes and criticism. Finally, Hal told me we were going to try it out in April, 2002 at The Goodman Theatre in Chicago.

But in January, Carrie got sick, with cancer. And then, she died. I was devastated; I didn't get out of bed for days; I didn't want to do anything. My husband finally said to me, "You've got to finish the play—for Carrie's sake." And, in a way, it saved me.

I went to Chicago; Hal had cast the show. What was wild, on the way there, on the plane, I said a prayer, "Okay, Carrie, let me know you're with me. We wrote together, and if I'm going solo, give me a sign. I need to know it's okay."

We checked into the hotel, and there was a beautiful array of Birds of Paradise flowers in the room; they had been Carrie's favorite flower. She had a tattoo of them on her right shoulder. The flowers were from Hal. I asked him later, "How did you know?" He said, "I didn't." It was a nice sign. The next night we went to dinner with Hal. The *maître d'* said, "I have a special champagne for you." On the label was the name, Louise. That was Carrie's middle name and my mother's name. Another sign. Now I'm crazy about rain; good things have always happened to me when it rains. Opening night arrived of *Hollywood Arms*, and it rained. Three signs, I felt very good. It was kind of nice. Now maybe it's all a coincidence, but I always feel there's something more to it than that.

Q What does it mean to you that there's such an outpouring of love from so many who watched and love your shows and now a new generation?

It's true. I get letters, since we're on YouTube and from the *Lost Episodes* DVDs of the show, from a lot of teenagers, and I could be their great-grandmother. What touches me is when those who write or tell me they watched the original shows and say that was a time in their lives when their families might be at odds—but for one brief hour, they were released from any fear that they were feeling, or from being sad—it may have been the only time the whole family would laugh together, and that really touches me. Young women tell me seeing what I went through and ended up doing gives them courage, and I feel so blessed.

And I'm thrilled about my newest book which is filled with anecdotes all about our guest stars, backstage stories, a lot of information about how things happened, being in such good company and notes about various sketches I performed with Harvey, Vicki, Tim, and Lyle on the show.

There were really only three TV channels in those days that everybody watched, and I was just so happy to go out and have some fun. ■

ELLEN BURSTYN

Ellen Burstyn's illustrious sixty-year acting career encompasses film, stage, and television. In 1975, she became only the third woman in history to win both the Tony Award and the Academy Award in the same year, for her work in Bernard Slade's *Same Time, Next Year* on Broadway and in Martin Scorsese's *Alice Doesn't Live Here Anymore*, also receiving a Golden Globe nomination and a British Academy Award for Best Actress. Ms. Burstyn has been nominated for an Academy Award five other times for *The Last Picture Show* in 1972, *The Exorcist* in 1974, *Same Time, Next Year* in 1979, *Resurrection* in 1981, and *Requiem for a Dream* in 2000. She became a "triple crown winner," receiving an Emmy Award in *Law & Order: SVU* in 2009, along with having won an Academy Award and a Tony Award. Ms. Burstyn also won an Emmy Award in 2013 for *Political Animals*. She has received Emmy Award nominations for her title role in *The People vs. Jean* Harris in 1981, her starring role in *Pack of Lies* in 1987, *Big* Love in 2008, *Flowers in the Attic* in 2014, and has also received a Screen Actors Guild nomination in 2015, and *House of Cards* in 2016. Her films include *Draft Day*, *The Calling*, *Interstellar*, *The Age of Adaline*, *Custody*, and *Wiener Dog*. She also appeared in the Broadway productions of *84 Charing Cross Road*, *Shirley Valentine*, *Sacrilege*, and the London production of Lillian Hellman's *The Children's Hour*. Ms. Burstyn was the first woman elected president of the Actors Equity Association from 1982 to 1985, and serves as the Artistic Director of the famed Actors Studio, and as co-president with Al Pacino and Harvey Keitel. She lectures throughout the country and her best-selling memoir, *Lessons in Becoming Myself* was published in 2006. Ms. Burstyn was inducted into the Theater Hall of Fame.

Q What do you love about creating on stage?

Well, the process of acting for me is amazing; there so many surprises. I love the whole process of digging into the play. These ideas may not be very developed at the beginning, but once I get into rehearsal, I love exploring in the rehearsal process—finding out meanings as the play is revealing itself to you. That to me is the richest part of being in a play.

Q Working on William Inge's play, *Picnic*, what kinds of things did you learn about Helen Potts, the character that you brought to life during the run of the play?

I kept discovering more about Inge and it affected my understanding of Helen. It gave me something concrete to play. I learned about what an unhappy life he had because he was a gay man in the 1950s. One did not "come out" then. Inge was a friend of Tennessee Williams, he was close to him; they were probably lovers but we can't verify it. Tennessee came out pretty overtly about his sexuality; Inge couldn't, he was so afraid of disappointing his mother. He couldn't face telling her so I found in playing Helen Potts that she is, in a sense, Inge's mother, and Inge is the one who keeps Helen from having a life of her own, controlling her life as given in the play.

As I read more about Inge, he actually said the character he identified the most with was Helen. I felt like she could observe without taking part in life. Yet because of her not having any life of her own, she invites into her life a young man and that has an effect on her.

Helen was in love once, but her mother weakened her. I think Helen just wants a male energy in her life. She wants to have men around. She enjoys their masculinity. It's Inge talking about his love in his life. The young man stomps in from the great outdoors, and brings that kind of energy into her house, and that's so lacking in her present life.

Q What is it that makes an ensemble work as well as it did in the production of *Picnic*?

It was that those individual actors dedicated themselves to the ensemble work. They worked graciously with each other: they weren't selfish, they weren't thinking about themselves, they thought about what would nourish the whole production. The cast was such a wonderful group of human beings.

I'm always tickled how theater is shown with dominating prima donnas, drunken egotistic directors or playwrights, or selfish actors. But I just never see that. It's so odd to me that that's how we're presented but it's not the truth.

With *Picnic*, that group of actors was kind, supportive. Before every performance we'd have a gratitude circle at five minutes to curtain on stage, and whoever wanted to would come and we'd hold hands and we'd say how much we were grateful. It was an opportunity to love and join together; and there was always laughing. It's what would send us on stage—a spirit of community.

Q I know you had a very special relationship with Eva Le Gallienne, one of the most celebrated actresses we've had in the American Theater. You had worked with her in *Resurrection*. What can we learn from Ms. Le G, as she was called, and what did she mean to you personally?

She wrote a couple of books on Duse. One of the most important is *The Mystic in the Theatre*. She also wrote her autobiography. She was a real giant in the theatre. It pains me when people don't realize their connection to such giants as Duse and Bernhardt. I have theatrical collections of their writing and their books. I believe this legacy is where we come from.

After Ms. Le G and I worked together on *Resurrection*, she showed me around her home. She had different artifacts from Duse, some that Duse had given to her personally. When Ms. Le G died, I was lucky enough to buy some of them. One is a ring which Duse's mother had given to Duse, and another is a ring Duse wore which she gave to Ms. Le G.

Whenever I'm in a show I always try and wear this ring. I wore it in *Picnic* for the first performance. After the performance, I thought it was totally inappropriate, so I didn't wear it again. I usually wear it throughout the production of a play I'm in.

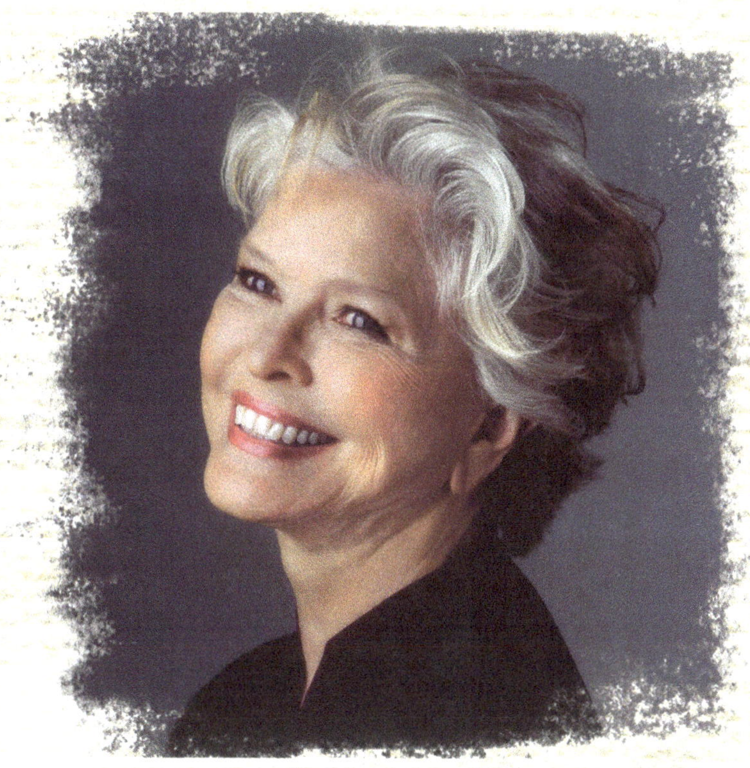

Ellen Burstyn photo: Howard Schatz

Q You've also been President of Actors Equity Association, and you're involved with giving yourself in service to others.
I've received so much from acting; it's my profession. It's also my art form, so I try and do what I'm able to. I also moderate sessions at The Actors Studio. I like to give as much as I can; to be in gratitude.

Q You became a member of The Actors Studio in 1967, and currently you're Co-President of The Actors Studio, alongside Al Pacino and Harvey Keitel. What sustains The Actors Studio in terms of the process of creating on stage?
That kind of work's been going on all these years at The Studio. It's the one place in the world where its members keep developing their craft between jobs. All other forms of art you can practice when you're not employed. An actor is the only one who needs to have a stage and an audience to keep developing your craft. The Studio provides that.

Q What makes audiences keep coming to the theater?
Great playwrights. You have to listen to what they say, if those who come have the ears to hear what's being shared. While some people come to be entertained and have a good time, others come with a focus, an attentiveness. If they really receive what theater artists are offering, then a transference of the message of the play will occur.

Q How do you stay open each day?
When I start the day I make sure the first words I say are, "I thank you." I'm thankful before I get out of bed. I just look at the incredible beauty of creation around me.

Right now I'm up in the Hudson, it's flowering with such splendor—magnolias, the parsippanies, hibiscus, and tulips. The light on the river. For me, it's staying connected to nature. It keeps me aware of the great blessing of living life. I believe we're all made out of the same stuff. It's the "God stuff" some people are aware of and some aren't. When people are in a difficult situation, that's when they're usually more aware of it. ■

LEN CARIOU

On Broadway Mr. Cariou starred in *Sweeney Todd: The Demon Barber of Fleet Street* opposite Angela Lansbury, receiving the Tony Award and Drama Desk Award; in *Applause* opposite Lauren Bacall, receiving a Tony Award nomination and a Theatre World Award; in *A Little Night Music*, receiving a Tony Award nomination, and the film version opposite Elizabeth Taylor. Mr. Cariou's other appearances on Broadway include *Dance a Little Closer*, *Teddy & Alice*, *Ziegfeld*, *Cold Storage*, *The Dinner Party*, and *Proof*. Mr. Cariou's television and film appearances include starring as Henry Reagan, Tom Selleck's father on *Blue Bloods*; as Judd Fitzgerald on *Brotherhood*; *CSI: Las Vegas*, *Murder, She Wrote*, *The West Wing*, *Star Trek: Voyager*, *Nuremberg*; as Franklin D. Roosevelt in *Into the Storm*, receiving an Emmy nomination; *About Schmidt* opposite Jack Nicholson, *Thirteen Days*, *Flags of Our Fathers*, and *Spotlight*. His Off-Broadway appearances include *Master Class*, and in three solo plays: *Broadway and the Bard*; as Ernest Hemingway in *Papa*, and in *Mountain* as Justice William O. Douglas. Mr. Cariou performed at the Stratford Shakespeare Festival in Ontario as Prospero, Coriolanus, Brutus, and Petruchio; at the Guthrie Theatre in Minneapolis as Iago, Oberon, Henry V, King Lear; and as Agamemnon in Tyrone Guthrie's production of *The House of Atreus*, receiving a Theatre World Award. In Canada, he played the role of Macbeth, Richard Nixon in *Frost/Nixon*, and performed many times at the Manitoba Theatre Centre. Mr. Cariou's voice-over includes many commercials, books-on-tape and films including *The Jonestown Flood*, receiving an Academy Award, and as Harry Bosch in Michael Connolly's well-known novels. Mr. Cariou was elected to the American Theatre Hall of Fame.

Q You have tackled some of the greatest roles ever written. Why were they important for you to take on?
Basically because they seemed to be the biggest challenge. When I went to the Stratford Shakespeare Company in my 20s, I had never done any Shakespeare. I soon realized how awesome, awe-inspiring it was. And that's the real challenge as actors—translating it, giving to the audience what Shakespeare intended, making it clear for them. Intellectually, physically, technically; you have to have the equipment. I was told by my mentor, "You're choosing the road less traveled, but don't forget the musicals, because you have that gift." And I've never forgotten.

Q When you take on a character who appears manipulative, totally ego-driven, and evil—how do you find a way to make him a human being we want to watch?
Basically, no matter what peccadilloes or strangeness they may have, it's up to me to find a way to make them human. To begin, I have to give him a point of view, a history. He has to become my best friend. Otherwise I can't play him with conviction for a long period of time.

Sweeney Todd was pretty easy to get over to the audience. He was screwed over by the judge, they took everything away from him, that was a great motivation for what he ended up doing. Figuratively speaking, if you've got to kill four people as a character on stage, you leave it there. You go home, and in a sense, turn it off. I find it nonsense to live as the character at home. The fact that I do what I do on stage can be a very cleansing thing as an actor.

Q How challenging was it for you doing *Sweeney Todd*?
Certainly from a musical point of view, it was a huge challenge for me vocally. But I went after it. I was coming from playing in classical repertory, doing Shakespeare, verse plays. I was in top-notch shape, physically, technically. But a singing voice is a different muscle. I worked with my singing teacher. I was going to give Mr. Sondheim two octaves, from a low G to a high G. And I worked until I could do it. We can do anything we set ourselves out to do.

Q Was the character as fully developed as you wanted it when you opened?
By the time the play is consumed by the audience, you do have to get it to a certain place; there is a very specific timetable. I had done Lear and Oedipus, so I had these roles in my quiver before *Sweeney Todd*, so taking him on seemed like a great marriage. And I also had to make this particular "grand guinol" style fresh eight times a week in *Sweeney Todd*. That was one of the proudest things for me over that period of time. We were borderline farce, Jacobean, blood and guts, walking a very tight line.

Angela (Lansbury) and I talked about it. We were most proud of keeping it fresh, of not going over the top. Without openly voicing it, we watched each other. It was a very narrow parameter; we couldn't go too far to the right or too far to the left. I had done two one-year runs before *Sweeney*, and I noticed something went strange eight or nine months into the run. I asked Ron Fields, the director of *Applause*, to watch what I was doing. He said, "I can't really see anything, it's a terrific performance, the only thing I can see is you're not listening as the character, you're listening as yourself." And that was it! So when I did *A Little Night Music*, I corrected myself.

Q What was the greatest challenge doing a one-man show?
The biggest thing is you're out there by yourself. When I did *Hemingway* and played William O. Douglas, I had to keep myself aware of the rhythm, the music of the piece, and moving it along. The audience gets ahead of you. Hemingway was pretty removed from the time I did him in, and Douglas was one of the most important people in our society, but nobody knew him as a person, just as a Supreme Court Justice.

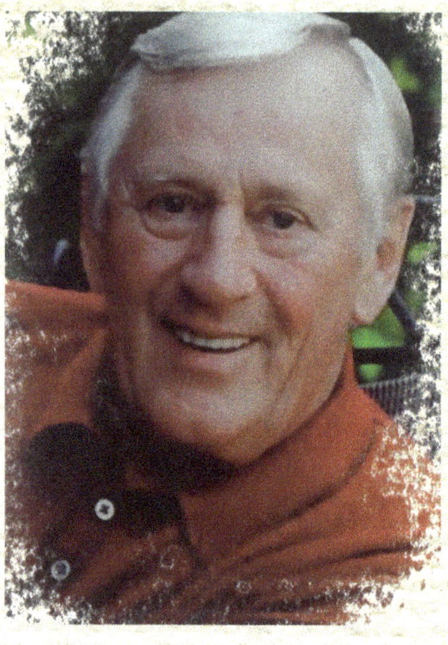

Len Cariou photo: courtesy of the artist

Q Do you act for the playwright, the audience, or yourself?
I think primarily for myself; I'm the one I have to satisfy. I want to use all my intelligence, all my gifts. Ultimately the playwright doesn't have a shot unless I do it right.

Q Has a character's passion ever overtaken you during a performance?
It doesn't happen that often. We're creatures of habit. Our discipline is to know exactly what we're doing every step of the way. But I've had those wonderfully exhilarating moments when you say, "Oh my God!" And you sit down and say to yourself, "I went someplace I've never been before. Now how will I do that again!" But once you start questioning yourself, asking "How?" you trip over yourself. The onus is on me to keep returning to the "well" for what I need—that's my job. ■

CAROL CHANNING

Ms. Channing created the role of Dolly Gallagher Levi in *Hello, Dolly!* on Broadway, receiving the Tony Award. She has performed in the musical more than five thousand times, both on Broadway and on the road. Her other memorable theatre includes receiving a Tony Award for her performance in *The Vamp*; *Show Girl*, receiving a Tony Award nomination; *The Millionairess*; as Lorelei Lee in *Gentlemen Prefer Blondes*; as Ruth Sherwood in *Wonderful Town*; *Lorelei*, receiving a Tony Award nomination; *Jerry's Girls*, *Legends*, and starred in the national tour of *Sugar Babies*. Ms. Channing's films and television includes *Thoroughly Modern Millie* with Julie Andrews, Mary Tyler Moore, and Beatrice Lillie, receiving a Golden Globe Award and an Academy Award nomination; *The First Traveling Saleslady* with Ginger Rogers and Clint Eastwood; *Alice in Wonderland*, *The Red Skelton Show*, and as Grandmama Adams in the animated version of *The Addams Family*. Ms. Channing has recorded ten gold albums, and the original cast album of *Hello Dolly!* topped the Beatles when it was released in 1964. She has received the Oscar Hammerstein Award, a star on the Hollywood Walk of Fame, Sarah Siddons Award, Oscar Hammerstein Award, and a Lifetime Achievement Tony Award. She was the first celebrity to perform in the *Super Bowl Halftime Show*. Her autobiography *Just Lucky I Guess* was published in 2002. A documentary about Ms. Channing, *Larger Than Life* was released in 2012. Ms. Channing was inducted into the American Theater Hall of Fame.

Q What did it mean to you when you were a presenter at the Tony Awards?
It was wonderful to be "back home" on the Tony Awards. I thought it was such an overwhelming show. And I went up the elevator with the Rockettes, can you imagine! Audra (MacDonald) won again! I gave her her first Tony for *Master Class*, and we've been friends ever since.

Q And you performed with LL Cool J—
Oh, he was so wonderful. Before we came out, he said to me backstage, "I'm going to give you a new name, it's 'C Low.'" We had this "rap bit" to do, and he told me, "The most important thing is for you to be relaxed. You don't have to remember the phrases. You be you and I'll be me." Rap is a whole language. During rehearsal he sang the rap with me and then we repeated it again together. He was so giving and generous.

Q You have certainly had a most amazing life.
I have a life in which I'm as happy as when I was twelve years old, I'm totally relaxed. When I was that age, I thought life would always be that happy, and it's back again. I'm so happy to wake up, to get started on the day.

Q You were very fortunate to have Gower Champion as your director on *Hello Dolly!*.
Absolutely! Gower had a talent for knowing just what had to be done, much in the same way Bob Mackie does it when he looks at Cher or Angela Lansbury. He sees the subject, he frames it, and then he can decorate it. Gower had that kind of talent. You just wanted to give yourself completely over to his ideas.

Hello Dolly! was originally going to be an intimate musical. There was only a chorus of four. But he took one look at it, and said, "We can't do it that way. Give me more waiters. The music has to be louder, the set has to be redder, the stairs have to be wider." And that's how it came to be.

Q How did you develop your character?
I found Dolly's "spine." I learned how to do it at Bennington College; I was taught the Stanislavsky Method. We were taught one had to find the spine for all the characters in the play. And when you discover it, all the characters come together. The spine was to rejoin the human race. I told Gower I had found it, and he saw it, too. The spine followed the plot; it raised the play.

Hello Dolly!'s not just about "production numbers" and "high kicks." Gower modulated the show, to allow Dolly to achieve her goal: to rejoin the human race. Isn't that something when you stop and think about it... isn't show biz thrilling!

Q And you played Dolly over five thousand times!
I have to tell you I never missed a show. Well, I did miss half a show, does that count? I had to do some shows in a wheelchair, and my right arm was in a sling for six months, my other arm was banged up, but I never missed those performances. I still went on. People must have thought it was an "interesting" way to play Dolly. I've had everything happen to me that could possibly happen.

Q You must also feel quite strongly about what happens between you and the audience?
Well that's why we're doing it! It's the "give and take" between the audience and the performer – it's a very healing experience. The audience gets excited and they give back to you. It heals, believe me! ■

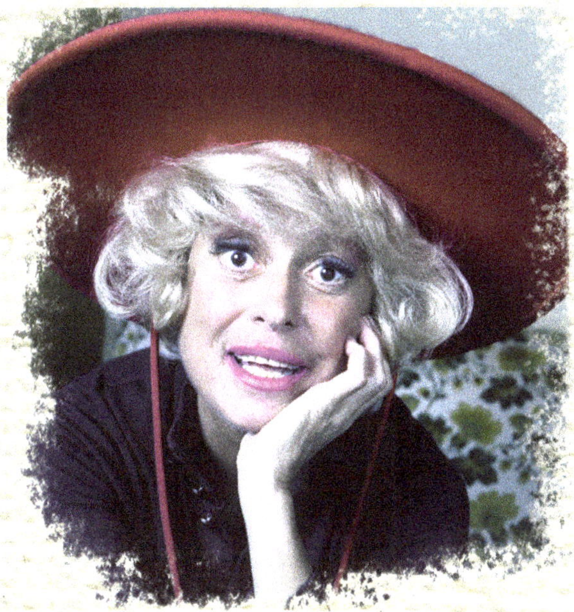

Carol Channing photo: Allan Warren, courtesy of Mr. Warren

TINA CHEN

A most gifted actress, director, composer and producer, Ms. Chen's films and television work includes *The Hawaiians* opposite Charlton Heston, for which she received a Golden Globe nomination; Arthur Penn's *Alice's Restaurant* opposite Arlo Guthrie; Sydney Pollack's *Three Days of the Condor* opposite Robert Redford; *Face* with Bai Ling; Albert M. Chan's *Descendants of the Past, Ancestors of the Future*, receiving New York City's Downtown Short Film Festival Best Actress Award; *Almost Perfect, Lady From Yesterday, The Ghost of Flight 401, The Potential Wives of Norman Mao*, narrated by George Takei, *The Streets of San Francisco, Kung Fu, The Tonight Show*, and *The Final War of Olly Winter*, for which she received an Emmy nomination. Ms. Chen has played several leading roles in productions on and Off Broadway, including in David Henry Hwang's *Family Devotions*, as the title role in *The Empress of China, The Love Suicide at Schofield Barracks, The Chang Fragments*, and *The Shanghai Gesture*. As a director, her work includes Lucy Liu's New York stage debut in *Fairy Bones, The Shining Queen, At A Plank Bridge*, and *Yin Chin Bow*. On Broadway, Ms. Chen also co-produced Peter Nichols' *Passion* starring Frank Langella, and *The Rink* starring Chita Rivera and Liza Minnelli, for which she received a Drama Desk nomination as part of the producing team. A gifted songwriter, she wrote the music for the song, "This Tree," with lyrics by Ruth Wolff, which premiered with the Hong Kong Children's Choir at its Silver Jubilee. Ms. Chen has delivered a lecture entitled, *Heroes of History: Legacy of My Chinese Family* to audiences across America. Ms. Chen has received Urban Stages' 25th anniversary award for Artistic Brilliance, the Women's Project's Women of Achievement Award, the Anna May Wong Award of Excellence and Pan Asian Repertory Theatre's Legacy Award. Ms. Chen volunteers for the Lighthouse Guild as a reader for the sight-impaired.

Q You began your study of acting with Sanford Meisner.

He was an amazing teacher. He taught me the essence of acting: "Acting is living truthfully in an imaginary circumstance." I will always remember an exercise from one of my first classes with him. We had to pick a word and repeat it over and over with a partner. After two or three minutes of this, I was surprised to find how many different ways, and with how many different feelings one word could be spoken. He was tremendous for my growth as an actress.

Q What roles have been the most rewarding?

I was fortunate as a young actress to play a very rewarding character opposite Charlton Heston in *The Hawaiians*. In the film my character aged from a teenager to an old matriarch!

The title role in the play *The Empress of China* stands out for me. The character was so different from me. To inhabit her and understand her, to make her believable and sympathetic was a wonderful challenge. She was ruthless and endlessly calculating, but she had to rule China, especially as a woman.

Q How are you able to get inside the characters you've played?

It's hard to articulate because it feels intuitive. I guess that's why I'm an actor! It's innate in me, as it is for many actors, to know how to inhabit someone you create from a script, to make it all your own. I do plenty of research on a role, the period of time. I try to be as open and receptive as I can be. I take chances and let the character blossom in ways that often surprise me. When I'm on stage acting, I become the person I'm playing. And I'm also able to switch it off when I finish.

Q What has it meant for your creativity performing and directing with the Pan Asian Repertory Theatre in New York City?

It's been immeasurable. Tisa Chang has given Asian American theatre artists an incredible, and much-needed gift. I've played some fantastic parts—from the title role of the Empress of China to Ying-Ying in *The Joy Luck Club*. Tisa also gave me my first opportunity to direct, and I'll forever be grateful that she took a chance on me. The play was Lawrence Yep's *Fairy Bones*, and I directed a young actress named Lucy Liu in her New York stage debut.

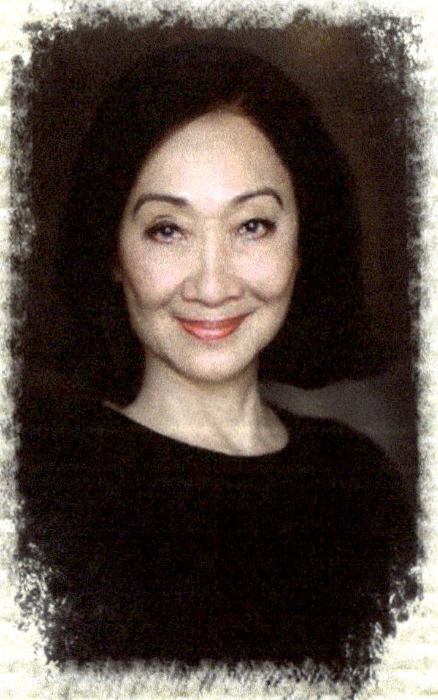

Tina Chen photo: courtesy of the artist

Q Your portrayal of Ying-Ying in *The Joy Luck Club* was a joy, especially how you brought out so many rich colors in the way you played her.

Thank you very much. Coming from you that means a great deal. She's a very complex character; someone I don't naturally identify with because she was a passive fatalist. But that's what made it such a rewarding challenge—to decide how to play her. In the play, Ying Ying finally woke up to help her daughter come alive and be strong. Once I had the time to get inside who Ying-Ying was, I found I admired what she was able to do for herself and for her daughter.

Q How rewarding is directing for you?

I love it. As an actor who has worked with many directors with very different styles, I like to think I know what works from an actor's perspective—how important it is to create the right environment for my cast and crew. I love stepping back and figuring out my vision for the play, and figuring out how to implement it. It's like conducting an orchestra; something I've never done but imagine myself doing. My family has always said I was born to be a director.

Q You're also a successful composer of several songs including "This Tree," which premiered with the Hong Kong Children's Choir.

I've always loved music. Ever since I was a child, I've heard melodies in my head. I would compose and play my own little pieces on the piano. When I was a teenager, I wrote a song called "Mother Life," a reflection of my struggles to choose between a "respectable" career as a scientist or the life of an actor. I've always been fascinated by science, and worked at the New York Blood Center's Serology and Genetics department for over thirteen years. I've also scored a flute piece for a Pan Asian Repertory production, and wrote a Hanukkah song, "Eight Nights." The lyrics are by my daughter, Yi Ling Chen-Josephson. I'm also currently writing a musical.

Q In your Lecture, *Heroes of History: Legacy of My Chinese Family*, you tell about the three generations of your mother's family and their extraordinary contributions to Chinese history. When did you first learn about your family history?

The Chinese are taught to be humble so no one at home ever mentioned my family's accomplishments. My first awareness of my maternal family's status was when I was six years old, when we moved to Taipei, Taiwan. My uncle was Chen Cheng, and the Vice President to Chiang Kai-shek.

During one official parade, our family was invited to be on the reviewing stand with the President and Vice President at the immense Presidential Building complex. I was lifted up by my father to see the tens of thousands of people gathered below. One of my favorite childhood memories was sitting on Madame Chang Kai-shek's lap, picking a dessert from a beautiful table.

My great grandfather, Tan Zhong-Lin, was Governor General of seven provinces under three emperors and one empress in the Ching dynasty. My grandfather, Tan Yen-Kai, supported Sun Yat-Sen who overthrew the Emperor's regime. After Sun Yat-Sen's early death, my grandfather became the first Premier of the first Republic of China. He was a great man who was ahead of his time. At a time when few women in China were educated at all, he sent his daughter—my mother, Tann Yuin—to Cambridge University in the UK for college.

A number of the members of the Tan family were also noted calligraphers. I have always felt a deep responsibility to follow in my forebears' footsteps; to use my talents as fully as possible.

Q How do you keep yourself growing as an artist?

I'm lucky to live in New York City. I'm always working on a new project, and have two or three in the works at the same time. I go to many concerts, operas, shows, plays, museums, lectures as I can. I think it's critical that I'm not afraid of failing; I'm always willing to attempt something new. So what if I'm not good at it! That's okay. At least I'll always know I gave it a try. ■

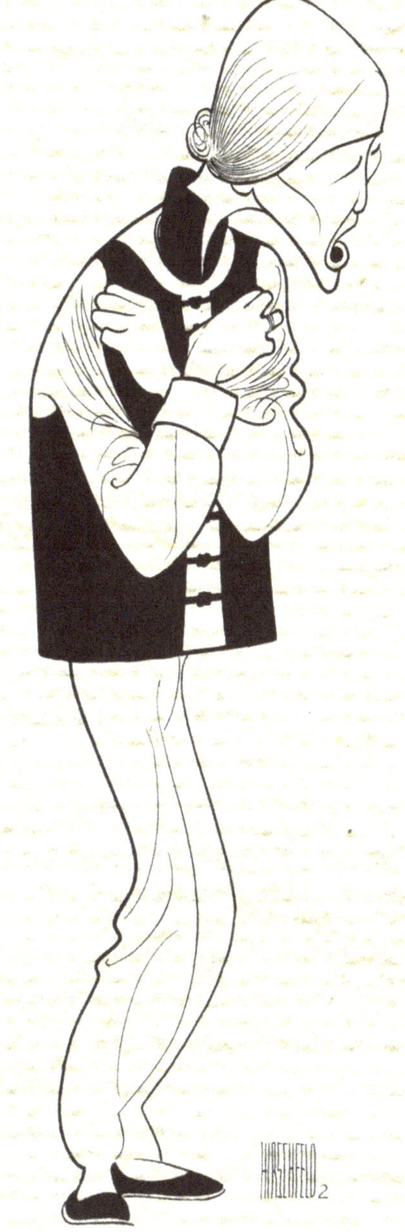

Tina Chen in "Family Devotions" by Al Hirschfeld © The Al Hirschfeld Foundation. www.AlHirschfeldFoundation.org

BRIAN COX

Mr. Cox's many stage roles include as a member of the Royal Shakespeare Company and London's National Theatre during the 1980s and 1990s in the lead role in *Titus Andronicus*, Petruchio in *The Taming of the Shrew*, as Burgundy opposite Sir Laurence Olivier in *King Lear*, and as *King Lear* at the National Theatre. He also played Inspector Nelson in *Rat in the Skull*, receiving the Laurence Olivier Award as Best Actor; on Broadway in *The Championship Season*; and in *The Weir* at The Donmar Theatre and Wyndham's Theatre. He began as a member of Edinburgh's Lyceum company, and the Birmingham Rep where he played the lead role in *Peer Gynt*, and Orlando in *As You Like It*. Mr. Cox's television and films include: as Sir Winston Churchill in Jonathan Teplitzky's film, *Churchill*, as Henry II in *The Devil Crown, War and Peace, The Prisoner*, as Leon Trotsky in *Nicholas and Alexandra, The Lost Language of Cranes*; as Hermann Goring in *Nuremberg*, receiving an Emmy award, Golden Globe and SAG nominations; *Frasier*, receiving an Emmy nomination; *L.I.E.*, receiving several awards including the National Society of Film Critics Award, and the NY Film Critics Award; as Jack Langrishe in *Deadwood*, receiving an Emmy nomination; *Zodiac, Doctor Who, Rob Roy, Braveheart; Adaptation*, receiving a SAG nomination; *The Ring, X2, The Bourne Supremacy, Red, Chain Reaction, Super Troopers, The Escapist, The Day of the Triffids*, and *Rise of the Planet of the Apes*. Mr. Cox has narrated several audiobooks including *Ivanhoe*, J.R.R. Tolkien's *The Silmarillion*, and *The Legend of Sigurd and Gudrun*. He was elected as Rector of the University of Dundee, and is an "Ambassador" for the Screen Academy Scotland. He received the Bradford International Film Festival Lifetime Achievement Award. Mr. Cox was appointed a Commander of the Order of the British Empire.

Q Why did you want to play Vladimir in *Waiting for Godot* at this point in your career?

I suppose the appeal of *Waiting for Godot* is that the play deals with the most fundamental issues of the human condition. A narrative unfolding within the premise of: for "Who, Why and What" are we waiting?

A profound questioning of humanity's purpose seen through the eyes of two travelling itinerant figures seemingly locked in a wilderness landscape, each encompassing the polarities of optimism and pessimism. Further polarized by the arrival of an archetypal master/servant duo, whose complex relationship undermines any notions of equanimity, which only exacerbates our duos' already questioning state. Questioning in a sometimes hilarious, sometimes poetic manner the validity of their lives.

The play from the actors' point of view made extraordinary demands on the range of my individual skills and demanded nightly a huge leap into the unknown. It is by far and away the most demanding play I've ever performed. For me, at this stage in my career, there can be no more profound resonance than the embracing of such a master as Samuel Beckett.

Q Did you have a desire early in your life to go into the theater?

I suppose my first experience of theater was as a small child aged about two, when my father put me on top of the coal bunker, in the window recess of our tenement apartment, in my home town of Dundee. At that ripe old age of two, I would perform to much applause the repertoire of Al Jolson with full actions and mimicry. I think this probably was my first taste of theatrical desire.

But honestly, I really can't remember a time when I didn't want be involved in some form of performance. The cinema was a huge influence on me as a child, and I suppose ultimately led to my desire to become an actor. I didn't experience the live theater till I was about fourteen. Then my desire was confirmed. From then, there was no looking back.

Q Who were some of the important inspirations for you when you began working?

I can consider myself incredibly lucky in the range of incredible directors, actors, and teachers who have inspired and mentored me throughout my career.

It was at The Royal Lyceum Theatre that I met my lifetime mentor—the Scottish actor Futon MacKay. A man of great insight and perspicacity, who always reminded me of the tremendous respect that is needed for the art and craft of acting. He used to say of my ambition, in his rooted Scottish vernacular, "Dinnae (Don't) worry about being a star, Brian. Just say your prayers and be a good actor." To this day it's the best advice I've ever had.

The great Lindsay Anderson and his great acting note to me in my debut at London's Royal Court Theatre in David Storey's family drama, *In Celebration*. He said. "Brian, don't just do something! Stand there!"

Michael Eliot, co-founder of The Royal Exchange Theatre in Manchester, a director of impeccable integrity and vision. He opened me up to the works of Ibsen with a zealot-like religious fervor which never failed to inspire to the highest degree.

Q Among the herculean roles you've assayed include Titus Andronicus and Petruchio, Burgundy opposite Sir Laurence Olivier as King Lear. Then you played King Lear at the National Theatre in London. How did these roles test your mettle and what did you discover about your craft?

As a result of my working partnership with Deborah Warner on *Titus Andronicus* and *King Lear*, I took a lot of risks in the creation of both roles. Risks involving a much deeper and profound sense of physical freedom. Creating a greater range in performance.

To be fair, the renaissance in my acting began six years before Deborah and I worked together. I was playing in *Macbeth* in India. A production that had begun at The Arts Theatre in Cambridge. When

I reached Bombay, a sixteen-year-old Katak dancer was assigned as my dresser. At every performance she would stand in the wings watching, nay, scrutinizing my performance. After the second matinee she approached me.

"Mr. Cox," she said, "may I say something about your acting?" I was taken aback, "Of course."

"When I watch you on stage, I feel you want to go further than you allow yourself. I feel you want to dance when you act. Your voice wants your body to move. To make the same movements in the air your wonderful voice makes."

I was shocked because she was searingly accurate in her observation. For years I had felt there was a barrier to achieving what I wanted to achieve as an actor. But I didn't know what that barrier was. From then on, at every performance, I had her observe and make notes for me. To the point where in Macbeth's "dagger" speech, I was virtually crawling all over the stage. And at every performance she would tell me to go further. Acting is a skill that you never ever stop learning and refining.

By the time I came to play Titus Andronicus, I was ripe to move into a whole new territory. This was a play that had defeated many actors over the years. Peter Brook had done a memorable production with Laurence Olivier in the mid-1950s. It was a production of inordinate depth.

The Titus of myself and Deborah was very much the product of a post-Becketian age, when a new mask has entered the arena of the theater. The mask of the ludicrous. In *Titus*, it is Shakespeare's embracing of the extremes of Titus's suffering that gives the play its extraordinary dimension and themes such as: grief, aging, madness, jealousy, self-obsession, treachery, self-righteousness. Of course, for the actor, it's a tremendous gift. Consequently, when I came to play Lear, Titus had already prepared me for the tragic path of the doomed and disillusioned King.

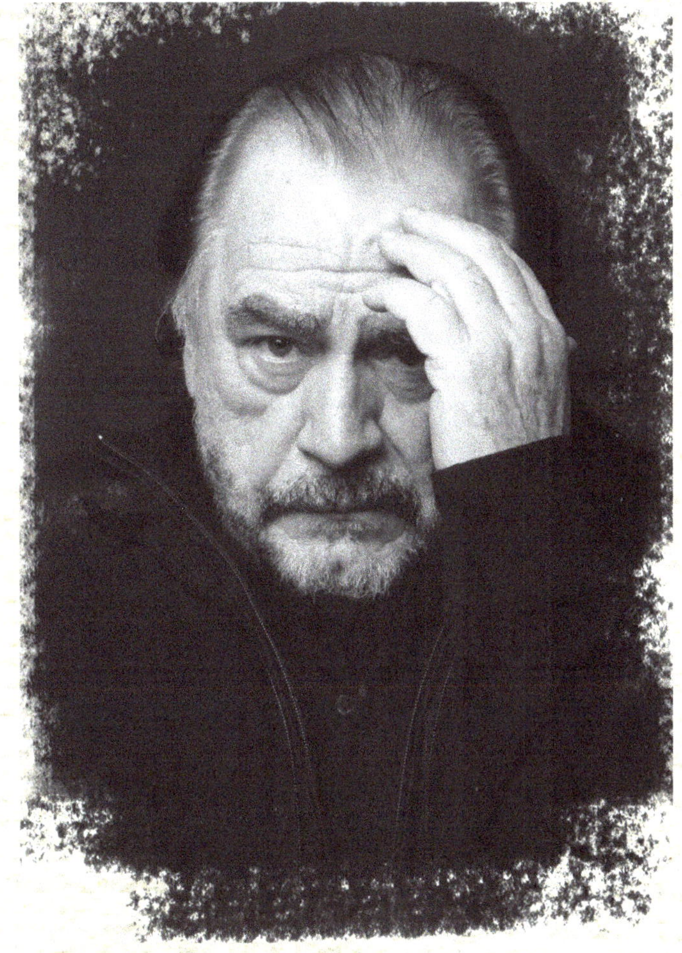

Brian Cox photo: courtesy of the artist

Q You have also created many memorable performances on screen. What led you to want to perform in film?

In the late 1990s, after performing in and out of theater for over thirty years, I decided it was time to professionally revisit my first love...cinema. In my home town of Dundee in Scotland when I was a boy, there were as many as twenty-one cinemas and between the ages of six and eleven I had visited every one.

The range of American Cinema was astonishing—the zany Marx Brothers comedies to Preston Sturges, the westerns of John Ford through Anthony Mann and John Sturges. The "noire" of Howard Hawks through John Huston, from Elia Kazan to Sydney Pollack. The advent of CinemaScope, Vista-Vision, and Cinerama. To be a child at such a time was a joy, and the cinema was the temple of that joy.

I made my first film in 1971, *Nicholas and Alexandra*, in which I played Trotsky, then *In Celebration* by the great Lindsay Anderson in the mid-1970s. I worked between theater and television until 1985, when I made a dual appearance in New York City in O'Neill's' *Strange Interlude* on Broadway, then at the Public Theatre in *Rat in the Skull*, and The Royal Court Theatre in London. From this, I was cast as Hannibal Lector in the film, *Manhunter*. This in turn led to many doors being opened for me in Hollywood. I was almost fifty when I made that decision.

Q I saw Jason Robards, Jr. in *That Championship Season*, and was fortunate to see your performance on Broadway in a revival of the play. What drew you to want to play the role of the coach?

For me, *That Championship Season* is one of the great American plays of the twentieth century because it tackles through a sporting metaphor the great archetype of "The American Dream." The great fear, that is surprising—central to American life—is not living up to expectations and the misery it creates in the American psyche: the pressure of too much early promise, and the deception that all too often goes with that promise. The play surgically examines it in great detail in a tremendously humanist fashion. The character of "The Coach," which I played, is in himself the false prophet of a better life to come. A great role in a great play.

Q You also acted in the TV series, *Deadwood*, with your wife, Nicole Ansari. I also saw you both in Tom Stoppard's *Roll 'n Roll* on Broadway, and I was fortunate to work opposite her in *Hamlet*. What has it meant for your life and work having Ms. Ansari as your partner and wife?

I regard myself incredibly lucky to have Nicole as my partner. Not just because she is a very loving, honest, caring, and empowering person, but also because she is a phenomenal artist. Both as an actor, and as a great discerner of talent—we're so much on the same page. In my life I have never been involved with someone so astute about their craft.

Q Why do you love Shakespeare as much as you do?

You simply can't get around Shakespeare. His writing covers the entire human experience. I was once in a production of a Shakespeare play. I won't say which one but I was very unhappy in it; I was committed to quite a long run of this play.

After my initial misery I decided that I would work through my unhappiness by a detailed study of the play. I compared it to doing a marathon run and that moment when you hit the wall and break through to a new energy. My understanding of the flaws in the production of course created bias. So I had to rise beyond bias to a more open understanding of the play's dramatic potential. This production had created in me an intense dislike for the play.

So as I was performing, I kept re-envisioning the play in a myriad of settings and scenarios, coming to the conclusion that the play's power superseded any inadequate production. As Hamlet so rightly says: "The play's the thing...." The circle was completed, when four years later, I directed this very same play to much success and satisfaction. The level of satisfaction in a fine production by this extraordinary playwright can be, at times, beyond words. ■

OSSIE DAVIS

In a celebrated acting career spanning eight decades, Mr. Davis began as a writer and actor with the Rose McClendon Players in Harlem in 1939. His Broadway appearances include *Jeb, Anna Lucasta, The Wisteria Trees, Green Pastures, Jamaica, The Zulu and the Zayda, I'm Not Rappaport*, and he wrote and starred in *Purlie* in 1961. His film and television appearances include with Sidney Poitier in *No Way Out, The Cardinal, I'm Not Rappaport, Twelve Angry Men, Do the Right Thing, Jungle Fever* and *Get on the Bus, Roots: The Next Generation*, Alex Haley's *Queen*, and he received Emmy nominations for *Teacher, Teacher, King*, and *Miss Evers' Boys*. He wrote *For Us the Living*, receiving the Neil Simon Jury Award, and with his wife, Ruby Dee, co-produced *With Ossie and Ruby*. As a director his films included *Cotton Comes to Harlem, Gordon's War*, and *Black Girl*. His books included *Escape to Freedom, Langston, Just Like Martin*, and he marked his 50th wedding anniversary to Ruby Dee with their joint autobiography, *With Ossie and Ruby: In This Life Together*. He received the NY Urban League Frederick Douglass Award, and he and his wife were named to the NAACP Image Award Hall of Fame, awarded the National Medal of Arts, and received the Kennedy Center Honors. He was inducted into the Theater Hall of Fame in 1994. Mr. Davis died in 2005 (this interview was conducted in 2003).

Q What drove you to write *A Last Dance for Sybil*, which Ruby Dee starred in?

I began to write this play originally in the 1960s. The questions I was writing about were before the black community. We didn't want segregation, we wanted integration. But we needed to ask ourselves: What do we mean by integration? Suppose we got integrated with organizations or companies or individuals that hold policies that we don't agree with—who should we be loyal to? It was not an abstract question in the black community, for our culture. It was a big debate. What would we be giving up by joining? What would we lose? And at what expense to who we were? Where does one put one's loyalties?

This play was a way to dramatize the debate. In a sense, because of the theater's natural geography—the life of the moment happening on the stage, and the people having a relationship to it in the audience, that geography provided the objectivity. Ruby, my wife and partner, was the leading lady and I was fortunate enough to have her share with me what she saw from an entirely different perspective.

Q You and Ms. Dee continue to have a most unique marriage and partnership, for over fifty years, which must naturally spur both of you forwards.

We have always been involved on stage and off in very important activities that required action on our part. Even while we may have been dealing with intense pressures of our own personal lives or our careers, because we were so involved in more important things than our own lives, we never thought about "being happy"—we were always on the run.

From my days in the army during World War II, the com-

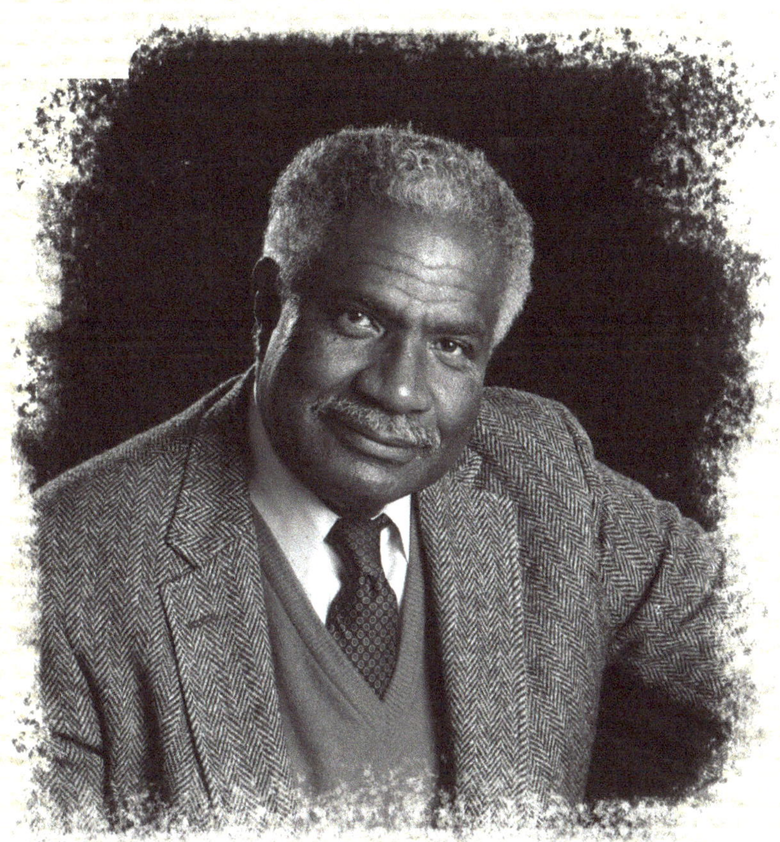

Ossie Davis photo: Davis Freeman

radeship between all of us in the company, knowing these guys had my back and I had theirs—that we had this bond let us know that we would fight to the death for each other. Ruby and I are like two soldiers, we share that kind of bond. And it's just as important as the marriage bond, the sexual bond, or becoming parents and having children. I know she'll watch my back, and I'll watch hers; we've learned to complement each other.

When we married in 1948, we were both fairly well-known. We did a national tour across the country, acted in films in Hollywood. We both acted in the first film Sidney Poitier made. New interest was being shown in the black performer at that time. And we expected there'd always be jobs for us not only on Broadway; theater was one of the first places to be integrated. But things turned out differently—the jobs weren't so forthcoming.

So to survive we began performing for black audiences at high schools, colleges, in churches, labor unions, theatrical settings. And we cultivated that audience over the years, applying all our craft and techniques as performers. It was the main reason we created our story-telling.

Q What impact did creating *Purlie Victorious* have upon your growth?

Purlie was the best thing I have ever done. At that time, I was working as the stage manager on *The World of Sholom Aleichem*, and Ruby was on stage in the play. I found time to begin writing. I wrote it sharp, bitter, angry, all about my experiences growing up as a boy in Georgia, all the racist things that went on. And I began to let all these passions flow onto the page. Well, when I read the play when I finished, it was so overboard I had to laugh. "Had it all been so bad?" I asked myself, "How did we survive?"

And little by little as I worked on it, this hot diatribe became a comedy. I became influenced from what I had watched on stage—the Yiddish comedy about Jewish life. *Purlie* allowed me to ultimately open up and fly. To do anything. All the fruits of freedom were handed to me. It was most rewarding.

Q How would you describe your reaction to what's happening today in the theater?

When I came into this business, there was passion and determination by the writers to produce new plays which explored new ways of looking at human beings. There were important artists like Paul Robeson, Canada Lee, and Lena Horne, who even in the face of segregation and hardship, expressed the human spirit. They were not only artists but activists. That's the kind of people they were. I was reared in that kind of political environment.

Now what has happened today? Little by little, the theater has drifted away from challenging us with what's important today. There needs to be more substance in what's being shown. Something is robbing us of our experience. I look, but I don't feel. I see, but I'm not touched.

We need again to see "larger than life" human beings clashing over big ideas, a sense of wonder in the work, of magnificence. That the life we're touching is human. That what we're writing about or portraying is throbbing, pleading life. We need to find our way back to the beginning of the human life.

Ruby and I have devoted our lives to telling human stories. And that's our function—yours and mine—to create humanity and to make it human. We've got to do it. We have no other choice. ■

RUBY DEE

Best known for originating the role of "Ruth Younger" in the stage and film versions of *A Raisin in the Sun* opposite Sidney Poitier, Ms. Dee received an Academy Award nomination and a Screen Actors Guild Award for the film, *American Gangster*. Her notable stage roles on Broadway and across America included *Anna Lucasta, A Long Way from Home, Purlie Victorious, Oresteia, Boesman and Lena, Hamlet, Zora is my Name, Checkmates, The Glass Menagerie, My One Good Nerve: A Visit with Ruby Dee, A Last Dance for Sybil,* and *Saint Lucy's Eyes*. Ms. Dee performed in lead roles at the American Shakespeare Festival as Kate in *Taming of the Shrew*, and Cordelia in *King Lear*, becoming the first black actress to portray a lead role in the festival. Her film work included *The Jackie Robinson Story, St. Louis Blues, Buck and the Preacher, Do the Right Thing, Jungle Fever,* and *A Thousand Words* opposite Eddie Murphy. Her television work included *I Know Why the Caged Bird Sings, Long Day's Journey into Night, Go Tell it to the Mountain, Gore Vidal's Lincoln, Having Our Say: The Delany Sisters First 100 Years,* and *Their Eyes Were Watching God*. She was an Emmy, Obie and Drama Desk winner. Ms. Dee also received a National Medal of Arts, Kennedy Center Honors, SAG Life Achievement Award, and was inducted into the NAACP Image Awards Hall of Fame and the Theatre Hall of Fame. She received the Grammy Award with Ossie Davis, the noted actor and her husband, for *With Ossie and Ruby: In This Life Together*. Ms. Dee and Mr. Davis were well-known civil rights activists. She was awarded—along with her late husband—the Lifetime Achievement Freedom Award, presented by the National Civil Rights Museum. Ms. Dee died in 2014 (this interview was conducted in 2002).

Q We continue dealing with finding ways to cope with everything going on, while continuing with our lives. What can the artist do at such a time?
One of the functions of the artist is to put our times into perspective, into context. The artist puts a divine spin on things, carrying us beyond where the five senses take us. I see there's all this unfinished business following us, through the spiritual growth of man. All these things are part of the long arc of history.

Here we are on this same planet, let us share. Let's not take what's not ours. If you wrong someone, make it right. We have to be patient with each other. There's always been a cost, a sacrifice with freedom. We have to stand back and look at ourselves. History has chosen us, at this time and place, in terms of aspirations. We do have a blueprint to get along, at least to begin it—the Bill of Rights, the Constitution. We have things that speak about how we should live with one another as human beings on this earth. I believe we have much to show the world. As God's children, we have to ask each other: How do we protect each other and love?

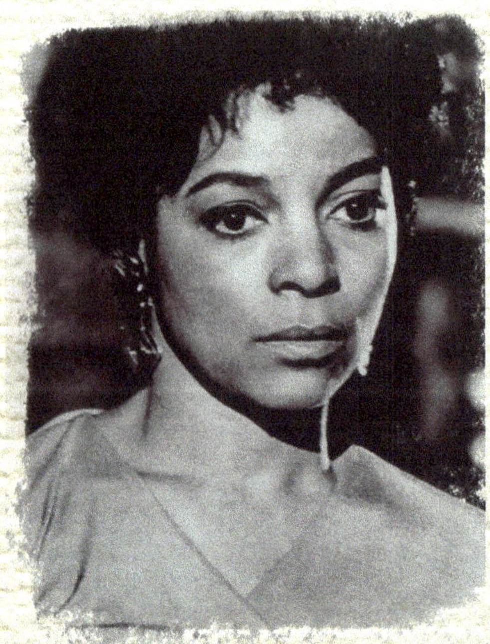

Q It was a great delight to experience your memorable performance in *Saint Lucy's Eyes*. What drew you to the play?
We're wrestling with so many things today we've never considered before. Abortion is one of those contentions. We're hearing all these discussions about stem cell research. One thing we need to realize is that God created an abundance of nature. It's people who cause scarcities. We're not endangered species. *Saint Lucy* dealt with second chances and forgiveness. It intrigued me because it dealt with the human condition.

Q You made history by being the first black woman to play lead roles at the American Shakespeare Festival. Have there been roles that presented such unique challenges that you wanted to keep working on them?
Gertrude, Hamlet's mother, was one. Sam Waterston played Hamlet, and for some reason it didn't click as well as I would have liked. With playing Mother Abigail in *The Stand*, the project was so big I just didn't have the time I needed. I wanted to encompass it, to let the role move into me, to get into the soul of it. Once that happens a role takes off. I felt that happened with Mary Tyrone in *Long Day's Journey into Night*, and all the others.

Q One of the delights audiences had was seeing your solo performance in *My One Good Nerve*.
I enjoyed performing it. It was a wonderful opportunity to pay homage to the ideas, to the language. It's a privilege to share the words and ideas, as they paint the time, like an artist with a brush, with the words as fluid as oil paint on a canvas. It comes from the knowledge of having absorbed everything, from my parents, my teachers, from history. I feel every sentence I say has its only little bit of information, and this stream feeds you.

You're never just saying words, it's what you're doing with them. It's a thrilling vocation, being a solo artist, through which doors fly open. And you let the subtleties, the music flow through you. You become the master of the ship by filling these words with the realities and the spirit they require. It's more than you who speaks. These ideas speak through you to live for others. ■

Ruby Dee artwork: Ruby Dee

RONALD RAND

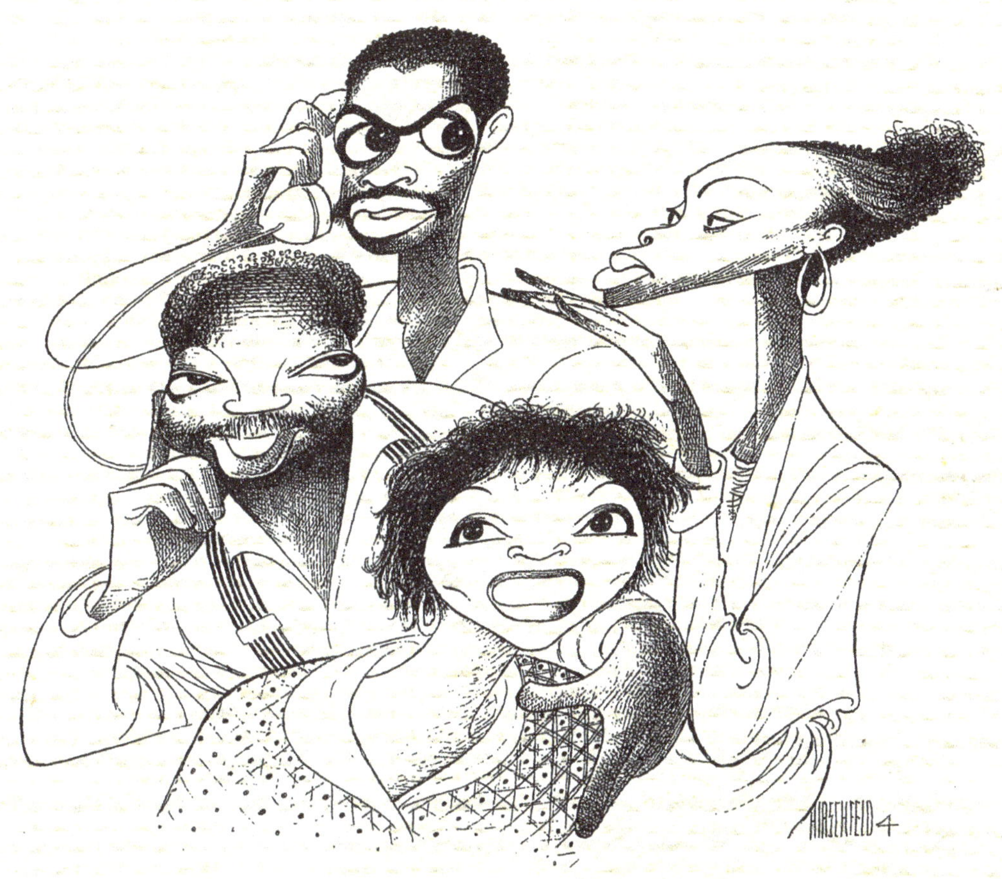

Ruby Dee, Denzel Washington, Paul Winfield and Martha Jackson in the Broadway production of "Checkmates" by Al Hirschfeld © The Al Hirschfeld Foundation. www.AlHirschfeldFoundation.org

ANDRÉ DE SHIELDS

In a career spanning forty-seven years, André De Shields has distinguished himself as an actor, director, choreographer, and educator. Mr. De Shields is best known for his performances in six Broadway productions: *Impressionism*, co-starring with Jeremy Irons and Joan Allen; the world premiere of Mark Medoff's *Prymate*, receiving a Drama Desk nomination; *The Full Monty*, receiving Tony, Drama Desk, and Astaire Award nominations, Outer Critics Circle and Drama League Awards; *Play On!* receiving a Tony nomination; *Ain't Misbehavin'*, receiving a Drama Desk nomination; and the title role in the musical, *The Wiz*. Mr. De Shields is an esteemed alumnus of the University of Wisconsin-Madison, 2004 Doctor of Fine Arts *honoris causa*, New York University's Gallatin School of Individualized Study. His numerous accolades include a second honorary Doctor of Fine Arts—SUNY-Buffalo State, an Obie award for Sustained Excellence of Performance, National Black Theatre Festival's Living Legend Award, a Fox Foundation Fellowship, Florida Atlantic University's Making Waves Award, the Theatre School at DePaul University Award for Excellence in the Arts, Riant Theatre's Pioneer of the Arts Award, three Chicago Joseph Jefferson Awards, and nine Audelco Awards. A triple Capricorn, Mr. De Shields is the ninth of eleven children, born and reared in Baltimore, Maryland (this interview was conducted with Mr. De Shields in 1999, when he served as Chair of Equity's Committee for Racial Equality). Ubuntu! I am because you are!

Q **You wrote an inspiring essay for Equity News: "Setting the Record Straight—Celebrating Duke Ellington," heralding his gigantic contribution and the influence of African American musicians from Bessie Smith to Lauryn Hill. In this age of synthesized computer-generated sound, how can a performer remain pure to their original vision?**

The age of technology, its influence, and way of informing theater do not surprise me. A perfect example was the production of *Closer* on Broadway which filled the stage duplicating a computer screen. Technology is the fastest growing art form. You can see the example of morphing in films and it's making that kind of effect in the theater. All my experience, all my feelings on the threshold of the 21st Century, indicates a new era when we'll feel much more at home communicating without seeing our partner. Old paradigms are no longer applicable. We've reached the point where the audience wants to come for an instant response. They've put their money down and, since the common denominator is technology, they expect the same in the theater.

Now theater is unique because it still demands the discipline of "You've got to go through this," not under it or around it. You've got to go through the four hours of *The Iceman Cometh*. The thrust of my article was to remind us of the invaluable contribution to world culture of Afro-centric personalities. It's long been associated with ancestor worship. It isn't as sophisticated as dogmatic religion, but it's part of our nation. We remain strangers in a strange world. It's no surprise we're still a splintered culture.

We have the responsibility to understand that those who existed before us are our soul, our essences. We have to revere the "God in everything, in a blade of grass, in a current of water, in a cloud." It's silly to think we can't communicate with a world of invisible spirits, it's a matter of being awake or asleep. Theater is a temple. If we could get back to this approach, then we'd have a more complex, intimate, intricate, truly fulfilling theater, which excludes no one.

But no theater will exist if there isn't an audience for it. Crossroads Theatre received a Tony for making exceptional theatre but it's an exception. To express the Afro-centric point of view of what's happening in this country requires a literate nation, the cultural discipline of going to the theatre. In the 1960s there were forty Black theaters alone resonating the theatre as a tool for resolving political and social concerns. We must graduate to the notion that the theater is necessary to the pursuit of happiness. "We hold these truths to be self-evident…"

Q What roles have allowed you to soar the most?

I'm blessed I haven't done any role that hasn't allowed me to soar, including the roles I had in *The Wiz*, *Ain't Misbehavin'*, and *Play On!* I've been able to become a master of "horizontal evolution." I subscribe to color-blind casting: for us to go into the canon of Shakespeare and rediscover these heroes from the other side of the color line.

When I performed as Willy Loman in *Death of a Salesman*, I had a white son in the play and my wife, Linda was white. What I did was tackle this universal experience and render it entirely universal, the audience of color

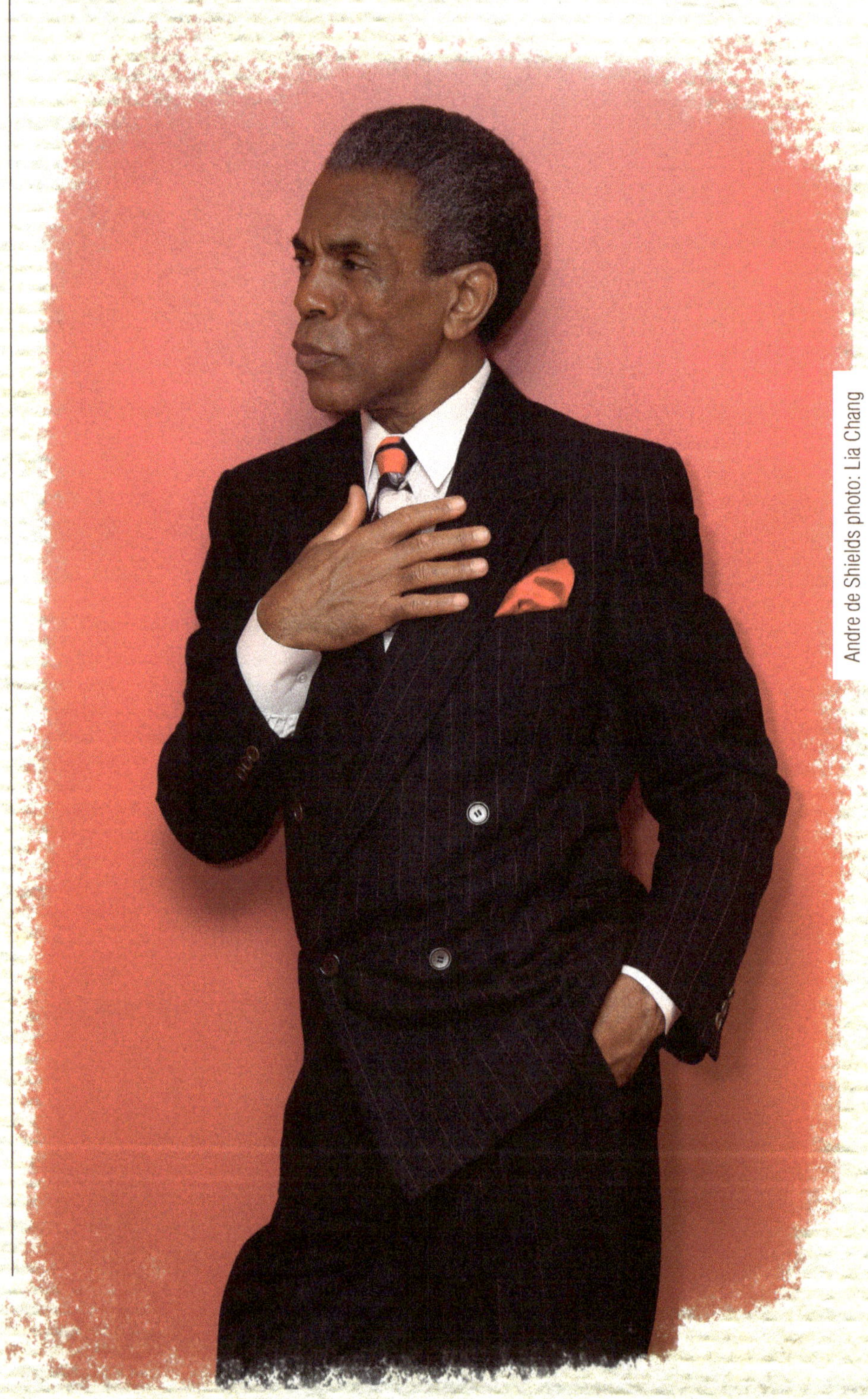

Andre de Shields photo: Lia Chang

were astonished. God is in the archetype; he is also in the stereotype. It's the diversity of experience that's part of the American dream.

Paul Robeson was one of our greatest artists who never stopped fighting for human dignity—because he understood the role of an artist as activist. He made his choices early in his life. He said an artist must fight for freedom. He was eternally a principled human being, an ethical politician, and a concerned artist. He was no saint, but he embraced his past without shame and without guilt. We're dealing with a generation that wants to obscure the past.

It's our responsibility to heal the wounds caused by America's historical racial divide. There needs to be racial healing in this country. We, as a nation, have to realize we're missing the power of our heritage. But the playwright can change this. They have the power to express America's multi-cultural society. We no longer need to accept the automatic separation of culture. I say—"put America on stage."

Q What keeps you creating and challenging yourself as a performer?
I'm a man of complex human emotions, and I can do more than sing my "money note" or do a split. Theater offers a greater opportunity to "exorcise my demons." It gives me the opportunity to express myself and invest myself in the lifetime of a character—I find it liberating as a human being. ■

OLYMPIA DUKAKIS

Ms. Dukakis began her illustrious career in the theater, receiving an Obie Award in 1963 for her performance Off-Broadway in Brecht's *Man Equals Man*. On Broadway she has starred in a one-woman play, *Rose*, *Who's Who in Hell*, and *Social Security*. Ms. Dukakis' film and television appearances include *Steel Magnolias*; *Moonstruck*, receiving an Academy Award, Golden Globe Award, LA Film Critics Association Award, and several other awards; in *Sinatra*, receiving a Golden Globe Award nomination; *Mr. Holland's Opus*; *The Cemetery Club*; *Cloudburst*, receiving a Seattle International Film Festival Award nomination; as Charlotte Kiszko in *A Life for a Life*; *The Event*, receiving a Genie Award nomination; *In the Land of Women*; *Mighty Aphrodite*; *Joan of Arc*, receiving an Emmy Award nomination; *Jane Austen's Mafia!*; as Anna Madrigal in *More Tales of the City*, receiving an Emmy Award; and starred in and executive-produced *Montana Amazon*. She directed the world premiere production of Todd Logan's *Botanic Garden* at Victory Gardens Theatre in Chicago. Ms. Dukakis appeared in the revival of Tennessee Williams' *The Milk Train Doesn't Stop Here Anymore* opposite Kevin Anderson at Hartford Stage. She also co-adapted and starred in the world-premiere of *Another Side of the Island*, at Alpine Theatre Project in Whitefish, Montana. Ms. Dukakis wrote her best-selling autobiography, *Ask Me Again Tomorrow: A Life in Progress* in 2003.

Q Why did you create the Whole Theatre Company in Montclair, New Jersey, which continued for nineteen years?
It allowed me to hang onto the continuity of my work. It also gave me a community, not only with other actors but with directors, set designers, and the audience. I got to feel they were a part of my life; I was a part of their lives, and the lives of their children, because they'd bring their children to see the shows, too.

Q You've also worked on stage with your husband, Louis Zorich, your brother, and your daughter, Christina, which must have had an effect on your work?
They're the people who love you and they're more honest with you; they dare to risk saying certain things to you. It's the trust factor, the intimacy, the vocabulary that develops because of the time you share on stage together. You fail, you prevail. We were always fighting to keep the company going, never taking anything for granted. We were keenly aware of how transitory it was. We didn't have a resident company; it was a revolving door. I felt all the different actors gave the company its signature.

Q You gave a memorable performance in Martin Sherman's play, *Rose*. What were some of the challenges you encountered?
It was an incredible challenge for me as an actress. First: The memorizing! I said, "I didn't think I could do it." Then I said, "I don't think I can do it," which developed into, "I can't do it," into, "Nobody can do it!" I kept taking small bites. I had to trust my sensibilities, my instincts, and put my willfulness behind me. Second: figuring out how to do it. A one-woman show I never aspired to do, neither did the director or the writer. We all found our way. I divided the play into seven sections; it felt like the seven gates in the Sumerian myth, pretty mystical. Third: holding it all together. You have so much information in your body. All I was able to do was drink water and eat yogurt.

And it was Rose's effort to know who she is in the world. What happens to her as a result of a telephone call. Everything is evoked in her, the past, the future is rattling about. She's a woman who never felt any one place; she felt separate, apart in her own family, wherever she was, in Warsaw, later when she was in the Holocaust, in America.

Q Who was the audience to you?
They were a group of people who came together and knew everything I knew. I counted on their

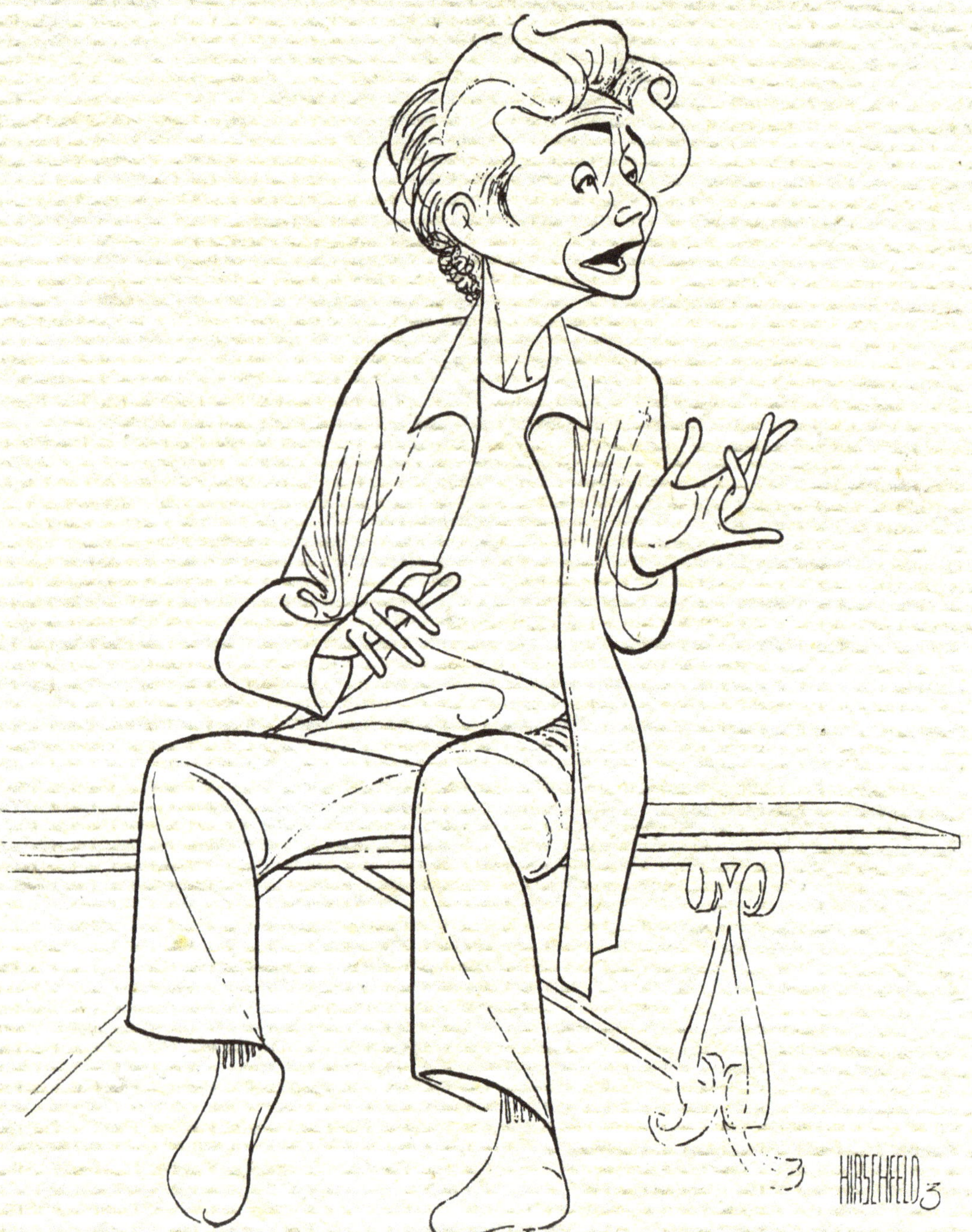

Olympia Dukakis in "Rose" artwork by Al Hirschfeld © The Al Hirschfeld Foundation. www.AlHirschfeldFoundation.org

knowing, on their coming with their feelings, their attitudes, their humanness, on their being informed. As a result, there's a tremendous permission to be intimate: what the evening is going to be about, what I'm going to do, where we might go.

Q You're a part of Touching Hearts, a national cholesterol campaign; a member of Broadway Cares, N.O.W., Women in Film, The Congress of Radical Equality, and Amnesty International. All these must mean a great deal to you.

Because I want to be a part of resolving something. I hesitate using the word "solving"; it's more to have some participation. I'm especially taken by the effort to present women with options—not only regarding their health, but issues involving their children, ways of seeing themselves in the world: not as secondary citizens or as victims.

The good news is we're calling attention to more issues. Many women today, professional women, women in the grassroots, are wanting to make their votes count, being involved in ways to improve their community. Women who have to get up every day and do several part-time jobs, they also try to do something at their children's schools, at their churches, their synagogues. I see that it's more enlivened by these sensibilities than twenty years ago. I think a lot has to change. I get discouraged and depressed, indeed I do. Women are dealt with as objects, trivialized, demonized, not only in this country but around the world. But there's been a spiritual awakening happening in this century: a female essence which is life-affirming.

Q Throughout your life you've worked with some of the greatest writers in theater.

I've never let go; I'm always wanting to act on the stage. I love acting. I love the process. I don't love the traumas that await me but one doesn't happen without the other—the dark and the light, the chaos and the order. I'm excited by the ideas, the depth of the characters, the writer. The people I'm going to work with; it's about the collaboration. With the right people, something lively's going to happen.

I love to go back to a play a second or a third time. You become more informed by life. Your vulnerability to the play deepens, your willingness to take in the play. We defend ourselves against the depth, out of fear of failing, wondering if we're going to land on our feet. I did Hecuba twice at A.C.T., and went on to do it a third time. Theater can be a way of evolving if you want it to be. ■

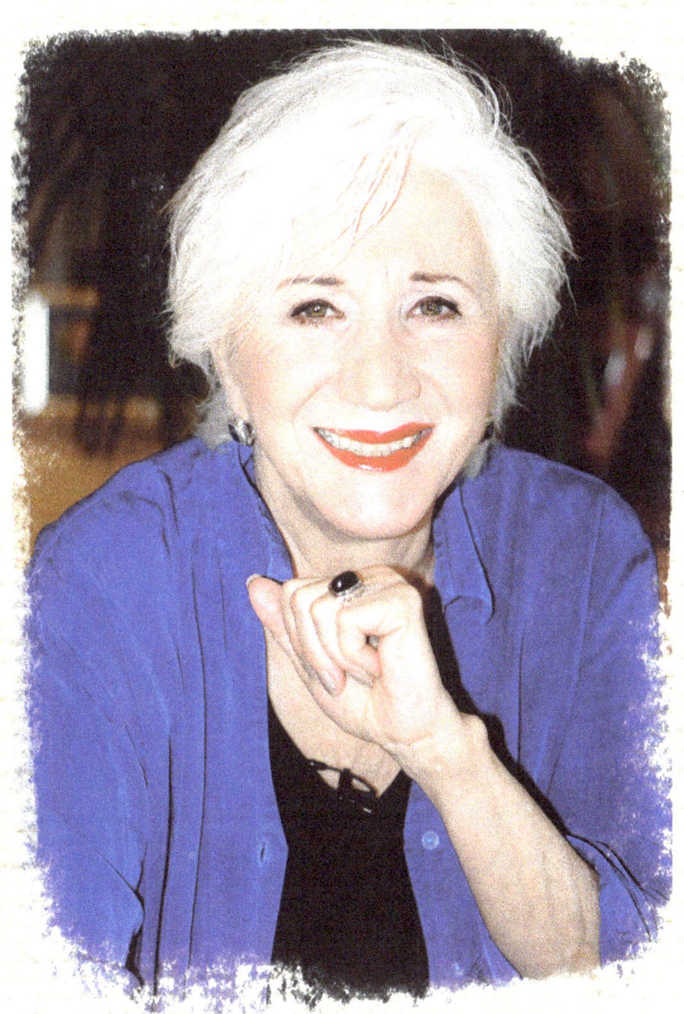

Olympia Dukakis photo: courtesy of the artist

BEN GAZZARA

Known for starring in *Anatomy of a Murder* opposite James Stewart and Lee Remick, directed by Otto Preminger, he also originated the role of Brick on Broadway opposite Barbara Bel Geddes in the original production of Tennessee Williams' play, *Cat on a Hot Tin Roof*, directed by Elia Kazan. Mr. Gazzara's other memorable Broadway appearances included Jocko in *End as a Man*; he received Tony Award nominations for *A Hatful of Rain* opposite Shelley Winters and James Franciosa; *Hughie and Duet*; and in Edward Albee's *Who's Afraid of Virginia Woolf*. Off-Broadway he played Yogi Berra in *Nobody Don't Like Yogi*. His other notable film appearances included as Jocko De Paris in *The Strange One*, *Husbands* with Peter Falk and John Cassavetes, *The Bridge at Remagen*, *The Killing of a Chinese Bookie*, *Saint Jack* directed by Peter Bogdanovich, *Voyage of the Damned*, *Inchon* with Laurence Olivier, *The Big Lebowski*, John Turturro's *Illuminata*, *Don Bosco*, *The Spanish Prisoner*, *Eve* with Lauren Bacall, and *L'onore e il rispetto*. His television appearances included starring in *Arrest and Trial*, and *Run for Your Life*, *QB VII*, *Colombo*, *An Early Frost* for which he received an Emmy nomination, *Hysterical Blindness* for which he received an Emmy Award, and *Pope John Paul II*. His autobiography, *In the Moment: My Life as an Actor*, was released in 2004. Mr. Gazzara died in 2012 (this interview was conducted in 2002).

Q You first starred on Broadway in Michael Gazzo's *A Hatful of Rain*, and then worked with Elia Kazan on *Cat on a Hot Tin Roof*.

I was a brave kid. I had made a deal to be let out of my contract with *Cat* after six months because I had promised my friend, Michael, that I'd be in his play first. Kazan could have very well have said "no," and not waited.

Q What did it mean to you acting in the original production of Tennessee Williams' *Cat on a Hot Tin Roof* on Broadway?

Well, to be a young actor and be directed by Elia Kazan, to act in a new play by Tennessee Williams, I was very flattered. Gadge (Kazan) was considered the "actor's director." I had done the play, *End as a Man* at The Actors Studio as a classroom project. Well, at the first performance at The Actors Studio, Williams was in the audience, and he was impressed enough with my work to offer me the part in *Cat*. When we did the production, the reviews couldn't have been better if I had written them myself.

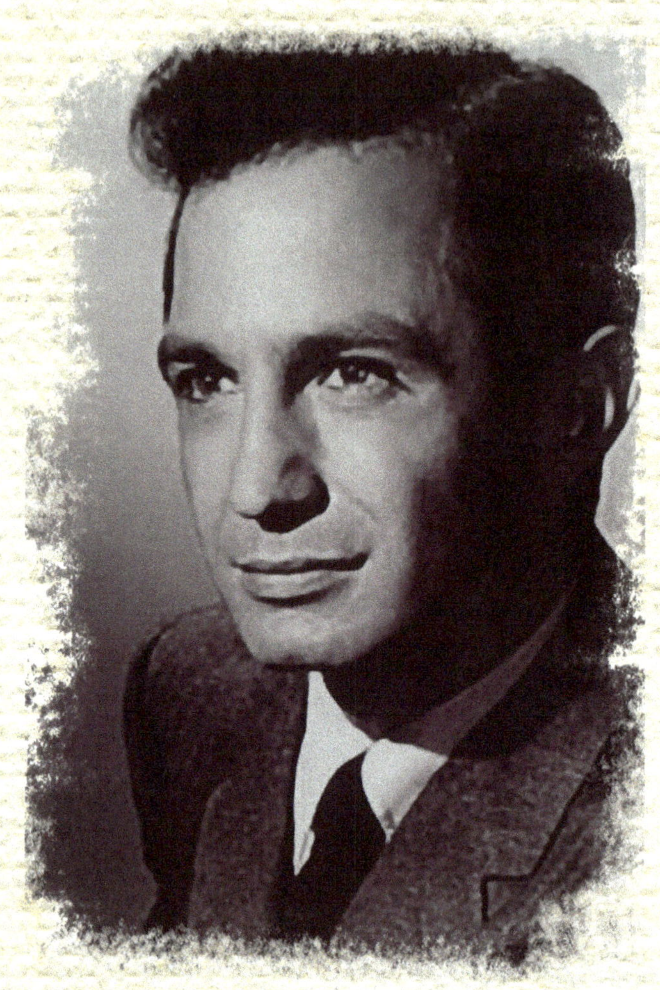

Ben Gazzara photo: courtesy of the artist

Q What makes Tennessee Williams' plays vital for us today?

His plays are poetic, they touch you, they're emotional. He wrote for the actor. To play these roles gives you the opportunity to show your wares. To act in his stuff, you don't really need to work so hard if you're in command of your craft. I've always believed in working with good actors, on the best material I could find; it can only draw the best out of you. When you're young, the sky's the limit, especially if you're a shy kid. Through acting I could show things I had always kept secret.

Q How did you begin to create the role of Erie Smith in *Hughie*?

I went searching for the man. I finally clued into the loneliness, his bravery, the "prince within him," his need to spin one yarn after another in order to keep his pipedreams alive. That touched me deeply. I went to work on him. I had had my years of drinking and carousing with a lot of losers, so I took something from that. A walk here, something else from there. That helped me find the man.

I'm also proud of my work in *Who's Afraid of Virginia Woolf*. There were very few people who thought I could play an intellectual. Only Albee did. He had seen me in *Strange Interlude* and called me. There again I worked on his walk. I made it more restrictive. Myself, I walk with a certain amount of pride; you know I'm coming. But George doesn't want to be seen.

I had no problem with Albee's language, the dialogue, the relationships. I tried to visualize the character. I saw him walking into the room and saying hello to me. I won't talk about the interior, that's private.

Q I understand you're writing–

A book, about my life. As a matter of fact, it's called *Only the Beginning*. I hope it is. ■

KELSEY GRAMMER

Most well-known for his portrayal as the psychiatrist Dr. Frasier Crane on the NBC sitcom *Frasier* opposite Jane Leeves, John Mahoney, Peri Gilpin, and David Hyde-Pierce, he was the first American actor ever to be nominated for multiple Emmy awards for portraying the same character on three different television shows—*Cheers*, *Frasier*, and *Wings*. Mr. Grammer also directed over thirty episodes of *Frazier.* On Broadway, Mr. Grammer originated the roles of Charles Frohman and Captain Hook in the Broadway musical, *Neverland*, directed by Diane Paulus. His other Broadway appearances include as Georges in a revival of *La Cage aux Folles*, receiving a Tony Award nomination; *Macbeth*, and in *Othello* with James Earl Jones and Christopher Plummer. Mr. Grammer's many television appearances included two miniseries, *Kennedy*, and *George Washington*, *Back to You* with Patricia Heaton; as Mayor Tom Kane in *Boss*, receiving a Golden Globe Award and also serving as an executive producer; *Star Trek: The Next Generation*, *Swing Vote*, *The Pentagon Wars*, *30 Rock*; *Partners*, on which he was also executive producer and directed two episodes; and as General S. Patton in *An American Carol*. His film appearances include *Transformers: Age of Extinction*, *Down the Periscope*, and *X-Men: The Last Stand*. He provided the voice of Sideshow Bob on *The Simpsons* for fourteen years, and created voices for many films including *Toy Story 2*, *Anastasia*, *Bartok the Magnificent*, and *Animal Farm*. Mr. Grammer's production company produces the sitcoms, *Girlfriends*, *The Game*, and *Medium*. He has won five Emmy Awards, three Golden Globe Awards, two People's Choice Awards, and a Screen Actors Guild Award. Mr. Grammer has received a Directors Guild of America nomination, a Tony Award nomination, and over forty-five nominations for major awards. Mr. Grammer received a star on the Hollywood Walk of Fame.

Q Is acting about the ability to tell a good story well?
I think it's understanding what story you're in—more selfishly than telling a good story, you've got to defend the character you're playing, bringing the rational to the irrational in the character—along with the intellect of the character.

Q What drew you to want to play Charles and Captain Hook in *Finding Neverland*?
I can't imagine not wanting to play Captain Hook; it's a terrific piece, especially in the "reveal"; I loved doing the show. From the very beginning, as a boy having read the story of "Peter Pan," it resonated within me, and that probably made me feel even more connected to the show.

Q Was it an exciting, creatively fun rehearsal period working on these characters?
Diane (Paulus) is so gifted as a director, and when we transformed the stage into a pirate ship—at my behest—it was thrilling. I used to go sailing, ever since I was nine, and it felt like I was really at the ship's wheel as Captain Hook. I could feel the wind kicking up, as we took off. I got a big kick from it every single night!

Q You also played Cassio opposite Christopher Plummer and James Earl Jones in *Othello* on Broadway.
The truth is Chris (Plummer) was very challenging as Iago, but it turned out being one of the best experiences I ever had. And he's the warmest person to get to know.

Q What do you keep learning from acting before a live audience?
You learn what's working. They tell you how you're moving through a particular section in the play. That way you learn how to survive a long run. Some actors become intimidated or they can become bored during a long run. You have to have a new experience every single night; it's probably the most immediate test of all, being in a long run.

Q You also brought Georges to life in a revival of the Broadway musical, *La Cage aux Follies*. Why did you want to take on that role?
I felt I could add something to it. When I had seen a production of the show in England I thought that Georges, who I eventually played, needed to be the "man" in the relationship, more like in the movie. And within the context between the two guys' relationship, as it played out as a traditional relationship, it wasn't really being held up in the show. So when I did it, I really enjoyed adding that element to the show. It was a fabulous experience doing that show. It was beautiful how they both cherished each other in the relationship. It was really about selfless love.

Q What did you relish the most in playing Dr. Frazier Crane for eleven seasons on *Frasier*?
That Frasier could go anywhere. I think it was Jorge Luis Borges who wrote that Shakespeare could toss all of these creations in the air, and that it was like a bauble. I felt that way playing him, it was all these human emotions that Frazier could go through—life was like a bauble to him; he could do anything. It just gave me the freedom to be even more silly; he was the most buffoonish sincerest character I ever played; he could do anything! Much in the same he was like Jackie Gleason and Walter Matthau, but it was even better since I had David Hyde Pierce and the entire cast to work opposite. They were always dealing with everything he did, and you could see it on their faces.

Q A lot of the comedy on *Frazier*, one could say, goes all the way back to commedia dell'Arte, the subtle work of Buster Keaton and slapstick routines of the Marx Brothers. What did you learn the most about the art of comedy?
The chief thing is you have to earn the laugh; that it's rooted in something indefinable but real to the audience. They're connecting to it through some emotional underpinning and once that happens, you can go anywhere. When you watch Charles Chaplin, you feel such great pathos. His creations always earned it. It wasn't just something that was added on to it. It was part of the art. That's

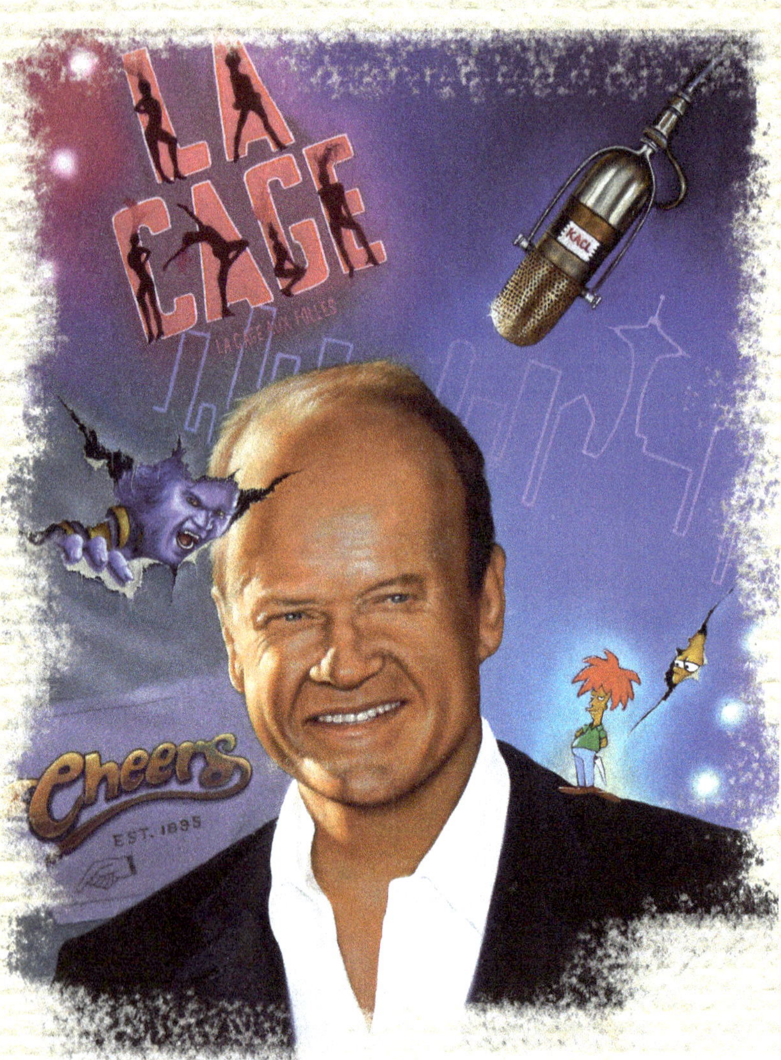

Kelsey Grammer artwork: Jim Warren, courtesy of Mr. Warren

where Frazier always ended up, with his deep-needed love. And it was never not funny, it just got better and better to keep him frustrated and searching for love.

Q Where do you find your greatest inspirations in life?
In all kinds of places. My greatest inspiration is probably from being with the children in my life. Life itself intensifies when it's connected with a respect for life, and I see such joy in the eyes of my children. It's the same child-like quality you have to bring to the work you do.

Q Drama and comedy have always helped heal ourselves and the world. How have you found the work you do to be that kind of universal healing force?
Laughter they say is always good for the soul as much as catharsis. I like to think that we were able to accomplish that with *Frasier*. There was a great love among the characters, an honest love that he felt for Diane, but while he loved her completely, she couldn't completely love him. But he kept loving her completely. And what became funny was that he could not love himself completely. But he had this desire to love fully.

Frazier was a lucky man and I have had the blessing that my work has helped many people. I've had so many people come up to me and tell me how it's made them so happy to watch the show, or I've received letters telling me it's been such a great joy and comfort for their mom or dad who were able to watch the show when they were in the hospital. That honestly means so much to me, that we were able to offer them this "look into life" with humor, and I'm thankful for that. ■

LEE GRANT

An Academy Award-winning actress for the film, *Shampoo* opposite Warren Beatty, Ms. Grant received Academy Award nominations for *Voyage of the Damned* and *The Landlord*. On Broadway she created the role of the shoplifter in the original production of Sidney Kingsley's *Detective Story*, receiving a Drama Critics Circle Award. Ms. Grant recreated her portrayal in the 1951 film, receiving a Cannes Film Festival Award and an Academy Award nomination. Her other Broadway appearances include *The Prisoner of Second Avenue* with Peter Falk, *Two for the Seesaw*, *A Hole in the Head*, and *All You Need is One Good Break*. Ms. Grant's films include *In the Heat of the Night* with Sidney Poitier and Rod Steiger, *Dr. T and the Women* with Richard Gere, *Airport '77*, *Portnoy's Complaint*, *Plaza Suite*, and *Valley of the Dolls*. Her TV appearances included *The Neon Ceiling* receiving an Emmy Award, *The Substance of Fire*, *Citizen Cohn*, *In My Daughter's Name*, *The Hijacking of the Achille Lauro*, *Mussolini: The Untold Story*, *Peyton Place* receiving an Emmy Award, and during television's "Golden Age," she appeared on *Studio One*, *Danger*, and *Kraft Television Theatre*. As filmmakers, she and her husband, Joseph Feury, have produced six documentaries for HBO, including *Down and Out in America*, which received an Academy Award, *Tell Me a Riddle*, *Bagdad ER*, *The Stronger*, *Tell Me a Riddle*, and over sixty intimate portraits for Lifetime TV; she received a Gilda Award for her interview with Madeline Kahn. Ms. Grant received the Director's Guild Award for *Nobody's Child*. Congress has recognized Ms. Grant for her work, and Women in Film honored her with their first-ever Lifetime Achievement Award.

Q When did you first know you wanted to act?

I started young. As a little girl, I was pulled by my mother into many of the arts. She had an immigrant's dream for her daughter; it was a romantic, unrealistic concept, and it made her euphoric. It started with dance. She put me into ballet class at the Met when I was four. Then I was sent to the Arts Students League when I was ten. I had no real talent for ballet but I had a gift from it. It gave me a strength, and a great appreciation of music.

But I was never built for ballet the way the "right" girls were. One out of the whole class was extraordinary, was made for dance. To me it was partly fun, partly an after-school chore, not something I loved. This was on 148th Street, where we lived, and my mother and I would trek down to the old Met after school; I was a tired child.

Acting came along when my mother took me to The Neighborhood Playhouse. I was impatient when I took my first class with Sandy Meisner; he told me I was spoiled. He gave me the exercise of looking for something. But I felt I was "home"—at home with the criticism, at home with the immersing myself in the situation. Acting became the religion for me. Sandy was "the Pied Piper" and all the things he gave me I have used all my life and I've tried to give them to other people.

Q Do you feel you have more to learn as an actress?

I do feel that. I had more to learn from Lee (Strasberg). I felt Sandy's (Meisner) specificity always; it always fed me. Taking me into the history of the character, and in writing it out—it gave me the boundaries—what I needed to make the character's reality my own.

At The Actors Studio there's a "dream" workshop. It gives another dimension to the work the actors bring into their scenes. I see them going places in themselves that I haven't seen before. It's something I'd like to do myself, just to see what the journey's like.

Q How did you create the role of "the Shoplifter" in the original production of Detective Story on Broadway?

The role grew out a speech exercise I was given at The Neighborhood Playhouse—to listen to people wherever I went, and to write down what they said phonetically. So it became like a script that you use. I wrote the sounds of how people spoke. There were two women talking in the seat behind me on a bus. And it became a very exciting thing to listen to—the way they spoke. I brought it into class; I think I was maybe seventeen at the time.

Well, when I was called in to read for *Detective Story*, Sidney Kingsley wanted me to first read for the role of the ingénue; she was a kind of an over-flowery young girl. Later I was asked to read the role of the old lady, who was the "shoplifter." She was described as forty years of age.

So I brought out one of those women I heard from the bus, and he loved it. I had been sent to him by Henry Fonda who had seen me in a Tennessee Williams play. So that's how "the Shoplifter" was born.

Q Did your expertise as an actress bring a lot to the way you work as a director?

First of all, it's how my favorite directors have worked with me; my favorite directors were Norman Jewison, Hal Ashby. They really wanted me to bring the character to them and then they could say "that's too much" or "that's not enough"—they loved working with me on the character. It made me very free and full of ideas, bringing in extremely exciting things. That's the way I approach my work with other actors.

Garson Kanin said "99% is in the casting." If you have a cast of actors who can bring you the most alive performances in their particular parts, then you're able to lean back and let them bring it to you. You certainly see that in the work at The Actors Studio. I don't work with the actors there as a director. Actors do their creative work by themselves and bring it to its essential. When I moderate at The Studio, what I talk about is everything related to the creative process, what the actors are going through on a role.

Q What has The Actors Studio meant to you personally for your creativity?

I think if you ask most of us at The Studio, we'll say: "It's a home." It's our home as an artist, which is just as important as this home we're sitting in now. It's something that I've been a part of since I was invited in after I did "Detective Story."

In California, when we didn't have an Actors Studio there, directors and actors like Jack Garfein, Martin Landau, Mark Rydell, Sally Field, Jack Nicholson, Bruce Dern, and Diane Ladd realized there was a need for one. That's when we started the West Coast Actors Studio, and it's still going strong. Here in New York and out there, it's where I go when I want to see talented work by my peers who have the guts to take on tough projects. Ellen Burstyn, Al Pacino, Estelle Parsons, Stephen Lang, Carlin Glyn, Harvey Keitel—I have such respect for them, and for the young actors starting out.

Q Is it the actor's humanity to communicate truth that propels us to go to those very personal places to create something unique?

I don't know exactly what impels an artist each time to take another chance to go deeper and to go farther, to explore those places that are mysterious. Acting is amorphous. We're not given notes to play like musicians, we're not given steps like a dancer. We're given words, and it's up to us to create the soul and the life of the person. It's a mysterious journey.

Q What keeps you honest in seeing truth?

I don't know how I know it. Acting first opened my eyes, opened my heart and soul. Don't forget that I was blacklisted very early, so I lost twelve years of my acting life; I was nineteen or twenty years old when the "Blacklist" hit. So I started teaching. That was my way to be connected.

I taught at HB Studio with Herbert Berghof and Uta. Herbert had been one of my teachers at The Neighborhood Playhouse. I taught by necessity. I was very fortunate to have had some very exciting actors come to my class. It was the beginning of a different part of my artistic life. It also led to my crossing the divide and going into directing, in working with actors in a room; I was lucky. Later on, I was in the first AFI Women Directors' Workshop.

Q How did you learn to deal with being nervous as an actress?

When I began, I think as far as acting was concerned, I was fearless. There was absolutely nothing I wouldn't take on. I did summer stock between my first and second year at The Neighborhood Playhouse, and played the mother in *Ghosts*; the next week, I did the little girl on the railroad tracks in Tennessee Williams' one-act, *This Property is Condemned*. I was out on a "tightrope" with absolute no fear. Fear came with success. The more successful I became, the more resentful I became, the more I felt invaded. I felt pushed into a place which I had to go through for other people, and my dream was really to be a part of a repertory company and play small parts and big parts all my life.

When I did *Detective Story*, I suddenly got all these great reviews on my first play. I had hoped to be hidden in this little part and to be found was not what I wanted. I left the play, even though it was a very big success, to take a chance in another one that turned out to be a total failure. But that's what I really wanted. I wanted the conditions I could fail in without anyone pointing a finger at me.

Q How important is "the moment before" to you when you're about to enter into a scene?

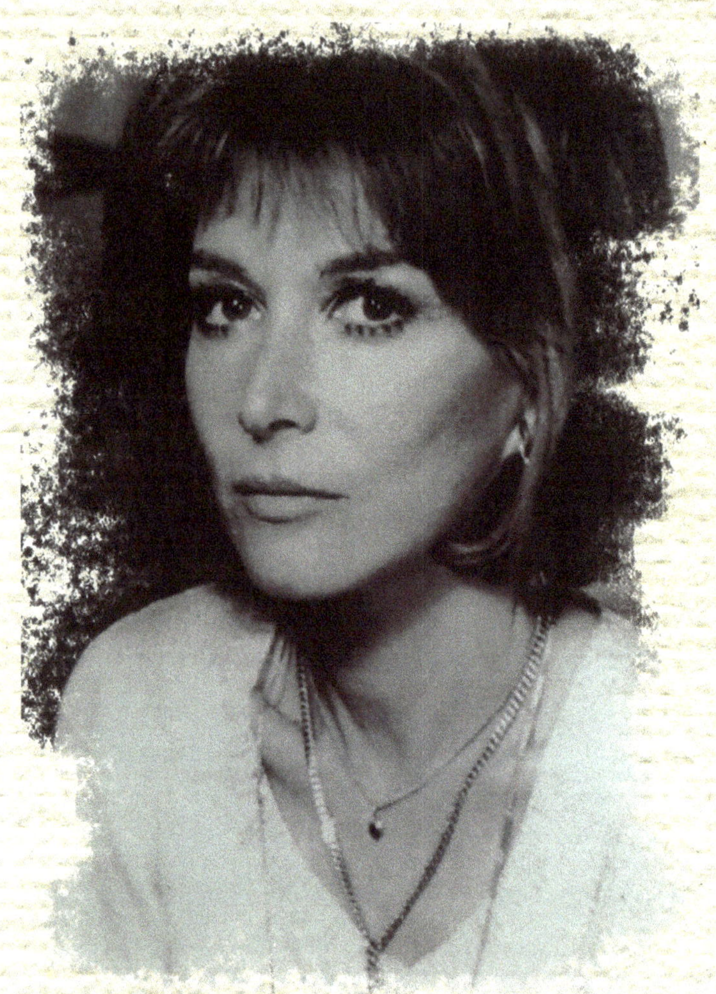

Lee Grant photo: courtesy of the artist

It depends on the kind of part it is. There are parts where you need to take a long time to get yourself into the right place. It might take many exercises, or privacy and people leaving you alone. There are other times, for example, when I was doing Neil Simon's play, and on opening night of *Plaza Suite*, that just before I went on stage, Mike Nichols (the director), said to me, "Just remember everything depends on you." It broke me up and it was the perfect thing to go on stage with. It took away the nerves; he was so right.

Q Is it important for an actor to take control of their own destiny?

What do we mean by the word, "destiny?" First of all, we have to recognize we're acting within a business, and you can't be in it and be totally deluded by what it is. It's as true of Broadway as it is in Hollywood. Any woman who works in film, they have to know that forty-years-of-age is a cut-off date for a fullness of a career.

Being in this business is about facing reality, with a strong sense of survival. That's one of the things that compels me to direct—my own need to keep working and doing things that excite me.

There is "our little tunnel" in breaking through it all, which I think is exemplified by the kind of things small theatre companies do, like Naked Angels or the Labyrinth; what Philip Seymour Hoffman did when he founded the LAByrinth company, and others have been doing at The Public, the Signature Theatre in New York City.

An actor/playwright brought in a play to the Playwright/Directors Unit at The Actors Studio. It went very well, so he invested in it and put it up, got a wonderful review in *The New York Times*, and guys from The Studio like Harvey Keitel and Robert De Niro went to see him. He had forged his way as an actor, wrote his own play, produced and acted in it Off-Broadway and that's what I see happening. Actors and writers are taking the "dirt out of their mouths." They have to follow their talent and respect their talent and push their talent to be seen.

Something's happening out there. At The Studio, it's a private place where actors and writers have their freedom in private to create. But I do want the work to jump outside the walls and find an audience.

Q How do you maintain your focus?
My focus goes to whatever my connection is on. I read *The New York Times*, I listen to NPR Radio. My focus is on: "What kind of world are we leaving for the children?"

All the sacrifices and fights we've put up to make this a better world make me wonder: How can what I see be happening? The people we elect—they're affecting the lives we're living, our children's lives. And I wonder: How can we take it back?

Theater has always had a history of touching people, and like the documentaries I've made, or the series of plays at The Public, we're all playing our part as we've always done historically—to awaken people, to seek them to take back the responsibility for the world we live in. ■

SPALDING GRAY

Mr. Gray is known for the autobiographical monologues that he wrote and performed for the theater in the 1980s and 1990s. His monologues included *Swimming to Cambodia*, which received a National Book Award, and was adapted into a film by Jonathan Demme; *Monster in a Box*, directed by Nick Broomfield as a film; and *Gray's Anatomy*, directed by Steven Soderbergh as a film. His film and television appearances included *Hard Choices, Beaches, Buckminster Fuller: Thinking Out Loud, Kate and Leopold, Saturday Night Live, Spencer: for Hire*, and *The Nanny*. In 1970, he joined Richard Schechner's experimental troupe, The Performance Group, and with actors including Willem Dafoe and Elizabeth Le Compte, helped to co-found the theater company, The Wooster Group in New York City. Mr. Gray appeared on Broadway in the role of the Stage Manager in *Our Town* for Lincoln Center Theater, and in *The Best Man*. His books include *Sex and Death at the Age of 14*, *A Personal History of the American Theater*. In 2011, *The Journals of Spalding Gray* was published. Steven Soderbergh made a documentary film about Mr. Gray's life, *And Everything is Going Fine*, in 2010. Mr. Gray died in 2004 (this interview was conducted in 2000).

Q You have that rare gift of storyteller to touch the nerve of the audience. How did this develop?
I think I began doing it around the time I was in Emerson college. I became more aware of it when I came to New York. I was in a job situation at a secretarial school. I started talking about my day to dish washers, the Irish cooks and they enjoyed it. So I naturally fell into it.

While I was living with Elizabeth Le Compte in the city, we had no television and I would do the story of my day for her. It was a natural thing at that time as we were being influenced by Grotowski and Artaud's work. I became extremely attracted to The Open Theatre, and I also took Joyce Aaron's Workshop. I was open to "jamming," a technique where you'd voice a stream of consciousness. I brought in "the story of my day" and Joyce asked me "Who wrote it for you?" I knew I had done something special. This was in 1959.

Then The Wooster Group encouraged me. They'd transcribe what I'd say and they became texts. Julian Beck said, "We have to be a lot like Columbus—to go out and discover and take our audiences on a voyage."

Q Who is the audience for you?
Being in front of the them to me is like a second home. Originally they were like a mother to me; I was infertilized by them. They're such a diverse body, from the age of six, like my son, to ninety! I've had ethnic-mixes, Puerto Rican audience members who would yell out in the middle of the show, all kinds. There's this dynamic "happening" occurring, a dialogue of understanding.

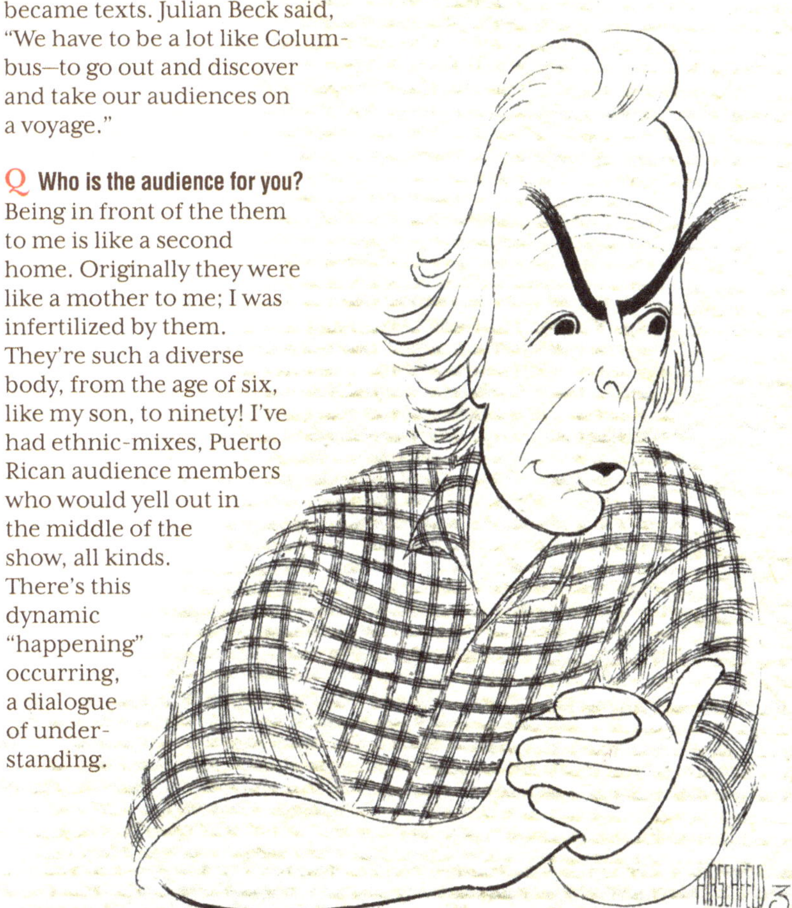

Q How did your extraordinary *Swimming to Cambodia* come about?
When I went to India in 1976 I started to keep a journal. I continued writing in it for seven years. *Swimming to Cambodia* was a good example of left-over energy. I was completely full of regret that I had to leave; I was haunted. These images would come up and grow out of it. When I came back, I sifted through my imagination, my fascinations, endless dreams. It was a real epic piece, a most complicated piece. It had to be.

Q How do you find a way of maintaining a balance between becoming discouraged and at the same time remaining open to finding new ways to express yourself?
I think I have found it. Twenty years ago this September it began. It led me to concentrate on producing good work. It's actually a discipline, a form of mediation, of feeling less threatened, of continual exploration. When I was doing research for *Gray's Anatomy*, I saw these psychic surgeons in the Philippines. Because of my research I was able to see things I wouldn't have normally seen. That's the kind of openness that's necessary.

We're taught almost from birth to strive for an elusive "pursuit of happiness." I'm reminded of what Joe Chaikin said: "We're made to cherish things we don't even care about and to give up things we fundamentally cherish." One could connect all of reality and our sense of reality to a certain transience in all of us. Life is change. We have this tremendous anxiety; we can't find our center. The quest is to find this feeling of silence in the middle of the motion. I labor with that in my material.

Q Why did you decide to confront mortality so deeply in your pieces?
It's so much in our conscience. It's denied so much of the time throughout our lives. It's the ultimate task of the poet, what any shaman's or priest's role should be. I like to hope I'm a poet, and I strive to combine it in a way that's not morbid. If my pieces are successful, they're hitting all the shakras, with chance endings that have been built into them.

To talk about death is what makes life so poignant, exciting. I wonder who doesn't think about death and how can we avoid not thinking about it. After all, it's the bottom-line reality. We should give ourselves permission to accept our neurosis. Culture is ultimately neurotic. ■

JOEL GREY

Best known for creating the role of the Master of Ceremonies in both the Broadway and film versions of the Kander and Ebb musical, *Cabaret*, Mr. Grey received the Academy Award, Tony Award and a Golden Globe Award for this role. On Broadway, he received a Tony Award for creating the role of George M. Cohan in *George M!*, created the role of the Wizard of Oz in the musical, *Wicked*, was Amos Hart in *Chicago*, for which he received the Drama Desk Award, and he has received four other Drama Desk Award nominations. On Broadway, Mr. Grey also starred in the revival of *Anything Goes, Come Blow Your Horn, Stop the World—I Want to Get Off, Half a Sixpence, Give Me Your Answer, Do!, Harry, Noon and Night, Goodtime Charley, Marco Polo Sings a Solo, The Normal Heart, The Grand Tour*, and *Herringbone*. Mr. Grey played the title role in *Platonov* at the Williamstown Theatre Festival, and Off-Broadway in John Patrick Shanley's *A Fool and Her Fortune*. His film appearances include *Remo Williams: The Adventure Begins*, for which he received a Golden Globe nomination, *Man on a Swing, Buffalo Bill and the Indians, The Seven Percent Solution, Kafka*, and *The Fantasticks*. Mr. Grey's television appearances include *The Muppet Show, Grey's Anatomy, Dallas, Star Trek: Voyager, CSI*, and he received an Emmy nomination for *Brooklyn Bridge*. He received a lifetime achievement award from The National Yiddish Theatre Folksbeine. A renowned photographer, Mr. Grey's book *Pictures I Had to Take*, coincided with his debut photographic exhibition at New York's Stanley Wise Gallery. His other books include *Looking Hard at Unexpected Things, 1.3—Images from My Phone*, and *The Billboard Papers: Photographs by Joel Grey*. Mr. Grey's work has been exhibited at the Museum of the City of New York, and has become part of the permanent collection of the Whitney Museum of Modern Art.

Q Did you know early on you wanted to perform in musicals?
I began at the Cleveland Playhouse doing repertory theater. I never thought I'd ever be in a musical, I thought I'd be a repertory actor. My role models were Laurence Olivier and Peter Lorre—real character actors.

Q Did you see a lot of theater growing up?
Oh yeah, it was my passion. I studied at the Cleveland Playhouse, then at the Neighborhood Playhouse, and with Wynn Handman.

Q You have worked a lot in television and film, including your mesmerizing performance in *Cabaret* with Liza Minelli. How did you learn how to act in front of a camera?
I learned it by trial and error. You think you know what to do and it turns into what "it" wants. And then the director comes along and he or she tells you "to go for more here," or you can "do a lot less." And you find yourself giving what the medium demands.

Q It was a joy to see the audiences respond to your work in such a big way as The Wizard in *Wicked*.
Isn't it why we do what we do? To give them a meaningful experience—to give joy away, especially in the times we're living through.

Q What drew you to want to play the Wizard in *Wicked*, and in playing him what did you learn about his nature?
I remember seeing the film with Judy Garland, and I wasn't really drawn to Frank Morgan who played the Wizard. When they called me for the role as the Wizard, I read the novel. It's rich, dark, political and very complicated, like life. But the Wizard is barely dealt with in the book; he's

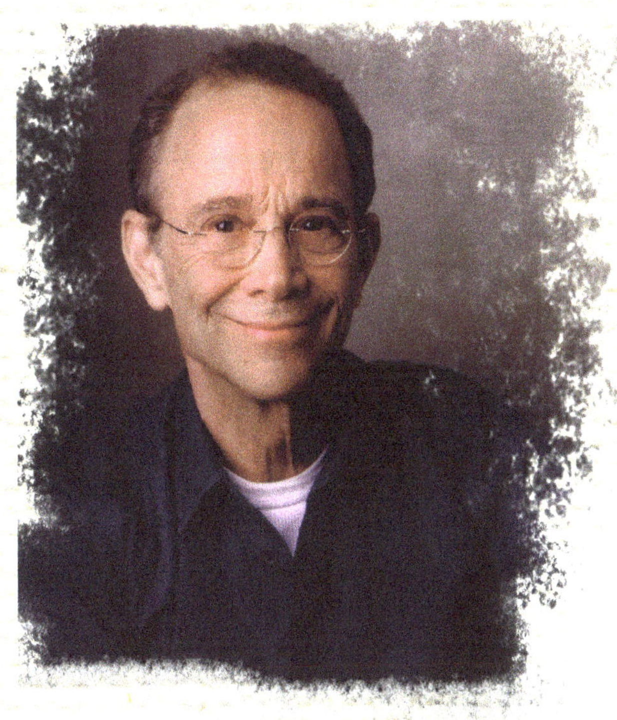

Joel Grey photo: Andrew Eccles artwork: by Joel Grey, from his fourth book of photographs, "Billboard Papers," courtesy of the artist

pretty much one-dimensional, he's seen as a villain.

When I met with the director and the creative team, we talked about the character of the Wizard, and I could see the direction they wanted to explore was "the father" concept. The arc of his character intrigued me. He's a sentimental man, and he does what he does because he longs to be a father. He just happened to have gotten stuck in Emerald City, and everyone thinks of him as so amazing, and when he realizes he can actually solve people's problems, it surprises him. Unfortunately, in the end he gets caught up in what he believes to be right. All he ever wanted was a daughter and he's really heartbroken, because his daughter, Elphaba, is banished, and in the end he's destroyed.

I think the audience is actually intrigued by the Wizard because they don't know exactly what to make of him. The story also continues to fascinate the public in a very big way. The theme of the book is really about "populism." Plus, it's amazing how Baum came up with all the names of the characters, like Elphaba, which came from his own name. There's an entire website devoted to all the "Oz-mania"—it's all kinds of fun.

Q How did the character of the Wizard reveal himself to you during rehearsals?

I kept my focus on telling his truth, even if it was "a lie." He gets so caught up in doing what he's doing, it doesn't occur to him that it could actually be harmful to others. The Wizard was a "pitch man," and the reason he ended up in a balloon, was he was out "pitching" for the circus, and it blew him to Oz. He's also the only earthling on the stage by the way, too. He's really a plain kind of guy.

I always do a lot of work. Finding out everything I can, creating biographies. I always do a lot of research. It's like a puzzle to me. I follow my instinct and assume that it will all come out in some way—it'll show up in my shoe, in the way I move.

Q You not only had some amazing actors to work opposite in *Wicked*, but the audience must have also given you a lot every night?

I was very fortunate to have as wonderful a cast as I did: Kristin Chenoweth, Idina Menzel, Carole Shelley, everyone—plus every single character has been realized beautifully, from Boq to Doctor Dillamond to Nessarose. The writers were very pain-staking, making sure they assembled the very best cast.

Of course, the audience is always important, especially in a musical. This particular audience every night is almost like a rock concert—there are so many young people. And they get caught up in the story. They identify with the girls, Elphaba and Glinda, and then they have to deal with the Wizard, but I don't think they really see him as a villain.

Q There are all sort of "ups and downs" in the life of an artist. What continues to give you the strength to keep creating?

The surprises. You wake up and find out the "flower has blossomed," from the day before. I speak of it metaphorically. You learn to take the good with the bad. It's all part of the adventure. ■

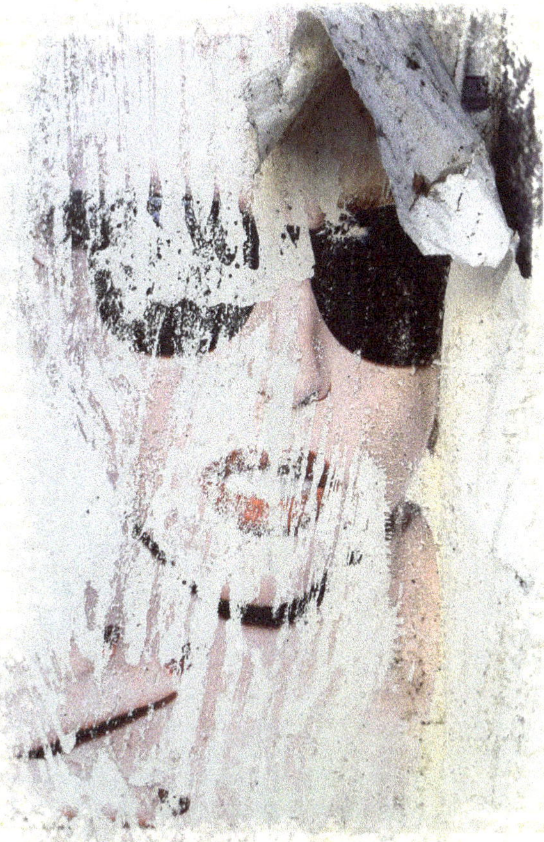

JULIE HARRIS

Considered the "First Lady of the American Theater," Ms. Harris won five Tony Awards, three Emmy Awards, a Grammy Award, and was nominated for an Academy Award. Among her many memorable performances on Broadway include: Frankie in *A Member of the Wedding* directed by Harold Clurman, Emily Dickinson in *A Belle of Amherst*; *The Playboy of the Western World, The Last of Mrs. Lincoln, A Shot in the Dark, Marathon 33, And Miss Reardon Drinks a Little, Forty Carets, The Glass Menagerie, A Doll's House, Lucifer's Child, The Lark* with Boris Karloff; *I Am a Camera*, and *The Gin Game*. Her film and television work included *East of Eden* opposite James Dean, *I Am a Camera, A Member of the Wedding, The Last of Mrs. Lincoln, Harper*, opposite Paul Newman, *Reflections in a Golden Eye, Victoria Regina, A Doll's House* with Christopher Plummer, and *Knots Landing*. She did extensive voice work for documentary maker Ken Burns including *Brooklyn Bridge, Not for Ourselves Alone: Elizabeth Cady Stanton and Susan B. Anthony*, and *The Civil War*. Ms. Harris was a Kennedy Center honoree, awarded the National Medal of Arts, and is a member of the American Hall of Fame. She received the 2002 Special Lifetime Achievement Tony Award. Ms. Harris died in 2013 (this interview was conducted in 1998).

Q I think it's fair to say you're a living reflection of what a true artist of the theater is all about, and what makes your art all the more amazing is how connected the audience becomes to your acting.

It's the storyteller's job—the involvement of what you have to be for that time on the stage. It's become more and more important to me as time has gone on, to become increasingly simpler and simpler. I strive for that simplicity in my work.

Q You were directed by Harold Clurman in the now classic play, *A Member of the Wedding*. What made him such a special director to work with?

I also worked with him on *The Young and the Fair, Mademoiselle Colombe*, and *A Shot in the Dark*. He was such a beloved man. It was always thrilling to hear him speak about the theater. He had so much passion. It was his energy.

When I worked on Frankie in *A Member of the Wedding*, I had to find out all about the wedding, what I was working on, helping with the cooking, the whole day in absolute detail. What color the washcloth was I used, it all helps so much in the reality. In rehearsals he always kept reminding me to remember where I was coming from for each scene.

Q I so enjoyed seeing your performances playing two extraordinary artists so memorably—Emily Dickinson in *A Belle of Amherst* and Isak Dinesen in *Lucifer's Child*. What attracted you to them?

It was their perception of life. Emily Dickinson led a very sheltered life while Dinesen's was sophisticated, and she fell in love with a white hunter. Their spirits talked to me, what they accomplished and the beauty of the writing of the plays.

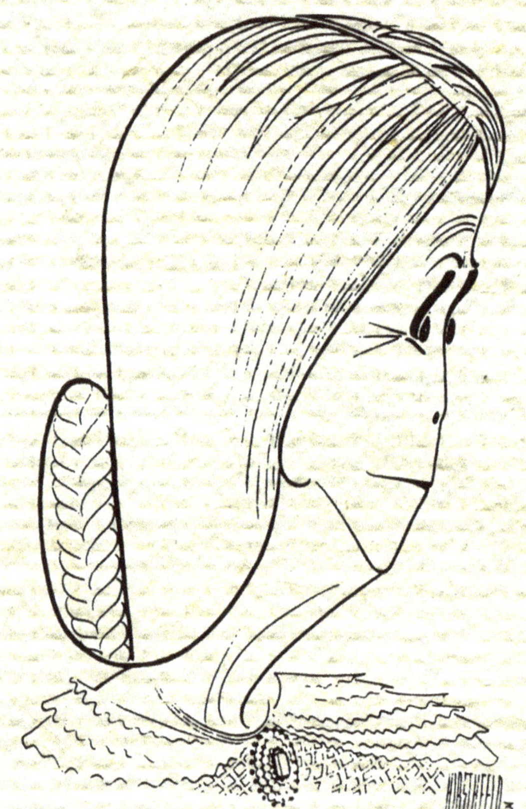

Julie Harris artwork: Julie Harris as Emily Dickinson in "The Belle of Amherst" by Al Hirshfeld © The Al Hirschfeld Foundation. www.AlHirschfeldFoundation.org

Q You also act in different regional theaters—

I find it exhilarating. This summer I'm doing two new plays, one in Seattle at A.C.T., *Scent of the Roses* by Lisette LeCat Ross, and a new play at the Victory Gardens in Chicago, *Winter* by Claudia Allen.

Q You're one of the few touring actresses who carries on the tradition of traveling across the country, bringing theater into the lives of the citizens of this great land. Why does it mean so much to you?

I so like acting in different theaters, and touring is fun. I just completed another tour with Charles Durning in *The Gin Game*; it's a play I love so much. I see the theater as a place that can reawaken our humanity, that's why it's so important for me to tour.

You know, I saw that wonderful RSC production of Nicholas Nickleby seven times and it was like re-discovering the theater all over again. Seeing both parts, spending the whole day at the theater it was such an enormous connection, so full of meaning. The theater has that power to reconnect us back to life. ■

STEPHEN HENDERSON

Best-known for his many roles in August Wilson's plays, Mr. Henderson originated the role of Turnbo in *Jitney*, receiving a Drama Desk Award, was Jim Bono opposite Denzel Washington in the Broadway revival of *Fences*, receiving a Tony Award nomination. He appeared in the revival of *Ma Rainey's Black Bottom* with Charles S. Dutton and Whoopi Goldberg; and starred in the premiere of *King Hedley II*, with Brian Stokes Mitchell and Leslie Uggams. He also played Van Helsing in *Dracula the Musical*, and *Drowning Crow* with Alfre Woodward. Mr. Henderson received an Obie Award and a Lucille Lortel Award for his performance in Stephen Adly Guirgis' Pulitzer Prize-winning play, *Between Riverside and Crazy*. His film appearances include re-creating his role as Bono in *Fences*, directed by and starring Denzel Washington; Steven Spielberg's *Lincoln*; *Tower Heist;* and in the 1989 version of *A Raisin in the Sun* with Danny Glover and Ester Rolle. His television appearances include Omar in *New Amsterdam*, *The Newsroom*, *Tyler Perry's House of Payne*, and *Blue Bloods*. He directed *Zooman and the Sign* for Signature Theatre and with the LAByrinth Theatre Company portrayed Pontius Pilate in *The Last Days of Judas Iscariot*. Mr. Henderson received the Actor's Equity Richard Seff Award, and has taught and lectured across America at many prestigious schools including The Juilliard School in New York City. He was the Chair of the Department of Theatre and Dance at the University at Buffalo, the State University of New York.

Q You were originally part of Group 1 at the Juilliard School Drama Division. Had you known what that training would be like?

I had no idea. I had been fortunate having a wonderful teacher, Gloria Terrell, who cast me in two productions of *A Raisin in the Sun*, and I got to play Karl Lindner in one and Walter Lee in the other. When I auditioned in Chicago for Juilliard, it was because of Gloria's belief in my abilities that made it possible. That first year at Juilliard was a culture shock for a young man like myself from Kansas. It turned out to be an incredible experience because of the teachers I had: Marian Seldes and Michael Kahn, Moni Yakim, Edith Skinner, and I was a part of an incredible first class wich included Patti LuPone, David Schramm, and Mary Lou Rosato.

Q What inspirations did you find in New York City?

It was 1968 when I came to New York. Of course, I knew of Sidney Poitier, Diana Sands, Ruby Dee and Ossie Davis—they were inspiring examples of great actors. Well, some of the great plays we went to see were James Earl Jones and Jane Alexander in *The Great White Hope*, Frank Langella in *A Cry of Players* with Anne Bancroft, and *Madwoman of Chaillot* with Katharine Hepburn—all quite inspiring. And I saw Athol Fugard's new plays; Woodie King had started touring new plays.

I think the person who was most encouraging for me was Amiri Baraka. I got to play the lead in his play, *Dutchman*, for a benefit, and Amiri read his poetry. He was most supportive, and when I told him where I was studying, he said, "Study the classics but don't let them cause you to lose your naturalness." His saying that freed me of my worries. It really made me aware that the classics prepare your instrument for whatever you choose to do.

Q What do you love the most about creating a role?

The first thing that occurs to me is the "belonging." In a play, you're a member of an ensemble; it's a form of a family, a community. You have a place in the telling of the story, and you're there to create that character in the midst of the story. So in that sense, it's being a part of that.

Q You had a special relationship with August Wilson. How were you first introduced to him and his work?

I met him in Pittsburgh, where

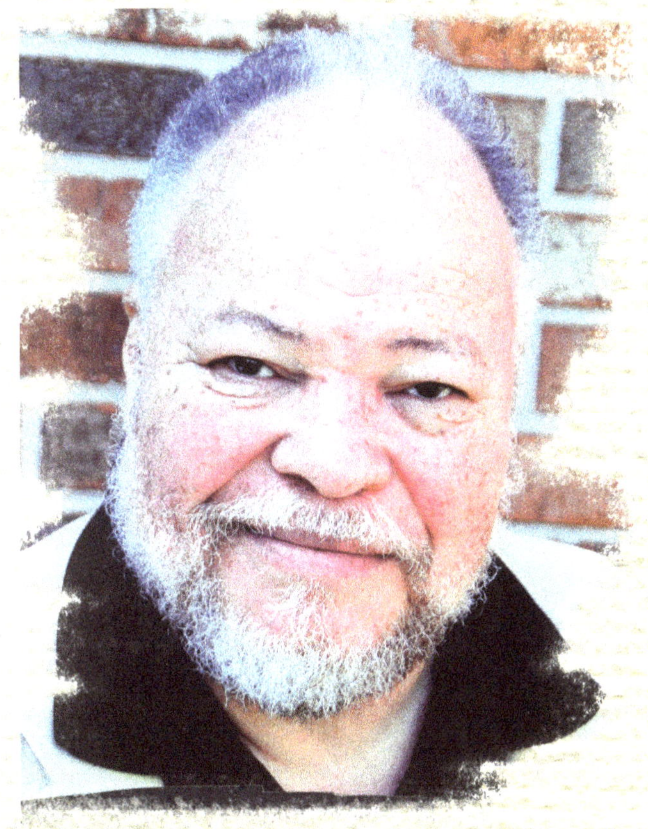

Stephen Henderson photo: Ron Wofford

I also filmed *Fences*. It was in the Hill district where I first met him on these streets. I did *Jitney* there in 1996 as well.

When I saw Lloyd Richards' production of *Joe Turner's Come and Gone* for the first time, I sat there absolutely completely spellbound. I realized that *Joe Turner* was a poetic, exalted text. I knew I was listening to a great poet playwright like Shakespeare or Tennessee Williams or Chekhov. I was thrilled by the language, the wisdom, the theatrical landscape.

Q How did you go about creating the role of Turnbo in the original production of *Jitney*?

For me, Turnbo was brilliantly drawn, yet he was not a sympathetic character. He had to be welcomed among those honorable men. I realized he was tolerated by Becker and the older guys and that they had known him for a long time; they knew what kind of child he was. I crafted into my characterization that he was an orphaned child, raised by elderly people as their own. It gave him a simpatico with seniors.

I told August (Wilson) that Turnbo was the child of a rape, that Turnbo had been left at the Irene Kaufman Settlement House. Turnbo was aware others knew this about him, so he wanted to have all the dirt he could find on others. He so wanted to belong, and in his mind, he finally belonged there at the Jitney station. It helped me embrace the distasteful parts of the character with relish. August used Turnbo to give background on other characters organically. Gossips are great for exposition at any time.

Q What made it special to perform in the premiere of August Wilson's *King Hedley II*?

It was my Broadway debut. If there was ever a role I would love to revisit, it would be "Stool Pigeon" in *King Hedley II*. I had done Turnbo for six years, and it was a joy to create "Stool Pigeon," especially since I got a kiss from Leslie Uggams in every performance.

When the Signature Theatre did the revival, I had the great joy of playing the role of "Elmore" opposite Lynda Gravatt, and also when Kenny Leon did his historic Kennedy Center stage readings of the Century Cycle.

Q You performed on stage opposite Denzel Washington in August Wilson's *Fences*, and also appeared in the film of *Fences*, directed by and starring Mr. Washington.

It was a joy doing that production on stage because Denzel is such a generous actor. He had seen me in *Jitney* and *King Hedley*, so he thought of me as a "Wilson actor."

A significant thing is that when Denzel was first asked to do the film of *Fences* in 2009, he told the producer Scott Rudin, that he had to do the play first. He remembered the impact of James Earl Jones who originated the role, and he said, "Before I can approach the character in a film I need to go to the stage." But they had no intention of doing that originally. He's that kind of artist.

Q You also had to audition for the film of *Fences*?

I was very glad to audition. There's only one reason to audition—because you want to play the role. So six years later, Denzel directed and starred in the film, and we had many of the original members of the Broadway cast, including Viola Davis, Mykelti Williamson, and Russell Hornsby in the cast. It doesn't happen that often.

Q You also played William Slade, President Lincoln's personal servant in Steven Spielberg's film, *Lincoln*, opposite Daniel Day-Lewis. How was that special moment at the end of the film created, when we watch Lincoln walk off to Ford's Theatre?

It was first because of Tony; he brought me to Steven's attention for the role. Next the generosity of Daniel Day-Lewis. Daniel had worked all day long on his other scenes, and when it came time to do that scene, he was willing to "take that walk" for as many takes as it took. Steven was inspiring, and very clear about all the things he was looking for in that moment. I once said to him, "Is that all?"

But to be trusted with it, to have it asked of you, to have everything around you replicated in such a way to respond to it all—and to share with Steven Spielberg that eventually one day, an African American President would be in that same White House was particularly significant to me— since I was watching, in a sense, the potential for that going down that hallway. It was a great blessing to know that.

Q Why did you want to teach the craft of acting?

I felt I owed it to a new generation because of those teachers who taught me. I've also been teaching occasionally at Juilliard which is an absolute joy, at The Actors Center with Lloyd Richards and Israel Hicks, and at Fordham. And I was on faculty for SUNY at Buffalo for twenty-nine years.

Q What has it meant to you to be a part of the ritual of theater?

I can tell you having been a part of some LAByrinth Intensives, their readings of *Between Riverside and Crazy*, all the leaps of faith with directors like Phillip Seymour Hoffman and Austin Pendleton, the heavenly ensembles at Atlantic Theatre and Second Stage, and when the brilliant Stephen Adly Guirgis won the Pulitzer Prize—from the ritual alchemy of it—I definitely know there is a spiritual core to the ritualistic nature of theater.

And I believe it must have existed in the hard work and magic that went through Lin-Manuel Miranda when he wrote *Hamilton*. He had to have become spiritually connected to Alexander Hamilton through the biography. I'm amazed by the genius of a storyteller who voices his story in many tongues. They create language from all those perspectives, and give actors a sacred place where a vision can find life. We breathe life into it, but we must have the text. ■

KIM HUNTER

Ms. Hunter's long and rich career included playing Stella in the original Broadway production of Tennessee Williams' *A Streetcar Named Desire* opposite Marlon Brando and Jessica Tandy, and in the film version opposite Vivien Leigh and Marlon Brando, receiving an Academy Award, and a Golden Globe Award. Her film and television work included *Deadline USA* opposite Humphrey Bogart, as Zira in the first three films of *Planet of the Apes* opposite Charlton Heston, *A Matter of Life and Death* opposite David Niven, *The Edge of Night*, receiving an Emmy Award nomination, *The Comedian* opposite Mickey Rooney, and *Backstairs at the White House*. Her final stage appearance was in the revival of Oscar Wilde's *An Ideal Husband* on Broadway. She also appeared Off-Broadway in the Colleagues Theatre Company's *The Madwoman of Chaillot* in 1998. Ms. Hunter received two stars on the Hollywood Walk of Fame. She died in 2002 (this interview was conducted in 1998).

Q You played Stella in the memorable Broadway production of Tennessee Williams' *A Streetcar Named Desire*. What made it such an important event in the American Theatre?
It was a bloody good play, that was the source. Each character Tennessee wrote was very much an individual. And Elia Kazan was the director, and *he* was brilliant. And the audience was just as much a part of it.

Kazan was constantly forcing us to find out about the character's needs and wants and the ways to go about it in the performance. He allowed us—Jessica (Tandy) and Marlon (Brando), Karl (Malden) and myself—to share in the process, in the activity involved. He was quite willing to listen to us but you still ended up focusing on only what his over-all aim was.

See, he'd get to know each of us and knew what button to push to make the character alive, and he was ruthless in getting it from you. But he always put the play and the character first above everything else.

Q How do you approach a role?
Basically I'm interpreting the role. Naturally there's some creating in a way going on at the same time; it's the nature of the beast. It's been true of every role I've played. It becomes a very personal and fascinating process.

I was delighted two years ago to be involved with Oscar Wilde's *An Ideal Husband* on Broadway. The audiences came, and we had such a good time. We just have to be willing to allow that kind of theater to happen much more often. ■

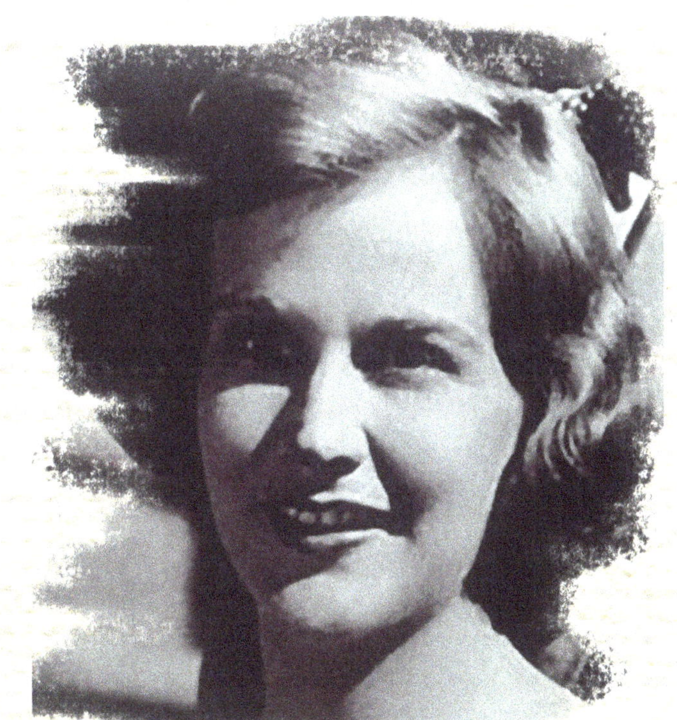

Kim Hunter photo: courtesy of the artist, 1951

DRAGAN JOVIČIC

One of the most gifted actors of Bosnia and Herzegovina, Mr. Jovičić was the Artistic Director of the famous Chamber Theatre 55 in Sarajevo for several years. He gained wide popularity from his television and film work including *Summer in the Golden Valley*, *Alena's Journey*, *Let u Magli*, the TV series *Porobdzije*, *Skins*, and *Aleksa Santic*. His memorable theater work began at the National Theatre of Bosnia in Banja Luka, including roles as Volodya in Drago Jančar's *Great Brilliant Waltz*, directed by Jovica Pavic, and as Ivan in *Metastable Grail*. At the Chamber Theatre 55, Mr. Jovičić's roles included Edmund Kin in Jean-Paul Sartre's play, *Kin*, the title character in Ahmed Muratbegović's play, *Hussein Gradaščević'*, the lead role in Ionesco's *Exit the King* directed by Dino Mustafic, Hasanaga in *Hasanaginica* directed by Mustafa Nadarević, in *Little Shop Around the Corner* directed by Francois Lunel, and as Machiavelli in *The Dialogue in Hell* directed by Aleš Kurt. He has co-starred with Selma Alisphasić in his award-winning performance for over a decade in Jose Sanchis Sinisterra's *Ay, Carmela*, directed by Robert Raponja and produced by the Sarajevo War Theatre-SARTR. Mr. Jovičić's acting awards include the Golden Laurel Wreath Award for Best Actor at the 35th International M.E.S.S. Festival, and the Sixth of April Award of Sarajevo for his enormous contributions to Theatre.

Q What first led you to want to act?
I had my first experience with acting at the age of seven, thanks to my teacher, Ms. Olga Istenic, who gave me a leading part in a play. Perhaps the decisive moment for my future profession was when I was supposed to unbutton my shirt to be examined by a doctor in a scene. However, the buttons on my brand new white shirt were sewn too tightly and would not unbutton despite all my efforts. I was in trouble. Was it a panic attack or epiphany, but I pulled apart the two firmly buttoned sides of my shirt with all my strength so that the buttons popped off and rattled all over the place. As I went on with my lines, huge applause thundered in my ears.

Q Did your love for art and painting begin very early?
Yes. I felt the urge to draw and paint, particularly as a teenager, as I was in search of answers to the big questions of life, meaning, and reason. I discovered art as a way out, to keep me busy and help me cope with the usual troubles of youth. At the climax of my passion for painting I almost ignored other subjects in school, imagining that I was an artistic genius. I've grown a little more realistic with age. Over the years, I have somehow neglected this early passion, and now that you have reminded me of it, perhaps it is time to go back to it.

Q During the historic three-year Siege of Sarajevo, I understand you stayed in the city and would perform at Kamerni Teatar 55 even though there was no electricity or running water. Those who stayed in the city as actors and audience would risk their lives from snipers to get to the theater and the citizens who stayed in the city would risk their lives to come with candles so there would be light in order to experience the plays. Why was it necessary for you to stay during the Siege?
It was indeed necessary that I stay. It was as though one day you wake up to a nightmare. We, the people of Sarajevo, found ourselves trapped and forced into a war because some politicians decided that we are so different among ourselves that, despite the tradition of our country, we could not and should not live together.

Actually, we did not look different, did not talk different, and it was impossible to tell who is who, but you could only get a vague idea when a person says his or her name. They decided, in my name, that I should hate my neighbor because of his name. They decided that I should leave my city and everything it stood for, including my friends and my theater, and go up to one of the surrounding hills from where I would have a better view of the city so as to be able to shoot and kill it.

All because, according to this insane division, my name-ethnicity-religion was what had determined me as a person. I could not let them categorize me or decide for me. They thought that my place was on the hills overlooking Sarajevo. I knew that my place was to stay there, come what may, and share my destiny with Sarajevo.

Being an actor, I realized that the times required that the theater pursue a higher mission, that of a spiritual survival. At a large scale, Sarajevo was the theater, and its people were the actors and the audience at the same time. At a smaller scale, my theatre, Chamber Theatre 55/Kamerni teatar 55, was a place of encounter where plays and other artistic events happened under the light created by the people who came in, despite the life-threatening ordeal that they had been facing, each bringing a candle as an entrance fee. This theater became a temple of spiri-

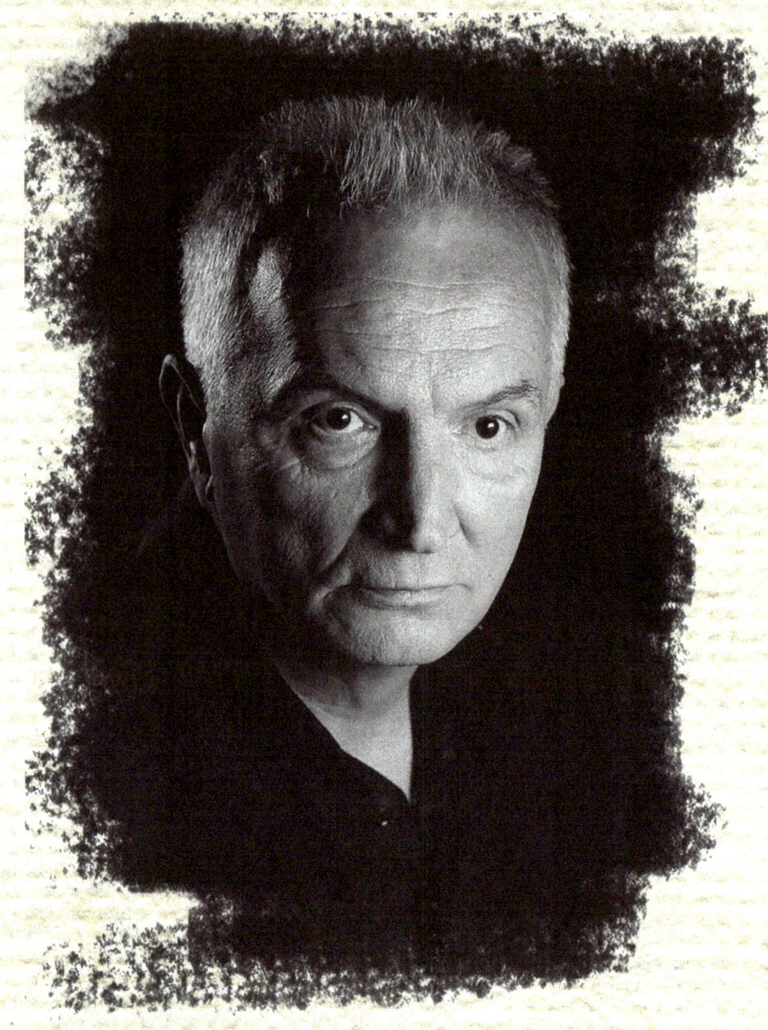

Dragan Jovičić photo: courtesy of the artist

tual resistance and recovery for all the people of Sarajevo, regardless of their religion, ethnicity or name. That is why I stayed, and it was worth it.

Q Running a theatre like Chamber Theatre 55 as its Artistic Director must have had its challenges and its rewards. You always worked to maintain great integrity for the work presented and also to create cooperation and collaboration across Bosnia in all regions, with all people. Why was this important to you?

Most of the challenges were related to the difficult situation in which art and culture have found themselves in these troubled times of post-war transition in my country. The social status and the perception of the importance of the theater in the actual political and economic context, the level of priority it is given by the state, the financial and regulatory restraints which discourage initiative in the theatre, and so on, have a huge impact on the work of any artistic director in Bosnia and Herzegovina, and that was the case with me, too.

However, I did my best to keep up to the standards and the reputation of Kamerni Teatar, and not to let the scarcity of funds cause the poverty of art. On the contrary, despite all the challenges, we managed to produce great, award-winning performances that continue to receive recognition.

I enjoyed the privilege of leading this great theater, being able to participate in the selection of plays and artistic teams who will bring them to life. It was a great pleasure to share our performances with the audience across Bosnia and the region. I have always believed that the theater has a noble mission of bringing people together and showing them all they share with one another. We, the theater people, have played and still play an important part in the process of healing and reconciliation.

Q During your time as Artistic Director of Chamber Theatre 55, you brought some guest directors from around the world to direct at the theater, including Ronald Rand and Francois Lunel. Why was this important to you and what impact did their work have on the actors they worked with and the audiences?

Collaboration and exchange are essential to art and culture in general, and therefore also to the theatre. The universal language of theatre speaks to the human spirit about common values that we all share, no matter where we come from. Our theater has a tradition of openness, and having with us our peers from other countries and cultures enabled us to benefit from their talent and knowledge.

It was a precious experience to have Ronald Rand and other guest artists with us, to learn from them not only about our art, but also about our humanity. From our side, we offered them what we had, and this exchange resulted in productions that yielded great success. For example, Murray Schisgal's *LUV*, directed by Mr. Ronald Rand, has been filling our auditorium to this day and bringing great joy both to the audience and the actors.

Q How did your working as an actor begin with Kamerni Teatar 55?

I started working in Kamerni Teatar 55 back in 1987, when I was invited to become a full time member of its ensemble and take the lead role in the play, *Don Juan Comes Back from the War*, written by an Austro-Hungarian-born playwright, Ödön von Horváth. And not even the war and all its calamities could separate us. It has always been a great pleasure and joy for me to act on that thrust stage that reaches out into the audience, helping me connect with it. After my term as the Artistic Director, I have felt that reunion even more intensely, almost like freedom regained.

Q You have also played some of the great roles by Bosnia's finest playwrights, including Safet Plakalo, some of Shakespeare's great roles, Ionesco, many other fine playwrights. Which were the most challenging for you?

It is difficult to choose. Be it Kin or Creon, Paulino or Scapino, Porfiry Petrovich or Prospero, no matter how big or small, each role I played had its demands and challenges. From each I discovered something about the human soul and nature, and each of them required my absolute devotion and commitment.

Q You have also been playing opposite the very fine actress, Selma Alisphasic, for several years in Jose Sanches Sinisterra's *Ay, Carmela*.

Yes, we have been performing this play for almost twenty years now; but to us, each time we play it is always new. I knew from the beginning that we had an extraordinary performance, but the utter excitement, joy, and elation with which it was received whether at home or abroad, was astonishing.

I feel like my actor's dream has come true. After each show, although soaking wet with sweat, I feel as light as a feather. One thing I know for sure: none of this would have been possible without this special partnership in acting between Selma and me.

Q Have you found the way in which you approach a role has changed over the years?

The forty-years-long experience has helped me approach a role with more serenity, maturity, and confidence. What I actually love the most working in the theater is the creative process, the birth of a performance, the weaving of the threads that each member of the team brings into a fine fabric of art.

Q You're also a passionate fisherman. What similar lessons can be learned from acting and fishing?

It is the focus and concentration that you need, being one with the fish/the role, clinging to it and diving into the deep waters. ■

RANDALL DUK KIM

On Broadway, Mr. Kim has performed in *The King and I*, *Golden Child*, and *Flower Drum Song*. In a career spanning nearly fifty years, his stage performances include with the New York Shakespeare Festival in *The Jungle of Cities* and *Pericles* and *Cymbeline*, *The Tempest* at Lincoln Center, *The Karl Marx Play*, and *The Year of the Dragon*, at the Jewish Repertory Theatre in *A Majority of One*, at Burlington's Champlain Shakespeare Festival in *The Taming of the Shrew, Titus Andronicus, A Midsummer Night's Dream and Richard III*, at San Francisco's American Conservatory in *King Richard III, The Three Penny Opera, Marco Millions*, at the Guthrie Theatre in *The Pretenders, Hamlet*, and *The Marriage*, at the Singapore Repertory Theatre in *Golden Child* and *ART*. In 1979, with Anne Occhiogrosso and Charles Bright, Mr. Kim co-founded American Players Theater in Wisconsin, serving as Artistic Director and performing as Puck, Titus Andronicus, Petruchio, King John, Shylock, Brutus, Falstaff, Prospero, Hamlet ,and King Lear; in Marlowe's *Tamburlaine the Great*, Chekhov's *Ivanov*, Sophocles' *Oedipus Rex*, Ibsen's *An Enemy of the People* and Moliere's *Tartuffe*. Mr. Kim's film and television appearances include The Keymaker in *Matrix Reloaded*, *Memoirs of a Geisha*, The Tattoo Master in *Ninja Assassin* and Master Oogway in *Kung Fu Panda*, BBC's *Prisoners in Time*, *The Lost Empire*, and as General Alak in *Anna and the King*. Mr. Kim is a recipient of an Obie for "Sustained Excellence of Performance."

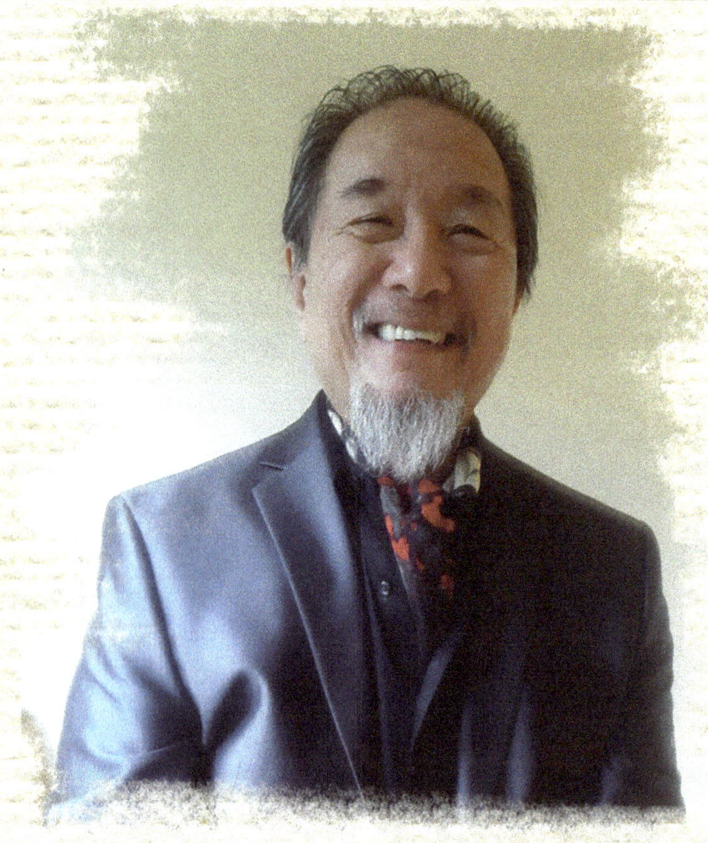

Randall Duk Kim photo: Doan Mackenzie

Q What has been the most challenging role you've played?
It's got to be Hamlet with all his complexity. I've been truly fortunate in that I've had the chance to play him on three separate occasions. My first Hamlet was a disillusioned, morally outraged, angry young man. First performances of great characters are usually done in broad strokes; depth and nuance need time, and an actor must make the attempt again and again if he or she wants to do the role justice.

When I met Hamlet for the last time, he was generous, humorous, and witty, a maturer man-kind, acutely aware of who he was as a human being, sensitive to the inner struggles of his conscience, and in the end, a man worthy of our respect, love, and loyalty—a man fit to be a leader. I think I got very close to the agonies of his tragedy.

In these my latter years, of course, it is King Lear I must reckon with. I've played him only once, most fortunately under the direction of Morris Carnovsky and Phoebe Brand. Their combined experience and insight provoked me to push beyond my boundaries and planted seeds for some future manifestation on stage.

Q What are some of the lessons you've learned working on the classics?
There have been many. I believe that an actor working on classical material needs to have an unquenchable curiosity about everything, and in particular, our species.

Zeami, the great Noh master, advised the actor to "Never lose the heart of a beginner." Being a beginner and asking questions go hand-in-hand. I believe another quality needed in working on these plays is empathy, with the non-judgmental capacity to "step into another's shoes." The great plays demand that the actor walks a most dangerous emotional tightrope if such characters as Oedipus, Antigone. Hamlet, Othello, or Lear are ever to live and breathe before our eyes.

Q But it happens all too rarely one has the opportunity to take on such roles.
Yes, it is a great sadness to me that actors have only the rarest opportunity to deal with classical drama in a repertory setting. To act in *Hamlet* at one performance, *Tartuffe* the next, or *Medea* followed by *Hedda Gabler*! This is theatre at its most challenging.

I believe that this system of production and performance, monumentally demanding as it is, can only serve to nurture masterful stage artists and craftsmen. It takes skill in communicating complex ideas and wisdom to avoid turning those ideas into clichés and great characters into cartoons. It takes skill to retain the complexity or ambiguity of a character, to hit the ear easily so that the thought is immediately accessible.

Sadly, too often performances are "frozen" after opening night and are expected to be exactly the same eight times a week. I think that truly great plays demand much more for a just and lively hearing. I'm afraid that because of the contemporary, commercial structure of "show business," we are seriously failing our fellow citizens. The theater could be of great service in such a time, providing the much needed space for deep reflection.

Q Why is experiencing great plays important?

Without hesitation, I can say that the greatest plays—those that have been universally passed on over the centuries—are important to the health and well-being of our society. These plays deal with some of the most important issues in being human. We in the theater continue to do the gravest disservice to our fellow citizens by denying them the opportunity to regularly witness these plays on the stage.

In the 1960s, the regional theater movement gave us great hope that in various parts of the country, communities would be able to see these plays as part of a repertory season. More than any other time, I believe that all efforts to strengthen real flesh and blood human contact are utterly necessary to our very survival, and play a very significant part in our healing.

Q What does our tradition of acting mean to you?

The American acting tradition is only part of a much longer tradition spanning thousands of years. When I reflect upon our tradition, as an actor I'm encouraged and strengthened by such a deep root system.

From the earliest shamans who bridged the living and the dead, to the ancient Greek actors tasked with some of the most profound tragedies ever conceived, to the players who traveled from town to town eking out a living, to the great luminaries of the last five hundred years: Burbage, Moliere, Talma, Kean, Rachel, Forrest, Booth, Bernhardt, Duse, and on Broadway, the inimitable Lunts. They were here before us. Who were they? What did they accomplish? What did they think about their work? I personally draw enormous inspiration in getting to know them. They set before us an ideal to reach for.

As a citizen of what Walt Whitman described as "the nations of nations," I claim a global inheritance from actors from other countries as my kinsmen, even teachers.

Q Who have been your greatest inspirations?

Among actors, Morris Carnovsky doing Shakespeare had the profoundest impact. I was eighteen and I saw him do Shylock, as well as Malvolio and Edward in *Richard III*, and it became the guiding light of my own efforts. When he was ninety years old, I had the opportunity to work with him. We had invited him and his wife, the fine actress Phoebe Brand, to our theatre to direct the company in Chekhov's *Ivanov*.

Two years later, we again invited them to direct our production of *King Lear*. Both Morris and Phoebe had been members of the groundbreaking Group Theatre. They were acutely aware of the truth necessary to be fully engaged and working out of the deepest part of themselves. Morris, of course, after the horrendous McCarthy blacklisting, had joined John Houseman at the American Shakespeare Festival in Stratford, Connecticut, and reconnected with an old love—Shakespeare.

Morris and Phoebe's many years of acting had brought them to a level of insight, an abiding respect for the art, and an understanding of the material which was incomparable and profound. To paraphrase Hamlet, "I shall not look upon their like again." They firmly set me upon the path I was traveling; to learn how to play these classical roles without manipulating them, to understand them on their own terms and render them using the very depths of myself.

Q We've also seen the loss of the true sound of the actor's instrument with the use of a microphone –

Yes, it separates me from the immediate contact with the audience, interfering with my task to "shake the air with the spoken word," and physically make contact with the audience's ear. On the stage the experience between me and the audience is immediate and palpable. Amplification is like having a strange third party between two people making love. The actor's voice—indeed his entire body—must be strong, flexible, and expressive, with the actor's inner self—heart, mind, spirit—fully and totally engaged.

Q How can that be cultivated?

Actors need to develop a vision of themselves as individuals living within the larger context of the world, the universe. Our educational system has a huge influence in how we see ourselves and the world. Through the theater, it can identify certain young people who have the appropriate drive, the curiosity, the "divine discontent"—to challenge, nurture and lead to a deeper understanding and awareness—and not simply to make a profit on.

Annie, my wife, continues to be my partner in this quest for great classical acting. We both share enormous curiosity and, when we work on a piece, we're like two obsessed detectives, digging into every bit of information we can find. It fuels our imagination and enriches the world we are to play in so the audience may witness these characters living out their destiny.

When I saw Morris as Shylock, he was not an actor merely playing a role; he was Shylock living, breathing, a man of flesh and blood susceptible to humiliation, capable of anguish and revenge. I saw the kind of acting that I would spend my life trying to attain. ■

JACK KLUGMAN

One of the pioneers of television acting in the 1950s, he is most known as Oscar Madison over five seasons on the television sitcom, *The Odd Couple* with Tony Randall, receiving two Emmy Awards and a Golden Globe, and as the medical examiner in his series, *Quincy M.E.* He appeared on several live TV dramas during television's "golden age" including *Inner Sanctum*, *Alfred Hitchcock Presents*, *The Twilight Zone*, *Naked City*, and *The Defenders*, for which he received an Emmy Award; later he appeared in *The Odd Couple: Together Again*, and *Diagnosis: Murder*. Mr. Klugman's films include *Twelve Angry Men* with Henry Fonda, *Days of Wine and Roses* with Jack Lemmon and Lee Remick, *Act One*, *The Detective* with Frank Sinatra, and *Two Minute Warning* with Charlton Heston. Mr. Klugman appearances on Broadway included *Golden Boy* with John Garfield, opposite Ethel Merman in *Gypsy*, *The Odd Couple*, and *The Sunshine Boys* with Tony Randall for The National Actors Theatre. Off Broadway, he appeared in *The Value of Names* with Dan Lauria, and in *Twelve Angry Men* at the George Street Playhouse in 2012. Mr. Klugman died later that year (this interview was conducted in 2006).

Q Who inspired you in the theater when you were beginning your career?
I saw *A Streetcar Named Desire* seventeen times; Marlon Brando was incredible as Stanley. I remember seeing the original production of *Our Town*, and *A Member of the Wedding*. The direction by Harold Clurman was magnificent, the acting by Ethel Waters and Julie Harris, and this little kid named Brandon de Wilde. I also saw Brando in his first big part before *Streetcar*, in *Truckline Café*. What he did in that seventeen-minute scene was unheard of—it blew me away! When I did *Gypsy* opposite Ethel Merman for two years, I have to tell you, I never worked with any star that wasn't more graceful; she was a pussycat.

Q How were you originally cast in Sidney Lumet's film, *Twelve Angry Men*, with Henry Fonda?
No one had to audition for *Twelve Angry Men*; Sidney knew everyone's work. But I didn't think he'd cast me. But Henry was producing the film, and he got the role for me. I had played with Henry in *Mr. Roberts* for six weeks, and we liked each other.

Making *Twelve Angry Men* was a labor of love. Every one of us was there every day on set. And what a cast—Ed Begley and Lee J. Cobb, E. G. Marshall, Martin Balsam and Jack Warden, all the others who were wonderful; we all knew each other from having done live television together.

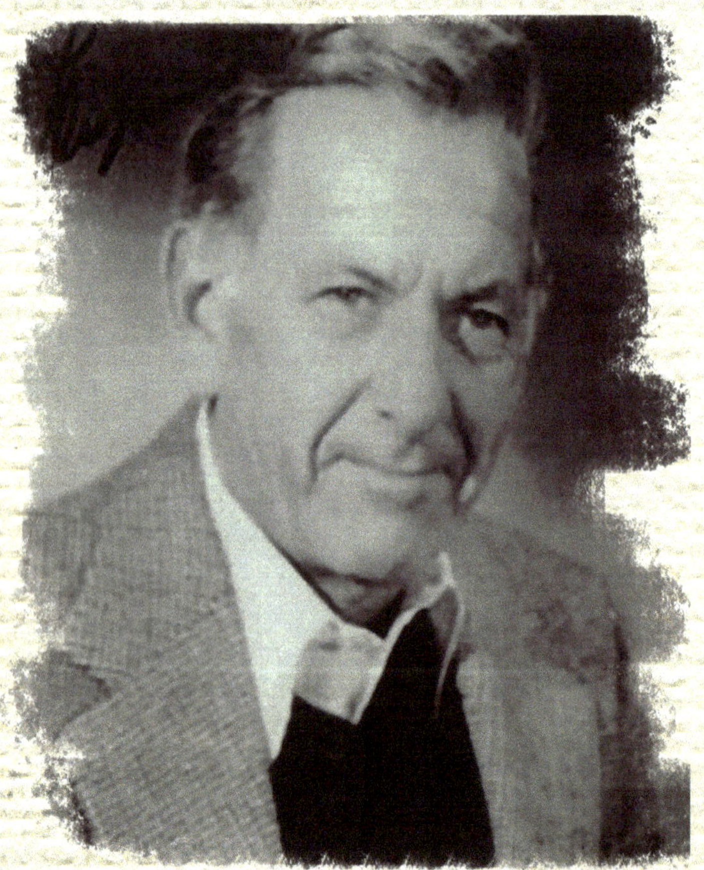

Q You also have had a very special chemistry with Tony Randall in *The Odd Couple*.
That was rare, Tony and I. You have to love what you're doing, that has so much to do with it. The cast and I also worked the same way in *Quincy* because we all liked each other so much.

Q *Did you ever think you'd return to the stage after your operation?*
After I had the operation on my throat, for three years all I could do was whisper. But then I met a guy who told me he could give me a voice. It wouldn't be the prettiest voice in the world, but I'd have a voice. So he gave me all these violent vocal exercises to do. I never thought I'd be back on stage.

Then Tony called. He told me, "I'm starting a theater. I want us to do one performance together of *The Odd Couple*." I didn't think I'd be able to do it. So we began rehearsing, and I was still not sure I could do it. Then comes opening night. The curtain went up, and I said my first line. I began to hear all this shuffling in the audience. I thought to myself, "I'll never be able to finish the night out." But after two minutes I heard them sit back, I balanced my voice and when the show was over, there was this immense standing ovation! Once the

Jack Klugman photo: courtesy of the artist

curtain went down, we all went to our dressing rooms. Then the stage manager comes back to tell us we have to go back on stage, they're still out there applauding. It was the greatest night of my life. And Tony gave it all back to me.

Helen Hayes told me in all her years in the theatre she had never seen such love in the theatre. I'm the luckiest guy in the world. The operation taught me so much about life. I learned I'm more resilient than I thought I was.

Q Why did you want to perform in Jeffrey Sweet's play, *The Value of Names*?
I loved playing this character. I found a freedom on stage I never found before. The play is all about the Hollywood Black-listing period in the 1950s, and I had been part of it. At the time I did *Golden Boy* with Clifford Odets, I saw the fear on the faces of the actors who were trying to get through it—Lee J. Cobb, John Garfield, so many others. It was terrible!

I grew up doing theatre, watching the Group Theatre actors on Broadway in their plays. Later, Bobby Lewis directed me in a production of *Twelve Angry Men*, and I also did a play with Luther Adler and Sylvia Sidney. I was Luther's understudy, and acted with Morris Carnovsky.

My first love was the stage. It's the only place you can learn how to use yourself. But you have to know how to use the rehearsal period. Selectivity is everything. An artist has so many different colors to draw upon. ■

SHIRLEY KNIGHT

Ms. Knight received the Tony Award on Broadway for her performance in *Kennedy's Children*, and received Academy Award nominations for the films, *The Dark at the Top of the Stairs*, and *Sweet Bird of Youth* opposite Paul Newman. Her other memorable stage performances on Broadway included *The Three Sisters* with Kim Stanley and Geraldine Page, *Landscape of the Body*, *The Man from Atlanta* with Rip Torn, *A Lovely Sunday in the Creve Coeur*, and Arthur Laurents' *Come Back, Come Back, Wherever You Are*. Off-Broadway, she starred opposite Al Freeman, Jr in the original production of Amiri Baraka's *Dutchman*. Ms. Knight's memorable regional work includes *The Cherry Orchard*, *The Glass Menagerie*, *Marriage Play*, and as Blanche in *A Streetcar Named Desire*. Her other films include *Dutchman*, for which she received the Volpi Cup, *The Rain People*, *The Group*, *Petulia*, *Juggernaut*, *21 Hours at Munich*, *The Defection of Simas Kudirka*, *Beyond the Poseidon Adventure*, *Playing for Time* with Vanessa Redgrave, *As Good as It Gets* with Helen Hunt and Jack Nicholson, *The Country Girl*, *My Louisiana Sky*, both *Paul Blart: Mall Cop* films with Kevin James, *P.S. Your Cat is Dead*, *The Private Lives of Pippa Lee*, *Redwood Highway* with Tom Skerritt, *Angel Eyes* with Jennifer Lopez, and *Divine Secrets of the Ya-Ya Sisterhood*. Her many television appearances include as Mrs. Newcomb in *Buckskin*; *thirtysomething*, *If These Walls Could Talk*, and *Desperate Housewives*. Ms. Knight has received three Emmy Awards, two Golden Globe Awards, and eight Emmy nominations.

Q Did you want to act at an early age?
I wanted to be an opera singer and went to Wichita State University in Kansas, that's where I'm from. I was doing some singing during the summer with the Central City Opera in Denver. Well, I went and saw Maria Callas in Kansas City, I was floored. I didn't know if I could do it that well. The turning point was my senior year when I started writing. I got a job to be an assistant to the society editor for the "Wichita Beacon," and I came across the magazine, "Theatre Arts." I had never seen it before. There was an ad in it: "For $250 take an Acting Course at The Pasadena Playhouse." This was the summer of 1958, and I thought it might be good for my singing.

Q Was there a theater department at the University?
No, not really, but they did put on plays. My boyfriend had been cast in one of them; he was going to be Romeo in *Romeo and Juliet*, and he convinced me it would be a good thing to try out. Well, I auditioned and didn't get Juliet, I got the Prologue. Then when I performed, I thought how much easier it was than singing.

Q Did you see much theater or films as a child?
I never saw anything. I was raised way, way out in Kansas. There was one church, one school, thirteen houses, a post office and granary, and that was it! We were rarely taken to a nearby town. I think I saw three movies as a child: *Bambi*, *The Wizard of Oz*, and *The Dolly Sisters* with Betty Grable.

I was very into paper dolls and costumes. So I got some cut-out dolls from "The Dolly Sisters," and on the back of the box, it read: "Costumes by Orry-Kelly." This was when I was twelve.

Years later when I did the film of *Sweet Bird of Youth* with Paul Newman, they told me to report to Orry-Kelly to be fitted. I couldn't believe it. This was the same name on that box. Orry-Kelly must've done five thousand movies; he was very famous at MGM.

When I took the train to Pasadena, my mother cried; it was the first time I had really ever been away. I did take the 6-week acting course at the Playhouse, and they divided you into two groups. I was in the "beginner" group, and I worked on *The House of Bernardo Alba*.

Q So you decided to stay?
I liked California. It was the first time I had seen an ocean. And I was a very practical girl. I applied to UCLA, but I had five weeks before it began, so my roommate

suggested we move to the Hollywood Studio Club. It was very well known. It was kind of like a dormitory. Marilyn Monroe and Kim Novak had lived there. Joanne Worley became my best friend, and she told me she had an audition at NBC and she wanted me to accompany her.

Well, I did and while I was waiting, I began wandering up and down the halls. One of the rooms was open and there was a young man playing a piano. He asked me if I sang, I told him I did, and he began playing "Smoke Gets in Your Eyes," which I knew, so I began to sing it. When I finished, I thanked him, and he complimented me on my singing, and he introduced himself: "Jule Styne." I told him who I was and then I went back to Joanne. I really had no idea who he was at the time.

Well, when we were about to leave, the casting director asked me to read. I said: "Oh no, I'm only here with my friend." But she insisted, so I did and this was for the lead role opposite Michael Landon for a new TV series. They called me the very next day and I got the part. They paid me $450.

Q Was that your big break?

No, what really set my career was studying with Jeff Corey. My classmates included Jack Nicholson, Dean Stockwell, Sally Kellerman, Bobby Driscoll and Robert Blake. And they wanted to do *Look Back in Anger*. So we put it on, and Robert directed it, and a lot of people came to see it, including Ethel Wyant, the head of casting at CBS. She really changed my life. She got me the best agent in L.A. and he took me to MGM and Warner Brothers who both offered me seven-year contracts. When I was offered a role in *The Dark at the Top of the Stairs*, I knew it was a great role, so I signed, and my work led to my being nominated for the Oscar.

Q One of your most memorable stage performances was in *Kennedy's Children*.

I loved that play and the part. It was a very different role for me; no one thought I could do it. I was always cast as sensitive, sweet demur victims, so playing it was wonderful in terms of the exploration. The role I had played before that in *Dutchman* was similar in some ways, in that it was very emotionally raw. It really fed me and helped prepared me for playing Carla in *Kennedy's Children*. She was like a flowing, soft piece of silk, and people kept grabbing at her. I did a lot of Grotowski exercises working on that role.Years before when I had played the role of Juliet, one of the things that always drove me crazy was watching actresses do the "poison scene."They'd talk, take the drink and pass out. I thought it was so wrong. So when I did it, I sipped the poison throughout the speech, so it began to affect her as she went on. It's very similar to Carla. She's taken forty pills before she comes into the bar, so she's really slowly falling into that dying. I loved doing that part.

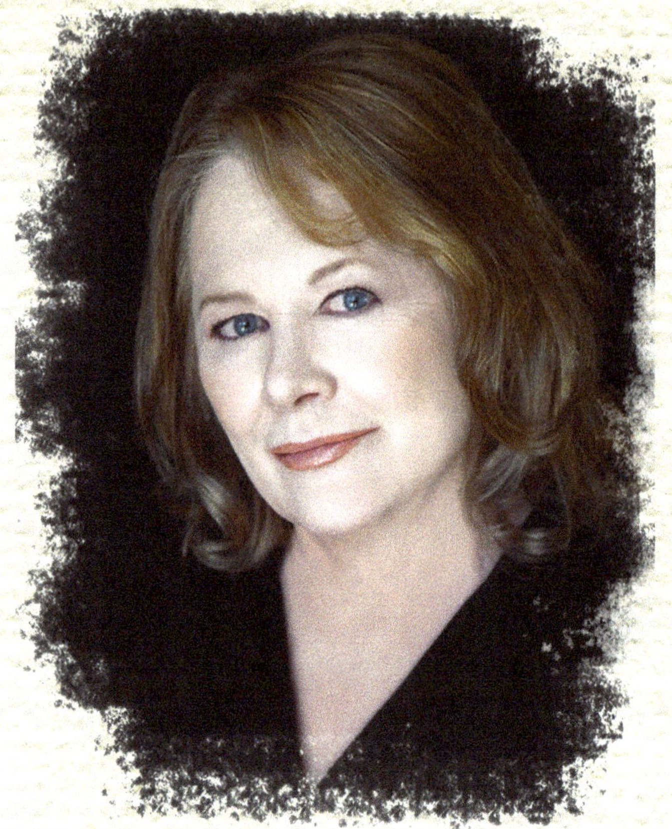

Shirley Knight photo: courtesy of the artist

Q How do you handle working on a play if the set's wrong or the director has a different take on your role?

There is a way to deal with it. You only focus on your part. You can't really change what another actor is doing, or change a director's interpretation. When I did *Landscape of the Body*, the set was going to be that set. What could I do? I went inside myself and the part. In that way, in the end I could win. I have no control over a set. I loved that role in *Landscape* and I worked very hard. You can't always do that in films.

Q What does it take to be a theatre artist?

You keep trying. Some of my greatest work wasn't in New York, like my work in *The Cherry Orchard* at the Arena Stage in D.C., or when I did Blanche in *A Streetcar Named Desire*. Tennessee Williams saw my work and wrote a play for me afterwards. You keep working and believe in the work. ■

STEPHEN LANG

Mr. Lang is widely known for his roles as Colonel Miles Quaritch in *Avatar*, Major General George E. Pickett in *Gettysburg*, Thomas "Stonewall" Jackson in *Gods and Generals*, and his one-man show, *Beyond Glory*. On Broadway, he played Colonel Nathan Jessup in the original production of *A Few Good Men*, *The Speed of Darkness*, and was Happy in the 1984 revival of *Death of a Salesman* opposite Dustin Hoffman, and in the television film. Off-Broadway Mr. Lang played Colonel Littlefield in John Patrick Shanley's play, *Defiance*, for which he received a Tony nomination, and in Arthur Miller's last play, *Finishing the Picture*, at Chicago's Goodman Theatre. He has performed his one-man show, *Beyond Glory*, for troops deployed overseas, and across America, receiving a Drama Desk nomination, and a Lucille Lortel Award for it. His film and television work includes the title role in *Babe Ruth*, *Manhunter*, *Last Exit to Brooklyn*, *Tombstone*, *Public Enemies*, *The Men Who Stare at Goats*, *Conan the Barbarian*, *Crime Story*, *The Fugitive*, *Terra Nova*, *In Plain Sight*, and *Into the Badlands*. He performed the narration for *The Gettysburg Story: Battlefield Auto Tour*, at the Gettysburg National Military Park. Mr. Lang was co-artistic director of The Actors Studio from 2004 to 2006.

Q What were your aspirations to be an actor?

I cannot remember a time when I did not want to be an actor. But I was sort of a "Peer Gynt"—I kind of lived in the dream of it; it was always in my future. As a boy, I watched films like *Robin Hood*, *King Kong*, *Frankenstein*, *Laurel and Hardy*, and I imagined myself into those stories. I remember being home sick from school watching a film called *The Long and the Short and the Tall* at least twice a day for a full week. I learned the script verbatim, and I imitated the dialects of Cockney, Aussie, Irish. I remember when I was eleven years old seeing Morris Carnovsky as Shylock, and he blew me away and broke my heart; I knew that was what I wanted to do. Years later, I was nominated for an award and Mr. Carnovsky was also a nominee; that was just an amazing moment of arrival for me, probably the first time I considered myself a true actor, and not an imaginary actor. What did I aspire to? I wanted to earn to right to call myself an "Actor."

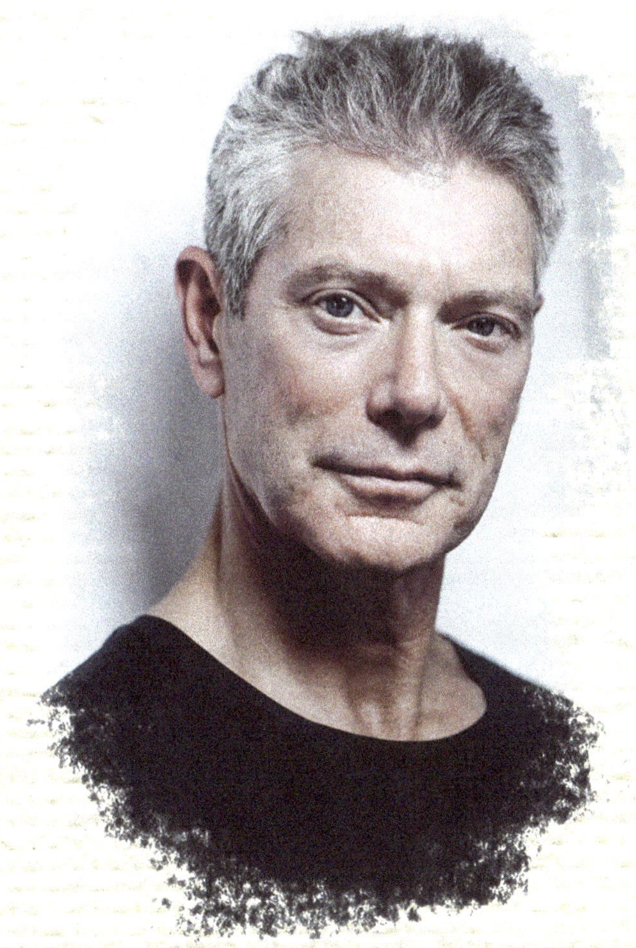

Stephen Lang photo: Jeff Vesta

Q Who are the strongest influences that have impacted upon your creativity?

I'm very impressed, and in a sense awed, by the immensity of talent out there. Specifically, I was inspired by Paul Newman. The way he practiced his craft, the way he lived his life, the diversity of his interests. As an actor he got better; he never stopped growing. Working with Dustin Hoffman as close as I did, was really what taught me the values of relentless probing and the pursuit never stops. Having worked with Robert Duvall, as Stonewall Jackson to his Robert E. Lee, he's one of the most extraordinary actors. When you look at the breadth of Meryl Streep's career, the scope of roles she has played both technically, the expertise and artistry it's required, and her rich soul, she stands as an absolute beacon to actors.

I admired Pete Seeger's commitment, his work politically. I do a lot of thinking about Abraham Lincoln. The thing about him that always strikes me is his tremendous humor, his sense of a deep self-deprecation, along with his fierce intelligence, and whatever he achieved was tempered by his humility. To me, he's something of a role model.

Q What led you to take on *Beyond Glory*, a solo play adapted from Larry Smith's book, portraying eight Medal of Honor recipients?

I wanted to take full responsibility for my life and my career. It's been a flat-out growing up experience. I felt the time had come to utilize my entire self. I wasn't sure I could do it initially. It's a great act of confidence and faith.

In the play I play an eighty-nine-year-old black man, Senator Inouye, and six other complex men; all eight characters requiring all my resources as an actor. The experience of going through what these men faced at these defining moments, again and again, in all states of exhaustion is highly energizing and thrilling. I allow the material to operate on me, and I've been surprised by what it takes to give it its full life and experience. I'm stirred, inspired, and humbled by the lives of these men. It's truly exhausting, but there's nothing more satisfying for me, and for those who come.

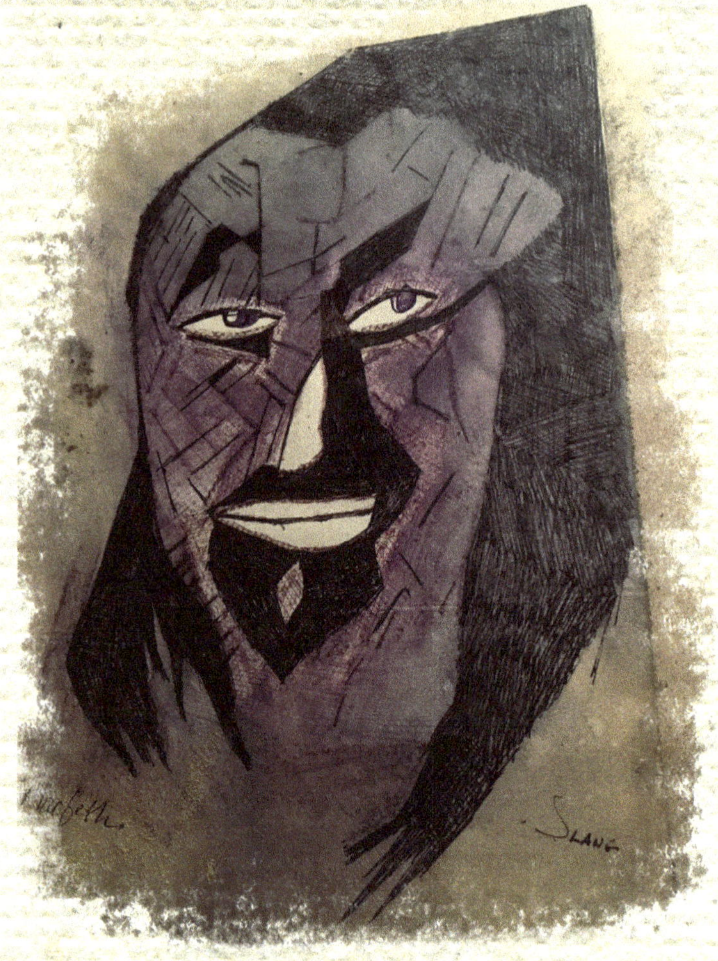

artwork: "Macbeth" by Stephen Lang, courtesy of the artist

Q You were involved in the world premiere of one of Arthur Miller's last plays at The Goodman Theatre, based on Lee and Paula Strasberg's relationship with Marilyn Monroe and her last film, *The Misfits*. Did you base your character of Jerome Fassinger on Lee Strasberg?

I tried to do via acting what Arthur was doing with writing, without impersonating or imitating. And God rest his soul, Arthur obviously wrote these characters based on Lee and Paula, but he clearly wrote different characters. I had studied with Lee in the 1970s, and as a member of The Actors Studio. I saw him teach many times, so I can't say I consciously did.

Arthur is one of my heroes. I love what he wrote; the way he changed the moral barometer of this country. Undeterred by any critical judgments of people, he followed his own path. Working with Arthur in the room was an immense experience again. Nothing he said went unnoticed. One of the first things he said was, "It's really a very funny play." Returning to work with him was a real full circle for me.

Q What does it mean to you when you return to act on stage?

The stage is my home. I feel I'm home in a theater. I love the cool darkness of an empty theater as much as I love the buzz of the crowd before the curtain rises. I find the ritualistic nature of theater comforting and reassuring, and at the same time each night is a new beginning, a new adventure, exciting and full of possibilities.

There is mystery in the theater as well, in the strange process of playing a role, of becoming someone else. And in the theater that process takes place over a sustained period, in increments, in moments of inspiration and epiphany and discovery. Working in film carries its own magic and demands, and I love it with all my heart; but returning to the theater is coming back to my roots, returning to the very fundamentals of acting.

I believe the impact we feel in the theater is immediate and electric; it's an experience of shared energy, passion, and intimacy: both private and public—it distills and crystallizes human experience. Theater, in Shakespeare's words, shows "the very age and body of the time, its form and pressure."

Q Have you found you share a "healing" experience with your audiences?

I think the short answer is absolutely yes. It's been beneficial to those who are a part of the shared experience. A couple of examples with my own show, *Beyond Glory*: I've been approached by vets or parents or children or spouses of vets, and they've talked to me about what the show meant to them. In many cases, it gave them an insight into what the veteran went through. For the vets, they find other men articulating feelings that they went through themselves. In many ways, the play helps healing to occur. To me, it's also an example of the power of the theatrical experience.

When I saw *Hamilton*, it also struck me as a "healing" work of art, articulating a story of our nation, which has been, in a sense, at war with itself, and the show makes it immediate for you. I remember when I did *Death of a Salesman* on Broadway with Dustin (Hoffman) in the early 80s, I could hear muffled sobs and groans from the men in the audience who recognized some chord deep inside, touching something in their own relationships.

Q Two of your most memorable portrayals are as Major General George E. Pickett in *Gettysburg*, as Thomas "Stonewall" Jackson in *Gods and Generals*. How much research did you do to create them?

Playing any role, fictional or historical, implies a contract between the player and the character. A contract to tell the truth, to represent honestly, to defend the role. I think there is a special responsibility when you play an historical figure. With both Jackson and Pickett there was an extensive historical record to draw from, and the reading and research was ongoing and fluid.

It was important to walk the ground they walked, to experience in a sensory way everything one can that duplicates or replicates the times and places in which they lived. And always to allow your imagination to roam, to travel to surprising places where surprising choices make themselves, but always observing fidelity to the man as you understand him to be.

Q What drew you to want to play Colonel Miles Quaritch in *Avatar*?

Ah, Colonel Quaritch! The world of Pandora, the scope of *Avatar*—what actor would not want to go there? The fluidity of that world, the spirituality, the wondrous beauty—and this is all lost on Quaritch. He doesn't get it. And that is incredibly interesting. His tension and conflict with the planet itself is tremendously dramatic. There is a journey, in every sense, for that character to take. It's going to be very exciting and demanding.

Q How would describe how you transform yourself into a character and the effect it has on your own growth?

I love being other people, to enter into them completely. The questions: How do I enter a character? Do I need red or blue, which color? That's how I began to work on *Beyond Glory* at The Studio. I have a maxim: "No rules beyond and above examination." It's a guiding principle for me. I have no fear opening up the world of possibilities that exist.

I think about what Daniel Boone said once: "Just because I don't know where I am doesn't mean I'm lost." The older I get, the whole phenomenon of "becoming" becomes all the more important for me. It's the only way I know to go about it.

T.S. Eliot defined poetry, and I may be paraphrasing, as a "state of complete and utter simplicity, costing not less than everything." I like to believe that my own direction and growth as an actor, and as a human, is embodied in those words. Simplicity and honesty achieved through hard-fought improvisation and imagination: rocky roads, tangled paths, dead ends, blind alleys that are to be explored, which will finally bring me to tranquil fields and shores of clarity and understanding. Or something like that. ■

LAURENCE LUCKINBILL

Best known for creating and performing his memorable one-man shows including *Lyndon* as *President Lyndon Baines Johnson*, which received an Emmy nomination on PBS; *Clarence Darrow, Tonight!*, which received a Dramatists Guild Award nomination and a Silver Gavel Award; *Teddy, Tonight!* as Theodore Roosevelt; and as Ernest Hemingway in *Hemingway*; all of these shows premiered in New York. *Hemingway* was commissioned by The Hemingway Foundation. All of his one-man shows were played at The Lyndon Johnson Presidential Library at the request of and for Ladybird Johnson. He performed *Lyndon* and *Clarence Darrow, Tonight!* at President Clinton's Second Inaugural Celebration. Mr. Luckinbill is well-known as Spock's half-brother, Sybok, in the film, *Star Trek V: The Final Frontier*. His theater career includes on Broadway in *A Man for All Seasons* with Paul Scofield; *The Shadow Box*, for which he received a Tony Award nomination; *The Boys in The Band*; in the first American production of Joe Orton's *What the Butler Saw*; *Chapter Two*; *The Electric Map*, for which he received a New York Critics Circle Award; *Poor Murderer*; at New York City's Public Theater in *A Prayer for My Daughter*; appearing as Bertolt Brecht's *Galileo* with his own company, The New York Actor's Theater; and he was a charter member of the four first-ranked American Repertory Companies in which he played many leading roles. His many television appearances include his own series, *The Delphi Bureau*; starring in James Ivory's *The 5:48*; and *Ike*. He also appeared in many films including *The Boys in the Band*; *Such Good Friends*, opposite Dyan Cannon; *Messenger of Death*, opposite Charles Bronson; *Cocktail* with Tom Cruise; and narrated Frank Thompson's documentary, *Moonwalk One*. He is married to actress Lucie Arnaz, and proud of his five children, Nick, Ben, Simon, Joe, and Kate.

Q Your performance as Clarence Darrow is an incredible tour de force. What compelled you to write, direct, and play this extraordinary "crusader of the common man's rights"?

It's been a transforming effort over the years. I was invited to play my solo performance as Lyndon Johnson in Boulder, Colorado for a Eugene McCarthy celebration, and I looked around for a "liberal" to write about and came up with Clarence Darrow. It piqued my interest, so I dug deeper into "The Story of My Life" by Clarence Darrow.

I learned that he had actually come to Pueblo for the Ludlow Mine Massacre trial, and in Boulder, I ended up meeting a 100-year-old gentleman who had attended the trial. I was worried that he would be critical of my performance, since he had been at the trial where Darrow appeared as a witness for the defense of the murdered miners.

But afterwards, all he said was, "You were wrong about one thing!" I said, "What?" He said, "Darrow never wore a white suit!" I actually was wearing a rented suit from the Mark Taper Forum in Los Angeles, which had been worn by Christopher Reeve when he did *Summer and Smoke*.

The theme of my play, *Clarence Darrow, Tonight!* is "What Is Justice?" Toward the end of his life, Darrow, who was not a rich man, went out to speak for small fees on the Town Hall and Chautauqua circuits, enduring long, hard train journeys to bring his message to those who would listen. He was often called "The Great Satan" for his agnostic views, which were intolerable, but fascinating to Americans stuck in Victorian moral codes, and racist attitudes.

He lectured on justice as a scientist, scouring his own experience to find out if it actually existed in this world or not. He was also called "The Defender of the Damned"—those who were seemingly indefensible, like Leopold and Loeb—or too poor to afford a lawyer. His passion was to find out the truth of why crime exists, believing that to understand "why" is to begin to be able to change society for the better. I think he was our greatest humanist.

Q What are some of the lessons you've learned from being on stage alone in a one-person show?

First of all, I've written my own shows, so I'm responsible for the stories I'm telling based precisely on the person's life. I call the series of four shows, *Great Americans*. Each man I've chosen—or, who somehow chose me—stood across his time as a Colossus. Each had ideas and beliefs about the nature of life, about politics and humanity that had to be dealt with by those in their time, and today in our time.

The struggles they faced were giant challenges and their responses against the odds were thrusts towards greater justice, and a better world for all to live in. They were witty, wily fighters, at ease in the constant conflicts they inherited. And each has been a great inspiration and a teacher of how we must make a better civilization.

Second, it was a huge surprise to find out that these shows, one by one, were going to free me from sitting by the phone waiting for some agent or producer to call me. I wrote, produced, and directed myself—for better or worse—and, as time went on, learned how to book myself everywhere I played. I was responsible for my own career. It has turned out to be a thirty-year odyssey with infinite possibilities.

Being alone onstage is always a problem; it can be lonely. So, I chose men who would, and could interact with those they were speaking to, and built in places in the script for that to happen. I eliminated distractions for the audience. I made bare evocative sets, isolated them in space, and was drawn into light or darkness as the story demanded, leaving only my voice and the words of these great men to guide them. I found that the audience can be a tremendously powerful force pushing the story along.

The imagination of a theater audience, once drawn into being by the actor, creates a collaboration. It becomes a great tango in which every move is instantly engaged, led or followed. Audiences have told me for years that they forgot that the one onstage was me—the actor—and believed

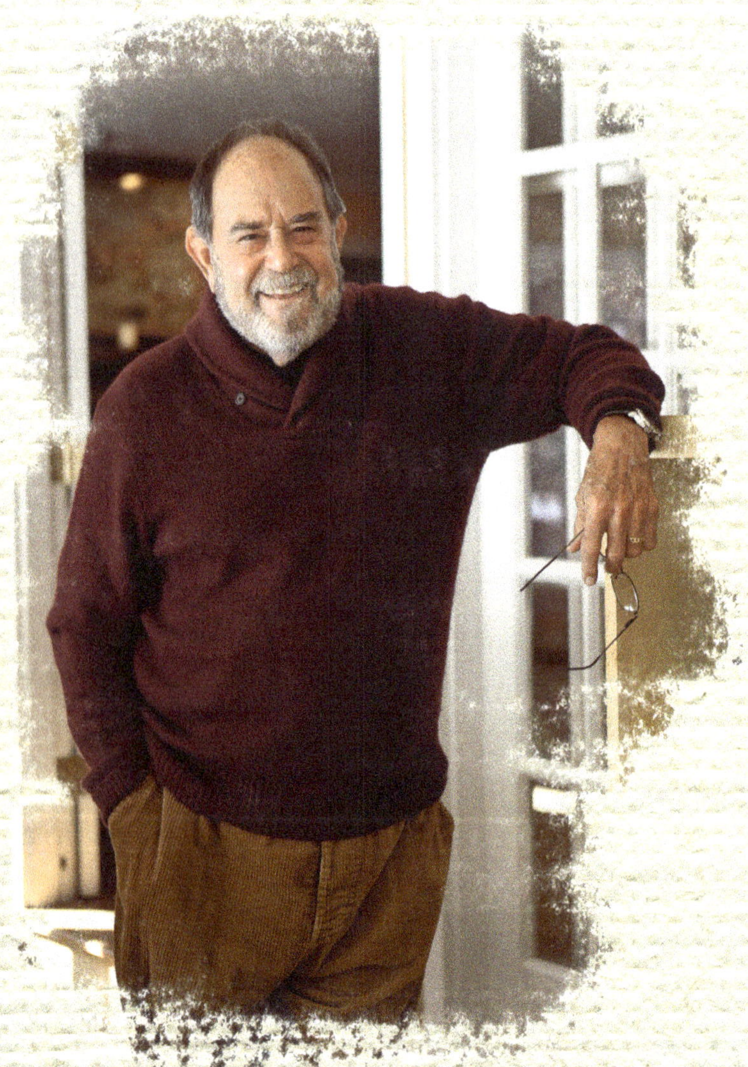

Laurence Luckinbill photo: courtesy of the artist

totally that I was "him," whoever "he" was. A great gift to an actor.

Q What have you learned about creating a role from performing as many roles as you have?

I'll tell you a secret: in a regular play surrounded by multiple actors, it takes 6 x 8, six weeks times eight performances, till you're actually alive onstage—really listening, really breathing—really thinking and feeling what the character is thinking and feeling. You exist, but as an adjunct to the character—as a facilit-ator. There is no difference between you and him. He is you.

In a one-man show, you rarely get a six-week run. It's often one-night stands. So, you rehearse, rehearse, rehearse. You do it for your family, your friends, for anyone who will listen, so you'll be prepared to give it the best you have "on the night."

The secret is the real joy that comes in giving it away! Only when you can play as if it is a free gift to the world in every performance, only then, in that purity, have you become the actor you have always wanted to be. ■

JUDITH MALINA

Ms. Malina, with her husband, Julian Beck co-founded The Living Theatre, a political theatre troupe that rose to prominence in New York City and Paris during the 1950s and 1960s. In 1945, she attended the New School for Social Research in New York City studying theater with Erwin Piscator. Ms. Malina and Mr. Beck worked in partnership to produce landmark plays including *The Connection*, *The Brig*, *Paradise Now* and *Dr. Faustus Lights the Lights*. Ms. Malina directed most of the troupe's shows. The company spent the five years touring in Europe, culminating in *Paradise Now*. Ms. Malina's film and television work includes *Dog Day Afternoon* opposite Al Pacino, *Looking for Richard*, *Awakenings*, *Enemies, A Love Story*, as Grandma Addams in *The Addams Family*, *Household Saints*, *Nothing Really Happens*, and *The Sopranos*. Ms. Malina's writings include her book, *The Enormous Despair*. Ms. Malina died in 2015. (This interview was conducted in 1999.)

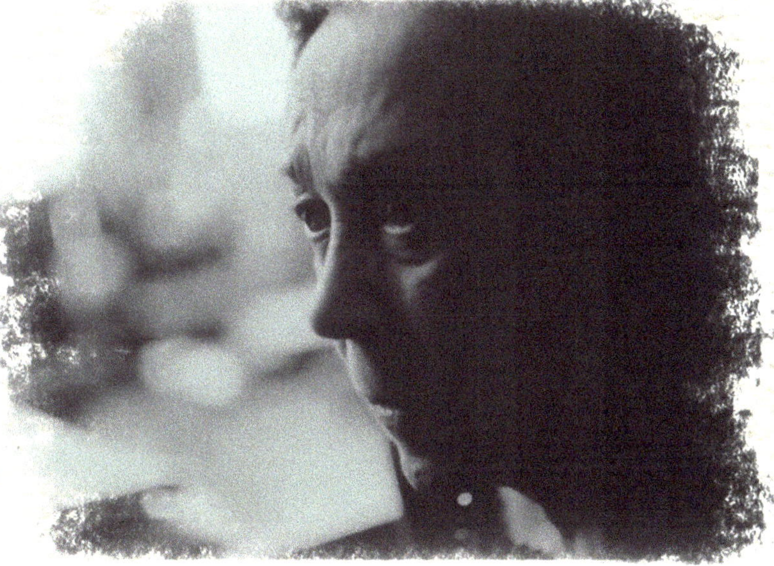

Judith Malina photo: Cordula Tremi

Q What would you describe as the role of the artist in society today?

I think the artist has an obligation to listen to the world's needs, through the seduction of the aesthetic, to change the world, to supply the needy of the world. Those being abused must be healed. The artist must suggest a better structure. The point is to revolutionize the structure.

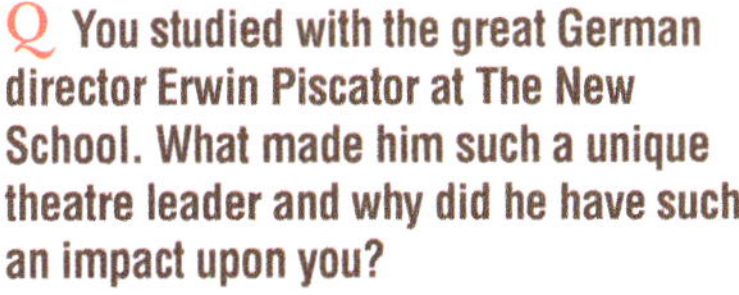

Q You studied with the great German director Erwin Piscator at The New School. What made him such a unique theatre leader and why did he have such an impact upon you?

He was a revolutionary. When I studied with him, I'd underline whole phrases in my notebook that he said, much like the Christians do with a Bible. The whole theatre would be more awake if he was around. Piscator wouldn't compromise like many artists. Maybe today we're ten to a hundred years closer to a true revolution with a world free of war, weapons, police, national boundaries, a prison society, a monetary system. If he were alive, he'd contribute to a greater understanding of our weaknesses, to show us how art is a useful thing, not just a decorative thing. Modern theatre has become too much about behavior and accepting things as they are.

Q When you spoke at the Fringe Festival Forum you said: "What we have today doesn't create a social change through the arts." What are we lacking?

We have no respect for the human mind. In Europe I'm considered an intellectual artist, but you can't say that here. These things are looked down upon and suppressed. Of course, Americans are vigorous, optimistic, thinking everything's possible, combined with real thought.

Look what happened in this country in the 1930s—we almost had a revolution. When the artists become intoxicated with the idea of ideas, things are possible. There's a big "swatch of cynicism" today, that's our biggest problem.

Q Are we making progress?

A favorite essay of mine is "Designing Pacifist Films" by Paul Goodman. He points out how so many film makers go out of their way to perpetuate the same myths in war films, showing the "thrilling" battle, heightened so the rush comes to the audience symbolically proclaiming "man is glorious" even while they say they want peace. The problem for the artist is to make "good as interesting as evil." Of course it's more interesting to show people fighting, but if were all share "goodness," that's "boring."

The Living Theatre has been trying to create the "great beauty play," to make the solution more interesting than the problem. If you want to raise eyebrows, try "goodness" and "kindness," "loving kindness." Why do we have "cynicism" gnawing away at us? It seems to be a character trait, a defense mechanism. Just as people are terrified to go unarmed in an armed world. We're afraid to be laughed at, we'll be thought of as "weak." It may spring from our having been invaders of another culture. And this "toughness" has become a feature of our society. We walk around with a certain amount of "hate" within us, but it diminishes our capacity to love.

Q And that's what you continue to work for?

I'm looking all the time for a vocabulary that's viable to the audience. The artist can't afford to act superior. If my audience doesn't get it, what am I not saying? Like the lover that strives to express the melody of love, this is the struggle of the artist—how can I go deeper? To make art to arouse people. I'm a committed optimist. We all have flaws, but I have seen the direct result of The Living Theatre's commitment for change. ■

JAN MAXWELL

Ms. Maxwell starred on Broadway as Elsa Schraeder in the first Broadway revival of Rodgers and Hammerstein's *The Sound of Music*, as Baroness Bomburst in *Chitty Chitty Bang Bang, The Dinner Party* opposite Henry Winkler and John Ritter, *Follies* with Bernadette Peters and Elaine Page, *A Doll's House* with Janet McTeer, *Coram Boy, The Royal Family, Lend Me a Tenor, Dancing at Lughnasa, Entertaining Mr. Sloane, Sixteen Wounded* with Judd Hirsch, *City of Angels, A Bad Friend, and The City of Conversation* at Lincoln Center Theatre. Ms. Maxwell has received five Tony Award nominations, won two Drama Desk Awards, a Lucille Lortel Award, Drama League Award, Outer Critics Circle Award, NYITT award, numerous award nominations, and she is the second actress to receive a Tony nomination in all four acting categories. Her Off Broadway appearances include: *My Old Lady, Entertaining Mr. Sloane, House and Garden, Scenes from an Execution, To Be or Not to Be, Victory: Choices in Reaction,* and *The Castle: A Triumph, Inside Out.* She performed at Carnegie Hall in the Stephen Sondheim concert, *Opening Doors.* At regional theaters across America, Ms. Maxwell has starred in *The King and I* opposite Richard Chamberlin, *The Seagull* at Washington, D.C's Kennedy Center, *Scenes from an Execution, Marvin's Room, The Marriage of Bette and Boo*, and *Snow White X.* Her film and television appearances include: *I Am Michael* with James Franco, Neil LaBute's Billy and Billie, *The Good Wife, Something Sweet, AIDS—Changing the Rules*, in four episodes on *Law & Order*, each time as a different character, and starring in the CBS series, *BrainDead* with Tony Shalhoub.

Q How would you describe your process as an actress?

I've never really taken an acting class. If you listen to me talk about acting, every theory would dissolve within five minutes. I really just dive in and see where it takes me. When I was in college, I was part of what was called "The StrawHat Players," and we'd put on ten plays in eight weeks. You did everything: lights, properties, act. That's really how I learned.

When I work on a script, I read it a thousand times. I usually go over my lines four or five times a day. Of course, there's always that danger of doing too much, so I have to know when to stop.

Q Does it help you working on a play with the writer present?

I love it. After all, it's his or her story, and whatever I can learn just helps me tell the story better. But I also have an irreverent quality towards the writer. My job is not to revere them. It's to play the character, to tell the story as specifically as it's been written.

My favorite directors are those who are focused, who know exactly where the eye of the audience should be. On one of the plays I did—*A Bad Friend*—Jerry (Zaks) had such wonderful energy. He wants it all to be wonderful, the best of all possible worlds. He gets so excited about what we're doing, it becomes contagious. It feeds you, you get giddy, you want to be a part of this collaboration. I so believe in collaboration.

Q Do you consider part of what you do is to present a particular point of view?

My job is not to "do something" to the audience. My job is to portray a character in a story. Now the writer may have had a specific idea of why he wrote the play, and what effect he's hoping it will have. But we're telling a story, plain and simple. You can't make it so important or righteous, or you'll bore people.

Q I remember when I attended one of the performances of *A Bad Friend*, the audience reacted out loud to what was happening on stage. Did that impact your performance?

It "jazzed" me. In that space, I had to have a thick "fourth wall" because the audience was so close. On the other hand, the lighting was so bright I also felt they were further away. It was sometimes difficult not to respond to what the audience said. When they reacted with laughter when I, as Naomi, was talking about my love for Stalin, I wanted to turn to them and say, "What's so funny!"

Q What did you learn about yourself playing Naomi in *A Bad Friend*?

That she was "closer to home" than I had originally thought. Naomi was a schoolteacher, so there was so much there for me, especially with how her mind worked. Her brain worked faster than mine, so I had to make sure I got out of her way.

When I was doing that particular show, every day I'd have strong reactions to what I read in *The New York Times*. I might be telling my son in the morning about something in the news, and he's jumping around, and out of the blue, I'd say, "Will you just stop and listen to me, this is important!" and my husband would turn and say, "Uh-oh, Naomi's here."

I've always been extremely interested in politics. Naomi was actually even more fervent in her passion. I based a lot of what I did in that role on my sister; she believed in many different causes. Jules (Feiffer, the playwright) told me that Naomi was all about his sister, that she would never doubt, even years later, even after what had happened became known.

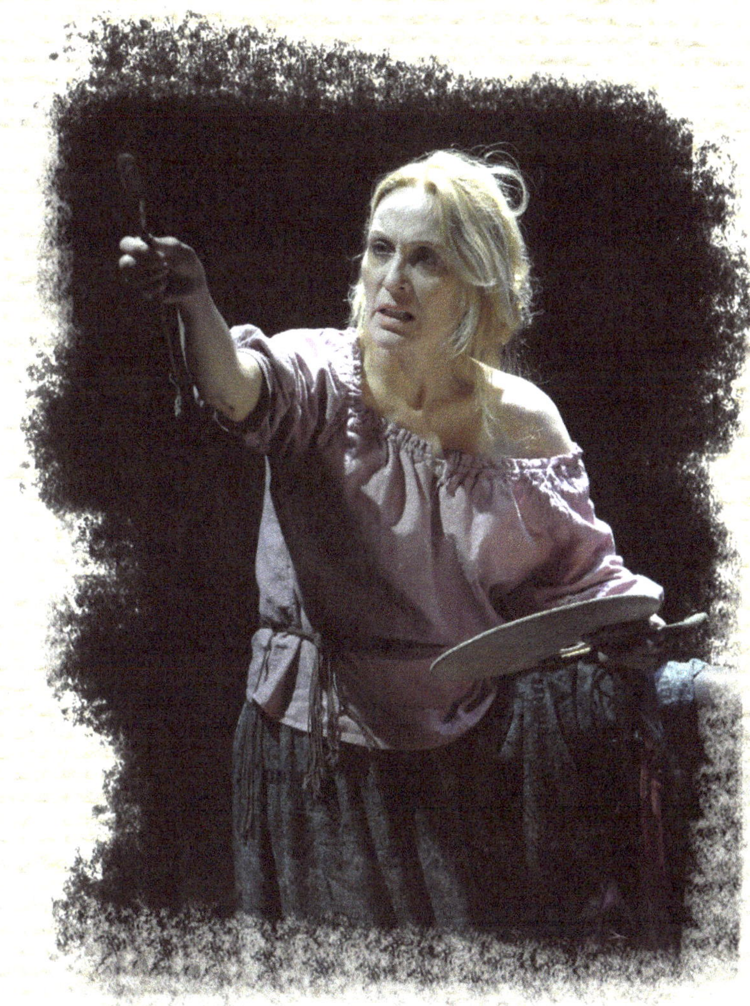

photo: Jan Maxwell as Galactia in "Scenes from an Execution" photo by Stan Barouh, courtesy of Mr. Barouh

Q What do you find most about exciting about being an actress and creating a role?

I really shouldn't be an actress! I don't like being told what to do. I hate changing clothes. I hate make-up. My favorite part is doing the research—going into all the history of the period, learning the culture, the language.

For example, when I first read the script of *A Bad Friend*, I immediately found a hundred things I had to look up. I was on the internet quite a bit—reading about the Scottsboro Boys, the Second Front in Europe, and Jules Feiffer was a well of information. *A Bad Friend* took place in the 1950s, which was an incredibly exciting time, and it wasn't that long ago. It's also quite a bit scary, when you think of what went on then, in relationship to everything that's going on now.

Q What does it mean being a part of the great acting tradition of the leading actresses in the American Theatre that stretches back to Charlotte Cushman and Minnie Madern Fiske, into the 20th and 21st century with actresses like Laurette Taylor, Ethel Barrymore, Rose McClendon, Lynn Fontanne, Ethel Waters, Uta Hagen, Geraldine Page, Kim Stanley, and Julie Harris, to mention a few?

I don't really put myself in that company. I really think of myself as simply an actress, and more times than not, the one who they'll say about, "Oh, she'll do anything." I suppose what it means to me is, when I watch colleagues of mine, the ones that stand out, I see truth and I think, "That's it!"

I also think of Eva Le Gallienne and Vanessa Redgrave. I would absolutely adore it if our society was able to provide such a thing as a National Theatre. It would be a wonderful and beautiful thing. I do feel such a loss that we don't have something like that.

I feel very fortunate to have strong family support, a supportive husband, and a good kid. I take solace in that. With everything that can happen, I think the best thing I ever did was have a child. Because when I go home and see my child, somehow everything else pales in comparison.

I really believe in the theater and that it will continue because of the love of the experience—of all the people gathering together, that they can feel each other next to them, feeling each other's breathing, and that anything can happen because there are live people in front of you. That's what's so incredible. You can't get that with any other medium. It's a very exciting feeling.

And for me that's what it is for me being on stage. It's so different from night to night. Probably what I love most about acting is empathy; that if everyone could put themselves into each other's lives, the world would be a better place. ■

RUE McCLANAHAN

Best known for her Emmy-winning role as Blanche Devereaux on *The Golden Girls*, for which she received an Emmy Award; as Vivian Harmon on *Maude*; and Aunt Fran on *Mama's Family*. Ms. McClanahan began her career on Broadway opposite Dustin Hoffman in *Jimmy Shine*. Her other Broadway appearances include *The Women, California Suite, and Wicked*. She received an Obie Award for *Who's Happy Now?* She performed in *Harvey* in London, *Lettice and Lovage* in Vienna, and in the New York and Los Angeles productions of *The Vagina Monologues*. Her television and film appearances include as Caroline Johnson in *Another World, Hogan's Goat, The Rimers of Eldritch, Colombo: Ashes to Ashes, The Fighting Temptations* with Cuba Gooding Jr. and Beyoncé, *Out to Sea* with Walter Matthau and Jack Lemmon, and as Matilda Joslyn Gage in *The Dreamer of Oz*. She received four Emmy Award nominations, and three Golden Globe nominations. Her autobiography, *My First Five Husbands...and the Ones Who Got Away*, was published in 2007. Ms. McClanahan died in 2010 (this interview was conducted in 2004).

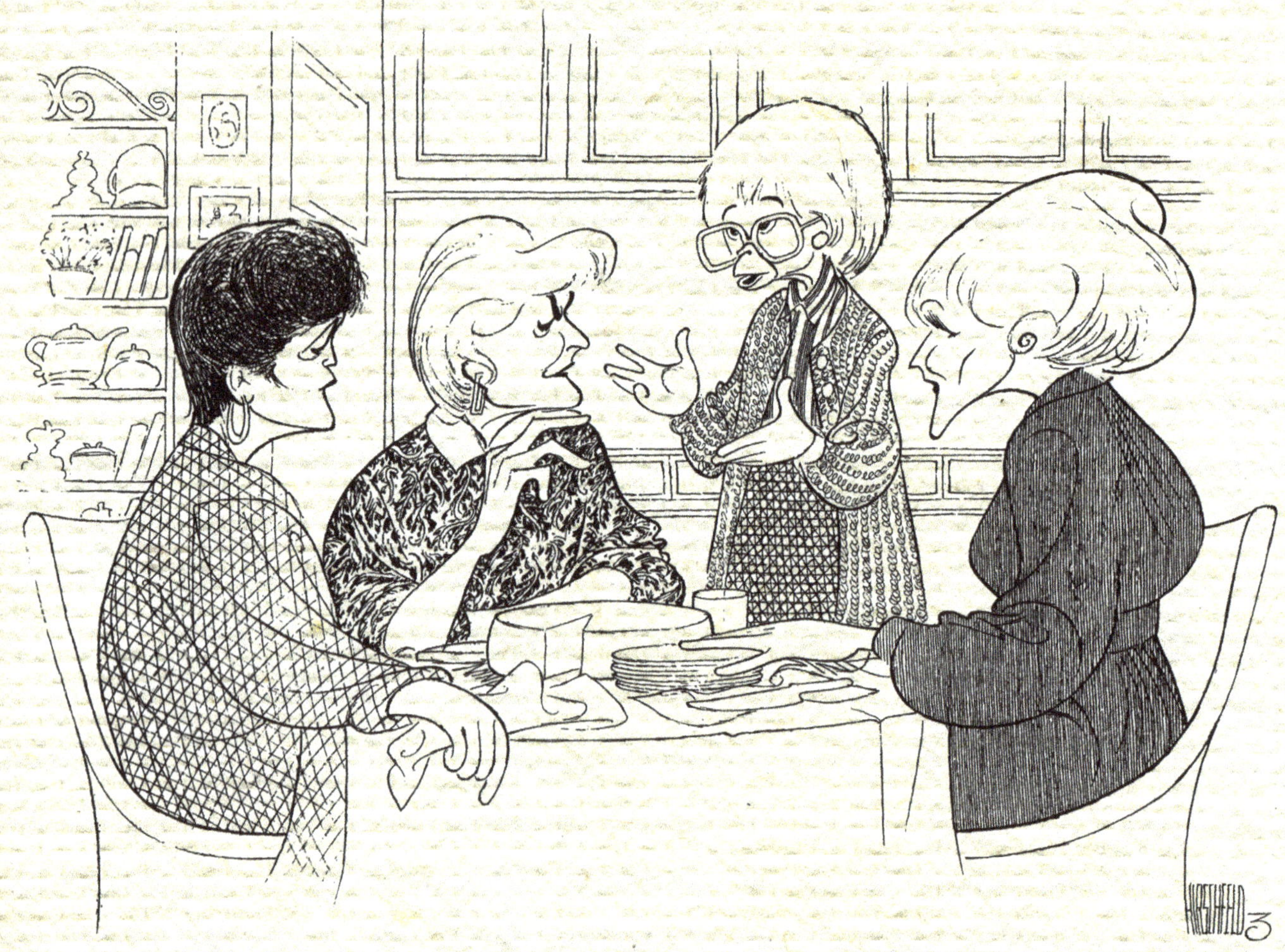

Rue McClanahan, Bea Arthur, Estelle Getty and Betty White in "The Golden Girls" by Al Hirschfeld © The Al Hirschfeld Foundation. www.AlHirschfeldFoundation.org

Q Was acting something you knew you wanted to do from an early age?

Only from about five. When I was two, I didn't know. When I was three, I refused to be a ring-bearer at a big wedding. I had rehearsed the day before but on the day I just panicked seeing all these people. When I was four, my mother lured me into tap dancing, but the noise was deafening so I dropped out. But at five I was in a play at kindergarten; I was one of the three little kittens. I thought, "This feels right, we're here to entertain."

Q Did you study to be an actress?

I had two very special teachers. Uta Hagen, when I first came to New York City. I was twenty-two, and I studied at HB Studios, and Ms. Hagen informed me that I hadn't really learned that much at the University of Tulsa. I took sixteen weeks with her. I remember doing a scene from *The Importance of Being Ernest* as Cecily, and Ms. Hagen pointed out to me, "What are you walking on? Is it pebbles? Where is the sun in the sky? Is it a warm day?" All these physical things I hadn't even thought about.

And I studied with Barney Brown at The Pasadena Playhouse on a scholarship. One thing he said to me made a deep impression: "You have to be brave enough to go way beyond what you think is safe—it's either sink or swim on stage."

Q I understand you also studied with Harold Clurman.

He was absolutely one of the most marvelous people in the world, the best lecturer who ever lived. I attended his 11pm class. You'd go in tired after having been in a show but once he started to talk, within five minutes, your fatigue was gone; you were brimming with enthusiasm. Two hours later you were so in love with the theatre you couldn't stand it! He was a phenomenal person.

Q Which actors inspired you?
I learned a lot from Bea Arthur on *Maude*. From her, I learned to go farther than I ever dared to go. I would have said, "It's too much," but I watched her and what I thought was too much, was so funny and so right. It was the same kind of extreme comedy you'd see from Bert Lahr or Zero Mostel or Lucille Ball.

I remember one very special moment in one of the *Maude* shows. After a party, Maude was cleaning up, and I went over to her house. And she was looking for her punch bowl. Maude couldn't find it and soon found out it was in pieces in a wastebasket. All the shards of the punch bowl were in there, and well, when Bea looked down into it, she didn't just look, she just completely bent herself over and just kept going down further and further down until her nose was in the wastebasket! It broke the audiences up to pieces.

Another time was when I had to come to the door dressed in plastic wrap. I think I realized it would be funny, but the moment when Maude and Walter looked at me—it had to have been one of the longest laughs we ever got on *Maude*. You learn from things like that.

Q What gave you the greatest satisfaction in working on *Golden Girls*?
It takes a certain kind of actor to really live through each show every week, learning a brand new script, being able to do it week after week. Naturally you never have enough rehearsal, you never really learn all those lines. Doing a sitcom is one of the most demanding experiences.

Blanche was one of my cherished characterizations. Betty White was going to play it. But after they saw me, and I read for them, they switched us. I just instinctively knew how to play Blanche. ■

PATRICIA NEAL

Ms. Neal was best known for her roles in *Hud* opposite Paul Newman, for which she received the Academy Award, BAFTA Award, National Board of Review Award and the NY Film Critics Circle Award; *The Subject was Roses*, for which she received an Academy Award nomination; *The Fountainhead* opposite Gary Cooper; *In Harm's Way* with John Wayne; and in Elia Kazan's *A Face in the Crowd* with Andy Griffith. Her other films included *The Day the Earth Stood Still*, *Breakfast at Tiffany's*, *John Loves Mary*, *The Hasty Heart* with Ronald Reagan, *The Breaking Point*, *All Quiet on the Western Front*; *Cookie's Fortune* and *Operation Pacific* with John Wayne. Ms. Neal's television work included *Little House on the Prairie*; as Senator Margaret Chase Smith in *Tail Gunner* for which she received an Emmy Award; *Joe, Murder, She Wrote*, and starring in *The Homecoming: A Christmas Story*, for which she received a Golden Globe Award. On Broadway her appearances included *The Voice of the Turtle*; *Another Part of the Forest*, for which she received the Tony Award; *The Miracle Worker* directed by Arthur Penn; *The Children's Hour*; and *A Roomful of Roses* directed by Guthrie McClintic. In London she performed in Clifford Odets' *Clash by Night*. Ms. Neal was inducted into the American Theatre Hall of Fame. Glenda Jackson played her in a television movie, *The Patricia Neal Story*. Her autobiography, *As I Am*, was published in 1988. In 1978, Fort Sanders Regional Medical Center in Knoxville dedicated the Patricia Neal Rehabilitation Center in her honor. Ms. Neal died on August 8, 2010 (this interview was conducted in 2006).

Q I'd like to begin with—
Are you going to ask me any sexy questions?

Q If you'd like—
I was just kidding.

Q But along those lines, how did you "fall in love" with acting?
It's what I always wanted to do. I "fell in love" when I started acting lessons when I was eleven. See, I went to this church and this woman was doing monologues and I'd never seen anything as exciting.

Q And when you first got to New York City—
You couldn't keep me home! When I first came to New York, two years after studying at Northwestern, I was nineteen. I got a job at a café cutting pies, scooping ice cream, and did the rounds. Probably not like it is today. Then I auditioned for *The Voice of the Turtle* and I got it. See, I adored the theater. It's all I wanted to be—a stage actress.

Q You seemed to have played some very self-motivated strong women—
I can't play anyone without any guts, and one of my favorite recent roles was a wonderful one in Robert Altman's film, *Cookie's Fortune*. What a sensational time it was, working with Glenn Close and Charles S. Dutton.

Q So Hollywood beckoned.
And they were such films to work on. I loved doing that role in *Hud* and working with Elia Kazan in *A Face in the Crowd*. He knew just what to do to get what he wanted. He tells you a secret and you'd do it, and it's so right. Working with him was very much like working in the theater. You know what I mean—"being alive" in the moment, having it "happen to you"—that's the key to everything. ■

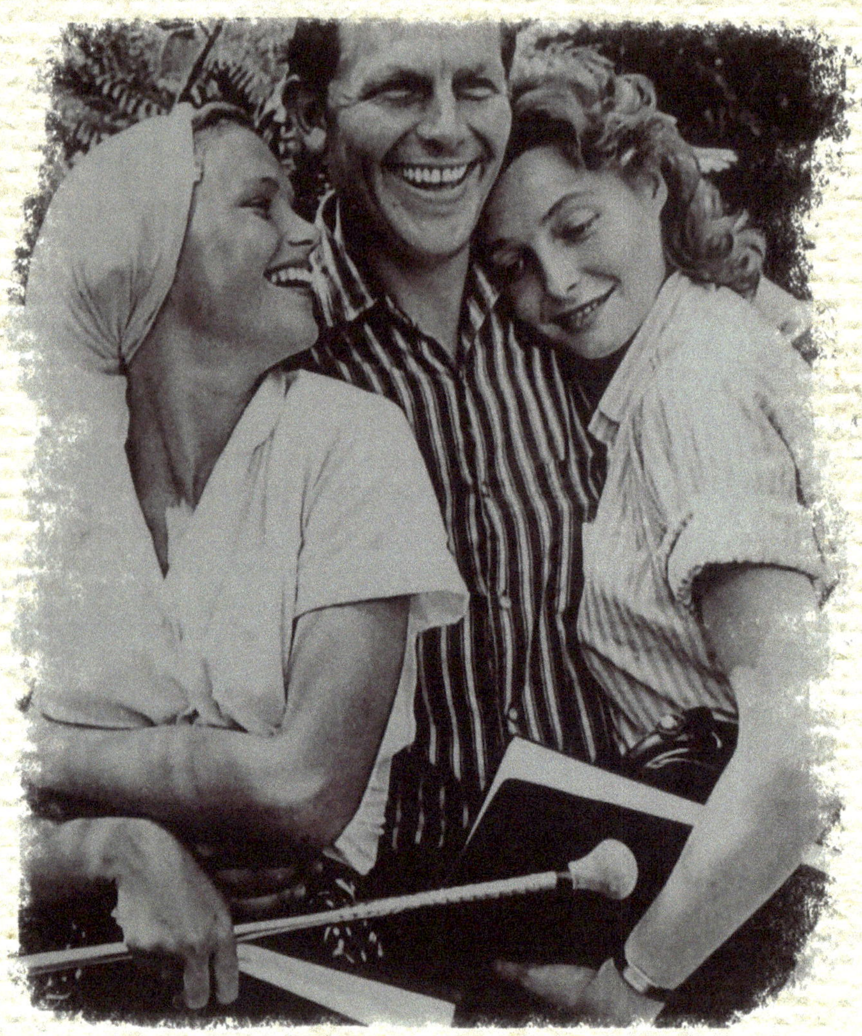

Patricia Neal, Andy Griffith, and Lee Remick on the set of Elia Kazan's "A Face in the Crowd," 1957, courtesy of the artist

JERRY ORBACH

Mr. Orbach was most well-known for his starring role as NYPD Detective Lennie Briscoe for twelve years on *Law & Order*, for which he received an Emmy nomination. He created the role of El Gallo in the original 1960 cast of *The Fantastiks*, the first to perform the show's song, "Try to Remember." He starred on Broadway in the original productions of *Chicago* as Billy Flynn, for which he received a Tony Award nomination; *42nd Street*; as Chuck Baxter in *Promises, Promises*, for which he received a Tony Award; *The Three Penny Opera*, *Carnival!*, *Guys and Dolls*, and a revival of *The Cradle Will Rock*. His film and television appearances also included *Prince of the City*, *Dirty Dancing*, *Crimes and Misdemeanors*, as the French-accented candelabrum, Lumière in Disney's *Beauty and the Beast*, *Chinese Coffee* with Al Pacino, *Golden Girls*, and *Frazier*. He was inducted into the American Theatre Hall of Fame, and was named a "Living Landmark" by the New York Landmarks Conservancy. A portion of New York City's 53rd Street near Eighth Avenue was renamed "Jerry Orbach Way" in his honor. Mr. Orbach died in 2004 (this interview was conducted in 2000).

Q **You began acting at the age of sixteen. What attracted you to the theater?**
Somehow the theater and acting in plays seem to come to me. I got picked to be in the school play and read "The Gettysburg Address" in a documentary. As a senior in high school I won the state singing competition, winning the gold medal in the baritone division. And then I went on as an apprentice doing summer stock outside of Chicago for $25 a week, and got my Equity card. When I was recently inducted into the Theatre Hall of Fame in my speech I said, "When I turned twenty-one, I was appearing in *Mack the Knife* opposite Lotte Lenya!"

Q **Who would you say you learned the most from as an actor?**
Well, my idols were Montgomery

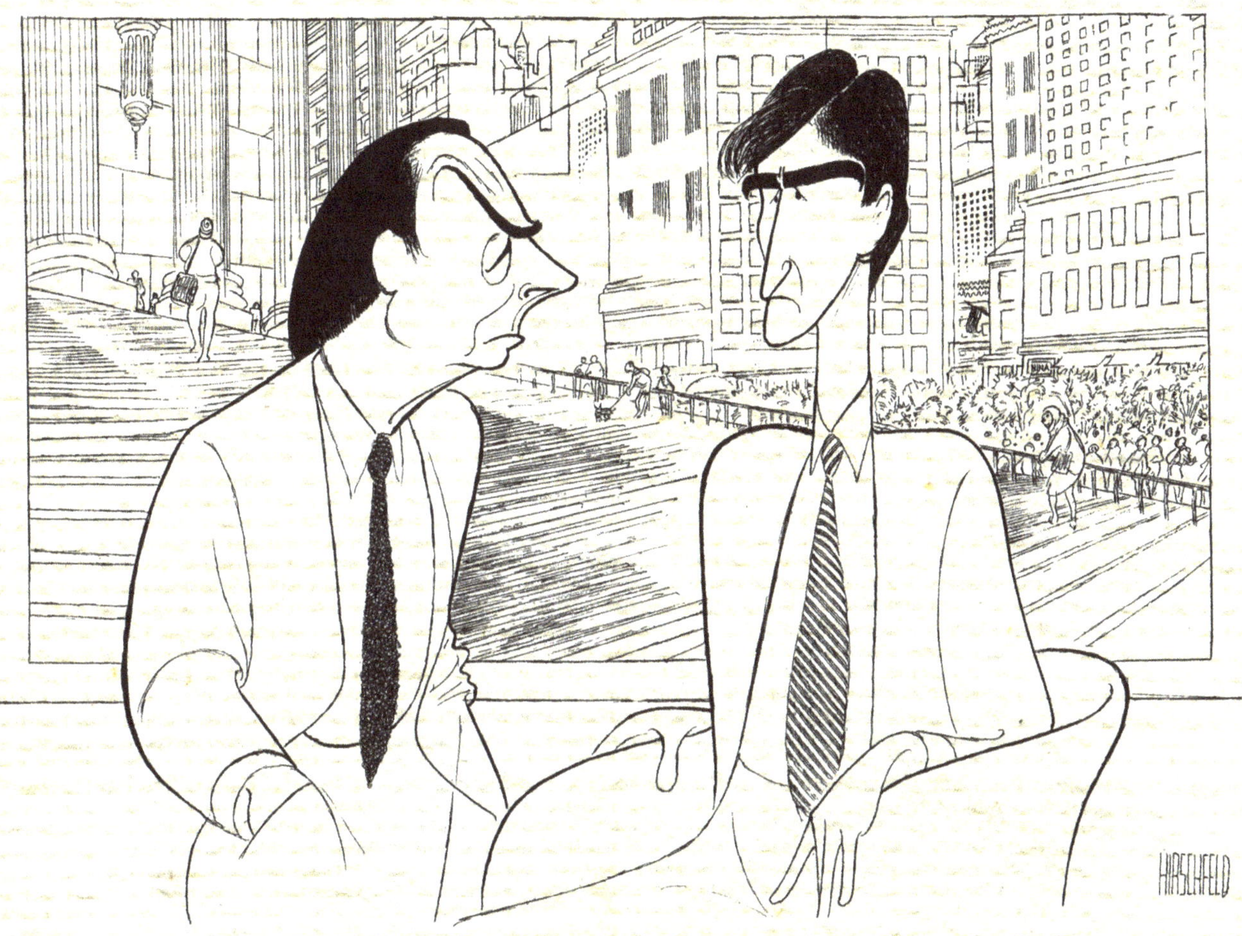

Jerry Orbach artwork: Jerry Orbach and Sam Waterston in "Law & Order" by Al Hirschfeld © The Al Hirschfeld Foundation. www.AlHirschfeldFoundation.org

Clift and Marlon Brando, whom I watched growing up. I also learned a lot from my teachers—Herbert Berghof, Mira Rostova, and Lee Strasberg.

Q You originated the role of El Gallo in *The Fantastiks* and joyously entertained *audiences in Carnival and Promises, Promises*, among others. Did it come easier to tackle roles in musicals than straight plays?

The difference was because I stayed, I got work here. My friends, Ed Asner, George Segal, Robert Loggia went to California. There was a lack of roles in plays, just like today, so they went to L.A. to work in film and television. There's never enough straight plays. I was a singer, so once I got my foot in the door I was able to work in musicals, and one thing led to the next.

Q You've been playing Detective Briscoe in *Law & Order* for several years. How do you continue to find ways to challenge yourself as an actor playing the same role?

Actually, I sort of have let my own life and Lennie Briscoe's become a part of one another. I walk in each day without studying the script the night before, coming in with no plan at all. So I'm wide open. I leave myself open to meet whomever I'm working opposite. So everyone I meet in the show is a new person, a character I'm meeting for the first time, just like in life. I'm flying by the seat of my pants.

Q One of the pleasures of watching you is your skill at making it look like you're not acting. Does that come from working opposite equally skilled actors or it something else?

Of course it's easier when the actors are skilled opposite you. You can't act in a vacuum. What it's all about is the illusion it's never happened before, making it look like the first time. That's the art. ■

ANGELICA PAGE

Ms. Page has toured in her acclaimed, award-winning solo play, *Edge*, as Sylvia Plath, around the world and across America, receiving an Outer Critics Circle nomination, and New Times Award. She has also appeared on Broadway in *Side Man* in London's West End and at Washington, D.C,'s Kennedy Center, receiving a Helen Hayes Award; in the national tour of *August: Osage County*, receiving a Helen Hayes Award nomination; and in *The Best Man*. Ms. Page's first professional debut was standby for the late Natasha Richardson on Broadway in *Anna Christie*. She played the lead in *Machinal* at The Actors Studio in New York City, and has appeared Off-Broadway opposite Elizabeth Ashley in *The Red Devil Battery Sign*, and regionally in Edward Albee's *Who's Afraid of Virginia Woolf*, directed by Michael Wilson, receiving a Carbonell Award nomination. Her television appearances include *Law & Order, The Sopranos, 100 Centre Street, Law & Order: Criminal Intent, Ruby's Bucket of Blood* opposite Angela Bassett, and in *Songs in Ordinary Time* opposite her cousin, Sissy Spacek. Ms. Page's films include *Nobody's Fool, The Sixth Sense, The Contender, Fast Food Fast Women, The Hungry Ghosts* directed by Michael Imperioli, and *Domestic Disturbance* opposite John Travolta. Her parents are Rip Torn, and the late Geraldine Page, whom she portrays in her new solo show, *Turning Page* directed by Wilson Milam.

Q What does it mean to you continuing the family acting tradition of your parents, Rip Torn and the late Geraldine Page?

I avoided acting for a long time, although everyone assumed I was going to act; except my father, he was full of many cautionary tales. I've always enjoyed being rebellious, and even now I often say, "I'm not an actress." But acting has helped me maintain my relationship with my mother after she passed away. She wanted me to be an actress and planted a lot of seeds in me to lure me in.

I've acquiesced to the fact that it's my duty to continue this style of work that my mother unearthed within herself and instilled in me. The more I work, the more I intimately understand my mother, and the more intimately I understand human beings. I grew up backstage with my mother and to have performed on Broadway, twice on 45th Street where my mother had such great success, that's very special to me.

Q You had a most unique experience playing two different roles at different performances in Warren Leight's *Side Man*. How did that come about?

I started with *Side Man* when the role of Patsy barely existed; I think she had four lines. But when Warren met me, he said, "I can write Patsy now." It took two and a half years of development out of town and Off-Broadway for the play to finally arrive at the Roundabout Theatre. And while we were running there, Edie Falco, who originated the lead role of Terry in *Side Man*, was cast in *The Sopranos*.

I offered to keep Edie's "spirit" in the show by playing that role when she was unavailable. I knew the part and the way she developed and performed it. The director, Michael Mayer didn't want to lose me as Patsy, but eventually the producers agreed that if they couldn't have Edie, I was the best alternate. It was such a demanding role, and it could be easy to get off on the wrong foot with the character, to make her a villain. But I didn't. I became the "sidewoman" of the cast.

I also had the opportunity to play two roles in Gore Vidal's *The Best Man*. I first created the luscious cameo role of Catherine then slid over to one of the female leads to replace Cybil Shepherd with eleven hours' notice. The characters couldn't have been more different. What fun!

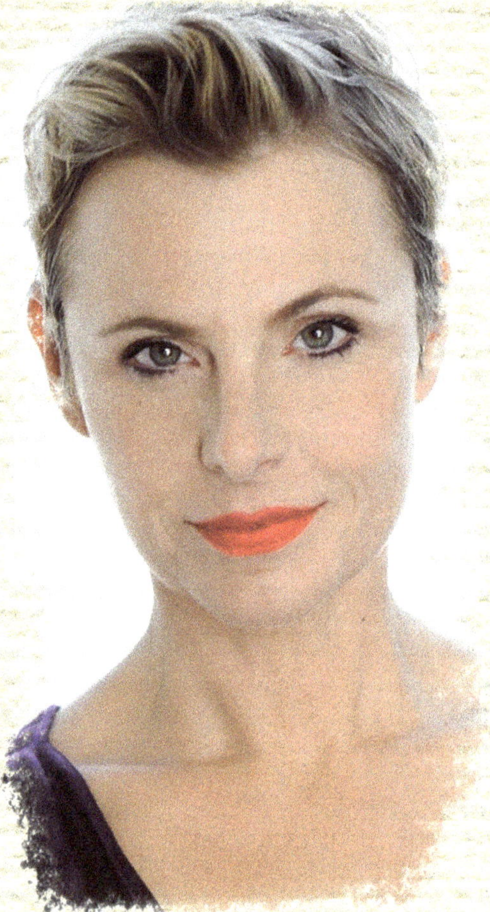

Angelica Page photo: courtesy of the artist

Q What similarities and differences did you find playing two entirely different characters in *Side Man*?

Actually Terry and Patsy are very similar women in some ways—the simple, pure core of their wanting to be loved, to be happy, to not wanting to settle for less. The main difference between them is that Terry is undone by her choices. Terry is destroyed by choosing a lifetime surrounded by jazz musicians while Patsy thrives within that atmosphere.

In all the characters I've played I try to come to their core, the soul. I mean, we all want to be loved, but we guard ourselves, and we hurt people at times before they hurt us. I think that's the most important thing to find—the humanity. To learn not to judge a character you're playing.

Q And *Side Man* won the Tony Award for best play of 1999 –

It was so exciting, incredible! I thought, "This is the way theater should be, for a play to start on such a small level and win the Tony!" I was so proud to be a part of it. If you choose art, art will choose you.

Q You also played Honey opposite Elizabeth Ashley in Edward Albee's *Who's Afraid of Virginia Woolf* –

It was a wonderful thing to happen. I first met Elizabeth when she was in *Agnes of God* with my mother and she scared me to death. After she saw my work we became fast friends. She said I should play Honey, and that intrigued me.

Edward Albee was very much involved in the casting of that production. There're so many ways you can go into a meeting. What I do is to hold myself up to the light in the most exposed and vulnerable way I can fathom. I also spent a fortune at Elizabeth Arden for the audition, having them give me a "Honey look"—the 1960s nails, honey-colored hair, everything. I went to a thrift shop and bought a mousy tweed dress.

Edward looked out the window the entire time I read during the audition. It could have seemed like he wasn't interested, but I knew he was listening intently to the words. You do not improvise Albee's work. If there's a period, they are there for a purpose. He gave me one note after I got the role—"That's not a dash, that's an ellipsis." He's a most talented writer, and that play is a masterpiece.

Q Why did you want to create your own solo play as Sylvia Path?

Sylvia has been on my radar since I was fourteen years old. I was captured by her unwillingness to mold herself into something convenient. I found her frightening and fierce, restless, misunderstood and vilified. I've had a past life regressionist tell me I was Sylvia in my last life. All this made the idea of creating a piece that would let Sylvia's spirit have her say, very challenging and that in turn, is very attractive to me as an artist. And perhaps I believed it might help put her ghost at rest somehow. She's always felt so not at rest in any way.

I've now been channeling her for over a decade and I've just been asked to play her in a film version. A woman in London approached me after a performance as if I was Sylvia: "I still don't like you but at least now I understand you," she said. I felt like that was a huge compliment. She had known Sylvia and was completely convinced that I was her.

My goal as an actress is never to worry about being liked but rather to allow the character to be understood. Now I'm playing my mother in my new show, *Turning Page*.

Q What gives you the greatest joy creating?

Inspiring others through my work. My mother said something wonderful about this that I keep with me always: "One should always be beginning to work—and then you allow others to dream." ■

CHRISTOPHER PLUMMER

Regarded as one of the most foremost Canadian actors of his generation, Mr. Plummer is probably best known as Captain Georg von Trapp opposite Julie Andrews in *The Sound of Music*. He received the Academy Award for *Beginners*, and an Academy Award nomination as Leo Tolstoy in *The Last Station* with Helen Mirren. He received Tony Awards for his performances in Anthony Burgess' musical, *Cyrano*, and as John Barrymore in *Barrymore*, for which he also received the Drama Desk Award and Outer Critics Circle Award. His Broadway appearances include opposite Katharine Cornell and Tyrone Power in *The Dark is Light Enough*, for which he received a Theatre World Award; *The Starcross Story* opposite Eva La Gallienne; *The Lark* with Julie Harris; *J.B.* directed by Elia Kazan; *The Royal Hunt of the Sun*; as Iago in *Othello* opposite James Earl Jones; *Macbeth* opposite Glenda Jackson; *No Man's Land* with Jason Robards, Jr. for which he received Tony, Drama Desk, and Outer Critics Circle nominations; *Inherit the Wind*, for which he received a Tony nomination and a Drama Desk Award; *The Good Doctor*; and in *King Lear*, for which he received a Tony nomination. In Paris, he appeared opposite Dame Judith Anderson in *Medea*. Mr. Plummer was a leading member of Britain's National Theatre under Sir Laurence Olivier, and the Royal Shakespeare Company led by Sir Peter Hall, where he performed in *Beckett*, receiving the Evening Standard Theatre Award. With the Stratford Festival of Canada, under Sir Tyrone Guthrie, he performed in many great roles, including Julius Caesar in Shaw's *Caesar and Cleopatra*, and Prospero in *The Tempest*. His films include *The Fall of the Roman Empire*, *The Night of the Generals*, *The Man Who Would Be King* with Michael Caine, *The Royal Hunt of the Sun*, *Murder by Decree*, *The Girl with Dragon Tattoo*, *Battle of Britain*, *Waterloo*, *Star Trek VI: The Undiscovered Country*, as Aristotle in *Alexander*, as Mike Wallace in *The Insider*, and *Remember*. Television appearances include *Hamlet at Ellsinore*, *The Thorn Birds*, *Nuremberg*, *American Tragedy*, for which he received a Golden Globe nomination; *Our Fathers*, for which he received an Emmy nomination; and he co-starred with Gregory Peck in *The Scarlet and the Black*. Mr. Plummer's autobiography, *In Spite of Myself: A Memoir* was published in 2008. Mr. Plummer has won many honors in Canada, the UK, America, and Austria, was invested as Companion of the Order of Canada, received the Governor General's Performing Arts Award, and was inducted into the American Hall of Fame and Canada's Walk of Fame.

Q What was the greatest challenge bringing John Barrymore to life in *Barrymore*?
The greatest challenge wasn't playing him, as much as giving the piece some substance. Bill Luce and I worked a great deal on creating a depth in the play. It was hard to find the pain he was in and put that on the stage. We both knew he never showed it but it was always evident. He was not an indulgent or self-pitying creature. We went as deep as we could to find the serious side of Icarus. I think we were successful; we worked hard on it.

Q Do you have to fall in love with the role you play?
Well, there's "falling in love" with the material, but one must guard against that. One must never indulge one's self. We're always inspired by great material; but it's a constant love and hate relationship. There's not a great actor who didn't have the "noble" temperament. They all had it: Irving, Salvini, Olivier. Think of Olivier's flair-up when he played Richard III.

Q What excited you about taking on Shaw's *Caesar and Cleopatra*?
It's such a marvelous role; it's a tonic of a play. It has glamour and sex, and that's very unusual for Shaw. And it's also very timely today, with Caesar occupying Egypt in the play. Caesar admitted he wished he hadn't gone there.

Q You've said that one must have a certain amount of contempt for the role, the writing, even the audience.
It's a wonderful contempt; in order to raise our profession to the dignity it does not deserve. You have love, and you have hate—in order to overwhelm those who come. We should, at times, be more like the poor actor, the vagabond, whom has never been accepted.

When Henry Irving was knighted, it changed everything. We had those polite, careful drawing room comedies, and the actor now had to be dignified to work on the stage. But an actor is really a vagabond. He was before, unruly and dangerous. I think it makes it all so much more exciting.

Q I understand you knew Harold Clurman.
Yes, I had gone to his classes, and he was interested in working with me. He had a particular play in mind. But unfortunately it didn't happen. I admired him greatly. I can't wait to see you in your play as Clurman.

Q You have had the extraordinary opportunity to work with several inspiring directors, among them: Elia Kazan, Tyrone Guthrie, and Theodore Komisarjevsky.
They all have the same attitude. Guthrie's attitude was the theater is like a three-ring circus, which had a large canvas on which he loved to work. He had an enormous sense of humor. Kazan was a very different fellow. He was wonderful at political drama, and he had his own set of immigrant background that spurred him on. They all were very exciting to work with—their great energy; Guthrie had more fun. They had the passion to get to the truth

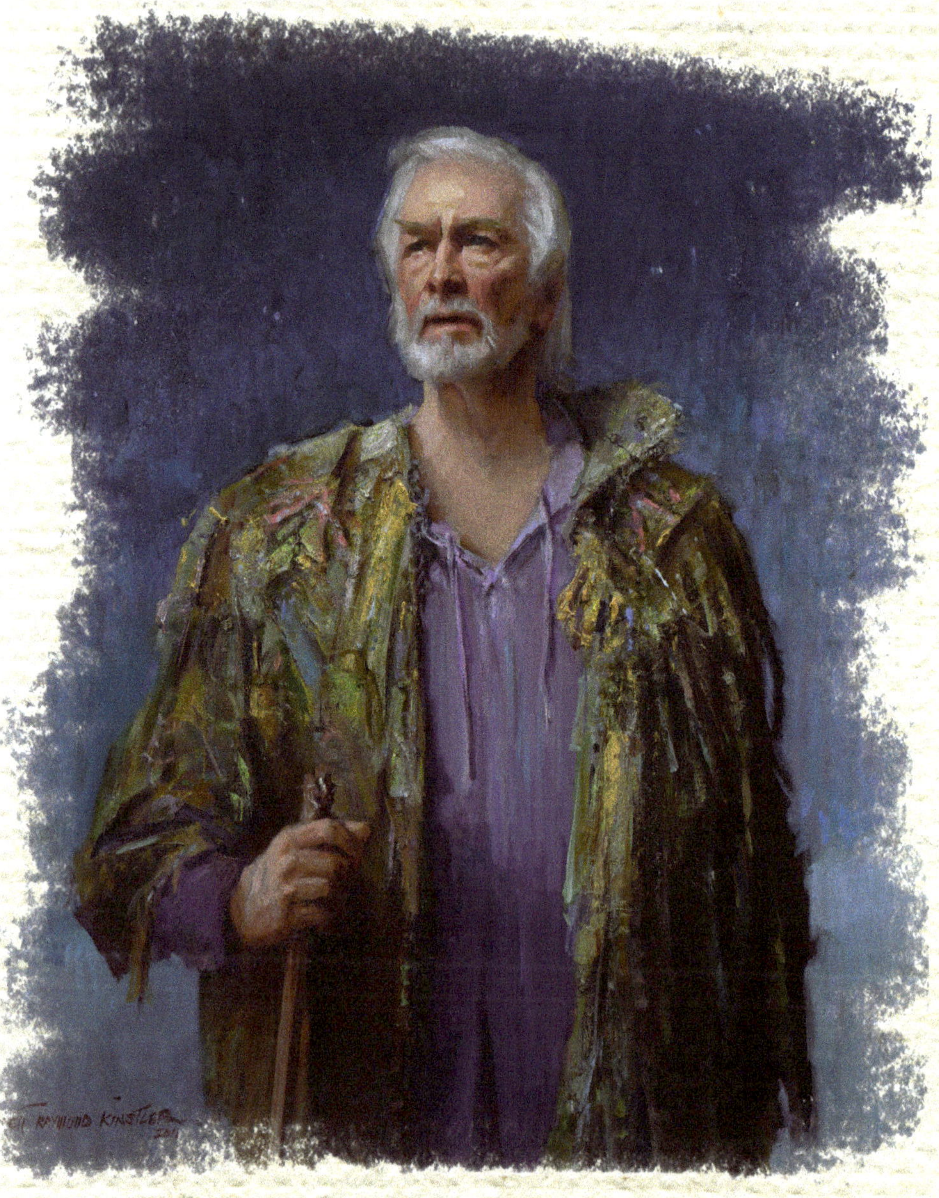

Christopher Plummer artwork: Christopher Plummer as Prospero in "The Tempest" by Everett Raymond Kinstler, courtesy of Mr. Kinstler

burning in them. None of them were infallible. They admitted their own mistakes, they were self-critical.

When I worked with Komisarjevsky, he had the other view, opposite than Stanislavsky, in his way of working. They all had basically the same passion for the theater, but just worked at it in their own different ways.

Q You do a great deal of film and television work, but constantly return to the stage. What makes theater important for you?

I put it in my book: I make my case. It's always been a place to go and hear ideas but today, unfortunately, not enough people want to think. We are unable to understand or appreciate the nuances and humor in language. It's a tough road for the theater today. Eventually, the actor comes back to the theater because he discovers he needs to experience this kind of work. It's where the imaginary forces work. And that is what the theater offers us.

Today you have everything spelled out for you in film, but you have to work in the theater as an audience and imagine what you don't see. That is the magical force. We need it. It will never go away. Also because the writing is so wonderful. We have the best writers and poets writing for the stage. There is always less dialogue in film.

I go back to the theater because I love the music of the words and the poetry. And it isn't always the theater for me. I adore painting and music, and the beauty of nature. I absolutely adore it. But I'm not pleased with what we're doing to it as a human species. I still have hope, though. There's an optimism boiling up inside of me. I want to do so much more. ■

BILL PULLMAN

Known for his memorable film work including as the President in *Independence Day* and *Independence Day: Resurgence*, Mr. Pullman also appeared on Broadway with Julia Stiles in *Oleanna*, opposite Mercedes Ruehl in Edward Albee's play, *The Goat, or Who is Sylvia?* at Second Stage in Edward Albee's *Peter and Jerry*, receiving Drama Desk nominations, and in *The Subject was Roses* at Washington, D.C.'s Kennedy Center. Mr. Pullman's other films include *The Accidental Tourist* receiving an Academy Award nomination, *Red Sky, Cymbeline, The Equalizer, LBJ, Rocket Gibraltar, Brain Dead, Home Fires Burning, Liebestraum, A League of Their Own, Crazy in Love, End of Days* miniseries, *Revelations, Ruthless People, Spaceballs, The Serpent and the Rainbow, While You Were Sleeping, Lost Highway, The Grudge, Scary Movie 4, Nobel Son, surveillance, Bottle Shock, Phoebe in Wonderland, Kerosene Cowboys, The Killer Inside Me, Peacock* opposite Susan Sarandon, *Lola Versus*, and *The Innocent*. His television appearances include *Night Visions, Tiger Cruise, Revelations, Too Big to Fail, Innocent*, as Oswald Dances in *Torchwood: Miracle Day*, and as President Dale Gilchrist in *1600 Penn*. Off Broadway, Mr. Pullman appeared as Wesley in a revival of *The Curse of the Starving Class* with Kathy Bates. At the Los Angeles Theatre Company, his appearances include *Barabbas, All My Sons, Demon Wine* and *Control Freaks*. As a stage director, Mr. Pullman directed and played the title role in *The Virginian*, which received the Wrangler Award for Best Picture. Mr. Pullman's play, *Expedition 6*, was performed at San Francisco's Magic Theatre and at New York Stage and Film's Powerhouse Theater.

Q When did you say, "I have to be an actor"?

I didn't know it until I was in college; that's when I knew I was hooked. I was in some plays, but that was it. Somehow I first got involved in a play in college with a very good director. I come from a small town.

Q What kind of acting fascinates you?

I think it's when there's a certain resistance to emotion—that captivates me. There's always something that's interesting it seems when a character is pushing away from something at a certain point, I find that interesting.

Q What did it mean for your growth bringing Peter to life in Edward Albee's *Peter and Jerry* at Second Stage?

It meant a great deal to me that Edward saw me in those plays. When I received the play I was really curious to see what he had done with the first act, since so many years had passed since he had written *The Zoo Story*.

During rehearsals, when I'd ask him a question about the play or Peter, from what he would say you'd realize there's much more information that I could find out. Edward said he wrote *The Zoo Story* because he had written one and half characters in *The Zoo Story*. So we're now able to see Peter at home, how he reacts to his wife; he supplied a full character.

I did learn the

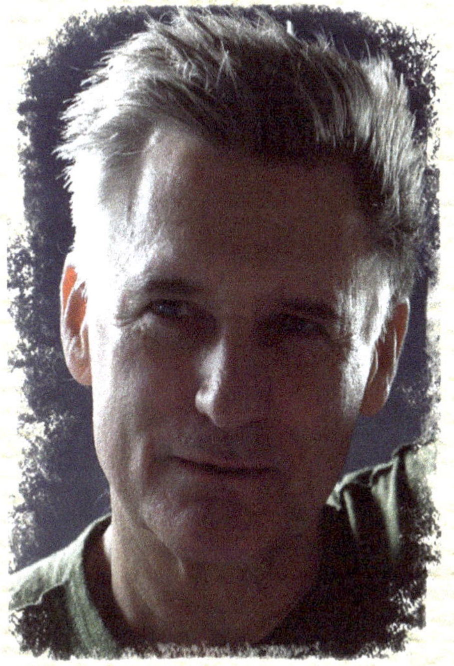

Bill Pullman photo: Claudia Barrius, courtesy of Ms. Barrius

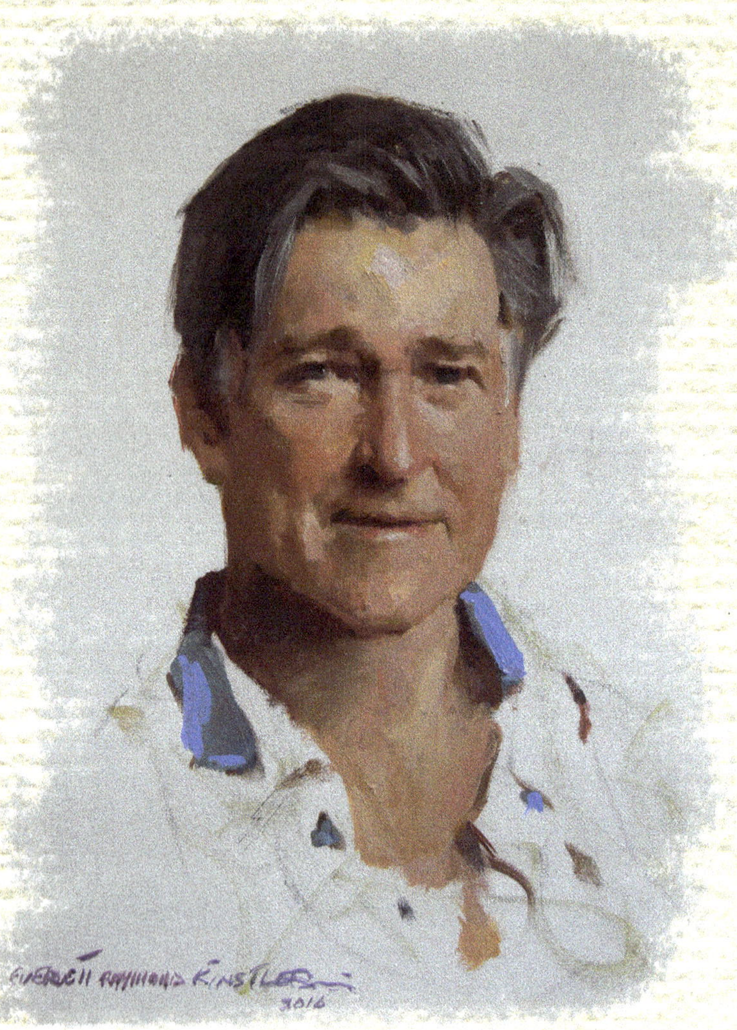

Bill Pullman artwork: Bill Pullman by Everett Raymond Kinstler, courtesy of Mr. Kinstler

power to carry something through the run of a play; to register in one moment what Peter is feeling and have it continue to resonate. And there's nothing like doing a play about New York in New York City.

Q What kind of research helped you find Peter?

Early on, it was important to me to not become too rigid in my body. I was very conscious of my breathing, and how Peter breathed.

Q How did you discover who he was?

I had lot to draw from. A certain amount of it came from listening to people; from watching how they listened to one another. Also from observing people as I took a walk from 33rd Street up Lexington to Central Park. There's a certain nature to the streets, and every person on them.

It says in the play that Peter lives at 33rd Street and Lexington Avenue. You can walk that walk as it's described in the play, and pass all these pit stops. For example, where he might get his haircut, buy his socks—as you're making your way to the jungle of Central Park. Of course what Central Park was when Edward wrote the play is not the Central Park we see today. It's a very different park than it once was.

On 33rd Street, where Peter might have lived, I tried to imagine which apartment house I would have been living if I was Peter at that time. It was an apartment clearly in the play that Edward had written about.

On my walk I did find an apartment house which had handrails with a metal squirrel at each end of them. This intrigued me. Peter says in the play: "Yes, we have two of each." So here were two squirrels.

I decided to knock on the door. When the door opened, a guy said "Hello." It was a bit awkward. I told him I was in a play and I was trying to imagine what it might be like in the play. And he said: "Come in and meet the owner." And the next thing you know, I'm sitting in the living room talking to her about the play, and she's telling me about the history of the house.

You never know where the "treasure hunt" will end up. It's a matter sometimes of not always looking directly at something. But you know there's something implanted in the play, and it's up to you to try to find out different things to get there.

Q How challenging was it for you performing in Edward Albee's *The Goat*, or *Who is Sylvia*? on Broadway?

The Goat was probably the most risky theatre I've ever been part of. As Martin, I was playing the riskiest role. It was big challenge to do as it was the first play I had done on Broadway. And to have these characters on the stage was very exciting. They'd respond to him making these hissing sounds. The other part of the audience would have some sympathy towards him.

The real challenge was to find out who Martin was. The way Edward built the play made it extremely challenging to find the right tone. If Martin is funny at the beginning, the audience might want it to be a different play. The stakes are very hard all the way through. It was also a tough thing physically on the audience, and on me.

I didn't completely realize how I was responding. I noticed I responded by curling in. My body had an animal reaction; I'd curl into a fetal position. It took a lot of determination to stay accessible.

Q Was part of the challenge being intimate while also making sure the audience never missed a word?
The theatre we performed in is a very small house on Broadway, only 800 seats. And I wanted people to not have to lean in to hear the dialogue, and still be able to hear these incredibly self-revelatory thoughts. Finding the right balance—that process was really interesting to me. The physical space was very awkward.

Every night you perform your body tells you different things, so you have to stay open no matter what.

I had spent a lot of time doing regional theater work. I did a lot of outdoor Shakespeare in Montana, while accomplishing certain vocal demands in the roles I played. You'd have planes going by and dogs yelping, so with all of that, you had to have a strong technique. But I just don't want technique to just kick in. The hardest thing is always staying open.

With Martin, I liked the clarity of a martyr walking into something when he has no other choice. He knows it's going to tear him apart.

Q You're also a playwright and your play, *Expedition 6*, focused on the story of the three crew members of NASA Expedition 6 who found themselves trapped aboard the International Space Station for six months following the Columbia's flameout. How has writing been a creatively fulfilling experience for you?
Yes, I've been lucky to be fulfilled by it. I look at plays all the time. I spent three years developing that play as a theater piece. It was worked on at the Kennedy Center, in Baltimore at Theatre Project and at The Magic Theater. Then we did it in New York.

Q As an actor, one of the greatest skills an actor needs to have is listening. I've noticed you have an uncanny ability to truly listen on stage.
That was one of the amazing things when I did *Peter and Jerry* that people told me about. Many people mentioned that, including one of the reviewers. It was a real compliment to the performance.

I don't really think of as a division of listening and talking. Sometime you have listen while you talk while you're listening.

Gertrude Stein wrote an interesting piece called "The Talking Being Listening." It's about listening while you're talking. I find it very true. Especially when you're talking, you're listening, and how that occurs is something that's important.

When I worked on *Nobel Son*, it was the second movie I had done with Alan Rickman. What a joy it was to get to do that kind of work with him and it turned out to be an 'intensely listening' experience.

But I don't really think about listening as something separate; it's such a uni-dimensional thing. No one in life is thinking about it, right?

What is an action of listening? Is it about hearing what's said or listening to the other person's action? You're really listening to what's going on, and all these things are happening at the same time, and that's what's important to me. It's all part of the creative act. ■

LUISE RAINER

Ms. Rainer was the first actress to win multiple Academy Awards consecutively; they were for *The Great Ziegfeld* starring opposite William Powell and Myrna Loy, and *The Good Earth* opposite Paul Muni, produced by Irving Thalberg. Ms. Rainer was trained by Austria's leading stage director, Max Reinhardt, becoming a distinguished Berlin stage actress with Reinhardt's Vienna Theater Ensemble. She appeared in several productions including *Saint Joan*, *Measure for Measure*, and Pirandello's *Six Characters in Search of an Author*. Ms. Rainer's other films included *Escapade*, *The Great Waltz*, *The Emperor's Candlesticks* with Spencer Tracy, *Dramatic School* with Paulette Goddard, and later in her life, *The Gambler*. Ms. Rainer's appearances in television over the years included *Suspense*, *Combat!*, *The Love Boat*, and *A Dancer*. She was married to the renowned playwright, Clifford Odets, for three years in Hollywood. Her other stage performances included *Behold the Bride* in London, *Saint Joan* in Washington, D.C. directed by Erwin Piscator, and on Broadway in *A Kiss for Cinderella*. She received a star on the Hollywood Walk of Fame. Ms. Rainer died in 2014 at the age of 104 (this interview was conducted in 2003).

Q It's a great pleasure to speak with you—as your memorable performances in several films, especially *The Good Earth* and *The Great Ziegfeld* touched me so deeply. As you know, besides acting, I also publish a newspaper about the art of acting.
Marvelous! You can be proud of your creation! And two more creations: You as an actor, and having written a full play as Harold Clurman, congratulations! But how can you possibly leave out Clifford Odets?

Q I haven't. He is in *Let It Be Art!*, along with several of those in my play about The Group Theatre.
Good—as they climbed up on the shoulders of Clifford. Without Clifford and his plays, *Waiting for Lefty*, to start with, there would not have been a real start for a "Group Theatre!" Harold hung on to him, as to dear life! I simply have to say this because I experienced it!

Q What led you to leave Hollywood when you did?
Really I was unprepared for it. I did several films but it was not where I wanted to be. The stories

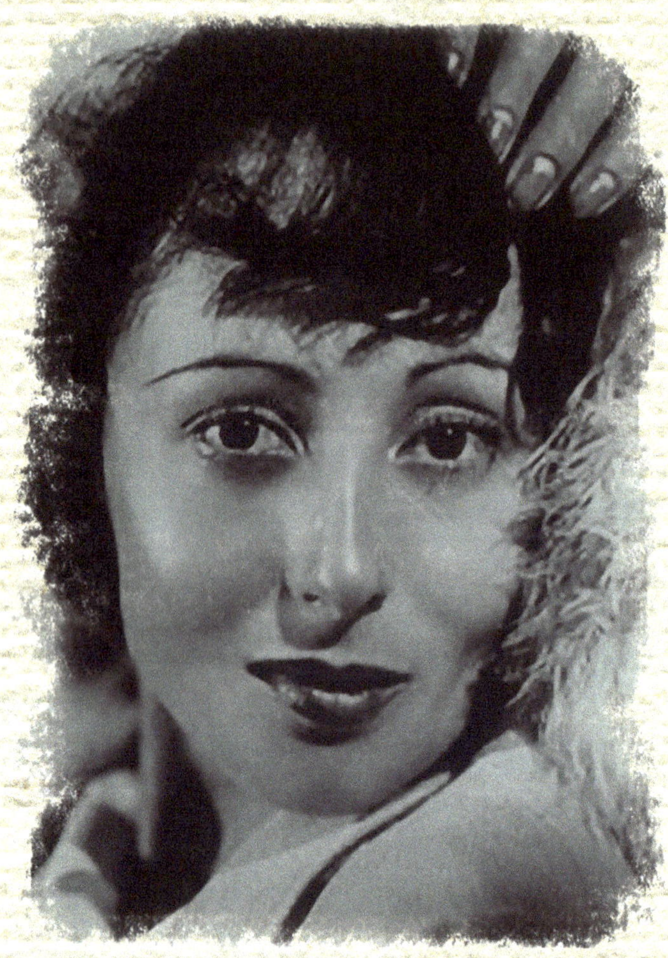

they wanted me do I did not like. I wanted to go back to Europe. I broke my contract with Metro. I was honest, I said, "My source has dried out." I wanted to finish. It was my life so I left.

Q We have seen great artists throughout history who have either destroyed the work they've created or even themselves.

Do we have to destroy the creativity within us? I don't think so. So many past artists have won the battle against the turmoil of life. Where would we be otherwise? Added factors within us lose what we have, make us destroy—those we should fight, not life!

We all have to walk erect to see the sky, to know how little we are and how great. To look outside and not always within: that should be our goal, and our health. Pain is a natural. It must be carried. ■

Luise Rainer photo: courtesy of the artist

TONY RANDALL

Mr. Randall is best known for his role as Felix Unger on television in *The Odd Couple* with Jack Klugman for five years, for which he received the Emmy Award. In 1991, he launched the National Actors Theatre on Broadway in New York City. Mr. Randall's Broadway appearances included *A Circle of Chalk*, *The Corn is Green* with Ethel Barrymore, *Candida*, *Inherit the Wind* with Paul Muni, *M. Butterfly*, and *Oh Captain!* For which he received a Tony Award nomination. Among the productions of the National Actors Theatre included *The Irresistible Rise of Arturo Ui* with Al Pacino and John Goodman, *Saint Joan* with Joan Plunkett, *The Sea Gull*, *Inherit the Wind*, *The Odd Couple*, and *The Master Builder*, which he directed; *The Flowering Peach*, *Night Must Fall* with Matthew Broderick, *Three Men on a Horse*, and *The Sunshine Boys* with Jack Klugman. His television and film work included *Mr. Peepers*, *Love Sidney*, *Will Success Spoil Rock Hunter?* with Rock Hudson and Doris Day, for which he received a Golden Globe Award; *Let's Make Love* with Marilyn Monroe and Yves Montand, *Oh, Men! Oh, Women!*, *Pillow Talk*, and *The Seven Faces of Dr. Lao*. Mr. Randall was nominated for five Golden Globe Awards, received New York City's Gold Medal Award, and was inducted into the Theatre Hall of Fame. Mr. Randall died in 2004 (this interview was conducted in 2003).

Q What led to you to create the National Actors Theatre?

I was trying to start a National Repertory Theatre—to have a permanent acting company to really build from, to perform our greatest plays. In the early years I tried to develop a cadre of actors, among them Maryann Plunkett, who was with us for five shows; Charles Durning was one of our regulars. I originally envisioned two acting companies, with the second being a junior company.

Q What made theater creatively exciting for you when you were young?

When I saw Olivier in *Othello*, it was the greatest stage performance I had ever seen. The presence of great acting can make a very big difference in the lives of young people. Also theatre dealt with political action in the past. In some ways The Group Theatre was that kind of a theater. Theater had something to say to what was happening in people's lives.

Q When we talk about the art of the actor—

And that's what it's really all about when everything is said and done. And there are all these ideologies, but it still remains about the art of acting. I've also heard opera discussed in hundreds of ways; volumes have been written about the meaning of Wagner, about what this means, what that means, but what opera is about is the glorification of the voice.

Q And acting?

There are countless books on the subject. Stanislavsky himself wrote *An Actor Prepares*, which discussed the inner world of the actor; *Building a Character*, which dealt with the external world, and *Creating a Role*. In those books are everything one needs to know.

I studied with Sandy Meisner; he's my authority. He said it's "fully living truthfully in the given imaginary circumstances." Now that can be explained, but what can't be fully explained is why one person can go on the stage and transmit a feeling, capture your entire imagination and soul, and transport you, and someone else can't. What Olivier did was great acting.

The greatest opera performance I ever saw was John Vickers. He went through a "transfer" from one human being to another, an entire transformation. Jose Ferrer once said to me, "What I do is come to the theatre, get out of my street clothes, get into my costume, put on my make-up, and do my part. I come to work."

Q What can we do to keep making the theater a vibrant experience for audiences?

We should keep the great plays alive for them. I have been striving to do that. All of art has a function in life. I think of the words of Bernard Berenson, in the forward to his book on Italian Renaissance art; it speaks to the heart of it. He said, "An artifact is not a work of art unless it humanizes us." The actor has the possibility of giving some of his humanity to every person—teaching him or her something—otherwise his work is just an artifact. And that's the real function of art. It should make us more human. ■

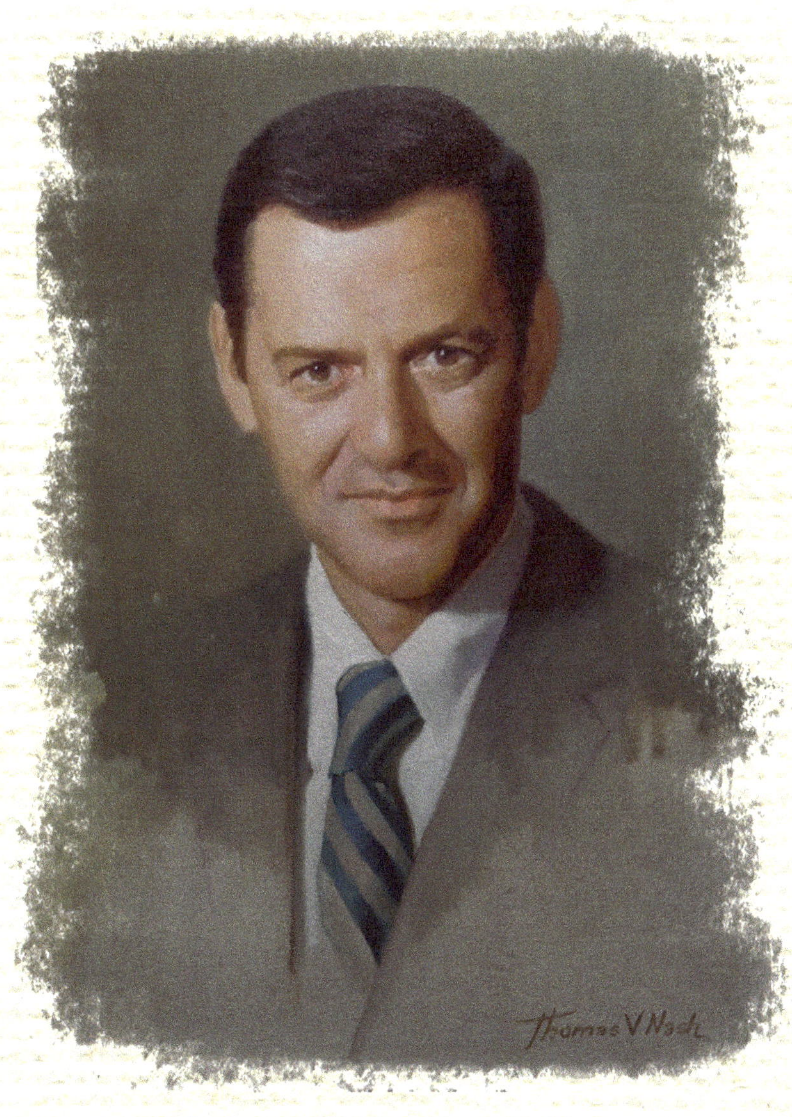

Tony Randall artwork by Thomas V. Nash, courtesy of Mr. Nash

PHYLICIA RASHAD

Recipient of the 2016 Lucille Lortel Award for Outstanding Leading Actress in a Play for her performance as "Shelah" in Tarell Alvin McCraney's *Head of Passes* at the Public Theater. Ms. Rashad has had an enduring career on stage, in television, and film. The first African-American actress to win a Tony Award for Best Performance by a Leading Actress for her riveting performance as 'Lena Younger' in Lorraine Hansberry's *A Raisin in the Sun*, Ms. Rashad also earned a Drama Desk award for that role on Broadway in 2004. Other notable Broadway appearances include *August: Osage County* as 'Violet Weston,' *Cat on a Hot Tin Roof* as 'Big Mama' opposite James Earl Jones, 'Aunt Ester' in August Wilson's *Gem of the Ocean* receiving a Tony Award nomination, *Blue, Jelly's Last Jam, Into the Woods*, and *Ain't Supposed to Die a Natural Death*. She has also appeared Off-Broadway in *Everybody's Ruby* at New York's Public Theatre; *Cymbeline, The Duplex*, and *Bernarda Alba* at Lincoln Center Theatre; *Helen*; *Puppet Play*; *Zooman and the Sign*; *Sons and Fathers of Sons*; *In an Upstate Motel*; *Weep Not for Me*; *The Great Mac Daddy* at the Negro Ensemble Company; and *The Sirens* at MTC. Ms. Rashad's regional work includes *Medea* and *Blues for an Alabama Sky* at the Alliance Theatre, *Every Tongue Confesses* at Arena Stage, and *Gem of the Ocean* at Huntington Stage. Ms. Rashad's best known television roles as 'Claire Huxtable' on *The Cosby Show* and 'Ruth Lucas' on *Cosby* receiving many awards and honors including NAACP Image Awards, People's Choice Awards, and Emmy nominations. Among her film appearances include Ryan Coogler's *Creed*, Tyler Perry's *Good Deeds*, and Tyler Perry's film of Ntozake Shange's *For Colored Girls Who Have Considered Suicide When The Rainbow Is Enuf*. As a director, she made her directorial debut at the Seattle Repertory Theater with August Wilson's Gem of the Ocean and has helmed productions at prestigious theaters throughout the United States including The Goodman Theater, Ebony Repertory Theatre, Westport Country Playhouse, the McCarter Theatre, and the Longwharf Theatre. In 2016, Ms. Rashad directed a production of August Wilson's *Ma Rainey's Black Bottom* at the Mark Taper Forum in Los Angeles, California.

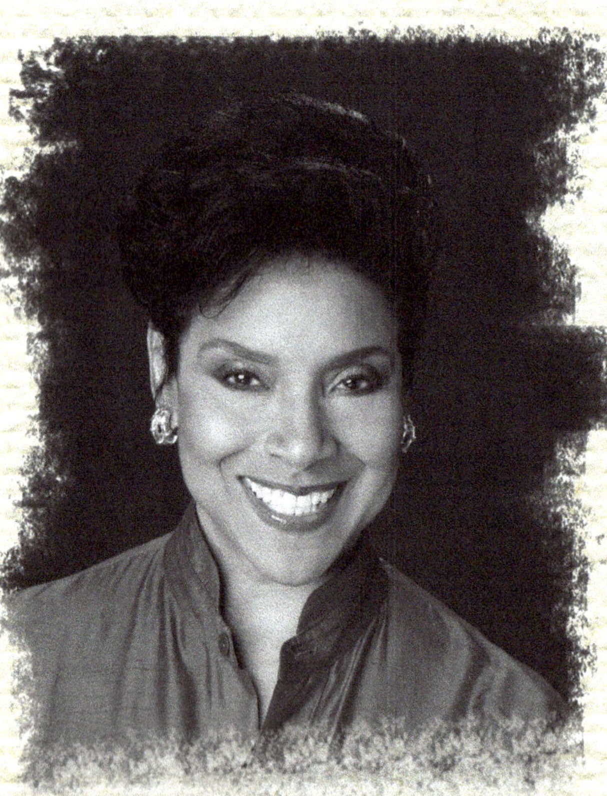

Phylicia Rashad photo: courtesy of the artist

Q What gives you the greatest satisfaction from the creative process of acting?

Collaboration. Theatre is not the result of a singular achievement. It's not the same as writing a poem or a novel or a symphony. You always have to compare it to dance and music and the visual arts. I enjoy the process of working as an actor working with the director, the playwright, with the cast, of working with the designers and the crew—it's a complete collaboration.

Q What is your approach as an actress to the first read-through of a play?

It varies; it's never just one way. Sometimes it's a completely new experience. That's always the fun when there are surprises. Discovering something, and even though I may have read the script at least once or twice, there are still surprises. We like the surprises; we want them to happen.

Q How different is your approach when you're directing a play?

As a director, what I do is listen. I am not having any expectations. I want to hear the words, the text through the actors' unique voices.

Q Among your memorable performances is 'Shelah,' the matriarch in Tarell Alvin McCraney's *Head of Passes*. What drew you to want to play her?

I like the playwright's work—his poetic text and how contemporary the play is. It's not set in 2016—the text and the times are regional—yet it's not so far removed from us today. He captured it very well. I love working in plays in which the playwright has captured the language, the characters through the speech.

Q It must have been a similar experience for you as Aunt Esther in August Wilson's *Gem of the Ocean*.

His texts are "living texts," they really are. It's a gift to have a text that is a "living text." At the very first day of rehearsal as we were doing the read-through, when I came to the passage when Aunt Esther describes the 'City of Bones,' I got caught up in it. I fell into the rhythm of August's writing; the rhythm carried me through. You just can't sit down and scan it. The writing is very organic. If you move into it, it will transport you. It took me someplace else.

Q Does it influence your creative process having the playwright in the room when you rehearse?

You can always ask them questions; that's very helpful in learning about the character, the playwrights intention. You don't have it working on a play by Shakespeare; he's not there. Yet, all the meaning is in his play.

Q Many plays deal with an enormous amount of history. How have you learned to deal with historical facts in a play?
An actor can't play history. The most important thing we do as actors is to connect with one another. I'm always looking for some truth of human behavior—that's what it's all about.

Q In the roles you've played, you've had to delve into the great realm of the mysterious, the great powers that exist between heaven and earth. How do you find your way to their depth and power?
It comes from the text itself, and with the help of the director—but all of it comes from the text. And then as you continue to work with it, subtle connections are being made for the character throughout the story, as presented through the play. This is the work. Every actor doesn't work in the same way. Each actor creates their own vocabulary which develops over time and through the work; it's very real thing, the different ways that actors work. It's one of the first things I learned as a director sitting on the other side of the table. I had never experienced the different approaches in which actors work on a play.

Q How does the creative process change for you when you direct?
When I'm directing what changes is that my scope becomes larger. As an actor I'm working with the character whom I'm portraying. As a director, now I'm concerned with an entire production, so I have to hold that vision, and line that up with everything that needs to be done, while making room for all the creative energies in the collaboration, and everything I haven't yet considered.

Q We're faced with great challenges today in our personal lives, in society. What role can the work we do help in the healing process?
I think there's always been pain in the world. You look back at history—when weren't there things like this happening? But we didn't have as easy access to the information; we couldn't learn about it so quickly. So now that we can, maybe together we can do something about it. We should all do what we can, to help in the healing that needs to take place. But the healing can take place in a classroom, it can take place in a grocery store—anywhere that people are conscious of one another—yes, healing can take place. ■

CHITA RIVERA

Ms. Rivera has won two Tony Awards as Best Leading Actress in a Musical, and received eight additional Tony nominations. On Broadway she starred in *The Visit*, the final John Kander/Fred Ebb/Terrence McNally musical directed by John Doyle; *The Mystery of Edwin Drood*; the Broadway and touring productions of *The Dancer's Life*, written by Terrence McNally, directed by Graciela Daniele; opposite Antonio Banderas in *Nine*; as Anita in the original Broadway and London premiere of *West Side Story*; and on Broadway and internationally starring in *Bye Bye Birdie, The Rink, Chicago, Jerry's Girls, Kiss of the Spider Woman*; and with the original Broadway casts of *Guys and Dolls, Can-Can, Seventh Heaven* and *Mr. Wonderful*. On tour, she also starred in *Born Yesterday, The Rose Tattoo, Call Me Madam, Threepenny Opera, Sweet Charity, Kiss Me Kate, Zorba,* and *Can-Can* with The Rockettes. Ms. Rivera was awarded The Presidential Medal of Freedom by President Barack Obama, and is the first Hispanic woman ever chosen to receive the Kennedy Center Honors. Great Performances aired the special *Chita Rivera: A Lot of Livin' To Do*, a retrospective on her life and career on PBS. She created a solo CD entitled *And Now I Swing*. Her most treasured production is her daughter, singer/dancer/choreographer, Lisa Mordente.

Q Does every cast you're a part of become, in a sense, like a family?
I know exactly what you mean. I have always felt that about every show I've done. That's the beauty of being there. You're in a magnificent space, for a certain time with the same people, and you're all together working on a wonderful show, which hopefully turns into a hit. I've been really lucky through my entire career to have worked with amazing people, and my shows have become real families. When I worked on *Nine*, that was one thing I missed badly, all the chorus boys. There was a lot of estrogen floating around, I have to tell you.

Q You did have a special actor, Antonio Banderas, opposite you.
That's true, but you were asking him to do a lot.

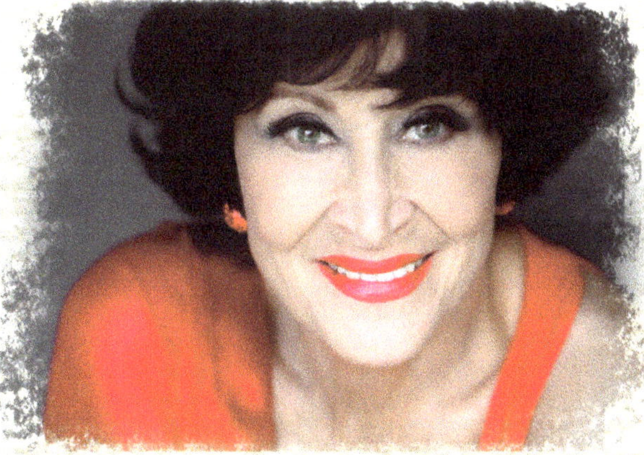

Chita Rivera photo: Laura Marie Duncan

Q You've spent your life performing in the theater. Does the audience play a large role in what you do?
Oh yes. It's all about communication, about getting the word out. Entertaining, hopefully inspiring them, energizing them. Theater's a beautiful form of communication. Without them you can't do anything, and

CHITA RIVERA

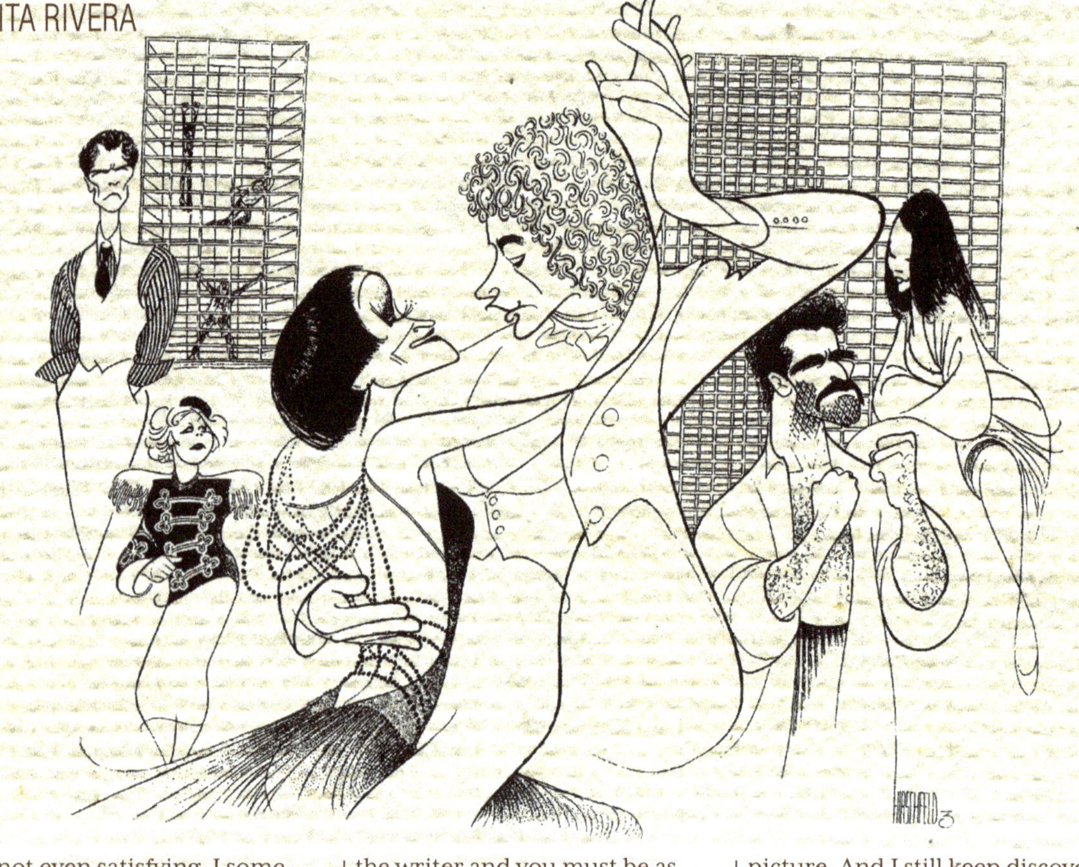

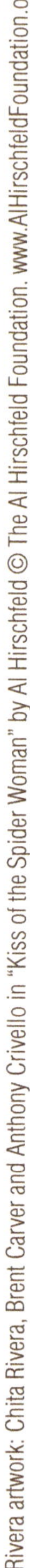
Chita Rivera artwork: Chita Rivera, Brent Carver and Anthony Crivello in "Kiss of the Spider Woman" by Al Hirschfeld © The Al Hirschfeld Foundation. www.AlHirschfeldFoundation.org

it's not even satisfying. I sometimes wish I could be like some people who can go off and work alone, but I always need someone there. It's all about really making it clear to the audience, so they understand what the playwright, the lyricist, the composer, the choreographer, the director, want to say.

Q What do you seek from a director?
What one expects from a director is to guide you to the root of the character's truth. The "okay" to explore—the freedom.

Q What was the experience for you working with Harold Prince on *Kiss of the Spider Woman*?
For me, it was very much like having a father figure to help me. In the case of *Kiss of the Spider Woman*, she was fragments, she was not easy to find. I'm here, and then I'm gone, and then I reappear. How to piece her together? It took all the rehearsals to do it and Hal was extremely open about it. He let me explore and let me find her.

Q How do you begin to create the world the playwright has created?
I think you really need to be open to the writer. You must be true to the writer and you must be as patient as possible. I always reach a point in my process when I think I know it and I substitute my words for the writer's words and then I come back to their words, and when they come out wrong, I throw the bloody script across the floor. That's part of my process. I get very impatient with myself. I always want to go into rehearsal knowing the words so that you have more time to explore.

Q How was your show, *Chita and All That Jazz*, created?
There was a process of shaping and re-shaping it. We were all really excited about working on it. It was in the hands of Terrence McNally. I had so badly wanted him to do it.

Q Did you have any kinds of fears when you began your career?
Always, oh gosh yes, and they're still there; they never seem to leave. Each time before I go out on stage is like the first time. You want to get it really right and be able to portray it the way the playwright intended, the way the lyricist, the composer, the choreographer intended—you want to get it right. They have a bigger picture. And I still keep discovering new things during every performance. Collaboration remains a necessity to create art and life on stage.

Q Why makes collaboration such a vital part of what you do?
Because we're all one piece of a big tapestry. We're all connected, and it takes time, respect, observation, and unity to do that. Working to find the find the right rhythm, and as Cy Coleman wrote: "Rhythm is a powerful beat." With unity you can get to the goal. You're also an enormously caring and giving performer, onstage and off.

It came from my upbringing. My father died when I was very young. My mother was a warm figure. She was an amazing woman, raising five kids. My family's still all alive and we still see each other at our powwows, and get together and talk. It's vital. It's a way of thinking I've always had towards my family, to the world.

After all, we're all in this together. I'm very aware of people who are kind and are giving. I mean, how can you not give back? It's a much better feeling. And laughing is a better cure any day. ■

ROY SCHEIDER

Instantly recognizable as Police Chief Brody in Steven Spielberg's *Jaws* opposite Robert Shaw and Richard Dreyfuss, and in the television series, *seaQuest*, Mr. Scheider was nominated for two Academy Awards, a Golden Globe Award, and a BAFTA Award. His many films included *The French Connection* opposite Gene Hackman, *52 Pick-Up*, *Klute*, *Marathon Man* opposite Dustin Hoffman and Laurence Olivier, *All That Jazz*, *Jaws 2*, *Blue Thunder*, and *The Russia House* with Sean Connery. He appeared on Broadway in Harold Pinter's *Betrayal*. Mr. Scheider's television appearances included *Jacobo Timmerman: Prisoner Without a Name, Cell Without a Number*, *RKO 281*, *King of Texas* with Patrick Stewart and Marcia Gay Harden, and he hosted *Saturday Night Live*. He helped to found the Hayground School in Bridgehampton, New York, with poet, Kathy Engle, dedicated to creating an innovative, culturally diverse learning environment for local children. Mr. Scheider died in 2008 (this interview was conducted in 2002).

Q When did you decide you would make acting your life?
By the time I did three and a half years of college theater, I knew this was something I could do well. I was around twenty-one, and I said, "Okay, this is what I do. I'm an actor." There was never any doubt in my mind.

Q There's always a deep personal stake in the truth in your work.
My father was a German Protestant, and had a very strong work ethic. He felt you had to do a dollar's worth of work for a dollar. There was never the idea of doing anything less than your best. He had a gas station, and when I worked there, he instilled in me a strong desire to do my job well.

Q What led to your studying with Harold Clurman?
I had auditioned as an understudy for a role in *Incident at Vichy* for the Lincoln Center Repertory Theatre at ANTA, and met Harold. Many of the actors in the company were already in his class. I asked him if I could join his class and he said, "Fine."

The classes met a couple of times a week at 11:30 at night; I was a part of them for two to three years. It was really a mature scene study class; about studying the play, dissecting a scene—how your character fits into the rest of the play. Harold felt you could play the most boring librarian dynamically, with a "dynamic ennui." Harold's main thrust was that the theater reflects better than any other art form—outside of music—the human condition. To Harold, the theater is medicine showing us how to be more compassionate human beings.

Q Harold Clurman chose you as part of his cast when he directed *Long Day's Journey into Night* for a tour in Japan.
I was delighted to have been chosen, along with Ruth White, William Prince, and Ira Lewis. He told us to not read anything about the play or see the movie. So, of course, we all immediately read as much as we could and watched the film. We had to immerse ourselves in the play.

At one particular rehearsal, and I had been working on my role a lot, and it was in the scene between the two brothers, Harold stood up and said to me, "Everything you're doing is fine and all, but you're boring me." And this was in front of everyone. Well, I was seething inside. So I went home that night, and I worked on that part, all through the night. And when I came in the next day, where I had gone right, I went left, where I had sat down, I stood up, I changed everything I did. When the scene was over, Harold

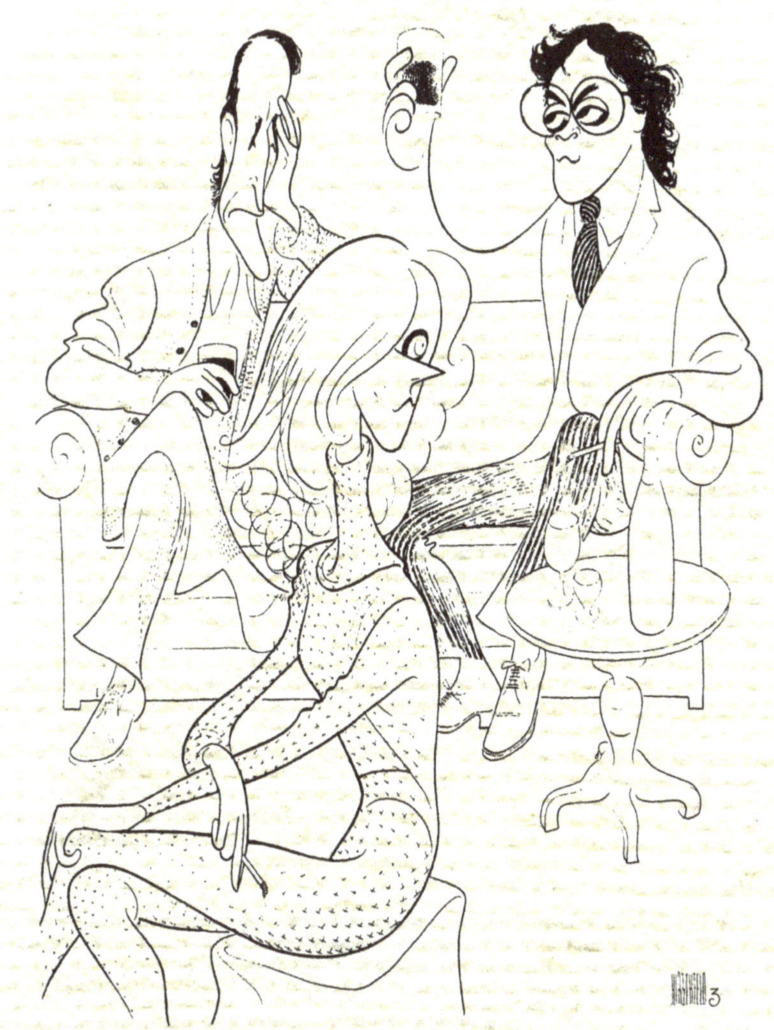

Roy Scheider artwork: Roy Scheider, Blythe Danner and Raul Julia in Harold Pinter's "Betrayal" on Broadway by Al Hirschfeld © The Al Hirschfeld Foundation. www.AlHirschfeldFoundation.org

stood up and announced, "I would just like to say what a privilege it is to work with as fine an actor as Mr. Scheider." But I was still steaming inside. But he had pushed the right button for me.

Q What led you to embrace the character so well in *All That Jazz*, directed by Bob Fosse?
I spent about two weeks reading the script with Bob, before we started filming. And we'd discuss similarities between his life and mine. He'd try to find experiences of mine that were in a sense close to his. The second week I began dancing, since we had no time for me take classes. The things we spent talking about together for hours were invaluable.

Q How different was it working with him from working with Clurman?
Harold was more intellectual and diagrammatical, Bob worked moment-to moment emotionally. Bob made sure I was absolutely honest. He'd whisper things in my ear. We would find ways to make it come alive.

Q You worked on a Hallmark Hall of Fame TV project adapted from *King Lear*. What drew you to want to do it?
It was a wonderful experience. The cast included Patrick Stewart, Marcia Gay Harden and Lauren Holly. The story has been set in 1842, in Texas, and it wasn't in Shakespeare's language. We shot it in three locations in Mexico. Lear's ranch was a famous ranch for raising fighting bulls; a marvelous expansive landscape all around us, with a dry and flat look that was perfect.

Gloucester has always been a fascinating character for me. The misguided father who doesn't understand the personalities of his own sons. One is ferocious and vigorous, while the other is gentle and quieter. He mistakes that for weakness. That's his lesson. And it parallels Lear's psychological lesson with his three daughters.

Q Why do you feel so strongly about teaching theater arts to young people?

A It gives them a sense of self; a chance to explore other people's personalities. When they get up, they can reveal parts of themselves in acting they wouldn't normally be able to. I see it in my son who's twelve, in his efforts to do Shakespeare. I can see he's touched by it.

Q You've always made acting look easy.
I work hard to make sure no one catches me acting; you can fail completely. Harold said in a career you need failure to learn from, to play parts you can fail in, and pick yourself up again. It's all about finding the notes to make it real for yourself. ■

MARIAN SELDES

Ms. Seldes' career spanned over sixty years. She appeared in 1,809 Broadway performances of *Deathtrap* on Broadway, a feat mentioned in the Guinness Book of World Records as "most durable actress." Among her Broadway and Off-Broadway appearances include *Medea* with Judith Anderson, *Ondine*, *The Milk Train Doesn't Stop Here Anymore*, *Tiny Alice*, *A Delicate Balance*, for which she received a Tony Award, *Equus*, *Painting Churches*, *Three Tall Women*, *The Play About the Baby*, *Ring Round the Moon*, *Father's Day*, for which she received a Drama Desk Award, *Painting Churches*, for which she received an Outer Circle Critics Award, *The Butterfly Collection*, and *Isadora Duncan Sleeps with the Russian Navy*, for which she received an Obie Award. She appeared in over a hundred and seventy episodes of the CBS Radio Mystery Theater. Ms. Seldes' film and television appearances included *The Greatest Story Ever Told*, *Town and Country*, *Mona Lisa Smile*, *Frazier*, and as Aunt Brooke on *Murphy Brown*. Ms. Seldes was a member of the drama faculty of The Juilliard School from 1967 to 1991. Her students included Kevin Kline, Christopher Reeve, Robin Williams, Kelsey Grammer, William Hurt, Patti LuPone, and Kevin Spacey. She also taught at Fordham University. Ms. Seldes died in 2014 (this interview was conducted in 2001).

Q You made your Broadway debut opposite Judith Anderson in *Medea*.
She was totally original, wonderfully instinctive. She used her body in every way. If you couldn't hear her, you would still know from her body what her character was saying. I had wanted to be a dancer and studied with Martha Graham at the School of American Ballet. The body is so underestimated.

Q Your artistry shows us the stillness in the soul of the character. How did this come to you?
Life teaches it to you. Julia Marlowe, one of the greatest actresses to grace the stage, once said, "There is grandeur in silence...it is the eye that is the mind's signal and the soul's interpreter."

Q Who have been inspirations for you?
Guthrie McClintic, because he believed in even my gray areas. He trusted me. His work was so beautiful, like his production of *The Three Sisters*. It changed my life. There was such unity, everything served the play, it was remarkable.

Kim Stanley's performances in *Cheri* and *Natural Affections*; I had to see again and again. She had this spontaneous ability of acting in the moment every time you saw her.

Q What led you to teach at Juilliard?

John Houseman told me I had to give back. When he began the acting program, he made up his mind that I would teach there. We had Michel St. Denis, Michael Kahn, and John. I learned endlessly about acting, about myself, from my students. It was tremendous, there was nothing like it. And when I act with my former students today or see their work, it means so much to me.

Q You were married to one of our greatest playwrights, Garson Kanin. What made him such a unique artist?

It was his writing. His play, *Born Yesterday*, is a classic comedy. It was his humor, his wit, his humanity. His characters are so real. He gave me the courage to be better, to be stronger. To believe in what I believe, to take chances.

Q Do you think today's actors understand their rich legacy?

People don't know enough about the history of our tradition. To learn something, you have to give it time. We're not used to doing that now. They want a "sound bite." You can't learn that way. In acting you have to make strong choices. It's extremely personal and time-consuming. Sandy Meisner said, "Life is life, and the play is theatrical life." His whole method is about behaving naturally in theatrical circumstances. Theater is not reality. It's the blending of the two.

Q How can today's actors protect their soul in the topsy-turvy world of show business?

I feel the New York theater community is very supportive of each other. I feel like a member of a wonderful family. The Arts are all intermingled. You make a choice to be in the theater, to battle for what you believe in; to learn to protect your soul from being unhappy or from despair.

The goal of great theater is always facing you. To reach up to it you can't give up. And if your work's not well received, it doesn't mean you're not good. It's all a matter of taste. It doesn't mean the work has any less value. It could be some of the greatest work you've done.

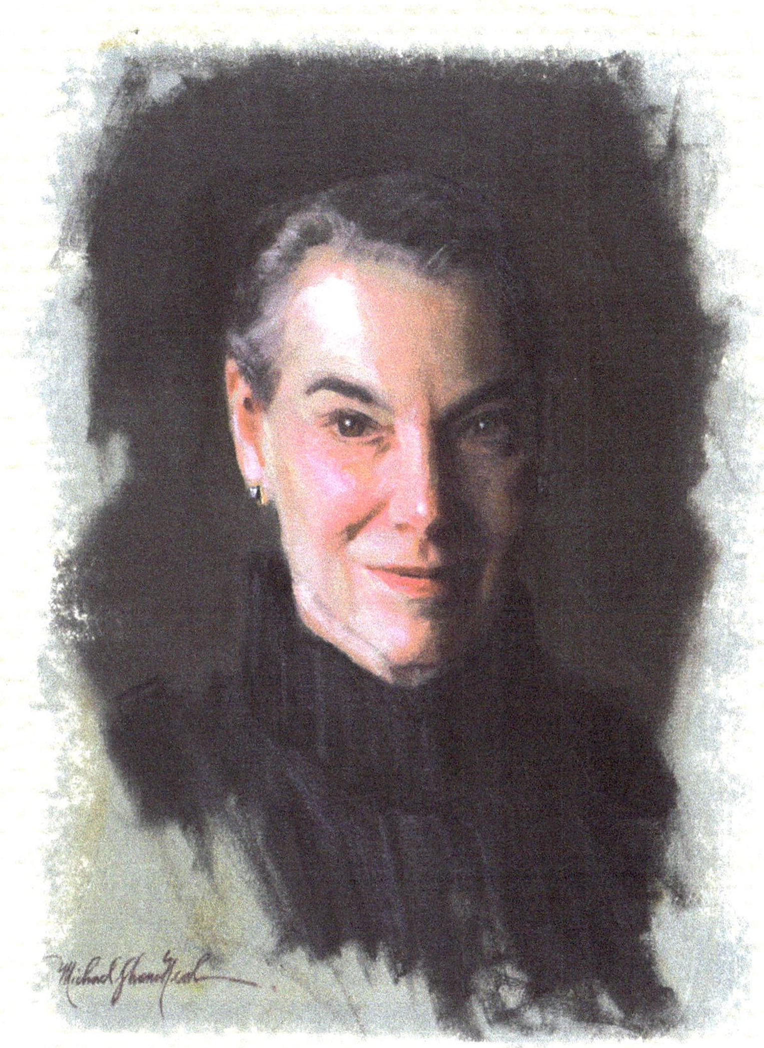

Marian Seldes artwork: Marian Seldes by Michael Shane Neal, courtesy of Mr. Neal

Q Is there a way you go about approaching a play by Edward Albee?

The words are like a musical score, so heart-fully chosen. The rhythms are so personal. I follow the text, and by doing so, it leads to a really pure performance. I've had the good fortune of having Edward direct me. It's like being in a room with Chekhov, it's both thrilling and daunting.

Q How do you prepare for a performance?

By being alone, if I'm lucky enough to have my own room at the theater. Being absolutely quiet. It's a letting-go of daily life, just being still. It's how you put on the clothes, the make-up of the character. I have to give it the time it requires. You can't "get going" on stage. The preparation must take place off stage. One has to take care not to waste time and energy on things that will diminish you. Go towards what will fill you; then you can pass that on and share it. ■

SABERA SHAIK

Considered one of the most versatile actresses in Malaysia, she has also acted in diverse roles on international tours in Singapore, India, Indonesia, England, and Bali. Ms. Shaik formed her own theatre company, Masakini Theatre in Kuala Lumpur, producing some of her own plays, new works, and one-woman plays, including *Lady Swettenham*, directed by Tage Larsen, which she performed in Holstebro and London, New Delhi, and at Mumbai's NCPA Theatre Festival; *My Bollywood Summer*, *Naga Women*, *In the Name of Love* by the acclaimed dancer Ramli Ibrahim, Alan Bennett's *Habeas Corpus*, and *Happy Days*. Ms. Shaik directed *Wayang*, with Chi Azim, the first shadow theatre in Malaysia, and directed and produced a new shadow theatre production, *The Story of Kuala Lumpur*.

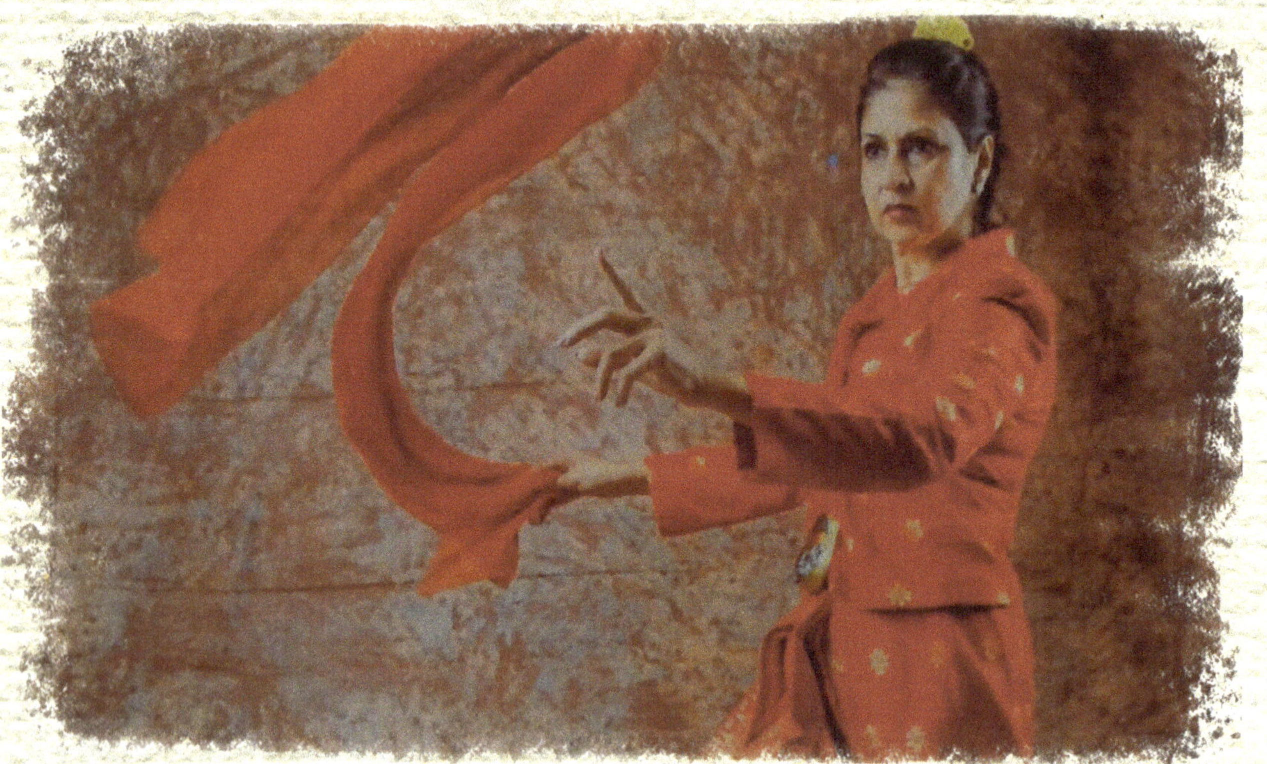

Sabera Shaik in "Stories from Dragon Women" courtesy of the artist

Q What first drew you to the theater?
Cantonese Opera! When I was perhaps thirteen years, television came to Malaysia and my father got us a set. Every afternoon I'd watch the Chinese Opera actors, in awe for an hour every day. I didn't understand a word of Cantonese but I quickly caught on to the conventions used and it dawned on me then that acting could allow you to be someone totally different from yourself. I was a shy person who wouldn't approach anyone.

As I grew older I told my brother I'd like to "go to Hollywood one day." That was my only way to explain a life in theater that I dreamed of. When I came to Kuala Lumpur in the 1970s for my undergrad studies at the University of Malaya, I never missed watching the operas that played in makeshift theaters by the roadside during the Hungry Ghost festivals.

Q How did you learn your craft?
We had a wonderful theater director for our lecturer during my undergrad days—Joy Zinoman of The Studio Theatre in Washington, D.C. She opened my eyes to the myriad possibilities of performance and storytelling. Her positive comments about my abilities were something I held dear for a very long time.

I performed a lot, producing works for my theater group, learning the rudiments of production. They were fun times, when friends and family chipped in to help us produce a play. I read books on acting and became enamored of the Russian teachers and actors and would try and use what they spoke about in my performances.

Q How was the solo play you've been performing, *Lady Swettenham*, created?
Lady Swettenham was first written in 1995, but it wasn't until 2009 that it evolved into a solo performance. Lady Swettenham came out of a chapter of Henry S. Barlow's book, *Swettenham*. A friend and a talented actor and director, Ramli Hassan told me about this woman who was rather misunderstood and mistreated by

her powerful and well-respected husband. We found her life fascinating. So we'd sit together over several weekends, while drinking copious cups of tea and white wine, to plot it out and write the script.

In 2009, itching to take *Lady Swettenham* on a solo journey, I asked Tage Larsen of Odin Teatret in Denmark to direct me. He gasped when he saw the forty-page script! We eventually pared it down to twenty pages, and within two weeks had the whole play worked out. I worked hard, sometimes alone in the Red Room at Odin from 8pm until 4 o'clock in the morning. Some nights would find me falling asleep only to be woken by the creaking of the huge tree near the door. The October wind howling outside made my imagination run wild!

Q What has been the most exciting for you directing the shadow theater production of *Wayang*?

Directing has allowed me to think of my audience and their need to understand what is happening on stage. This year I directed my fourth *Wayang* or shadow theatre piece. Working with professional dancers for shadow is a real treat as they dance our traditional dances and then slowly or quickly morph into an animal or a sea urchin! What's most heartening is when children as young as seven years old come to our productions year in and year out.

Q How did you create the script for your memorable performance as the princess from Kelantan in *Puteri Saadong*?

I had only one sentence to work on—The princess who killed her husband with her hair pin! Legend? Myth? Truth? However, there is a Puteri Saadong in the history annals of Kelantan where I was born. There have been numerous depictions of her by different theatre groups but never a solo piece. In Kelantan I went about reading every story about her by different writers, getting some idea of who she was as a child.

I went away, immersing myself in her character, and began to write about a fifteen-year-old princess who marries an older man she loves. Creating "real" rather than "dreamlike" sequences, I added lines from Aeschylus, from Shakespeare's Lady Macbeth's famous speech. Some days it sounded good, some days it was awful. Many drafts later, with Tage Larsen's help, the final script was born.

But one day, after two performances in Penang, I wrote to Tage, "I'm changing the whole piece into something of my own." Tage wholeheartedly agreed. I incorporated my new dialogue into the script and was utterly happy. No one, including myself, missed Lady Macbeth!

Q How did you decide to include the musicians as your chorus?

My director and I both had the same thought, that they should be incorporated as a device to string the play forward as a chorus, like in Greek theater. It was a deliberate decision to have them play traditional music.

Q What gives you the greatest joy being a creative storyteller?

The greatest joy is when audiences come and listen, laugh at the right places and are engaged, even though they may not understand the language I'm speaking. Then I know my acting can tell the story with only physical movement and sound. It gives me great joy to watch audiences open up, to give them a feeling of freedom, to expand their vocabulary. Putting together a whole production gives me great pleasure. Yes, it's always worth the sweat and agony. ■

SYLVIA SIDNEY

Best known as a film heroine of the 1930s, she received an Academy Award nomination *for Summer Wishes, Winter Dreams*. Ms. Sidney's films included Josef von Sternberg's *An American Tragedy*, *City Streets* opposite Gary Cooper, King Vidor's *Street Scene*, *Dead End* with Humphrey Bogart, Fritz Lang's *Fury* with Spencer Tracy, *You Only Live Once* opposite Henry Fonda, Alfred Hitchcock's *Sabotage*, *The Trail of the Lonesome Pine* with Henry Fonda, *Blood on the Sun* with James Cagney, as Fantine in Les *Misérables*, *One Third of a Nation*, *Raid on Entebbe*, *Beetlejuice*, *Used People* with Shirley MacLaine and Marcello Mastroianni, and *Mars Attacks!* Her television appearances included *Naked City*, *Magnum, P.I.*, *Fantasy Island*, *The Shadow Box*, and she received a Golden Globe Award for *An Early Frost*. Her Broadway appearances included *Gods of the Lightning*, The Group Theatre's *The Gentle People*, *Vieux Carré*, and *Barefoot in the Park*. Her touring and stock theater performances included *The Madwoman of Chaillot*, *The Importance of Being Earnest*, *The Glass Menagerie*, *Cabaret*, *Butterflies Are Free* and *'Night, Mother*. She received The George Eastman Award in 1982. Ms. Sidney died in 1999 (this interview was conducted in 1998).

Q You have a role in the new television series, *Fantasy Island*—

Isn't that crazy! A contract for seven years at the age of 88!! They're flying me to Hawaii for an episode, too.

Q Are you looking forward to working in television?

Honey, whatever it is, acting is acting, I'm happy to be paid!

Q What originally made you choose acting?

I had no choice. It was the only thing I could do. I hated school and when we got to calculus, I was dead! But in the theater I didn't have to be me. See, my father was a regular theater goer and he'd come back and talk about it. And I was lucky. When I became an actress at sixteen in 1925, the show I was in became a big hit on Broadway, and then my salary went up like crazy.

Q Then you went out to Hollywood—
Why not, I thought I'd work more and make more money and I did. But I wanted to do what I wanted to do.

Q One of the films I enjoyed you the most in was *Dead End*.
They didn't know what to do with me, I was an ugly kid.

Q You also returned to the theater appearing in The Group Theatre production of *The Gentle People* with Franchot Tone—
I married one of its stars, Luther Adler. He was one of our greatest actors, the original Golden Boy! You see, kid, when I started in the theater, I had to fence three afternoons a week; I don't know if today's actors do enough of that. They don't know how to use their voice, their diction, everyone wants to mumble, to imitate the "speech of the streets." Everyone says "gonna" instead of "going to."

Q What would you tell a young person who wants to act?
Listen, the only way you learn is by working. Either you know how to act or you don't. But, listen, I mean really listen, that's what I learned from George M. Cohan, and make mistakes or you don't learn a thing. ■

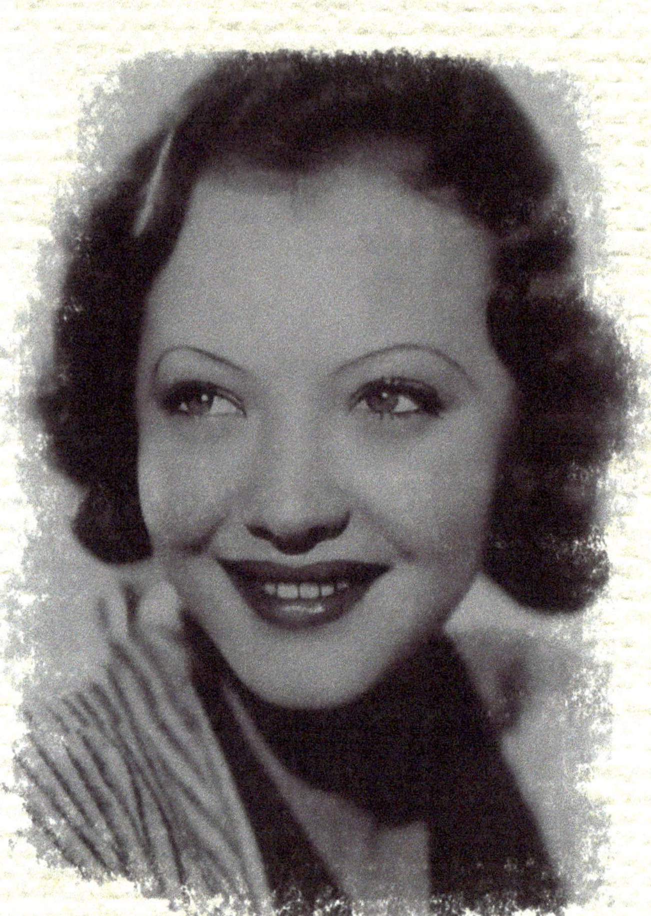

Sylvia Sidney photo: courtesy of the artist

KATE VALK

Kate Valk has been performing in New York City with The Wooster Group at the Performing Garage, a New York-based theatre collective started in 1974, for nearly four decades. Her first performance was in *Route 1 & 9*, a version of Thornton Wilder's *Our Town*. Appearing in over twenty-five Wooster Group productions, Ms. Valk's Wooster Group performances include *L.S.D. (...Just the High Points...)* based on Arthur Miller's *The Crucible* in 1984; Mildred Douglas in Eugene O'Neill's *The Hairy Ape, Brace Up!*; Chekhov's *Three Sisters* in 1991 and 2003; *House/Lights* based on Gertrude Stein's *Dr. Faustus Lights the Lights* in 1998 and 2005; Eugene O'Neill's *The Emperor Jones* in 1993 and 2006; *Hamlet* in 2007 as Gertrude and Ophelia; *Poor Theater* in 2005; *To You, The Birdie! Phèdre* from 2001 to 2006; *North Atlantic* in 2010; Tennessee Williams' *Vieux Carré* in 2010-2011; and *The Room* in 2015-2016. Ms. Valk also participated in the production of The Wooster Group's four video features, an opera, three radio shows for BBC-3, the film *Wrong Guys*, a CD of songs from the Group's *To You, The Birdie! Phèdre*; and the interactive video installation *There Is Still Time... Brother*. She was Associate Director to Elizabeth LeCompte for The Wooster Group's collaboration with the Royal Shakespeare Company on *Troilus and Cressida*, as part of the World Shakespeare Festival. In 2014, Ms. Valk directed the Wooster Group's *Early Shaker Spirituals: A Record Album Interpretation*. She founded and serves as the director emerita of two arts education programs with The Wooster Group, an in-school theater curriculum at Dr. Sun Yat Sen Middle School in Chinatown, and The Wooster Group's Summer Institute, a free three-week workshop for public high school students. She recently became a 2016 Guggenheim Fellow, and served as a mentor for the Rolex Arts Initiative.

Q You have said you found your artistic home with the Wooster Group.
Through New York University's undergrad drama department, I studied for two years with Stella Adler. She was a fabulous teacher, a great persona. But when I completed the program I knew I didn't have the kind of ego that's necessary to be "in the business." I couldn't imagine myself getting a picture and resume; I was looking for a place to go. I had one semester left, so I went into the Experimental Wing, and that's where I met Liz (director Elizabeth LeCompte) and Ron (Vawter) and Spalding (Gray). They were teaching there for one semester so I got to work with them. I went to see performances

of their trilogy: *Three Places in Rhode Island*: *Sakonnet Point*, *Rumstick Road*, and *Nayatt School*. I had never seen art work like that before on a stage. I volunteered to do anything for them. I could sew at the time so I offered myself up as a seamstress.

Q You first performed with The Wooster Group in *Route 1 & 9*, a version of Thornton Wilder's Our Town.

Yes. Liz was working on that new piece after *Point Judith*. I was her assistant, I was making props and costumes, whatever was needed. I was transcribing and editing texts; I transcribed the Pigmeat Markham routines.

Q Is there a way you begin to create?

I like working with a mask. I like wigs and costumes and transforming. It's where I found my power—in the mask. That's what theater is about for me.

Q How would you describe how a piece is created at The Wooster Group?

We find the play together; it all happens very organically in the room. Liz is making a world, and I'm making a being to exist in that world.

Q What is necessary for the process to occur?

Time. Some pieces happen quicker, others can take a long time depending upon the text we're working on. If the text is dense, then it can take a longer time. It's all part of the conscious, the unconscious, living with it in our collective imagination. Certain impulses might present themselves, and you follow through with them during the next rehearsal process.

Q From what I understand, the creation of a performance at The Wooster Group is an entirely collaborative effort including the technical part—

Yes—the technology is a very important part of the work—the receivers, the audio recordings, the visuals: video and film inputs—we're impulsing off the technology. Being an actress is not separate from the work with The Wooster Group. I am not an actress separate from the "dance" I do with the technology. I'm a performer with the Wooster group, working, developing this aesthetic in the room with the Liz for the past thirty-eight years.

We use audio and video recordings to affect our performance; sometimes we're "channeling" directly the material. The performers, and all the technical artists of the sound, the video, everyone is in concert with each other. I'm dependent on the technical artist to activate the visual and aural cues for me to move through the space, speak the text. The mechanism is something similar to the way the No Theater performer works with the singers and the musicians.

We've had actors come and try and succeed at our methods who normally perform in more traditional productions of plays. But I can't be in a naturalist play; it's not how I'm activated as a performer. My shortcomings probably led me to these devices.

But I have to say, everything I learned from Stella Adler in her classes, plays right into what I'm doing now. Stella Adler encouraged actors to know and use the physical circumstances. I never

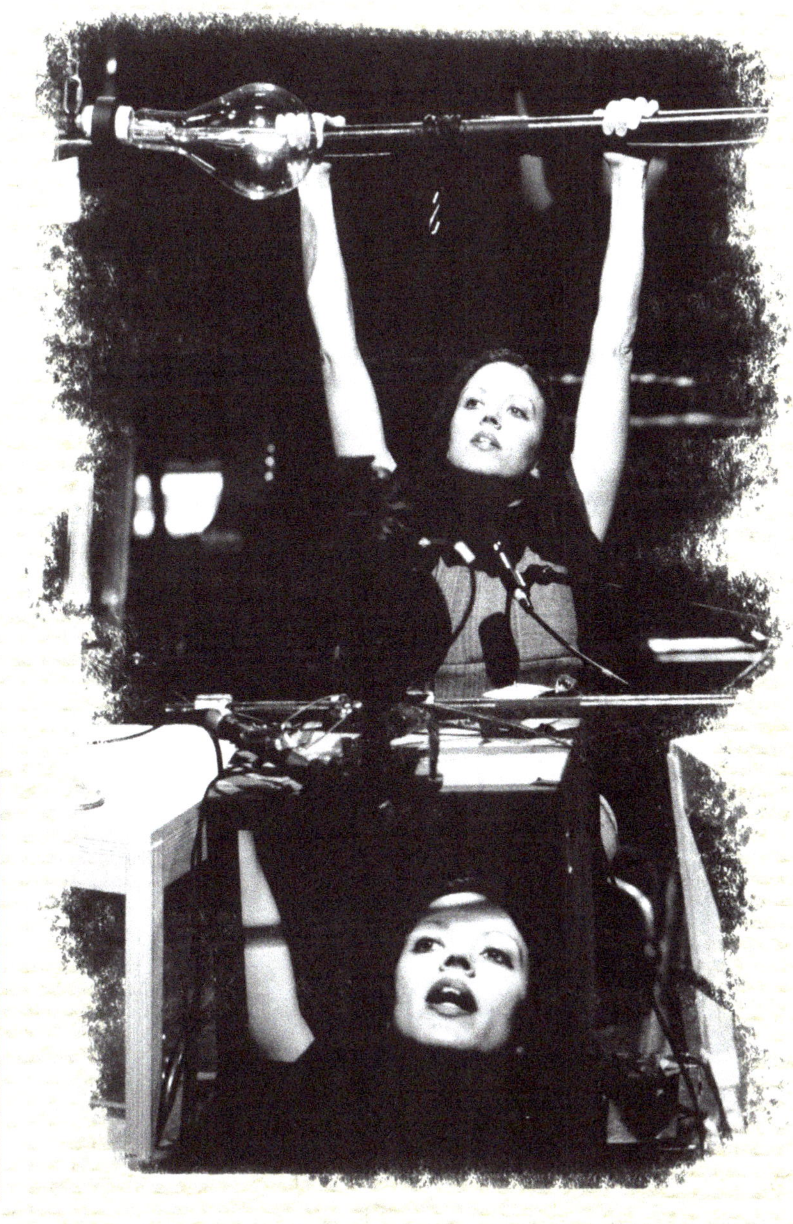

Kate Valk photo: The Wooster Group's "House Lights" with Kate Valk © Mary Gearhart

really understood "emotional recall." I wanted to get away from myself. And Liz is so into the architectonic elements of what she is making, the physical circumstances. It's about navigating the architecture of the space. The TV screen and the camera are very important to the work. They are part of our acting.

Q What compelled you to direct *Early Shaker Spirituals*, with a cast that included Frances McDormand, Elizabeth LeCompte, Bebe Miller, and Suzzy Roche? I understand it was inspired by a 1976 recording by the Maine-based Sisters of the United Society of Shakers.

The record had been in our collection for thirty-five years and I have always loved it. It had particular resonance for me. I looked around and saw we had the perfect complement of women to do it. I thought it would be a project we could do, and it went over well; people liked it.

I feel so lucky to have a situation where I can work like this. I think about people who have an impulse to want to make something but then they wonder, "How can I get a place to work?" I'm fifty-nine-years old, and I've been working here for thirty-eight years. Believe me, I take less for granted now than ever. My impulse now, more than ever, is to keep The Performing Garage going and to do the work that I can do *now*. I have a great compulsion for the work, and it's different than my youthful enthusiasm.

Q You also founded two different arts education programs. An in-school theatre curriculum at Dr. Sun Yat Sen Middle School in Chinatown, and an arts education summer program for high school students. When you're working with young people, do you have a particular approach in engaging who they are in bringing out their potential?

I like working with kids, that's why I started the program. I wanted to do workshops but I'm not a teacher. I got other actors to come in and teach and then I'd make something with the students. I think it's because of the program that I got into directing. I was running the room and could try something and fail, and figure out how to make it better. It's was a great workshop to find my voice as a director. I'd work on texts, getting people present in their bodies, connected to their voices, engaged with the material. Sometimes I have to face failure, but it's theater, so you keep going. Always remember though, you could be making a "turkey."

Q Yet you keep going—

Because I love it. I'm deeply committed to making performance. I feel like I've picked up a few things over the years by osmosis that could be useful. It's been an incredible experience working with Liz all these years. Why quit now? ■

BEN VEREEN

A Tony and Drama Desk Award winner for his renowned performance in Bob Fosse's *Pippin*, Mr. Vereen's Broadway appearances include: *Wicked, I'm Not Rappaport, Chicago, Hair, Fosse, Jelly's Last Jam, Jesus Christ Superstar*, and *A Christmas Carol*. Mr. Vereen completed a successful run in the world premiere of *Fetch Clay, Make Man* directed by Des McAnuff at the McCarter Theatre. Mr. Vereen continues to tour throughout the United States with his concert act, *Steppin' Out with Ben Vereen*. His notable film appearances include *Rocky Horror Picture Show* directed by Kenny Ortega, *Time Out of Mind* with Richard Gere, *Top* Five with Chris Rock, *Idlewild, All That Jazz, Sweet Charity, Funny Lady* receiving a Golden Globe nomination, *Why Do Fools Fall in Love, Once Upon a Forest*. His television appearances include on a new Amazon series produced by David Shore and Brian Cranston, the miniseries *Roots, Hot in Cleveland, How I Met Your Mother, Grey's Anatomy* receiving a Prism Award, Tyler Perry's *House of Payne, NCIS, Law and Order: Criminal Intent, An Accidental Friendship* receiving an NAACP nomination, *Tenspeed* and *Brown Shoe, Louis Armstrong - Chicago Style, Ellis Island* receiving a Golden Globe Nomination, *Feast of All Saints, Zoobilee Zoo* and *Star Trek - The Next Generation*. Mr. Vereen is one of the nation's most requested motivational speakers delivering talks on Overcoming Adversity, A Trip Down Broadway, Black History, Arts and Education, Substance Abuse, and the Art of Physical and Occupational Therapy. He led the American athletes into the Los Angeles Coliseum for The Special Olympics. Mr. Vereen has created the Ben Vereen Awards and the newly formed organization, Wellness Through the Arts, benefiting young people across America. He directed the musical, *Hair* at Florida's Venice Theatre in Florida and will perform on Broadway in the new musical, *From Brooklyn to Broadway*. Mr. Vereen has become an advocate for Americans for the Arts, the largest advocacy group of the Arts in America, and spoke at the Democratic Convention in July 2016. He has received a number of awards including Mr. Vereen has received the Broadwayworld.com Cabaret Award Best Celebrity Male Vocalist, Israel's Cultural and Humanitarian Awards, three NAACP Image Award, three NAACP Inage Awards, an Eleanor Roosevelt Humanitarian Award and a Victory Award. Mr. Vereen was the first recipient of the Walk of Fame Award from the LaGuardia School of Performing Arts, and has been inducted into The Theatre Hall of Fame, the National Museum of Dance, and the Dance Hall of Fame.

Q As a humanitarian and arts advocate you have spoken about the "breath of creativity...for the need of more arts in schools for our children who can make a better difference in our world...to give them the tools that they need." Making a difference in other's lives—was this something that was impressed upon you as a young person?

Life is an art form; we have forgotten that. It's all in The Good Book as a spiritual understanding, based on faith. A spiritual understanding, a seeking to understand, to understand the power, call it Jesus, God, Buddha, Krishna, one power and we're trying to understand that awesome power. In the beginning a power was created, a creative power. I say: Why don't we use this creative power to come together instead of separating ourselves.

I started Wellness Though the Arts with the idea for young people to talk about obesity, low self-esteem, how to live with one another. These are the topics we need to discuss, to put them on the table, to dissect them. We've all been bullied, so many of us are living with obesity, have diabetes: I have diabetes. I teach master classes, do workshops, get these kids to start talking about themselves and with one another. I want these young people to get out there with purpose. They write essays to workshops. I put them with a music person or a drama person, and we put together a show about the essay they've written, bringing art into play, and we act their stories out on stage so they can see the arts, to touch their fears, to embrace their fears. Inside those fears are our strength.

What it is for me in the performing arts is that it's life itself. Any art form is life. It's a creative expression of who we are, and that creative speak is working towards the good in us. It allows you to express whatever avenue you want to go down in a positive way. If there's anger you're feeling, it's been created but we can take it and entwine it into a way to learn how to live, a way to learn to live with one another. Each breath we take has been given to us, and we have to accept that out of that breath all of us are given an opportunity to bring creativity into the world.

When I was about twelve-years-old, I was living in Brooklyn. I grew up in the Pentecostal Church; I was a kid in a poor family, and I couldn't afford to go to the theater. It was also a time of great crisis, there were riots in Harlem. I remember I was traveling in a subway train returning to where I lived, and the riots had started in my neighborhood; it was in flames. It was the time of Martin Luther King, Jr., Malcom X, Huey Long, Dick Gregory. I learned from them that we're here to make a difference in the world. I was part of that generation when it was hard for me to sit still, and in the arts, I found a place where I could tell stories, to take the places I was feeling my anger in my heart, and to make something productive out of it. To be something that could heal people, to be someone that could heal our nation, especially today when we need that more than ever. We need a coming of togetherness. Never mind what political party we're a part of; we have to get it together. We need to love one another.

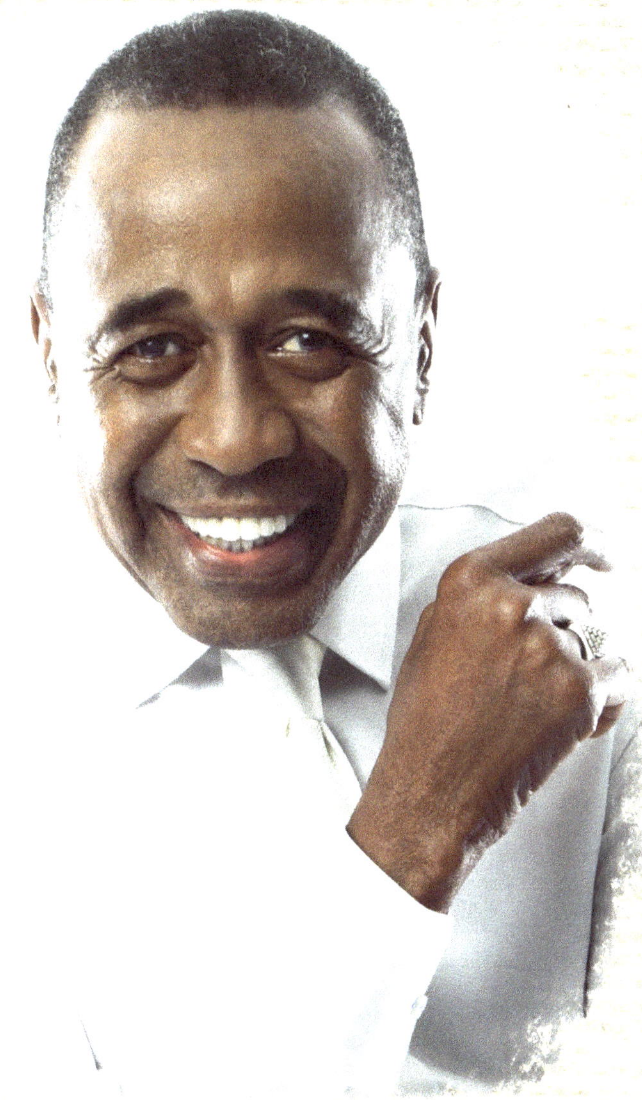

Ben Vereen photos by Isak Tiner

Q You studied under world-renowned choreographers, Martha Graham, and George Balanchine and Jerome Robbins, and was directed by Bob Fosse, among many other extraordinary artists. What were some of the great lessons that have stayed with you over the years?

Fosse gave me style. He wanted his work done well. He gave me a discipline from his experience. He'd say: "You're free to do this," and he'd brings things out of me and then he'd shape it. Balanchine and Martha Graham were adjudicators at the High School of the Performing Arts. It's also where I saw the first modern dancer—Norman Walker. The way they danced; it blew my mind. I had so much passion and there were all these great teachers there that set me a foundation.

Working with Tom O'Horgan gave me freedom. And before everyone there was Ira Aldridge, an African-American actor who escaped slavery and changed the face of doing Shakespeare on this planet.

Q You continue to tour the world with your one-man show, *Steppin' Out with Ben Vereen* which receives rave reviews internationally, which I experienced in Detroit. Why did you originally want to create your own show and what has it meant to you?

The "ham" in me. We sing, we act, we do it because we need more love. My love was so big I had to get it out. When I did the shows I did they were a part of my life. I've been doing the show telling the spirit of my journey. When I did *Jesus Christ Superstar*, working with Tom O'Horgan, singing "Corner of the Sky" from *Pippin*, *Sweet Charity*, the Sammy Davis songs, *Wicked*. All the songs have a personal vibration inside me.

So I started singing back then. I decided to put my act right together right after *Pippin*. It's my gratitude show. I get to share with the audience where we've been together, and to thank the audience for being here with me, in the moment.

Q What continues to give you the greatest joy in life and on the stage?

In my life, it's seeing my children blossom and grow. To see how young people, grow through art. So many people come up to me and tell me: "How wonderful it is to meet you. You changed my life," or "I saw you in *Pippin* or you taught a master class and it changed my life." This is why we do what we do. We like to get paid but the important thing is like the legacy you're laying down with this book. The real payback is beyond any monetary reward, it's the gratitude, the recognition that you touched somebody's life and made a difference. ■

ELI WALLACH

A founding member of The Actors Studio, Mr. Wallach received an Honorary Academy Award at the age of 94. His many Broadway appearances included his Tony Award-winning performance in *The Rose Tattoo* opposite Maureen Stapleton, *Mister Roberts*, *The Teahouse of the August Moon*, *Camino Real*, *The Cold Wind and the Warm* directed by Harold Clurman, *The House of Blue Leaves*, *The Price*, and *Rhinoceros*, opposite Zero Mostel. On stage, he often co-starred with his wife, Anne Jackson the two became one of the best-known acting couples in the American Theater, playing in *The Typists and The Tiger*, *Waltz of the Toreadors*, *The Diary of Anne Frank*, and *Cafe Crown*. Mr. Wallach's Off Broadway appearances included *The Chairs*, *The Lesson*, and *Visiting Mr. Green*. His notable film and television appearances included *Baby Doll*, for which he received a Golden Globe nomination, *The Magnificent Seven*, *The Good, the Bad and the Ugly*, *The Godfather Part III*, *Wall Street: Money Never Sleeps*, *Tough Guys* opposite Burt Lancaster and Kirk Douglas, and *The Misfits* co-starring with Marilyn Monroe, Montgomery Clift and Clark Gable, *The Poppy is Also a Flower* for which he received an Emmy Award, as Mr. Freeze in the *Batman and Robin* series, and *Highway to Heaven*. Mr. Wallach died in 2014 (this interview was conducted in 1998).

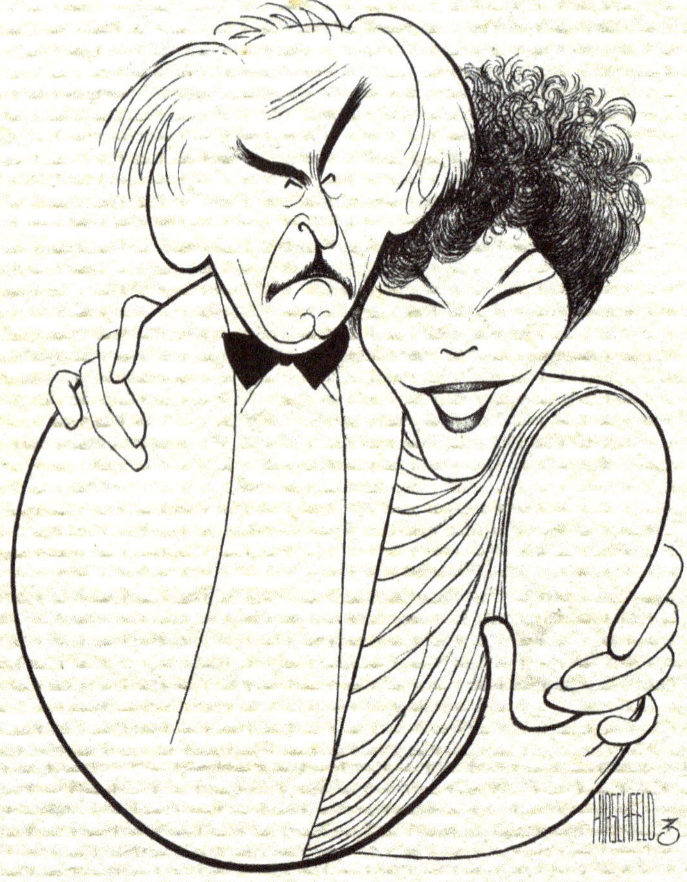

Eli Wallach artwork: Eli Wallach and Anne Jackson by Al Hirschfeld © The Al Hirschfeld Foundation. www.AlHirschfeldFoundation.org

Q How did you end up playing in Tennessee Williams' *Camino Real* on Broadway?

It was a great role! I was in *Mister Roberts* with Henry Fonda on Broadway, and Elia Kazan who knew me and my work wanted to experiment with fantasy. So we worked together in a scene from *Camino Real* at night and then showed it to Tennessee. Tennessee liked it so much he said, "I'll expand it" Then he said, "You have to play the role."

Camino Real took a while to get the money together, and at the same time I had auditioned and was offered the role of Maggio in a new film, *From Here to Eternity*. But then the money came through and I had to choose whether to do the play or the film. I chose Tennessee's play and it was the greatest experience of my life! I did the play for a year and a half, first in Chicago, then on Broadway and on tour.

It reminds me—because Frank Sinatra just died—and he

got the role in *Eternity* and went on to win an Academy Award. Whenever I'd meet him afterwards, he'd always say, "Hello, you crazy actor."

Q You've etched into our memory characters from many memorable films, including *The Good, The Bad and the Ugly*. Is there something you do differently in film than on stage?

It depends upon the characters. When I did *The Good, The Bad and The Ugly*, I had no idea what to do. It was the third in a trilogy of westerns that Sergio Leone had done. He had seen me in *The Magnificent Seven*, so that's what must have drawn him to me. But it was a challenge."

You know, another interesting character that I've received more mail about was playing "Mr. Freeze" in the TV series, *Batman and Robin*, and I only received three-hundred fifty dollars. Arnold (Schwarzenegger) got twenty-two million for playing that part in the movie, so my wife said to me, "You should have lifted weights!"

Q Why did you want to do Jeff Baron's play, *Visiting Mr. Green*?

He was a wonderful character to play. The man is fearful, living in a cocoon, doesn't want to be bothered, but he's awakened. That's what intrigued me. We played for eight months at the Union Square Theatre, and also in Florida and Massachusetts.

It's a first play by an American author. We're a disposable society, that disturbs me. In 1947, I was in the American Repertory Theatre that Margaret Webster, Eva Le Gallienne, and Cheryl Crawford founded, and we did five productions a year and tickets were only $4.80. It's appalling to me that this country doesn't have a real budget for the arts!

I wrote a letter to the President—I told him, "For the left wheel of a stealth bomber, you could send a marvelous musical like *1776* to every hamlet in this country! This city, this country has a great sense of cultural need and hunger for theater and it needs to be fed!" ■

FRITZ WEAVER

Mr. Weaver made his Broadway debut in *The Chalk Garden*, for which he received a Tony Award nomination and a Theatre World Award. His other Broadway appearances include *A Shot in the Dark*, *A Tale Told*, *Angel's Fall*, *Protective Custody*, *Miss Lonely Hearts*, *All American*, *Lorenzo in the White House*, as Sherlock Holmes in *Baker Street*, *My Fair Lady*, *Absurd Person Singular*, *The Price*, *Ring 'Round the Moon*, and *Child's Play*, for which he received the Tony Award. Off-Broadway he appeared in *The White Devil*, receiving the Clarence Derwent Award; *The Power and the Glory*; *Peer Gynt*; a solo play as *Lincoln*; *Love Letters*; *Don Juan in Hell*; *A Life*, receiving a Drama League nomination; *Trying*, receiving a Joseph Jefferson Award; and *The Voysey Inheritance*. His television work included starring as Josef Weiss in the miniseries, *Holocaust*, receiving an Emmy nomination; *The Martian Chronicles*, *Twilight Zone*, *Mission Impossible*, *L.A. Law*, *Star Trek: Deep Space Nine*, *The X-Files*, *Frasier*, and *Muhammad Ali's Greatest Fight*. Mr. Weaver acted as Hamlet in 1968; Richard II, Henry VI, and Macbeth at the American Shakespeare Festival in Stratford, Connecticut; and as King Lear at the Shakespeare Theatre in Washington, D.C., in 1991. His film appearances include *Fail-Safe*, *Day of the Dolphin*, *Marathon Man*, *A Walk in the Spring Rain*, *Black Sunday*, *Demon Seed*, and *The Thomas Crown Affair*. Mr. Weaver was inducted into the Players Hall of Fame and Theatre Hall of Fame. Mr. Weaver died in 2016. (This interview was conducted in 1999.)

Q You played a most unusual character, Messerchmann, in an enchanting production of *Ring 'Round the Moon* on Broadway. Was it as much fun as it appeared to be?

Can I spot a good role or what? It was fun when it went well. I don't think of *Ring* as an anti-romantic piece, but perhaps my role was, at its heart. But I hadn't finished my study of Messerchmann when we closed.

Q As one of our finest classical actors, why was it important for you to take on some of the great roles in the Shakespeare canon?

I've played twenty-two Shakespearian roles and failed in most of them. But if you're lucky enough to be offered them, you mustn't, as some of my colleagues have done, turn them down. How else are you going to learn what you have to do?

No one told me in advance that, in order to play Hamlet, you must have the body of a ballet dancer, the vocal resources of an opera singer, and the stamina of a champion athlete.

I had been working on that role for decades, and you can't talk about your interpretation, and yes, I had one—without an instrument to express it. Imagine trying to sing Verdi, without years of severe training.

Q You were part of the Stratford Shakespeare Festival and many other fine ensemble companies. Which roles have been the most satisfying for you?

What's your favorite letter in the alphabet, your favorite wave in the ocean? That was Henry James' answer when he was asked which, among his novels, were his favorites. I wouldn't have missed any part. And the chance to work with theatre artists like Uta Hagen, Joe Buloff, Morris Carnovsky, so many others, has been priceless to me.

Q What kind of a challenge was it for you working on the TV mini-series, *Holocaust*, in 1978?

The challenge was to try to imagine what it was like to be a Jew in Germany in those years. Of course that's not possible, but until more people try to imagine it, the lessons will not be learned.

I leave you to imagine—after days of filming in a real death camp, what the company bus ride back to Vienna was like...

Q You certainly have a magnificent vocal instrument as an actor. How did you originally work on your voice?

My voice is a large animal that needs to whipped, cajoled, and goaded—and it's never enough for

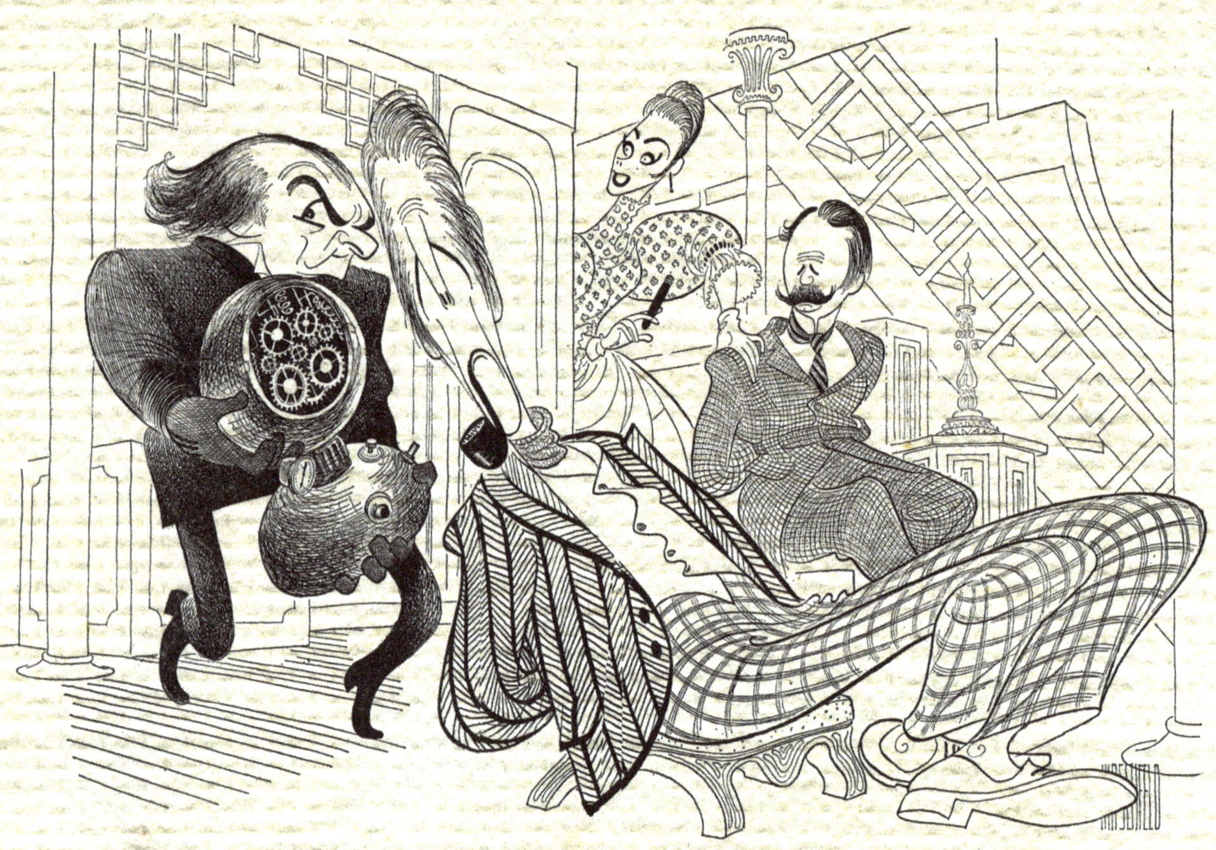

Fritz Weaver artwork: Fritz Weaver, Martin Gabel, Peter Sallis and Inga Swenson in "Baker Street" by Al Hirschfeld © The Al Hirschfeld Foundation. www.AlHirschfeldFoundation.org

what I want from it. The first review I ever got said, "Mr. Weaver was completely inaudible as Antonio." That's when I got to work. The goal is never a beautiful voice.

The American actor Joseph Jefferson said, "A good voice has ruined more actors than booze." What is wanted is an athleticism of speech, that is tuned to the finest nuances of the soul. ■

ARTISTS AND DESIGNERS

MARTHA CARPENTER

Considered one of the premiere portrait artists of America, Martha Carpenter's paintings are permanently exhibited nationwide, in private homes, institutions, and corporate offices, her career involving numerous exhibitions, publications and recognitions. As a participant in a Salon des Nations Exhibition promoting independent American artists, five of her paintings were accepted and exhibited at the Centre International D'Art Contemporain in Paris. For the major part of a forty-year career in the field of portrait painting, Ms. Carpenter has enjoyed affiliations with the nation's foremost portrait agencies which she credits as being instrumental in her pursuit of artistic and personal accomplishments.

Q How did it happen that you began painting?

It was a gift that I discovered when I was a child. I still consider it a gift, and I'm continuing to discover it more every day.

Q When did you know you wanted to be a portrait painter?

When I was a young child I drew people; I don't know why. Sometimes I think about that. I wonder about my quest for painting portraits. Because I'm a little bit of an introvert, maybe it's my way of communicating.

Q How did you develop your style?

If I have a style it's not by design. It's just the way my hand moves across the canvas, the way my eyes see the subject matter, and how it's translated onto the canvas. I like the painting to have a fresh quality. Sometimes I strive to leave certain brushstrokes unhampered and not manipu-

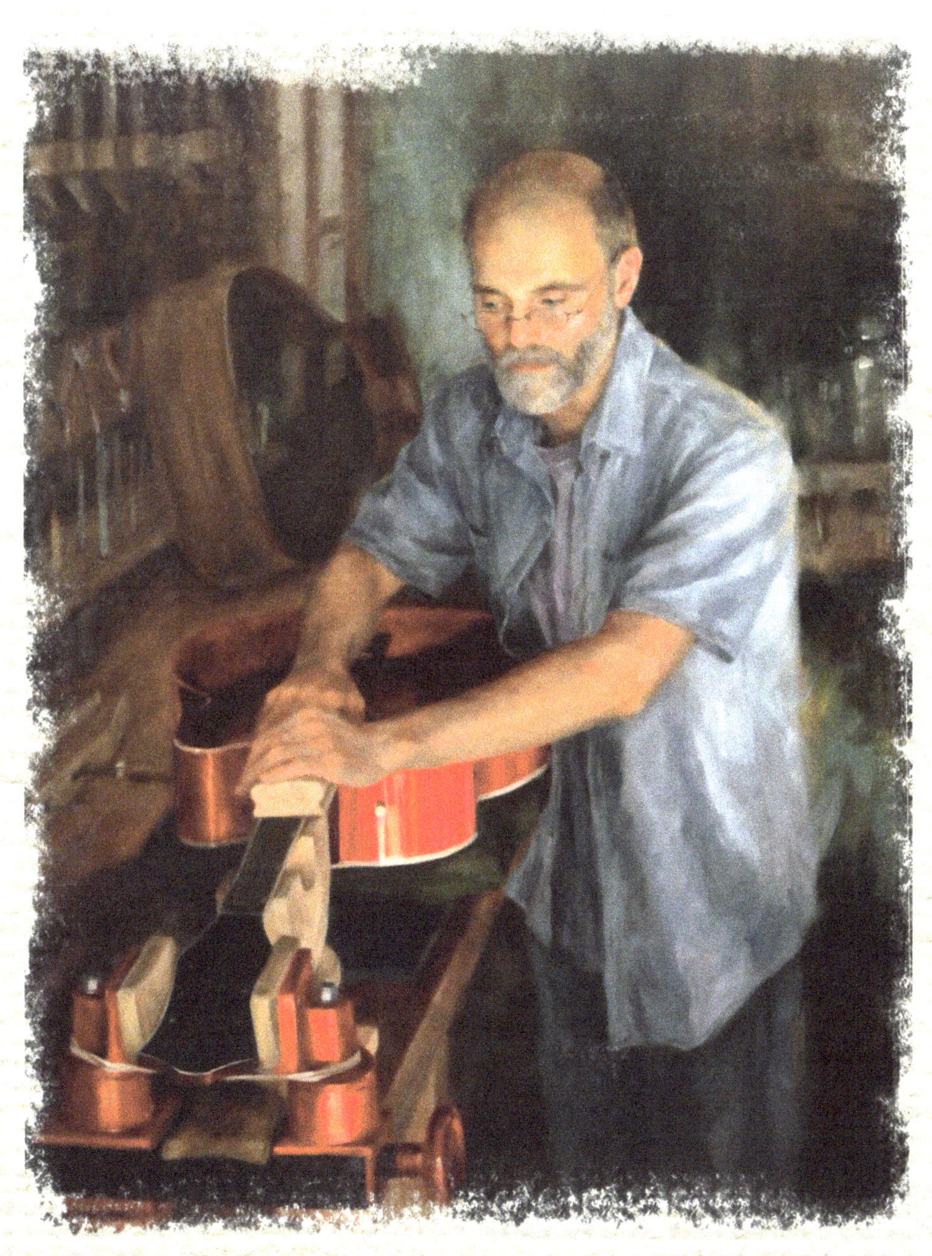

"The Luthier" by Martha Carpenter, courtesy of Ms. Carpenter

lated after they have been applied to the canvas.

A lot of master painters have practiced that effectively. I'm a student of John Singer Sargent. I've been inspired by certain artists who painted a certain way. Every individual artist will inevitably have what one would call style. I don't know if it's always intentional; it happens by nature.

Q What do you find in John Singer Sargent's portraits that make such a deep impression on you?

I am intrigued by his superior skills as a painter, and the longevity of his artistic journey. Standing before one of his paintings is captivating, as his subjects are portrayed in a magical way. His composition and lighting, the scale of the paintings, the way he connects with the viewer, all have an impact ,as well as does his mastery of the medium.

For example, Sargent's use of color value. One day I was viewing one of Sargent's paintings of a woman in white. She wore a dress which appeared to be of a satin material. It was a gorgeous rendition of this white garment in the painting. I took a white envelope from my purse, and I held it up in front of the white in his painting, to discover the color in his painting was closer to gray. However, stepping back, the painting clearly portrayed a woman wearing white. I aspired to achieve that amazing illusion by using color intensity and color value.

Later that day while examining a painting by Sargent of a lady standing in the outdoors, I witnessed fiery brush work throughout the painting, which contrasted with sensitive refinement around the facial area. In the same painting there were paint brush bristles imbedded in the dry paint. It's all there like a time capsule. I took that as a license to follow in suit.

Q Are there certain artists who have influenced your work?

Yes—many artists—some are living today and some have long passed. I look at art books studying other artists' works, and am strongly influenced by other portrait artists of today.

Q On what canvas do you prefer to paint and what brushes do you use?

I use a Belgian linen canvas on which a particular priming technique has been used. The primer on a canvas affects the way the canvas receives the paint when a brush stroke is made. The linen comes from the flax plant, and the fibers are long, making it a much stronger fabric and giving more longevity to the painting.

Most of the brushes I use are bristle filberts. The brush ends are curved and work well in painting the curvilinear form of a human subject.

Q Do you normally paint your paintings with the person sitting for you?

I've done a multitude of portraits from life, which is preferable. The reason the old master works are so incredibly convincing is that they were painted from life. In doing a painting from life, all the information is right before the artist's eyes.

However, I have done a great deal of portraits by means of photographic reference, which I execute myself. If the painting is to be done using photographs, it's better that the artist controls the photography because it creates the design of the painting. Still, a photograph is an illusion, not to scale, and two-dimensional; whereas the real human form is three-dimensional and full-scale.

Q Your paintings must hold great meaning for those who have commissioned you—

A mother commissioned me to paint her daughters; while later traveling with her daughters to Chicago for a doll show by train there was a terrible tragic crash. Two of her daughters were lost. Later, I was informed the parents had done a television interview, which I was able to watch. They discussed what helped them get through their grief. Their young daughters were very beautiful. As the mother was interviewed, she spoke about her faith in getting through this terrible tragedy. The paintings were shown on the screen and the mother mentioned how much the portraits meant to her. Hearing this made me feel very worthwhile and gave a whole new meaning to me of what my work can mean for others.

A similar experience happened when I was commissioned and had painted individual portraits of four children of a family who, while on a safari in Africa, were killed in a plane crash. The grandfather had chartered a tour by plane for him and the entire family. Only one child who was too young to go, and stayed behind with the nanny. When this child was left orphaned, she was adopted by family members. The commission to paint this last child in the family had already been contracted, so I was fortunate later to also paint her portrait. Portrait paintings are a very effective way to document a life; a very humanistic art form.

Q What does it take to be a painter of portraits?

Sacrifice. When a portrait painter enters the studio to put in a day of work, and reports to the easel to do a commissioned painting, there is a realization of the lack of ownership of the painting. The assignment is to accurately portray an individual, whether it's a child with a puppy dog or the President of the United States. A down payment has been made and it's the client's painting from the start. A certain amount of artistic freedom is sacrificed and a different faculty of the mind is employed.

Also, the art form requires patience. I am an academic painter and sometimes I need more patience than I think I have.

Q What gives you your greatest joy in painting?

The fulfillment of a successful painting. The fact that it's all I am. It makes me feel grateful, blessed. I was given this chance to paint

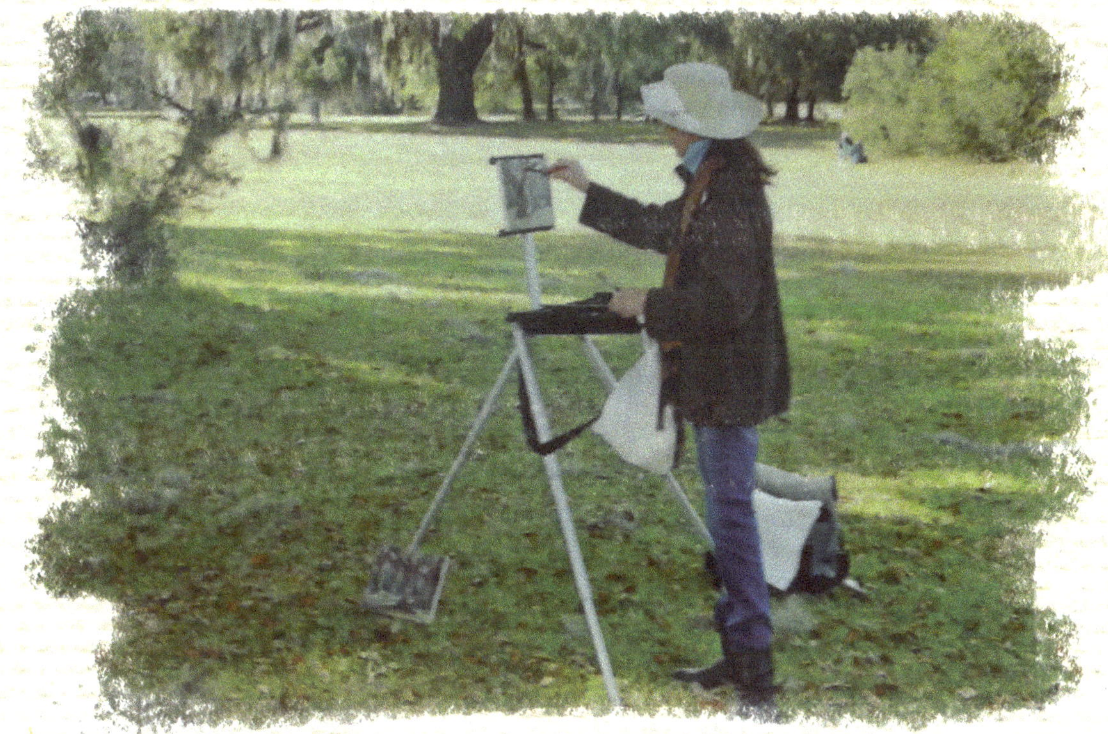

Martha Carpenter photo: courtesy of the artist

and it's been there as my companion, my livelihood. Sometimes I compare academic painting to the sports world. When one performs well, there is a sense of joy. Whenever I place a painting in a home or an institution, I know it will be appreciated and hold meaning for someone; that gives me gratification.

Recently I ventured into a non-commissioned painting. The content told the story of an artisan in his craft. The subject was a luthier, one who crafts and repairs string instruments. This painting was refreshing and energizing and I consider it to be the beginning of a series.

Q Is there a way to develop one's appreciation or taste for art?

I think Harold Clurman had it in a nutshell when he wrote in a commentary about the theater when asked, "Is it a good play?" The essence of his answer was that if it touched people it was a good play. It's very relative, isn't it? They say beauty is in the eye of the beholder. Some may see it in a Rothko or a Picasso, which are entirely different from a Botticelli or a Michelangelo. A person can be affected by the skill level or the conjured-up emotions and it gives tremendous meaning to the viewer. When I see a painting by John Singer Sargent, my senses react in a great way and I'm amazed at how he achieved what he did.

Sometimes the appreciator and the artist don't see "eye to eye." For example, there's a painting I was commissioned to do of a young girl of the age about twenty. Everything about the subject was quite ordinary including her attire. But I consider it one of my most successful paintings. I, the artist, and not necessarily any viewer of the painting would be the only one who would make that observation.

The reason for this has to do with my artistic experience while doing the painting. The consistency of the paint, the way the canvas received the paint, and the way magic seemed to happen with each brush stroke. There was a purpose behind each contact that the brush made with the canvas. The result was a fresh, painterly final affect.

I can think of paintings with tremendous brush work: works by Goya, Velázquez, John Singer Sargent, William Merritt Chase. I'm inspired by these artists and many more who invested a lifetime in their art form. If one is able to do that in a serious nature, not for recognition or fame, it will inevitably prove to be a worthy investment, whether it's dance, music, theater, visual art—it's about the process—that's what makes art great.

Q What makes creating art important in your life?

In my case, it's always been a good friend, a child, a companion, and a partner. I think an artist is born with a need to create and a quest for beauty—be it a poet, a writer, an actor, a musician, a painter, all the artistic disciplines—in pursuing an art form. It helps us ride above the normal circumstances of the day. We have a God-given opportunity, and if we can take advantage of it throughout our lives it gives us a sense of worth. And it does take a lifetime. An artist doesn't just get up one day and acquire the skill to produce a great work of art. Creation takes a lot of willpower, effort ,and in most cases, a great deal of time.

When I haven't painted for a while, the sensation feels unnatural. I have heard my fellow artists express the same thoughts. And when we get to a certain point where we have a lot of work behind us, we're at a level which allows us to either teach and share what we've been given—or venture into a new level of expression. It's how we live. To an artist, it is life. Our art forms become our life. ■

ALVIN COLT

Mr. Colt was one of the American Theater's leading costume designers. He made his Broadway debut with the original production of George Abbott's *On the Town*, choreographed by Jerome Robbins in 1944. He designed over two hundred productions for Broadway, in film, and television. Among them included the original productions of *Guys and Dolls, Fanny, Li'l Abner*; *The Lark* with Julie Harris and Boris Karloff, for which he received the Tony Award; *Top Banana* with Phil Silvers; *Wildcat* with Lucille Ball; *Sugar, Finian's Rainbow, Lorelei, Destry Rides Again*; Rodgers and Hammerstein's *Pipe Dream*, for which he received the Tony Award; *Fanny*, directed by Joshua Logan; and *Waiting in the Wings* with Lauren Bacall and Rosemary Harris. Off Broadway, he designed several shows including *Forbidden Broadway: 2001 A Spoof Odyssey*. His costume designs for films and television included *Top Banana, Li'l Abner, Kiss Me Kate, The Night of 100 Stars*, fifteen Tony Award shows, and *The Adams Chronicles*, for which he created more than two hundred costumes for the thirteen episodes. He designed sixteen plays for the Phoenix Theatre, including *Mary Stuart* with Eva Le Gallienne and Irene Worth, John Houseman's *Coriolanus*, and *The Sea Gull* with Montgomery Clift. In 2007, the Museum of the City of New York presented the exhibition "Costumes and Characters: The Designs of Alvin Colt." He was inducted into the Theatre Hall of Fame. Mr. Colt died in 2008 (this interview was conducted in 2002).

Q After attending Yale Drama School you pretty quickly began designing for Lincoln Kirsten?

While I was still in school, I began working at a summer theatre in Maine, and at the end of the season a small company of dancers called "The Ballet Caravan" came, headed by Lincoln. This was long before he established the New York City Ballet Company. I got to know him, and he told me when I got to New York to look him up and I did. I must have walked around the block six times to get up my nerve to see him.

When I did, he gave me introductions to Aline Bernstein, Irene Sharaff, Robert Edmund Jones, and Lee Simonson, all top designers in the theater. A lot of their advice was, "Go back to Kentucky, you don't want to work in this terrible business." But I stayed and look what happened!

Finally, Lincoln invited me to design the costumes for one of his ballets, *Charade*, as well as the set. One day he introduced me to Barbara Karinska, who revolutionized the making of costumes in this country. Coming from Russia, she was extraordinary in how she handled fabrics. Lincoln also introduced me to the great Russian painter, Pavel Tchlitchew and he became my mentor. He taught me so much, I also learned a lot from Lincoln—that you learn by doing.

Q You then designed Massine's *Saratoga* for the Ballet Russe de Monte Carlo at the Metropolitan Opera House, with Oliver Smith doing the scenery.

Massine contacted Lincoln and said he wanted to do a ballet with an American theme even though his company was all Russian. He wanted American designers, so Lincoln got it for Oliver and me. It was Oliver's first set. I then did Michael Kidd's *On Stage* and Balanchine's *Waltz Academy*. Then came *Fancy Free*, which I didn't do, but it evolved into *On the Town*, which became my first Broadway show. We were all scared to death before it opened, nervous wrecks. But George Abbott, our director, was the guiding light. He knew what was funny, what dragged, what should stay in, what to cut. It was the first show with Jerome Robbins' brilliant choreography and Lenny Bernstein's magical score.

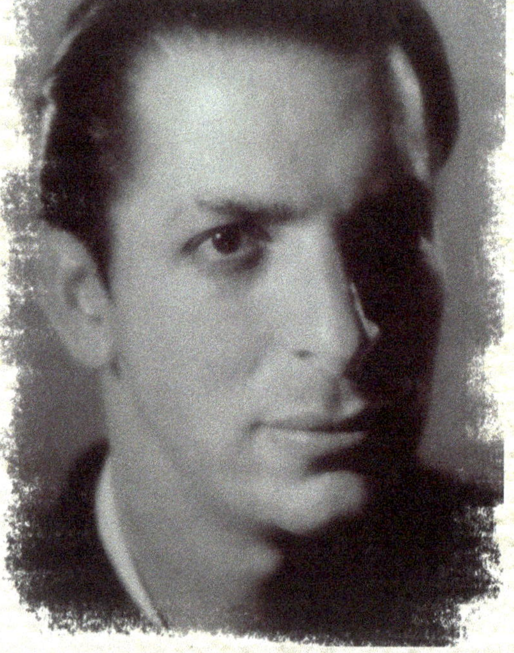

Alvin Colt photo: courtesy of the artist

Q How did you end up designing the original Guys and Dolls, capturing

Runyon Damon's characters so beautifully?
I think it was Abe Burrows who wrote the book, who said, "Get whoever did *On the Town*, they look like New York people." I read Damon's stories, and always think: if it's in the script it must be on the actors' backs; that's my main approach.

Q You also worked with Eva Le Gallienne and Orson Welles.
It was a great privilege to work for Miss Le G. She was challenging and what a wonderful woman; so knowledgeable about every phase of the theatre. When I did *Mary Stuart* with her and Irene Worth, I researched a number of paintings of the period, and the director, Tyrone Guthrie, was a tremendous help. I remember at a photo call at the Phoenix Theatre, when Miss Le G. entered in a costume that must have weighed a ton, she strode up and down on stage; there was an awesome silence. Then she stopped, and said, "Thank God, I've got strong legs." What a joy it was to do *The Seagull*, *A Doll's House*, *The Trojan Women*, and *Ring Round the Moon* for Miss Le G.

Orson had come to Tchlitchew because he wanted to design *Around the World in 80 Days*, but Tchlitchew wouldn't do it; but he said, "I have someone who will and I'll watch over him." Of course I was thrilled. We had five shops making hundreds of costumes, and Orson ended up being in the show besides directing it. It was a lot to do but Orson always knew what he liked and didn't like. He was a dominating man but I didn't have any trouble with him. It was one of my favorite shows.

Q And you designed for Tallulah Bankhead, and *The Beauty Part* with Bert Lahr.
I first met Bankhead at her Murray Hill town house. She said, "What did you say your name was?" I told her, "Alvin." She said, "Don't be ridiculous, darling, no one can be named Alvin." She was wearing a long mink coat. She told me she was going to have her hair different for the show, but when the curtain went up, she was as glamorous as always.

Bert was such a personality. He played five or six different characters in the show, and was brilliant. When I first went to see him in his apartment on Park Avenue, he answered the door in an Indian blanket bathrobe with a cord and tassel belt. He took me into the living room, which was very, very elegant. I turned around and on the wall was a full length oil portrait of him as the Lion in *The Wizard of Oz*. I couldn't get over it and almost began to weep. He was so easy to work with, a real pleasure.

Q How did you approach designing *Forbidden Broadway*, including their 20th Celebration?
Well, it's a satire of many Broadway shows—very tongue in cheek. I first saw it performed in a basement on a very small stage with lots of talent, wit, and audience appeal. Over the years, it's been built up to a full-scale production. I had designed costumes for four actors with about sixty costumes and wigs; the quick changes are not to be believed.

I truly feel it's unfortunate that people today never saw the shows of the famous Golden Era. They don't know what they've missed, they really should take the time to research them. To work in the theater is such a rich and rewarding experience, producing something every night that's magic for an audience. One must always keep learning by doing and never give up! ■

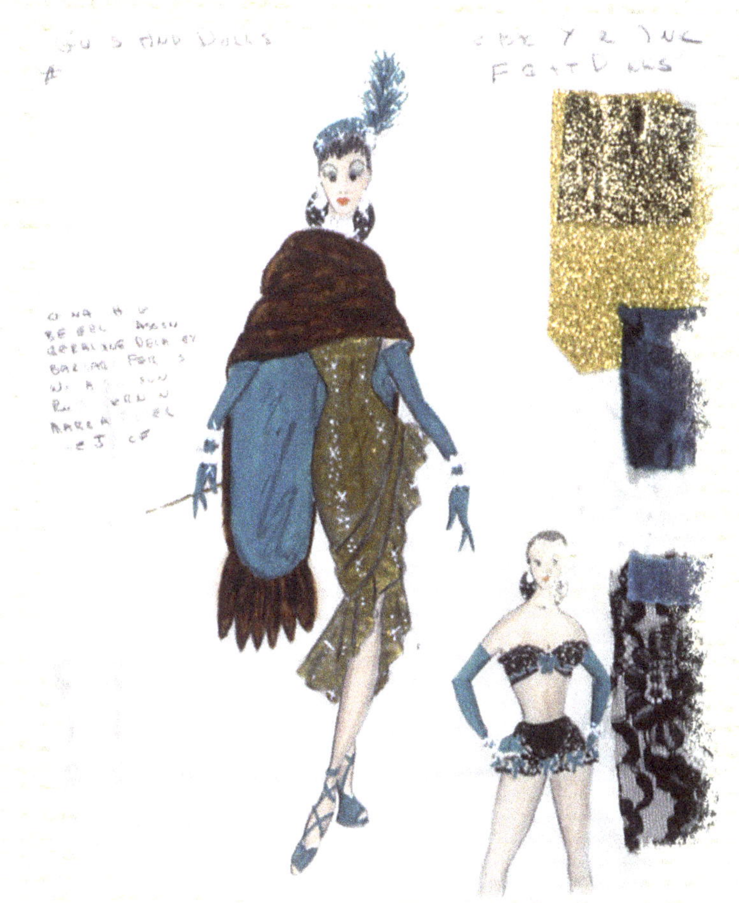

Alvin Colt's design for Adelaide's costume in the original Broadway production of "Guys and Dolls," courtesy of the artist

AL HIRSCHFELD

Al Hirschfeld's drawings stand as one of the most innovative efforts in establishing the visual language of modern art through caricature in the 20th century. A self-described "characterist," his signature work, defined by a linear calligraphic style, appeared in virtually every major publication of the last nine decades, including a seventy-five-year relationship with *The New York Times*, as well as numerous book and record covers and fifteen postage stamps. He is represented in many public collections, including the Metropolitan, the Whitney, the National Portrait Gallery, and Harvard's Theater Collection. Mr. Hirschfeld authored several books including *Manhattan Oases* and *Show Business is No Business*, in addition to ten collections of his work. He was declared a "Living Landmark" by the New York City Landmarks Commission in 1996, and a "Living Legend" by the Library of Congress in 2000. Just before his death, he learned he was to be awarded the Medal of Arts from the National Endowment of the Arts and was inducted into the Academy of Arts and Letters. The winner of two Tony Awards, he was given the ultimate Broadway accolade on what would have been his 100th birthday in June, 2003: The Martin Beck Theater in New York City was renamed the Al Hirschfeld Theater. Mr. Hirschfeld died in 2003 (this interview was conducted in 1998).

Q What has been your most important aim as an artist?
To capture what the playwright intended, what the character is portraying. The actor is important but he changes from play to play. But the intent of the playwright, that's what I try and concentrate on.

Q And the time you spent in Bali changed you profoundly—
In 1931, when I was there, I realized the sun bleached out color and left everything in black and white, and that's when I became influenced in *pure line* and how it communicates.

Q You've certainly experienced most of the greatest performers and actors of our time and you've drawn them!
It's always the last drawing I do that I remember with the most intensity.

Q Are there any who stand out?
Always the bigger-than-life

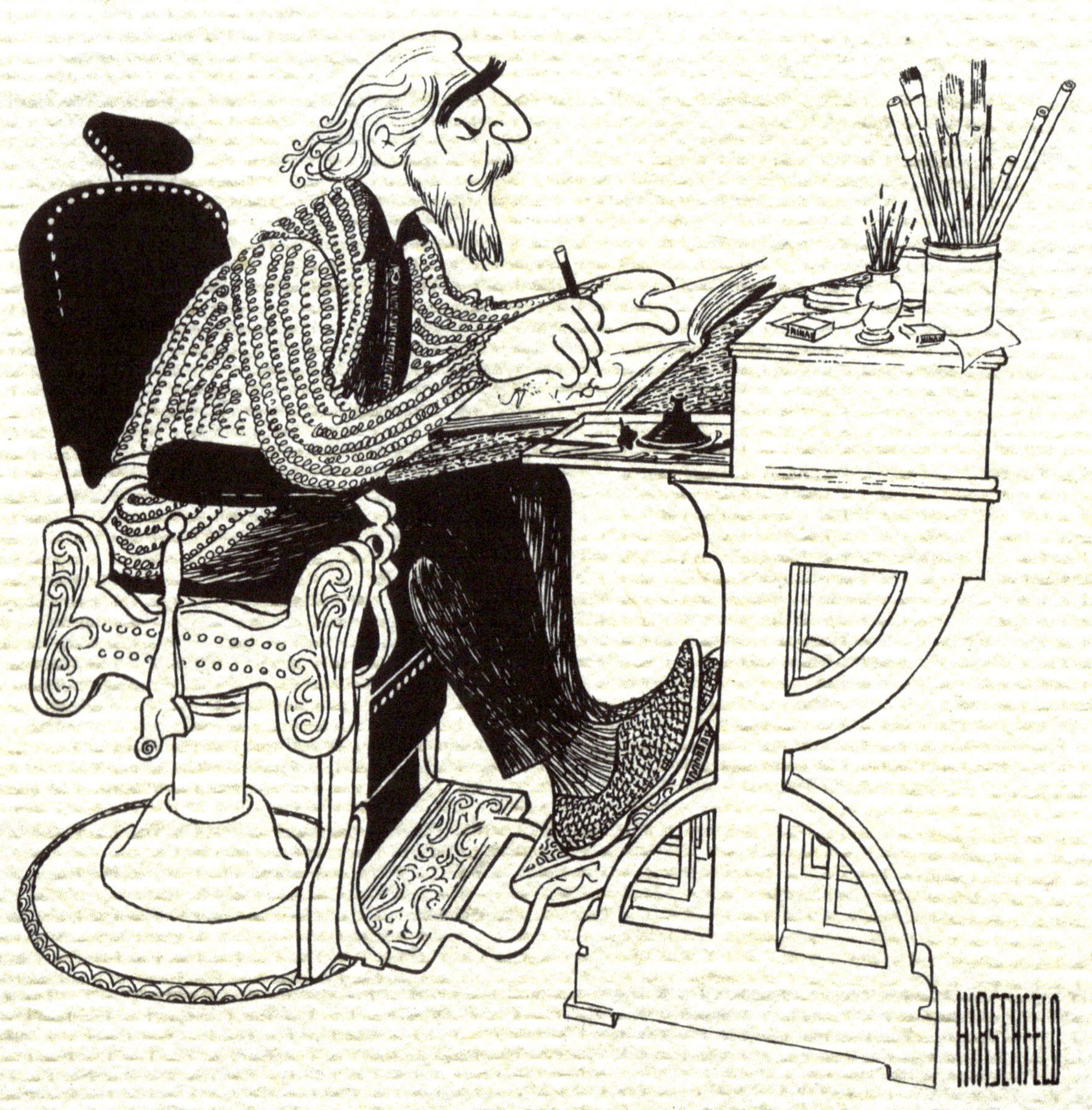

Al Hirschfeld self-portrait by Al Hirschfeld

personalities, the explosive actors who could communicate to the last row of the second balcony, who were trained to communicate at a great distance. Today the intensity of the playwrights has changed, so the actor has changed.

Then there were those so powerfully, wonderfully inventive, like Helen Hayes, the Lunts, and most of the comedians—Zero Mostel, W.C. Fields, Jimmy Durante, Buster Keaton, Chaplin, Carol Channing.

Q The artist must be supported, but this country appears unsympathetic in fighting for the arts. What happened?
Well, if you look at what came out of the WPA, what the Federal Theatre produced in the 1930s, a whole group of talent was creating art and theater and its influence on the country was dramatic! The Living Newspaper, Orson Welles, Martin Gabel, Joseph Cotton, Arlene Francis, Abe Feder. But with the death of the Federal Theatre, and when The Group Theatre closed down...still their profound influence can't be measured. Nobody can finance it like today—except for the government.

Q But still the artist –
Will do what he has to. Art's a "luxury," they'll tell you, "No one needs it." But the artist knows there're no rules in art. It's such a personal thing. But it's not "work." Work is something "you don't like to do." If you don't have financial backing, you should go into the delicatessen business. However, anything you like to do, you're going to do no matter what. ■

EVERETT RAYMOND KINSTLER

One of the nation's foremost portrait painters, he studied at the Art Students League, where he later taught from 1969 to 1974. Mr. Kinstler's more than twelve hundred portraits include Tony Bennett, Carol Burnett, James Cagney, Betty Ford, Gene Hackman, Lady Bird Johnson, Paul Newman, Peter O'Toole, Gregory Peck, and John Wayne, as well as writers including Arthur Miller, Ayn Rand, Tennessee Williams, and Tom Wolfe; Supreme Court Justices Ruth Bader Ginsburg and Harry Blackmun; business and government leaders, among them: John D. Rockefeller lll, Senator Daniel Patrick Moynihan, six U.S. Governors, four U.S. Secretaries of State, and the presidents of universities and colleges including Brown, Harvard, Oklahoma, Princeton, and Yale. He has painted over fifty cabinet officers, including Presidents Richard Nixon, Gerald R. Ford, Jimmy Carter, Ronald Reagan, George H. W. Bush, Bill Clinton, and George W. Bush. Mr. Kinstler's portraits of Ford and Reagan are the official White House portraits. His portraits of Katharine Hepburn, James Cagney, Christopher Plummer, Jason Robards, Jr., Alfred Drake, and Jose Ferrer can be found on the walls of The Players in New York City in The Kinstler Room. More than fifty of his works are in the permanent collection of The National Portrait Gallery, and his work is also in the Metropolitan Museum of Art, Brooklyn Museum, among others. The National Portrait Gallery acquired seventy-five original works for its permanent collection. Mr. Kinstler received the Copley Medal from the Smithsonian National Portrait Gallery.

Q I understand you grew up in New York City.
Yes, I was born on 105th Street. I went to public school here in the city. I have to tell you, theatre has always been a great passion of mine. I actually studied to be a musician, but I left Music and Art High School at fourteen years of age.

Q You began at age sixteen drawing comic book covers including *Zorro*, *The Shadow*, and *Hawkman*, and others. What influenced what you put on the covers?
I had been fascinated at five or six years old by the great illustrators who were all major personalities in those days. The field of illustration flourished at the turn of the century. You had such great illustrators like Rockwell, Parrish, Pyle, Gibson, Flagg. There were over a hundred and fifty pulp magazines in those days like the ones you mentioned, plus *Dime Detective*, *Doc Savage*, *Tom Mix*—I drew the covers for all of them.

See, I was trying to tell a story. The key to me was the cover had to have a heart and soul. The illustrators were storytellers in those days, glorious artists. And I saw the great silent movies: *The Thief of Baghdad* with Douglas Fairbanks, Sr., all of the great ones. I created the Zorro character for the comic books based on Tyrone Power and the two Fairbanks. I'd get movie stills from a store on 42nd Street; they were 5 cents apiece, and base a lot of my drawings on the movie stars in those stills.

Q You were also fortunate to have James Montgomery Flagg as a mentor.
Monty (Flagg) was a great looking guy, a big fellow, such a personality. I cared about him deeply. I would see him every week in his studio. I worked as an apprentice for fifteen years. You see, training didn't exist in those days. It was an extraordinary opportunity for someone with the inclinations, and I worked hard. I was very lucky to be able to pursue a career in a field that really doesn't exist today. It was a totally different world.

I've been in this building fifty

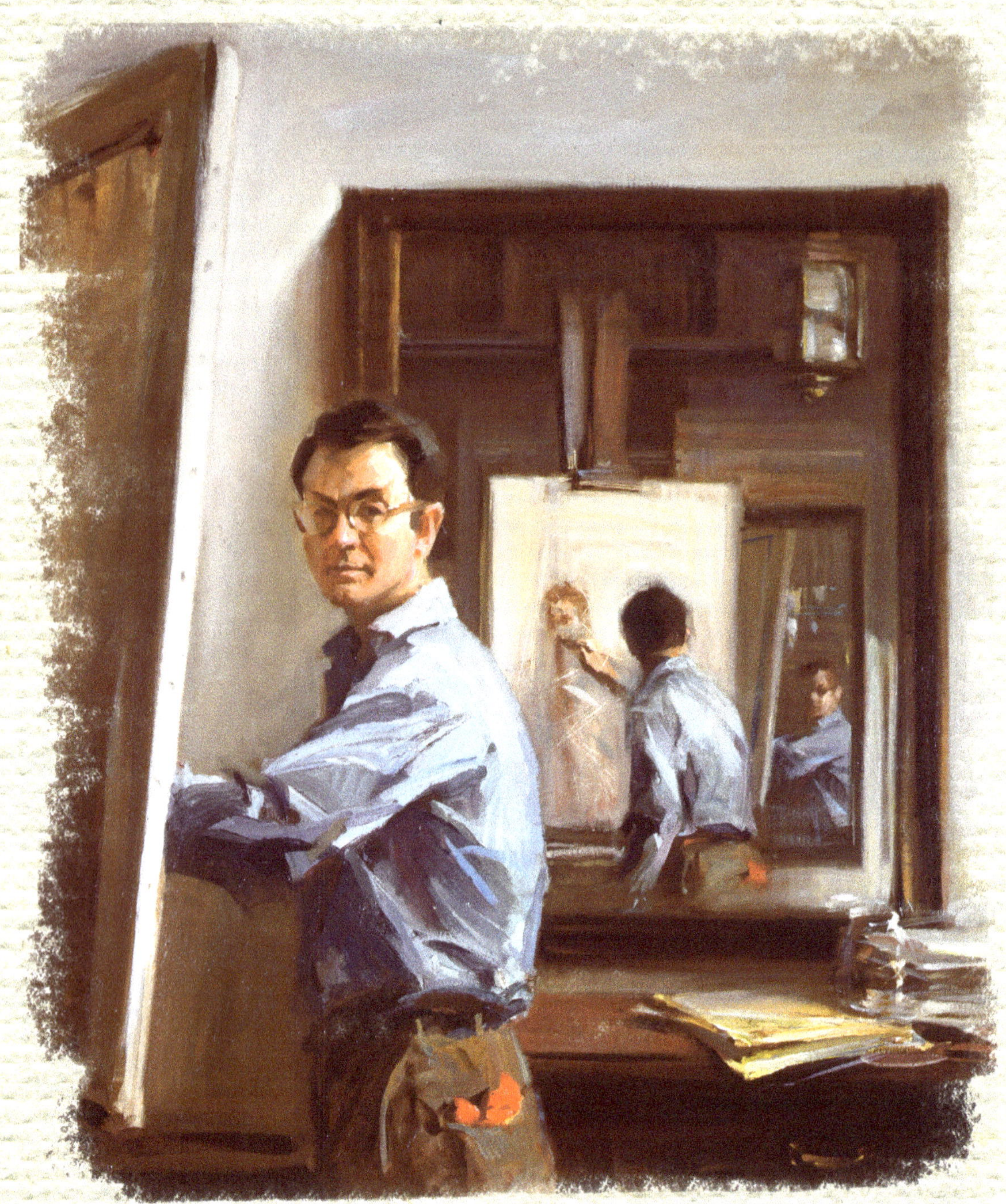

"Mirrors: a Self-Portrait" by Everett Raymond Kinstler artwork: "John Wayne" 1978, by Everett Raymond Kinstler, courtesy of Mr. Kinstler

years (Kinstler's large apartment and art studio overlooks Gramercy Park in New York City). John, who was also known as Jack, Barrymore lived down here at Gramercy Park. That sword you see at the fireplace was his; Jack use to pose for me, too.

I'll tell you an interesting story. He used that sword when he was rehearsing for *Macbeth*. You see, Monty and Jack were very good friends. He adored Monty's work. But Jack's wife began seeing Monty, and one day, she showed up at Monty's flat, and told him, "Jack is coming and he swears he's going to run me through!" So Monty, of course, lets her in, just as Jack shows up, sword in hand. His hair is all tousled, extremely drunk. He hollers through the door, "You've been living with my wife and I know she's in there! She hasn't been true to me!" Somehow, Monty was able to cool him down. Finally, Jack says, "Well, Monty, I couldn't blame you," and Monty was able to get that sword away from him. And that's the same sword.

Q Over the years, you've painted some of the most unforgettable stage and film stars.

I've been very blessed. So many of them I saw in the movies, and then I was able to draw them years later. You were telling me about The Group Theatre and The Theatre Guild. Well, I drew Robert Edmond Jones, he sat in this studio. When I met John Carradine years later, I told him, "You were my villain for all the *Zorro* covers I did." I also painted Douglas Fairbanks, Jr., the two Barrymores (John and Lionel), Bert Lahr, Katharine Hepburn, James Cagney; these were all people I grew up admiring. And I painted several of our Presidents.

When I drew Cagney, he was working on the movie, *Ragtime*, and I'd go on the set and show him my sketches. He would say to me, in that unique voice of his, "You're my boy, and anything you want to do is okay with me!"

With John Wayne, I actually had to fly out to California to meet him; he was seventy-two at the time. I later went to his home and he had a sculpture on one of his tables, of his famous pose in *The Searchers*. He told me, "There's a story about that pose." I told him I knew about it. He said, "What do you mean?" I told him I had seen the John Ford documentary. "That's right," he said. "The movie ends," he went on, "with this long shot, and I didn't know what to do with my hands. And Harry Carey, the director of photography on the film, had this mannerism of putting his hands on his hips. So when the camera started shooting, that's what I did." Wayne was pleased with the final painting I did. He told me, "I like that fellow—he's ready!"

Q How did you first meet Katharine Hepburn?

The first time I met Katie Hepburn was in her upper Eastside townhouse. Now on a side table, there was a framed reproduction of a charming painting of Ethel Barrymore by John Singer Sargent, and naturally I was drawn to it. Sargent has meant more to me than most painters. And Katie says to me, "Sargent drew that and it doesn't look a thing like Ethel!"

Q You're also a member and several of your gorgeous paintings including Jose Ferrer, Jason Robards, Jr., Katharine Hepburn, Dennis King, and Alfred Drake can be seen on the walls at The Players in New York City in The Kinstler Room named after you.

The Players has meant a great deal to me. It was Stotts Cotwell who first got me interested in the Club. Stotts was "the glue of the theatre." He had wanted me to do a portrait of Dennis King. When Dennis came to my studio the first time, he brought with him a manila envelope, and took out a photo of himself entirely in costume, and told me, "I want this to be your portrait." Of course, I painted him entirely different.

When I painted Alfred (Drake), I unfortunately hadn't seen him in all of his great productions like *Kiss Me Kate*, and when I told him this, he ended up singing all the numbers from all of his shows as I painted him. With Jason (Robards), I wanted to do something related to his work with O'Neill. So I portrayed that aspect of him.

Q I imagine you paint every day.

Every day. I get up at 6 o'clock in the morning and wait for the light to break. I'm a creature of daylight. I'd be pretending to say I "catch the soul" of a person. And "making a statement" is best left up to the political caricaturists. My role is to record, hopefully, with insight and some talent. I try and develop a point of view about a person. All an artist has is a point of view. My life is richer because of all the people I've painted. ■

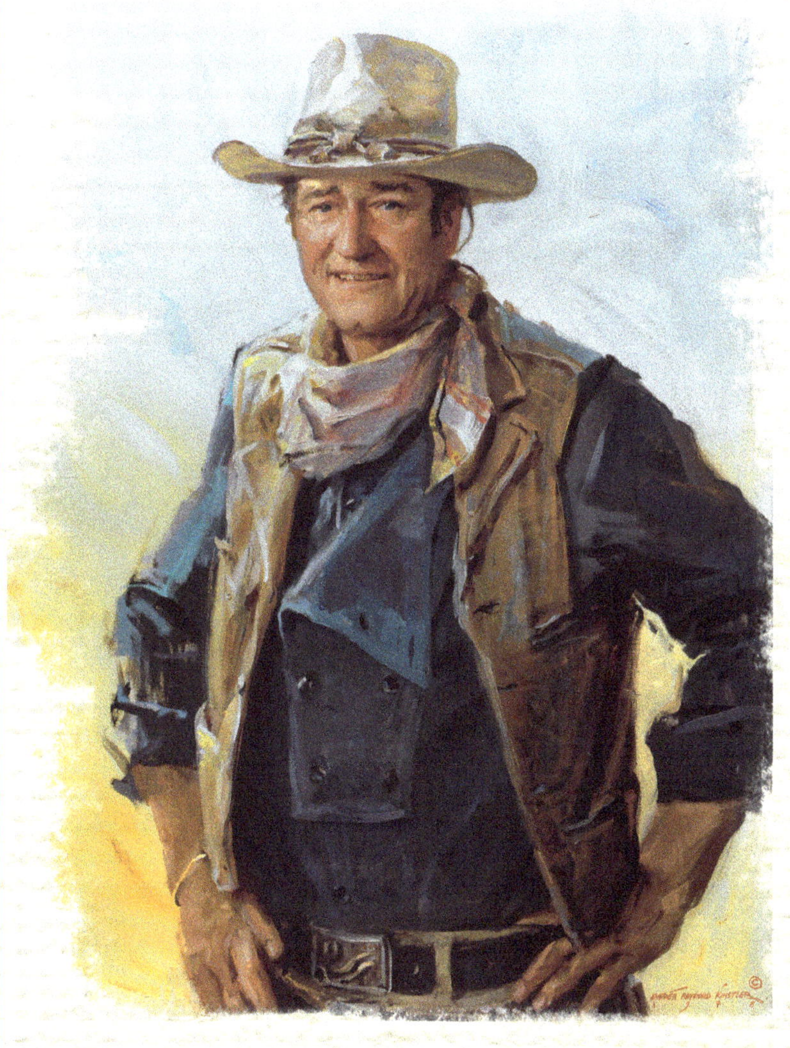

"John Wayne" 1978, by Everett Raymond Kinstler, courtesy of Mr. Kinstler

PARISH KOHANIM

Named one of the "World's Top 100 Photographers" for three consecutive years by Graphis, Mr. Kohanim has been a successful photographer for thirty years. In 2004, he opened his own Fine Art Gallery in Atlanta. He has been a Canon "Explorer of Light" since 1994 when the program was initiated worldwide. His Fine Art images were part of an exhibit of American artists shown at the Taylor Foundation in Paris, and are now in a permanent collection in Barbizon, France, and in several galleries across America. He has created a unique collaboration with Cirque du Soleil performers. Mr. Kohanim's ad photography has appeared in many national magazines including *Vogue, Harper's Bazaar, Forbes, Time, "Newsweek.* Mr. Kohanim's work has been featured on the covers of *Graphis Nudes, Communication Arts, Professional Photographer, "Digital Photo Pro*, and featured articles about his work. His clients have included many of the Fortune 500 companies including IBM, AT&T, Coca-Cola, Hanes, and Kimberly Clark. Mr. Kohanim is the recipient of many awards over the years.

Q How would you describe the influence where you grew up had upon your way of seeing light, color, and nature?
It goes back to where I was born—in the city of Shiraz; famous wines come from that area. It's in southern Iran, over five thousand feet above sea level, like Santa Fe, New Mexico. A pristine crystal blue sky, millions of stars at night.

I attribute a lot of my appreciation to nature to my parents; they were deeply connected to nature. We never had a TV. We'd travel into the mountains on vacations. Family unity was very important, and also very nourishing. We'd hike a lot of places where it was filled with flowers

When I came to the U.S., I fell into art. It was a very important part of our culture (in Iran) but if you became an artist there, there was a huge stigma attached to that. Here in America, I got a lot of encouragement.

Q What led you to photography?
My father was an amateur photographer, and had a darkroom. I never took an interest in it but I was fascinated and connected to it, eventually taking photography classes; photos spoke to me. It was my language. I think our values, our artistic vision, is based on what we experience in our childhood.

Q What do you find in nature that fuels your creativity?
When I'm in a landscape, up in the mountains, I'm like a little kid running through the fields; there could be snakes or bears but I have no fear. I'm a very visual person and when I'm there, in that moment, all my senses are awake. I feel the wind on my skin; I'm electrified by all the sounds and sensations.

Q How have you learned to trust your inner voice to what is possible in a photograph?
In the creative process, it's effortless. I'm on a higher level of being. I have a mission to do. When I'm in the process, I'm connected to the journey, and the journey is connected to me. I strive to capture every detail in front of me and that respect elevates my spirit.

The gift of photography allows me to become astonished with beauty, the designs before me. I fall in love in the process of capturing an image. Everything is ephemeral, it all goes so quickly. But the process elevates my spirit. Photography frees me from my incessant reptile mind. I trust my intuition, and it proves to be right on a lot of things; I have never questioned it.

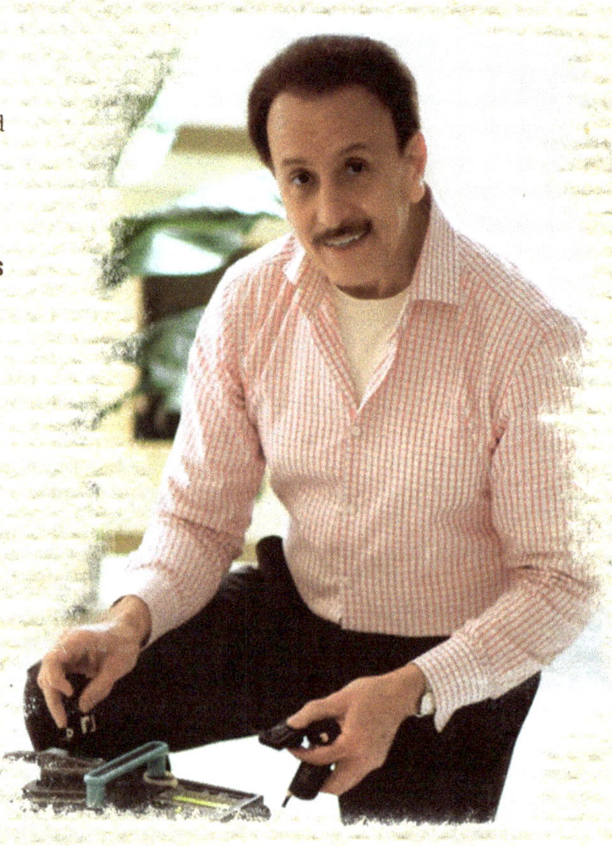
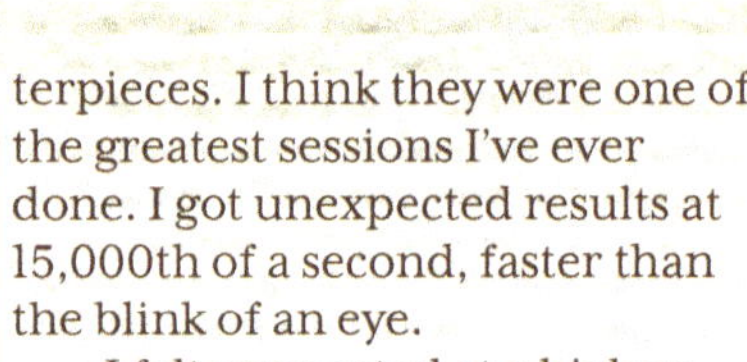

Parish Kohanim photo: courtesy of the artist

Q You've created several masterpieces involving Cirque du Soleil performers. Where did the sessions take you in terms of creating new ways of seeing the shape of the human figure?
Thank you for calling them masterpieces. I think they were one of the greatest sessions I've ever done. I got unexpected results at 15,000th of a second, faster than the blink of an eye.

I felt connected at a higher level with the performers. What they call "total synchronicity": you know it when it happens. I felt a much bigger force was directing us.

The performers never repeated their body language or their positions; it was absolutely extraordinary what they did—their quest for perfection. They must have done their movements more than fifty times. They were probably in pain but they appeared to be on a mission, and I had to get that perfect shot. The photos synchronized with the energy they were transmitting aesthically. I could feel their level of wanting to get to their perfection and that fired me. I was just an instrument as a photographer.

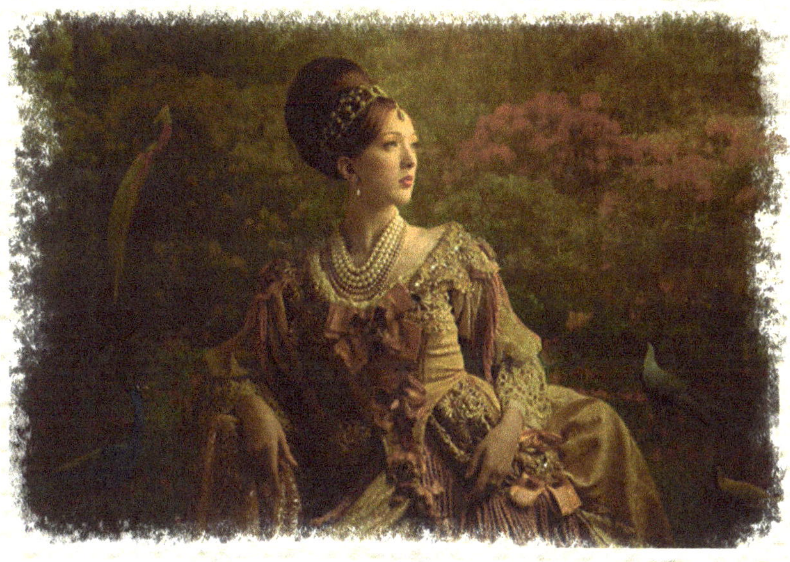

"Portrait" by Parish Kohanim, courtesy of Mr. Kohanim

Q What was the process to create your luminescent floral photographs?
It was first just curiosity. I never had any formal training in painting other than doing abstracts. This kind of "painting-realistic photography" opened up a new channel. I used a different tool—electronic pens. I found I could experiment, exploring through my imagination. That was the catalyst to experiment, not knowing what I'd end up with. It was a surprise as they evolved into something wonderful.

Q What have you learned from teaching?
I learn a lot. One of the greatest of gifts has been the gift of friendships. I have met people from all walks of life and they have become friends which no amount of money can bring you. I get to hear their life stories and it has a profound meaning for me. I feel we're all artists. A plumber who is skilled can call himself an "artist," as he uses his intellect and skills to find a leak, and then the solution.

Q I understand you have a special room in your studio where you go to listen to music.
It has a tremendous influence. Ever since I was a kid, music was tremendously important in my life. My mother would play classical opera, and my father played Iranian classical music.

I have found everything in life has its own rhythm, as our heartbeat does. We connect to it in a profound way. It helps in our connection in art. Not only visual artists fire my imagination but musicians. Rachminoff and Beethoven are so incredibly inspiring.

The full impact of the music really dissolves my anxieties and frustrations, and in the long term refuels my energy. When I take photographs there's always music in the background which is a catalyst helping me to complete the pictures. I'm sure as an actor you have to have a tremendous amount of this energy flowing to transform yourself when you become someone else.

When you learn an art, it really defines you. I never define my own art; it's up to the viewer to determine if they feel it's art. What gives it its value is the emotional impact it brings. ■

MING CHO LEE

One of the world's pre-eminent scenic designers, Mr. Lee has designed nationally and internationally for fifty years, for opera, dance, Broadway, and regional theatre. He designed the sets for over twenty Broadway shows including *K-2* for which he received the Tony Award, *Two Gentlemen of Verona, Mother Courage and Her Children, King Lear, The Shadow Box, The Glass Menagerie, For Colored Girls Who Have Considered Suicide When the Rainbow is Enuf,* among others. He was the principal designer for the New York Shakespeare Festival from 1962 to 1973 for more than fifty productions including *Peer Gynt*, and *Hair*, and virtually all the Shakespeare canon. He has also designed for Martha Graham, American Ballet Theatre, Joffrey Ballet, thirteen productions for the New York City Opera, eight productions at the Metropolitan Opera, Arena Stage, Mark Taper Forum, and the Guthrie Theatre. Mr. Lee is the former co-chair of the Design Department of Yale School of Drama, and holds the Donald Oenslager Chair in Design. The recipient of the National Medal of Arts, his other awards include the Mayor's Award for Arts and Culture, Tony Award for Lifetime Achievement, Helen Hayes Award, Drama Desk Awards, Outer Critic's Circle Awards, and the TCG Theatre Practitioner Award. He was inducted into the American Hall of Fame. Mr. Lee's work was given a retrospective at the New York Public Library for the Performing Arts, Yale School of Architecture, in Taiwan, and China. A book, *Ming Cho Lee: A Life in Design* written by Arnold Aronson was published in 2012.

Q You had the opportunity to learn from two of the greatest theater designers—Jo Mielziner and Boris Aronson.
To begin with, I think it's important to realize the tradition of apprenticeship in the theater design field, similar to the artisan guilds of the middle ages. Donald Oenslager taught forty-six years at Yale, and he and Jo Mielziner worked for Robert Edmond Jones, the pioneer of new theater who had been influenced by Appia and Gordon Craig.

Jo Mielziner was my mentor when he was doing over half of the shows on Broadway. Boris came from an entirely different lineage, the post-revolution Russian theatre of the constructivism, of Meyerhold, and especially Alexandra Exter. So I had two experiences poles apart which gave me something unique.

Q You have said, "Truly strong theater is dangerous."
Can you imagine theater not being dangerous? Theater examines human issues in a non-conformist way, destroying preconceptions, dealing with dissatisfaction, exposing the corruption of what's around you, challenging the status quo.

But I don't mean serious theater needs to be earnest or lacking in a sense of humor, with no capacity to be irreverent. We need to poke fun at things. But theater's not worth its salt unless it examines human life and all its issues.

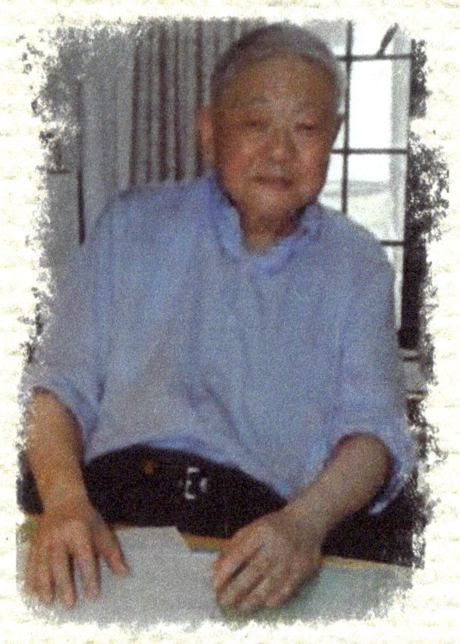

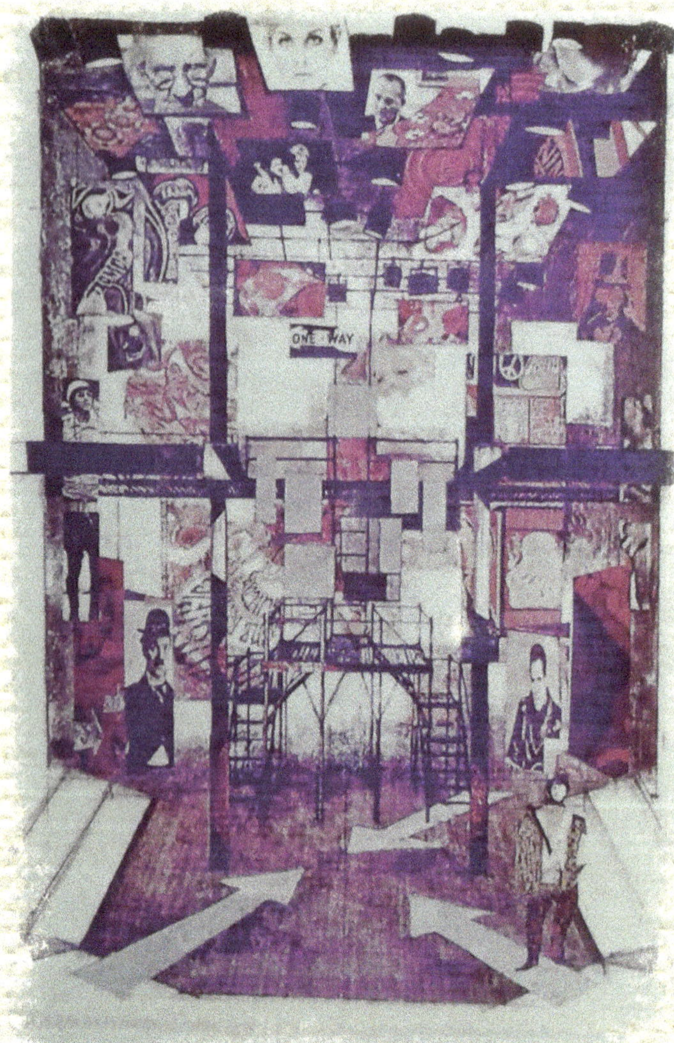

Q How were you able to ground yourself working in so many different styles?
When I was young, I didn't have the luxury of refusing a show and didn't necessarily want to. Whatever show I worked on, I owed it to myself to find the core of the work and how it related to myself. I did almost all of Shakespeare's plays because of Joe Papp—a truly remarkable person.

Every encounter with Martha Graham—a giant of modern dance—led me into unfamiliar territory. Everything she did had a kind of reservoir that I couldn't find a bottom to. It changed my way of looking at the world. It changed me as a person.

We need to realize that theater and art, like education, are an important and necessary part of the fabric of a democracy. We should speak out and do whatever we can, using all our resources, to allow theater and its artists to seek truth in all its forms. ■

Ming Cho Lee photo: courtesy of the artist   artwork: set design for "Hair" at New York Shakespeare Festival, courtesy of the artist

CAROLYN D PALMER

An accomplished sculptor, many of her works are displayed in prominent museums and public venues as well as in various private collections across America and the world. Ms. Palmer's work includes bronze busts of Franklin and Eleanor Roosevelt in the main lobby of the Franklin D. Roosevelt Presidential Library and Museum in Hyde Park, New York. She also created a marble bust of Pope Francis displayed in the entrance of the Papal Residence in New York City for his visit to the U.S. in 2015. The Holy Pontiff performed a special benediction over the sculpture. Her first bronze edition of Pope Francis is in Saint Patrick's Cathedral in NYC. Ms. Palmer also created sculptures of Thomas Jefferson for the prestigious Jefferson Center in Syracuse New York, and sculptures of Orville and Wilbur Wright at the Sanford Orlando Airport in Florida. She also sculpted a life-size bronze figure of Lucille Ball for Lucy's hometown in Jamestown New York. Ms. Palmer's sculptures can also be seen in the television series, *Madam Secretary*.

Carolyn D Palmer photo: Carolyn D Palmer working on Lucille Ball for "Lovable Lucy" sculpture, courtesy of the artist

Q When did you first know your path lay in creating sculptures?

While growing up in Orange County, NY, we'd vacation at my grandparents in Florida where I'd sculpt sand people on the beach. I was so young, yet I had this huge passion for creating faces and figures. People gathered in amazement watching my little hands sculpt. I didn't feel the faces were that good, but their reactions gave me a clue that I had some kind of innate gift.

First I became a portrait painter, and in 2002, a friend, who owns the Thomas Jefferson Center in Syracuse, called asking about a painting of his son. He also asked if I could find someone to sculpt a bronze Jefferson for his building. I was so excited that I asked if I could first take a shot at the sculpture with a preliminary clay model for his approval. I said, "If you don't like the figure, you don't have to pay me." This was my first statue so it was thrilling, yet extremely intimidating. Every now and then, he would stop by to see the sculpture in progress and thankfully he was very happy about how it was coming along.

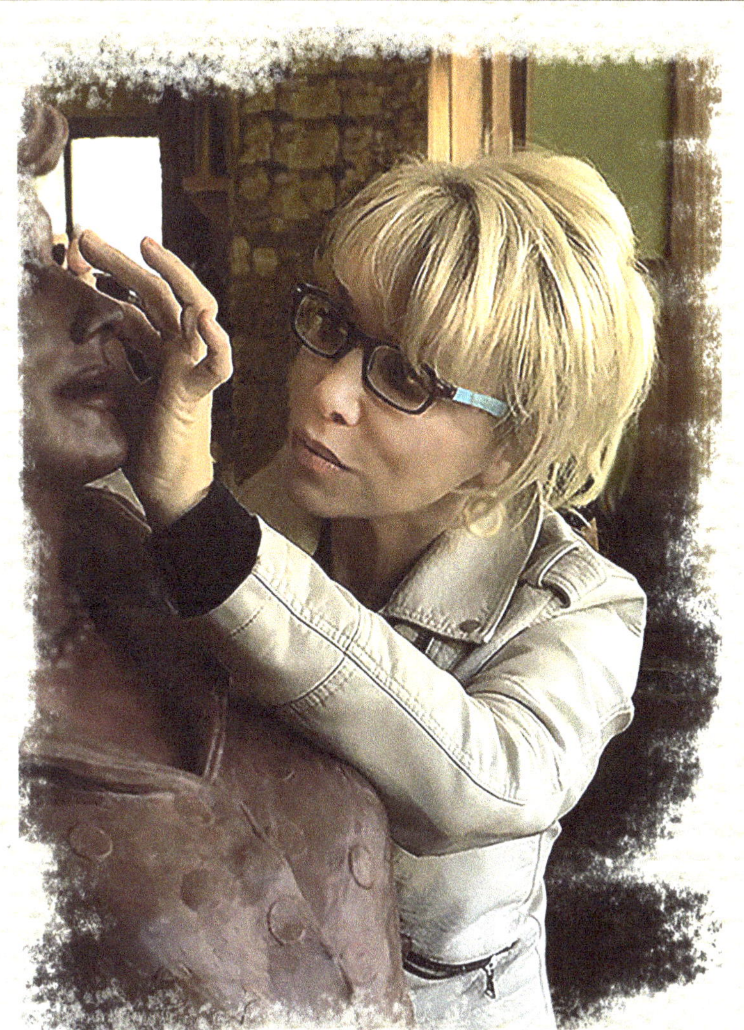

There were no photographs of Jefferson so the only available images were from the paintings created by other artists. I wanted to research and create my own rendition based on how Jefferson was described in books: it was said that he stood six feet-two-and-a-half inches tall, was strong as a horse, with a powerful square jaw. The profile on the nickel was another reference along with how other sculptors portrayed him. The French sculptor, Houdon, actually had Jefferson sit for him but I liked Rudolph Evan's rendition at the Jefferson Memorial because it was closer to how Jefferson was described by his peers. When the sculpture was finally completed, I received tremendous positive feedback which brought a big sigh of relief!

I had no idea my future would be as a sculptor. I just had a huge passion to create this Thomas Jefferson and it seemed like other commissions just sort of found me so I went with it. Now I can't imagine a life without sculpting. You wonder what path you will go down and mine was found a little late in life, but I guess you can say we all leave our own "fingerprints in the sand."

Q I understand you make only nine molds of each sculpture. Is that part of a tradition?

The traditional sculptor typically made just one mold from their original sculpture, and from that one mold they would create an edition of nine castings and keep a few artist copies for themselves. I like following that tradition unless I'm commissioned to create a "one of a kind" sculpture where the mold is basically destroyed. But a limited edition that is numbered gives a sculpture a certain prestige; gives it a rare quality, especially when there are only nine in the entire world.

Q You created masterful sculptures of President Franklin D. Roosevelt and Eleanor Roosevelt displayed in the renovated lobby of the FDR Presidential Library and Museum. What kind of preliminary work did you do?
For the Roosevelts, I researched their personalities and various moods found in countless photos. I felt Eleanor was such a special lady exuding inner beauty. Although her mother and others commented on her homely looks, I focused on Eleanor's compassion and honesty along with her determination. Eleanor was actually quoted as saying, "No matter how plain a woman may be, if truth and honesty is written on her face, she will be beautiful." I aimed to give Eleanor that very beauty she spoke about.

I used many reference photos, studying the light and shadows on their faces and then I'd simulate the same lighting in my studio. For example, if FDR had lighting from the left, I would aim my studio lighting form the left to study the lit up facets of his face and its shadows. I then sculpted to create shadows exactly where they were in the photographs.

Q I understand you also made the sculptures touchable for the blind.
Yes. This was such a powerful gift! When I was first commissioned, the Director of the Library asked if it was okay for the blind to touch them. I was thrilled and it opened up a whole new dimension to my work. While sculpting, I would periodically close my eyes to feel each sculpture in a more sensitive way. I began to feel with both hands and could easily discern the nuances of the anatomy or feel if the planes weren't symmetrical. I started to call forth their likenesses just by feeling with my hands.

Now, from that point forward, whenever I work on a sculpture, I'll close my eyes and feel the forms and textures of various parts of the body to see if it feels like a real face, arm, or an authentic leg; it's truly been a gift of sight!

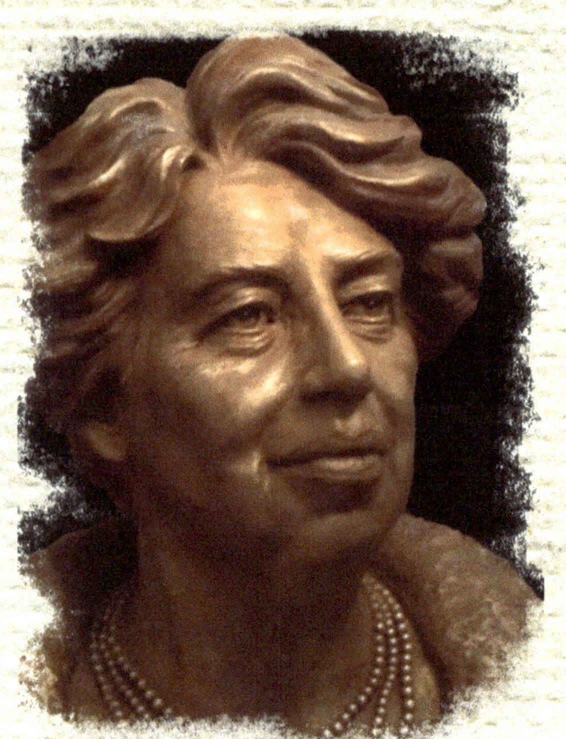

Eleanor Roosevelt Bronze by Carolyn D Palmer at Hyde Park, New York, courtesy of the artist

Q How long did it take you to create your memorable sculpture of Pope Francis for the Papal Residence in New York City? And as you worked on it, did you have music playing to help create a certain mood?
It took me about six months to sculpt the Holy Father. To create the mood, I played lots of chamber and spiritual music; in particular, classical choral pieces by a group called "The Priests." I spent days looking at photos of Pope Francis. It took longer than expected for me to be pleased but he finally showed up in a way that I liked.

When I complete a sculpture, it's really open for the viewer's interpretation. I'm never totally satisfied with a piece and if there wasn't a deadline, I would never find completion. It's as Leonardo da Vinci said, "Art *is* never finished, only abandoned." I always feel that way.

Q What were you seeking to include of Lucy's personality when you created your sculpture of Lucille Ball?
I wanted to portray the glamorous Lucy exuding confidence with a little bit of her playful side. My vision was to have her walking onto her Hollywood star saying, "Here I am!" I think "peacocking" her dress with her right hand adds a certain playfulness to it, while the left hand sits confidently on her hip, dangling a purse.

Also, I wanted to show the stylish Lucy; collar turned up and scrunched up sleeves, with pleated and signature polka dot dress. I gave her a pearl necklace and earrings. She even has a petticoat showing. Sculpting her face to find the spirit of Lucy was both fun and challenging. I endured many sleepless nights. You just hope the public is pleased with your work.

Q Of course, sculpture has a long lineage stretching back thousands of years to the Greeks and the Egyptians and no doubt even further back to the dawn of man, and whether one is enthralled either by Michelangelo's Pieta and his David, or work by Rodin, Houdon, Elisabet Ney, Jo Davidson or modern sculptors including Louise Nevelson, Alexander Calder, Louise Bourgeois, and Isamu Noguchi, sculpture is a great expression coming from

an artist's vision. How was your vision shaped and what are your greatest goals in creating life in a sculpture? In Hinduism, the embodiment of a god or a person can live in a sculpture, they call it a "Murti," and this is also practiced in many cultures around the world. I really believe a statue can touch the viewer with its inner spirit. While sculpting, I am always thinking of the person's spirit, probably more than their personality.

My goal is for the viewer to have an emotional experience of that person. I'm learning all the time not just by studying people but also by studying others that came before me. When I look at a bust by Jo Davidson or *Jean-Baptiste* Carpeaux, I feel moved, especially by Carpeaux, in the way he captured movement and people's personalities, which is all so inspiring to me.

Overall, I believe our love and passion for a piece of art creates a special bond or communication between us and what we're viewing. When art moves us, a shift occurs that brings us to a higher plane. I think of all good art as spiritual experiences.

What I do, I do mostly for others, not for myself. My creations are a way of contributing to the world—and to hear people talk about how they're moved by viewing a sculpture I've created—I feel humbled, and ecstatic; that's the greatest gift of all. ■

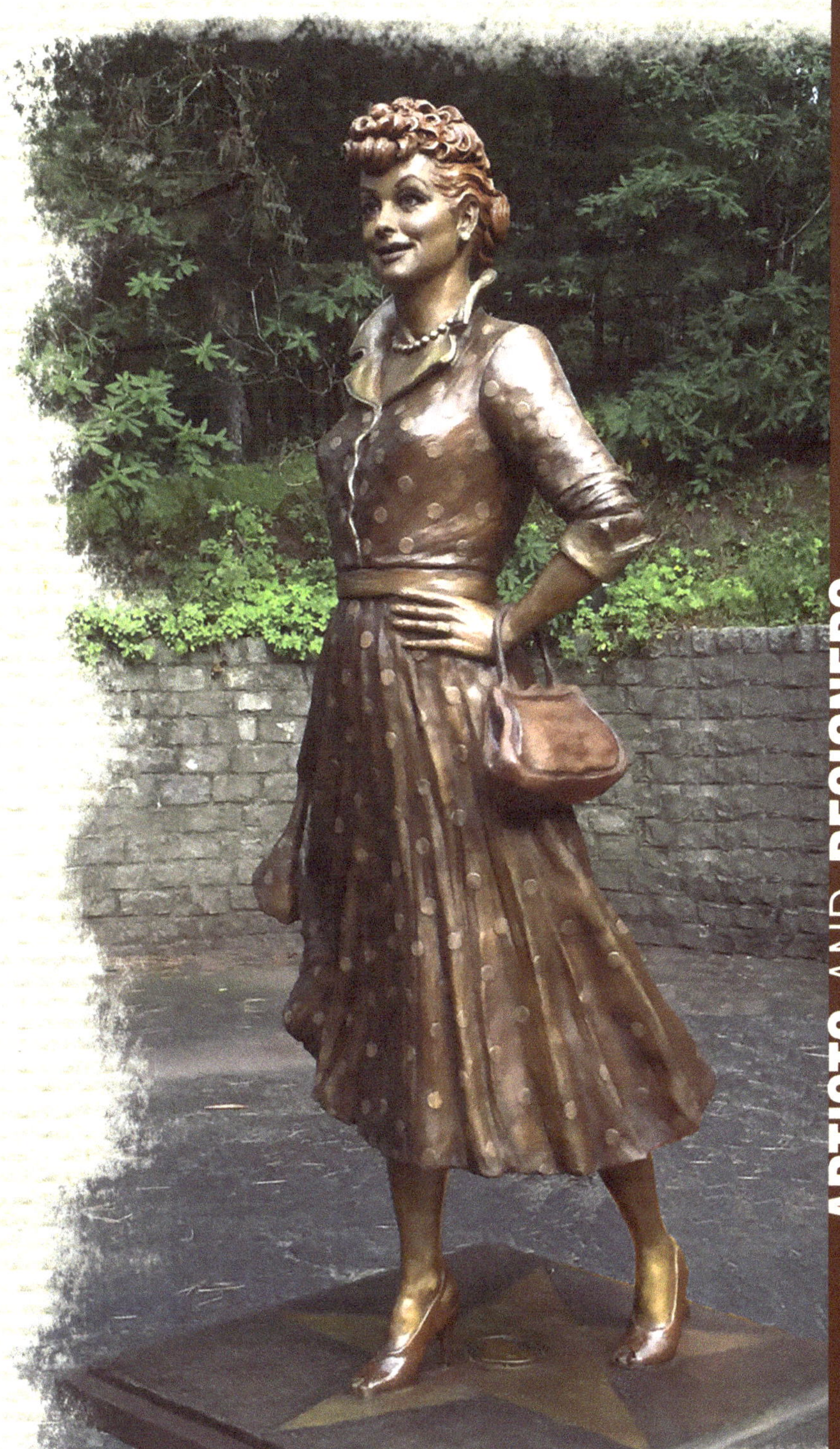

"Lovable Lucy" by Carolyn D Palmer for The Lucille Ball Memorial Park, Celeron, New York, courtesy of the artist

TARA SABHARWAL

An acclaimed artist, Ms. Sabharwal was born in New Delhi, and currently resides in New York City. She has had solo exhibitions of her paintings and prints around the world, including in New Delhi, Bangalore, London, New York City, Dusseldorf, Orvieto, Katsuyama, Karachi, Mumbai, Konstanz, Leeds, Newcastle upon Tyne, Darlington, Versailles, and Portugal. Ms. Sabharwal has taught art at the Guggenheim Museum, Cooper Union, City University of New York, the Rubin Museum of Art, and in New York City public schools as a teaching artist. Her work is in the collection of the British Museum and the Victoria and Albert Museum in London, New York Public Library, Boston's Peabody Essex Museum, and the Library of Congress in Washington DC. Ms. Sabharwal has received several commissions and grants, and most recently, the 2015 Joan Mitchell "Creating a Living Legacy Grant," and the 2015 Gottlieb award.

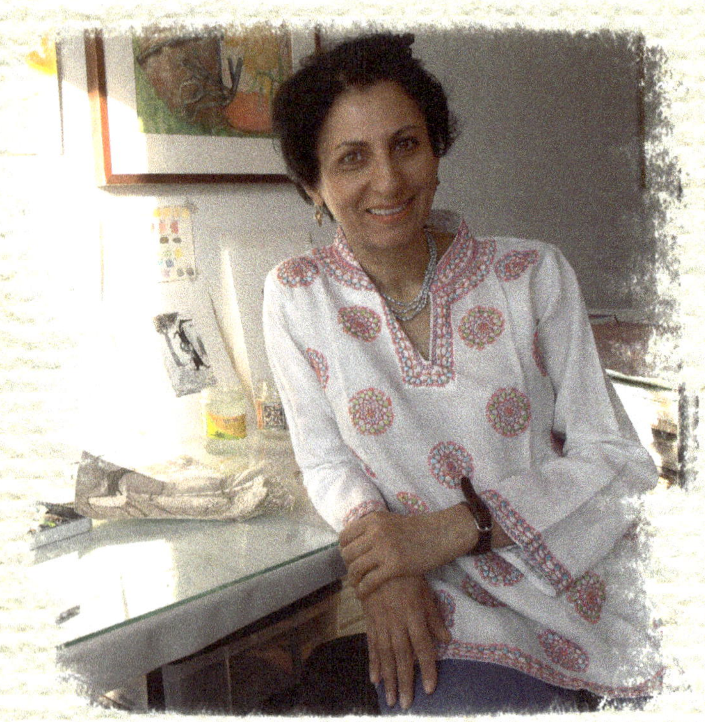

Tara Sabharwal photo: courtesy of the artist

Q When did you first know you had to express yourself creating art?
I was thirteen years old; it was a moment in my life when things were up in the air. My parents had recently gotten divorced; it was rare in India those days. It was a big shock, and then on top of it, I had an accident playing basketball and suffered a head injury. I was in the hospital and missed school for five months.

I remember the day I started drawing. I saw the raindrops through the rain, and I thought it was the most incredibly beautiful thing. That was the moment when I drew a glass of water and I knew, "This is my life." I drew the reflections, looking at what was inside and outside. The whole world was in it; it was very exciting. I wanted to be a painter but my father insisted I go back to school, which I did. I think I was angry for a long time, but I'd draw constantly, sitting at the back of the class.

Q Then you went to Baroda Art College—
Yes, it was a college unique in its emphasis on both Indian and Western art and aesthetics. I had a wonderful drawing teacher, Nasreen Mohommedi, who inspired us to be honest, to find the correct relationship between objects and space. Around that time there was a festival—Navaratri, a celebration that lasts nine nights. Everyone dances a lot, and something was released in me. Slowly I made color arrangements along with my drawings.

Q What artists' work touched your creativity?
Munch resonated within me, how he captured deep emotions, moods, and anxieties in people, in the mountains and fjords of Norway. I also liked Piero Della Francesca's paintings, which are graceful, sublime; and Blake, Bonnard, and Paul Klee.

All these amazing artists made me realize that there was so much more I could do with what was inside my dreams. I was influenced by the delicacy of Indian miniatures. At that time in India, I pretty much saw only small reproductions of art by the masters, and the work of my teachers.

Q How did you learn the art of etching and woodcut?
Etching was one of the subjects I had in college; I always loved making prints. When I went to Japan, I learned to make woodcuts.

Q How did your getting a scholarship to go to London influence your art?
I was very lucky, I got solo exhibitions, and The Victoria and Albert Museum bought my work. So it was a really wonderful time. I got grants to go to Italy, France, Netherlands, Germany, New York City, and Norway. I saw medieval art, discovered Redon, Goya, European painting, certain forms of Romanticism and Expressionism, all stimulating and enriching my pictorial language.

The Indians' style is flattened out, with surfaces stitched together. Now I saw deep space, and began to include perspective in my work. I think, in my work, there's an engagement between the contradictions between the Indian and European visual language, and I try to assimilate the two so these two strains can express and celebrate as they unite and separate only to meet again as a distinct identity.

When I returned to India, I began doing small watercolors that were much more psychological, figurative, but the essence was always abstract. A microcosm of worlds within worlds, color itself expressing emotion.

Sometimes I think I'm cursed and blessed at the same time. I paint to get in touch with who I am, to find some stability. For example, the other day while I was painting I had a feeling, so I put a mark on a canvas—which was floating. So I put another mark on the surface to anchor it. But I can't rely on it, it's an illusion. It's like a feeling one feels early in childhood when everything is shaky; a very disconcerted feeling.

I have a feeling everything is made out of quicksand, yet I like the constant search. All the time, one is a beginner. In London, I had a very wise teacher who said you have to make your own language. I throw myself into the orbit to find my own balance.

Sometimes I may succeed. I always say that an artist prays for years.

Q How did you develop your own personal way of seeing?

Visual memory is a gift I've always been blessed with. Some image from the past will flash in my head: I see back in time into my grandmother's house; I see the light of the place, clouds passing, like I'm transported to an oceanic moment, and I express it through color and form.

Right now I'm doing work which is neither a painting nor a print. I take a plexi glass, 30 inches by 40 inches and make marks on it, add color and solvents. When I'm done, I put paper over it, take it through the press and make a mono print, which I then bring home and work on as an oil painting. I've made thirty of these kinds of large paintings about movement, abstract large fields of colors, closer to dancing and being free with movement. I don't know where it will take me. I also made a large sculpture for the first time.

Q How has being in New York City shaped your work?

It's definitely changed my art. There's so much vitality here, so much art to be explored. It impacts on me—meeting lots of other artists, trying new experiments.

I'm enthused by the architecture; the cityscape finds a way into my work. Here, I also get a sort of feeling of not knowing where I belong. My dreams may be set in London or in India, or what has happened in my life, then I may have a feeling of being nowhere. At one time, my husband had a heart problem and I started seeing scans of the body. I did a whole series of pictures located in a landscape inside myself, inside the blood vessels.

Q How would you describe your role as an artist?

I hope to create work that's honest and emanates from a deep spring inside. The other role I might play, being an artist constantly moving between three countries, is cross-fertilization, as a window for other artists.

I also teach art to poor inner city public school kids, and when they learn how to mix colors, they jump for joy; they'd rather paint than have a new IPad. They realize how colors can express happiness or anger. Art makes their lives happy, and at the end of the day if I can bring them joy, it becomes a balancing point for me.

Having a child was also a good experience for me, connecting me to the city and the world more than I could have ever imagined. I think before that I was too much into being an artist. I try and broaden myself on many levels, reading philosophy, sociology, literature. I have to keep opening up to life. ■

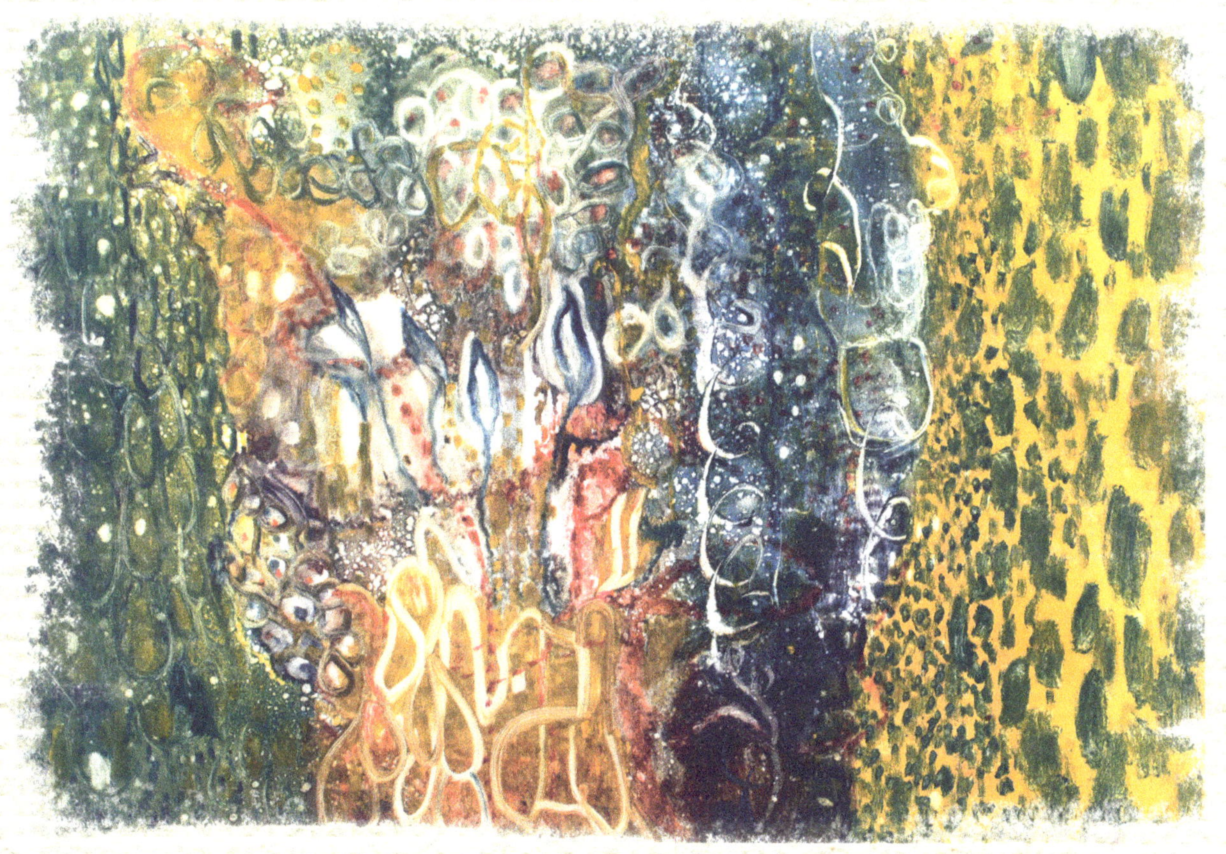

artwork: "Sparkle" by Tara Sabharwal, courtesy of the artist

TIM STEVENSON

One of America's finest landscape painters, he has been painting for over forty years in the tradition of the "Old Masters." A native-born Alabama artist, he began by "drawing pictures for cookies" at age three. His intermittent excursions into art have included cartooning, advertising, illustration, and billboard painting along the way. Mr. Stevenson's most recent works featuring the peaceful vistas of the Tennessee Valley, vivid still life and thoughtful figurative paintings in watercolor and oil were seen in a solo exhibition at The Carnegie Visual Arts Center in Decatur, Alabama. For nine years, he taught painting and drawing at his namesake art studio and school, and now teaches a small group of students twice a month in Tuscumbia.

Q You wrote, "I have found over time the true value of art lies in its effect on the human heart and mind, its inherent soulfulness and its ability to stimulate thought." How does one begin to see? To understand color and light?

Scrutiny. This is antithetical to modern life. We've been going through a time, which began back in the 1980s, with MTV videos and film clips, now the internet, where everything's spliced into split seconds, guided by speeded-up opinion. We've become a culture taught to not stop and think and allow time for things to resonate.

Looking implies solitude, time to analyze what's before you. Writers, actors, musicians, painters—we have to go off by ourselves, and spend time in solitude. That's when the good stuff comes.

Given we have a fantastic ability to comprehend color and light; we have a hundred million receptors in our eyes making sense and meaning out of what we see. Our understanding has to do with our education from our teachers, from reading, conversations with other artists, from our native intelligence, or from just looking.

The real test of an artist is to comprehend the input. It's takes a lot of patience and determination to learn all that's needed to make great art. I spend weeks and weeks on a painting. Each day I might do a few square inches; it's a slow process but one filled with a fuller comprehension.

I actually haven't painted for a month right now, which is very unusual. Before that, it had been ten years since I took a month off. I did it to think.

Q I understand as an art student at the University of North Alabama, you painted in a modernist style.

That's a story I'm fond of. Revolutions often leave fires in their wake. Mine was a personal revolution. In 1978 I burned four hundred and fifty abstract paintings of mine and told myself, "I'm starting all over." It felt great, it

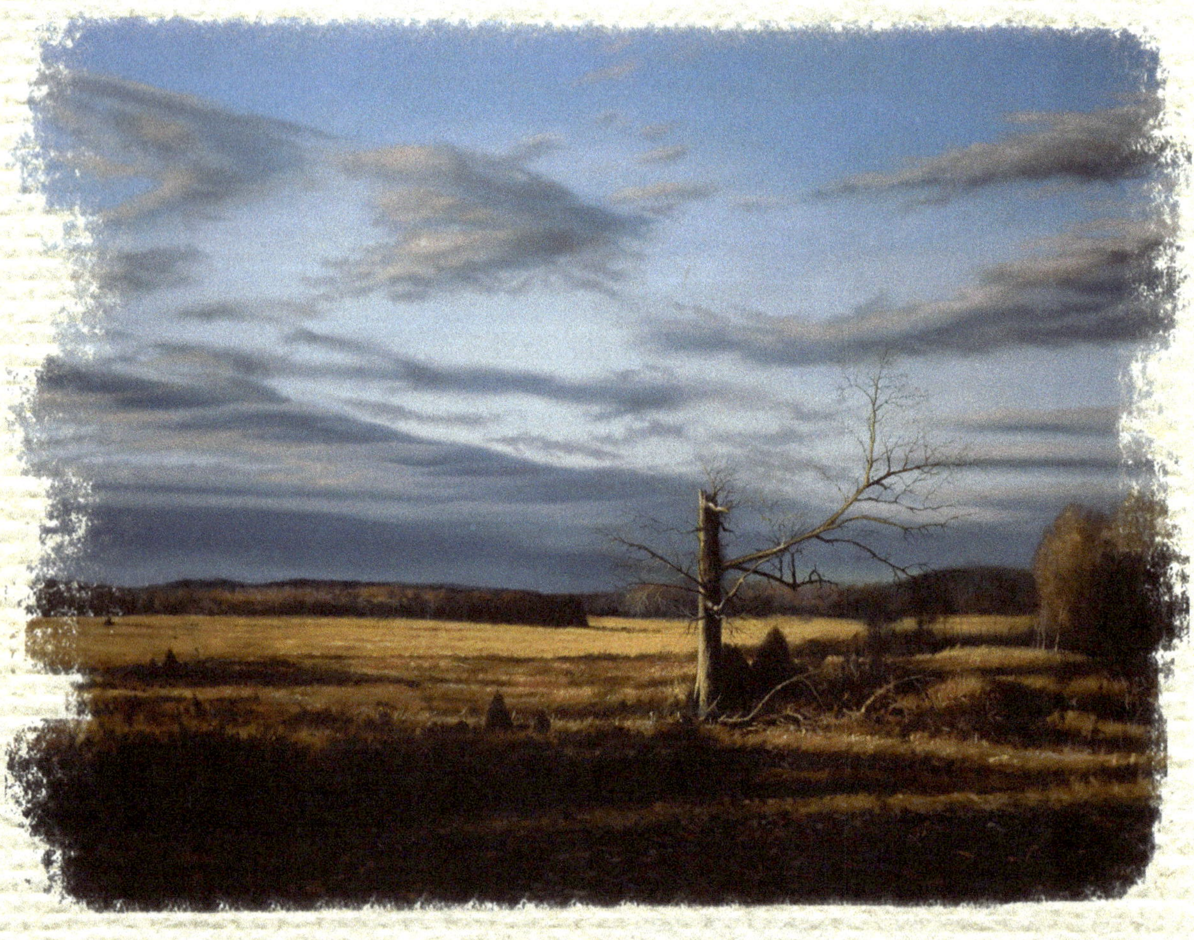

artwork: "Snow Front" by Tim Stevenson, courtesy of the artist

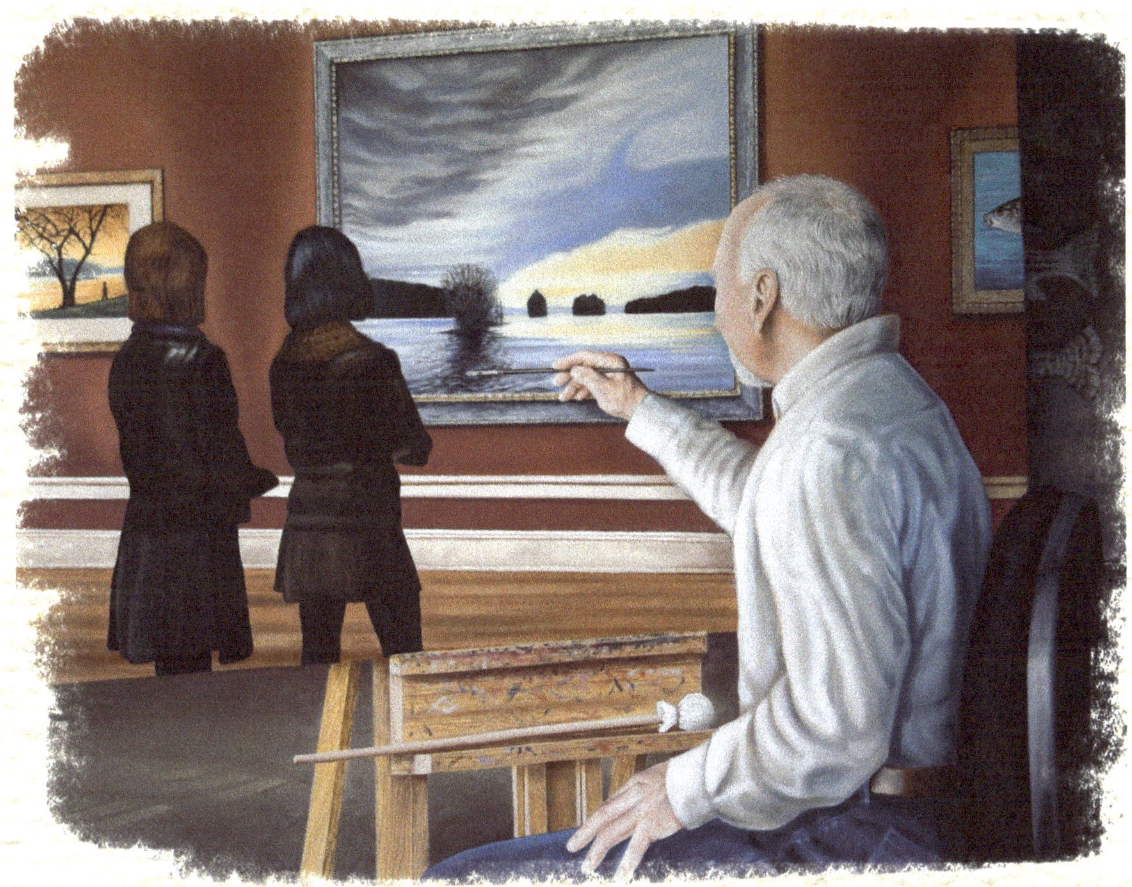

artwork: "Self-Portrait" by Tim Stevenson, courtesy of the artist

was a cleansing—like finding a new purpose in life.

Prior to that, I was thinking—y'know—of being famous. And fame is a four letter word, according to Mr. Rogers. So I began to think more about my purpose than the accolades, and often there's a price to be paid for doing that. As a good friend reminded me, "Sometimes you're the only one who cares about what you're doing." I made the decision to focus on purpose and my own voice, however the chips might fall.

Q How did your work in illustration and billboard painting contribute to your skill?

It all contributed tremendously. For instance, in billboard painting, it's purely a skill painting a thirty-foot long car or a fourteen-foot tall peanut butter parfait with a cherry on top of ice cream. You learn the skills of representation, of accurate color, of accuracy in a nutshell. Your client is paying so you have to paint it as *they* see it, very realistically. I painted over two thousand billboards seen by thousands of people on a daily basis. Michelangelo did that kind of scale with the Sistine Chapel.

Q Were there artists you were drawn to when you began?

As a student I was impressed with Matisse, partly because of his color. I studied artists' work, particularly the late impressionists, the fauve painters. Later on, I got to the Americans: Winslow Homer, Hopper, and Wyeth who had a lot of heart, and were skillful at telling the story they wanted to tell.

Q Is there a particular time you paint?

I like having a certain moment in the morning when I have a brush in my hand. I'm asked, "How can you be so prolific?" It's simply getting up and going to work every day. For many years I only worked in watercolor, but over the past ten years, the hands have tightened, a quality of vision is diminishing. So I've shifted to oil painting. Watercolor painting's unforgiving, requiring a certain type of precision, a clarity of vision. Oil painting allows you to paint over what you've done.

I'm also a studio painter, so I can keep a regular schedule on rainy days; I've never been a plein air painter. I have eight windows in my studio so I can balance the amount of natural light with artificial light.

Q Some of the great landscape artists through the ages included Turner, Innes, Constable, Monet, Homer, Cezanne, O'Keefe, Rembrandt, Bierstadt, Sargent, Cole, Sisley, Church, among many others. What do you think makes an artist's style and vision unique?

A sense of place. That's a simple answer to a complicated question. Every place has its own locale. Painting in this river valley, I understand it more as I continue.

I actually don't remember

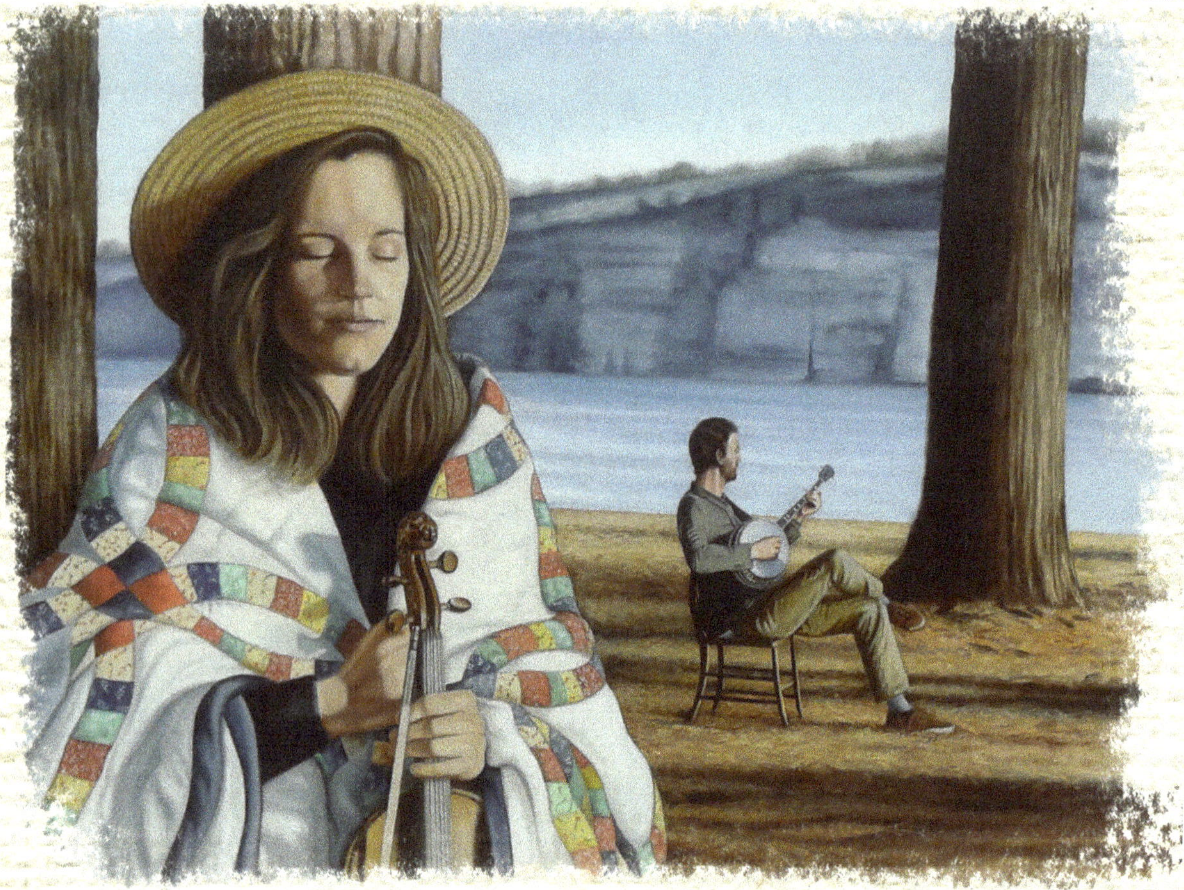

"The Moment The Music Begins" by Tim Stevenson, courtesy of the artist

learning to swim. My brother also told me he didn't remember learning and I once asked our father if he remembered teaching us to swim. He said, "I just pitched you and him in the river, but don't tell your mama. And you swam like a fish." That happened when I was a baby.

I grew up with the river a part of me, so it comes from something deeper than memory. If you're a landscape painter, that wellspring is the land that informs you for the rest of your life.

In American mythology, the river played a large social role in books like Mark Twain's *Huckleberry Finn*. The Hudson River School of painting is another example. I tried starting a Tennessee River School but so far I'm the only one.

I've been watching these clouds out the window, and they're speaking to me about the time of the year, the change in the weather. I'm dissecting the colors, the different values, the birds flying by and soaring up. They're like a message I'll remember when I go to sleep tonight. I have a phrase I use: "Take it to your pillow."

Q Why has teaching become a large part of your life?

I was reluctant at first. I just wanted to paint. But my wife, Carol, encouraged me. She said, "You've spent all these years acquiring all this knowledge and to not pass it along..."

At first I started with one class with just six people, but within six months I had thirty students. I've really enjoyed watching people grow, and being able to share concepts and philosophy about art. I tell my students it's a good thing to trust the gut. Actually I think I'm just reminding them what they already know and that's why it resonates.

Q How can art help us at a time like this?

It's a reminder of another way of experiencing the world and we desperately need that. The paintings I painted were found in solitude; therefore, the spirit will hopefully have something to do with a state of mind. The paintings are quiet, not crowded with other thoughts. They hold a "deep breathing."

We're kindred spirits, you and I. Essentially we try to bring something good into the world. Sometimes it can be disappointing or frustrating but nevertheless we go back over and over again "to the well." That's our mission.

I think it's necessary to find the better qualities in one's self. It's easy to separate and go to the lower nature. You see it in politics, various aspects of American life, when people are being divisive, hateful, but there's the superior aspect of human kindness, an inherent goodness. It's our ability to paint a good painting, write a good chapter, to act really well, even cause people to laugh. Having a sense of humor is the greatest thing. If you can laugh, you have it made. I want to learn how to paint laughter. Now that would be quite an accomplishment. ■

PAUL TAZEWELL

Mr. Tazewell received the 2016 Tony Award for best costume design for Lin Manual Miranda's Tony Award production of *Hamilton* on Broadway, and he designed the costumes for *The Wiz Live!* with Queen Latifah, Mary J. Blige, and Chanice Williams on NBC. He has been designing costumes for theater, dance, opera, and film for over twenty-five years across America, and around the world. His designs on Broadway include *Dr. Zhivago, Side Show, Jesus Christ Superstar, Memphis, In the Heights, Lombardi, A Streetcar Named Desire, The Color Purple, A Raisin in the Sun, Caroline, or Change, and Bring in 'Da Noise, Bring in 'Da Funk.* He has designed productions for many prestigious institutions including the Metropolitan Opera, San Francisco Opera, Pacific Northwest Ballet Company, English National Opera, Bolshoi Ballet, Guthrie Theatre, Washington D.C.'s Arena Stage, Stratford Shakespeare Festival, and the Kennedy Center. Off-Broadway his designs include *Hamilton, Flesh and Blood, Harlem Song, One Flea Spare, Blade to the Heat, Henry V, Purlie, Lost in the Stars, Little Me, Boston Marriage, Venus, It's a Bird, it's a Plane, it's Superman*, and *Fetch Clay, Make Man*. He has given numerous master classes at universities across the country. He has also taught costume design as a guest instructor at NYU, and was on the faculty at Carnegie Mellon University from 2003-2006. He has received six Tony Award nominations, a Drama Desk nomination, two Lucille Lortel Awards, four Helen Hayes Awards, and he received the Princess Grace Statuette award. The Metropolitan Museum of Art also invited him to participate in *The Artist Project*.

Q What brings you the greatest joy in creating costumes?

I think overall, it's bringing an idea to life with three-dimensional reality. I'm really excited about the element of research that is involved, the drawing out of an idea, the collaboration it takes, the types of fabric I use. It all feeds me; it's a good matchup with who I am.

Q Do you consider yourself a storyteller?

Absolutely. In giving characters the clothing they wear, I'm giving an audience the first impression of who they are. It sets a tone for the rest of the story. It can either be a subtle message or a broad message as to how the characters may feel emotionally. It adds to how they physically move, leading to creating an emotional arc through the story-telling, creating a poetic through-line as the characters reveal themselves.

Q When did you first begin to see yourself as a costume designer?

It was probably in high school. I grew up in an artistic family; music as well as plays and theater were a big part of our lives. My mother made puppets, and we were constantly making crafts around the house; I took that on myself. When I saw a production of *Oklahoma* in high school, I fell in love with what they were doing, and as the years went by (even though initially I had thought I'd be an actor), and because of my interest in creating clothing, I started to design costumes for the shows. By the time I went to the North Carolina School of the Arts for undergraduate school where I majored in costume design, I had found my path.

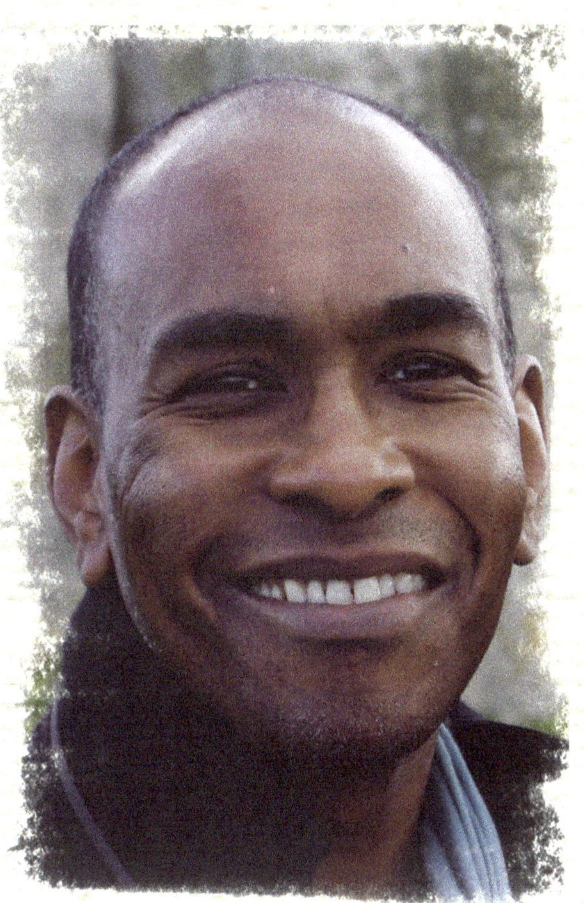

Paul Tazewell photo: courtesy of the artist

Q With *In the Heights*, and in many of your shows, your use of color, the way you capture the rhythm of the person is evident in your costumes. Do you recognize it in the script or does the director point you in a specific direction?

I would say it's all of that. Going into a production, I normally will read the script a couple of times to familiarize myself. I listen to the music if it's a musical, or see an early un-staged reading. After that, we launch into talking about the show—the director, the set designer, the lighting designer, the choreographer—discussing the qualities of the piece and how best to tell the story

During the conversation I start developing a concept. I'm always being informed by the way the director tells the story—tapping into reading minds, trying to create a visual assemblage of all the metaphors—how the director wants the story to be told. It brings out my own visual sensibilities of how I might see a scene.

Speaking of *In the Heights*, what the audience first sees is the opening number, all the activity of that neighborhood of Washington Heights in New York City. They had to see the bright color of the neighborhood in what the characters wore; then it shifts to the fourth of July when everyone's celebrating in red, white, and blue. But the thing is to not "be on the nose." Just enough of a hint. Then it shifts into a nightclub scene, in which I carried a feeling of the mood into their clothing, staying true to the urban Latino culture.

The show ends with the opening of the fire hydrant because it's so hot. I wanted to carry the metaphor of water in air, which was important to me, into the type of cotton clothing they wore, how the color of water moves, and how that movement was coming from the dancers. It all helps the audience feel what the water feels like. I'm always working with the choreography, and the mood which the lighting designer is creating, to help carry the audience into that whole world.

Q When you were first introduced to *Hamilton*, what was exhilarating for you, and what did that particular period of history mean to you?

The reason I wanted to do it was I knew it would be an exciting experience creating and working with a writer like Lin-Manual (Miranda), with the choreographer, Andy (Blankenbuehler). Most of all when Tommy (Thomas Kail), our director, proposed it to me, I thought to myself, "What an odd topic but I'm game." Then I went to see a reading, and the piece spoke to me very strongly. It's an emotional story, even though it's about American history, it takes on a life which feels very universal. It's very touching and very poetic.

What became daunting was how to create that world in a respectful way; I wanted to make the absolute right choices for the production. We all met and talked a lot, and I pulled together a lot of different images—paintings of our forefathers, Washington, Hamilton, reams of pictures of the American revolution, and pictures of the uniforms. The question was: How much do you want to be beholden to the actual period and yet do it as a contemporary telling of the story? I looked at the fashion then and now, and we agreed we wanted to do something that felt modern.

When we did the staged reading at The Public, because I had access to their wardrobe warehouse, I was able to use uniforms from other previous productions: white corsets, breeches—trying to create a look that would hold together visually but it wasn't the full design. I needed to transform the clothing to help the actors in the way they moved. I put the sisters in period dresses; I tried to find an authentic weight for the uniforms. When we moved to Broadway, they were made with a lighter wool, and I was able to expand on what I had first come up with.

The question was how to acknowledge who the contemporary actors were while letting the play, play out and make it appropriate for the characters. It became a marriage of those two qualities. Lin-Manuel's main request was that Hamilton be dressed in green, the color of money. Another element was to start out doing the costumes in a cream, more of a neutral, color—which gave us a blank slate, and then as each principal was identified, color was added when they changed into another character.

Q When you designed the costumes for The Wiz Live! you've said you were trying to see through the eyes of Dorothy, a teenage girl—

It was more about what the expansive nature of a teenager's mind might create if she imagined who the Wiz is or Emerald City or Glinda. This fantasy world was conceived as being seen through the lens of a young girl and all that she has been exposed to in her life. She might imagine a magical witch with a bright yellow fiber-optic dress which lights up—and all these fantastic lovely people in crazy hip clothes.

Q You chose Anthony van Dyck as part of The Artist Project for The Metropolitan Museum of Art. Do you find a lot of inspiration in paintings?

Especially if it's a period piece I'm working on. I'll examine the paintings from the same period to see what people wore, how the clothing was worn, and what it's saying about the person in the painting. Before photography, painting was the most accurate way to document clothing and style. Painters through their ability to paint can show us the quality of silk or satin, what the fabric felt and looked like. They understand how light works off materials, and why it transcends beyond just what they're wearing. For more contemporary projects, I'll look at photos. For any period where clothing still exists, I examine vintage clothing; that is the ultimate source of reference. But it then is on me to make the character choices along with the accuracy of the period, and blend that with the idea of how to interpret the characters. I try and encapsulate all that into my costume work.

Q How did you develop your eye to see how clothing reflects color and light?

I started painting and drawing from an early age. As a family we'd see films like *Mary Poppins*, a lot of the Disney features. Other kinds of fantasy films; it all went into a kind of "bank" I can now draw from when I'm thinking about what I'm designing; it comes in a visceral way. As all designers, my visual experience allows me to provide something for the lighting designer, the set designer, the director, the cast, so we're all going towards the same result. ■

CHOREOGRAPHERS AND DANCERS

LORI BELILOVE

Founder, Artistic Director, and choreographer of The Isadora Duncan Dance Company and Foundation and Soloist, Ms. Belilove is recognized as a premier interpreter and ambassador of the dance of Isadora Duncan. Among her teachers were first-generation Duncan dancers: Anna Duncan and Irma Duncan. Ms. Belilove is the lead dancer in the award-winning PBS documentary, *Isadora Duncan: Movement from the Soul*, narrated by Julie Harris. Touring extensively internationally, she created an affiliate Duncan school and performing company in Brazil. The Isadora Duncan Dance Company performed at the Moscow International Performing Arts Center and the Great Tchaikovsky Hall. She staged and danced as Isadora in *Isadora... No Apologies* at New York City's Duke Theater, and her creations include *The Red Thread* at Alvin Ailey Citigroup Theater, *The Art of Isadora* at Judson Dance Theater, *Isadora Goes Downtown* at Dance New Amsterdam, *Isadora into the 21st Century*, *Perfumes of the Night*, and *Wind Sail*. As a master teacher, she has taught across America and around the world. She maintains a studio and school in New York City. Ms. Belilove has received the Mills College Distinguished Achievement Award.

Q Did the way in which you were raised affect your becoming a dancer?
I was sort of a tomboy growing up. My mom was a gestalt therapist and a great homemaker. My dad was a businessman, and also sang opera. So my brother and I were raised in a way that allowed us great exploration. Isadora Duncan said she danced in the womb, having been nourished on oysters and champagne. I guess I'd say I began dancing to the music of our player piano, exploring "movement for movement's sake." I spent a lot of time in our gardens, exploring everything.

Q When did you first learn about Isadora?
When my family and I went to Greece; I felt so at home. The Duncan family had also come to Greece to make their pilgrimage. While I was there I met an older gentleman, whose name was Vassos Kanellos. He told us he had been a member of her troupe, and talked about Isadora Duncan and showed me a locket which held a lock of her hair. He said to me, "You are the next Isadora," and gave it to me. He said, "You need to come back and study with me when you're ready." I was in heaven.

I began to learn everything about Isadora, and began to develop a classic understanding of beauty and harmony. At that time, there was a lot of unrest in Berkeley, and it was getting really rough socially and politically. My mother thought I should go to a small Quaker boarding school in the country for two years. I started to study the dancing ideals of Isadora.

I decided to go back to Greece and studied seriously for two years with Mr. Kanellos. Besides daily dancing and singing lessons, he introduced me to classical studies, Greek Mythology; we visited Delphi, Olympia, Sparta.

When I returned, I began studying with others in the Duncan community, meeting dancers who had worked and

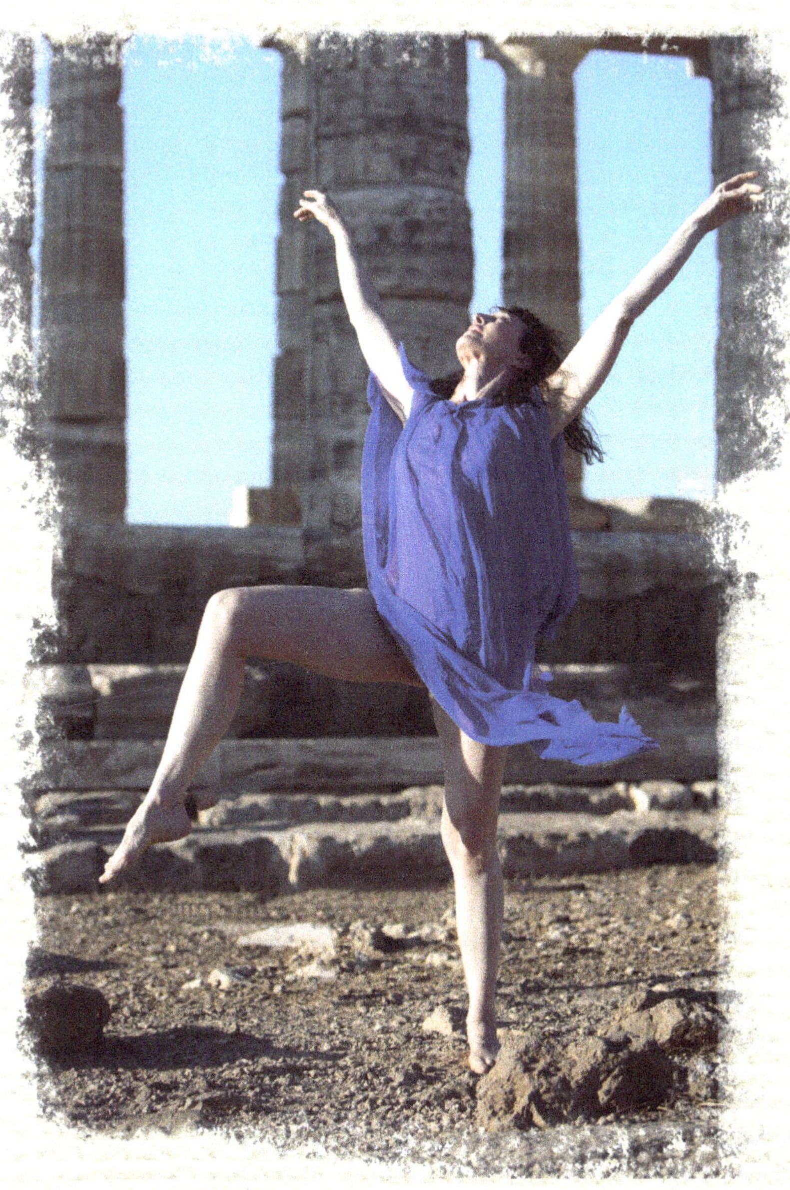

Lori Belilove photo: Rose Eichenbaum

studied with Isadora, coming upon fragments of her choreography.

There came a knock on the door. A woman was standing there. She introduced herself as "Mignon Garland." She told me she had actually been in Isadora's troupe, and then said, "The gentleman you studied with in Greece is an imposter. He had never been with Isadora. Maybe he had thought everyone was dead so he could get away with it." I was shocked and confused. She told me she was interested in keeping Isadora's work alive because there was no Isadora dance school, as so much had been lost.

Later, I discovered that Mr. Kanellos has indeed studied with Duncan, but it was before Isadora had opened her first school, so few people had heard about him. I then studied with Mignon, and eventually met the "Isadorable" Irma Duncan, and the New York followers of Isadora. I was embraced by them, but they were teaching in small studios. I wondered, "There's a technique with over eighty dances...where is the legacy?"

Q Is that when you decided to keep Isadora's spirit alive through your re-creations and your teaching?

Yes, I began to figure out how to teach it. I eventually created a way to teach, linking the present into modernity, linking art and dance, sculpture to painting, philosophy to music, as she wanted all the arts to move with one another. Basically, the mantle folded onto me.

Isadora's passion for living offers a pathway for living spiritually with compassion and physically, allowing dance to occur through natural movement. Her dance style comes from the breath, and the solar plexus located in the chest at the base of the sternum. The movement of the torso becomes the inner motor allowing for huge emotional expression and power.

Isadora had gone back to the Greeks, to bring an open-ness to the movement of the body. The public of her day thought she was mad to show loose breasts and naked legs. Her dances express the human condition. I love her work. It feeds and churns inside of me.

Q How do you create new work using Isadora's choreography?

It may take me six months or more to create a new piece, exploring ideas. I had the great fortune of receiving a residency in Florida at the Atlantic Center of the Arts to create new work for three weeks. That's when *The Every Woman* series emerged into a fuller form.

Q What is it like entering into a state of creativity creating a new dance?

It's very consuming, engaging my entire being. The act puts me in a state of complete playfulness. I see variations of things stumbling upon themselves. Usually in the deep hours of the morning, something comes and triggers something deep inside. It becomes like a faucet—synapses snap, one thing leads to another—in one fleeting moment structure and patterns converge—the story comes. It becomes clearer during rehearsals.

When I get into that creative state, it's a fun state. I like to be there more than anywhere else. Once you're there, you're not afraid of who you are. You're skimming along a wave, on top of the water, there may be a splash. I may find myself in another place and time.

Samuel Beckett said, "Strictly speaking, we can only remember what has been registered by our extreme inattention and stored in that ultimate and inaccessible dungeon of our being to which habit does not possess the key, and does not need to." ■

JACQUES D'AMBOISE

Mr. d'Amboise is recognized as one of the finest classical dancers of our time. In 1976, while still a principal dancer with New York City Ballet, Mr. d'Amboise founded National Dance Institute. At the age of eight, he studied at the School of American Ballet with George Balanchine, Anatola Oboukhoff, and Pierre Vladimiroff. At age twelve, he performed with Ballet Society, the immediate predecessor to New York City Ballet. Three years later, he joined New York City Ballet and the following year made his European debut at London's Covent Garden. As Balanchine's protégé, Mr. d'Amboise had more works choreographed specifically for him by The Ballet Master than any other dancer, including the ballets: *Stars and Stripes*, *Tchaikovsky Pas de Deux*, *Episodes*, *Figures in the Carpet*, *A Midsummer Night's Dream*, *Jewels*, *Raymonda Variations*, *Meditation*, and *Brahms-Schoenberg Quartet*. He is best known for his roles in such distinctly American dance works as *Filling Station* and *Western Symphony*. He has also danced in several movies, including *Seven Brides for Seven Brothers* and *Carousel*. As a choreographer, Mr. d'Amboise's credits include almost twenty works commissioned for New York City Ballet. His ballets include *The Chase*, *Quatuor*, and *Irish Fantasy*. *He Makes Me Feel Like Dancin'*, a 1984 PBS documentary film about his work with NDI, won an Academy Award, six Emmy Awards, the Peabody Award, the Golden Cine Award, and the National Education Association Award. Mr. d'Amboise's many awards include the Capezio Award, the Governor's Award of New York State, The Mayor's Award for Arts and Culture, The National Medal of Arts, The Fred and Adele Astaire Award, and the Kennedy Center Honors.

Q What is the significance of dance for our cultural understanding and harmony of the world?

If it's true that dance does have the power to change lives, you first have to ask: What is dance? You have to ask: What is art? How can we prove it has an effect beyond one's own personal culture? Dance, like everything else in the universe, is a form of architecture; that is, an ordering of matter and material. You have musical composition, an ordering of sound, an ordering of movement. These all entail choices and time. Just as a painter has to decide what colors he or she uses on a canvas. Do I use a brush or work on wood? They are all choices.

The universe is a form of ordering of matter; you have galaxies, solar systems in different patterns and shapes. The arts—dance, music, art, theatre—spring from this ordering of matter. Even if I were to meet an alien, I could communicate through dance and music.

In 1993 on Christmas Day I was in a remote village in India, and I met and watched a group of children were who studying the art form of the Kathakali dancer. They had never seen a TV in their entire life. I didn't speak their language; they didn't speak English. Yet we were able to communicate through our movements together.

The last day I was there, I was walking down a dirt road as I was leaving, and out popped all these teenagers and they started yelling, saying goodbye. And then they began doing their version of Michael Jackson's "moon walk" for me. Where did they get it from? Probably some college students had come through and showed it to them, and here they were doing it for me. I believe you can win over any person in any culture by eating their food, singing their songs, and getting up and dancing with them. You share photos of each other's families. The arts allows you to cross bridges, through storytelling, you communicate emotion.

Q You were drawn into dance at a very early age.

I was just a "street" boy. My introduction to the arts began on a "high" level by age seven. Balanchine chose me at age eight to be Puck in his *Midsummer Night's Dream*. Cecil Beaton helped put on my make-up. By seventeen I was a principal dancer. I was blessed. I realized arts are transforming. It's that aspect that develops in a human organism. It starts with our birth. And then it's what we do with the time allotted to us. That's why it's important to give your best. It's the material you work on that forms your soul.

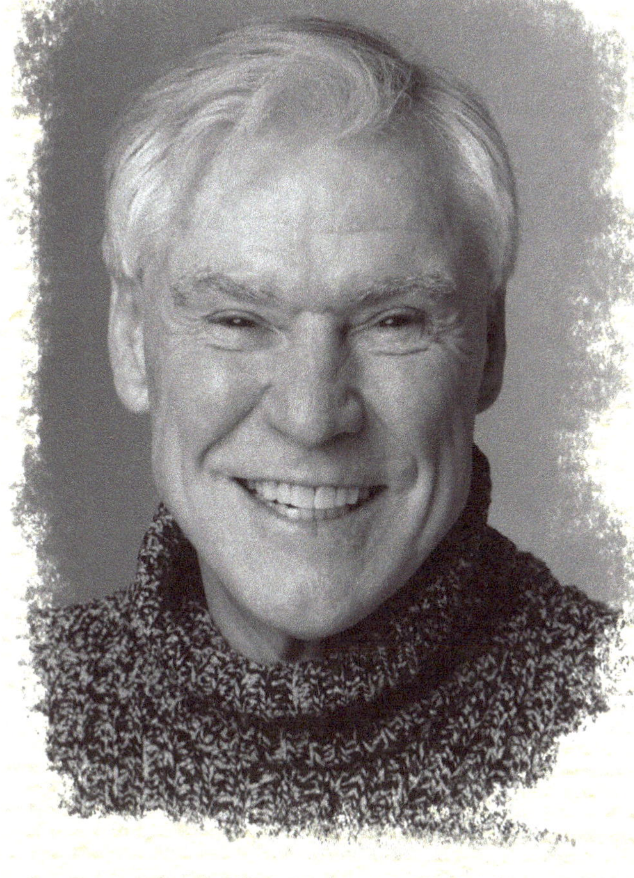

Jacques d'Amboise photo: courtesy of the artist

If, when you're young, you work on material that hampers your soul, it can become injured. If you're involved with good stuff, your soul can become positive. Over time, I was able to experiment. I found I needed to express myself and I wanted children to experience discovery by learning through the arts. The National Dance Institute was started because I felt all children should be involved in the arts. I knew what we do here would transform the lives of children. They're really "light bulbs." They become transformed by those who teach them through their passion.

Q What did working with Balanchine mean for your growth as an artist?

Balanchine was a consummate "master of music." His inspiration was music and dance. There were no demands. You knew he wanted excellence, it was expected; you wanted to please him. We never did anything less than a hundred percent. It was always about how do you get better as an artist. The early days under Balanchine can best be described as a passion for the art of dance.

Q It must have been quite different dancing in the movies?

When I went to Hollywood and did *Seven Brides for Seven Brothers*, I'd come on set at 7:30 in the morning to start my first day of shooting, and there'd be no one there. I thought to myself, "I'll be ready," so I warmed up. At 9 am a stagehand came in, around ten, the other dancers arrived.

Then Michael Kidd arrived. We started working at eleven o'clock, then there's a coffee break, at 1pm we're in the commissary having lunch. At two there's a rehearsal; between three and five maybe we'd get something done. There was no performance at night!

Q With Balanchine it must have been entirely different—

Balanchine would come in, every day, right on time. We'd rehearse all day. There would be an hour break. Then you'd warm up for the performance that night.

When I'd stand in the wings right before the curtain would go up, in that moment, the whole world became the dimension of the stage. I'd stand there, in this shadowy space, and I'd be visited by unseen forces. It became the "passion of the moment." Then when the performance would finish at 11pm, I'd be exhausted, thrilled, exhilarated. Everything I did during the day, my performance on a great stage, with an orchestra, the excitement! For me, all it was about was: How can I be better the next day? This was my life every single day.

Today when I watch my daughter, Charlotte, when she dances, never have I seen the exact same thing. She always brings something new. Always with such passion! It thrills me!

Q What makes the arts vital for our lives?

People need to eat, buy clothing, have a bed, a roof over their heads. We can't avoid the necessities of life. But we're more than an organism. We're human. So how do we define what makes our humanity? Through the expression of our arts, our games, and play. We have our scientific curiosities, we love to play, we have our games of competition, we've learned how to survive. The artist expresses the wonder of being a human being.

I think we live in a culture where greed has become fashionable. The different mediums and certain celebrities express this greed, and yet... there is something "dark" about this. The accumulation of more goods, leading up to the paying of water and air rights. I believe it's become something terribly destructive to what we call "humanity." It's affected our nature, our lives, and it's almost uncontrollable.

I try and spend all my time with people who give me joy. I read things with nobility. I invent theatre games to see if I can make them happen. Yes, I have to pay bills, but I try and put my energy into the art. Every artist should. Nothing is exciting for me as being involved in art all day!

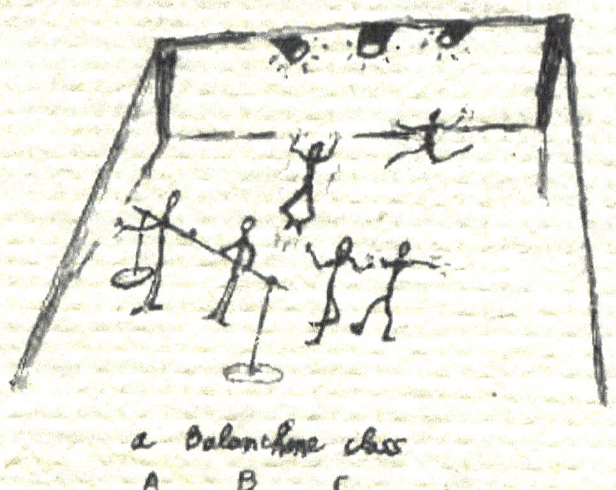

artwork by Jacques d'Amboise, courtesy of the artist

Every single day we write a new chapter in our lives. Every day we create every single moment, and every moment brings exciting, thrilling moments. They all make us who we are. What I find incredible is what an adventure life is. Even if we're tired and we rest—what dreams will visit me tonight? Will the night bring me the most amazing visions? Who knows? Every single moment for me is thrilling, but I don't think about it. I just do it! ■

GRACIELA DANIELE

As a dancer, Ms. Daniele first appeared on Broadway in *What Makes Sammy Run?, Here's Where I Belong, Coco* with Katharine Hepburn, *Chicago* with Chita Rivera and Jerry Orbach, and in *Promises, Promises* opposite Jerry Orbach. As a director-choreographer her work on Broadway includes *The Most Happy Fella, The Pirates of Penzance, A History of the American Film, Chita Rivera: The Dancer's Life, Annie Get Your Gun, Marie Christine* starring Audra MacDonald, *Once on This Island, Chronicle of a Death Foretold, and Dangerous Games.* As a choreographer, her work includes *Pal Joey, The Pirate Queen, Ragtime,* for which she received the Astaire, Ovation, and Callaway Awards, *The Goodbye Girl, Zorba* starring Anthony Quinn and Lila Kedrova, *The Rink* starring Chita Rivera and Liza Minnelli, *The Mystery of Edwin Drood, and The Visit* starring Chita Rivera. Ms. Daniele conceived and directed *Tango Apasionada.* Ms. Daniele also choreographed *Hello Again, The New Brain, The Glorious Ones, Bernarda Alba* and *Dessa Rose* at Lincoln Center, *Little Fish* at Second Stage, was the first to direct William Finn's *March of the Falsettos* and *Falsettoland* at Hartford Stage, *Naughty Marrietta* at City Center, and *Joseph and the Amazing Technicolor Dream* for the Brooklyn Academy of Music, *Die Fledermaus* for the Opera Company in Boston, *Alice in Concert,* a musical starring Meryl Streep at New York City's Public Theater. Her film and television work includes *Pirates, Bullets Over Broadway, Mighty Aphrodite,* for which she received the Fosse Award, *Everyone Says I Love You,* for which she received the Fosse Award. Ms. Daniele has received ten Tony nominations, and six Drama Desk nominations, and was inducted into the American Theater Hall of Fame.

Q What do you love about creating a new dance?

Right now I'm at home working on a new production, listening to the score, reading the script, making notes, dreaming of every single moment. I think because I was a dancer, then a choreographer, and then a director, I love trying to use the language of dance, especially in the musical theater. It's entirely another language to tell a story, to define character through movement. For me, it's not only about the steps. Of course, that's what dances are, but for me, the story we're telling is so much more important.

Q You grew up in Buenos Aires. How did the culture and tango play a role in how your talent blossomed?

I was born there, and I entered the Teatro Colon as a ballerina at seven years old, and years later I graduated. It was a very rigorous discipline, a wonderful school, very strict. I was always into classical music, not so much tango.

My mother loved tango. I remember as a little kid I learned the steps with my feet over her feet; she showing me the steps. What's interesting is there was one person's music I loved at the time—the composer Astor Piazzolla. His music was a mixture of tango combining compositions of baroque and jazz.

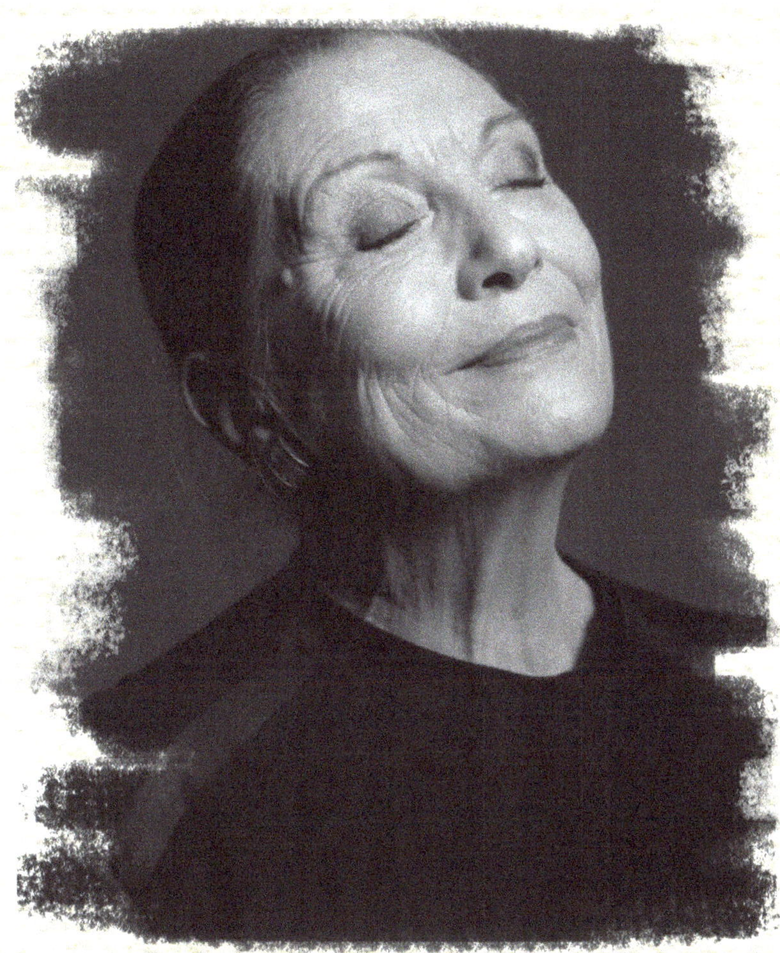

Graciela Daniele photo: Walter Kurtz, courtesy of Mr. Kurtz

Q You then went to Paris?
I had gone to Europe as a ballet dancer and lived and worked there. It was in Paris that I saw *West Side Story* for the first time. Jerome Robbins is my icon. What I admire the most about Robbins is that he was a master in very simple movement. He could express so much of the character's inner states. I was enthralled as I watched the dancers in the show walking, trying to keep their cool, then all of a sudden explode into dance—explosion, explosion! Seeing the fury inside them. After three years I then returned to New York City to study jazz.

Q Is that when you studied with Martha Graham and Merce Cunningham?
When I came to this country, I kept taking ballet classes; it's tremendously important as a basis for the dancer. I asked my teacher who I should study jazz with, and started with Matt Mattox in the fall of 1963; he was a disciple of Jack Cole. Cole really had created the idiom of jazz dance as an art in this country. I asked Matt about other teachers to continue studying. He recommended Martha Graham and Merce.

So I began to take classes with Martha. I adore her work, but when I was doing it, it didn't connect with me. Every time, after I left the class I'd feel contracted and compressed, in pain. I respect her work but it just wasn't for me. I told Matt and he said, "Maybe Merce is for you." And I tell you the first day, when Merce had us run across the studio, I thought, "This is it!"

Q How did you become Michael Bennett's assistant on *Coco* and *Follies*?
Matt was choreographing *What Makes Sammy Run* and asked me to be in it. Two months later, I had my debut on Broadway. Then just a few years later, I was in Michael Bennett's *Promises. Promises*, and after that, in *Coco* and *Follies*. That's when I became Michael's assistant on both of those shows.

Q What led to your creating *Tango Apasionada*, based on three short stories and a prose poem by Argentine writer, Jorge Luis Borges?
When I had the opportunity to choreograph at INTAR, the Latino Theatre here in New York City, they asked me, "What would you like to do?" No one had ever asked me that before. I am used to having scripts sent to me. Now I was being asked what I would like to do. It opened the door to the universe. So I said, "Astor Piazzolla."

So they said, "Well, that places it in the tango society, Argentina and Borges." So we developed the piece, Jim Lewis and I, with the help of a dramaturg. And as it turned out—I met with Astor Piazzolla. I couldn't believe it!

He came to my home and I sat at his feet. He was crucial to me. I told him my ideas, the story of the show. He said, "No, don't tell me. Tell me the color or a word, that's all I need." I learned so much from such a great master. It was really my first introduction to tango; his music inspired me. I really love the street tango, and I was able to explore his music. That's when I really fell in love with tango.

Q Do you seek something different from an actor, a dancer, and a singer during your auditions?
I seek the same thing from a

creative actor that I do from a dancer or a singer; I don't separate actors from singers or dancers. First, I expect to see a strong technique. As a director I can't teach technique in the six weeks of rehearsal. I expect them to have a strong base in ballet, their technique should be exceptional or we can't work together. When I give dancers a combination in an audition, I'm also asking them to express something of themselves, an openness, to act the movement. Those who do, they're my favorites.

With actors, if they have questions I'm willing to listen; I try and answer their questions if I can. I look for a great deal of freedom. I'm expecting them to explore and come up with many different choices. I work to create a romping room to experiment in. It may not necessarily be improvisation we're doing, but we take a scene and explore ways into the character, trying to expose all the different colors of a rich, more human characterization. I want them to express themselves through their talent.

With a singer, I'm looking for them to perfect their voice, to be free physically, and to also explore choices. The most extraordinary actor I've worked with would have to be Kevin Kline, when we worked together on *Pirates of Penzance*. He came up with so many different choices. He would say, "I can either stab my toe or kill the parrot," and it went on from there. He would keep coming up with so many choices, he just never stopped.

Q You have worked with Chita Rivera on many shows, including *Chicago, The Rink, The Visit*, and of course her own show, *Chita Rivera: The Dancer's Life*. Have you developed a special way of working together?

She is like my sister now, after so many years. We've known each other since I worked with her in *Chicago*, and even before that we worked together on a show at the Waldorf Astoria. With *Chicago*, I was one of the girls in the show, and with each show, I've gotten to know her better. Yes, we did *The Rink*, and on and on, so many years. To me, Chita is not only a dancer, a singer, an actor, a performer—she's a force of nature.

I might come to the studio for rehearsal to work with her, and my energy might not be where it could be, but when she walks in, my entire body rises up three inches, from my toes to the top of my head. She brings in such an incredible amount of energy. I just adore her talent, and as friends we talk often. We have a great affinity with each other, not only in what we believe in our work, in our passion, but what we believe in as a positive approach to life.

Q How did you immerse yourself into the time period of the turn of the century, when you worked on the musical, *Ragtime*?

I do a great deal of research. When I was younger I'd go to the library for days to study the period before I started anything. Now it's so much easier because of Google.

With *Ragtime*, first I read Doctorow's novel; it's such a great classic. I always love reading stories from the past. I've lived in so many different countries, and speak four languages. I loved all the jazz of the period, all the music. I knew the director, Frank Galati, from before, and the whole team was just terrific to work with together.

Q You started out dancing at an early age. How important is it for children to have the opportunity to express themselves through dance?

Extremely important. I think it focuses them in expressing themselves creatively, by putting certain demands, a discipline in regard to shape and structure, it's also very liberating how you use that freedom creatively in dance. I was trained in ballet, which was extremely disciplined. I think it helped me not only for my work but for everything in my life. It's given me a certain self-assurance in everything.

Q Where do you find your inspiration in life to renew yourself?

Inspiration comes at my age from my life experiences, the teachers I've had, the people I work with—all of those inspire me. I keep absorbing so much.

When I did *The Visit* with John Doyle, I came to the studio when he was directing the actors. He asked me what I was doing there. I told him, "It's an opportunity to learn." To work with such a brilliant director was the best school.

I do have to say it's a busy hectic life, with all the pressures and stress. When I finish a show, I run to the country to seek a total communication with nature. I'm an avid gardener; I enjoy it the most.

In both the theater where I create, and in gardening, there is a result that comes, but it is different in my garden. Yes, both are inspiring, but in my garden, there comes that moment when nature takes over and... it's ten times better than I could have ever done. I'm always happiest when the first flower comes—there's such a world of beauty. The colors, the complexities, the smell— I love it! I think of what e. e. cummings wrote: "...faces called flowers float out of the ground." I love it, I love that line by him so! ■

KATHERINE DUNHAM

Considered "The Grand Dame of American Dance," Ms. Dunham had one of the most successful dance careers in American and European theater of the 20th century. Ms. Dunham's Technique is now part of the American dance vocabulary. For almost thirty years, she maintained the Katherine Dunham Dance Company, choreographing more than ninety dances. Her major ballets include *Negro Rhapsody*, *L'Ag'Ya*, *Rites de Passage*, *Shango*, and *Southland*. In 1945, she established the Dunham School of Dance and Theatre, influencing Peter Gennaro, Marlon Brando, Walter Nicks, Chita Rivera, and Eartha Kitt. Her dance students include Louis Armstrong, Canada Lee, and Langston Hughes. During 1943-1965 she toured the U.S. and fifty-seven countries; on Broadway in *Cabin in the Sky* staged by George Balanchine, *Pins and Needles*, and *Bal Nègre*. Her films included *Sharp as a Tack*, *Pardon My Sarong* with Abbott and Costello, *Stormy Weather*, *Mambo*, and *The Bible*. She directed Scott Joplin's opera, *Treemonisha* at Atlanta's Morehouse College. She enjoyed a long association with the Southern Illinois Performing Arts Training Center. The Katherine Dunham Museum is located in East St. Louis. Among the many awards Ms. Dunham has received are the Dance Magazine Award, Albert Schweitzer Award, Kennedy Center Honors, and the National Medal of Arts. She was inducted into the National Museum of Dance. Ms. Dunham died in 2006 (this interview was conducted in 2001).

Q What makes you want to keep creating?
I find I cannot keep myself from either choreography or a rhythmic motion if I hear a certain music or a sound that has a deep meaning, although it's been harder for me now to give myself to the stage as much.

It's also very important to keep teaching. I believe if the very young are not taught everything available, they're deprived of their adulthood. I'm very interested in prenatal communication. My feeling is that the more the fetus learns, the more the baby will have, and the more the baby has, the more the adult will give in life.

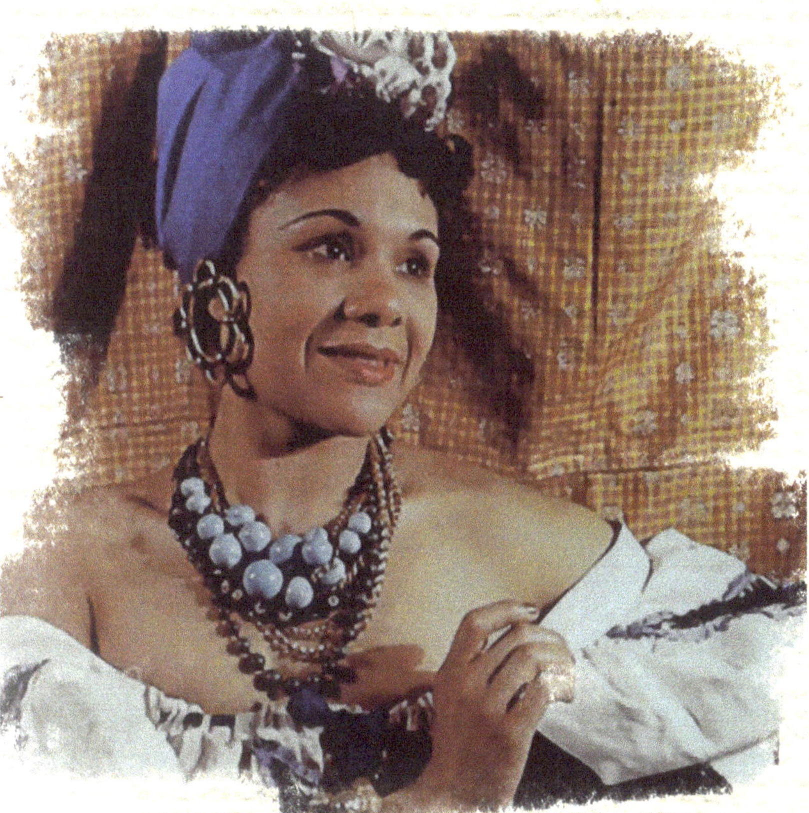

Katherine Dunham photo: courtesy of the artist

Q Did your parents encourage you?
My father was a singer and he sang bass. In the 7th and 8th grade I was down in the bass register. My parents were astounded at the idea of showing yourself on stage. But it wasn't enough to stop me.

Q Do you keep learning something new every day?
We, as thinking people, should never stop learning. I'll be ninety-two years of age my next birthday. I couldn't possibly stop learning new things every day.

Q What interests you the most each day?
Form and function—it's our relationship to practically every living being. I don't know what a cat feels. When it leaps, when it plays with a ball of yarn. It's serving a need for the cat. It's gets to be quite fascinating, the intricate activity.

Q What gives you the greatest joy as a teacher?
Seeing a movement completed with the meaning it was intended for. What you do as a teacher is enable the student to recognize the relationship between themselves and form and function. Then the student will demonstrate his own recognition. I say, "I want to know what you want to do with it." I want them to take it on an inward journey.

Q What is the role of the artist in society?
To make people aware of the artist's intention. We all hope what we do will come from the heart, for love, and all those things. The artist tries to make other people see what he sees; although if he tries to impose it upon his audience, it's a mistake.

He should just put it out there, and it's up to the audience to take it. It takes a generous, giving person, a considerate person, to keep society in mind, with an understanding of what society doesn't have and would like to have.

Q Is this country growing up?
The kinds of things we emulate, our icon figures, what we're producing, not just from the artist, but as a people, makes me wonder if we are. Are we advancing as we could be? Technology seems to never stop. To grow up you have to be in the stream of life.

Q So you remain optimistic as we enter a new millennium?
Even if one's spirit is down, or you become disappointed, there is inherent in the expression of people, an unquenchable fire, a realization. The happiest artist is he who could always do better. ■

ANNA HALPRIN

Ms. Halprin's career has spanned the field of dance since the late 1930s. In 1955 she founded the groundbreaking San Francisco Dancer's Workshop, and the Tamalpa Institute in 1978 with her daughter, Daria Halprin. Her students include Meredith Monk, Trisha Brown, Yvonne Rainer, Simone Forti, Dohee Lee, Dana Lova-Koga, Shinichi Momo Lova-Koga, Isak Immanuel, and G. Hoffman Soto, some of whom were involved in the Judson Church Group. Over the years, her famous outdoor deck has been an explorative haven for numerous dancers and choreographers, including Merce Cunningham, Eiko and Koma, and Min Tanaka and Anne Collod; composers, including John Cage, Luciano Berio, Terry Riley, LeMonte Young, and Morton Subotnick; visual artists including Robert Morris and Robert Whiteman; poets including Richard Brautigan, James Broughton, and Michael McClure. Ms. Halprin is an early pioneer in the expressive arts healing movement, leading numerous collaborative dance programs with terminally ill patients. For the past decade, she has led Circle the Earth, a contemporary community dance ritual to confront real-life issues facing participant communities around the world. Her *Planetary Dance: A Call for Peace* was staged in Berlin, commemorating the 50th anniversary of the signing of the Potsdam Treaty ending World War II, and involved over four hundred participants. Ms. Halprin works also include the award-winning videos *Returning Home*, *Song of Songs*, *Spirit of Place Intensive Care: Reflections on Death and Dying* at the Festival D'Automne in Paris, and *Seniors Rocking*. In 2006, The Museum of Contemporary Art presented a major one-woman exhibition of her life's achievements. Ms. Halprin is the author of three books: *Moving Toward Life: Five Decades of Transformational Dance* with Rachel Kaplan, *Dance as a Healing Art*, and *Returning to Health: With Dance, Movement and Imagery*.

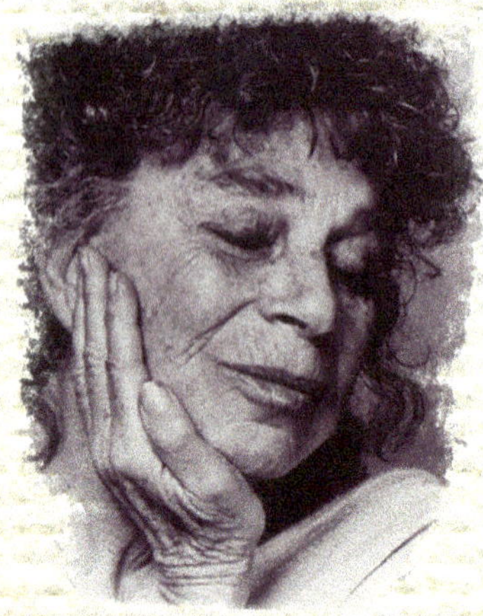

Anna Halprin photo: courtesy of the artist

Q What are some of your recent creations?
I completed a new version of *Parades* and *Changes* at the Berkeley Art Museum, which has been referred to as "a performance that changed the definition of dance." I was also arrested at that performance for indecent exposure.

I've been focusing on a new piece that is part of a trilogy called *Remembering Lawrence*, about my husband. The first part of the trilogy was called *Spirit of Place*, and was performed at a site that Lawrence designed a park, an amphitheater in San Francisco, called Stern Grove.

The second piece was a series of events at Larry's sites that he designed at the campus of the University of California in Berkeley, and started creating the third part called *Beyond Death*.

Q What have been some of your strongest discoveries in creating dances for those facing life-threatening illnesses?
What I discovered is that there is a difference between curing and healing. I feel that dance, because our bodies are our instruments, has the opportunity to heal but not necessarily to cure.

In the twenty-five years that I have worked specifically with people with life-threatening illness, I have realized the need for people to keep physically fit, to learn how to develop an internal awareness of their physical bodies, and to be able to express themselves through their bodies.

Whether the expression is one of fear, hope, loss, enlightenment, regrets...whatever someone is feeling, when movement and feelings are expressed freely, there is a deep sense of satisfaction, release, change, and fulfillment.

Another healing is the opportunity to be with like-minded friends who are able to appreciate, share their deepest feelings, and work together for each other's healing. I created three videos that show the healing effects of dance, *Positive Motion*, *Dance for Life*, and *Breath Made Visible*.

Q How have you learned to quiet your mind to allow true expression to occur?
I developed a series of processes to guide students into internalizing this, involving a series of exercises. Awareness exercises that

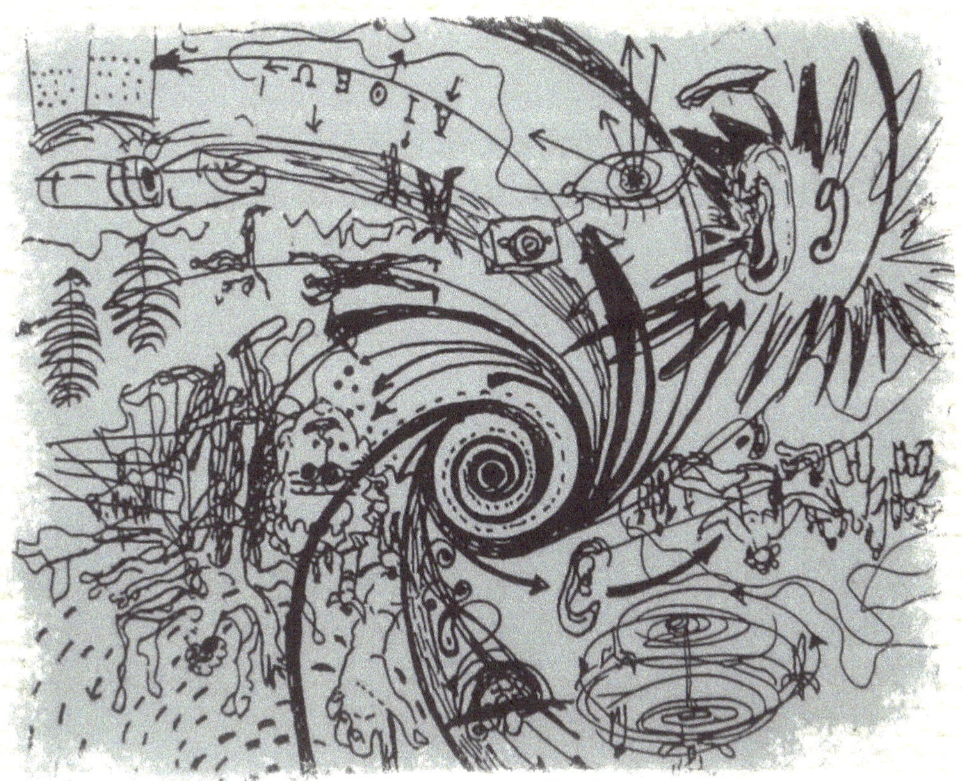

drawing by Anna Halprin's late husband, the celebrated landscape architect, Lawrence Halprin. He drew this portrait of her, courtesy of Ms. Halprin

focus on breathing, hearing, relaxing, facial expressions, the sensation of and sound of birds, smell, and so forth. They take anywhere from ten to thirty minutes before the student is ready to dance.

Another good way to internalize is shaking movements, giving you time to get out of your head. You instantly start feeling your body. There never is just one way to do something, to achieve a particular result.

Q What are some of the most valuable things you learn from your students?
I learned how normal, easy, and important it is for them to generate their own creativity. I like to leave a class saying to myself, "Wow! How inspirational these students are!" rather than "What a good class I taught."

Creativity for me is the key word and it's exciting because what they do is original and uniquely their own. I am always amazed by the diversity and uniqueness of each student's creative expression.

This is the most valuable thing I have learned from my students—the life affirmation of each individual's stunning creativity. On a more self-serving level they respond to my stories in a way that provides me with new and fresh resources and ideas that I would never have imagined, so that I get as much from a class as I give to them. ■

BILL T. JONES

One of the world's extraordinary dancer/choreographers, Mr. Jones created with Arnie Zane, the Bill T. Jones/Arnie Zane Dance Company in 1982. He also co-founded the American Dance Asylum in 1973. He has created more than fifty works for his own company, and for the Alvin Ailey American Dance Theatre, Axis Dance Company, Boston Ballet, Lyon Opera Ballet, Berkshire Ballet, Berlin Opera Ballet, among others. He directed and performed in *Degga* with Toni Morrison and Max Roach at Alice Tully Hall, collaborated with Jessye Norman in *How! Do! We! Do!* as part of Lincoln Center's Great Performers New Visions series. Mr. Jones also directed Derek Walcott's *Dream on Monkey Mountain* for the Guthrie Theatre. His work on TV includes *Fever Swamp* for PBS Great Performances, *Untitled*, *Last Supper at Uncle Tom's Cabin/The Promised Land*, *Still/Here*, and his *D-Man in the Waters* aired on PBS in the documentary *Free to Dance*. A 1994 recipient of a MacArthur Fellowship, he also has received three Bessies, an Izzy Award, the Dorothy B. Chandler Performing Arts Award, Dance Magazine Award, and served as the 1998 Robert Gwathmey Chair at Cooper Union. His memoir, *Last Night on Earth*, was published in 1995.

Q The first time I met you was when you celebrated your 50th birthday with a memorable collection of your extraordinary dances at the New Victory Theatre in New York City. What had that evening meant to you?

It was an important personal marker for many reasons. I come from a "wild" generation and I never believed I'd be fifty. When we began, we were very much an improvisational generation; we weren't interested in the future. I see now we've built an institution. The evening reminded me of our original dreams, our original themes, and that it has continued to go forward. I received a lot of love that evening, and that was very precious to me.

Q What would you say made your unique collaboration with Arnie Zane "fly," and continues feeding you?

It's a mysterious thing, as all life's gifts are. It was a real American story. Here was this New York City-bred young Jewish Italian man, Arnie Zane, and he wanted specific things from the American dream. He was a sensitive man who believed in love and poetry, and these two things congealed when he met me.

I was a young African American dancer, born of migrant workers, and I wanted to experience the world and I really didn't have enough skills. I was posing as a rebel, a holy man. He demanded complete discipline and commitment from me, and together we had desires and dreams and realized that those could be realized. It became an engine that we still feel today.

Q What is it in dance and what you bring to it that speaks a universal language?

Well it's not always universal. There have been gaps, but I believe there is an openness, a willingness to share in dance, about what we don't know. To show we love, with the community of people who are there. It's a metaphor, that hopefully they'll receive the same hope and love we all experience through this ephemeral art.

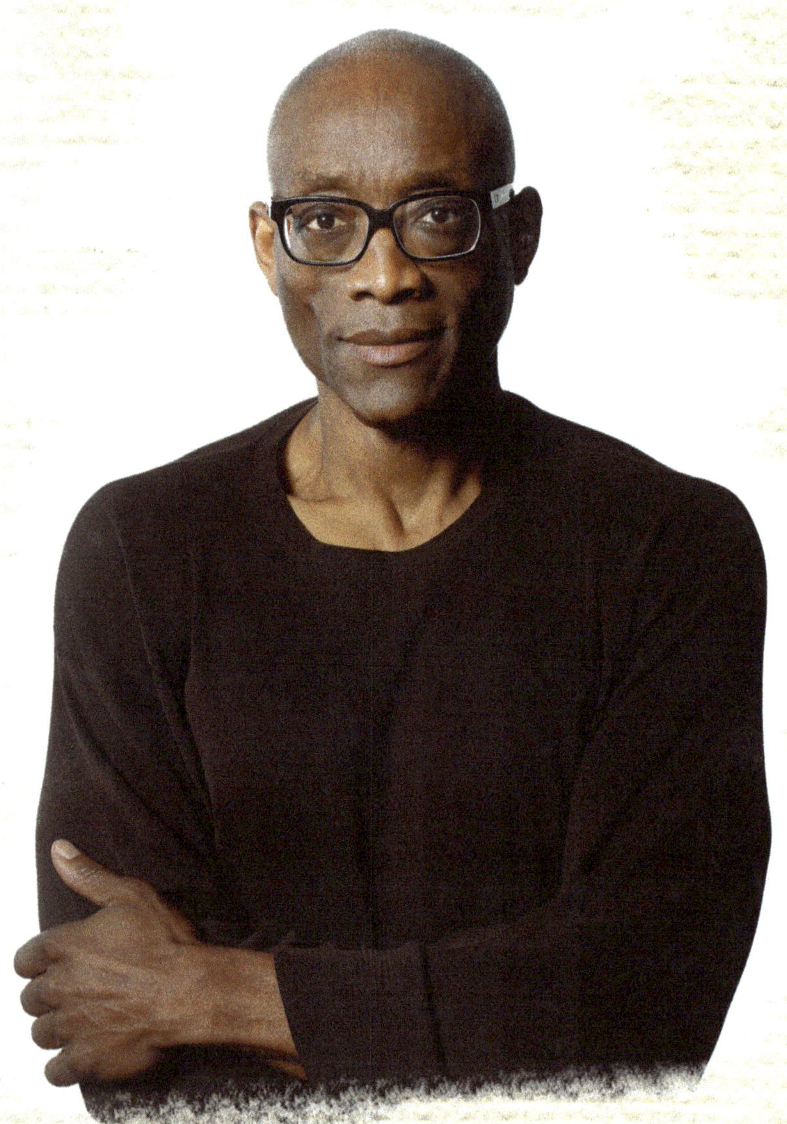

Bill T. Jones photo: Philip Habib

I believe in the fragile body we all have, that it's capable of communication and responding to what is worth doing. And that the dance experience isn't dance until there are those breathing people out there watching and responding to those performing onstage. Live theater and live dance are experiences that have to be witnessed, allowing the expansive domain of the imagination to come forth.

At one point I was involved with Riverbed Productions, two young artists who use digital equipment, applying motion sensors on my body, generating images to be seen on the computer, but it isn't dance. Dance has to be alive, just as it was done thousands of years ago by the ancient Greeks.

Q What is the biggest challenge in maintaining your expertise?

The biggest challenge is to live in the instrument, with clarity and sensitivity. As one ages the joints get stiffer. I have to blend mind, body, and "soul," so that it reflects an emotional re-affirmation. I have to keep up with my dancers, and they're in their twenties! I've returned to dancing more, and dance is also an internal art that keeps the body enlivened, to live in a correct way.

Q What kind of an experience was it directing Derek Walcott's *Dream on Monkey Mountain*?

It was a very challenging experience. Derek is a fabulous poet, and his plays are overly generous. I was also fortunate to have a great dramaturg, Jim Lewis. Jim has also worked with the White Oak Project and Philip Glass, and he was instrumental with *Dream on Monkey Mountain* in how to think about the dialogue, in trimming the words to get to the depth and richness of the material. It was an amazing experience for me, having come from a nonverbal art form, to fall into this cauldron of words.

Q What inspires you to create?

I actually have quite eclectic tastes. Of course, my favorite choreographer is Merce Cunningham. I also love to read; I'm constantly reading new books. I love architecture. I'm constantly trying to understand human thought, and the human mind. In terms of that eternal question of what comes first—the chicken or the egg? My first epiphany was reading Proust; it was a whole world of how one can be a looking glass through one's time.

My first theatrical experience was watching my mother pray on Christmas morning. She would get up and in the midst of the lights coming from the Christmas tree, she'd transform herself. I was a small five-year-old, and I'd watch her transform herself into this seer!

Q With a new piece, are you inspired by specific music or does an image come to your mind?

Well, for example, I had embarked on a new piece with a contemporary company in Dayton, Ohio—the Dayton Contemporary Dance Company. They had commissioned me to create a piece for them. I usually have an image, a dream. It can also be a line from a book, a piece of music. It has to strike me. It invites me to have a dialogue. I look for a clear structure rhythmically, an evocative phrase that will lend itself to be transferred to a dance movement. I begin to have a love affair with it. In a sense, the piece is inventing itself.

I remember reading what Alice Walker said, "The characters write themselves." I come into rehearsal with basic dance phrases, and once the dancers absorb the movements, new questions come. And I've got to be ready for those sparks, and then they sink in, creating all new questions.

Some days I may become discouraged with my art form... from the problems one encounters, from the lack of funding. I feel, "Why am I an artist?" But I am encouraged by all the young energy I see. I want to participate in the world, in the world of ideas, in this great universe. ■

ALONZO KING

Mr. King serves as Director of the international touring company for his LINES Ballet, located in San Francisco; the Alonzo King LINES Ballet BFA resides at Dominican University of California, and Dance Center. Mr. King's works are in the repertories of the Swedish Royal Ballet, Frankfurt Ballet, Ballet Bejart, Les Ballets de Monte-Carlo, Joffrey Ballet, Alvin Ailey, Hong Kong Ballet, North Carolina Dance Theatre, and Hubbard Street Dance Chicago. He has worked extensively in opera, television, and film. Among his noted works include *Shostakovich, The Steady Heart, Concerto for Two Violins, Figures of Thought, Writing Ground, Wheel in the Middle of the Field, Scheherazade, Refraction, Dust and Light, The Steady Articulation of Perseverance, Rasa, High Sky, Migration, The Moroccan Project, Satoh, Before the Blues, Resin, Rite of Spring, The Patience of Aridity, Heart Song, Syzmanski's Vibraphone Quartet, The Heart's Natural Inclination, Klang, Sacred Text, Handel Pas de Deux, Rock, String, Fallen Angel, Awake in the Dream, Ligeti Variations, Reoccurrence, Prayer, Stealing Light,* and *Ictus.* His collaborations and seminal works include *People of the Forest* in 2001, choreographed with Baka artists from Central African Republic, and *Long River High Sky* in 2007, *China's Shaolin Monks,* with actor, Danny Glover, legendary jazz saxophonist, Pharaoh Sanders, Hamza al Din, Pawel Szymanski, Jason Moran, Charles Lloyd and tabla master, Zakir Hussain. Mr. King is a former commissioner for the city and county of San Francisco, and a writer and lecturer on the art of dance. Renowned for his skill as a teacher, Mr. King has been guest ballet master for dance companies around the globe. In 2012, he was awarded the Lifetime Achievement Award by the Corps de Ballet International Teacher Conference, and many prestigious awards, including the first ever Barney Choreographic Prize from White Bird Dance, Jacob's Pillow Creativity Award, U.S. Artists award, Bessie Award, the Doris Duke Artist Award, and the Los Angeles Lehman Award. He was named a Master of Choreography by the Kennedy Center, and the Dance Heritage Coalition named Alonzo King an "Irreplaceable Dance Treasure."

Q You have called your works, "thought structures, created by the manipulation of energies that exist in matter through laws, which govern the shapes and movement directions of everything that exists." How do those who dance your work learn this way of working?

All life processes have an underlying mathematical description and possess intelligent self-organization. We look for and study them, in everything that we observe. The manner in which clouds form and dissipate, the patterns on the skins of animals, ferns, leaves, ice crystals, sea shells; similar patterns repeat themselves in exhaustless invention. These patterns are mathematical, symbolic, and index fingers pointing to the Spirit and Nature conundrum, as exemplified in ancient architecture and sacred geometry.

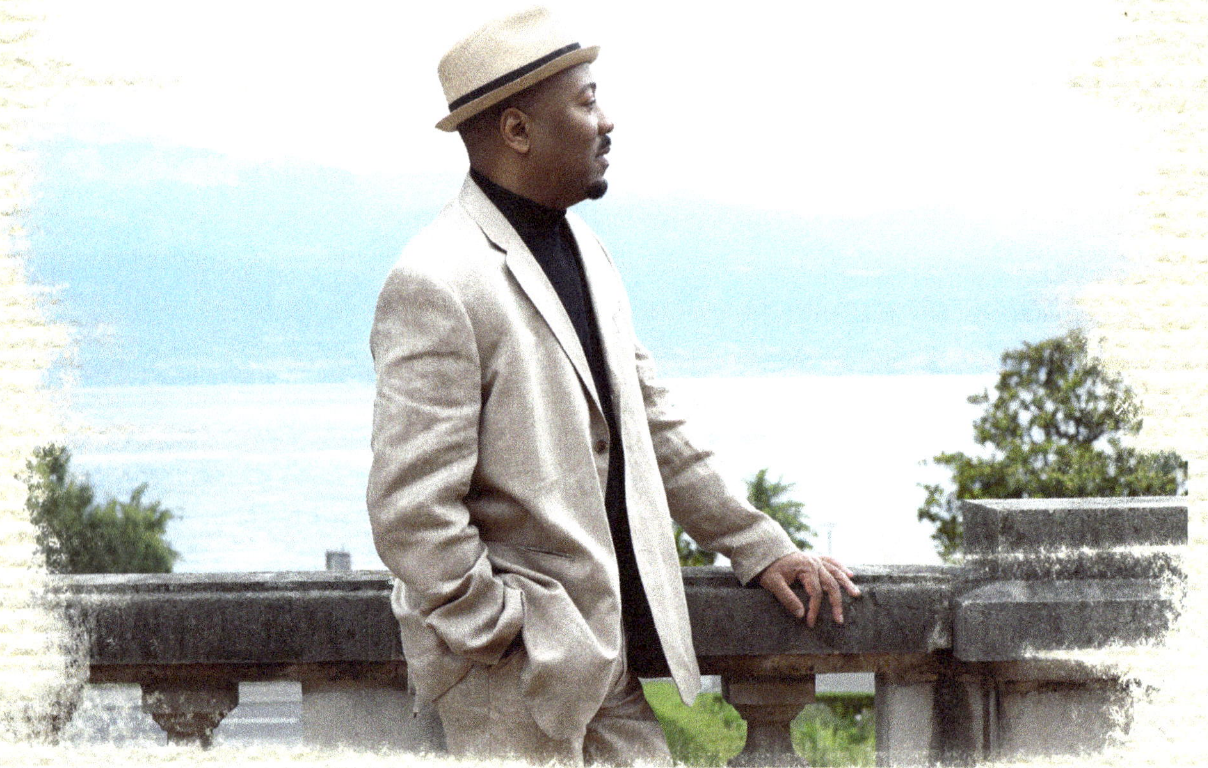

Alonzo King photo: Franck Thibault

Choreography is thought made visible. Literally taking vibratory blue prints from the ideational world and birthing them into form. The dancer has to understand what is being expressed and communicated in choreographed forms. Keen intelligence is not enough. It has to come from an inner knowing by inhabiting the movement forms and listening to what those physical structures are saying. The dancer has to step into the consciousness that emanates from those physical forms and by absorption, become them.

"You have to become the horse before you can paint the horse." To imitate or mimic the horse, or merely draw the horse's likeness misses the mark. You must inhabit and become the object of your concentration. Two becomes One. The query presented to the dancer is to answer what these shapes mean, and on multiple levels present their exegesis. The dancer answers those questions through their understanding. As the singer interprets and brings life, meaning, and understanding to lyrics; the dancer does the same interpretation, singing in the language of movement.

The way the body works is in coordination with the working principles of how everything works in the world. The knowledge of those mechanics and primordial truths inform the way we work. There is no single force in the universe. We live in a world of duality where joy and sorrow, pain and pleasure, sickness and health, attraction and repulsion work together; you can't have one without the other. Darkness and Light are needed to tell the story. Everything that is put out is returned. Diversity is a trick. As fascinating as diversity is, particularly when you consider the mind-boggling variety of life beneath the ocean, it's still a guise.

Science is now in agreement with the ancient rishis of India, concurring that all things are born from the same Source, and only appear different because of their different rate of vibration. We study and are aware of the oldest and latest discoveries in science, as well as our own personal observations in nature. The play with gravity, the perennial hide-and-seek, thrust and parry, the tension jack-in-the-box release, the karmic boomerang of cause and effect, salmons returning upstream to give up their lives and regenerate new life. These are movements and contemplations on how life works.

Q How instrumental were those you studied with and danced with, in the development of your strengths during your

time in New York City before you arrived in San Francisco?

Although I had the privilege of studying with the large name institutions and extraordinary teachers, what catapulted my learning was sharing the room with the high level of artists that were drawn to those centers, more than the centers or teachers themselves. Observing each individual carving out their unique voice and particular strengths, plus the unified striving and focused energy in the room was an instructor. It was that gathering of artists from around the globe who were at the highest levels of the discipline who, for me, were the real transforming presence. "Environment is stronger than will power."

Q In LINES each dancer is encouraged "to push past individual comfort zones to find new ways of moving fluidly from the traditional geometric designs associated with classical ballet, into varied non-Western movement disciplines." Is this an entirely new way of thinking of ballet?

One of the fascinations about movement exploration is this insatiable attitude about discovering endless ways that the body can be manipulated. The geometric designs generally employed through classical ballet are not western. They are universal forms and archetypes that are part of the science, art, folklore, astronomy of all large civilizations and world cultures. They are part of the vast intelligence placed in form that you find globally. The mathematical precision and symbol that you find in pyramids, and at the Cathedral of Chartres, are the same mathematics and symbol that you find in the human body. Straight line and circle encompass all forms.

What is specifically different at LINES is that the meanings of those symbols, and their origins in nature, are taught. The new way of thinking about ballet is approached in several aspects. We think of the body as a field of energy to be manipulated, and the artist as chiseler, sculptor, engineer, and architect. The task is to live through transitions and to inhabit moving shapes as living vibratory ideas. The process is akin to condensation and evaporation. The solid form melts like ice in varying degrees, moves into liquid, is evaporated or disintegrated and then congeals back to hard form. This is a process that is musical and based in phrases.

Every step or movement is a pyramid or wave, where there is a genesis, peak, and dissolution—and then a rebirth or new idea. Men and women often share roles. There is an emphasis on complex rhythms, and the dancer is thought of as a poet. When the making and doing that we humans participate in is brought to the highest levels, regardless of the activity, it becomes a kind of poetry. The dancers aim for a living experience. They are dancing treatises, theorems, paintings, songs, and stories. As we understand more about what humanity is, and what bodies are—dancing changes.

Q You also have a most unique collaboration with composers, musicians, and visual artists—including commissioning music from the table master Zakir Hussain for Scheherazade, and Sephardic music with Judeo-Spanish songs by Jorge Savall. How has this kind of music fueled your work? And are you hoping that we, the audience, open ourselves to a new way of experiencing what's possible?

We have been fortunate to commission and work with some of the greatest musicians on the planet. Even those who have passed away, and their music continues to live. For this I am deeply grateful. Music is another fascination with dance makers because music and dance are the same. Dancers are musicians and great musicians are dancers. You have to move something to make sound, and when a dancer is moving they are making their own music with the audible music. Vibration is sound and movement. They are inextricably linked.

If you have the choices of masterful composers from around the globe, why would you limit your choice to one genre? I adore the musical masters of all traditions and all cultures. A lament is a lament regardless of its country or culture of origin. The tuning fork vibrating with the harmony of truth is where I want to live and work. Incredible expressions of the heart and mind through music are magnetic and can change our being.

Q Another of your collaborative projects was *Long River, High Sky* exploring the fusion of elements of classical ballet and the movement traditions of Shaolin monks. What led you in that direction and what kinds of discoveries did you make?

Initially the monks refused to touch the women in the company. It was forbidden in their discipline. After rehearsing for a while they realized that it was solely about the communication of ideas and it became okay. What was also fascinating was their ability to jump right into the dance forms. They saw them not as scary unfamiliar propositions, but as other ways of shape making. They were quick and wholly involved. When they made mistakes they didn't go through ego disappointment; they laughed at themselves and then continued to do the work. It was also a breakthrough into a wider palate for the members of the company to build their warrior power.

Q You definitely encourage your dancers to understand their history, to learn about art, philosophy, religion... how does this ultimately play a role in the way in which they dance?

The dancer dances their consciousness. You dance who you are, there is no escaping that. Your dancing is your understanding. When the understanding is vast, or expanded, there is greater depth in the dancing. It is wisdom that we want to behold. The more wisdom, the more light. The more light, the more perception and clarity for the viewer.

So many questions we ultimately may never have answers to—yet we must go forward. What gives you your greatest joy in creating new work?
We aren't here just to be born and die. We must find a deep purpose to our lives and bring effort towards expansion. To watch the people you work with transform themselves into masters is a joy to witness. Everything that exists is trying to expand itself, to enlarge into some form of non-stop existence. Everything is reaching for omnipresence, gems, trees, mountains, shooting stars, volcanos, and human beings.

When you look back on your life, you want to have a view that shows that you have come a long way, that you went far and discovered much, and are changed. Moving forward into new work, is really working on yourself. It is about self-expansion, and when that happens there is a joyous satisfaction. ■

PEARL LANG

Renowned dancer, choreographer and teacher, she was known as an interpreter and propagator of the choreography style of Martha Graham. A student of Martha Graham and Louis Horst, she joined the Martha Graham Dance Company, and danced as a soloist from 1942 to 1952, and as a guest artist from 1954 through the late 1970s. She was an original cast member in *Deaths and Entrances, Punch and the Judy, Land Be Bright, Imagined Wing, Diversion of Angels, Canticle for Innocent Comedians, Dark Meadow, Night Journey*, and *Appalachian Spring*. On Broadway, she danced in *Carousel, Finian's Rainbow*, and *Peer Gynt*. Ms. Lang created her own dance company in 1952, and choreographed sixty-three works for film, opera, and television. Her works were performed by the Dutch National Ballet, Boston Ballet, and the Batsheva Dance Company of Israel, and included *Song of Deborah, Rites, And Joy is My Witness, Black Marigolds, Tongues of Fire, I Never Saw Another Butterfly, A Seder Night, Kaddish, Song of Songs*, and *The Time is Out of Joint*. Ms. Lang taught at Jacob's Pillow, the Julliard School, Yale School of Drama and in many dance festivals in America and abroad. Her students included Madonna and Pina Bausch. Among her many awards included two Guggenheim Fellowships, the Martha Graham Award, the National Foundation for Jewish Culture's Cultural Achievement Award. She was inducted into The Dance Library of Israel's Hall of Fame. She died in 2009 (this interview was conducted in 2001).

What makes the Martha Graham Technique so unique?
Her movement is an exploration and an enhancement of aspects of human experience. One of the principles of the technique she evolved is a visceral inner movement of the muscles of the torso and pelvis, which automatically reacts to coughing, sobbing, or laughing. She used it as the source movement of the center. It is called contraction and release. It begins the movement, which then travels out to the arms and legs and extremities, and into space. It can then return back to the center and create a deep passion and dynamism of movement.

In addition, the technique includes a series of different kinds of falls and recoveries, a daily phenomenon of living, even if the falls aren't always physical. This, in addition to the legwork for stretching and jumping.

Most of her repertoire is based on world literature and drama, as well as dance movement works, and they also reflect a dramatic imagination. I feel very fortunate to have been able to dance such a variety of her roles: as "the Bride" in *Appalachian Spring*, the "Three Aspects of Mary" in *El Penitente*, and again in *Primitive Mysteries, Herodiade*, "Jocasta" in *Night Journey, Clytemnestra*, and "Emily Dickinson" in *Letter to the World*.

Where do you draw your inspirations from?
All my work has been inspired by all types of music—folk, baroque, classical world-wide contemporary composers, Biblical, Jewish, holocaust literature, the poetry of T.S. Eliot, and Shakespeare.

How do you teach actors the value of having an expressive body?
A lot of actors think they don't need it. But the stage is first a visual experience for the spectator. I teach stage movement for actors and directors. That was my course at Yale University and the Neighborhood Playhouse. I try to make them aware of the potential and importance of body movement in creating a role. Every role demands a physicality—a size—a way of moving—a posture—not to diminish, but to enhance the scene and the word.

What drew you to create a new version of *The Dybbuk*?
I was born into a Jewish immigrant family, and had an extensive Yiddish education of literature, Bible history, along with an emphasis on the arts, music, theater, and dance. Since *The Dybbuk* is the most beloved play in Jewish dramaturgy, I heard about it at an early age.

I actually saw it in New York when the Habimah Theatre brought it from Israel. It is set in a Hassidic community. The piece is nurtured in ecstatic piety, out of the feeling that if you imagine and think with an inner melody, it is purer than even the words of a prayer. The spirit moves the body. It was believed that "if you jumped high enough, God would reach down and lift you higher."

Those are the dancer's words.
Yes, I choreographed a three-act dance-drama called *The Possessed*, based on the play, *The Dybbuk* by

S. Ansky performed in New York City in the 1970s and then toured it. I feel *The Dybbuk* resonates in all cultures, and begins and ends with "Why, oh why, from the highest heights to the deepest depth has the soul plummeted; within the fall, resides the power to rise again." The energy for survival is in that phrase.

Q You also choreographed a fascinating dance, *Shira*.

Shira means "song" in Hebrew. The dance is based on a parable by Rabbi Nachman Bratslav: "At the end of the world stands a high, high mountain and from it flows a spring. At the opposite end is the heart of the world. The heart of the world keeps the spring ever in sight. If, for one moment it loses sight of the spring, it loses, in the same moment, its life; and the spring endures only as long as the heart of the world looks towards its source.

"At the close of the day, the spring calls to the heart of the world in a song, and is answered in a song from the heart. And out of their song, shining threads come forth and fasten onto the hearts of all of the world's creatures. There is a righteous and benevolent man who goes to and fro over all the earth's surface, gathering up the threads from all the hearts. These he weaves into time, and when he has woven one whole day, he passes it over to the heart of the world, which passes it over to the crystal spring, and so the spring achieves another day of life, and thus the world continues."

Of course it is a symbolic tale. The heart of the world is man and the ever-flowing spring from the mountain is the refreshing, refining element always to be strived for, which is the work of all artists. In dance, it is the silent soul that sings through the body. ■

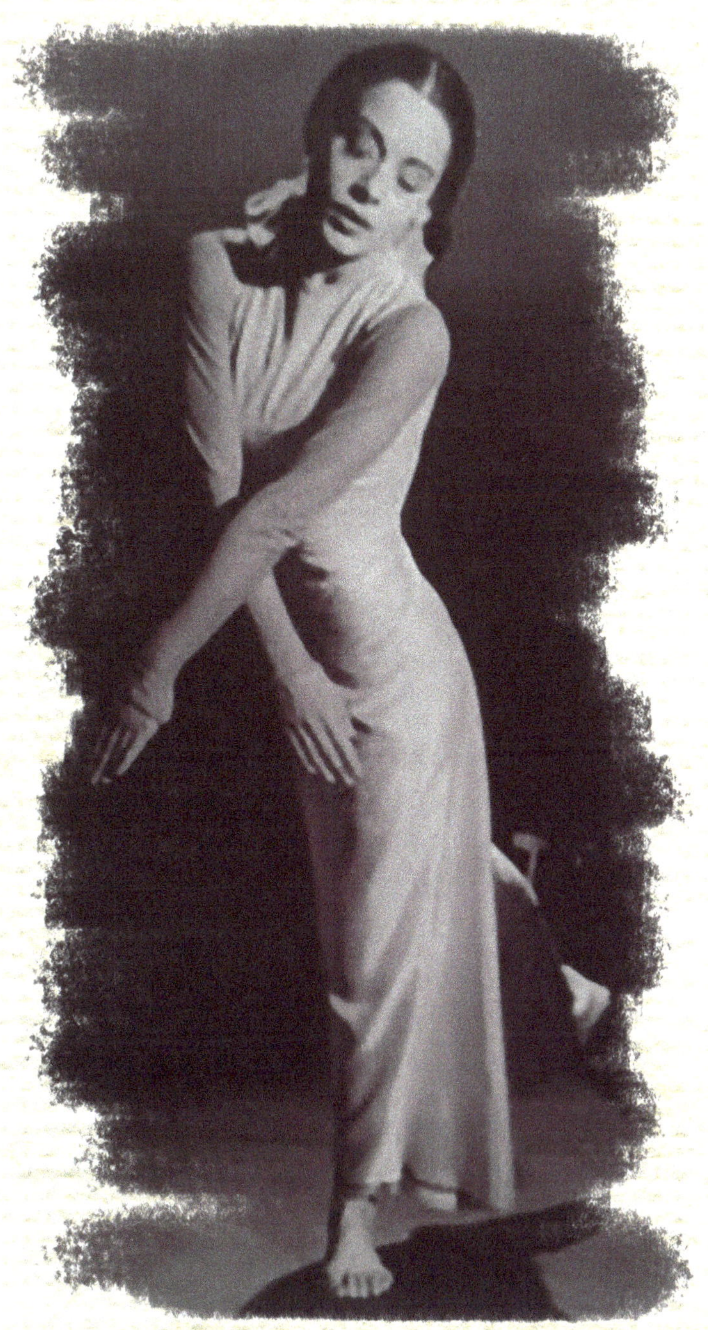

Pearl Lang photo: courtesy of the artist

PILAR RIOJA

Considered one of the world's pre-eminent Spanish flamenco dancers, Pilar Rioja has thrilled audiences around the world in many countries including the United States, Russia, Argentina, Spain, Colombia, Canada, Austria, and a dozen other countries. Ms. Rioja performed in New York City at Repertorio Espanol for thirty-three seasons beginning in 1973. Ms. Rioja dances included *Bulerías, Jaleo, Farruca, Boccherini's Fandango, Habanera, Sevillanas Moriscas, Grave Assai, Tangos Andaluces*, and *Carretero*, set to music by Cuban composer Guillermo Portabales.

Q How young were you when you were first introduced to dance?

Six years old. I was born in the north of Mexico. My parents were from Spain, and I'd go to parties, get-togethers, and there was dancing. This was the atmosphere I began in. From there, I began dancing at Red Cross benefits. Later on I was taken to Mexico City to study ballet. My father also taught me a form of dance—matador. He was not a bull fighter but he liked the movements.

Q What did it mean to you to return year after year to dance at Repertorio Español in New York City?

It was like a home to me. I performed there for thirty-three years consecutively. It was very important to me. Spanish dance is intimate, it is very expressive and to have been able to dance in a small house, where they can see your face, it was good.

Q What has Flamenco meant for you?

It's very, very important. You can relate it to everything, what you're feeling as you're dancing. It has its rules, but at the same time you can break away from the discipline. It's a contrast to the very strict 18th Century school of Bolero. For the Europeans, the footwork is very important. For the East, it's always the hand. For the Africans, it's the muscular movement of the body. For Flamenco, it's a mixture of all these. That's why I love it. It's very personal—you can do whatever you want, improvising within this structure. The hand movements, "braceo," are beautiful.

These days, the feminine quality of dancing Flamenco is being lost, in terms of competing with men. There's too much emphasis on the footwork. For me, it is a combination of the foot and handwork, without losing the feminine side. There's too much emphasis on technique today, forgetting the emotional side, how important it is communicating with the audience. Of course, technique for me is very important; it's a means to express emotion. But you have to forget technique when you dance.

Q Your dancing is also stunning because of the moments of stillness you create.

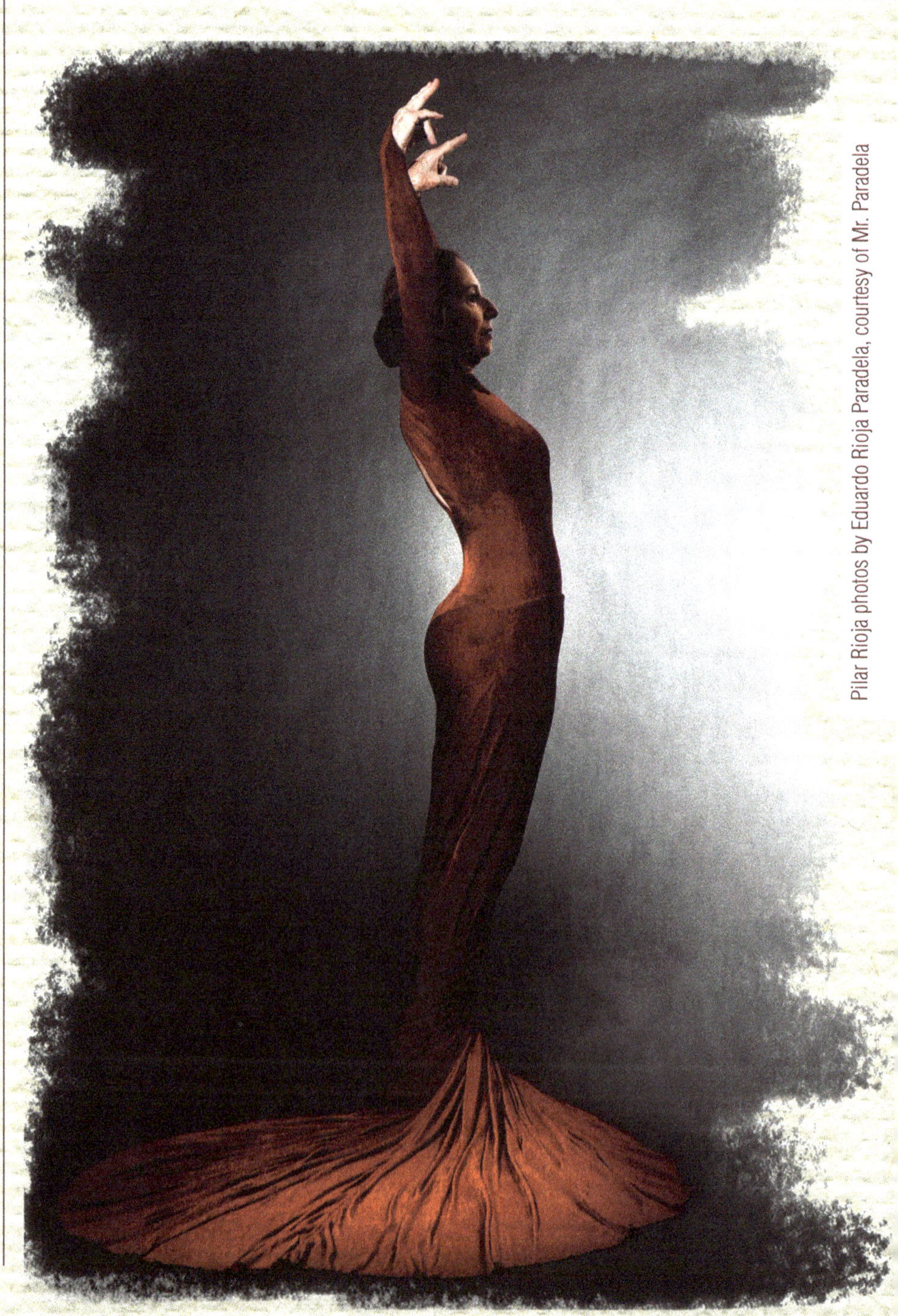

Pilar Rioja photos by Eduardo Rioja Paradela, courtesy of Mr. Paradela

Nureyev would come out and stand still, without doing a lot and it said so much. It's more difficult to be still, to simply lift an arm or to walk around.

Q How important is the audience for you?

Very important. In Flamenco, the dancer has to have "duende"—feeling. So the public feels what she's feeling. Similar to what Stanislavsky talked about between the actor and the audience. A ray of communication has to exist. A communion between the two.

Q What were the greatest challenges performing such physically demanding dances?

I have lost certain things as the body ages, yet the expression continues. I have to concentrate more; it's the same as for the actor. You do all these preparations and exercises when you're younger and you think about entertaining more. As I've matured, I've drawn experiences from life; I take it and express it more simply.

Q Where do you find your inspiration?

Nature, music, poetry, all of these. My husband, Leon Felipe, was a very good poet. He had a great impression upon me. I absorb from everything. Life is the best teacher. I see a lot of theater, dance, art, sculpture; I read a lot of books.

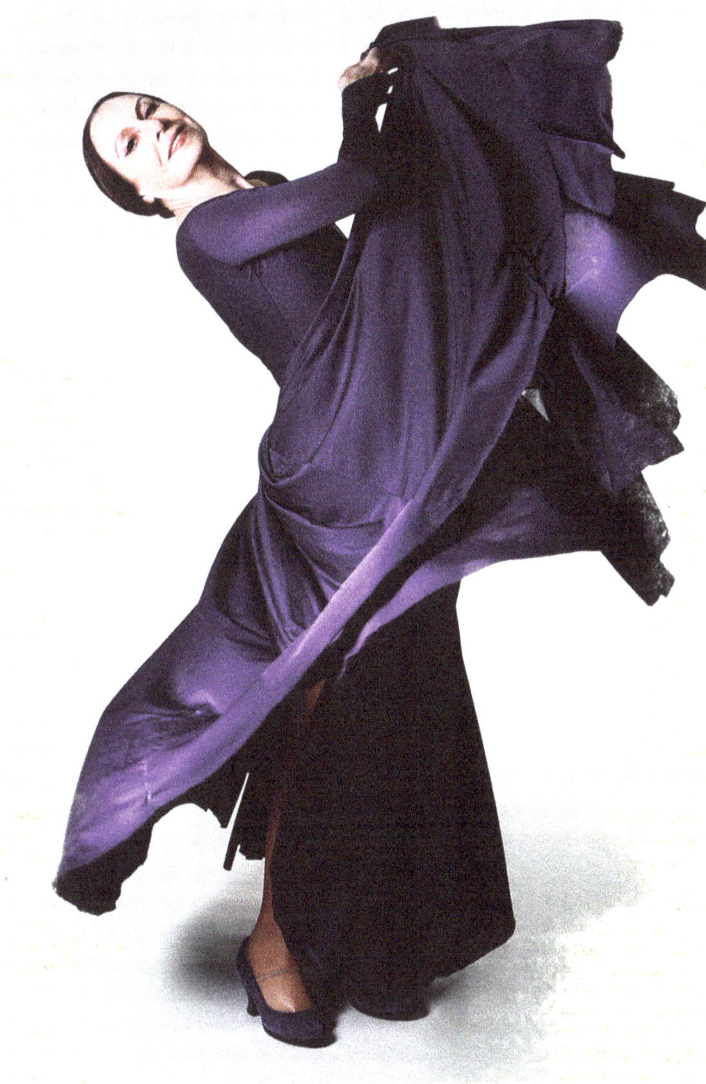

Pilar Rioja photos by Eduardo Rioja Paradela, courtesy of Mr. Paradela

Q You've also taught around the world.

It's a very large responsibility to teach. When I do, like I just did to the Bolshoi Ballet, I teach posture, Spanish dance, the twirling with the fan, using the shawl. I like to combine the schools of dance; the differences between the Bolero school, the classical, and the Flamenco.

Q Watching you dance Flamenco, one gets such a feeling of "life and death" –

It has that. That's what life is about. Lope de Vega has that in his poetry. Life has those contrasts. It is life and death, love and hate, night and day, good and bad. On stage I'm accompanied by singers clapping their hands while they are singing, finger snapping, shouting, tapping by canes, pounding hands on drums.

Q How do you keep your focus?

By concentrating a lot in each dance. In Flamenco, the musicians change rhythms. That's the beauty. I'll change, too, so the guitarist has to focus on what I'm doing. It's not like in classical dance. The musicians and I have to be in concert, understanding each other's changes.

I have to concentrate and motivate myself as if it's the first time I've ever done this dance, just like in the theater. If not, I become cold, stagnant. Then it becomes like work and art is not work. Many say artists have to suffer, sacrifice. When I love something, it's not a sacrifice, it's a joy.

Q When you dance and you're taken over by "duende," is it ever too overwhelming?

I like to continue with that feeling. I feel the public and I'm not thinking about what I'm doing. It's as if this spirit is directing me, everything comes from inside. Of course, I'm afraid of that, too. ■

TOMMY TUNE

Known as one of the most prolific director/choreographers of the twentieth century, he has received ten Tony Awards, which includes the 2015 Tony for Life Achievement in the Theatre. He is currently touring the country in his one-man show, *Taps, Tunes and Tall Tales*. Mr. Tune began his career as a dancer on Broadway in *Baker Street, A Joyful Noise*, and went on to appear in *The Best Little Whorehouse in Texas* and *How Now Dow Jones*. He received Tony Awards for his work either as a director or for performing on Broadway in *Seesaw, My One and Only* with Twiggy, *A Day in Hollywood/A Night in the Ukraine, Grand Hotel, The Will Rogers Follies, Nine*, and *Grand Hotel*. In 2015, Mr. Tune appeared in the Encores! production of *Lady, Be Good!* at New York City Center. His film appearances include *Hello Dolly* opposite Barbra Streisand and Walter Matthau, directed by Gene Kelly, *The Boyfriend*, and *Mimi Bluette... fiore del mio giardino*. In 1999, he made his Las Vegas debut as the star of *EFX*. Mr. Tune is the recipient of the National Medal of Arts, honored with a star on the Hollywood Walk of Fame, designated as a Living Landmark by the New York Landmarks Conservancy. He was awarded eight Drama Desk Awards, three Astaire Awards and the Society of Directors and Choreographers' George Abbott Award for Lifetime Achievement.

Q What gives you the greatest joy today in the work you're creating?
The audience, without a doubt. It's all about their reaction to the show. Each audience is different. It makes me think of a Japanese saying: Each step is a building block; each performance is a stone in the path.

Q When did you decide to create your current show?
It happened when I realized it was my 50th year anniversary being in show business! I had gotten my Equity card in Dallas doing musicals during the summer musicals. And I thought it was time to look at what I had done in terms of telling *my* story—who I was and how I got here.

Q How did you put it all together?
People ask me how I chose all the songs I sing in the show, and I tell them I'm doing these songs from all the shows I've done during my life, and then there are also songs from shows I like, like *Promises, Promises*, a Carole King song, one by Green Day.

Still, mostly they're the songs from the "sound track of my life." And they're not necessarily shows I was in but they tell my story and they're attached to every important event in my life. The hardest part was deciding what to leave out.

Q What does it take to stay physically and mentally in tip-top shape, and diet-wise to prepare yourself for each show?
I do some important physical exercise every day. It can be yoga, movements, but I need to do something every single day. I also have rehearsals, voice classes. Not a day goes by where there isn't some kind of class or physical warm-up for the maintenance

I also have a special diet. I'm very strict, disciplined, because, as a dancer you have basically your talent, and the main thing is to establish a balance, as with anything. When you're putting together a show, some songs are slow, some are fast, and your heart is in every note. So there are certain things you have to do to be in balance. You have to know what is feeding your instrument.

Q At the beginning of your career, you appeared in the film, *Hello Dolly*, with Barbra Streisand and Walter Matthau. How did you get the role and what kind of an experience was it for you?
It was thrilling to get that. At the time I was dancing in the chorus on Broadway in *How Now, Dow Jones*, and I was covered while I was flown out to Hollywood for the screen test. I was the only person from New York flown out there, and I tested along with twenty other guys for Roger Edens.

There are no "accidents," so the idea of getting the job was wonderful. I actually didn't find out until about two to three weeks later. I was doing a show and was in the dressing room along with everyone else in the chorus, and we're tightly packed in there, and I heard, "There's a phone call. They want *you*." So I climb over everybody at our dressing room table, and hear on the other end of the phone, "How would like to come to Hollywood and make a movie?"

I had never made a movie; I need an audience. It's definitely not the same thing to have a machine filming you. I personally prefer doing a whole show from start to finish. You can't stop if you don't get it right.

When I worked in the film with Gene Kelly, he pulled me aside after one of the takes and he gave me the greatest bit of advice I've ever gotten—"dance better."

One thing that I'm reminded of, by your giving me this stone that you've painted with this beautiful sea turtle on it, which I just love, was when we were shooting *Hello Dolly* on location in Garrison, New York, and something that occurred, and I haven't thought of it since that day.

Well, we were on location—it was up on the West Point campus, near Poughkeepsie, and here we were shooting in this location—and someone in the crew said to all of us, and we're in our costumes in the middle of shooting, "You've all got to see this."

So we step over and look over a fence, and there's a giant sea turtle in what you could describe as sitting in loam, and she had somehow come down a tributary from the sea, and came through the grass, and had made her way into this vegetable garden, and there she was, digging a hole for her eggs.

Here she was, in this garden, with all the corn growing, and we all just stood there in our costumes and watched her bury

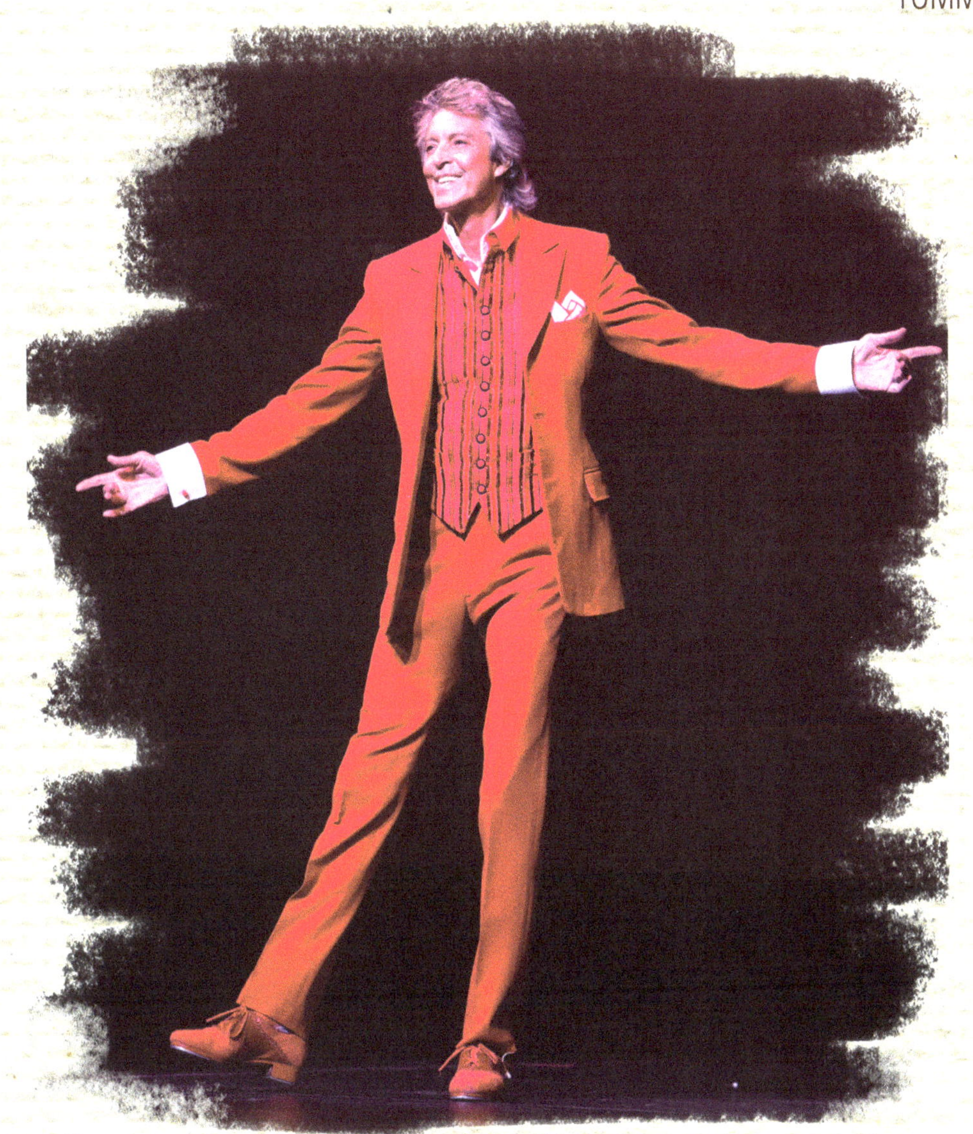

Tommy Tune photo: Franco Lacosta

her eggs. Of course, what happened to her offspring, who knows? You just sort of hope they made their way back to the sea somehow.

Q Your carry on the tradition of several great musical directors including George Abbott, Joshua Logan, Katherine Dunham, Harold Prince, Jerome Robbins, Martha Graham, to mention a few. What does it mean to you to be a part of that kind of tradition?
I'm proud to be a part of it and to include me with that list, it's flattering. I guess that's a question I can't answer because when you're in the midst of creating and bringing yourself to art and bringing art to others, I think we're lucky to be able to do it. It's really a collective process. I feel we're all just working the best we know how, serving the greater god of the arts, using the gifts we've been given.

Q You're also a painter. How have you allowed yourself to keep seeing with new eyes to create art on stage and off?
Well, each day I start with a thank you and a prayer. In a way, it's "cleaning the canvas," which I do each day when I begin a new painting. And when I begin I just never know what's going to happen.

A few days ago I began to paint and allowed whatever wanted to come. Well, I've never been a big fan of cubism, but once I began it became a cubistic painting.

Now if you look close up at either a TV screen or a computer screen, it's always moving since it's all pixels, cubes, and dots. So in a way, pointillism became cubism, and we're surrounded by cubism, especially when you look at the buildings in this city. It's a Euclidean derivation of what we see. We may not consciously see it, but cubism is surrounding us, in front of us, and affecting our subconscious.

Ultimately I think to create anything, the magic ingredient is love. That's the highest source, the main ingredient. Right now I'm still doing what I'm doing on stage because when it hits you, you know you're working in a state of love with what you're doing. And if not, change it because the world needs all the love it can get. That's what it's all about. ■

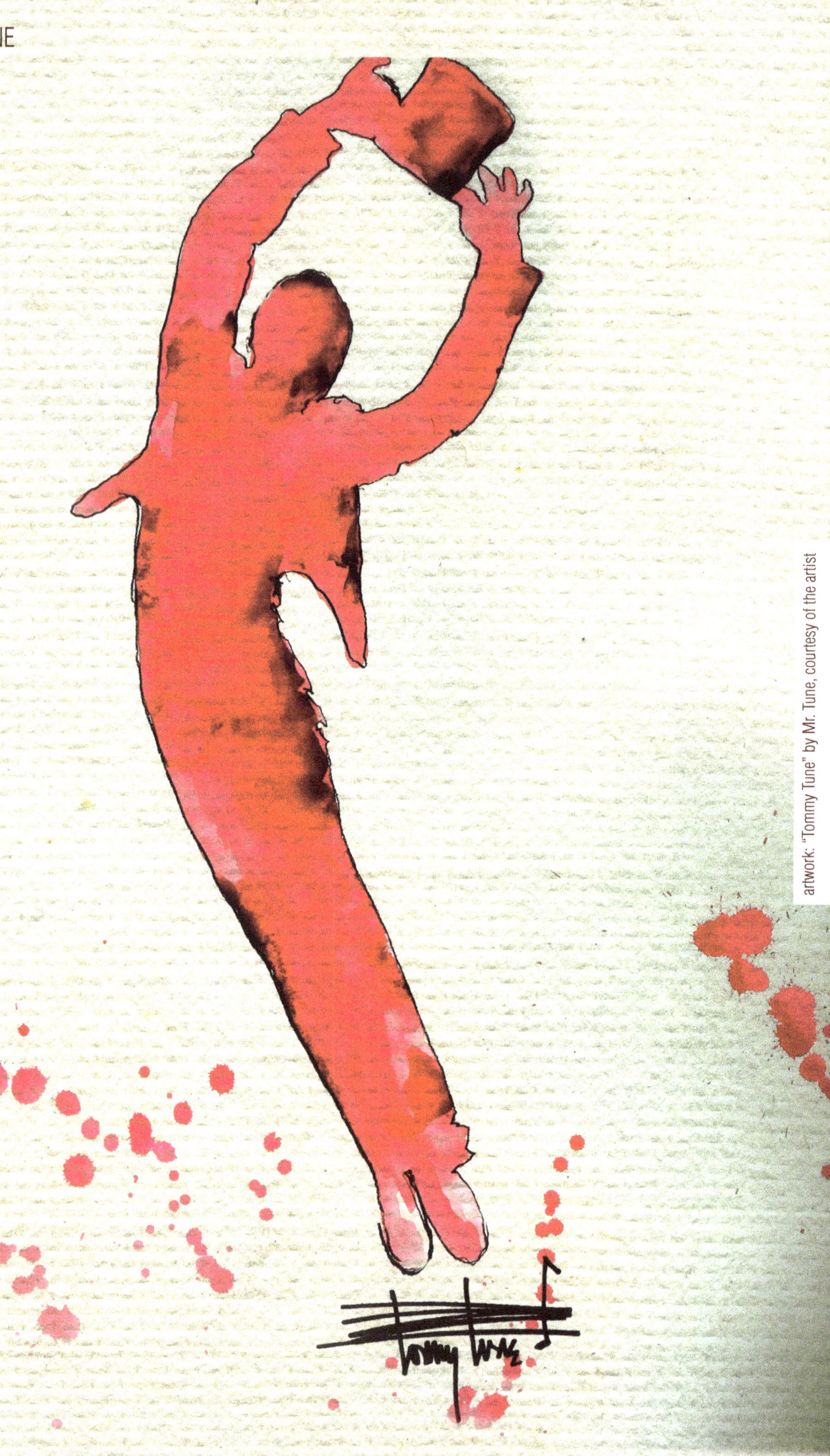

artwork: "Tommy Tune" by Mr. Tune, courtesy of the artist

CLOWNS, MIME ARTISTS, AND PUPPETEERS

GREGG GOLDSTON

For over forty years, Mr. Goldston has toured his solo art of mime performance across the U.S., Asia, and Europe. He is the creator and co-artistic director of The School of Modern Mime, an annual summer intensive in Warsaw, Poland. He developed BalletMime, a new vocabulary of ballet mime acting, which premiered in BalletMet's *Romeo and Juliet*. Mr. Goldston performed as Marcel Marceau's assistant on his 2000-2002 U.S. tours, and took on lead roles with Mr. Marceau's Nouvelle Compagnie De Mimodrame at the American Repertory Theater. He has presented his work Off-Broadway in New York City. Mr. Goldston has appeared on *The Daily Show*, *Law & Order*, *PBS online*, *The Early Show*, and created projects for F.A.O. Schwarz as "The Mechanical Man." As a mime coach, he worked with Anne Hathaway on *Ella Enchanted*, and with Julie Harris. Mr. Goldston is a recipient of two N.E.A. choreography fellowships, and also creates pen-and-ink drawings, and stainless steel and bronze sculptures.

Q What led you into the world of mime?

I grew up in Los Angeles, where my father was a carpenter. In high school, I went from metal shop to sculpture, and then fell into a sketch improv group. I first saw Marcel Marceau in 1975 when I was eighteen years old; it was actually the first time I had ever been in a real theater. The most creative thing in our house was Elvis Presley's Christmas album.

Q How were you drawn to mime?

Like so many others, it was Marceau. After seeing him, I took my first mime classes with Richmond Shepard. He was one of the first mimes in America, and he had taught Shields and Yarnell and Lily Tomlin. After a few months with Richmond, I moved to Salt Lake City, which at that time was very supportive of mime. There I was mentored by Joan Woodbury, an early Graham dancer and a modern choreographer; she had a big influence on me. Within a few years, I had created a two-hour solo mime performance, and began touring.

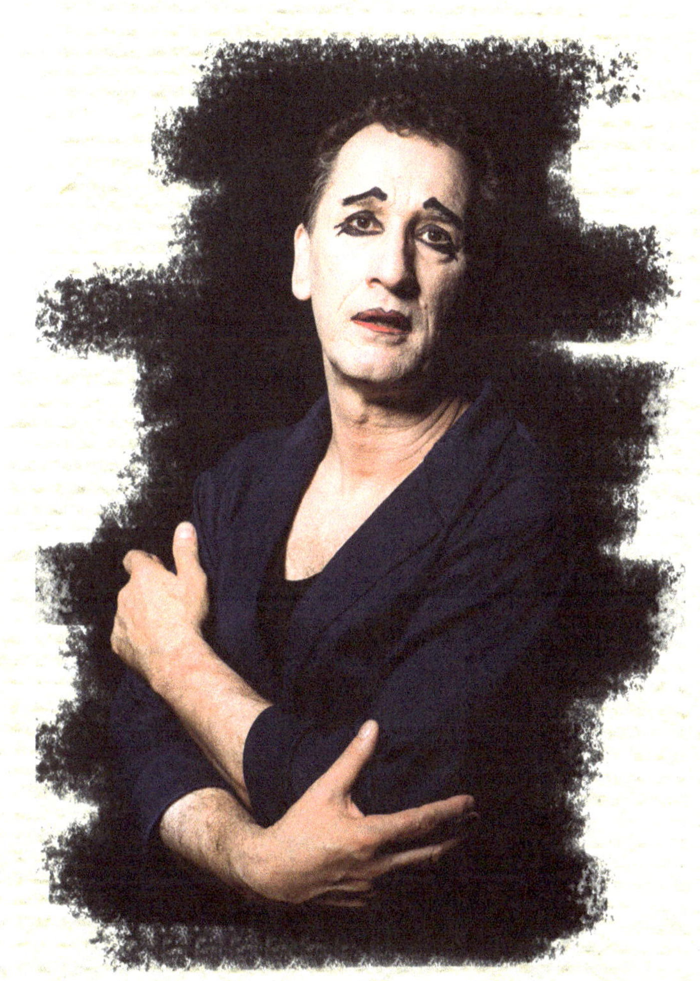

Gregg Goldston photo: Kasia Chmura-Cegielkowska

Q When did you first meet Marceau?

It took me ten years, though I tried to meet him every year he was on tour. Once, I actually had a birthday cake made for him designed like his Bip Hat, but to no avail!

I finally met him in Berkeley where he was performing. I went backstage, and when we saw each other, we locked eyes immediately. After a short talk, he invited me to come and meet him in Ann Arbor where he was holding a summer workshop. We bonded quickly in that one week.

The following summer, I invited him to teach a two-week seminar, which I hosted as a part of my School for Mimes summer intensive. We shared a very close relationship for twenty-one years, until he passed away in 2007. Marceau would often say to me that he was the older brother I never had.

Q Mime has been around a very long time—

Yes and no. It can be traced back to the Greek and Roman amphitheaters, but actually what we know as mime today was created in the 1940s. Marceau even perpetuated the "oldest art" rumor. He said he did this to give his new art a history.

This art of mime, "modern mime," as we call it, was created by Etienne Decroux who was Marceau's teacher. He created it with Jean-Louis Barrault, and was later joined by Marceau. Once

Gordon Craig discovered Decroux, everyone said that this had never existed before—the rearrangement of attitude, gesture, and movement.

Chaplin used a lot of mimetic elements in his work, but Chaplin was not a pure mime—we could call him a "mime of film." At first glance, one would think the biggest invention of modern mime was the invisible world—like the wall or the rope. But what modern mime truly gave us is the grammar to show the non-verbal "thought process."

For me, what made Marcel Marceau such a great mime artist is that he had a mind in the genius realm, like Einstein. The amount of information he could absorb was stunning—about painting, art, history, politics. He could speak five or six languages. He loved telling jokes; he'd invent fantastic comedic stories after dinner. He also loved to play chess and prided himself on the fact that he once played with Bobbie Fischer. His interest in the world, in different cultures, in humanity and humor all made him a great artist.

Q What do you think drove him to create as an artist?

During World War II, Marceau was sixteen, and living in France when the Germans invaded. His family was Jewish, and his older brother, Alain, was an important figure in the French underground. The Germans captured Marceau's father and tortured him to death, trying to get him to reveal the location of Alain. Alain had actual hid Marceau in a basement, along with other Jewish children. Alain believed Marceau had great talent, and told him that someday say he would be an important person in the theater. This obviously had a big impact on Marceau, on his commitment and devotion.

Q What does it take to be a mime artist?

If you take ballet and list all the techniques you need, and put mime next to it, they would be very close. Then add acting technique as well. Mime also requires a large amount of choreography to make it successful. For example, if I turn at a certain speed, the audience will feel one thing; if I turn at a different speed, they will feel something else. Mime is about emotion and thought.

A mime is a type of magician, but not of an illusionary world; rather, of the mind of an audience. I not only make the audience see what's not there, but I create a dialogue within their own mind. I sculpt time and space in a way that no other art does. This is actually necessary because it's essential how I cause viewers to write their own words to the plots they see.

Q You have a very special relationship in Poland, appearing annually at the Warsaw Mime Festival.

In 2000, I was invited to perform at the first International Mime Art Festival in Warsaw; that was my first real visit to Poland. Since then, it's as if I've been adopted by them. I've now been a part of it almost every year. In 2008, I created a summer Intensive there that still continues today. I founded it with Bartlomiej Ostapczuk, the Artistic Director of the Mime Art Festival. We fashioned it after the School for Mimes, which I created in Ohio that he had attended.

Like France, Poland has been one of the most influential countries in the development of modern mime. Henryk Tomaszewski was one of the most famous ballet dancers in Poland and had a vision to start something new that was physically-based. In Wroclaw, Breslau, a cultural city, actually the same town where Grotowski came from, Tomaszewski began to invent very large mime works.

Q What gives you the greatest joy creating mime?

When I'm involved in creating, it's mesmerizing. Each time I begin creating a new work, I fall in love again with the symbolism to communicate the concepts, presenting a series of images, like viewing a series of impressionist painting in a museum.

Consequently, mime transcends culture, age, and social boundaries of all kinds. It allows me to penetrate the heart in ways that words cannot. As a performer, I strive to create the moment when the audience is laughing and crying at the same time. As I often say, when the audience is transfixed, mime is the loudest silence you will ever hear. ■

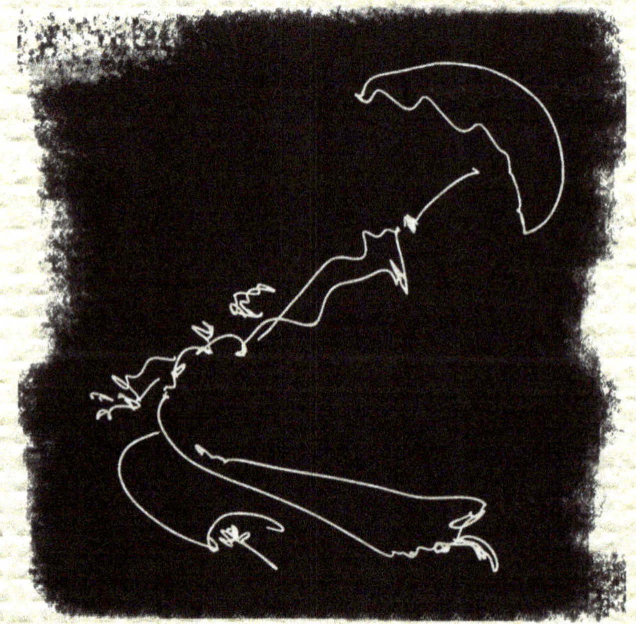

Gregg Goldston artwork: "Gregg Goldston" by Mr. Goldston, courtesy of the artist

BARRY LUBIN

Known as "Grandma," Mr. Lubin graced New York's famed one-ring circus, Big Apple Circus, with his delightful antics for twenty-five seasons, where he became the "Face of the Big Apple Circus," and was featured in its 20th anniversary production. Before that, he spent five years with the Ringling Brothers and Barnum & Bailey's Clown Alley. He has appeared in the International Circus Festival of Monte Carlo twice, the only American clown to have received this honor. He has also appeared in the International Circus Festivals in Hungary, and in Izhevsk and Moscow, Russia. Mr. Lubin is one of only two American clowns to appear in the 80-year history of prestigious Wintercirckus of Circus Krone in Munich Mr. Lubin was in the films, *Big Top Pee-Wee* and *My Life*. Mr. Lubin was featured in the PBS mini-series, *Circus*. He starred in *Stars en Der Manege*, *Circo Massimo* in Italy two times, and numerous other international television appearances. His television appearances include *Prime Time Live*, all of the morning programs on NBC, CBS, and ABC, PBS's *Evening at Pops*, *Late Night with David Letterman* four times, and PBS's mini-series, *Circus*. He served as writer/consultant for CBS's *Circus of the Stars*. Mr. Lubin is the first performer in history to perform a running headstand onto a whoopee cushion on the hallowed stage of Carnegie Hall. Barry was inducted into the International Clown Hall of Fame in 2002, and the Sarasota Ring of Fame in 2012, the highest honor in American Circus. He received the Lou Jacobs Lifetime Achievement Award in 2007. He was a featured character in fifteen appearances both live and on NBC in the seventy-five-year history of Macy's *Thanksgiving Day Parade*. Mr. Lubin was inducted into the International Clown Hall of Fame, and the Sarasota Ring of Fame—the highest honor in American Circus.

Q What led you to decide to become a clown?

I had gone to Emerson College to be a television director, but after three years I took a year off to try to determine what direction I wanted my career to go. I ran into someone who had gone to Clown College. It fascinated me. To hear that you could be paid to travel and make people laugh, it sounded fabulous. So in 1974, I auditioned for The Ringling Brothers Clown College at Boston Garden. They walked me through different routines, doing a pantomime of a wire-walker, and then we were paired off with a professional clown. The more he talked the more I was intrigued by it all. Three or four months later, I was driving a cab when I received a call—I had been accepted. As a boy, I hadn't really grown up going to the circus. I lived in Atlantic City, and the Steel Pier had a water circus, with a few clowns, but that was about it. I had never seen The Ringling Brothers Circus until I joined the Clown College.

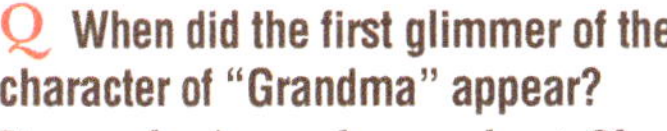

Q When did the first glimmer of the character of "Grandma" appear?

It was during rehearsals at Clown College that I first came up with her character. She got immediate notice, and a lot of audience attention. That's the first step towards getting a laugh. Now, a lot of the audience looked like "Grandma" because here we were in South Florida. I wanted it to seem as if she had just wandered in, like she was an audience member. In classes you work on character development, trying to come up with a specific character that makes your clown unique.

Q How did you develop "Grandma"?

She developed as I performed with The Ringling Brothers Circus doing about six hundred shows a year. During the "come-in" before each show, I would perform a forty-five-minute improvisation with the audience. I'd stay true to her character, while I made people laugh. From day one, I kept in mind to do it with a

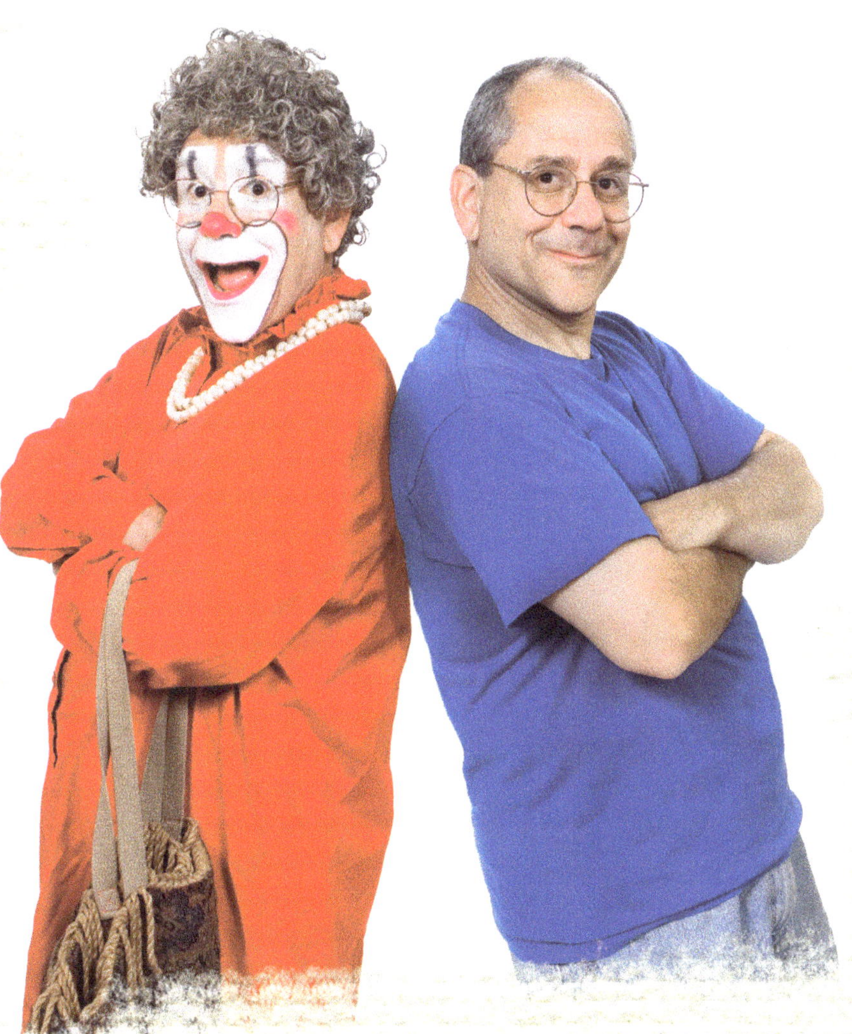

Barry Lubin photo: Maike Schulz, courtesy of Mr. Schulz

lot of love, and not make fun of elderly people. I cherish the memory of my grandparents.

Q How did you find the ease with which you perform?
At the beginning, I treated each performance like an acting exercise. But through the years I've cut away the excess. The line to get into character has become cleaner. I also concentrate like hell!

When I teach I tell my students the clown is really an extension of yourself. Who the character is and all the fun comes out of who you are. I've learned to get out of my own way. Achieving a relaxed concentration, being in the moment, has come from doing so many performances a year. I'm not a great improviser, I know my limitations. But I gave myself the opportunity to improvise because you never know what someone in the audience will do.

Q What did the relationship you had with The Big Apple Circus mean to you?
There was a real feeling of home. I loved being there; it was a very comfortable place. Paul Binder and Michael Christensen, the two founders of Big Apple had been clowns themselves, and when they decided to create their own circus, they had decided the clown would be the centerpiece of their show. I had been encouraged to do my work in this kind of atmosphere. My heart and soul was really there.

Q You visited thousands of patients with the Big Apple Circus Clown Care Unit, traveling to hospitals—
There's nothing more fulfilling than going to the bedside of the ill, and taking them out of their pain for a moment and making them laugh. To touch someone on a one-to-one basis is unbelievable. Michael founded the Care Unit, and it's been an incredibly successful arm of The Big Apple Circus.

Q Do you feel a kinship to the tradition of clowning which has existed since the Greeks and Romans? In America we've had extraordinary clowns like Emmett Kelly, Red Skelton, Jonathan Winters, just to mention a few.
I'm very influenced by the clowns I've seen. I'm aware of the tradition. And I remember when we acted together we attempted some Commedia dell'Arte in Goldoni's *The Liar*. Yes, I have drawn from all those influences.

I remember when I was a kid, about seven years old, my father, who was a great lover of silent comedy, rented a theatre in one of the large hotels now torn down, and he would show silent movies every night during the summer. I'd be in the booth, helping him load the films, and I'd watch, through the small smoky glass, the great clowns like Chaplin, Lloyd, Keaton, countless others. They were doing this incredible classic non-verbal silent comedy, and their art was derived from the ancients. It was an incredible education. Later, when they showed all those films at Clown College, I knew them all by heart.

Q How did you keep every performance fresh?
From every performance, with every audience, I learned something new. Things would pop up, like in the show you saw. That's what I aim for. There's always constant change and I'm always making adjustments. That's what always keeps me on my toes. ■

CRAIG MARIN

Puppet Master, Mr. Marin, with his wife and partner, Olga Felgemacher, created The Flexitoons; they performed the Juke Box Puppet Band on Nickelodeon's inaugural series, *Pinwheel*, for 260 episodes, appearing alongside George Carlin and Ringo Starr, on the Emmy-winning *Shining Time Station*, on PBS. They pioneered interactive television, performing *Goin' Up* on Channel 13/WNET. Mr. Marin has also portrayed *DJ Kat* on Fox Television. Their *Tide Talking Stain* is one of the Top Super Bowl Commercials of all time, and was voted the funniest office commercial in the world. The live Flexitoon Puppet Theatre has toured domestically and internationally, and is New York City's only permanent, professional institution dedicated to the puppets arts. Flexitoon received a Henson Foundation and a UNIMA Award for Outstanding Puppetry.

Q When did you know you had to create as a puppeteer?
My father was a cartoonist in vaudeville, for Minsky's and comedians like Phil Silvers, and I remember watching Paul Winchell at age three. He had this puppet on his knee and he was making him "live." I said to myself, "I want to make other children feel the same way he's making me feel."

So I started doing ventriloquism as I was learning to talk. Paul was amazing, he was the voice of Tigger in *Winnie the Pooh*. Later when we worked together, I told him, "You're my inspiration." He said, "You're the result."

Q That was your childhood—
In one word,

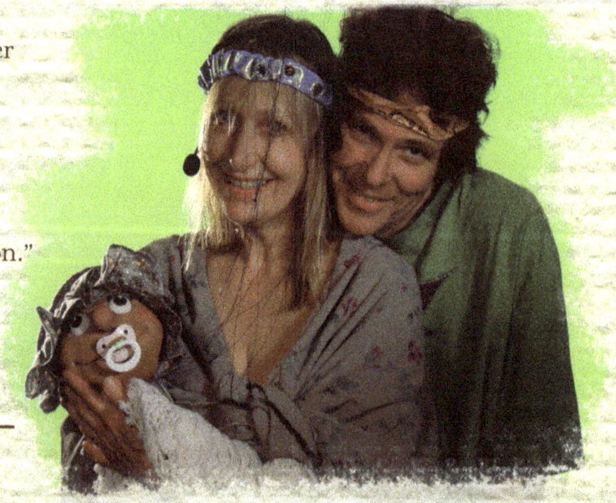

Craig Marin photos: courtesy of the artist

yes. I started making puppets. I'd watch phenomenal talents on local TV, Sandy Becker, Chuck McCann. When I saw Bill Baird, it was the best. Finally, I began to appear on local shows. When I was fifteen, I also worked at CSC for a year, as the scullery boy in the New York premiere of Anouilh's *The Cavern*. But I never really had the hook in me; I wanted you to look at my puppets instead.

Q So you found the magic of puppetry?

Exactly. I was fascinated by the fantasists, like Lewis Carroll and Frank Baum. So, I began writing my own shows in high school. I toured across America for three years, playing at colleges. I decided it was a greater responsibility to teach children, so I began doing other's people's shows. That's how I met my wife and one of the most famous female puppeteers, Olga Felgemacher. We began working together and created our own company, creating the first show ever for Nickelodeon, *Pinwheel*.

Q Why do you feel puppetry is valuable for all of us?

Alfred Jarry wrote for puppets, Edward Gordon Craig understood their significance, he wrote about the "Uber-Marionette." Punch and Judy in England was a reflection of its society. During World War II in Czechoslovakia, marionettes voiced the political opposition.

Puppet Theatre is a reflection of a nation growing up. Sesame Street, Kukla Fran and Ollie, Shari Lewis and Lambchop, Mr. Rogers, to mention a few, and The Bread and Puppet Theatre in this country, which have their roots in medieval pageantry. They're been carrying the torch for years. I've yet to see playwrights dedicated to the infinite possibilities of puppetry.

Q What does the magical world of puppetry mean to you?

You see a story like *Star Wars*, it carries the human story to another galaxy, it has profound messages, making great use of puppetry, like Yoda. It all comes down to our depth of perception. Either you look at a tree or you look at the space between the leaves. I want to bring the puppet sensibility back to us. After all, we all once played with puppets as children.

Q How did your success with *Shining Time Station* occur?

We proved our ideas could be done with a modern sensibility, with a band that lives inside a juke box. They said, "But you can see the rods of the puppet." I told them, "You see the lines in a drawing." We ended up doing sixty-five half-hour shows and ran for six years. It led directly to my dream—my own show on Fox-TV.

Q So your dreams are connected to –

Going over the rainbow. Puppets are a dimensional representation of our ages. We all once sang, "Puff the Magic Dragon." Why put it away? Why have those colors fade away? Once ventriloquists made stone idols speak. Puppetry is a true alchemical force in theatre. Look at what Julie Taymor has done. It is a distilled essence of truth in the hands of a real puppeteer. To transfer vision—to make you see—because the real artist is of his time because *we* define the time. ■

ROB MERMIN

In 1987, Mr. Mermin founded the award-winning international touring company *Circus Smirkus*, which has had cultural exchanges under the big top with over thirty countries, earning it the title "The United Nations of the Youth Circus World." Mr. Mermin ran off to the circus in 1969, clowning with various European circuses including Britain's *Circus Hoffman*, Sweden's *Cirkus Scott*, the Hungarian Magyar *State Cirkusz*, three years with Denmark's *Circus Benneweis* in the famous Circus Building by the Tivoli, and throughout the former Soviet Union. He trained with mime masters Marcel Marceau and Etienne Decroux. Mr. Mermin co-founded Canada's Paul Gaulin Mime Troupe, appeared for two seasons on Denmark's popular weekly show, *TV 1 Teltet*, and toured Europe with the Sandglass Puppet Theater. He was Dean of *Clown College* for Ringling Brothers and Barnum & Bailey Circus, President of the All-Youth Blackfriars Summer Theater, and is Artist-in-Residence for the Vermont Arts Council. Mr. Mermin currently tours with a series of autobiographical one-man, multi-media shows at universities across America. He has written two books: *Circus Smirkus: True Tales of High Adventure* and *Low Comedy*. Among Mr. Mermin's awards include Copenhagen's World Star-Time Clown, Vermont's Bessie Award, Russia's Best Director Prize at the International Festival on the Black Sea, and the Governor's Award for Excellence in the Arts.

Q What are the ingredients you've learned from watching and working with master clowns?

Working with the great European circus clowns—Francesco Caroli, Charlie Rivel, Karl Kossmayer, Buby Ernesto, Popov, Toto Chabri, and Joe Jackson, Jr.—I learned how to slow down the gags so there's time for laughter to build up during a routine, to not just aim for the one-trick laugh. Running into the circus ring for the first time, I knew I needed to relate to the audience differently—relax into my character, improvise the timing, to think on your feet, and let go of any clever technique. To get out of my own way and let my trained body do the instinctive physical comedy. I learned a repertoire of tricks up my sleeves—juggling, wire, acrobatic, and equestrian skills which

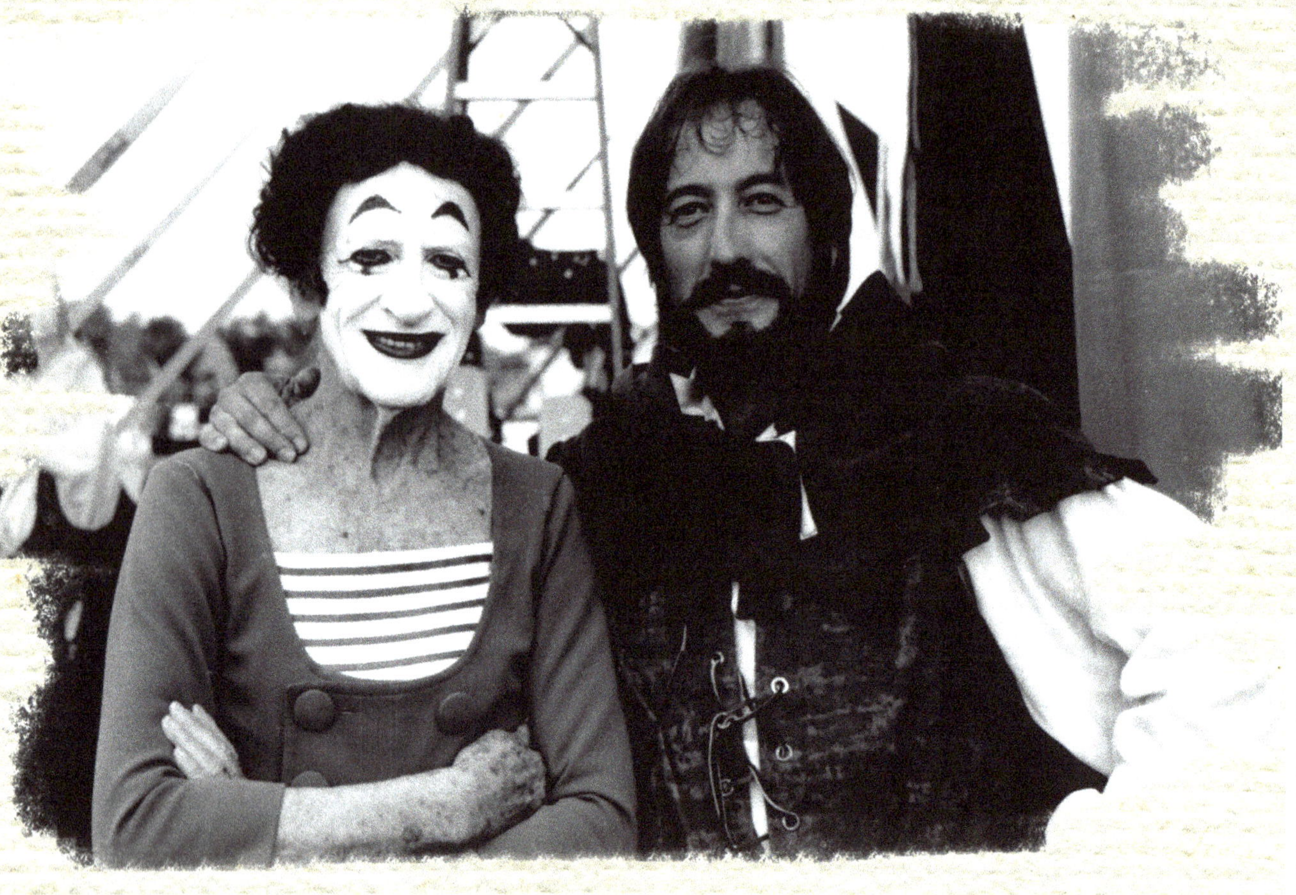

Rob Mermin photos: courtesy of the artist

became part of my arsenal.

My mentor, Marcel Marceau, taught me the importance of timing, rhythm, clarity of intention, projection of character, and the absolute power of silence.

By watching the great silent clowns—Charlie Chaplin, Buster Keaton, Laurel and Hardy, Harold Lloyd, Harry Langdon—I learned that the best comedy comes from a kind of seriousness of the heart. They took laughter seriously. I think laughter is perhaps a kind of survival technique of the human species.

Q What does it mean to see how Circus Smirkus continues to touch so many lives?

Circus Smirkus is a bridge linking the itinerant lifestyle and traditions of the small traveling tent show to the creative style and energy of contemporary circus. We aim for a variety of styles in clowning—knockabout, slapstick, solo, silent, short reprise gags, and longer group entrees.

Smirkus, in a way, shares the best of who you are. I created Circus Smirkus because I wanted a way for American kids to share my own experiences of seeking adventure, living an unconventional lifestyle, and finding a greater community in the circus world.

It's hugely gratifying to see the company continue to grow and touch lives for three decades. I think it's because the kids and the public get the spirit of what we do. Smirkus troupers from thirty years ago are now sending their kids to Smirkus.

Q What are some of the life lessons young performers gain by being a part of Circus Smirkus?

They come to us as kids and teenagers molded by the propaganda of mass media and pop culture, and they leave as young people ready to face the world with a sense of their own worth and abilities, confident, with a strong work ethic.

It is a hugely moving experience to witness the transformative power in the ring. I try to impart a philosophy, and how to live with tolerance in a tight knit community, to share the best of themselves with a real generosity of spirit.

Mime was my first love because it taught me new ways to perceive the world; circus taught me a way to live in the world between sawdust and the canvas, between the earth and the sky. Those who are a part of Smirkus are a part of our history each time they help raise the big top and step into the magic of the ring. ■

DAVID SHINER

One of the world's great clowns, Mr. Shiner is also an acclaimed actor, playwright, and director. On Broadway, Mr. Shiner and Mr. Irwin's two-man wordless show, *Fool Moon*, featuring music by the Red Clay Ramblers, ran for eight years, receiving a Special Tony Award for Live Theatrical Presentation, a Drama Desk Award, and an Outer Critics Circle Award. Together they also appeared in their award-winning production of *Old Hats* at the Signature Theatre in New York City. Mr. Shiner originated the role of "The Cat in the Hat" in the stage musical, *Seussical*. He worked for various circuses including *Cirque de Demain*; the German troupe, *Circus Roncalli*; and the Swiss National company, *Circus Knie*. With *Cirque du Soleil*, he co-created and performed in *Nouvelle Expérience*, touring for nineteen months throughout Canada and the United States, and was the writer and director of *KOOZA*. Mr. Shiner's film and television appearances include *Lorenzo's Oil*, *Man of the House*; opposite Bill Irwin in Sam Shepard's film, *Silent Tongue*; and numerous appearances on *The Tonight Show* with Johnny Carson and Jay Leno. He has also mentored and guest directed at Lilalu, a German youth circus program.

Q When you began as a mime, were your parents supportive of your creativity?

My parents were always supportive. I come from a family of eight children and they couldn't always keep track of all of us. When I went to Europe early in the 1980s, I would improvise in the street but I never considered myself a mime. I really taught myself by constantly improvising; it became part of my physical vocabulary.

Q Were there clown and mime artists who inspired you?

I was enamored by Marcel Marceau and that whole movement; they were great, great people. There was Claude Kipnis, Robert Shields. And when I was in Geneva in 1982, I saw the Swiss circus *Knie*; that changed everything for me. I thought, "Now that's real clowning."

Q Were there other clowns you were attracted to in the movies?

My heroes very early on clearly were Charlie Chaplin, Buster Keaton, and Laurel and Hardy. Chaplin intrigued me; it was the poetry of his movement, his storytelling. His film, *City Lights*, is my favorite. It's just brilliant—the idea of creating a powerful character only through a little movement, a little costume and makeup. I wanted to do that but I didn't know why.

Q What has given you the greatest joy performing *Old Hats* with Bill Irwin at the Signature Theatre Company?

At this stage in my life I think it's that I'm able to make people laugh—and working with Bill, and with Shaina Taub, she's an incredible talent, the whole band, with everyone involved with the production. We're all on the same wave length, we support each other, and I respect Bill as much he does me. It's really the whole experience at the Signature, what they manage to do, how supportive they are. I've never experienced anything like it anywhere else.

Q What led to this show originally being created?

Jim Houghton said to Bill and I, "Why don't you both get back together?" So we said to each other, "Let's spend a week together and see if we can come up with some ideas." Jim kept after us. He'd bring us back together for two weeks at a time, and we'd spend time in the studio finding out what we could come up with. After the second meeting, we said to each other, "We'll do a show."

Originally we had ended up working together on Sam Shepard's film, *Silent Tongue*, and came up with a clown routine instantaneously, which we both knew was special.

Q How do you teach what makes a good clown?

That's a difficult question because there are many different styles of clowning. When I teach at the Acting Academy in Munich, I work with young German actors, and what I teach them doesn't have to do with a clown technique. I help them find out their own creativity, inspiring them to find their own voice, to face their fears, to do things they wouldn't normally do, to trust their own instincts. I always ask, "What is the fool? What is the essence of a clown?" It's basically transforming pain into laughter. It's also the ability to improvise, to have good ideas so that at the end of the day you can ask, "What is the core thing that makes me communicate the way I do?"

Q Before you joined *Cirque du Soleil*, you were also a part of several different circuses.

I learned so much with the first circus I worked with in Germany. We'd do twelve shows a week and because I was doing so many shows I kept learning and experimenting. I had three numbers, so I was forced to stick with my routine, but in the afternoon shows I'd experiment. So I began to understand what worked. With the *Circus Knie*, I learned how to listen to a paying audience, which was very different because when I performed on the street, I had to make sure they stayed and watched, so my character would change dramatically.

Q With *Cirque du Soleil*, you co-created and performed in *Nouvelle Expérience*, and you also created *KOOZA*.

Performing with *Cirque du Soleil* was just a great experience. I wrote a lot for the company, directed some of it. My character was featured. Everyone was wonderful to work with. It was a really creative time—the "fervent years"! It was also the first time people saw me in America.

Q Your wordless show, *Fool Moon*, with the Red Clay Ramblers enchanted audiences for years. Did it change over time?

You're always perfecting the numbers, but there comes a point where you've been doing eight shows a week, which takes a lot of energy, you calm down. Bill and I would dare one another. I actually think I'm doing my best work now.

It's interesting—you hit sixty years of age and you realize you don't need to prove yourself any longer. It's wonderful when the audience applauds but it's not about getting a standing ovation. They will either like it or they won't, so it's very freeing. It gives me the freedom so I can improvise. At an earlier point we're all terrified about what others will think: and ask, "Am I funny enough?" But then you reach a certain period when you realize you just want to go out there and have fun.

Q You also originated the role of "The Cat in the Hat" on Broadway in *Seussical*.

I think it was a lark. They called me in and I had never auditioned for a Broadway show, and they gave me the part. I was surrounded by so much tremendous talent. People who can really sing and dance, all these great composers, lyricists, all exceptional talents. I think I did a good job. My wife said to me, "It's not for you, you're a clown," but I got to try it.

Q Does the audience play a part in what you create?

Honestly, it really doesn't have anything to do with the audience when you're creating. You create what you want to create, what you have to create. You figure out the timing and once you're on the stage the audience will let you know if you're flying or you're sinking.

At this time in my life what is important is telling stories and staying true to my vision. Filling those who come with a story that has a lot of heart and soul. I'm literally on a search through the story with a deep longing to find hope, to search for meaning, a quest for understanding. It's what everyone is longing to identify with.

Q How do you begin creating what the story of a show will be about?

I start with one idea. Let's say it's about this guy who has a problem, he's trying to reconcile his place in the world. As he's trying to solve the problem he meets another character who can either impede him or help him in his search for something that's luminous, with a longing to rise above the agony and pain of this earthly existence. I think everyone can identify with the idea that there has to be something more. So I want to do stories that have to do with love and hope, overcoming fear, fighting against the dark forces.

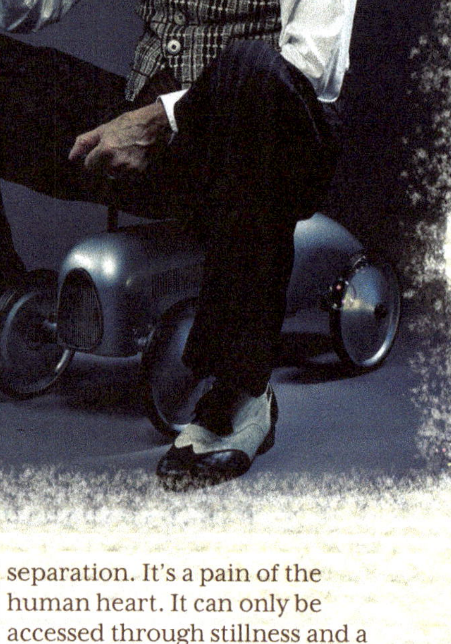

David Shiner photo: York Hovest

My favorite book growing up was *The Lord of the Rings*. It's the story of a young man with a true heart triumphing over extremely powerful forces of darkness. I feel that way about life. We need to have more innocence and hope, compassion; I believe tenderness will always triumph.

Q I remember watching Emmet Kelly and Red Skelton, two of our greatest clowns. They also made a deep impression on you.

Yes, Red Skelton had that great Hobo piece. My hobo piece is not finished. It's basically Emmet and Red Skelton. Skelton also did that wonderful character, Freddy the Freeloader. It was all quintessential Americana. I always wanted to do the "sad figure."

I'm always trying to challenge myself to make the audience laugh and cry, to feel the loneliness deep inside of us—the pain of separation. It's a pain of the human heart. It can only be accessed through stillness and a quiet mind.

My feeling is that what exists in the human heart would stagger the imagination. We spend so much time in our daily lives giving into fears. We forget to return to our heart. It's there all the time but life seems so dangerous, so a lot of the time we shut down.

I play the fool, so at the end of the day I can help others realize we can also sometimes act like fools when we take ourselves too seriously. The moment we think we know what we're doing, we can become foolish. It's all relative, knowing deep down there's something so much better.

Every second we're alive, the challenge is to embrace the moment with all there is. We're all here for a reason. Something's beating in all of us. That intrigues me more than anything else—the human heart. ■

COMPOSERS AND LYRICISTS

GRETCHEN CRYER

Best known for the pioneering musical, *I'm Getting My Act Together and Taking It On the Road*, which she performed in at The Public, and Circle in the Square in New York City for three years. Ms. Cryer is part of one of the most successful collaborations in musical history, having worked with Nancy Ford for over sixty years. When they began they were the only female composer-lyricist team in New York theater. They began writing together as freshmen at DePauw University and produced three shows in college before coming to New York. Their New York productions include *Now is the Time for All Good Men*; *The Last Sweet Days of Isaac* with Austin Pendleton and Alice Playten, which received the Obie, Drama Desk, and Outer Critics Circle Awards; *Shelter* on Broadway; *Anne of Green Gables* for Theater works USA *Eleanor*, *The American Girls Revue*, and their new show *Still Getting My Act Together*, which premiered at the Laguna Playhouse last fall. Her newest play, *Changing*, is scheduled for its debut at the Intiman Theater. Ms. Cryer appeared as a performer on Broadway in the original productions of *Little Me* with Sid Caesar, *110 in the Shade*, and *1776*. Ms. Cryer was a Jonathan R. Reynolds playwright-in-residence at Denison College, an adjunct professor at Colorado College, and presently teaches solo performance in New York City.

Q Did you begin writing at an early age?

I grew up in the country, forty miles east of Indianapolis. I was five years old when I wrote my first play. It was called *The King and the Fairy*, and my brother was the king, a non-speaking role; I was the fairy and had all the lines. I made the costumes out of Kleenex and scotch tape. Mom and Dad were our audience and they had to pay a nickel to see it. In school I was in a lot of plays, although I never considered that it would be my profession.

At DePauw University during my freshman year I met Nancy Ford; she was studying to be a composer. Every year we'd put on an original musical, and Nancy and I wrote three shows together. I got my license to teach, thinking I'd be an English teacher. My husband was going to be a minister, but after a year at Yale Divinity School, he decided to leave the ministry to go into show business.

When we moved to New York City, I decided to go into show business as well. Once here I began getting acting work, which led to a job on Broadway in *Little Me* with Sid Caesar. While I was in the show, I was pregnant with my first child; I kept working for seven and a half months until our stage manager said, "I think it's time." I was growing out my costume. After that, I was in *110 in the Shade* on Broadway, had another baby, and then in the musical, *1776*.

Q Have there been actors who have been inspiring for you?

When I saw Michael Redgrave in *Hamlet* in London, I understood every word, every nuance, what was going on at every moment. He made everything absolutely clear; it was an extraordinary performance. Seeing Vanessa Redgrave in *Long Day's Journey into Night* on Broadway, I felt I had seen a life-altering performance. A father and daughter gave me two of my most memorable theater experiences.

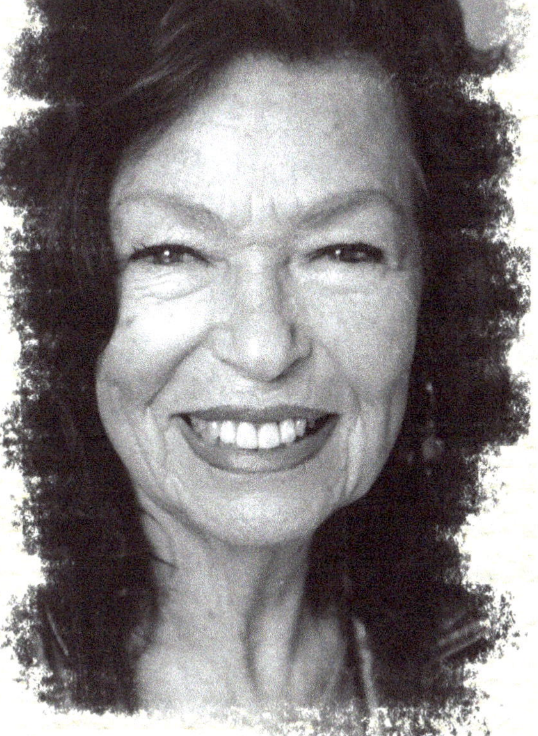

Gretchen Cryer photo: courtesy of the artist

Q So you continued writing with Nancy?

Oh yes, we wrote *Now is the Time for All Good Men*—our first show produced in New York City. I wasn't going to be in it, but a week before we opened, our lead actress got ill and I took over the part. I changed my name to Sally Niven so it wouldn't be a vanity production. So Sally Niven ended up getting wonderful reviews, and the show and Gretchen Cryer got terrible reviews.

I was also working on a musical with Austin Pendleton about Junius Booth, which he eventually did as a straight play with Frank Langella. At that time Nancy and I were writing in the "Rodgers and Hammerstein mode." We broke out of it with *The Last Sweet Days of Isaac*.

Q How do you begin creating a musical?

It nearly always begins with a fascination of some sort, then the idea becomes character-driven, the characters take over. I write out of the worlds I know. I'm always very interested in themes. Marshall McLuhan's work propelled me to write *The Last Sweet Days*.

Now is the Time for All Good Men was inspired basically by pacifism in "small town America. My brother was a pacifist. He was vilified by the conservatives in our small town, and I felt compelled to write about that. He went to prison for four years. He had burned his draft card and was called a traitor. The whole idea of the play was driven by that.

Getting my Act Together and Taking it on the Road was autobiographical. My newest play, *Changing*, was inspired by an article in *The New York Times*. A guy had a sex change in his 40s, then went back to Harvard for a reunion with his football buddies. He had been a football player and went back as a woman. I took that idea and ran with it, imagining what that reunion must have been like.

Q What makes a good collaboration work?

You have to have a similar sensibility with your collaborator. I have collaborated mostly with Nancy, but I've also collaborated with Austin Pendleton on one show. I also wrote five industrials with John Dumke.

With Nancy, interestingly enough, we work separately. I write the book and lyrics, she takes the script with her, works on the music by herself, then we get together. With *Anne of Green Gables*, I gave her the whole first act. In our sequel, *Still Getting My Act Together*, we probably have been thinking about writing it for thirty years. It's about the same characters as in *I'm Getting My Act Together and Taking It On the Road*, taking place thirty years later.

Nancy and I also wrote a couple of shows for the American Girl Company. They built theatres into their retail stores, and we made shows based on the American girl books called *The American Girls Revue*.

Q What led you to teach?

I started teaching solo performance about ten years ago. When I taught my workshop in Colorado, they asked me to create a course on solo performance. It was very successful so I've continued. I tell people they can incorporate whatever their talent may be. One person did a whole piece performing on rollerblades. My students aren't just actors: they're midwives, computer specialists, ministers, nurses, nuns—all have stories to tell.

As we work on them I have living room readings here in my apartment. I fashion exercises that foster a certain kind of analytical thinking. It's the most amazing thing seeing people discover what they can do with their talent, to come into their own.

In my own writing I wrote intuitively; but after teaching all these years, I've become much more aware of structure and technique; it's actually helped my own writing process.

Q How would you describe your joy of creativity?

When I'm writing, it's very rejuvenating. I feel happiest when I'm doing it. I've learned the reward is the writing; it's very tough. I love the theater because it's a live experience. The extent to which we are living our lives electronically today is scary. It's so important to have a live experience to maintain our humanity. ■

ERVIN DRAKE

Mr. Drake's most well-known songs included "It Was a Very Good Year" recorded by Frank Sinatra, Robbie Williams, recently by Ray Charles and Willie Nelson; "I Believe (For Every Drop of Rain)" recorded by Barbra Streisand, LeAnn Rimes, and Frankie Laine; "Good Morning Heartache," recorded originally by Billie Holiday, then Diana Ross, Tony Bennett, and Sheryl Crow; "Tico Tico," "A Room Without Windows," "Perdido," and "Al Di Là." He also wrote the musicals *What Makes Sammy Run?*, *Sophisticated Lady*, and *Lobster Alice*. Mr. Drake wrote, composed, and produced hundreds of television shows and films including *Yves Montand on Broadway*, *To Mamie Eisenhower with Music*, *The Bachelor*, for which he received the Sylvania Award, *Ethel Merman Special*, *Radio Days*, *Fabulous Baker Boys*, *Sinatra*, *Sex and the City*, and *The Sopranos*. Mr. Drake received the ASCAP Award, and was inducted into the Songwriters Hall of Fame. The Ervin Drake Music Scholarship is presented annually by Townsend Harris High School and Five Towns College. Mr. Drake died in 2015 (this interview was conducted in 2001).

Q How did the times you grew up in play a role in the music you wrote?

It was the time of the Great Depression, and I grew up on the upper Westside of Manhattan. My parents had three sons and a daughter; Dad was in the wholesale furniture biz. To get to my high school, the subway fare cost ten cents there and back. As to writing songs, I started really young, when I was twelve. One of my brothers was already writing songs. My younger brother became a renowned comic book writer.

I was greatly influenced by George Gershwin, Cole Porter, Rodgers and Hart, Kern and Hammerstein, and Johnny Mercer. I knew Johnny later when I was President of the Songwriters Guild. I listened to Bing Crosby, who established the style of singing called "crooning." Some called it "groaning."

I remember The Group Theatre's outstanding productions such as *Waiting for Lefty*. In 1945, with everything going on in the South, I wrote "There are No Restricted Signs in Heaven," and Johnny Mercer heard it and told me, "I love it, I'll record it on the Capital label." My publisher and I were terribly excited. But then we got the word that he couldn't do it. His partner, Glenn Wallichs, the business head of Capitol told him, "We're a brand new firm, and if we record this, we'll lose our Southern distributors and goodbye Capitol." That's how it was in those times.

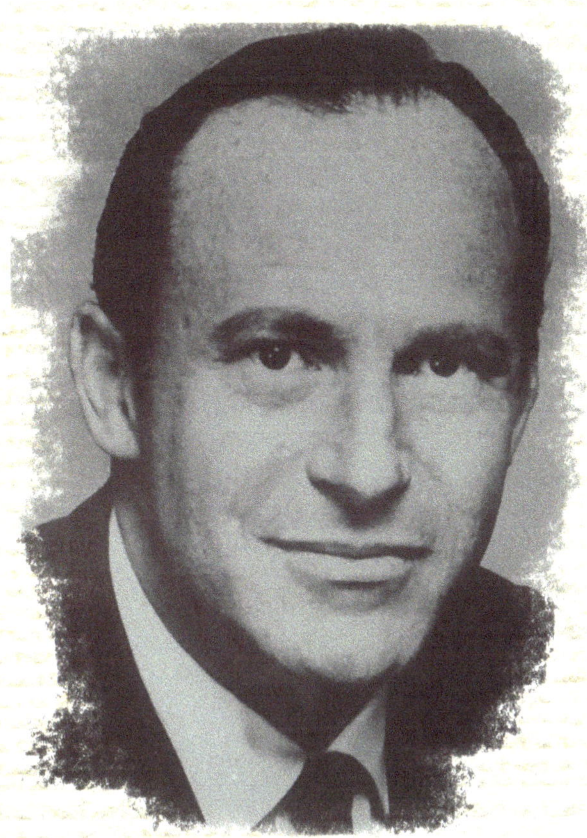

Ervin Drake photo: courtesy of the artist

Q You also had Billie Holiday record one of your early songs?

To have Billie record your song I learned was a great advantage. Not only was she a marvelous stylist, but often Billie's recordings actually became big "underground" hits. I wrote "Good Morning Heartache" due to my unhappiness when my girlfriend, Edith, "dumped" me. It was in my depression that I wrote the song. Strangely, thirty-three years later, her husband and my wife, Ada, both died. Edith looked me up when she saw a notice in *The New York Times* about the passing of Ada and phoned me. Now I've been married to this wonderful woman for twenty-two years.

Q How did your song, "I Believe," come about?

There were four of us, we were the songwriters for "The Jane Froman Show" on CBS, and had to come up with a song that Jane would record and make into a hit. We thought, "What do we write?" And as it turned out after we broke for dinner, Jimmy Shirl and I were left with the task. At that time, it was 1952, and we were still in the war against North Korea and were sustaining heavy losses of troops. Only faith was keeping many mothers and fathers from totally breaking down. So Jim and I decided to write a song of faith.

When we finished, it was unlike anything we had ever written before. Well, the next day I'm at the piano, and I play it and sing it for Jane. She said, "Play it again." I asked her, "Do you like it?" "Like it?" she said, and she pulled her sweater sleeve back, and said, "Look, I've got goose pimples all over." I asked her, "Then you'll record it?" "No, it's not 'commercial' enough." How wrong she was. Frankie Laine turned it into one of the biggest successes in song history, selling twelve million copies.

Q What led to Frank Sinatra recording "It Was a Very Good Year"?

I was walking through the halls early one morning in a Broadway building next to Tin Pan Alley. The door to a music publisher's office opened and a friend of mine, Arthur Mogull, who ran the music business of the recording group, The Kingston Trio, called to me, "Bobby Shane, of The Kingston Trio, needs a song as a solo. Do you have one?" "No." "Could you write one?" "Take me to your piano room." First I phoned home to my wife to tell her I'd be a bit late for dinner. Then I sit down at the piano, pulled out my diary. I keep a new one and write down lots of ideas for possible songs.

I looked through it and found an idea. A note read, "The story of a guy's life told in wine vintage terms. Neo-folk." That was it. Why quibble? And for one of the few times in my career, the words and the music came together; most unusual. After creating it, I wrote it out on a lead sheet so that I wouldn't forget the music the next morning. A bit later, Bob Shane came in and listened, liked it, it was recorded, and over the next four years, more groups recorded it. Among them: The Turtles, Johnny Mann Singers, Modern Folk Quartet, and Gaslight Singers.

It's four years later, I was in London, and I called my British publisher. He said, "Listen to this!" So I'm standing there in my hotel room, the phone in my ear, and I hear the most unusual recording—Frank Sinatra singing "It Was a Very Good Year." I tell him, "Play it again!"

I had to wait until I returned to rush to a record store, get the LP, and take it home. Sinatra read the lyric, like the great actor he was, phrasing the music so that it reaches me deeply to this very day. That day I must have played it at least 30 times!

Later, when Frank and I became friendly, I asked him, "How did you first get to hear the song?" He told me, "I was driving from LA through the desert to my home in Rancho Mirage with the radio on and I hear the Kingston Trio singing it, and I thought, this would be perfect for my comeback album, 'September of my Years!'" It was absolutely pure luck he happened to hear it!

Q Do you believe in "luck"?

Yup. Both kinds, the good and the bad. A few years back, I was interviewed and I was asked, "Is there anything you would wish for your songs that you'd care to mention?" I said, "I've always wanted Willie Nelson to record 'It Was a Very Good Year.'" And now, this recent duet between Willie and Ray Charles, on Ray's "Genius Loves Company" has come out and I'm thrilled. As I've always maintained, "You've got to be there when the band starts playing." ■

MARVIN HAMLISCH

His groundbreaking show on Broadway, *A Chorus Line*, received the Pulitzer Prize. On Broadway he also wrote the music for *They're Playing Our Song*, *The Goodbye Girl*, *Sweet Smell of Success*, *Jean Seberg*, and the *Nutty Professor Musical*. He was the composer of more than forty motion picture scores including his Academy Award-winning score and song for *The Way We Were*, his adaptation of Scott Joplin's music for *The Sting*, for which he received his third Academy Award. His prolific output of scores for films include original compositions and/or musical adaptations for *Sophie's Choice*, *Ordinary People*, *The Swimmer*, *Three Men and a Baby*, *Ice Castles*, *Take the Money and Run*, *Bananas*, *Save the Tiger*, and *The Informant!* And *Liberace—Behind the Candelabra*, starring Michael Douglas and Matt Damon and directed by Steven Soderbergh. Mr. Hamlisch was Musical Director and arranger of Barbra Streisand's 1994 concert tours and her television special, *Barbra Streisand: The Concert*, for which he received two Emmy Awards. Mr. Hamlisch was the principal pops conductor for the Pittsburgh Symphony Orchestra, Milwaukee Symphony Orchestra, Dallas Symphony Orchestra, Pasadena Symphony and Pops, Seattle Symphony, San Diego Symphony, The Buffalo Philharmonic, and The National Symphony Orchestra in Washington, D.C. As composer, Mr. Hamlisch received three Academy Awards, four Grammy Awards, four Emmy Awards, one Tony Award and three Golden Globe Awards. Mr. Hamlisch died in 2012 (this interview was conducted in 2006).

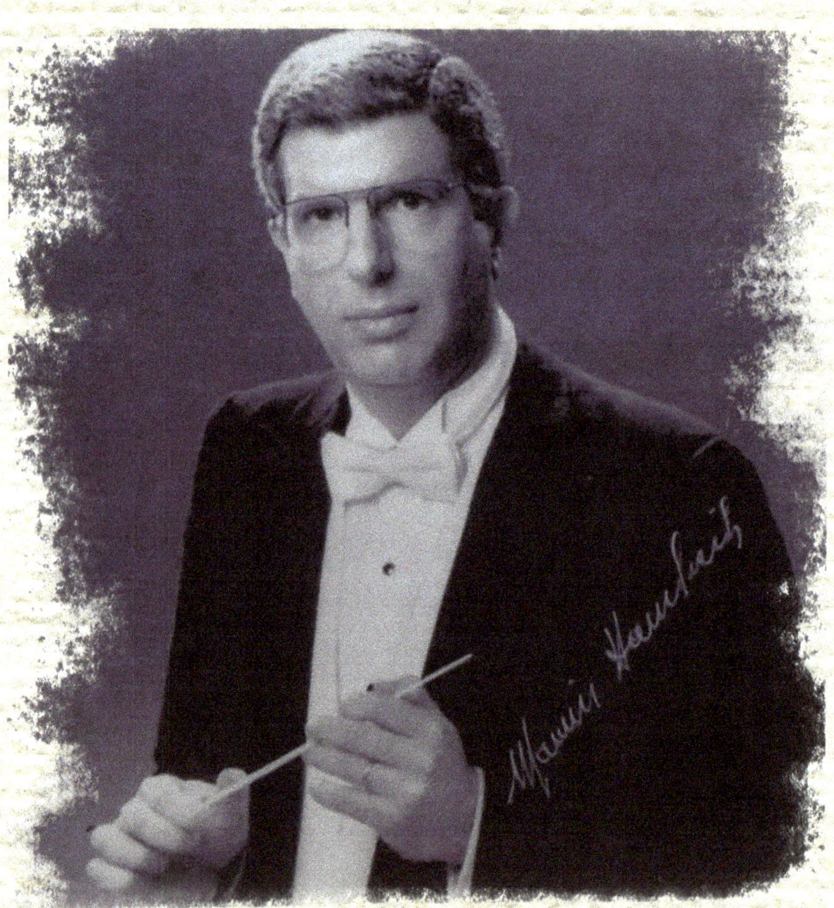

Marvin Hamlisch photo: courtesy of the artist

Q I understand you're working on a new revival of *A Chorus Line*?

The original *Chorus Line* had risk-taking orchestrations, and we've decided to use that as our philosophy. If the show was being written today, what would have to be different? We're adding synthesizers to the orchestra. Over the last thirty years, things have gotten more complex and "smarter."

Q Did you see theater growing up and begin playing music at an early age?

I started playing music at six years old and was accepted at Juilliard at six and a half. In New York as a student, I saw a lot of theater, rubbing shoulders with a score of actors; I went "nuts" for it. My parents were very supportive; my father was a musician.

Q What makes collaboration work for you?

Collaboration is one of the keys to success in the theater. When you get three or four people together they have to answer together: What is this show about? You get lots of different answers but everyone has to be on the same page. They're the pilots of the plane, and you can't be going to four different places.

A chemistry has to happen. Obviously, you're dealing with different personalities in a collaboration. Most of us can't accept it when personalities clash. But if you have faith, if the person has a major talent, if it's Jerome Robbins screaming at you, then you listen and find a way to work together.

Q How do you go about creating music for a film?
With movies, even if I read the script beforehand, and it may be a complicated script, it's not going to tell me what makes it interesting until I see the film. Once I see a movie I get a sense what to add to it. *The Sting* was one of those perfect films, and you have Paul Newman and Robert Redford. The music is there is to tell the audience this is a caper, in other words: "Don't take it all too seriously."

With *The Way We Were*, you have Streisand and Redford, and the film takes off from a college, and for two and a half hours, we're mainly entrenched in a major love story; we care about these two people. That's important to know. I tried to bring nuances, painting "white on white," adding something to the "wall" that isn't there.

Q You were the musical director and arranger of Ms. Streisand's concert tours and her television special. How did you remain open to what she brought to each song, while also staying true to what you feel would work?
That's the game. To make it possible for Streisand to sing the truth; and that's also part of the joy I have. It's most important, not just what notes she'll sing, but I want to put her in as comfortable manner as she can possibly be in.

Q You've talked about "music being an international language, a way of expanding this communication."
I feel very strongly that young people in America and around the world need to know who Cole Porter is, who Copland and Gershwin are. To get this kind of music out there. Where are they going to hear it? On TV? There's no *Ed Sullivan Show*; they don't hear it on the radio. The whole experience of a live orchestra is one of the greatest experiences you can have in this world. I want it to be seen and heard by as many families as possible—for it to be a part of their lives. ■

SHELDON HARNICK

One of this country's most prolific lyricists, Mr. Harnick is best known for his collaborations with composer Jerry Bock for his musicals, *Fiddler on the Roof*, *The Body Beautiful*, *Fiorello!*, which received the Pulitzer Prize for Drama, *Tenderloin*, *She Loves Me*, *The Apple Tree*, and *The Rothschilds*. Mr. Harnick contributed a song to the revue *New Faces of 1952*, his Broadway debut. Besides his work with Jerry Bock, Mr. Harnick has worked with Joe Raposo on the musical *A Wonderful Life*; with Richard Rodgers on *Rex*; and with Arnold Black on *A Phantom Tollbooth*. He provided an English translation for Michel Legrand's *Umbrellas of Cherbourg*; the librettos for several operas with composer Jack Beeson: *Captain Jinks of the Horse Marines*, *Cyrano*, and *Dr. Heidegger's Experiment*; the librettos for two operas with Henry Mollicone: *Coyote Tales* and *Lady Bird*; and the book, lyrics, and music for the musicals, *Dragons* and *Malpractice Makes Perfect*. His work for television and film ranges from songs for the HBO animated film, *The Tale of Peter Rabbit* with music by Stephen Lawrence, to lyrics for the opening number of the 1988 Academy Awards telecast. He wrote the theme songs for two films, both with music by Cy Coleman: *The Heartbreak Kid* and *Blame It on Rio*. Mr. Harnick has won three Tony Awards. His many other honors include: The Johnny Mercer Award presented by the Songwriters Hall of Fame; the Marc Blitzstein Memorial; being honored at the Annual William Inge Theatre Festival; and Mr. Harnick and Jerry Bock were presented with the York Theatre Company's Oscar Hammerstein Award.

Q What first drew you into the theater?
I'm from Chicago and my uncle was involved in The Mummers. I'd see the plays he'd perform in; it was very exciting. In school I had hoped to be a violinist. I was also a good sight-reader so I was invited to play for various Gilbert and Sullivan productions. I was dazzled by the virtuosity of the patter songs in *Pirates of Penzance*. So I began writing parodies, and that's when it all began. I really didn't go to the theatre until I was in the Army. As a going-away present, I was given tickets to a touring Broadway play.

In the Army I wrote songs, performing them at various bases. After seeing *Finian's Rainbow* by Yip Harburg on Broadway, I thought, "If I could do what Yip Harburg does, that would be a career worth pursuing."

Q What was your experience from the success of *New Faces of '52*?
First of all, I met other writers like Ronny Graham and Mel Brooks. Second, it confirmed I had a future in the business. I wrote a song for Alice Ghostley, and when she stopped the show singing it, I wept. It was an important validation for me.

Q What are the chief qualities a lyricist must have?
A good sense of rhythm, a love for words and sound. He or she doesn't have to be a trained musician. Mostly it's a feeling for words, and how they relate to music. You have to care for that relationship.

Q As a new show of yours gets closer to opening, have you learned to deal with the pressure?
I haven't; I get very anxious. I talked with Richard Kiley and he told me that after he had opened in *Man of La Mancha*, he was at a party and heard a dreadful review, so he stopped reading

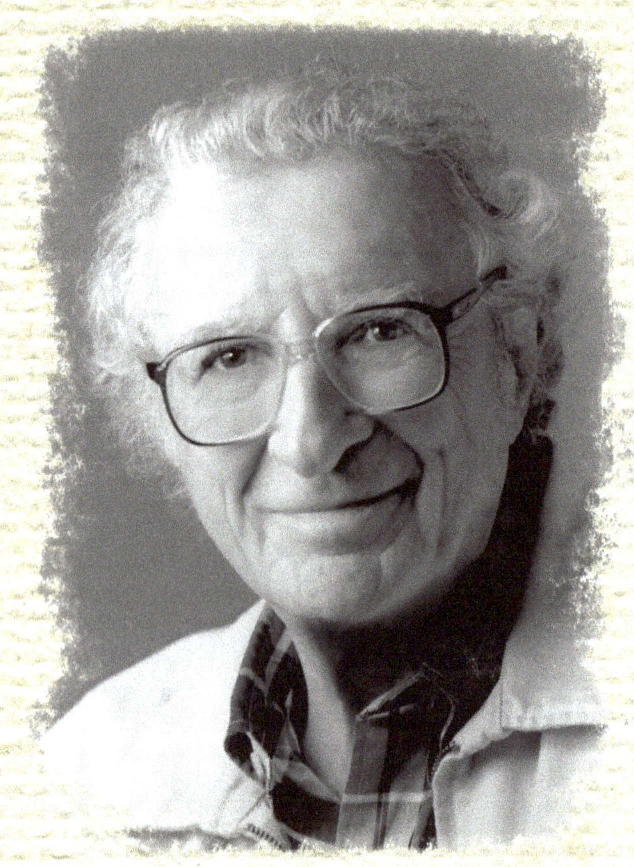

reviews. I now ask my wife. I'm very thin-skinned.

Q You had the opportunity of collaborating with Richard Rodgers—
Yes, on *Rex*. At that point, he had been assailed by serious illnesses and while we were in pre-production, he had his larynx removed. But his fight to continue working made me love and respect him even more. Whatever happened to him, he just accepted it and moved forward. He was a very strict editor. I discovered he had to have all the lyrics first which was a challenge for me. I had to make sure they had rhythmic variety.

Before our first performance in Wilmington, we were optimistic. Nicol Williamson was the lead, playing Henry VIII, but when he came offstage, he said, "They hate me." That wasn't a good sign.

Sherman Yellen and I have thoroughly revised *Rex*. The new version was presented at The York Theatre and it went extremely well. There was no budget, but it was great fun.

Q How did *Fiddler on the Roof* occur?
Somebody loaned me a novel by Sholem Aleichem about a Yiddish theatrical troupe, thinking it might make a great musical. Jerry Bock and I read it and showed it to Joe Stein. He realized it was too big, too sprawling. So we looked for other works by Sholem Aleichem, and found "Tevye's Daughter." We felt that what Sholom Aleichem had written was universal, and that's the way we approached the show.

Q What were some of the greatest lessons you've learned?
From watching Jerome Robbins I learned how dance can sometimes tell more than the words. We had a four-minute song for Perchik and Hodel that worked quite well. But Robbins said, "I want to try something." He created a little dance for them and accomplished in thirty seconds what we were trying to say in four minutes of singing. And I learned how ruthlessly objective one has to be.

Robbins had this ten-minute ballet with Tevye going blindly throughout the town after his daughter has married out of the faith. The audience was baffled. He trimmed and trimmed, and when he finally got it down to two minutes it worked. He was very much like George Abbott in that he did everything he could to keep the storyline clear and swift.

Q Who are your inspirations?
Stephen Sondheim is an inspiration to me for three reasons: his formidable gifts, his integrity, and the shows he chooses to do. They're all an attempt to say something important. Yip Harburg was one of my heroes; he was a mentor for me. Then there are individuals like Gandhi and Harold Clurman—what they stood for.

I didn't know that much about Fiorello La Guardia until we did a show about him. I learned to respect his integrity and his drive. He could be a ruthless man, but it was all in the interest of helping people.

Q How do you remain optimistic when there're so many ups and downs?
I think I've been blessed with an optimistic temperament. Intellectually, I may be pessimistic but I'll find myself whistling. What keeps me going is that I love the theater and I love to write lyrics for it. It's all about, "How do I know what I think until I hear what I say?" That's how I remain cheerful. ■

Sheldon Harnick photo: courtesy of the artist

CHARLES STROUSE

One of America's most successful musical theater composers, his music has been recorded by Barbra Streisand, Frank Sinatra, Tony Bennett, Bobby Darin, Harry Connick, Jr., Jay-Z, Louis Armstrong, Nina Simone, and Duke Ellington and his Orchestra. He has received Tony Awards,two Emmy Awards, his cast recordings have earned him two Grammy Awards. Mr. Strouse has written scores for over thirty stage musicals, fourteen for Broadway, including *Annie*, starring Andrea McArdle; *Bye Bye Birdie*, with Lee Adams, starring Dick Van Dyke and Chita Rivera; *Applause*, starring Lauren Bacall; *Annie*, with lyricist Martin Charnin and librettist Thomas Meehan; *Golden Boy*, an adaptation of Clifford Odets play, starring Sammy Davis Jr.; *Charlie and Algernon*; *Rags*, with Stephen Schwartz and Joseph Stein; *Nick and Nora* with Richard Maltby, Jr. and Arthur Laurents; *All American*, with a book by Mel Brooks, starring Ray Bolger, directed by Joshua Logan; *It's A Bird... It's A Plane... It's Superman*, produced and directed by Harold Prince; *I and Albert*; *A Broadway Musical*; *Bring Back Birdie*; *Dance a Little Closer*, with Alan Jay Lerner, a musical adapted from Paddy Chayefsky's film *Marty*; *The Night They Raided Minsky's*; and an adaptation of Theodore Dreiser's *An American Tragedy*. Mr. Strouse wrote both the music and lyrics for Off Broadway's *Mayor*, and with Martin Charnin created *Annie Warbucks*. His film scores include *Bonnie and Clyde*, *There Was a Crooked Man* with Henry Fonda and Kirk Douglas, *The Night They Raided Minsky's*, *Just Tell Me What You Want*, and *All Dogs Go to Heaven*. His film and television musicals include *Bye Bye Birdie*, with Jason Alexander, Vanessa Williams, and Tyne Daly; *Annie*, directed by John Houston, starring Carol Burnett, Albert Finney, and Bernadette Peters; *Alice in Wonderland*; *Applause*; and *It's a Bird... It's a Plane... It's Superman*. His song, "Those Were the Days," launched over 200 episodes of *All in the Family*. Mr. Strouse wrote the music, book, and lyrics for *Nightingale*, an opera performed in London with a cast that included Sarah Brightman. Mr. Strouse wrote *Concerto America* to commemorate 9/11, which received its world premiere from the Boston Pops Orchestra. His anthem, "On This Day," written for the White House Commission on Remembrance, was performed on Memorial Day, May 26, 2003, in front of the Iwo Jima Memorial in Arlington, Virginia. He has been inducted to the Songwriters Hall of Fame and the Theatre Hall of Fame.

Q What did it mean to you being inducted into the Theatre Hall of Fame?
For most of us, there's that shiny city—creative success. And on the way it feels like you're having all these stones thrown at you. For example, when you see those people at a marathon and along the way they're holding out cups of water for the runners, receiving awards like the Tony, they're like getting those cups of water. I've been fortunate to have had my share. Receiving that honor was like getting a nice glass of egg cream soda. It's wonderful being connected to all those already in the Theatre Hall of Fame.

Q When did you discover your path led in this direction?
I showed an aptitude for music early, so when I was fifteen I went to a musical conservatory, the Eastern School of Music. When I began composing music for shows I thought how different it was and what fun. I also had wonderful private teachers, Nadia Boulanger and Darius Milhaud. I studied with Aaron Copland for three years.

Q I see you have a program on your wall for *Shoestring Revue* with George Grizzard.
That was one of my first attempts with Lee Adams, on the road to musical theater, almost fifty years ago, along with *A Pound in Your Pocket*.

Q What led you to want to create the ASCAP Musical Theatre Workshop?
Everybody I knew went to the BMI Lehman Engels Workshop. As a member of ASCAP, I thought ASCAP ought to have its own workshop. I met with the Board, broached the idea, and they gave me permission to begin it. It's became quite popular. I directed it for about fifteen years.

Q How would you describe how you've composed with some of the theater's greatest lyricists?
It's been easy and tough. It's like a marriage—the viscidities of the getting on with another person. You have to want to bring out the best in each other and they have to want to do the same for you. I've been very fortunate to have worked with some of the best. I'm a very good collaborator. I love the process.

Q One of your musicals, *Golden Boy*, came from Clifford Odets' powerful play.
I spent about two and half years with Clifford at his home in Los Angeles; he didn't like to fly. When I read Harold Clurman's book, *The Fervent Years*, it was exciting for me. I also felt Clifford was like the character he had written in his play, *The Country Girl*—a left-wing writer who has a feel for money in his pocket.

When I knew Clifford, he'd tell me about flying in Frank Sinatra's plane, his relationships with people like Marilyn Monroe and Danny Kaye. He was a total contradiction. He had this "fire" in him against injustice, but with a bug of wanting to be loved by people.

When I worked on the musical, I was highly connected to Clifford's vision of his play as well as his ideas of racial balance. But that was also one of the right/wrong things with the musical. That whole Group Theatre period fascinates me. It sliced right through a juicy period of American political thought. The Group Theatre had this great ambition of "theater for the people."

Q I understand that when you were originally told the idea of making Annie Warbucks into a musical, you thought it was a terrible idea. But you changed your mind.
I've learned to not always act on it. I did feel turning Annie Warbucks into a musical was a stupid

idea, but I hadn't seen it theatrically in my mind yet. Sometimes thinking logically or gut reactions can be wrong. Some of the ideas that have given me the most fame, I first thought weren't terrific ideas; *Annie* being an outstanding example.

I love to write, but I can't just sit down and write; I need a commission. I thought *Golden Boy* was a wonderful idea, and what greater story is there than *All About Eve*, which became *Applause*? With *Bye, Bye Birdie*, we were all young men, and I had a feel for rock & roll. But I'm not a rock & roller, I just was able to do it. I feel *Rags* was one of my best scores, and I wanted to do something with undertones. *I and Albert* was another of my best scores, although the English didn't go for it. All I know is that I just love to write notes.

Q Does knowing you're writing for a particular performer, like Sammy Davis, Jr. or Lauren Bacall, influence how you write?

We all knew Sammy Davis, Jr. would star in *Golden Boy*, and he was one of the biggest performers in the world. So yes, it did.

By the time Bacall joined *Applause*, we had finished most of the score, but we hadn't finished the book yet. You just wanted her to look good, and if she looked good, you knew you would, too. She was very musical, very challenging and wonderful.

Q Have you thought about what it means being connected to the tradition and history of musical theater?

I have thought about it—the idea of the connection to certain composers whom I admire. Of having had teachers like Aaron Copland, and Leonard Bernstein. Harold Arlen was a good friend to me. When I started out, I even wrote a nightclub show for George White; it was my first job. As for composers knowing they're forging a new path, they're rare. Maybe Wagner did, and Beethoven, and Mozart. Gershwin may have. In the theatre, for actors, it's probably even more ephemeral.

Q How do you maintain your open and positive enthusiasm for what you do?

You can either despair or be cheerful about life. It's a human condition. My family has given me great support. I've despaired, gone through everything. Ultimately, it's thinking about others, although I know I can't control them. But the next day, I go back to what I thought was bad and find a seed in it for something better. ■

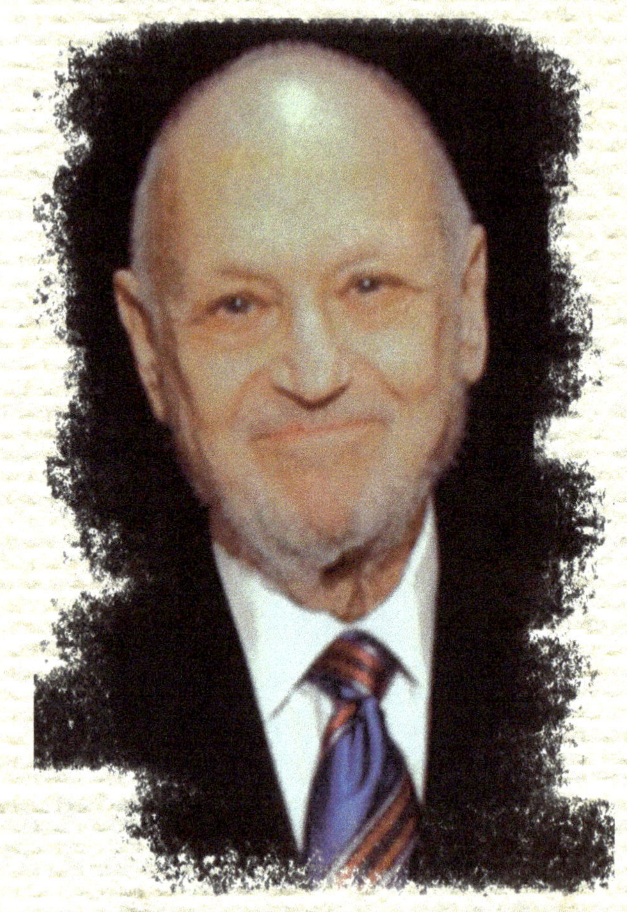

Charles Strouse photo, courtesy of the artist

JEANINE TESORI

Ms. Tesori won the Tony Award for Best Original Score with Lisa Kron for the musical, *Fun Home*, on Broadway. She also wrote the Tony Award nominated scores for *Twelfth Night* at Lincoln Center, *Thoroughly Modern Millie* with lyrics by Dick Scanlan, *Caroline, or Change* with lyrics by Tony Kushner, *Shrek The Musical* with lyrics by David Lindsay-Abaire. The production of *Caroline, or Change* at the National Theatre in London received the Olivier Award for Best New Musical. Her 1997 Off-Broadway musical, *Violet* with lyrics by Brian Crawley opened on Broadway in 2014 and garnered four Tony nominations, including Best Musical Revival. Ms. Tesori's operas include *A Blizzard on Marblehead Neck* with a libretto by Tony Kushner performed at Glimmerglass, *The Lion, The Unicorn, and Me* with libretto by J. D. McClatchy, performed at Washington D.C.'s Kennedy Center. Her music for plays includes *Mother Courage* directed George C. Wolfe, with Meryl Streep and Kevin Kline, *A Free Man of Color* directed by George C. Wolfe at Lincoln Center Theater, and *Romeo and Juliet*. Ms. Tesori wrote songs for *The Emperor's New Groove 2: Kronk's New Groove*, *Wrestling with Angels*, a 2006 documentary about Tony Kushner, *Shrek the Third*, and three animated Disney DVDs: *Mulan II*, *Lilo and Stitch II*, *The Little Mermaid: Ariel's Beginning*. Her film scores include *Nights in Rodanthe*, and *Every Day You're Not You*. She was cited by ASCAP as the first female composer to have two new musicals running concurrently on Broadway. Ms. Tesori is the founding artistic director of *Encores! Off-Center* at New York City Center, and a lecturer in music at Yale University. She is the proud parent of Siena Rafter, a senior at LaGuardia High School for the Arts.

Q What do you love the most about creating a new show?

I love "putting the concrete" in with the abstract; creating the architecture to a show. I have to figure out what that is. I need to always have the "beginners mind." No matter how good you are, you have to remember that *this* show has never been done by *you*. It's like a giant crossword puzzle, and I have to figure what works. That's part of the mystery, and the joy.

Q *Fun Home* is a thoroughly amazing experience. How were you first introduced to the Alison Bechdel's book? What made it most exciting and challenging in the development process working with Lisa Kron?

Lisa sent me the book and asked if I would be interested in writing the music. When we met, I said: "I have no idea how this can be a musical." She thought I was turning it down, but that was the reason I wanted very much to do it.

Q As you and Lisa Kron worked on *Fun Home*, was the development process challenging?

Once we began working on it, I knew it would have to be about the bridge between the gap of what people want and what the world will give them. There's so much one does in that gap. I knew the show would "sing," but I didn't what form it would take. The actual book is like a labyrinth. Alison builds the story in her novel like a corn maze, there's so many places you jump, its maddening. It was definitely challenging.

I keep learning not every story has to fit in a classic mode. The show will eventually tell you how it should be told. "The form," Sondheim said, "is dictated by the context."

Fun Home is non-linear; things can happen at any time. She can be eight years old or jump to forty. It was like grabbing a slippery fish. It came from a lot of experimenting. When we finally saw what we were doing, it came into place. Everything led to the car ride. The narrator becomes involved in the narrative.

Q How did the performers who included Beth Malone, Michael Cerveris, Judy Kuhn and Sydney Lucas, enrich the musical?

The great thing about Michael (Cerveris) and Judy (Kuhn) is that they do so much new work, they ask questions during the process as we're putting it together. Michael understood when he signed up, that the part wasn't completed. That can be very difficult for a performer. I knew in my heart that the part wasn't complete so we played some of it for him.

I needed it to be clear in the show that Bruce (the father) is a tragic figure, not a villain. If you don't write him responsibly, he can be reduced to something unsavory, terrifying. In denying who he is and who he was, tragedy happens. Everywhere today tragedy can become a legacy. A parent who commits suicide leaves a trail of tears.

Q I understand you began early playing the piano, but were on your way to a career in medicine.

I began playing the piano at age three, and had formal training at about six years old. I took lessons until I was fourteen, then I quit. My mother was a nurse, and my father was a doctor; his office was connected to our home. I loved science, and still do. Musicals actually have a lot of science in them.

When I actually began seeing a lot of theater and coaching at a kids' theater camp in the Catskills, I went into music. After a year and half working as a pianist and an arranger, I had those moments when I thought: "I can do this." I felt happy but I didn't know you could make a living doing it.

Q Were there specific writers that inspired you as you developed your craft?

Well, Sondheim is number one. He's a great composer and playwright. I studied him and still do. I was classically trained, and then went on to play a ton of pop and R&B on a lot of albums when I was working in Nashville for ten years with my mentor. My training was from all over the place; I studied with some wonderful people. I think my ear is very non-judgmental. How I was trained is very helpful for what I do. I love Stravinsky and Sondheim. Stephen Schwartz who wrote *Godspell* and *Pippin* was one of the first to put piano-based grooves in a Broadway show and I can still play most of them. I started doing summer stock shows, then Gypsy, *Secret Garden* and *Tommy*.

Q Then you had to write *Violet*?
I left the city for ten months in order to stop working as a music director. It was hard to say "no" to work. You're tempted to say "yes" to every gig. Suddenly I was asking myself at twenty-eight, twenty-nine years old: "What do I do now?" It was very hard to "escape to a lighthouse," but I went away to see if I was going to be able to use unstructured time in the rehearsal room. I had to create my own syllabus, to not rely on anyone's past work. And I needed a deadline so I made one for myself.

Q How have you learned to handle what critics say about your work—and your own "inner critic?"
I think I learned a lot from *Violet*. One review sank it. I was in bed for three days; I was devastated. It changed me. Everything was riding on that one show, and I saw what that did to me. I swore I'd never let that happen again. I swore I'd always have other things in my life, another show, a life, the passion of activism and the love of friends and family.

Q Did you particularly feel you were tapping into a deep well inside your creativity?
I think it started with *Twelfth Night*, and definitely with *Violet*. It became: How to use time to write quickly. In musical theater, you have a lot of lead-up time and then you have only three weeks. You have to be a marathon runner and a sprinter.

Q You've had some wonderful collaborators, including with Lisa Kron, Dick Scanlan on *Thoroughly Modern Millie*, Tony Kushner on *Caroline or Change?*, and I imagine it was also a bit challenging with your approach on *Shrek* with David Lindsey-Abaire.

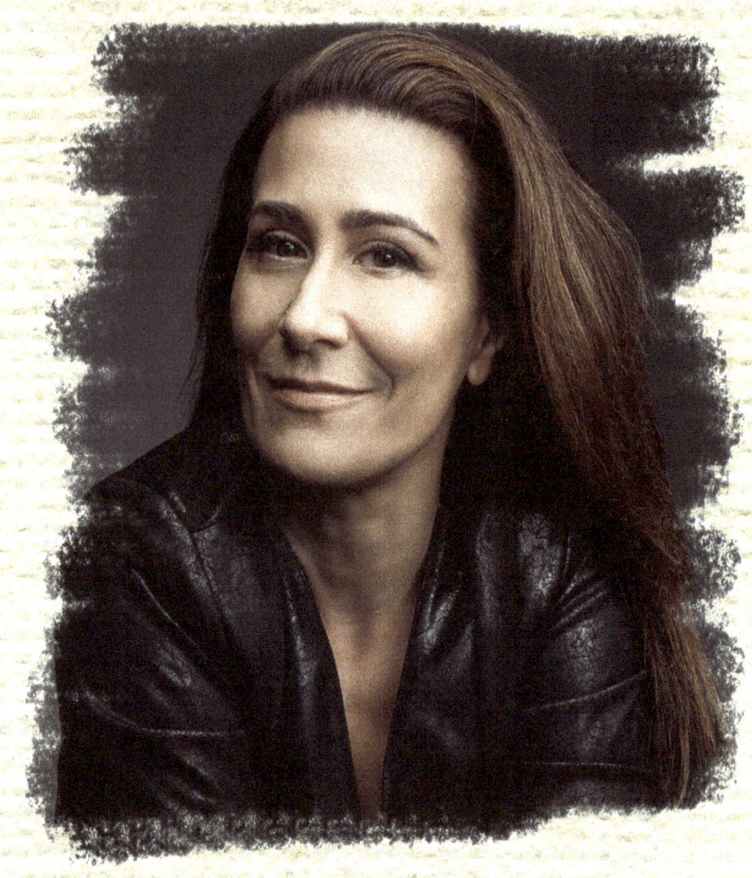

Jeanine Tesori photo: Rodolfo Martinez

Every collaboration reminds why I hate to work alone. You hopefully impress on each other to be better. I like working with a lot of different writers. I'm working with David on our next show and I'm still nervous, tackling and grappling with it.

When David and I wrote *Shrek*, we took on a great hero story, a quest story but the hardest thing was this: Shrek doesn't want anything. Or at least he doesn't *think* he wants anything. His essence was that of a prince, but his identity was that of an ogre, an ogre who is perfectly happy being alone. But we know that's a lie, and we travel with him as he finds out the truth, and his true love.

What also made it challenging was we were writing a story that everyone in the audience already knew, so you have to manage their expectations. Yet, we had a really good time working on the show.

Q You must also get an enormous amount of satisfaction sharing what you've learned so far leading the *Encores! musical theater series Off-Center*—
A hundred and fifty percent! I love what I do more than I ever. Being at City Center, championing new work, being an advocate for other people's work, mentoring and teaching is so meaningful. Students always have a lot of questions and there is so much more that is quantitative... pitch, harmony, tension, but then there's the qualitative parts. It's up for grabs how someone sees the world, and that's the complete joy of it! ■

MELVIN VAN PEEBLES

Mr. Van Peebles is a composer, actor, director, screenwriter, and playwright. He wrote the musical book and score for *Ain't Supposed to Die a Natural Death* on Broadway. His albums include "Brer Soul," "As Serious as a Heart Attack," "What the...You Mean I Can't Sing?", and "Ghetto Gothic." As a director, his films include *Pickup Men for Herrick, La Permission, Sunlight, Don't Play Us Cheap, Identity Crisis, Gang in Blue, Vroom Vroom Vrooom, Bellyful, Watermelon Man, Powder Ridge Rock Festival, Confessions or Ode of an Ex-Dufas Mother*, and *Sweet Sweetback's Baadassss Song*. His son, Mario van Peebles's film, *Baadasssss!* tells the story behind his father's film. As an actor, his appearances include *O.C. and Stiggs; Jaws, the Revenge; Sonny Spoon; Terminal Velocity; Posse*, based on his novel, *Panther*; as a screenwriter, actor and producer, *The Shining*, and *Melvin van Peebles' Classified X*. Mr. Van Peebles is the subject of a documentary, *How to Eat Your Watermelon in White Company...and Enjoy It*. He made a double album with Madlib. He also appeared in *Philip Glass: Einstein in Concert* at Carnegie Hall.

Q How did it all start for you?

I had a spatial knack. That allowed me to go to school with a scholarship, so I took it. I come from a very non-elitist background; I never thought about being an artist. I didn't know what I was going to be at that time. I knew I was going in the military; the draft was on. I had plenty of time to think and I gravitated to what I could do easily. Later on I did things that were more difficult.

I was in the Strategic Command for three and a half years, based in Riverside, California and in those days, we did globetrotting missions going up the coast to Japan, Hawaii, then skirt the coast of Russia, staying 300 miles off the coast in international waters, in case they launched an attack. Then I'd head home; I had mid-air fueling. This was at the end of the Korean War. I was in the service from 1953 to '56.

Q Were you thinking about making your life in the arts around that point?

I was just thinking about getting out alive. Once I did, I moved to Mexico. In Mexico, I supplemented my income with portrait painting. Mario, my older son, was born in Mexico. People think he's Italian but he was born in Mexico. Then I moved to San Francisco.

Once I was there, I thought the greatest job to do was to work on the cable cars in San Francisco, so I did. And as I was driving my cable car, people were always getting on, but there wasn't anything to buy except for a little bronze replica of a cable car. I said "Hmm..." Now I didn't know the

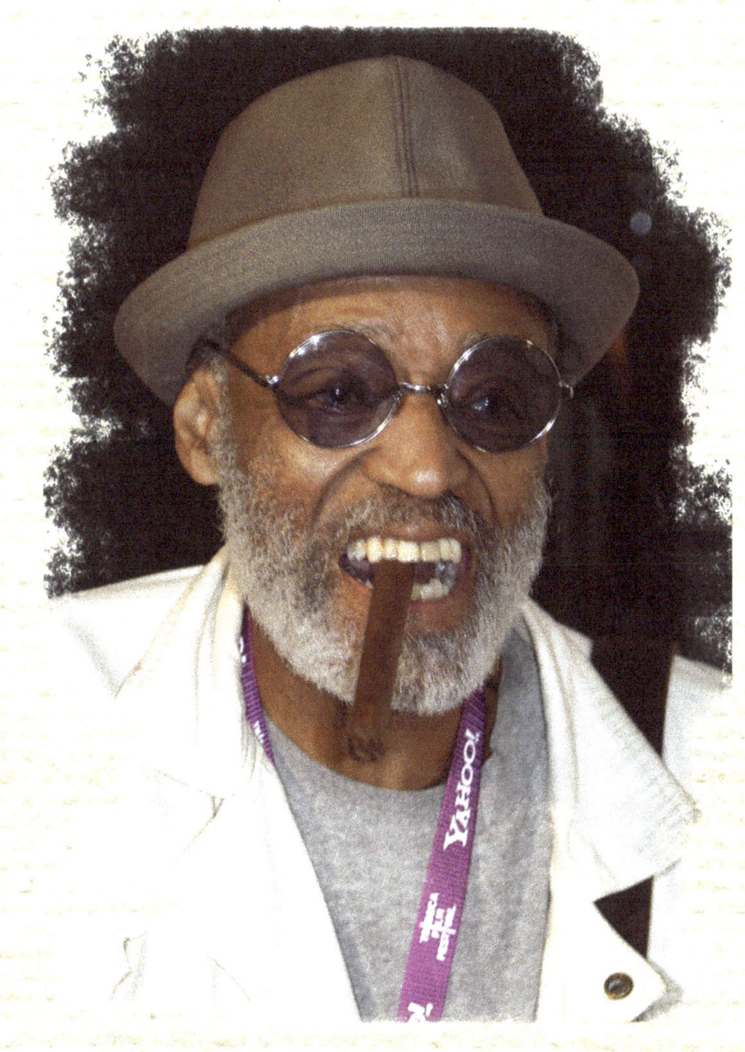

Melvin Van Peebles photo: David Shankbone

genre of the time, but I recognized a market opportunity.

So I wrote a little book about the life of a grip man, and I thought people would like pictures so I found a photographer, took pictures, and one day the book got reviewed. One day I get on my cable car and a fellow on board told me how much he loved it. He told me, "Your book is just like a movie." And that's how my first movie in 1958, *Three Pickup Men from Herrick*, came about.

Q How did you develop your take on life?

For me, I'm not on introspective terms with myself; I take what life tells me. If I got two or three days to put together a "short" film, tie it all together, then that's what it's about. There's an expression, "If it ain't broke, don't fix it." What do I know? I like what I like.

When I started making movies out in San Francisco, a guy introduced himself and he said: "I hear you're working on a movie. I want to welcome you to the Bay Area Film Society. And he started asking me all these questions about filmmakers. "Who do you like? Kurosawa? Orson Welles? I didn't know any of them. I had never seen *Potemkin*, *Citizen Kane*, or *Seventh Samurai* yet.

Q You've also created a lot of music which seems to be popping up all over these days.

Yeah, someone spoke about a song of mine that Grace Jones is doing called "Apple Stretchy." That song came about because I saw some winos fighting in Union Square and it all came into my head. When people quite honestly ask, "Well, what's it like?" I say, "It's not like anything else." You have to make it like that. Some hip hop guy comes and tells me we're using some of your music—well, that's okay with me.

Q How would you describe your attitude towards creating each day?

I'd have to quote Edward G. Robinson's character, Johnny Rocco, in the movie, *Key Largo*. Bogart said to him, "You have everything, what else do you want?" And Rocco tells him, "I'll tell you what I want—more! Yeah that's right, I want more!" I feel the same way. I'm not needy, I'm greedy. That's what I love about life! Bring it on! More! Keep moving! Keep moving! ■

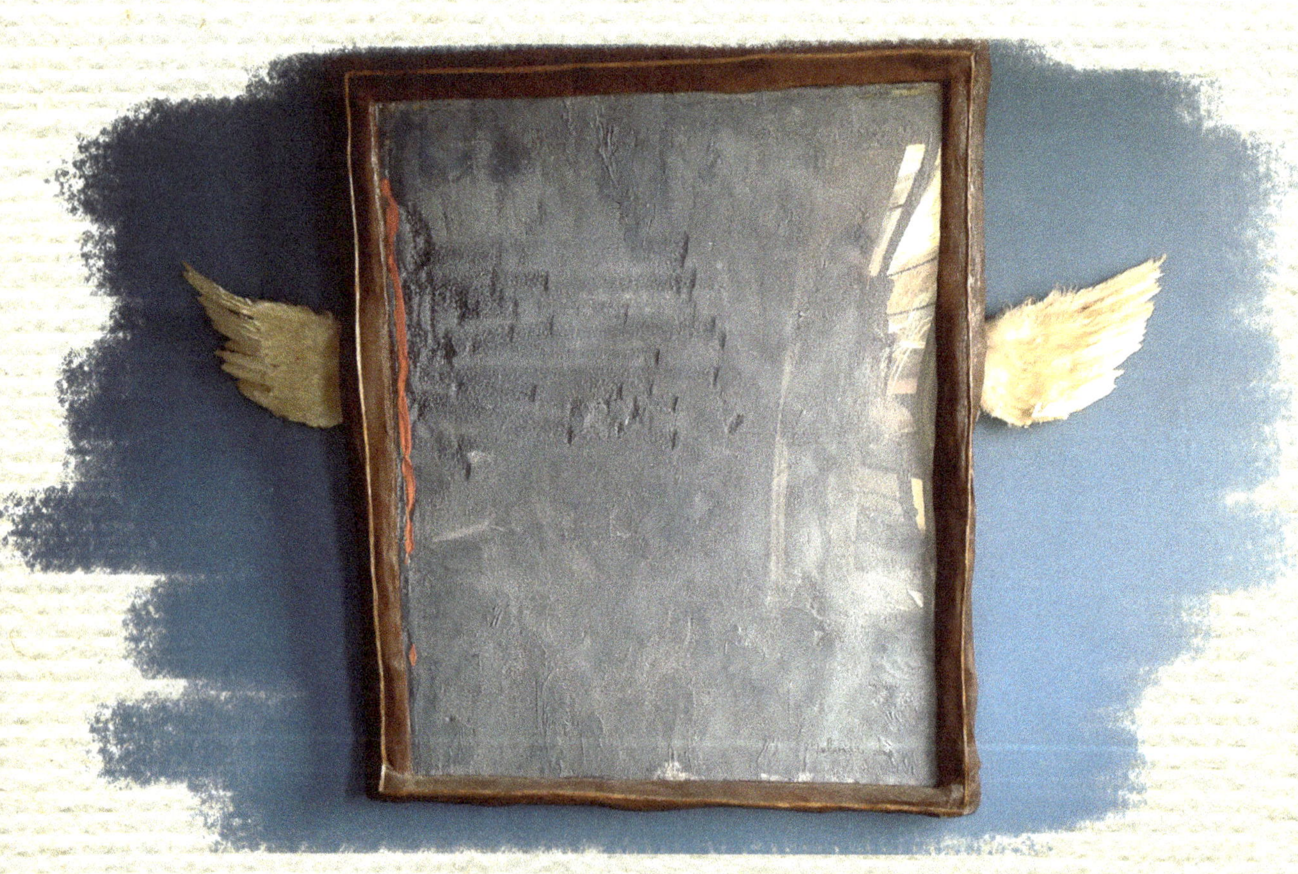

artwork: "Ex-Voto Monochrome (A Ghetto Mother's Prayer)" by Melvin van Peebles, courtesy of the artist

DIRECTORS

EUGENIO BARBA

Mr. Barba is a Theater Director, author, and founder of Odon Theatre in 1964, and the International School of Theatre Anthropology, located in Holstebro, Denmark. He has directed more than seventy-five productions with Odin Teatret and the Theatrum Mundi Ensemble, some of which have required up to two years of preparation, and include *Ornitofilene*, *Ferai*, *Min Fars Hus*, *Brecht's Ashes*, *The Gospel According to Oxyrhincus*, *Talabot*, *Itsi Bitsi*, *Kaosmos*, *Mythos*, *Salt*, *Great Cities under the Moon*, *Andersen's Dream*, *Ur-Hamlet*, *The Marriage of Medea*, *The Chronic Lie*, and *Don Giovanni all'Inferno* in collaboration with Ensemble Midtvest. Since 1974, Mr. Barba and Odin Teatret have devised their own way of being present in a social context through the practice of theatre barter, an exchange through performance with a community. His books include *Grotowski In Search of a Lost Theatre*, *The Paper Canoe*, *Theatre: Solitude, Craft, Revolt*, *Land of Ashes and Diamonds: My Apprenticeship in Poland, followed by 26 letters from Jerzy Grotowski to Eugenio Barba*, and in collaboration with Nicola Savarese, *The Secret Art of the Performer* and *A Dictionary of Theatre Anthropology*. Mr. Barba is the recipient of the Danish Academy Award, Mexican Theatre Critics' Prize, Pirandello International Prize, and The International Association of Theatre Critics' Thalia Prize.

Q What does the beginning of a new millennium mean to you?

For many people, this millennium is something important, but I feel the thirty-five years of Odin Teatret's existence is just pushing me forwards. As we move in this direction, it will continue to give meaning to all our beginnings.

Q You joined Jerzy Grotowski in 1961, as his assistant, and then became instrumental in raising the world's consciousness of Grotowski's amazing work in Poland. What can we learn about Grotowski's work, his teachings, and his influence today?

Here is the example of a theater artist who built a theater, which became a phenomenon. Grotowski is an example of a constructor. In such a country like Poland, in order to evade the norms of socialism, it was his adherence, his ideals, and how he worked with his actors for it to become an ensemble, which is inexorable. This is what we can learn.

Q Why does the theater continue to remain necessary for us?

A theater is a social situation in which human beings gather to face questions on western civilization.

Q In the play, *Mythos*, which I saw at La MaMa, the questions were asked: What is the meaning of cruelty? Why is Oedipus punished?

The reason for theater is to ask questions. Theater gives us the possibilities to reflect on our own experiences, to reflect upon our own lack, on the illusion of ideas.

Q The Odin Teatret, along with Grotowski's Laboratory Theater, are considered among the most important influences in the modern European group theater movement. Your exploration into your training can be read in your book, *Theatre-Solitude-Craft-Revolt*. The actor is at the center of Odin Teatret's work. How much has the study of acting changed over time?

Enormously. The art of acting changed at the beginning of the 20th Century with Stanislavsky, with Meyerhold. A new approach developed dealing with a new set of rules, in regards to characterization. The old was washed away, and we started having actors be creative.

The twentieth century was the century of theater schools. The skills of actors have had to adapt to new mediums: film, television, so the actor's work based on one's self became narrower. When one thinks of the great actors in the past, with their voice alone they could control the spectator.

The eternal dilemma remains: How to teach without teaching? How to discover one's own rules without imposing a general rule?

If you have the need to be an artist, you will do whatever it takes, even out of your own pocket, if it's what you need to do. Expect indifference. Only if you can manage to gather those around you, those who have the same affinity, then you can do this work. This was the beginning of us—of Odin Teatret—a common horizon. This was very important for us to recognize. ■

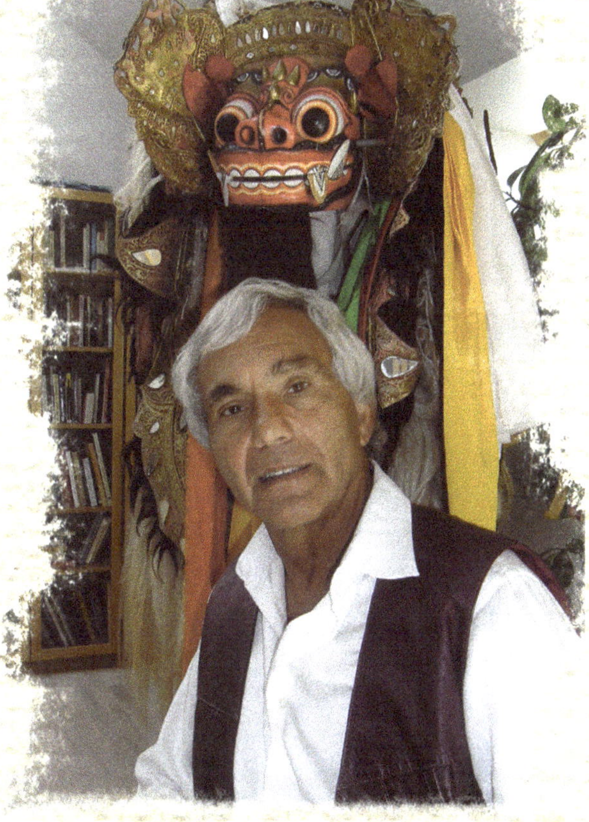

Eugenio Barba photo: Rina Skeel

ANNE BOGART

Ms. Bogart is the Co-Artistic Director of SITI Company, which she founded with Japanese director Tadashi Suzuki in 1992. She is the recipient of a Doris Duke Artist Grant, a USA Fellowship, a Rockefeller Fellowship, and a Guggenheim Fellowship. SITI's works include *Persians, Steel Hammer, Café Variations, Trojan Women, American Document, Antigone, Freshwater Under Construction, Who Do You Think You Are, Radio Macbeth, Hotel Cassiopeia, Death and the Ploughman, La Dispute, bobrauschenbergamerica, Room, War of the Worlds, Cabin Pressure, The Radio Play, Alice's Adventures, Culture of Desire, Bob, Small Lives/Big Dreams, The Medium*, Noel Coward's *Hay Fever* and *Private Lives*, August Strindberg's *Miss Julie*, and Charles Mee's *Orestes*. Operas include *Norma, Carmen, I Capuleti e i Montecchi, Nicholas and Alexandra* at the Los Angeles Opera; *Marina: A Captive Spirit* at American Opera Projects; and *Lilith and Seven Deadly Sins* at New York City Opera. Ms. Bogart is the author of five books: *A Director Prepares, The Viewpoints Book, And Then, You Act, Conversations with Anne*, and *What's the Story*.

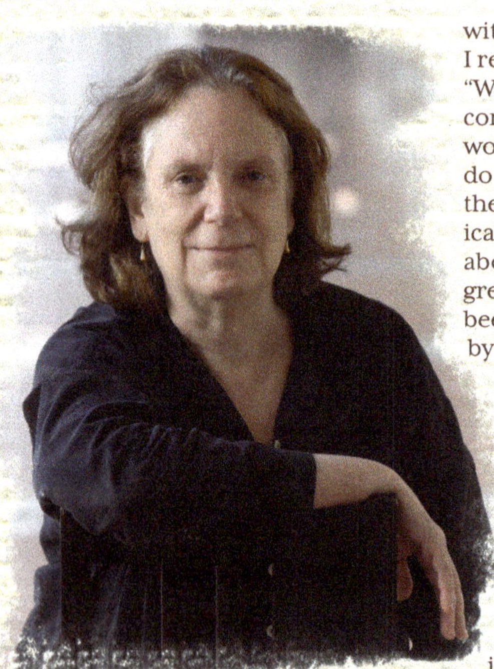

Anne Bogart photo: courtesy of the artist

Q After an amazing century of progress and evolution, where do we go from here?

Because of media's impact, which has swallowed up the actor, the stage is going to have to adapt. The actor will have to become more humane, more poetic, television has stolen the obstacle; like a horse galloping towards a raised barrier, the jumps for the actor have become too low.

Actors want to take large leaps, to answer the big questions. We see the reaction to our work at SITI. So many people want to take our classes because they want to use their voices, their emotions, their bodies totally to attempt extraordinary human activities.

Q How did the idea originate to create your own company?

It came out of conversation I had with Ariane Mnouchkine. I remember asking her, "What about creating a company to do this kind of work?" She said, "You can't do something like that there," (referring to America); but the more I thought about it, I realized every great thing that's ever been done has been done by a company, from the Moscow Art Theatre to the Group Theatre to the Living Theatre, to The Open Theatre. It's what I tried doing at Trinity Rep.

Q And that's how the SITI company came about?

It was Tadashi Suzuki's idea. He came to me with the idea of a fellowship. He said, "I'll help you for five years," and so we spent half our summers in Japan. Finally, we made our home in Saratoga Springs, New York. Once we began performing in New York City, we realized it could be a reality to also have a home in the city.

Q Can we recognize a certain evolution in the course of actor training and performance through the course of the twentieth century?

I feel no matter how chaotic it is, there has been a shift of interest. We see it shifting from what we call "the disease of Freud": the misunderstandings of Stanislavsky's System of Acting. I gain a lot from looking at his late discoveries. You have to realize he changed with his times.

The danger is becoming "set," being too dogmatic in any one theory. I've had students with viewpoints, who have come for solutions. They say, "This is it." I say it's a process. You look at it and make it work for you now.

Q How did the concept of your production of *A Streetcar Named Desire* come about?

I was invited to stage a production for the international branch of Theatre Artists but when it didn't work out, there were a lot of funds remaining and they asked me, "What would you like to do?" I told them, "I'd like to do *Streetcar*." So with a large group of actors who continued on, we began to work on the play. I always wondered, "How do you deal with Marlon Brando? How do you deal with all that baggage and history?" I ended up having twelve Blanches, eight Stanleys, four Mitchs and one Stella!

Q What do you consider your relationship to the actor to be?

I really see it like this rocket ship blasting off and someone stays in the control room on the ground—that's me. The actor is like an astronaut out there in space going, "Whoooooah!!" I'm their connection to land, and I try to support their flight.

Q Does the future hold for you a certain special allure?

I don't think about looking forward. I think about and look at the past. When you think about what Heisenberg said, "By standing on the shoulders of the giants, I can see further"; it's never been my intention of being avant-garde or innovative. I gain my greatest inspiration from using the things we've been handed down. ■

JOSEPH CHAIKIN

Mr. Chaikin is the Founder of the Open Theater, one of the most influential experimental theater groups that existed in the United States. In the early 1960s, he performed in the Living Theater's landmark productions including *Man is Man*, and *The Connection*, directed by Julian Beck. Among the fourteen productions of the Open Theatre, those that Mr. Chaikin directed included *The Serpent* and *America Hurrah* by Jean-Claude van Itallie; *The Mutation Show*, for which he received a Drama Desk Award; *Nightwalk*; *Viet Rock*; and *Terminal*, which toured to Iran's Shiraz Arts Festival and prisons in the U.S. and Canada. As an actor, his performances included as Hamm in *Endgame* with Peter Maloney, and *Woyzeck* at The Public Theatre in New York City. Mr. Chaikin, with Sam Shepard, wrote *Tongues* and *Savage/Love*, which he starred in; *The War in Heaven*; and *When the World Was Green*, for the 1996 Olympics. He performed in *Struck Dumb*, which was written by Jean-Claude van Itallie and Mr. Chaikin. Mr. Chaikin's productions as an actor/director included *Electra*, *The Dybbuk*, *The Bald Soprano*, *The Glass Menagerie*, *Medea*, *The Seagull*, and *Happy Days*. In 2000, he co-directed *Shut Eye* with Dan Rothenberg at Pig Iron Theatre Company. Mr. Chaikin received the Vernon Rice Award, six Obie Awards, including one for Lifetime Achievement. His book, *The Presence of the Actor*, was published in 1972. He was the subject of the documentary film, *The Presence of Joseph Chaikin*. Mr. Chaikin died in 2003, and was inducted, posthumously, into the American Theatre Hall of Fame (this interview was conducted in 2000).

Q You began as an actor with Julian Beck and Judith Malina—

Yes, performing with The Living Theatre in *Many Loves*, and *The Connection;* I was so happy to be in *Man is Man* with them. To travel throughout Europe, such an interesting experience.

Around this time, I began to ask myself, "Who am I on stage?" I met with Gordon Rogoff, the drama critic and dramaturg, and he introduced me to Jean-Claude van Itallie—The Open Theatre was born. We went to work—*The Serpent*, a process of six months. Very exciting, such applause for it. It was performed in Europe, London. In the summer of 1968 we returned to New York; even Walter Kerr, drama critic of *The New York Times* loved it, surprisingly.

Q Your next play was *Terminal*—

I wanted to concentrate on dying. We focused on illness, the bed, the dread of dying, what it means to us. James Frazier's idea was, "The animal inside the animal, the man inside the man, is the soul." With Joseph Campbell's mythology, it became a dramatic piece, very difficult. Very successful in performance. Heart problems occurred again. I had rheumatic fever as a kid. We shifted –

Q To *Mutations*—

Working with humor, dealing with human mutations, the experience being torn away from ourselves. If we permit ourselves to be, the more we learn. A window opened to a lot of new ideas. We did political stuff. It became a real effort for me. It felt like I only had one more year to live because of my breathing.

Our last play, *Nightwalk*, was successful enough to bring to Europe. I began working also with Sam Shepard. But I had to have a heart valve changed, a pig valve. This was it. The end, goodbye forever. But...I recovered, very slowly.

Q Then you felt the urge to be on stage again?

Joe Papp said I could do anything. I decided to act in *Woyzeck* at the Public. But again, heart problems, a new valve. I was better again, but endless recovery. I directed *The Dybbuk* at The Public. I was invited to the Habima Theatre in

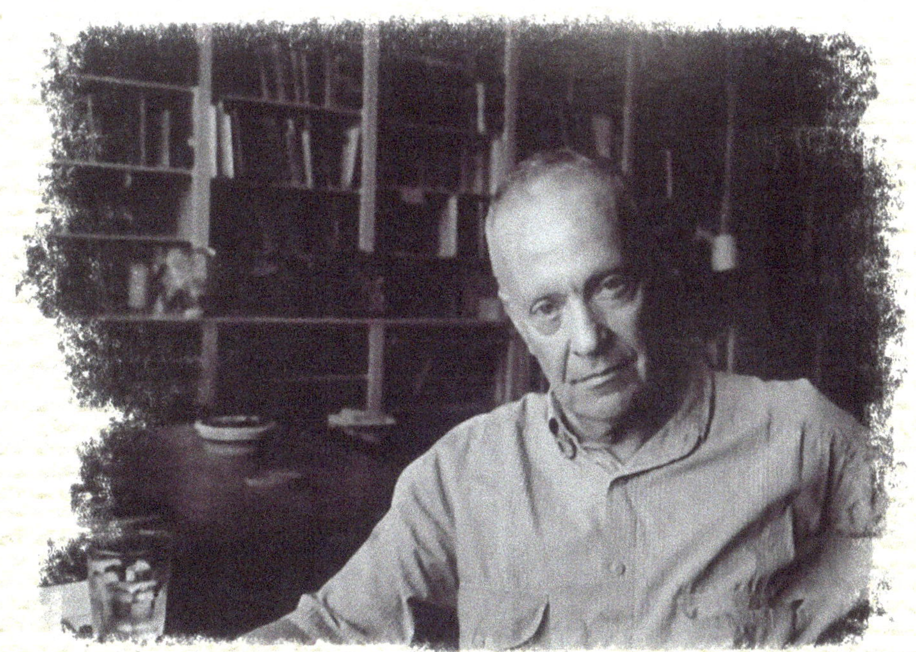

Joseph Chaikin photo credit: Jason Frank Rothenberg

Tel Aviv. I enjoyed directing very much.

I now corresponded with Samuel Beckett; I knew Beckett was in Paris and traveled there. Thrilling to meet him. He was so sweet and kind. We had coffee together. I told him I wanted to do *Texts for Nothing*. He said, "Anything you want to do; you have carte blanche." I had done *Endgame* before.

The valve problem again. Afterwards I couldn't talk at all, I had a stroke. I could only say, "Yes." Speech therapy for six months to learn to say "no." I was very articulate before. New work. Sam Shepard and I wrote *The War in Heaven*; then collaborating with Jean-Claude van Itallie on *Struck Dumb*.

Q You told me you still want to direct *Medea*?

When I was a kid, I heard a recording with Judith Anderson, it still haunts me. I'm crazy about the Greek playwrights. I directed *Electra*; also *Antigone* at The Public.

Q I felt blessed to have studied with you, and be directed by you, working on *Endgame*. Why did you choose O'Neill, Beckett, Shakespeare, and a new playwright, John Belluso for your workshops?

John Belluso was a student with Tony Kushner at NYU. He's in a wheelchair, a wonderful writer. Why Shakespeare? I love his words. I learn from O'Neill. Beckett is a teacher for me. I'm still obsessed by Beckett. After my stroke, he wrote a poem for me: "What is the Word"—the last thing he wrote.

Q Why was it important to perform *Struck Dumb*?

So important to put it in my brain. Aphasia today affects one million Americans. To focus on disabilities, handicaps, is so important. We all can learn so much. So glad to live, to teach, travel. The joy and wonder. Myself often like Beckett, I was pessimistic. Now... so much more... so many questions. ■

TISA CHANG

Artistic Director of Pan Asian Repertory, Ms. Chang, who is originally from Chongqing, China, directed her first production in 1973, the Peking Opera's *The Return of the Phoenix*, at La MaMa in New York City for Ellen Stewart's Chinese Theatre Group. She also produced bilingual versions of *A Midsummer Night's Dream*, and *Servant of Two Masters* in Mandarin and English at La MaMa. In 1977, Ms. Chang created the Pan Asian Repertory Theatre, and over its forty-year history, she has directed many acclaimed productions, including *The Joy Luck Club*, *Rashomon*, *The Empress of China* with Tina Chen, and the world premiere of *Shanghai Lil's*. As an actress, she has appeared in several Broadway and Off-Broadway plays including *Lovely Ladies, Kind Gentleman*, *The King and I* with Yul Brynner, Stephen Sondheim's *Pacific Overtures*, *Flower Drum Song*, and *The Basic Training of Pavlo Hummel* with Al Pacino. Her film and television work includes *Ambush Bay*, *Greetings*, *Escape from Iran: The Canadian Caper*, *A Doctor's Story*, and *Year of the Dragon*. Ms. Chang has received several awards, including a Theatre World Special Award, Organization for Chinese Americans Lifetime Achievement Award, League of Professional Theatre Women Lee Reynolds Award, the New York City Chinese American Cultural Pioneer Tribute, and the Barnard Medal of Distinction.

Q What originally drew you to the theater?

I started seeing theater at a very early age. I had piano lessons, ballet; I knew there was a world out there beyond what I saw. When I arrived in America, I was "a little China doll." I felt a great deal of separation, isolation, but my mother's influence helped me. I studied with Uta Hagen and appeared in several shows including *Flower Drum Song* and *The King and I* on Broadway. What helped shaped me was seeing great work. It makes a difference when artists have profoundly moving experiences in their early years.

Q What led you to create Pan Asian Repertory?

I believe in an ensemble, so in the 1970s, I directed a bilingual production at La MaMa Theatre, adapting a Peking Opera with only five actors, using parallels between Shakespeare and Commedia dell'Arte. It put us on the map. Within the next five years, we did our ground-breaking *A Midsummer Night's Dream* and *A Servant of Two Masters* productions.

Ellen Stewart said to me at that time, "You should become your own company." We were working on a shoestring budget, and as the manager I was responsible for everything; it felt like the same kind of company Moliere or Shakespeare had started with. I believe artists should take on responsibility. I decided to create a repertory that would dignify Asian-American artists. It's been wonderful to stick with it for forty years; there's still so much more to accomplish. I look at it as a continuous spiral, like wine, artists getting better all the time.

Q How did you go about directing Susan Kim's adaptation of Amy Tan's novel, *The Joy Luck Club*?

I read the script, avoiding going to any other source; I wanted to see it in an individual way. I knew the strength of this piece was in the four mothers, the daughters are a reflection of them. Because of the wide appreciation of the novel, I wanted a total complete stage production, an absolute original creation. I sculptured the piece like a musical theater work, where the "hush" points are, allowing the audience to breathe in the valleys.

Q Should the artist play a greater role in what kind of theater we have?
We have to become more empowered; it is we who care the most. We have to rise to another level of maturity. I was first a performer, working for other people, then I took on more responsibility. I believe in self-reliance, leadership. Accepting more responsibility is a way to expand, it insures my own growth.

I expect to accomplish a great deal in the 21st century. You have to say to yourself, "What do I want to accomplish in five, ten, twenty, fifty years?" An artist has to have a philosophy, standards, values, so you're not jerked around. It's an adherence to an artistic excellence. This we must strive for, because I look and always ask, "Where is the art?" ■

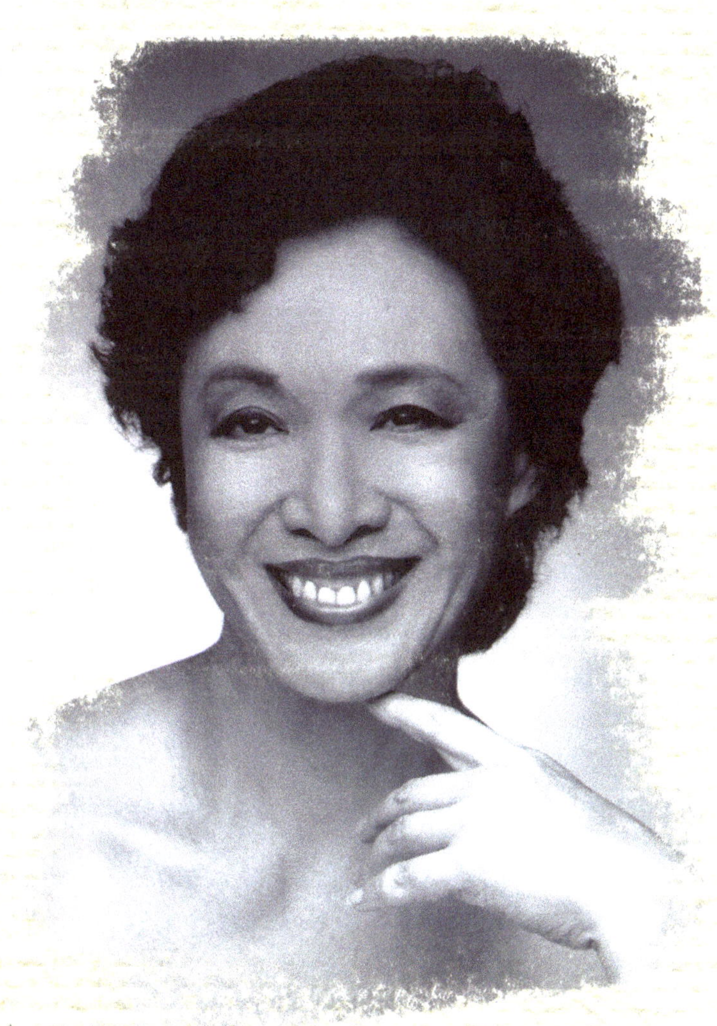

Tisa Chang photo: courtesy of the artist

PING CHONG

Theater director, playwright, choreographer, and video and installation artist, Mr. Chong is a leading contemporary theatre artist and a seminal figure in the Asian American Arts Movement. Since 1972, he has created over thirty-five works, including *Noserafu, Angels of Swedenborg, Blind Ness: The Irresistable Light of Encounter, The Undesirable Elements* series and the acclaimed *East-West Quartet*; *Obon: Tales of Rain and Moonlight*; *Edda: Viking Tales of Lust*; *Revenge and Family*; *I Will Not Be Sad in this World*; *Sacred History*; *Cathay: Three Tales of China*; *Beyond Sacred: Voices of Muslim Identity*; and *Collidescope: Adventures in Pre- and Post-Racial America* with Talvin Wilks. They have been performed at major museums, festivals, and theatres throughout the Americas, Europe, and Asia. His puppet theatre work, *Kwaidan*, premiered at the Atlanta Center for Puppetry Arts, was presented at La Mama ETC as part of the 1988 Henson Int'l Festival of Puppet Theatre, and toured in the U.S., London, and Japan. Mr. Chong received two Obie awards, his second for sustained achievement. He has also received six NEA fellowships, a Playwrights USA Award, a Guggenheim fellowship, two Bessies, and the National Medal of Arts from President Obama.

Q Did your grandparents and parents being producers and performers in the Chinese Opera affect your path into the arts?
My father's closest friend was a painter in the Chinese Opera and he saw that I was interested in visual arts, so he gave me woodcuts, by the artist Hiroshige, of *Gray's Anatomy*, European and masters' art copies. It all interested me. My father was a librettist, a producer and director. He'd also go to China to bring talented artists back. That's how he met my mother. She had joined the Chinese Opera in her teens. So I grew up seeing Chinese Opera every time a troupe would come over to perform. I also grew up on Chinese films; cinema is another great love of mine. I love film, because I love light. It's all about light for me.

Q Why did you decide to use puppets in your work?
A hundred years ago, Gordon Craig talked about the "divine puppet" as "the last echo of some

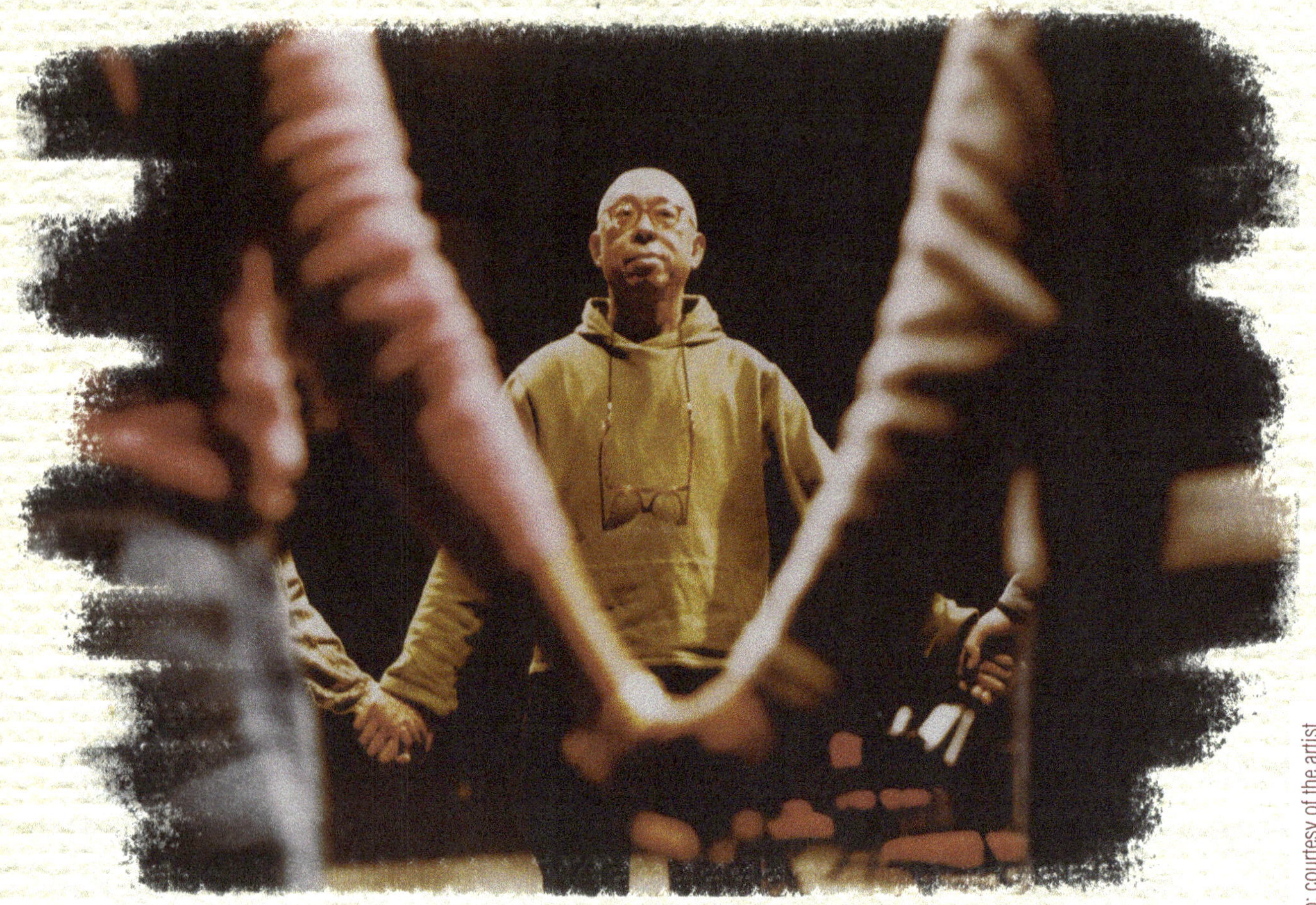

Ping Chong photo: courtesy of the artist

noble and beautiful art of a past civilization." There's always been a puppet presence in my work. I came out of a visual arts school and never intended to go into the theater. I thought I'd be a visual artist or a filmmaker. But I thought, "There are really no Chinese filmmakers"—this was in 1969. But I wasn't aggressive enough, I've never been able to sell myself; I'm a craftsman.

After I graduated, I studied dance, then hitchhiked across America. It was the 1960s. I still had no plans to be a performer. When I returned to New York, it so happened I was crossing the corner of Houston and Broadway and ran into Meredith Monk. She told me, "There's a workshop tonight." It was fate. I was meant to be in this field. In my earlier work, I was accused of using actors like puppets, but for me, it's a collaboration. I'm an artist in the theater; I'm not a theatre artist.

When The Center of Puppetry in Atlanta called me up to do a full-length show with them, that was a turning point. I welcomed it. *Kwaidan* had sat dormant for fifteen, twenty years.

Q How do you approach creating?

It was Thornton Wilder who said in *Our Town*, that we realize too late how precious and how vibrant life is. It's usually only the philosophers and artists who look at how the world is, in a sense, through the eyes of a child. So we act out, like children, in our creative lives, as adults in our adult lives. Artists have somehow retained this ability.

At times it becomes harder and harder to keep my perception pure today, aware of everything that's affecting what I do, remaining open. There's a lot of "smoke and mirrors" affecting us, and we don't always see it. The important thing as an artist is not to repeat what's been done before. So I try as best as I can.

Q What led you to create your theater piece, *Secret History*?

It actually has two different names. Its original name was *Undesirable Elements*. I began the project in 1992, the summer before I taught conceptual scenic design in Holland. It was a ten-week intensive workshop with international students. There were only two students from America, and everyone else was from around the world. We'd all have lunch together, and as the students would get drunker on wine, they'd speak in their native tongues. I just loved the sound of the human diversity of language. I wondered if it was possible to do a piece with multiple languages.

When I came back to New York, I created an art installation called *A Facility for the Containment and Channeling for Undesirables* at Artists Space. The director of the space, Carlos Gutierrez-Solana, asked me to do a performance in my installation. I wondered, "What would we talk about?"

When I brought my first participants together, I was flabbergasted at the richness when they talked about their lives. We first did a forty-minute version about the stories of their lives, about their customs, language, then expanded it. It was structurally unlike anything I had ever done before. But it now has the longest "legs" of any of my pieces; it's up to its eighteenth production.

Q What role can artists play at such a time as this?
For me, it's never a question. I'm doing what I should be doing—work that is trying to make people socially connected. Every artist should do what they can. I know I need to, in my soul. We have to continue to do what we have to.

Q Is there a way to encourage young people to attend the theater?
It's the failure of modernism, it all gravitates towards the mind. It's become all about "concept." You can't compete with TV and film. Theater should open new insights. When people don't make a habit of going to the theater as a part of their lives, it becomes like going to the moon. Unless it's accessible, unless it connects to their experience, they won't come.

There should be all kinds of theater. You have to respect all forms, you don't have to love them, but theater should be life-affirming. You have to ask, "What are you bringing that's new?" And we have to be generous, to allow things to flower. It's that simple. ■

JACK GARFEIN

Mr. Garfein made his Broadway debut as a director with *End as a Man*, starring Ben Gazzara. He had survived eleven concentration camps, and lost his entire family in the Holocaust. He received a scholarship to study with Erwin Piscator at the Dramatic Workshop at the New School for Social Research in New York City. While there, he performed in *The Burning Bush*, directed by Piscator. As a director, his productions on Broadway and Off-Broadway included *The Shadow of a Gunman*, *The Sin of Pat Muldoon*, *The Lesson* with Joseph Wiseman, *Kurt Weill Cabaret*, *Endgame*, *The Beckett Plays*, *Anton Chekhov Sketchbook* with Joseph Buloff, and *Rommel's Garden*. Mr. Garfein produced Arthur Miller's *The Price* and *The American Clock* on Broadway, and directed the French premiere of *Master Harold and the Boys* in Paris, and the world premiere of Beckett's *Night and Space* in Austria. His documentary, *The Journey Back*, chronicles his return to Auschwitz. His films include *The Strange One*, and *Something Wild* starring Carroll Baker. On television he directed *The Marriage* with Jessica Tandy and Hume Cronyn. He created The Harold Clurman Theatre on Theatre Row in New York City. In 1966, in collaboration with Paul Newman, he created The Actors Studio in Los Angeles. He co-produced, with Rita Fredricks, Ronald Rand in Rand's play *Let it be Art! Harold Clurman's Life of Passion* at the Filmothèque du Quartier Latin in Paris. Mr. Garfein created the book, *Life and Acting: Techniques for the Actor*, and currently teaches in Paris at Le Studio Jack Garfein and in New York City. He was awarded the Masque d'Or, and voted best acting teacher in France.

Q When did you know your path led into the theater?
After the war, having been liberated in Bergen-Belsen, I was taken to Sweden for recuperation. There in the DP camp, we put on a play for the Swedes about the life in the camps. I suddenly realized that the horror I've been through could bring some meaning to people. I was also astonished at the realities that came back to me while playing in it.

Q You directed *End as a Man* on Broadway. What drew you to Calder Willingham's novel?
It was a compulsion, as much of creating art has to be. I learned to use the limitless resources in an actor's imagination to discover the character in rehearsal; to create conditions to let the character emerge.

Q You also worked with Samuel Beckett.
Beckett gave me the last play he wrote. He wouldn't give it to National Theatre. He said to me, "I cannot say no to you." So I went to Paris to meet with him. He told me, "I've done my work, now you do yours." When I asked him things about the play, Beckett said, "Now Jack, I can tell you the intention but not the meaning." Alan Schneider asked Beckett, "Did God ever show up in *Waiting for Godot*?" Beckett told him, "Alan, if I knew, don't you think I would have written it?"

Q Harold Clurman made a deep impression on you.
Harold said. "We're a country without memory." He was a force of life. He had a remarkable sense of living, of coping, always going with life. I loved his stories. At the beginning of my career in New York, I directed a play on Broadway; it didn't get very good reviews. Harold said to me, "So how do you feel, Jack?" "How do I feel?" I replied. "I have a flop on Broadway!!" Harold said, "Jack, you have a flop on Broadway!" I thought of Beckett when he said, "I can't go, I go on."

Q Erwin Piscator's work also influenced you.
I wrote in my book about the way he worked as a director. Before Peter Brook, before Beckett, Piscator had a sense of the possibilities of the stage, especially technically. What he did was amazing. He had a sense of how to engage the audience. Some of the productions at the President Theatre and the Rooftop Theatre in New York City were astonishing. He had Bea Arthur, Elaine Stritch, Eli Wallach, Walter Matthau in them.

Q Who have been inspirations for you as an artist?
Of course, the great playwrights. The novelists: Proust, Lawrence Durrell, Henry Miller, and Mark Twain. Directors, including Piscator, Harold Clurman, John Ford, Elia Kazan, George Stevens, Ingmar Bergman, Carl Dreyer, and in the beginning of my work, Lee Strasberg's remarkable appreciation of what an actor can accomplish in revealing the hidden aspects of a play. The actors: Sir Laurence Olivier, Lee J. Cobb, Nuria Espert, and Edwige Feuillere.

Q In your new book, *Life and Acting: Technique for the Actor,* you wrote, "I define something that hasn't been defined before—things an actor can grab onto. I'm very aware of what the actor's problems are."
Many actors don't know how to read a play. I try and give them courage. You can't teach anyone how to act. You can't give anyone talent. As an acting teacher, I point out what an actor is doing. The confidence comes from the discovery of what's inside you, what you have to offer. I say, first a human being, then an actor.

Q What is it that sustains theater in a culture?
The need to grasp the goings-on beneath the surface of life. There have been many inroads by technology into the theater, but the real power of theater remains great storytelling. It's the revelation of the mysterious complexity in the human soul, which is fathomless. It also has the means to take the kinks out of the human psyche.

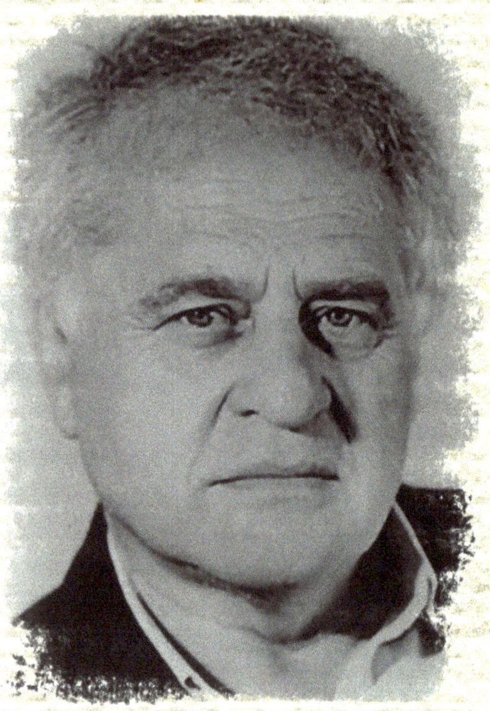

Jack Garfein photo: courtesy of the artist

Q Does the theater change society?
I don't believe so, or else all the work of the great playwrights, actors of the 19th century, couldn't have led to the nightmares of the twentieth. The artist's first responsibility is to descend deeply within himself to awaken the slumber, the pain in himself, and through that, make others see the hidden reality. ■

ANDRE GREGORY

World-renowned theater director, Mr. Gregory, was the Artistic Director of The Manhattan Project, a New York theater collective that performed in New York and all over the world. He is the author of the play, *Bonesongs*, and Mr. Gregory has performed it at the 92nd Street Y and at Redcat Theatre in Los Angeles. His production of the Obie-winning *Alice in Wonderland* ran for five years in New York City, toured Europe, the Middle East, and South America. In 1975, he directed *Our Late Night* by Wallace Shawn, and later starred in and co-authored the popular film, *My Dinner with Andre*, with Wallace Shawn. Mr. Gregory's directing includes *Endgame*, *Our Late Night*, *The Master Builder*, Shawn's *Grasses of a Thousand Colors*, performed at London's Royal Court Theatre and New York's Public Theater, and Mr. Shawn's *The Designated Mourner*, also presented at the Public Theater. A long-running workshop of *Uncle Vanya*, adapted by David Mamet, which rehearsed for over four years with Mr. Shawn and Julianne Moore, later became *Vanya on 42nd Street*, a film directed by Louis Malle and Mr. Gregory. Mr. Gregory's film work as an actor includes Peter Weir's *The Mosquito Coast* and Martin Scorsese's *Last Temptation of Christ*. In 2014, Mr. Shawn and Mr. Gregory's production of *A Master Builder* was made into a film by Jonathan Demme. A documentary about his life and work, *Before and After Dinner*, directed by Cindy Kleine was released in 2013. Side by side with his work as a director, he began to draw and paint over a decade ago. Mr. Gregory has had two shows of his work at the Jason McCoy Gallery in New York City. Mr. Gregory is directing a new production of *Hedda Gabler*, and with Todd London, completing a book on his life and work.

Q When did you think about being a director?
I'll tell you something Harold Clurman said about me: "Andre Gregory is like me. He'll go anywhere in the world to see great theater. He's like the Mexican pilgrims who go on their bleeding knees, crawling up steps, to worship at the altar of theater." It's true, I'll go anywhere.

As a young man I searched out Grotowski in Poland, Brecht in Berlin, and Planchon in France. Clurman also said, after *Alice in Wonderland* had opened, and critics were using the word "genius," in their description of the work I did, "When one uses the word 'genius,' I would like to think of that word as describing Michelangelo or the genius of Beethoven. Why do you have to go and destroy a talented young man by calling him a genius!" When I terrifyingly, delicately, with great awe, thought of being a director, I thought the best preparation would be like being "a captain of a ship," knowing everything about every part of a ship.

When I got out of college, I did a lot of sneaking into the second act of Broadway plays seeing new plays by Anouilh, Giraudoux, Christopher Fry, T.S. Eliot, Williams, Osborne, Arthur Miller, Inge; seeing Laurence Olivier and Vivien Leigh in *Caesar and Cleopatra*, and in *Anthony and Cleopatra*! Off Broadway there were new plays by Genet, Ionesco, Beckett, and Albee.

Compare it with the kind of plays we're seeing today. There's a lot of activity, but no culture. Today it seems many new plays are being written as a way to break into television and film; so many young actors and directors have no sense of history. Often they don't know the work of Stanislavsky, Vakhtangov, Meyerhold, Brecht. How can you work in the theater with no sense of your lineage?

It would be absurd for a painter not to have heard of Michelangelo or a pianist not to have heard of Bach. When I did a workshop in Canada a while ago, the students asked me if Grotowski had come before or after Stanislavsky, as if he had been dead for a hundred years. I told them he had "definitely come before Stanislavsky." When I told Grotowski, he laughed. But it's an extremely serious dilemma.

Q What do you wish to be revealed as a director?

I'm seeking, waiting, with great enthusiasm, year after year to see what will be revealed, what will appear, with great patience I expect the unexpected. When you direct a play in the commercial theatre you have four to six weeks. Your task is to decide before you go into rehearsal what you want to say, and then in rehearsal, find out the most articulate way to say it. My rehearsal process is about waiting, unmasking, self-revelation—stripping away layer upon layer in an attempt to get closer to the essence.

Q And what is that essence?

That's hard to answer. Artistically, it's about simplicity for the actor. It's about having courage, to be as deeply revealing as the author. It's about clarity, about taking the time to make each moment an illumination, a crystal. If you're working with a group of actors who are spiritually seeking themselves through their work, it's a wondrous thing. You might say we're doing a form of research on ourselves. We come to our work every day, not unlike the way the monks go to their devotions every day.

Take for example, a play like Ibsen's *The Master Builder*. It's a play in which Ibsen has gone to some very deep places within himself to reveal himself. The actor has to be given the same time to be able to find those places, to access all those different things inside himself or herself, relating to the needs of the role. You never know what actors will find.

What Wally (Wallace Shawn) did in *Uncle Vanya* reminded me a lot of the Howard Beal character in the film, *Network*. Wally was that man on the fire escape, screaming, "I'm mad as hell and I'm not going to take this anymore!" He had to find that rage within himself in order to play it.

Q What do you do when you don't know how to continue?

You wait. We each have a thousand selves. I come up against "walls" of all kinds—psychological, spiritual, physical. In relationship, in the process of psychotherapy, we often don't know how to continue; but we must take the time and have faith. Did you see the documentary about breaking the sound barrier? The first jets that tried kept exploding. And what happened when they came so close? The plane would start shaking violently, and the pilots would slow down. But the pilot who had the impulse to go faster when the shaking began, he broke the barrier. It's a natural impulse, a natural resistance to put the brakes on when you come in contact with the unknown.

Einstein talked about the three "b"s. His version of the three "r"s—reading, writing and arithmetic. He said, "You have to work and work and work, and suddenly you're in bed, in the bath, or at the beach, and it reveals itself."

Someone asked Grotowski, "What is it you love so much that you have to keep going into the unknown? You keep talking about the need to go into the unknown." He answered, "Did I ever say I loved it?"

My rehearsals are noted for a lot of laughter. Every time I see the truth in an actor, I roar with laughter. Laughter is a form of support, an encouragement to dare the actors to go a little further, to be fully present, completely simple. I never judge the actor. I encourage the actor not to judge himself.

I remember how moved I was by seeing Andy Rooney and Ann Miller in the later years of their lives, perform on Broadway in *Sugar Babies*. I loved watching them because they seemed to have "one foot in the grave, and the other on a banana peel." And although they were in their 80s, their craft was more precise and more perfect than most actors that are sixty years younger.

Q How would you describe the nature of collaboration between a director and an actor?

We tend to forget that the director entered the picture only a hundred years ago. Actors had been doing fine without a director for two thousand years. I think a director is like a gardener. First he or she creates the right soil appropriate to the play being rehearsed; that's the atmosphere specific to the rehearsal of this one play and no other. When the earth is in place, he drops in a few seeds, we call that casting. It's very, very, very important. Then you water the earth, water the seeds, and you bring out as much sunshine as possible into the room; it's really very simple.

As a result of my directing, I was able to act in about fourteen movies. It was the first time I was

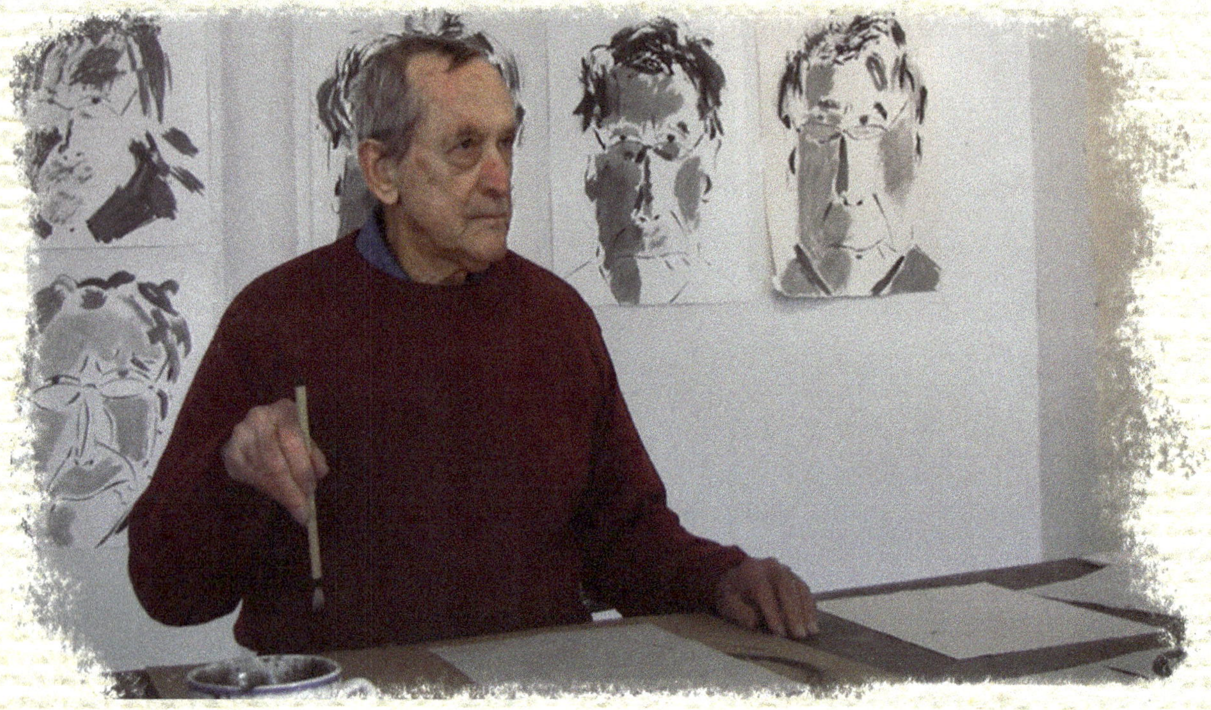

able to watch other directors direct. Two of them were truly great: Peter Weir and Martin Scorsese. On the whole, I have found most directors don't really know "how to drive." As a director since 1970, the plays I've done average out to be about one play every five years. Directors like Kubrick or Malick did the same in film. Grotowski only did a handful of plays.

Q How do you begin?
I begin by reading the play every day for about a year, but I never think about the play intellectually; I just listen to it, like music. I choose each play the way we choose a life partner, with a sense of deep commitment, deep passion. We don't need to know why we fall in love but we sure know it when we feel it.

Q How important is it for you to know your actors well?
I never audition my actors. Some actors can be really great in an audition, but they don't know how to truly work at a rehearsal. I generally have many meetings with the actor. I have to fall in love with them for us to go on this journey together. I'm asking my colleagues to go further into the unknown, into themselves, but I have to be sure I'm working with as pure, as objective a loving spirit as possible.

When Grotowski talked about the work of the actor, he said, "An atmosphere must be created, a working system in which the actor feels that he can do absolutely anything. It is often at the moment when the actor understands this that he reveals himself."

I intuit where most actors would like to go, but I never manipulate them to work faster. I want them to work in a way that's organic to them. A human being is like an iceberg; ninety percent of it is underwater. We sense, from the little we see, the depth of what's underneath. A tree isn't always telling us how expressive it is, it's simply there. Simple.

Q Where did you first glimpse this way of working?
When I was twenty-four, at the Berliner Ensemble. The simplicity of their work was stunning. I watched them take weeks to find one brief moment in a scene. Brecht would always attempt to find the one gesture that told the story. I didn't speak a word of German when I went there. I hadn't read Brecht's plays. I was very ignorant, yet in spite of this, I understood ninety percent of what I had seen.

Q Do you consider yourself continuing the tradition of the way in which these masters worked, like Brecht and Grotowski?
I like to think I'm a son of Brecht and Grotowski, a grandson of Vakhtangov and Meyerhold. They were seekers; all dealt with the actor in depth, with a heightened reality, which we would call "style." And they all took a great deal of time.

Q You co-founded Seattle Repertory Theatre, then you were Artistic Director of the Theatre of the Living Arts, then founded The Manhattan Project. What kinds of lessons did you learn creating The Manhattan Project?
In the regional theater, I learned about organization and fund-raising. I learned about working quickly, and I realized I wanted something different. I wanted an actor "who could fly," who could "be the scenery." But I didn't know what that meant.

Then one day, Ellen Stewart came down to my theater in Philadelphia. She told me about a young actor in Grotowski's company who could do this. I went to Poland to see for myself, but Grotowski wasn't there. So I went to

Andre Gregory photo: courtesy of the artist

Edinburgh, and saw twelve of Grotowski's performances. I was staggered. I was literally stunned. I thought to myself, "I'll never be able to do this with a group of actors in America. Maybe I should give up the theater and become a therapist." I joined Grotowski's workshop in France for three weeks.

Four months later, inspired by that, I came back home and found the courage to bring together a group of actors who had just graduated from NYU. Armed with what Grotowski had given me, my group and I began the journey of creating an actor "who could fly." This was how The Manhattan Project came to be.

Q I understand you worked on a play of your own for a long time.

Yes, it's in verse—*Bonesongs*. It was inspired by my losing my first wife from cancer; we were married for thirty-three years. It took exactly twenty years to write it. I did a workshop with Sam Waterston and Diane Wiest at one point. Julie Haggerty became a part of the project; it was directed by Liz Sherman. It's an odd cabaret, a kaleidoscopic collage of love songs, scenes, soliloquies, and stories. I believe, as it says in the Song of Psalms: "Love is stronger than death."

The value for me in writing the play was to let my wife move on, to allow myself to move on. Tibetan Buddhists feel that for the soul to move on, you have to let the loved one go. You have to make peace.

I can't believe I wrote it, because I'm not, of course, a playwright. Henry Miller, in the last part of his life took up painting, and wrote a book, *To Paint Is to Love Again*. It's about that divine place that exists in each one of us, that some of us might call "amateurish." Each one of us, I feel, is like a child, with a certain naivety at our core, and if we can connect with that place, we can create with the same kind of joy that many children do.

When I performed in an A.R. Gurney play, Stella Adler came to see it. She told me at the end, "Do you know, darling, why the audience loves you? It's because you're an amateur. They really wish they, too, could get up on stage and do what you're doing and lose their inhibitions." I think of myself as an amateur, a dilettante. And the root meaning of the word, "dilettante," in Latin, is a mix of dilletare, "to delight in." In Sanskrit, they use a certain term, and taken together, it means, "He of many talents, who dips his hands in the earth and releases the waters of life." That should be on my gravestone.

I think for me, the artist is an antenna in a desert, picking up these vibrations which come through us. Our job is simply to keep our antennas in working order, to make sure they don't get rusty, through whatever it takes—therapy, meditation, learning—to be open to receive what is out there.

From Hamlet to Hamm, Masha to Peer Gynt, many of the great characters in dramatic literature attempt to come to terms with the great unknown—one's own mortality. It's certainly one of the largest questions we face, as well as what comes after.

Q Has this "great unknown" played a role in your approaching theater pieces, especially *Endgame*?

What comes to my mind is when I visited the wonderful actress, Ruth Nelson. She was performing in the production we were doing, *Uncle Vanya*, right up to the end of her life. She was clearly dying. I asked her, "Are you afraid?" She replied, "No, dying is the same

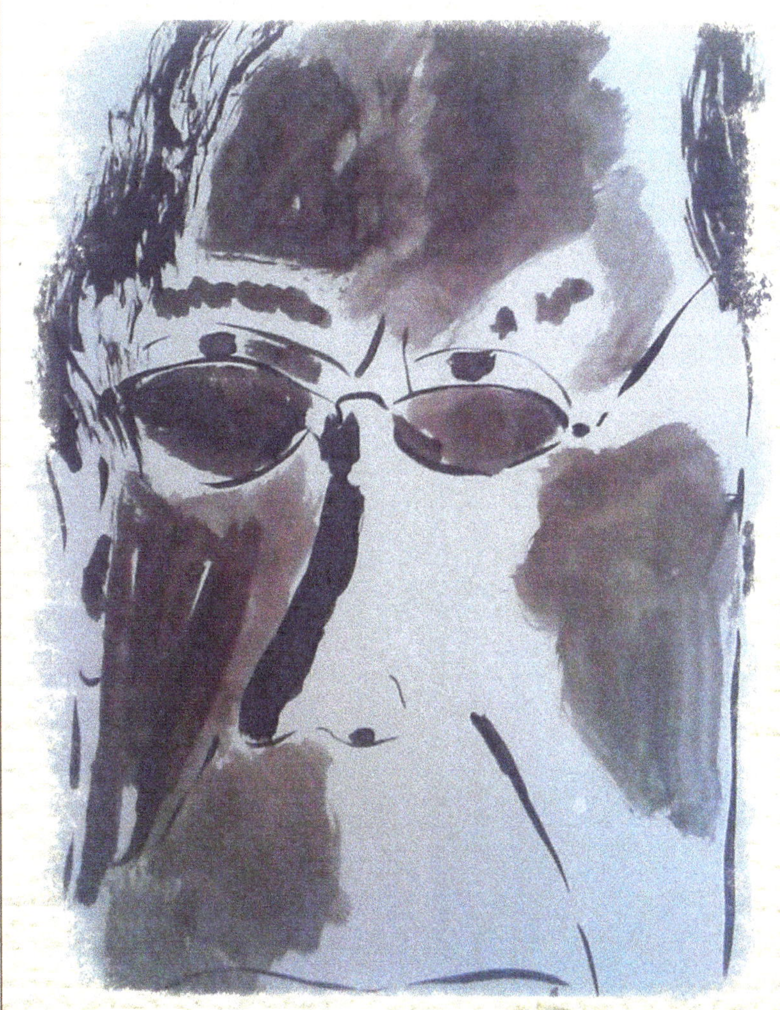

artwork: "Self-portrait" by Andre Gregory, courtesy of the artist

process as the work you and I do. We live moment to moment without asking what the end will look like." When you work, as I do on a play only in the moment, there's no past, no future.

At my age, the whole issue of leaving is a big one. I'm having such a good time; I'd like to be here forever. The most important issue is letting go when it's time. I have a feeling I've already done much of my work; I've already experienced most of what I can do as a director. Even though I've not stopping directing, I have a feeling my real work may be the peace movement now. I want to do something, in some small little way, to leave the world in a better way for our children and our grandchildren.

When we had the performance of the Peace Movement's program of *Poems Not Fit for the White House* at Carnegie Hall, it was unbelievable. I feel the peace movement is vitally important to the future of democracy in this country. A veil of illusion is being stripped away. We're being forced to face many of the terrible things America has done in the past. We have to be willing to face the truth about ourselves. The key is to be more open, vulnerable. When I was younger, I was a closed-off frightened angry person, so I had to learn to be open. Being a director, a teacher, has taught me how to be more open.

Q How would you describe your way of teaching?

I don't have a method or a way. Every new actor I work with comes with his or her own history, their past, their desires, blocks, and so forth. My task is simply to help them go further than they imagined they could.

On stage you may ask: What is my objective? Yet in life we never really know what we'll do, we think we do. Your objective may be at an office to get a job, but you might pass the water cooler, meet someone, and fall in love. You don't know what you're doing, but that becomes your objective. Hilda's objective in Ibsen's play, *The Master Builder*, is to get him to leave his wife. But then she gets him to go up on that high tower, and to die in a moment of ecstasy. She "wants her kingdom."

When I watched the great Polish actor, Ryszard Cieslak rehearse, each moment became a moment of risk; like the way a river flows, every moment it flows in a different path.

Q How can we cultivate a greater moral responsibility?

All of us suffer from moral laziness; it's easy to turn away from the genocide around the world, in Rwanda, in Cambodia, in the Balkans. It's easy to pretend it's not happening. To be an artist means you're willing to stand up for life. But it's not just the artist; everyone should hate death and killing. Some artists are shamans. They pick up the "darkness" and respond.

In *My Dinner with Andre*, I talked about New York City becoming a new model where the inmates become the concentration guards themselves. That was written over twenty-five years ago. Artists often see what's coming.

When I had lunch with Louis Malle about a year before he died, we talked about *My Dinner with Andre* again. Initially when he had seen the film, he empathized with Wally's character, and thought my character and a lot of what I said, absurd. Then he later realized, he confessed to me, that the things I had said back then had come to pass. We also wondered if either of us would have become directors, if we were young now. I said, "I think I probably would have become a therapist." He said, "I might have been an anthropologist."

I felt I could change the theater. He felt he could change cinema.

Clifford Odets in his diary, *The Time is Ripe*, reflects that "All great playwrights had the same path of travel in the continuity of their work. They all went from naturalism to a sort of poetic symbolism, dealing in the end with very lofty abstract themes: Ibsen, Gerhart Hauptmann, Strindberg, Maxwell Anderson, O'Neill, Sean O'Casey."

Jung said the first half of our life is the process of building our ego, and the second half is letting it go. It's an act of surrender, in a sense, in an attempt to get closer to the light, to the mysterious. I've been influenced by the Bal Shem Tov, St. Francis of Assisi, Martin Luther, Jr., and my own guru. My journey now is a journey of an ecstatic. Towards the light, always with joy and love. Wake up!!!!

Each of us can make a difference, we have to remember that. Stokowski said, "Art is like a high mountain which one keeps climbing with never the top in view. An artist reaches a plateau and thinks it is the top. He rests there and stays there for the remainder of his life, but it is not the top at all." We have seen examples of searching, probing artists like Grotowski, Stanislavsky, who seem to never rest.

I feel each artist has some fundamental questions he or she is trying to answer. We try through our work again and again to see if we can find the answer. There's something going on in the artists working today that gives me a great deal of hope. I find more and more young people are committed to the theatre, and not necessarily thinking about getting rich. They're not obsessed by possessing things, and seem to truly love the theatre. God bless them! ■

SABRA JONES

Artistic Producing and Artistic Director of The Mirror Repertory Company, she co-founded the Mirror in 1983, with Geraldine Page, Eva Le Gallienne, John Strasberg; it's located in New York City and Greensboro, Vermont. Through thirty years their productions included Eve Le Gallienne's *Alice in Wonderland* on Broadway, which received a Tony Award nomination, followed by sixteen other plays in alternating repertory in New York City. Ms. Jones' directing at the Greensboro Arts Alliance and Residency in Vermont includes *Hamlet*, *Our Town*, *The Seagull*, *The Three Sisters*, *You Can't Take it with You*, *The Fantasticks*, *Peter Pan*, *The Sound of Music*, *The Music Man*, and *The Miracle Worker*. As an actress her appearances include *Butterflies Are Free* on Broadway, *Six Degrees of Separation* at Lincoln Center, *Nightflowers*, *The Balcony*, and *The Rehearsal*. With the Mirror, she appeared opposite Geraldine Page, Michael Moriarity, and F. Murray Abraham in several plays including *Rain*, *Paradise Lost*, *Clarence*, *Hasty Heart*, *The Inheritors*, *Joan of Lorraine*, *Children of the Sun*, and *The Seagull*, directed by Robert Lewis; in fifteen other plays regionally; and in *La Fille du Regiment* and *Les Troyens* at The Metropolitan Opera. As the daughter-in-law of Lee Strasberg, she taught at the Lee Strasberg Institute, Pace University, and at Manhattanville College.

Sabra Jones photo: courtesy of the artist

Q What led you to a life in the theater?

In the deepest sense, a hunger to feel alive. But historically, when I was young, I really didn't understand what the theater was about; I grew up in a very small town, very close to Los Angeles. When I was nine, I was part of a summer children's theatre program at San Fernando State College, and played Cinderella.

My father ran the largest mental hospital in California, and when a television documentary was being made about the mentally ill children in the hospital, my father allowed me to "play" a pyromaniac, playing with matches, have temper tantrums, kicking adults; I thought acting was the most wonderful thing in the world.

Later on, they built a theater on the grounds for the patients to act in. When it was dedicated, the actress Billie Burke came to speak. She was very old but so beautiful; I had never seen anyone so elegant. She talked about how the magic of theater could "heal wounds and help people's souls." That made a deep impression on me.

Q I understand your life changed after you were cast in *The Rehearsal* in Boston.

Yes, after that I did *Pony Girl* in Cincinnati; I actually was supposed to go to NYU but I was cast as the second actress after Blythe Danner to play Jill in *Butterflies Are Free* on the First National tour. They asked Eileen Heckart if she would do the "confrontation scene" with me on stage at the Booth Theatre between the Saturday matinee and the evening show. I think they really needed to see if I would cave in under pressure. Eileen was very strong, really came at me. After I read, Milton Katselas, the director, asked Eileen what she thought. She answered, "The kid can do it." I toured with Eve Arden, and then with Gloria Swanson.

Q What was it like working with Eve Arden?

She was just incredible. She taught me so much about how comedy works. One thing I learned was the "rule of three" from her; it's an old Vaudeville technique. Eve noticed something I did on stage got a laugh, and she said, "Do it twice more and you'll get a bigger pay-off each time you do it. Three is the top, though, no more."

Years later I was driving Eli Wallach and Anne Jackson home

from New Jersey and Eli was talking about the show they had just done and he said, "Rule of three. Works every time." That is the sort of thing that can only be learned from oral tradition—from actors sharing stories and experiences—from practicing one's craft.

Q How did you meet Lee Strasberg at The Actors Studio?

When I was living in the East Village and finally got to NYU, I'd always see this young guy going up Second Avenue on his bike with this great big dog running on the sidewalk.

Well, someone asked me to play a part in a one-act in The Playwrights Unit at The Actors Studio. We performed it for Lee Strasberg. That was the first time I saw this "living legend." He was very pleasant and flattering to me, and I enjoyed working for him.

Afterwards this same young guy whom I had seen with the bike and the dog came up to me and introduced himself. "Hi, I'm John Strasberg." Soon after, we were married.

Q What led to your teaching acting?

Lee asked me, John helped me. I was incredibly honored and quite awed by the responsibility, but Lee told me I could do it because I reminded him of Kim Stanley. He said I seemed to understand aspects of The Method even though I had never studied it. I didn't know who Kim was until Lee and John told me about her; oral tradition again. One day I actually met her and we talked about acting.

Q How did you meet Harold Clurman?

Harold Clurman was a special part of my life. I first met Harold at a party in Bel Air. People were skinny-dipping in the pool and I was too shy so I went into the library. There in the cool, dark, book-laden room was a gentleman in a summer white suit. He turned to me and said, "You can't take the skinny-dipping either? Let's talk!"

Oh, how Harold could talk! I loved him dearly; his soul was truly so large. When he talked about art and the theater he would became so inspiring. I thought of him as the "eternal light" of our theater. He didn't just talk about art, he lived it. In his critiques, he would talk about what the play required—what the message needed to be. He was a great critic, someone who really understood the art of the theater. Worldly, eloquent, and so funny!

Q Who were some of the other artists who inspired you?

Stella Adler was a revelation to me; her understanding of a playwright's work was profound. So was Robert Lewis, and Ellis Raab.

Geraldine Page, whom I also loved dearly, was marvelous because her humanity and generosity were truly inspiring. She used to say that critics should have bios under their reviews, just as artists have bios, to show they had credentials to write an opinion the public should take seriously. The three years I shared a dressing room with her showed me her truth, devoid of pretension or vanity. She could get fifty meanings out of a single word.

Q What led you to create The Mirror Repertory Company?

Lots of people contributed to creating the Mirror. We have a fine Board and exciting artists. My motivation was simply: to bring artists together to, you might say, "save the world." I believe by presenting human beings who are striving to say truthful things in plays of great meaning, it will enable us to become more humane—that we can learn from our shared human experience, discover common truths all over again. We need evolved artists, who have struggled not to become famous but who want to share their knowledge and compassion with the world.

Q What have you learned it takes to keep a theater creatively growing?

I think it's a matter of collaboration; that becomes the over-riding aim in fostering great tradition. Many creative people in the theater desire it, to learn and create together in such an environment. It's a matter of finding a balance between freedom and responsibility.

It's also a constant struggle to find the right material that enables a theater company of artists to grow and experiment, to push the envelope, to present the work truthfully, with humor and love. So the audience finds themselves caught "off-guard" by a new experience, by something they didn't anticipate, by something that satisfies their souls. I've also learned what happens between those on stage and the audience allows for a unique bond of energy to be created, a cosmic space that is most precious, transcendent; it is a life lesson.

Theater is a particular magic where a brave actor on stage brings home the true drama and courage of life. It's stunning. It's revolutionary, and profoundly mysterious. Life is all so precious! ■

MICHAEL KAHN

Artistic Director of The Shakespeare Theatre Company in Washington, D.C. for over thirty years, Mr. Kahn was the Richard Rodgers Director of the Drama Division of the Juilliard School from 1992 to 2006. A world-acclaimed director, his Broadway, Off-Broadway, and regional productions include all of Shakespeare's plays, *Showboat*, for which he received a Tony Award nomination, *Whodunnit*, *Cat on a Hot Tin Roof*, *Hedda Gabler* at the Roundabout Theatre, *Mother Courage and Her Children*, *The Government Inspector*, *Richard II*, *Volpone*, *The Way of the World*, *Cyrano*, *Peer Gynt*, *Mourning Becomes Electra*, Camino Real, *Sweet Bird of Youth*, *Old Times* at The Goodman Theatre, *A Touch of the Poet* at Arena Stage, *The Duchess of Malfi* at The Guthrie Theatre, *Torchsong* at the Studio Theatre, a new adaptation of the world premiere of *Lorenzaccio*, and David Ives' adaptations of French comedies, *The Liar*, *Heir Apparent*, and *Metromaniacs*. His other notable productions include the original productions of van Itallie's *War* and *America Hurrah*, Kennedy's *Funnyhouse of a Negro*, *Helen*, *The Rimers of Eldritch*, *Death of Bessie Smith*, *Measure for Measure* for New York Shakespeare Festival in Central Park, and he directed over twenty plays as the Artistic Director of the American Shakespeare Festival in Stratford, Connecticut. including *Merchant of Venice* with Morris Carnovsky; *Three Sisters* with Marian Seldes and Kate Reid; Jane Alexander and Sada Thompson in *Mourning Becomes Electra*; and *Othello* with Moses Gunn. Mr. Kahn directed Bizet's *Carmen* at Washington Opera, Barber's opera; *Vanessa* at Kennedy Center, Houston Grand Opera, and City Center Opera; Adamo's *Lysistrata* at Houston Grand Opera and NYC Opera; and Guunod's *Romeo and Juliet* at Dallas Opera. He was the Producing Director of McCarter Theatre Center from 1974 to 1979, Artistic Director of The Acting Company from 1978 to 1988, and founder of The Chautauqua Theater Company and the Institute's acting training program. He directed *The Oedipus Plays* at The Athens Festival in Greece. Mr. Kahn has received Drama Desk Awards, a Joseph Jefferson Award, seven Helen Hayes Awards, was inducted into the American Theater Hall of Fame, and honored by Queen Elizabeth II as an Honorary Commander of the Most Excellent Order of the British Empire.

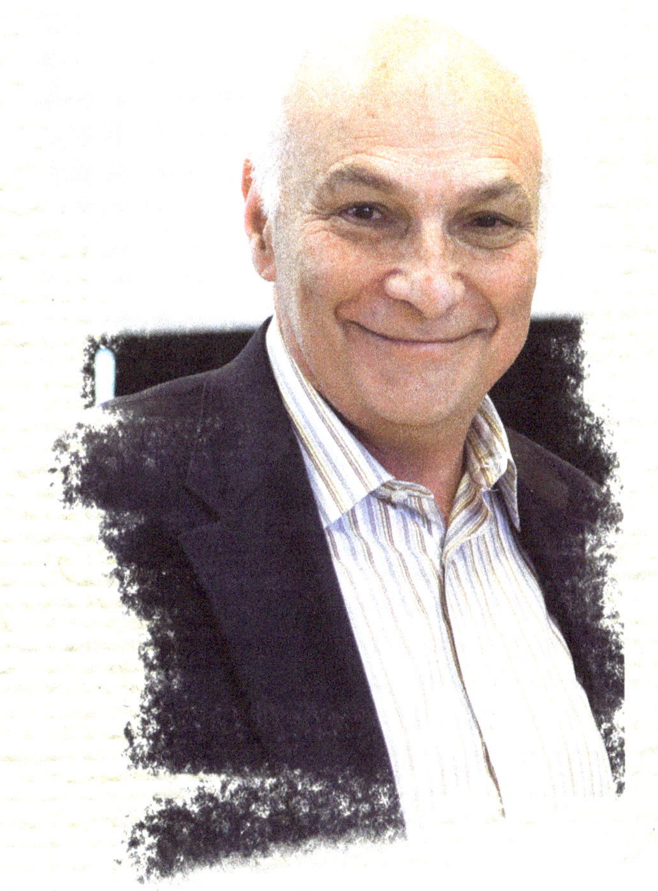

Michael Kahn photo: courtesy of the artist

Q How were you drawn into the theater?

I was lucky; I went to see theater when I was very young. At age five I knew this was what I wanted to do, at age six I wanted to be a director. I went to a Quaker school, and they allowed me to direct at that age. While I was going to the High School of Performing Arts, I would go to the theater all the time. I saw APA/Phoenix's *Coriolanus* with Robert Ryan, Donald Madden, Rosemary Harris, and Fritz Weaver, and Laurence Olivier in both *Caesar and Cleopatra*, and in *Anthony and Cleopatra*; Maurice Evans as Hamlet; George C. Scott and Colleen Dewhurst doing Shakespeare in Central Park.

Q How did directing plays by van-Itallie and Kennedy affect your approach working on Shakespeare's plays?

I enjoyed doing those plays. I was considered, what you might call, an avant-garde director. So when Joe Papp asked me to do Shakespeare's *Measure for Measure*, he asked me what I was interested in; I was working with concepts, the symbolism in the play, and how I could make the play visually work on stage. I brought everything I had known into what I did. I was also influenced by those European artists who had come to America at the time, like Peter Brook, Strehler, and also by Elia Kazan's work. I was also inspired just as much by seeing Martha Graham and Paul Taylor.

Q What touched you in Kazan's and in Brook's work?

It was Kazan's sheer theatrical power and emotion that he created on stage. Peter Brook for conceptuality that totally illuminated the play, and the same can be said for Strehler. Seeing Kabuki theatre was important for me, too, and reading about Brecht's work. I've also been influenced quite a bit by Ingmar Bergman. I learned from him—you should do what you feel is true—to trust your insides, your imagination.

Q Has your directing changed over the years?
I now think less of myself; I'm more interested in the complexity of the play. Earlier on, I thought each production had to make a point. I'm now more interested in dealing with all the many sides of the issues within the play. I'm getting better at being a better storyteller. I've also been teaching all these years, and that's had a great influence in how I work with actors. I've become more aware and more responsive to the different ways actors work.

Q What if their interpretation of a character or their take on a play may be very different than yours? How have you learned to foster a meaningful, creative relationship with the actor?
I don't think I've ever cast an actor who had such a different interpretation that was against what the play was about. If an actor feels a certain way about their character, or they need to go in a certain direction, I've learned ways of dealing with it. I'm most interested in finding out in rehearsal what I don't know, as much as the actors are. I don't like an actor who has decided it all before we begin to work.

I like actors who have ideas; I live off new ideas. They'll spark something else for me I may not have originally thought of. I love actors who have opinions and make choices. It can be a drawback at times, if a director has become a "smart" or a "strong" director, the actors then abdicate making choices; I'm not for that. I need something to bounce off in rehearsal. I may have my own strong opinions, but I'm flexible enough to know when a better idea comes along.

Laurette Taylor said, "We create in the imagination the character we wish to express." I don't know what I'd do without my imagination. I actually plan less these days. I think the best rehearsals happen when I allow my imagination to work, and allow things to just happen; I enjoy that the most.

Of course there are those days when I have to rely on my technique to get through; I have my skill to fall back on. I think if I have any faults, it may be that I'll see something so wonderful, that I want to set it too soon. I do demand whatever is done is based on the text. There is a certain logic being expressed in the play—we can come up with different meanings—but it still remains, the meaning is the meaning. You have to make the play as clear as possible. You need to love the text, and see it as a vehicle of expression.

Q What has drawn you to direct Shakespeare as much as you do and how do you find a way into his plays?
Shakespeare asks us questions, in a form, that also celebrates the highest potential in mankind through language and thought. That's what it's all about. For me, the most exciting thing I can see in the theater is a wonderful production of Shakespeare. His plays affirm our lives, they provoke us, stimulate us, taking the best measure of man. They're a celebration of what we're always in need of.

And for the actor and audience, they're the "Olympics" of participation. I read the play again and again, and let Shakespeare talk to me. I know why a character is saying what he or she is saying, emotionally. I "talk" to Shakespeare, in order to know the world that is going on within the play.

Michael Chekhov once wrote. "Listen to your bodies and they will interpret the movement of your inner impulses." But you can't think about the impulses, you just have to let them come by reacting physically, as free as possible. And it can't happen if you're in your head. Acting is doing, reacting—you have to be willing to let go.

Q You were at the very beginning of Juilliard's Drama Division. How would you describe its mission?
I had taught there from the day it opened. The basic tenants of Juilliard is the synthesis of what's really fantastic about American acting—its honesty, reality, physical life, subtext, truth, a real use of internal life, and working on the voice, body and the text. They're still the basic challenges.

What I feel I did the most was to rejuvenate new ways of thinking, introducing more directors who came from different schools of thought into the school. We opened the school to playwrights, creating the Play and Director Department. It was necessary to reflect the student body and to continue bringing to the student's attention what is most exciting and challenging to be an actor. To help the students maintain their artistic ideals in a materialistic society. To foster the idea that the artist is an essential part and a contributor to American life.

Q Is our society making progress in recognizing the value that theater plays in our lives?
Some do. But there're still so many who remain oblivious to the role it plays in their daily lives. We still remain a country founded by the Puritans, who didn't like dancing, music, art. We haven't totally surmounted that, or that way of thinking. There is so much more of a need for theater today than ever before. The theater reminds us of our common humanity, our relationship to the world. And that's why I love what I do. I love getting in the rehearsal room, working on a great play, and not knowing where I'll be at the end of the day! ■

WOODIE KING, JR.

In 1970, Mr. King founded the New Federal Theatre, and has produced nearly two hundred theatre productions, presenting over five thousand performances, introducing many playwrights, including J.E Franklin, Ron Milner, Ed Bullins, Amiri Baraka, Ntozake Shange, David Henry Hwang, Genny Lim, and Laurence Holder. Mr. King's directing includes *Appear and Show Cause*, for which he received an Audelco Award; *Checkmates* on Broadway with Ruby Dee, Paul Winfield, and Denzel Washington, for which he received an NAACP Image Award; *James Baldwin: A Soul on Fire*; *Splendid Mummer*; *Robert Johnson: Trick the Devil*, for which he received an Audelco Award; *A Raisin in the Sun* at Atlanta's Alliance Theatre; *The Taking of Miss Janie* and *Joe Turner's Come and Gone* at Brooklyn College. Among plays Mr. King produced were *Black Girl*, *Medal of Honor Rag*, *What the Winesellers Buy*, *Sizwe Banzi Is Dead*, *For Colored Girls Who Have Considered Suicide When the Rainbow Is Enuf*, and the musical, *Reggae*, on Broadway. Mr. King's books include *Black Theatre: Present Condition*, *Voices of Color*, and*The Impact of Race*. His collection of essays, *Black Theater: Present Condition*, was published in 1981. Mr. King founded the National Black Theatre Touring Circuit, presenting *Boogie Woogie Landscapes*, among other plays. Mr. King received an Obie Award for Sustained Achievement, Paul Robeson Award, Rosetta LeNoire Award, and he was inducted in the American Theatre Hall of Fame.

Q You grew up in Detroit and first began as an actor. What prompted you to create Concept East Theatre at that time?

I couldn't get roles; it was a very difficult time for black artists. I had just gotten out of Wayne State, and I came in contact with Guthrie McClintic and Harold Clurman, and hearing what they said inspired me. So I started Concept East doing plays like *Krapp's Last Tape* and *A Raisin In the Sun*.

Q You spearheaded the Black literary renaissance of the 1960s by establishing the National Black Touring Circuit, making us aware of playwrights like Baraka, Shange, Bullins. Are we doing enough for our new voices?

There are a lot of new voices today, but we hear them much more in television and in the movies. You know when I first came to this city, I hitchhiked my way here and saw Jason Robards, Jr. in *The Iceman Cometh* at the old Circle-in-the-Square, and Fredric March in *Long Day's Journey into Night*, and Sidney Poitier came and he broke the mold of what was before. Those were inspiring performances. Over a hundred and twenty-five theaters were born because artists wanted to say things in the theater.

Black Theater has a very important responsibility to project positive images and we've been exploring what's happening today here at the New Federal Theatre, about what we can contribute as a people. We've always been working on important new projects. Some of the exciting plays we've done here, and with the National Black Touring Circuit, included *The Trial of One Shortsighted Black Woman Vs Mammy-Louise & Safreeta May*, by Marcia L. Leslie, and plays on Zora Neale Hurston and Paul Robeson.

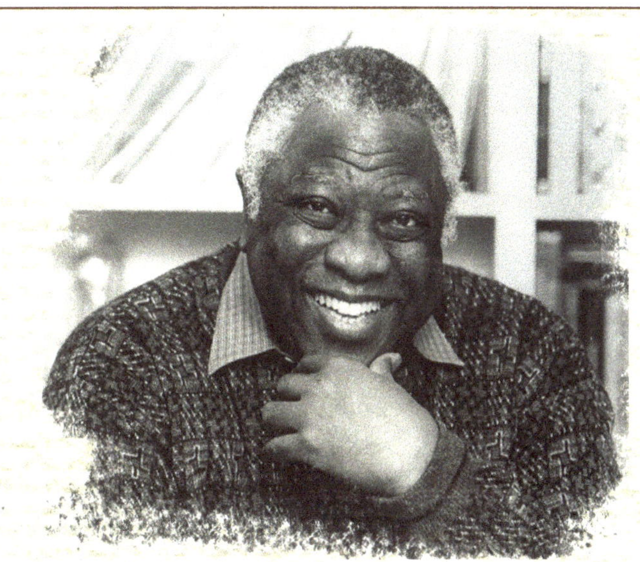

Woodie King, Jr. photo: courtesy of the artist

Q How did the National Black Touring Circuit come about?

We started it in 1975, and toured across America, to Washington, D.C, to Philadelphia, Chicago, and Detroit, to festivals in Ghana, all over Europe. We went to colleges with plays about Black American heroes in jazz, shades of Harlem, a lot of biographical plays.

Q Why did you choose a name similar to The Federal Theatre which was involved in bringing free theater to people across America during the Great Depression?

The Federal Theatre tried desperately to do theater to make people aware, to bring theater to those who had never seen theater before. When I began this theater in 1970, I was influenced by Hallie Flanagan, in a way, to pick up the tradition, providing free theater. I was moved by the Black Theatre Unit in Harlem that was part of the Federal Theatre. To put the Black artist to work and provide engrossing plays for our audiences—that's vital to me.

Q What do you want to say to the young actor of today?

You must be prepared—and to Black artists, study! Remember, sometimes you get only one or maybe two chances, and if you're brilliant they embrace you, so work and study. Study to keep your craft sharp! ■

ROBERT LEPAGE

One of Canada's most honored theatre artists, he is the founder of Ex Machina, a multi-disciplinary company which tours internationally. Among the productions he has created at La Caserne, a multi-disciplinary center in Quebec City are *The Seven Streams of the River Ota*, *Elsinore*, *Geometry of Miracles*, *The Far Side of the Moon*, *Lipsynch*, *Playing Cards*, *The Image Mill*, celebrating the 400th anniversary of Quebec City, *Eonnagata*, *The Blue Dragon*, *The Nightingale and Other Short Fables*, *887*, and *Quills*. When he was with Théâtre Repère during the 1980s, he created *Circulations*, *The Dragons' Trilogy*, *Vinci*, *Polygraphe*, and *Tectonic Plates*, and toured around the world. He was the artistic director of the National Arts Centre's Théâtre in Ottawa from 1989 to 1993, and staged *Needles and Opium*, *Coriolanus*, *Macbeth*, *The Tempest*, and *A Midsummer Night's Dream*. Mr. Lepage directed Strindberg's *A Dream Play* at Stockholm's Royal Dramatic Theatre. As a director, his films include *Le Confessional*, *Le Polygraphe*, *No*, *Possible Worlds*, and *Triptych*, an adaptation of his play *Lipsynch*. As an actor, he has appeared in *Jesus de Montreal*, *Stardom*, and Martin Villeneuve's *Mars et Avril*. He was the director for Peter Gabriel's *Secret World* tour and *Growing Up* tour. Mr. LePage has directed several operas, including *Bluebeard's Castle* and *Erwartung* for the Canadian Opera Company; *The Damnation of Faust* in Japan, Paris, and at New York's Metropolitan Opera; Richard Wagner's *Der Ring des Nibelungen*, Stravinsky's *The Rake's Progress* in Brussels; Lorin Maazel's *1984* at the Royal Opera House; *The Tempest*, and *L'Amour de Loin*. Mr. Lepage created the Cirque du Soleil show, *Ka*, in Las Vegas, and their touring show, *Totem*. Among his many awards include the Legion d'Honneur, SORIQ Award, Medal of the Officers of the Ordre national du Quebec, Denise Pelletier Prize, Stanislavsky Award, Governor General's Performing Arts Award, the Compaqnon des Arts et les lettres du Quebec, and the Glenn Gould Prize.

Q To sit through your eight-and-a-half-hour performance of *Lipsynch* was one of the most amazing, transfixing journeys I've ever experienced in the theater. How did it first come to you?

I was on a plane trip. I was sitting in business class, and in front of me towards the front of the section of the plane there was an opera singer; she was trying to practice her music. And at the back, behind me, there was a baby screaming, crying, very loudly. There were these two different voices. I could see the opera singer and she was becoming more and more upset. She couldn't continue so she got up. I could see this from where I was sitting; I was between these two entirely different voices. So when I heard it, when I saw what was happening, it struck me. I thought this could be something for a show. The voice of the singer in the front, the baby's raw voice behind me. I took the fuselage of a plane, and cut it in half to explore where the voice goes.

Q What needs to happen to engage an audience?

You need to trigger them. It can be with sound, it can be with objects or with images; so in this way you trigger their thoughts.

Q What do you expect from the actors you work with?

That they will be intelligent, that they will know how to get the words out to act the part—that they will be real.

Q What does it mean for you when you come to America and bring your work here?

It means a great deal because they're very involved here at BAM; they're very engaged. I'm glad to be here, the audiences they listen, they're a good audience. ■

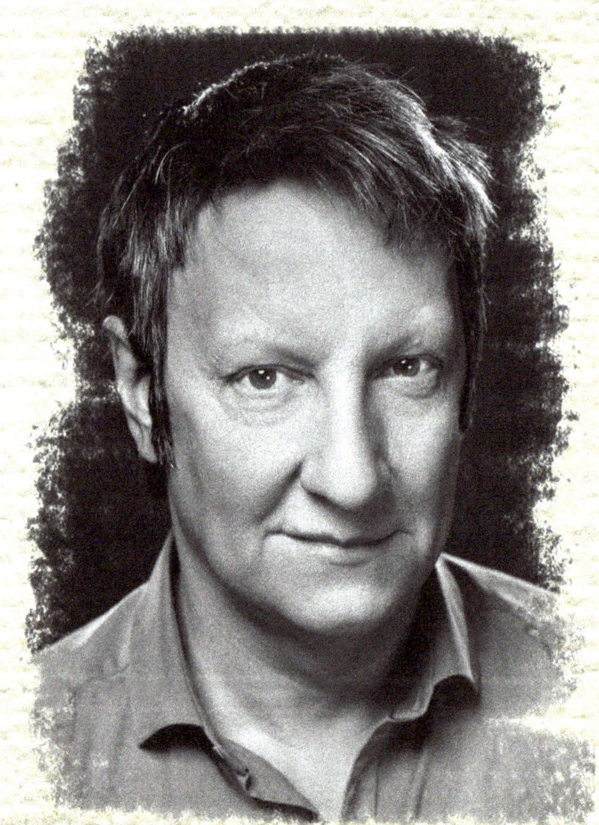

Robert Lepage photo: Jocelyn Michel, courtesy of Consulate of Canada and Mr. Lepage

EMILY MANN

One of this country's most gifted writer/directors, Ms. Mann is the Artistic Director of McCarter Theatre. On Broadway, she directed *A Streetcar Named Desire* with Nicole Ari Parker and Blair Underwood. Ms. Mann wrote and directed *Having Our Say*, receiving three Tony Award nominations and the Hull-Warriner Award; premiering at the McCarter, on Broadway, a national tour and in Johannesburg. Ms. Mann also wrote the teleplay for *Having Our Say*, receiving the Peabody Award, Christopher Award, and a Writers Guild of America nomination. Under Ms. Mann's leadership, McCarter Theatre commissioned, developed, and premiered Christopher Durang's Tony-award winning play, *Vanya and Sonia and Masha and Spike*, and the McCarter Theatre received the Tony Award for Outstanding Regional Theater. She has directed the world premiere of Nilo Cruz's Pulitzer Prize-winning and Tony Award-nominated *Anna in the Tropics* at The McCarter and on Broadway, and his new play, *Bathing in Moonlight*; Edward Albee's *All Over* with Rosemary Harris at the Roundabout Theatre, receiving an Obie Award; *Romeo and Juliet*; *The Tempest* with Blair Brown, and *Antony and Cleopatra*. Ms. Mann also directed *The Cherry Orchard* with Jane Alexander and Avery Brooks; *Miss Julie* with Kim Cattrall and Donna Murphy; *Uncle Vanya*, *The House of Bernarda Alba*, and *Baby Doll* with Dylan McDermott, all of which she adapted; *A Doll's House* with Cynthia Nixon, directed and co-authored by Ntozake Shange; *Betsey Brown*; the world premiere of Edward Albee's *Me, Myself and I* with Tyne Daly and Brian Murray; *The Glass Menagerie* with Shirley Knight and Dylan McDermott; *Cat on a Hot Tin Roof* with Pat Hingle and JoBeth Williams; *The Three Sisters* with Frances McDormand, Linda Hunt, and Mary Stuart Masterson. Ms. Mann directed the world premieres of *Twilight: Los Angeles,1992*, *Miss Witherspoon*, *The How and the Why* with Mercedes Ruehl, *Phaedra Backwards*, *Five Mile Lake*, and Danai Gurira's *The Convert*, which received six Ovation Awards. She wrote and directed *Meshugah* with Elizabeth Marvel; *Execution of Justice*, receiving a Drama Desk Nomination; *Greensboro: A Requiem*; *Still Life*, receiving six Obie Awards; *and Annulla, An Autobiography*. Ms. Mann received The Helen Merrill Distinguished Playwriting Award and the Margo Jones Award given to a "Citizen of the Theater who has demonstrated a lifetime commitment to the encouragement of the living theatre everywhere."

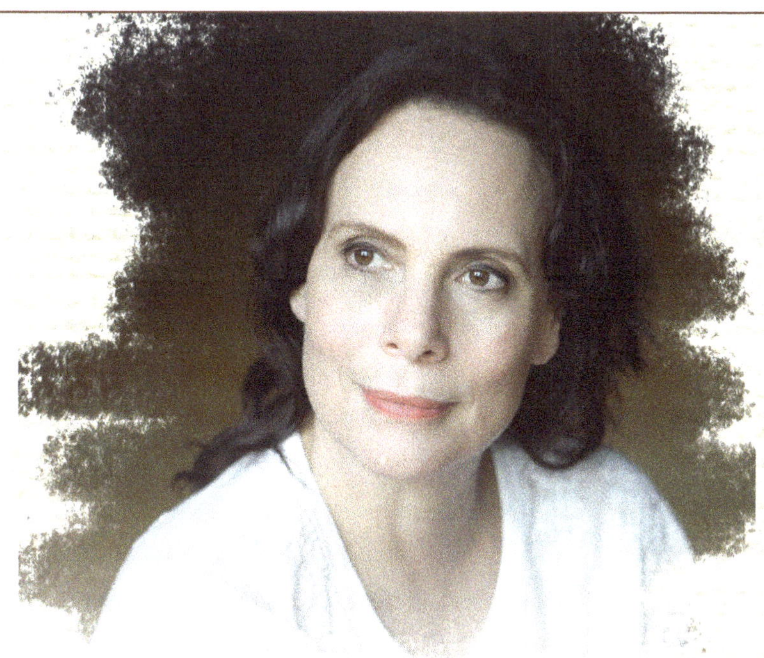

Emily Mann photo: courtesy of the artist

Q Why did you want to write your own adaptation of *The Cherry Orchard*?

Well, it's one of my favorite plays. I see it as a metaphor, shockingly close to the American experience. Serfdom in Russia was about the ownership of people, like the slavery we had in America. I looked at the play anew instead of as a musty period piece about Russia. I used a lot of imagery from W.E.B. DuBois and I was fortunate to have Avery Brooks and Jane Alexander, and it worked very well with a mixed cast.

Q The McCarter Theatre is one of the world's most important theatres and a lot of it is due to your twenty-six years as its artistic director. If you could point to certain things that continue to make it work so well, what would you say they are?

It started with having an amazing managing director. Jeff Woodward was my partner; he's a great man of the arts, and we shared a common vision. The two of us thrived on harmony. We have a loving respectful theatre. I trained at the Guthrie Theater, I learned what was necessary. Like the Guthrie, we have a terrific shop here, and designers from across the country come to the McCarter because of it. I'm also a writer and we have a very fine resident dramaturg. My managing partner now, Tim Shields, like Jeff did, shares my vision for the theater.

We're absolutely dedicated to every writer who comes to the McCarter, to their process. We've done new plays by Cruz, Fugard, Durang, Gurira, a lot of emerging and established writers. I'm also a great believer in the classics. We've developed very strong relationships with some of the finest directors in the country, like Stephen Wadsworth, and we attract the very best actors. You might say, an informal true ensemble is created every time for each production.

Q One of your greatest gifts as a writer is taking an historical event and creating an unforgettable play. What were some of the influences that shaped you as a writer?

Oddly enough it wasn't so much influences like Brecht or Piscator. It was more from being the daughter of a history teacher. I read a lot of oral history when I was young, and I found this particular form of story-telling, true and dramatic. Each time I did a new documentary piece I developed a new form.

Q What has made it such a fruitful experience working with Nilo Cruz?
We're both writers and he knows I respect, understand, and love his work. He knows I'm looking out for him on every level. He and I also share a love for Nilo's greatest influences—Federico García Lorca and Tennessee Williams. I've directed those writers' works as well. They exemplify a particular sensibility that I resonate to. When I direct Nilo, I live inside an intoxicating poetic world.

Q Are you seeking something specifically from actors during the rehearsal process?
I like working with very talented people who have done their homework. That's what I expect. I'm interested in artists bringing a lot to the process, that they're not blank slates. I want to see emotional fearlessness—open to whatever I'll give them—coupled with actors whose craft is first rate.

Q What makes theater necessary for our lives today?
There's more need now than ever before for art, for beauty, for tough real questions about what it means to be alive. This is the moment to be reminded of our humanity. ■

DIJANA MILOŠEVIĆ

Co-founder and artistic director of DAH Theatre in Belgrade, Serbia, the first theatre laboratory in her country, Ms. Milošević co-founded Natasha Project, an international theatre network, the Association of Independent Theatre Groups in Belgrade, and currently is the Director of Institute for Actors and Directors of DAH Theatre. She tours with her work, giving lectures and workshops around the world, writes essays for different national and international publications and magazines, and has worked on issues of violence against women with the activist group, Women in Black and Act Women, performing stories of women from Kosovo, Bosnia-Herzegovina, Serbia and Croatia. Ms. Milošević has taught across America at different colleges and universities.

Q When did you begin thinking about creating your own theatre company?
My need to create a group started very early in my childhood. It was not a conscious idea to create a theatre group but a group of the people with whom I would go through different adventures. In my imagination they were very concrete people with special skills, in my mind it was very real. I was fortunate to have an older neighbor, who, unlike my parents and older sister, listened every day about my adventures. So, every day I'd knock on his door and tell him about my adventures. He was my first spectator, and thanks to him the idea became real. Later, when I understood my path, I realized how much it had formed me and my vision of the theater company.

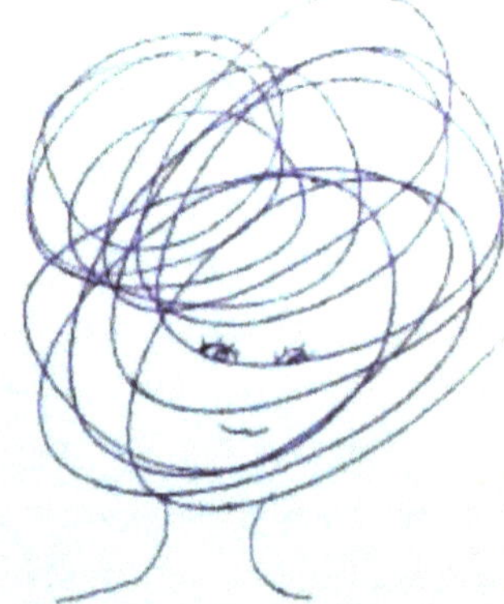

"Portrait of Dijana Milošević" artwork: N. Paripović, courtesy of N. Paripović and Ms. Milošević

Q Who have been inspirations for you as you created your work?
The first big inspiration in theater was Polish director Jerzy Grotowski and his book, "Towards the Poor Theatre," which blew my mind away when I read it for the first time. My other big inspiration, and someone I consider my master is Eugenio Barba, and his actors, especially Torgeir Wethal, who was a formative member of Odin Teatret. Another big source of inspiration for me is the work of my partner Nesa Paripovic, a renowned conceptual artist.

Q How would you describe the main reasons you co-founded DAH Teatar with Jadranka Anđelić?
We wanted to create a theatre laboratory to have a much longer period to devise and create our pieces—to develop constantly as artists and as human beings with the group of people—to perfect our skills and techniques on the every-day basis and create our own conditions. To establish different, more human relationships then relationships in institutions. To create a space free to experiment, a space of freedom in the broader sense. We were aware of the paradox that in order to create the space of free-

dom we had to construct very strict rules, with a work ethic. But as we started, the Civil War broke out in our country and our theater laboratory became really "a breath of life in that time." A platform from which we were able to speak openly and publicly, to oppose the war and violence and insanity of our government then, as well as the madness of the world politics.

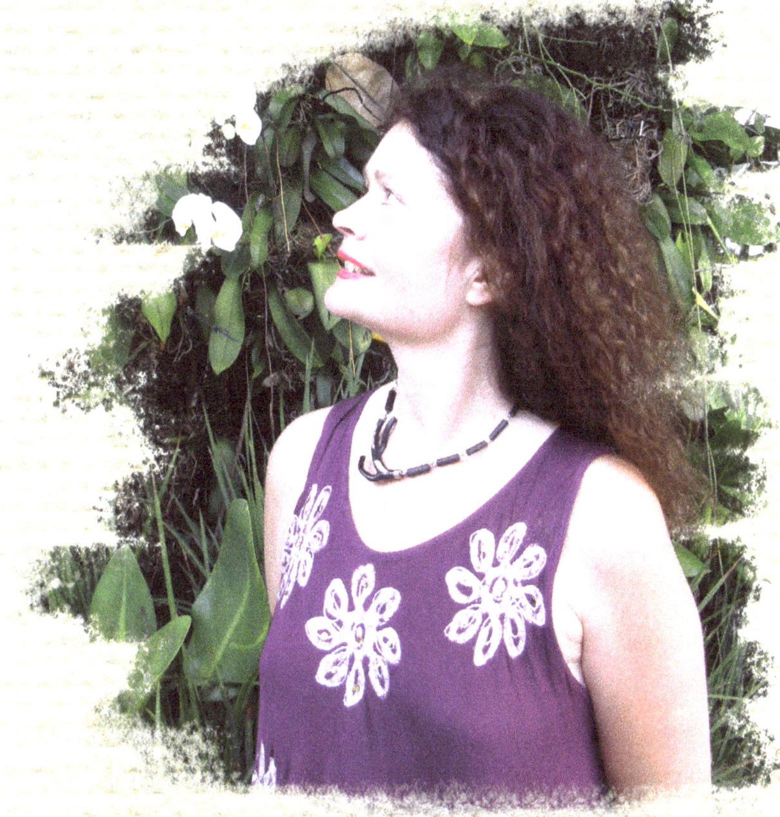

Diljana Milošević photo: courtesy of the artist

Q Your earlier performance work, Gifts of our Ancestors, led to your first performance piece, This Babylonian Confusion, based on the songs of Bertolt Brecht, who also spoke out strongly against war after World War I. You have said two questions led DAH Theater: "What is the role and meaning of theater? What are the responsibilities and duties of artists in times of darkness, violence and human suffering?" As you've continued creating new theater have you been able to approach some answers?

We realized that the only way to oppose destruction is to create. So our performances, have as their main theme, the relationship between the individual and history, while becoming a powerful celebration of life. By helping to remove barriers between people, theater nudges us to face the truth—to meet the fear, anger, prejudice, pain, and suffering we all feel—to feel the suffering of others, contributing to reconciliation. Influencing profoundly without political pressure or propaganda through the dancing, singing body of an actor the energy of life can be manifested and help us smile together.

Every country in our region faces the same important questions: Can we create a shared space? What would it take? So many people have stories to be told, and through creating together, new meaning can come to help heal the loss people experienced. Using humor to "speak truth to the power" can re-frame events and experiences, making it possible to find a "shared wisdom." Through our touring, we meet people from other ethnic communities and work to build a basis for exchange and collaboration.

Q How do you keep up your spirit and energy?

Very early on, during our first anti-war performance on the streets of Belgrade, I realized how our words and actions were needed as much as food and water. This gave me energy to continue through all the hardships and constant financial insecurity. The idea that we can make our society, our world a better place is not a naive utopia for me. It is something I constantly choose to practice through my work, something that I share with my colleagues, and in return, I get a lot of energy from that.

Q Are you currently working on new theater pieces?

Yes, for DAH's 25th Anniversary, I am composing a new piece from real stories from the past twenty-five years in the context of what doesn't exist anymore in my country. How every moment is colored and marked by the political and historical situation in a very direct way.

Another piece called *Decades*, is based on interviews with elders. The project was initiated by Ruwanthie de Chichera, an actress and director from Sri Lanka. She started a project, Dear Children Sincerely initiated by Stages Theatre Group in Sri Lanka, collecting stories and experiences of the elders, taking them to young people through story-telling performance. She asked through her show: "Eight decades of this world. Of change. Of experience. Of loss and gain. What have they learned? What do they regret? What do they want to say to us before they leave?"

The elders in my country experienced and witnessed the failure of the idea of Yugoslavia as the "most just country in the world" and all its horrific circumstances. They might have something to tell us about how to build the future.

Q What have you discovered about the art of story-telling that makes it such a universal language?

Within a circle storytelling happened for the first time. That lives in all of us. Storytelling touches something very deep human in us, creating community, a shared space and a shared moment in real time—a live experience that cannot be replaced. ■

DIANE PAULUS

Ms. Paulus is The Terrie and Bradley Bloom Artistic Director of the American Repertory Theater at Harvard University. She was selected for the 2014 "Time" 100, "Time Magazine's annual list of the one hundred most influential people in the world. Ms. Paulus received the 2013 Tony Award for Best Director for *Pippin* on Broadway. Her other Broadway productions include *Waitress, Finding Neverland*, the Tony Award-winning revivals of *Pippin, The Gershwins' Porgy and Bess*, and *Hair*. At the A.R.T., she directed Eve Ensler's *In the Body of the World*, Matthew Aucoin's opera, *Crossing, Waitress, Finding Neverland, Witness Uganda, The Gershwins' Porgy and Bess, Prometheus Bound, Death and the Powers: The Robots' Opera, The Donkey Show, Best of Both Worlds, Johnny Baseball*. Ms. Paulus directed Cirque du Soleil's *Amaluna*, currently on a world tour. As an opera director, her productions include *The Magic Flute*, the complete Monteverdi cycle, and the trio of Mozart-Da Ponte operas. Ms. Paulus is the Professor of the Practice of Theater in Harvard University's English Department. She was awarded the 2012 Founders Award for Excellence in Directing from the Drama League.

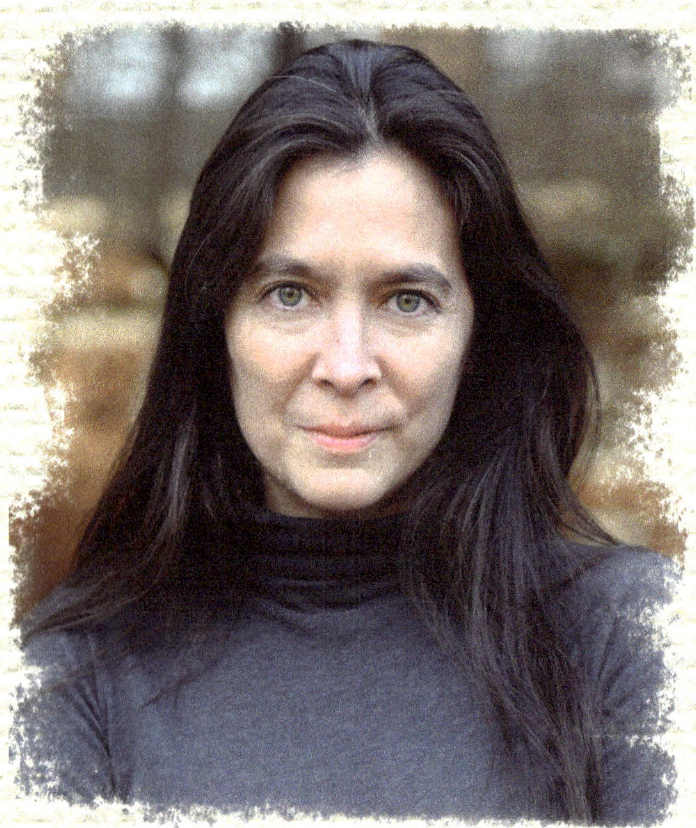

Diane Paulus photo: © Susan Lapides

Q In the face of the challenges we're continuing to face in our society, how can art help heal us?
I'm deeply moved by the potential of the theater to be a community that is defined by its diversity. We see many who are speaking up for tolerance, as well as for freedom of expression. These are the values that define us; what it means to be an American. It's the reason why I keep at it—the possibility that the arts can play a critical role in protecting and curating tolerance. It's also the resilience of the arts, and the role of the artist to heal and transform us. The arts can do a great deal to galvanize the community to understand how precious we all are—to help us wrestle with the big questions.

Q When did you know that you wanted to direct?
When I was in high school, I was politically active—I marched for the ERA movement and nuclear disarmament, and I lobbied for Planned Parenthood. When I went to college I thought about a career in politics, believing the world could be a better place; that if we were politically motivated we could make a change.

I had an epiphany moment after my freshman year, when I worked for Ruth Messinger, a Councilwoman for the Upper West Side of Manhattan. She sent me to represent her at a meeting for the Coalition of the Homeless. I remember being fascinated by the plans to get the food out, all the van routes and diagrams, of "being in the trenches." That's what I wanted—to be in the trenches. To roll up your sleeves and work directly with people. After that I searched my heart and realized that theater was what I really love—physically, emotionally, intellectually. It drives me on all cylinders.

Q Who were inspirations and influences for you in your life, and in the theater when you began your career?
I studied ballet as young girl and thought I wanted to be a ballerina. I appeared with the New York City Ballet as a child. The first ballet I ever did was Stravinsky's *Firebird*; I was a flower pot at the end of the ballet—but the power of that music marked me. It was the 1970s—George Balanchine was the head of the New York City Ballet, and amazing ballerinas like Suzanne Farrell and Patricia McBride were in their prime. Everything about Balanchine was so artistic; and he knew how to reach an audience, especially with his story ballets. And when Baryshnikov came, I was there as a little kid and danced with him in *Harlequinade*.

When I studied theater at Columbia University, I had two great mentors—Anne Bogart who taught directing, and Andrei Şerban who was head of the acting department. Anne and Andrei are both world-class directors and forces in the theater. Being at their side, not only did I learn about directing, but I learned about being committed to excellence in the way you work, and I also saw how they pushed the actor to places they've never been before. And by assisting Andrei on Massenet's *Thais*, I was introduced to the world of opera.

Q Two of your earlier successes, *The Donkey Show*, and *Sleep No More*, both engaged the audiences in unique ways, shattering expectations, encouraging greater participation.

Donkey Show was really a labor of love. I was a young grad student, and we first rehearsed it in the lobby of Columbia University's School of the Arts after hours. It was born of an interest in investigating *A Midsummer Night's Dream* in a way that we don't normally experience it. We are used to seeing Titania playfully putting flowers into Bottom's head when he has been turned into an ass, and the impression is lovely and sweet. Randy Weiner and I wanted to reveal a darker telling in a more visceral Artaudian way. The show was set on a pulsing 1970's disco dance floor—our version of the enchanted Athenian woods. We wanted to break all the rules and have the audience stand and dance to actual disco music.

With *Sleep No More*, I was in London directing an opera, and everyone was talking about Punchdrunk, the company that created it. I decided to bring Punchdrunk to America for their U.S. premiere as part of my first season as Artistic Director of the A.R.T. We mounted a new production of *Sleep No More* in an abandoned school in Brookline. There was an unbelievable response to the show—it became a phenomenon—and then moved to New York City, where it continues to play today at the McKittrick Hotel. People were crazy for it because it was so challenging. I remember the early previews thinking: "Maybe we need to make a map" then realizing that would be the exact wrong thing. You couldn't understand it with only one visit, which meant you had to come back. It treated the audience like a detective. It was as if a gauntlet was being thrown down for the audience, to make them want to know more, to go down one more hallway...

Q How has it fed your creativity being the Artistic Director of the American Repertory Theater at Harvard University?

The mission at A.R.T. is to expand the boundaries of theater through the great classics of the canon, and the new voices of tomorrow. It was this mission that drew me to the A.R.T.—I knew I could throw myself into this job with my entire heart and mind. As an undergrad at Harvard, I had seen the great work done at A.R.T. under Robert Brustein with Andrei Serban, Robert Wilson, JoAnne Akalaitis, Julie Taymor. I ushered at the theater, and often snuck into the back of the auditorium to watch the second acts. The poster of Joanne Akalaitis' controversial production of *Endgame* that I stole as a student is now hanging in my office at the A.R.T.

What I love about being at A.R.T. is that it constantly pushes me to expand the boundaries of theater as a director and as a producer. This mission has had a profound impact not only on the art created on the stage but also on how we build relationships with the audience. During my past eight years, I've worked intensely on engaging audiences, using theater as a fertile hotbed to communicate ideas, to generate debate around the most pressing issues our time.

Q What makes the process most exciting for you directing a revival, and you've directed several musicals on and Off-Broadway, including *Finding Neverland* and *Waitress*?

For many years when I did revivals, I'd always question the notion of what a "revival" is. When we do a production of *Hamlet*, we don't consider it a "revival." What motivates me in directing a revival is to create in the present, afresh and anew, what made the show so exciting when it first premiered. In the same way, when *Don Giovanni* premiered—what made it so alive when it was first performed? I want to find that out, and then create that same effect for a modern audience.

When it's a new musical, I'm focused not only on the production questions, but at the same moment, on building the story, making sure the structure of the musical works, changing songs, rewriting the opening number etc. In a new musical, you're constantly in a state of flux, you're tweaking, changing things up until the opening. The real discovery happens when the audience comes. There's nothing like a first preview of a new musical. It's a magical moment when you think—let's see what happens! Then you learn from that audience, and make more changes. I'm addicted to working on musicals; they require the most selfless collaborative effort, because there are so many moving parts.

When I was working with Kelsey (Grammer) on *Finding Neverland* or with Andrea Martin on *Pippin*, I felt like I was in comedy school. They have impeccable timing, and are master comedians. I loved working with Kelsey; he's such an accomplished performer—he can quote Shakespeare at the drop of a hat! In *Finding Neverland* rehearsals, he would watch scenes he wasn't in, and be totally moved by his fellow performers; I attribute it to his generosity as a performer.

Q What do you consider your biggest task as an artist?

My job as an artist to ring "that bell" and send those vibrations into people, to, in a sense, rattle people's bones to be present in the moment. That's what makes me tick and keeps me going as an artist. It's vital to being awake to what's happening every moment, to our planet, for our future. ■

MICHAEL PRESSMAN

Mr. Pressman was the co-executive producer of the award-winning *Blue Bloods* starring Tom Selleck and Len Cariou, and the executive producer/director of *Picket Fences*, receiving two Emmy awards. His directing on television includes *Damages, In Treatment, Justified, Law & Order, The Practice, Boston Legal, The Closer, Weeds, Chicago Hope*, for which he received a Directors Guild Award, *Saint Maybe* starring Blythe Danner, Ed Hermann, and Mary Louise Parker, *To Heal a Nation* with Eric Roberts, and *A Season for Miracles*. Mr. Pressman's film directing includes *The Bad News in Breaking Training, Some Kind of Hero* starring Richard Pryor, *Teenage Mutant Ninja Turtles II: The Secret of the Ooze*, and *To Gillian on Her 37th Birthday* starring Peter Gallagher and Clare Danes. A noted stage director, his productions include on Broadway *Come Back, Little Sheba* with S. Epatha Merkerson, Kevin Anderson, and Zoe Kazan, the West coast premiere of *To Gillian on her 37th Birthday, The World of Sholom Aleichem*, the world premiere of *Days and Night Within, Love Letters* with Kathy Baker and Tom Skerritt, and *Frankie and Johnny in the Clair de Lune*. His film, *Frankie and Johnny are Married* about that experience, received the Ashland Film Festival's Best Acting Ensemble Award, and Ft. Lauderdale Film Festival's Renaissance Award. A graduate of the Film School at California Institute of the Arts, where he was also a Board of Trustee. Mr. Pressman has taught at Pittsburgh's Carnegie Mellon.

Q What led you to your deep love for theater and filmmaking?

It was a convergence of a lot of things. First and foremost, I loved acting. I began acting onstage as a child in *A Thousand Clowns* in summer stock theatre, Off-Broadway in *Emil and the Detectives*, and played Bottom in *A Midsummer Night's Dream* by the age of fourteen.

When I was eight years old, I remember standing backstage on Broadway watching Jason Robards, Jr. as the character, collapse at the end of *The Disenchanted*. He'd jump up as soon as the curtain fell, and greet my father, who had directed him in the play. It was a life-changing experience for me—watching the transformation from the character back to the actor getting ready for his curtain call.

I learned a lot from my father—David Pressman. He was a natural, born teacher. He'd share stories with me, his feelings about what acting is. I think the greatest thing was his enjoyment of always seeing something new. My father lived to ninety-six, and both my father and my mother were great models, with an ageless look at the world.

When I fell in love with films, I studied with Alexander McKendrick in film school; his most famous film was probably *Sweet Smell of Success*. I found my career then—movie making. The first film I made was for Roger Corman.

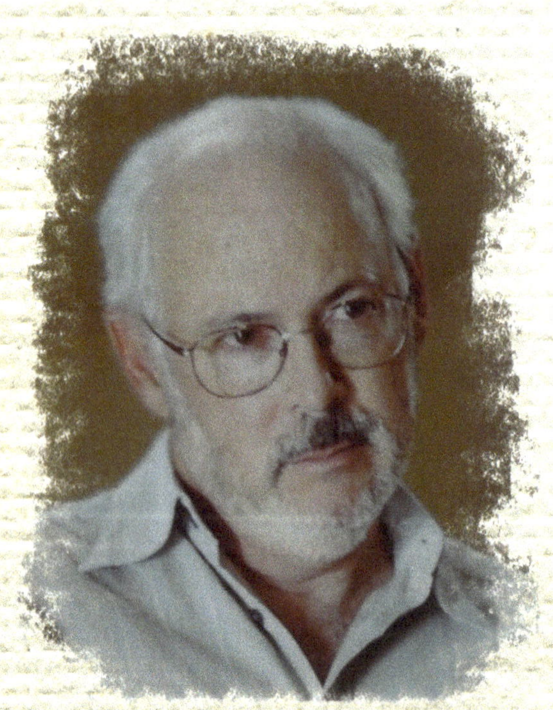

Michael Pressman photo: courtesy of the artist

Q You have a very strong feeling about the actor's contribution.

It never comes alive until the actor inhabits the character in the work. That's where the work begins, regardless of the visual style, all the details of movie-making. In that respect, I feel every director should get up on stage and act.

Q Your film, *Frankie and Johnny Are Married*, was based on your experiences putting on a theatrical production in Los Angeles.

Yes, I wrote, directed, and had the audacity to star myself in the film. It's a personal look at marriage and the theater, humorous and uplifting about all the pitfalls, dramas, and disasters that go on in the creative journey. The film also starred Lisa Chess, whom I was married to at the time, a fabulous actress, and Alan Rosenberg. It took a year of planning, actually doing the production of Terrence McNally's play, *Frankie and Johnny*—a year to write the screenplay, a year to make the film. It was my ninth feature film. I can safely say with pride, I feel I got it right.

Q What would you say that means?

When all the elements come together, and a little bit of magic happens, which lifts the experience to another level. It's the key to the creative process. It takes the confidence to do it, a little bit of madness, and a desire to tackle the impossible.

Q How challenging was it for you directing and acting in the film?
I protected myself as a director with a cameraman I trusted and had worked with on many films. By shooting it digitally I was able to look at the playback, and analyze the work. Acting in the film was hard, but nowhere as terrifying as getting back on stage after thirty years. Besides the sheer terror, was the concentration of my "instrument," having not been onstage for thirty years. I didn't know if I could stay in character, and get rid of my stage fright, but acting with Lisa, who was my wife at the time made it safer. I also got help from having a co-director, Steve Gomer. It was a wonderful growth process. I wish I could have played the play many more times. As I got stronger, I felt less afraid.

Q What kind of an experience was it directing Richard Pryor in *Some Kind of Hero*.
It was a large life-changing moment. Richard very rarely improvised a line, he said every line written in the script. But he had the ability to make the whole thing seem improvised because he was so present. I witnessed his live stand-up act which was all rehearsed. The night before, I saw him rehearse his act, and watched him work out the smallest detail of his act. He had an extra ability which separated him in the heat of an electric moment.

Q How do you know when something works?
It's the audience reaction. And when I view a film of mine, I can discover, "Oh my, we stayed at that party too long," in a scene. It definitely falls in the area of trust, confidence, critical judgment. It's knowing the "when and when not to."

Q Why do you feel theater can be empowering?
It's the nourishment of our souls, pure and simple. The live experience cannot be replaced. There remains an incredible urge to see something live. I watch young people who have had no education in theatre see a show for the first time, and it's a life-changing experience for them. When a play is over, I believe the audience should be changed. I trust that kind of energy life force will live on in generations to come.

Q What keeps you creating?
As long as I can continue to do my work, and my craft improves, maybe I'll get to the point where I can do something that will make a difference in the world. That's the spine that carries the artist forward. It doesn't mean I'll change the world tomorrow, but maybe I can make a difference. I think you learn through art how to do that. ■

HAROLD PRINCE

Recognized as one of the most creative and innovative figures in theatre, Mr. Prince's shows on Broadway have included the original productions of *The Pajama Game, West Side Story, Fiddler on the Roof, A Funny Thing Happened on the Way to the Forum, Cabaret, Company, Follies, Candide, Pacific Overtures, A Little Night Music, Sweeney Todd, Evita, Bounce, The Phantom of the Opera, Parade, The Petrified Prince, Whistle Down the Wind, Prince of Broadway*, and *LoveMusik*. Among the plays he directed were *The Great God Brown, 3hree, The Flight of the Lawnchair Man, Hollywood Arms, The Visit, End of the World, Play Memory*, and his own play, *Grandchild of Kings*. His production of *Don Giovanni* is in the repertory of the New York City Opera. Mr. Prince's opera productions include *Ashmedai, Willie Stark, Madame Butterfly*, a revival of *Candide, Turandot* at the Vienna State Opera, and have appeared at Chicago Lyric, the Metropolitan Opera, New York City Opera, San Francisco Opera, and Buenos Aires' Theatre Colon, among many others. A recipient of a National Medal of Arts, he has received twenty-one Tony Awards, more than any other individual, including eight for directing, eight for producing the year's Best Musical, two as Best Producer of a Musical, and three special awards including a Tony Award for lifetime achievement, and was a 1994 Kennedy Center Honoree. His memoir, *Contradictions: Notes on Twenty-Six Years in the Theatre* was published in 1974.

Q Were you interested in theater at an early age?
I read a lot of plays in high school. I owned a stage when I was young, and I would put on plays. Later on as I got older, I'd work the plays I read out in my head. It's funny, but I didn't see any musicals at that time. They weren't that exciting for me—the lyrics and music didn't seem to reflect the book. The only musicals that excited me were *South Pacific, Porgy and Bess*, and *Showboat*. There was a lot of other more goofy stuff, too, that didn't excite me. Our period today is very similar. It's like a pendulum that swings. But there's always room for everything.

Q I notice among your theater books behind you that you have books on the great directors: Meyerhold, Vakhtangov, and Piscator.
I've seen a lot of theater in foreign countries. I love Russian theater, the classics and modern work. I love German expressionism and traditional Japanese theater. I've interpreted these versions of theater in my work.

I have to tell you, at one time I was lucky to meet Joshua Logan, right after he had done *Mr. Roberts* on Broadway. I thought his direction for that play, for *Charley's Aunt*, for *South Pacific*, were as good as any I had seen. We

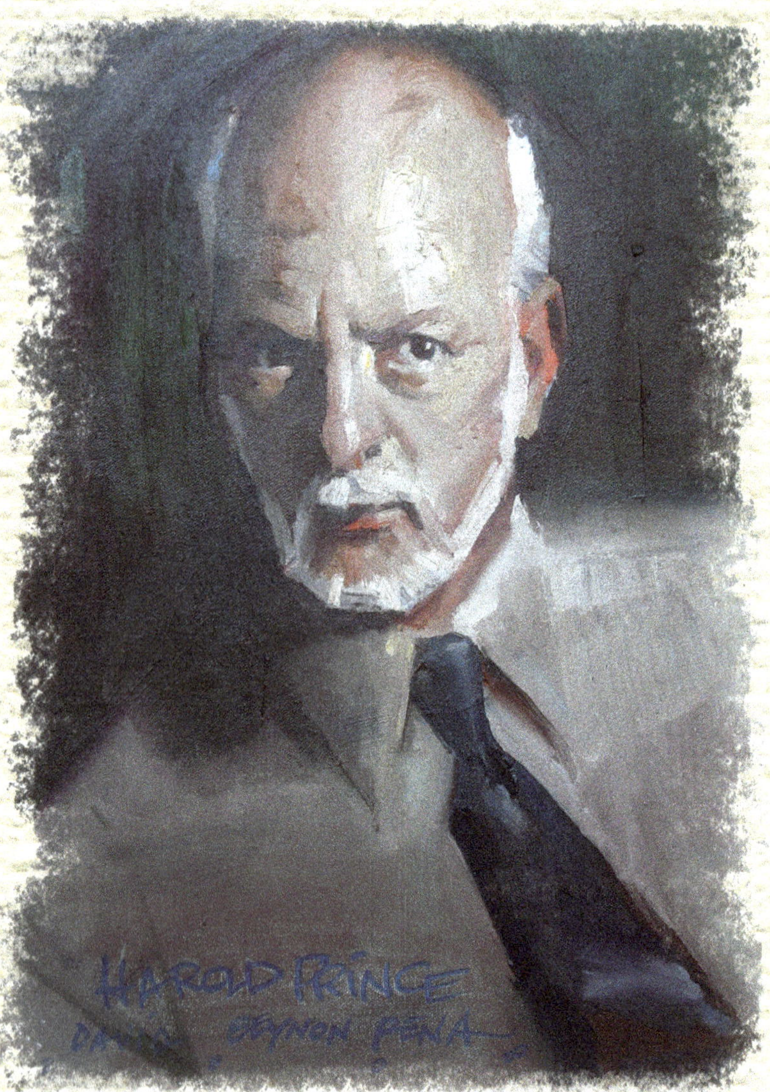

became close friends and he told me all about his having traveled to Russia and his studying with Stanislavsky. He also told me my directing was very similar in style to Meyerhold's. He said, "You work very much like him. Your work is reflective of his style."

I really didn't know that much about Meyerhold, but when I read everything about him, I was surprised to find out the way in which I had begun my "game plan" for *Pacific Overtures* was very similar to how he had worked on his production of Dos Passos' *D.E. in Moscow*. It was bizarre.

Later when I did *Evita*, I realized during rehearsals a number was desperately needed to introduce Peron. I recommended to the authors that they write a musical scene, in which colonels and generals sit in chairs in a row, and as the scene progresses, the chairs are removed until only one chair is left with Peron. I said, "Furthermore, why don't we make them rocking chairs." Well, later on I received in the mail a photo of a Meyerhold production in which he had a scene of rocking chairs. It was like "something had whispered in my ear."

Q What leads you to choose a particular project?

It's sort of a hydra-headed thing. I'm an audience, too, and I want to see things that I'm not seeing. And from out of the process of preparing the play, working with the author, the scenic designer, the actors, I derive a huge amount of joy. I'm never happier coming home than when I've been rehearsing, and have a large problem to solve whatever it is. It's me expressing myself towards an end result that I'm waiting to explore, to behold. Theater operates in trends. And sometimes these plays you see speak to you, or sometimes they elude you.

Q You directed Carol Burnett's play, *Hollywood Arms* on Broadway, with a cast including Linda Lavin, Frank Wood, and Michele Pawk—

I did it because I loved the material, the story, and the cast we were able to put together. It was exciting to go to work every day. The play is about a very loving family. The portrait can be very funny at times; it can also be very serious and upsetting. The idea that Carol Burnett could tell this story honestly and still love all these people affected me greatly; she just didn't paint a pretty picture. My guess is, she knew, instinctively, that if you can still love those around you, under these kinds of circumstances, these incredibly difficult situations, and manage to share a bond of laughter and music, you'll survive. That's why the show moved the audiences who came to see it.

Q What inspires you?

Optimism and denial. They go hand in hand. The irreconcilable difference between the two. I don't want to retire, nor am I ready to retire. I want to maintain the quality of my work for as long as I'm pleased with it. I like to communicate to an audience. Numerical age is irrelevant. Yet I know people at sixty who just stop, and decide that's it. I work on Saturdays and Sundays. For me those days are choice days rather than a day of rest or respite.

Q Who have you learned the most from that you've worked with?

From a whole lot of different people. I learned from George Abbott how to organize work. How absolutely necessary it is to be truthful in whatever style you're working. That if the actor responds honestly, whether it's even slamming a door, there had

Harold Prince artwork: David Pena

better be a good reason. And if it's appropriate and honest, the audience will respond. When the audience heard the noise of the door slamming at the end of *Sweeney Todd*, I knew they'd shiver. They had every reason to. I also learned from Abbott that I could direct. That's what every aspiring young artist needs to hear from an experienced person.

When I was stage manager, I'd watch Abbott and Jerome Robbins, they were both giants, and yet they were both entirely different. When there was a production in tryouts, and they'd run into a problem, I'd go home that night and try to solve it. And the next day I'd come in and see what they did. And it wouldn't be anything at all like what I had come up with. I'd anguish over what they did. Why had I been so wrong? But slowly I began to realize it wasn't that I was wrong, I had just come up with a different solution. So when I began to direct, I realized that's what made my work uniquely mine. I've learned to want to aspire to, and to want more in what I do.

I've learned from my wife, from Boris Aronson, and from Stephen Sondheim. All three had intellect and taste, and a degree of impatience.

Q As you've traveled around the world, what theater have you seen that stirred your creativity?

I learned a lot from seeing plays like *Ten Days that Shook the World* at the Taganka Theatre in Moscow; *The Three Sisters* performed by the Moscow Art Theatre, which was the best I've ever seen; the Japanese No Theatre, it fascinated me; from various operas I really loved; I learned a lot from Joshua Logan's work on *South Pacific* on Broadway; from Elia Kazan, on many projects, no question. That work was hugely encouraging to watch. It was definitely very much larger than life. I learn and continue to learn from travel.

Q What fuels a rebirth of creativity in theater?

What fuels each generation to regenerate the theater is isolation; the need of isolated, young, lonely people to create some fantasy into which they can escape. And I find when I talk to or listen to older artists, like actors, conductors, opera singers, the one thing they shared in common, was the need to fantasize. They all seem to have had solitary-ness in their youth. ■

NANCY RHODES

Artistic Director of Encompass New Opera Theatre, Ms. Rhodes staged the world premiere of Kirke Mechem's *Tartuffe* for San Francisco Opera, Virgil Thomson's *Lord Byron* at Alice Tully Hall, *The Astronaut's Tale* at BAM, and new operas for the Brooklyn Philharmonic Orchestra and Opera Theater of Pittsburgh. Internationally, she directed *Death in Venice* in Stockholm, *Carmen* in Oslo, and *Happy End* in Finland. She staged *West Side Story* and *Kiss Me Kate* at Tirana's Albanian National Opera, the first American musicals staged in Albania, and musicals for the Turkish State Theatre in Ankara and Istanbul. She directed *Eccentrics, Outcasts and Visionaries: A Century of American Opera* for the Holland Festival in Amsterdam. Her production of Grigori Frid's opera, *The Diary of Anne Frank*, toured Cleveland Opera receiving wide recognition. Ms. Rhodes has staged over fifty-five operas at Encompass, including Virgil Thomson's *The Mother of Us All*, Blitzstein's *Regina*, Richard Pearson Thomas's *A Wake or A Wedding*, Evan Mack's *Angel of the Amazon*, and George Antheil's *Transatlantic*. Ms. Rhodes co-conceived and directed *Only Heaven*, based on poetry by Langston Hughes, and created the *Paradigm Shifts: Music and Film Festival*. As a U.S. Delegate and Vice-President of the International Theatre Institute, Ms. Rhodes has conducted workshops around the world. Her opera, *The Theory of Everything*, was performed at New York City's Skirball Center, CUNY, and Symphony Space. Opera America honored Nancy Rhodes and Encompass for "25 Years of Dynamic Leadership."

artwork: Nancy Rhodes, courtesy of the artist

Q How young were you when you were first introduced to opera?

I'm one of those people who grew up in a musical family. My father played the trombone and the piano. His sister was a concert pianist, and I studied piano with her starting at age five. Every holiday, we'd have family musicales. We lived in a small town, in Chambersburg, Pennsylvania, near Gettysburg. There was always a lot of music—church and school choirs, bands and orchestras, but we had no opera. I didn't see my first opera until I was sixteen years old, in Washington, D.C. I also remember seeing the national company of *The Sound of Music* around the same time. I was on the edge of my seat; the story never left my mind. I think it was then that I decided to go into the theater to be a director.

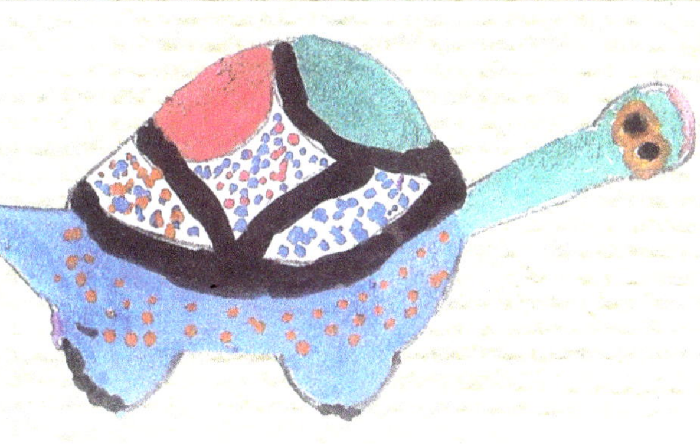

Q How did directing your first opera come about?

The first time I was hired it was to direct a production of *The Mother of Us All* by Gertrude Stein at the American Theater Festival. Then I got a frantic call, "We thought it was the play version, but it's an opera! Can you change it?" I really needed the job, so I said, "Yes, I'll make an adaptation," and got a music director. A friend told me I should get in touch with Virgil Thomson, the composer of the opera.

Virgil was a living legend; he had written two operas with Gertrude Stein. Their masterwork, *Four Saints in Three Acts* played on Broadway with an entire African-American cast in 1934. So I called him at the Chelsea Hotel. He said, "Come on over." When I arrived, he invited me to sit on his velvet settee surrounded by paintings by Matisse and Picasso. Then he jumped up and began playing through key sections of the music, singing some of it, and we enthusiastically exchanged ideas. He said "Yes" to some of the unusual staging ideas I had.

A master saying "yes" to a young artist was an extraordinary gift, which I will always cherish. I was twenty-two years old, he was eighty-two, and we hit it right off. He changed the course of my life from that day on. When we did the production, Virgil loved it. My producer, Roger Cunningham, said, "Let's do the whole thing as an opera," and that's how Encompass began. Virgil was behind us for the last ten years of his life.

Q Why did you want to create Encompass New Opera Theatre?

At that time, there wasn't an opera company that exclusively focused on American opera composers who wrote about the coming together of what we call "America." One of the things I learned from Virgil was that it was pretty rough sailing for American composers to get their works done in the United States in major opera houses because the emphasis is on performing the masterpieces of 19th Century Europe.

When Virgil recommended us to the Holland Festival, we did seventeen excerpts of American opera, which I titled "Eccentrics, Outcasts and Visionaries." After that I stayed in Europe, and for the next ten years, I directed throughout Europe and parts of Asia.

Q Who have been inspirations to you?

Certainly Virgil Thomson—Sheldon Harnick and Charles Strouse, and Robert Ward. I learned so much from working with the great writer, Michael Stewart, and Estelle Parsons. Martha Coigney of the International Theatre Institute gave me many opportunities outside the U.S.

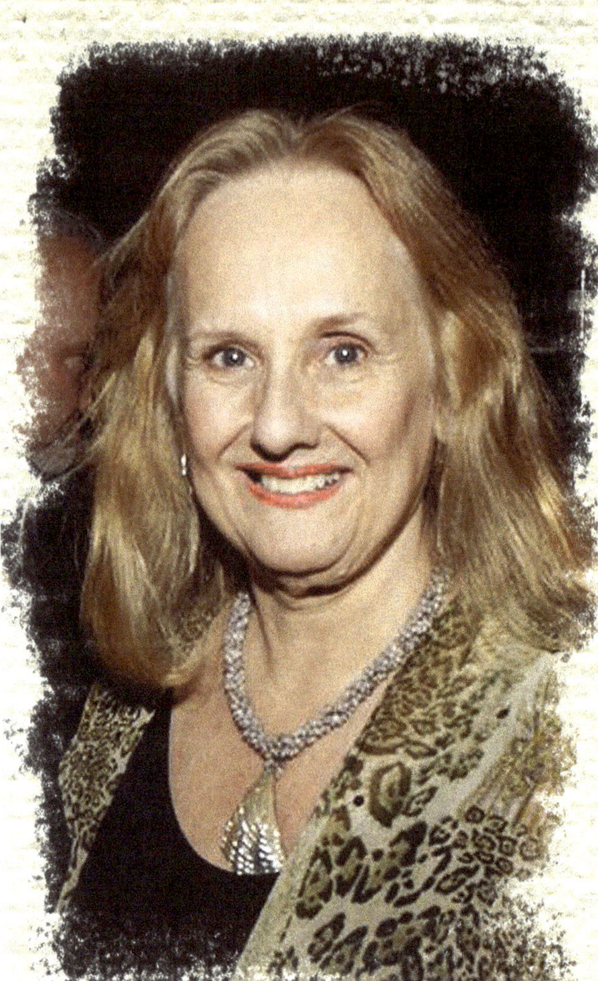

Nancy Rhodes photo: courtesy of the artist

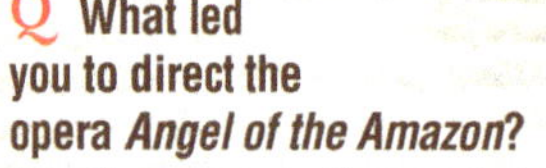

Q What led you to direct the opera *Angel of the Amazon*?

I've been an artist-activist for as long as I can remember. I grew up close to nature as a child; it's so much a part of me. I'm aware of the terrible scars of colonialism that affect the world today, and I believe in speaking truth to power, we can understand all human beings and cultures.

I had been wanting to do a "rainforest opera" for years. One day it came in the form of a handwritten letter and a tape through the mail. I listened to it, and saw a big talent, and an opportunity to combine music and theater with what's going on environmentally in the world.

Evan Mack was finishing up his doctorate at Cincinnati Conservatory when he heard the story of Sister Dorothy. She had gone into the rain forest to help gain land rights for indigenous families and he learned about the terrible tragedy that befell her in the Amazon Basin of Brazil. In a white heat of passion, he wrote *Angel of the Amazon*. I directed the premiere, with Mara Waldman as music director, at The Baryshnikov Arts Center in New York City in 2011.

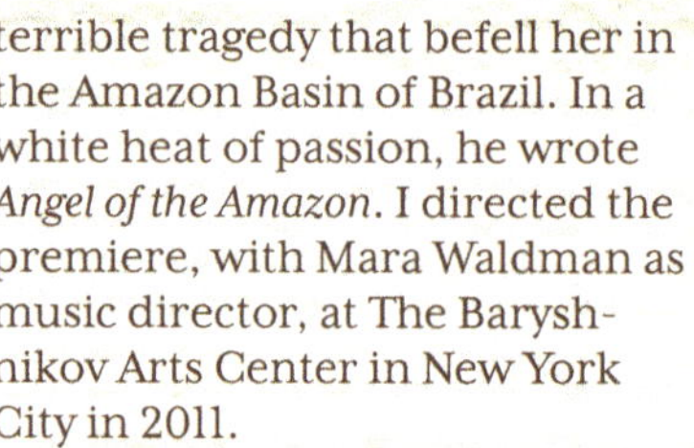

That led to my coming up with the theme for a Cultural Event we produced—Paradigm Shifts - dealing with issues of science, arts, ecology, philosophy, indigenous cosmology, and exploring them through music.

Q What led you to create your opera, *The Theory of Everything*, with John David Earnest?

John wrote the music; he's a deeply spiritual person, a Buddhist and a first-rate musician. It's been a productive and enriching collaboration.

As I was developing my character of a Brazilian quantum physicist in the book of the opera,

I came across David Bohm's life. I also learned about the Native American dialogues in New Mexico at the SEED Institute. Leroy Little Bear, an Elder who taught Native American studies at Harvard, had read the writings of David Bohm, and realized they expressed exactly what Native Americans had already known and understood for thousands of years. We're "a map of the world."

I went and visited the Navajo nation. I immediately sensed the influence of Tibet all around me. I learned that the Navajo traced their ancestry back to Tibet. The heartland of America is rich in ancient cultures, ancient history. I've gone out to Albuquerque twice for the "talking stick dialogues" with Native American physicists and western scientists. Many people I met knew Bohm, and all of it has figured into my opera.

Physics and science have always been interests of mine since I was a child. I had become inspired by long walks through nature with my grandfather, who was a physics teacher. He taught me how to observe and analyze and appreciate the invisible forces.

In 1987, I had a dream in the middle of the night. When I woke up, Act I, Scene 1 came to me, taking place in a planetarium. Thus began *The Theory of Everything*. The journey of writing reminds me of portals that continue to manifest and unfold—just like William Blake's poem, which I used in the libretto:

To see a world in a grain of sand
and a heaven in a wild flower,
Hold infinity in the palm
of your hand,
and eternity in an hour.

Q How would you describe the power of creativity—and how music feeds that creativity?

I once jumped into a taxicab, and as soon as I got in, I was amazed. The driver had decorated the ceiling and sides of the cab with beautiful photographs of the sea, waterfalls, three-dimensional flowers, gorgeous trees and foliage, and for the duration of the ride I was transported into a breathtakingly delightful world of nature and water. The driver was expressing his creativity by making a beautiful environment with the tools and skills that he had.

Composers and writers are compelled to express something about being human, to delve into what is happening in the world today or in the past, and bring it into focus. Plato wrote, "Music is a moral law. It gives soul to the universe, wings to the mind, light to the imagination, and charm and gaiety to life and everything."

In bringing new opera to life, we embrace ideas that broaden the scope of human potential and human experience. Music is a meaningful and a soothing expression in our fragmented and uncertain world. Leonard Bernstein said, "This will be our reply to violence: To make music more intensely, more beautifully, more devotedly than ever before."

We've often elevated the word, "creative," sometimes imbuing it with the sense that only certain people or certain powers can create. However, every living person is creative. Every day of living is a creative opportunity and act. The only difference comes in how we express our creativity. ■

LLOYD RICHARDS

In 1958, Mr. Richards became the first Black director of a Broadway play with his production of Lorraine Hansberry's *A Raisin in the Sun* starring Sidney Poitier, Ruby Dee, Claudia McNeil, and Diana Sands. He also introduced August Wilson to Broadway, directing *Ma Rainey's Black Bottom*. Mr. Richards directed and collaborated on five other plays by Mr. Wilson—*Fences*, *Joe Turner's Come and Gone*, *Two Trains Running*, *Seven Guitars*, and *The Piano Lesson*, which he directed on CBS and which received eight Emmy nominations. Mr. Richards received Tony nominations for Best Director for three of his six collaborations with August Wilson, and won the Tony Award for *Fences*. He also directed *The Yearling*, *The Moon Besieged*, *The Long Dream*, the musical, *I Had a Ball*, and a 1977 production of *Paul Robeson* with James Earl Jones. He produced seven of Athol Fugard's plays. Mr. Richards taught acting under Paul Mann at the Actor's Workshop in New York; among his students was Sidney Poitier. He was Head of the Actor Training Program at New York University's School of the Arts, Professor of Theatre and Cinema at Hunter College, Dean of the Yale School of Drama, and Artistic Director of the Yale Repertory Theatre from 1979 to 1991. Between 1968 until 1999, he was Artistic Director of the National Playwrights Conference at the Eugene O'Neill Theatre Center. He helped develop the work of Wendy Wasserstein, John Guare, Charles Fuller, Christopher Durang, Lee Blessing, and David Henry Hwang. Mr. Richards' television work included segments of *Roots: The Next Generation*, *Bill Moyers' Journal*, and *Robeson*. He received the Audelco Pioneer Award, Actors' Equity's Paul Robeson Award, and the National Medal of Arts. He was inducted into the Theater Hall of Fame. Mr. Richards died in 2006 (this interview was conducted in 2001).

Q You made your debut directing an amazing cast in *A Raisin in the Sun* on Broadway, one of the great theatrical events of 20th century theater. What were some of the greatest challenges you faced?

We were all baptized through that experience. I got the job through Sidney Poitier. We were both struggling actors, poor at that time, and we'd hang out at a beanery and talk; it was called an "after-class." At that time, actors like Paul Robeson and Canada Lee showed us what could be done in a major way. Now Sidney told me, "If I ever do a major play on Broadway, I want you to direct it."

Well, Sidney called me from Hollywood—he was working on *Porgy and Bess*—and he said, "I

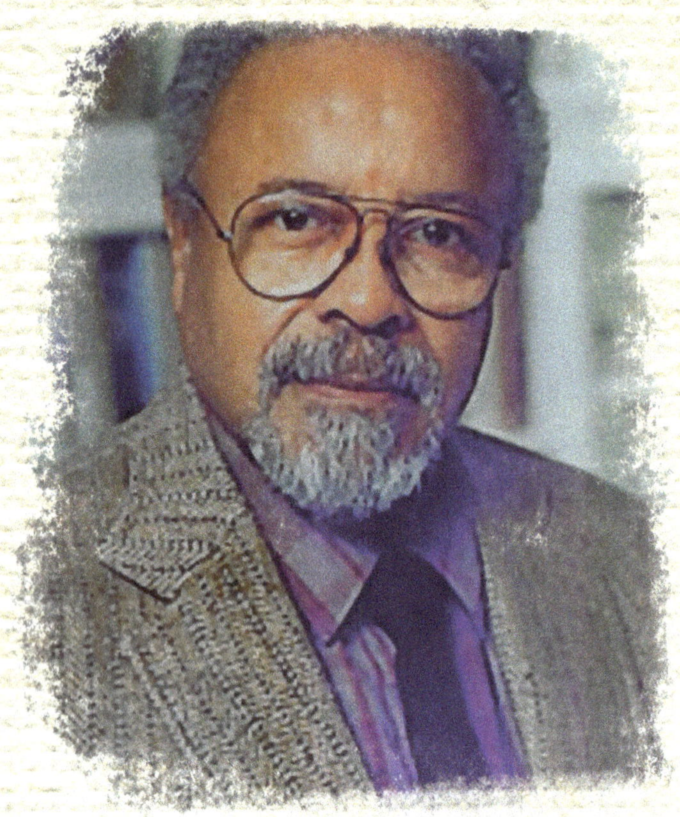

found the play and I want you to meet the producer, and the playwright, her name is Lorraine Hansberry." I meet both of them and we hit it off.

I worked with Lorraine every week for almost a year while Philip Rose tried to raise the money. The word in New York was, "They weren't ready for a play about a black family." We couldn't get a theater. We did readings again and again, and just kept trying to raise the money.

Q How did you work with Lorraine Hansberry on the script?

Lorraine was intelligent, articulate, with very strong beliefs. She was writing about something personally meaningful to her and socially important. Her idols were O'Casey, Ibsen, Shaw, all who had a strong command of language, metaphor, and a concern for social issues. She understood what I'd point out in the script, and she'd address the problem and find her answer. I don't want to be the playwright. I want to provoke the playwright, encourage what the writer wants to say.

When we went into rehearsal we still didn't have the money. Eventually it came. Our biggest investor was Harry Belafonte. We only had two out-of-town bookings, in New Haven and Philadelphia. But when word started to go out once the show opened, theater owners came to see it. Finally, the Shuberts booked us at the Blackstone Theatre in Chicago. But it was still touch and go. Then we came to New York.

Q You also had an amazing collaboration with August Wilson.

Well, I first met August at the Playwrights Conference at the O'Neill Theatre Center. He was a poet who was trying to become a playwright. He had been rejected five years in a row. The man couldn't write dialogue. Someone told him, "If you can't write dialogue, you listen." Well, the year he was accepted was with his play, *Ma Rainey's Black Bottom*. The readers told me, you've got to read it. When I did, I knew all the characters. I met them all in the barber shops when I was a kid, arguing about baseball, politics, religion.

Q The Playwrights Conference at the Eugene O'Neill Theatre Center is a very special place.

It's a place where attention is paid to the development of a new play; the playwrights are the future of the theater. In the old days, plays would evolve under the wing of the producer/manager. When I first went to the O'Neill, it was called "TryOut USA."

Those who work in the theater, and give their lives to it, exemplify a spirit of why we all went into the theatre in the first place. It's a matter of paying attention to its playwrights, and through that caring, new voices can emerge.

Q You produced several of Athol Fugard's plays. Why is his work vital for our culture?

He was in the middle of racial strife and conflict and he had a point of view that was contrary to the accepted political point of view. He chose to address it. I've been involved in several plays that have had a social concern. For me, that is my way of addressing the problems I see in our society. I'm also attracted to the theatre because of its use of language. What words can say and how they affect people.

Q You also value Harold Clurman's writings.

I had great respect for him. As a critic he was never in competition with those he wrote about. Many people write how they perceive, not with the understanding of what these people are really about, in a particular play.

Q How is theater a reflection of our society?

Theater has always been a reflection of our times. A lot of things have happened in our country's history that shaped the theater, its voices. Major issues through our history have galvanized us as a people, like a war, a depression, a movement. They affected our writers. So much of our good theater comes out of societal confrontations. It's almost too easy to survive. What will make theater important again will be issues. ■

Lloyd Richards photo: courtesy of the artist

MARK RYDELL

An Academy Award-nominated director, Mr. Rydell's films have throughout his career received twenty-six Academy Award nominations. His films include *The Fox*, which received the Golden Globe Award; *The Rievers,*; *Jeremiah Johnson*, as producer; *Scarecrow*, as Producer, for which he received the Palme D'Or; *The Cowboys, Cinderella Liberty, Harry and Walter Go to New York*; *The Rose* with Bette Midler; *On Golden Pond* with Henry Fonda and Katharine Hepburn; *The River* with Sissy Spacek; *For the Boys, Even Money, Crime of the Century*; and TNT's *James Dean*, for which he received the Directors Guild Award, directing himself in the role of studio mogul, Jack Warner opposite James Franco. As an actor, Mr. Rydell made his Broadway debut in *Seagulls over Sorrento* with Rod Steiger; appeared opposite John Cassavetes and Sal Mineo in *Crime in the Streets*; in *The Long Goodbye*; and Woody Allen's *Hollywood Ending*. His directing career on television includes *Ben Casey*, the first episode of *I Spy* starring Bill Cosby and Robert Culp; more than fifty episodes of dramatic television, including an award-winning episode of *Gunsmoke*. Mr. Rydell played the lead in *Moving Right Along*, by Elaine May and Jan Mirochek, at San Francisco's Magic Theatre. Mr. Rydell, with Martin Landau and Lyle Kessler, produced *The Total Picture Seminar*. Mr. Rydell is an accomplished jazz pianist.

Q Your initial training was in music.

I grew up in the Bronx; my father was a Wall Street stockbroker. I studied piano and became a jazz pianist. I used to go and listen to jazz at The Three Deuces, the Downbeat, and listened to people like Art Tatum. I'd get home three in the morning; music was an escape for me.

When I decided to be an actor, I was interviewed by Sandy Meisner, and he gave me a scholarship. It changed my life. Sandy was an idealized father figure for me. He was an artist. He was encouraging, a supportive teacher guiding me. He also sent me to an analyst. Everything he told me, it changed my life completely. He was one of the strongest influences on me, along with Gadge (Elia Kazan), and Clurman.

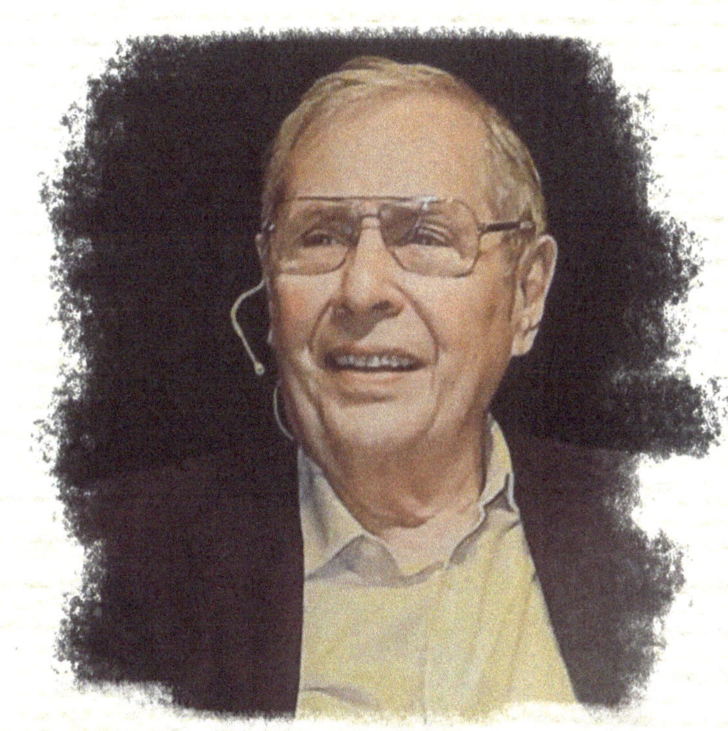

Mark Rydell photo: Gene Egan courtesy of Sedona International Film Festival

Q I understand you were in Harold Clurman's late night acting classes.

I was in his midnight class till four in the morning; it was a great class. It was the 1950s, and Harold was inspired. He would get so passionate that he would stutter like Marchbanks in the Shaw play to get all his ideas out. Harold was so exciting when he was passionate; he influenced my life.

Kim Stanley, Brando, George C. Scott, Colleen (Dewhurst), Eli (Wallach) and Anne (Jackson), Maureen (Stapleton) were all there. I'll never forget watching him when he would talk about the work; he had such a commitment. I actually met my first wife in his classes.

Q Has being an actor informed your work as a director?

I think I inherited my father's leadership with all the realities that go with it. I wanted to be a conductor early on; that led to the idea of my being a director. Some people are propelled to follow, others are comfortable guiding others.

Every director should be forced to take acting classes to realize what it takes to create real behavior. It's a skill most directors don't understand at all. They learn how to work with a crew and the camera and with scripts. All my acting has been a critical element for my directing. I believe in craft, because art isn't an accident. It's about making choices.

Q What led to your directing in television?

In those days in live television there were a lot of great directors: Sidney Lumet, Frankenheimer, Arthur Penn, and really great writers: Chayefsky, Rod Serling, Reginald Rose.

Well, Sydney Pollack and I were very close friends. At that time Sydney was doing TV in California and suggested I come out. He spoke to the executive director of *Ben Casey*. Well, I came to California, and suddenly I'm working on *Ben Casey* for a month as an assistant, and I've never stopped. I was lucky.

Q You've directed many talented actors, including John Wayne. How do you prepare with actors before the camera rolls?
I love directing and helping people reach their capabilities to achieve their best work. I insist rehearsing on every film I direct; studios object to it. They have to pay the actors. Those of us in the theater, we know how important it is to go over each scene in detail—what the characters are striving for, to accomplish what they want to do—the why.

Once the confidence happens within the actor, they're able to do the work. Each actor has their own way of working. When I worked with the Duke (John Wayne), he was one of the nicest, most generous men I've ever known, very dedicated.

Q Your film, *On Golden Pond*, had a most memorable cast which included Henry Fonda, Jane Fonda, and Katharine Hepburn. How did you decide what needed to be said during filming?
I rarely talk about this but what I learned from being in therapy was how everyone has to be treated differently. There's a lot inside of us that needs to be released. I try to provide a "lubricant," in a way, so actors can do what they do well.

Working with Fonda and Hepburn was glorious, and I also had a chance to work with Jane. We knew each other from The Actors Studio. Jane had bought the play as a gift for her father as an effort to reconstruct their relationship. They hadn't talked in years. Thank God, when Henry agreed to do the film, he said, "Get Mark Rydell." I had met with him before, and we had a great time together. He was not easily approachable, as was Hepburn.

Once we were on the set, it was just a great experience all together. Hepburn was all over the place, and Henry warmed to her. Also what happened in the film literally helped Jane's relationship to her father. They hadn't spoken in a quite a while, and to have them together was very special. She spent a lot of time working for his understanding, and he reluctantly submitted to her. It was quite an experience. It was like "art imitating life."

Q You also directed James Franco in TNT's *James Dean*. Why did you want to tell that story?
I knew Jimmy (Dean) very well when we were young actors. We acted together on the first teleplay by William Inge for Omibus. *The Glory and the Flower*, with Hume Cronyn and Jessica Tandy. I was close to Jimmy. I felt I could do him justice; it meant a great deal to me.

It was a great experience with Jimmy Franco. I wanted to capture Jimmy's essence, and Jimmy (Franco) was able to embrace a lot of things that made it all come together.

Q How does art soothe our struggles?
We live in a democracy. That's had a lot to do with conditioning us to pursue the dollar. It's been the nature of American culture for a long time. I can't imagine what the world would be without the arts existing. It appeals to the perceptive and sensitive area of human development; it's food for a hungry nation. But most people don't recognize it. I've been thrilled to have a very productive life creating work with some of the greatest people in the business. ■

ANDREI ȘERBAN

A major name in twentieth-century theater, Mr. Şerban is renowned for his innovative and iconoclastic interpretations and stagings. At La MaMa, E.T.C., he directed *Fragments of a Greek Trilogy*, receiving an Obie Award and international awards; he performed at more than twenty festivals. He worked with Peter Brook at Brook's International Theatre Institute in both Paris and Persepolis. He directed Aeschylus' *Agamemnon* and Chekhov's *The Cherry Orchard*, adapted by Jean-Claude van Itallie, at Lincoln Center for the Performing Arts with Irene Worth, Raul Julia, and Meryl Streep, receiving a Tony Award for Best Revival. Mr. Şerban was the General Director of the Romanian National Theatre, and has also directed at Yale Repertory, the Guthrie, Circle in the Square, Delacorte, A.C.T., London's National Theatre, Schauspielhaus Bochum, Comedie Francaise, Metropolitan Opera, Seattle and Los Angeles Operas, at the Paris, Geneva, Vienna, and Bologna Opera Houses, Covent Garden, and with Tokyo's Shiki Theatre Company. Mr. Şerban's directing includes *Cleansed* in Romania, *Lucia di Lammermoor* at the Paris' Opera Bastille, *Hamlet* starring Liev Schreiber at New York's Public Theater, a modern Kabuki at the National Theatre of Korea, *Arms and the Man* at St. Petersburg's Maly Theatre, *Carousel* at Bucharest's Bulandra, and *Angels in America* at Budapest's National. For more than twenty years, Mr. Şerban has been associated with the American Repertory Theater—his directing includes *Lysistrata*, *Merchant of Venice*, *Three Sisters*, *The Miser*, *Sweet Table at the Richelieu*, and *Pericles*. Since 1992, he has been Professor of Theater at the Columbia University, and has also taught at Yale University, Harvard University, Carnegie Mellon, Sarah Lawrence College, Paris Conservatoire d'Art Dramatique and A.R.T.'s Institute for Advanced Theater Training. In 2006, he published his autobiography. Mr. Şerban has received the Elliot Norton Award for Sustained Excellence, SSDC's George Abbott Award, Romanian National Foundation for Arts and Sciences, and the Romanian Academy's Prize for Excellence in Romanian Culture.

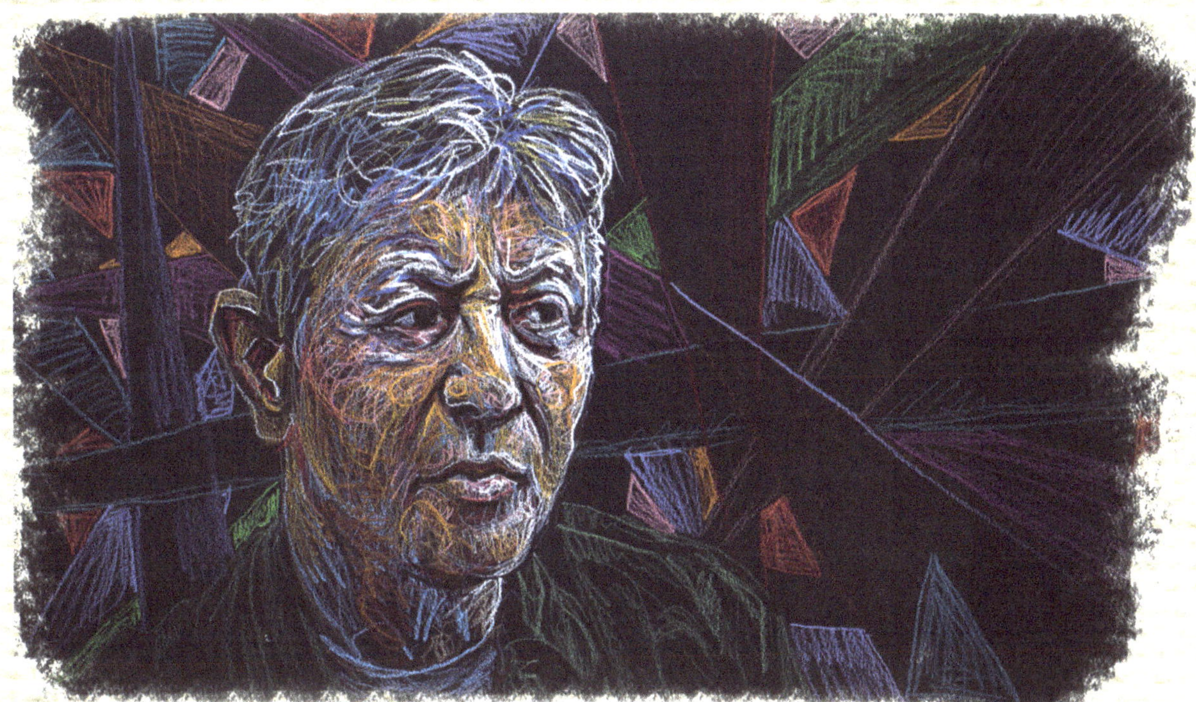

Andrei Șerban artwork: Fred Hatt for A Film by Fred Hatt for American Montage, Inc. on La MaMa, ETC

Q Who were inspirations to you when you first came to America?
First, when I arrived in the city after landing at JFK Airport, it was at the Chelsea Hotel that I met Andy Warhol filming in the lobby. It was my first discovery of America at the age of twenty-six, coming from Communist Romania. Then at La MaMa and Ellen Stewart, where I found my first artistic home, with all chaotic, idealistic, undisciplined freedom contrasting with my rigid, solid structure I had acquired in Eastern Europe.

Harold Clurman was a big influence. As a critic, he saw my productions at La MaMa, and wrote about my work which helped me to understand myself. Peter Brook was a great influence. I went to Paris to be a part of his International Centre of Theatre Research. It changed my life. Until then I was doing theater out of pleasure, the pure joy of being alive, but from Brook I learned the importance to endlessly ask questions, and never be satisfied with answers. Not to seek applause but to look for something deeper, a hidden reality.

Then Joe Papp invited me to Lincoln Center, where I did two radical interpretations of Chekhov and Aeschylus; one, a huge success—*The Cherry Orchard*, the other—*Agamemnon*, a wonderful failure, from which I learned a lot.

Robert Brustein, the Dean at Yale, later at Harvard, besides offering me many opportunities to direct with his company, introduced me to the academic world and I was able to learn how to teach, that opened the possibility much later for me to start an acting program at Columbia.

Then when my career took me to the opera: from Placido Domingo to Sir Colin Davis to Phillip Glass, and my life changed again.

Q I was fortunate to study with the great Polish director, Jerzy Grotowski. How would you describe the effect Grotowski had on you?
I didn't really work with him directly, except I met him several times. He was a good friend of Peter Brook. Grotowski was an extraordinary human being. He shaped the destiny of the late twentieth century theater more than anyone. He was never satisfied, always defining himself through his discoveries. When he presented his work in New York City, he received an extraordinary reception and was considered a guru. He transformed the state of the theater with such a radical approach.

But at the top of his glory, he returned back to Poland and started new experiments in nature, looking for new ways to communicate outside of expected conventions. Was he in search of new forms? I doubt it. What interested him, I think, was the evidence of a deeper reality, an invisible truth. He dedicated his life to searching.

Q In 1971, you staged *Medea* at La MaMa E.T.C. Three years later, you directed *Fragments of a Greek Trilogy* which included Medea, *The Trojan Wome*n, and *Electra*. In 1987, was your remarkable revival, which I experienced. In your memorable collaboration with Elizabeth Swados, who created the music and what did you draw upon from Euripides and Sophocles?
These authors are our contemporaries. They touch in us with the same human dilemma that existed two thousand years ago, the

same unexplained aspects of the mysteries and contradictions of life. Touching the essence of existence. We can interpret them again, make them "modern" and try endlessly restaging them. They will still sound both new and familiar.

With composer Elizabeth Swados, what we did together, was a continuation of the work with Brook—using ancient sound vibrations to tell the story. They hold universal emotions that are just as powerful today as they were two thousand years ago. We tried an experiment to tell the story via non-verbal communication, beyond logical spoken language.

The human voice has the potential to touch directly the inner being, the soul. We learned from Grotowski about resonators that are in us, not used, therefore mysterious. In doing this work, one discovers the language of the subconscious, an opening to a different way of acting—Artaud was a strong inspiration. This was extraordinary material to work on, to communicate to a modern audience. Like in opera, the audience receives an emotion with the help of music, more powerful than any intellectual exchange. A language that proves quite universal!

Q You directed a memorable production of Jean-Claude van Itallie's translation of *The Cherry Orchard* at Lincoln Center with Irene Worth and Meryl Streep in the cast. Did you give the actors a lot of freedom to explore?
Always in the theater one cannot find this freedom alone. We need to remember we depend on others; I am part of a team. My work improves better having the opportunity to create something with others.

The Cherry Orchard production at Lincoln Center was one of the most extraordinary experiences I've ever had, working with great "others": Irene Worth, Meryl Streep, Raul Julia, and "other great ones". The better the quality of each artist, the richer the ensemble.

I never have an idea how to stage a play before I come to rehearsal. I discover in the room because of the people present there that inspire me. For example, at the end of the play when the cherry trees were gone, there was this empty white stage covered with snow. The Vivian Beaumont stage is a wide open barn. How to fill that space?

After all the characters leave at the end of the play, George Voskevec as Gaev remained onstage, then Ranevskaya played by Irene Worth decides to also stay. They had to go to the station, the train was leaving, but they couldn't. The actors began improvising, imagining when they were children. Suddenly the ghost of their mother appeared, leading their steps. It was such a stunning moment to remember—these two old actors circling the white empty stage, calling the past, holding onto one another, refusing to leave their home, and in the process becoming young again. A great sense of renewal, not at all the sad melancholic exit so often seen in Chekhovian productions.

Q What led you to want to direct a production of *Hedda Gabler* in Romania?
Because it is the opposite of a Greek drama: it is a tragi-comedy about living one's life with a lie. I was interested to work with Hungarian actors from Cluj, this medieval town in Transylvania, northern Romania, where I could concentrate exclusively on doing theater. With Ibsen, like with Chekhov, I tried to free the acting from a tendency towards heaviness and sentimentality, more natural, against a humorless, stiff, and physiological approach. I wanted to find out what creates the sense of this disturbing comedy, because it is a comedy of cowardice and lack of courage.

We discovered that Ibsen's world is so absurd and horrible. We look at these people and we can recognize ourselves and so find how laughter accentuates the tragic aspect of the human condition, as we are caught in a maze of false ideals, crushed by vane ambitions of materialism. Laughing at ourselves can lead to a certain sense of freedom. Humor becomes a kind of medicine.

Q Did you want to teach to find something out?
It sounds like a cliché, but it's true—I teach in order to learn. Our students at Columbia are increasingly demanding, especially when they have to pay these outrageous sums of money to study acting. They ask of me to improve, to be better all the time, to re-invent myself. No clichés allowed, no deja-vu, no imitation of what has been already done, but questioning, inventing, risking all the way. It is like an ideal theater: one can live as if you are on Prospero's island, protected, and feel free to experiment and discover, to make mistakes and start again.

Yes, I discovered a new energy in myself due to the inspiration coming from the students. They have no preconceived ideas of how theater should be. I can be relaxed enough to say, "I don't know myself"—to do things with them I've never imagined before. After so many years in the theatre it is another chance to surprise myself, and curious.

Q When you directed Liev Schreiber in *Hamlet* at The Public, at one point he was in the audience and delivered the "O, what a rogue and peasant slave" soliloquy in the aisles, with the house lights up. Is staging scenes about getting the audience to experience something they've never experienced before?
That's my hope; it doesn't always work. It depends on how sensitive the spectators are. It enters my mind every time I direct. The drama always happens in the audiences' mind. In the theater all we can hope is to try to change the state of being of the spectator. They come in one state of mind, and a change can take place, when the old catharsis occurs. This possibility to transform ourselves, even for five minutes, is the real potential of the theatre, the reason theater did not die.

No other art can replace theater, because it is only there

that we all breathe together the same breath—the present instance—when we are linked suddenly by a current of energy that lifts our inner tempo. These plays are all about us being alive, and maybe even learning who we are.

When I go to the theater I want to leave touched by catharsis, in other words with more energy than when I came in. You watch Greek tragedy about wars, death, destruction, and you are moved by the horror and the pity. You have a chance to better understand yourself and the world. Theater can give you the appetite to develop as a person—to remain free on the inside, in order to understand each other—to have a more real, more positive relationship. Theater must affirm, not deny life. This is our role to play. ■

ELLEN STEWART

Founder of La MaMa, E.T.C. (Experimental Theatre Club) in New York City in 1961, Ms. Stewart created a theater with Paul Foster and others, which became one of the most successful Off-Off Broadway theatrical companies. While working as a fashion designer during the 1960s and 1970s, she brought to the forefront new generations of American Theatre playwrights, including Sam Shepard, Lanford Wilson, Harvey Fierstein, Maria Irene Fornes, Adrienne Kennedy, Jean-Claude van Itallie; performing artists, including Meredith Monk, Tan Dun, Joel Zwick, Mike Figgis, Jackie Curtis, Blue Man Group, John Kelly, David and Amy Sedaris; actors, including Al Pacino, Robert De Niro, Harvey Keitel, F. Murray Abraham, Olympia Dukakis, Richard Dreyfuss, Bette Midler, Diane Lane, and Nick Nolte; composers, including Elizabeth Swados, Philip Glass, and Stephen Schwartz; directors, including Robert Wilson, Tom O'Horgan and The La MaMa Troupe, Richard Foreman, Joseph Chaikin, Lee Breuer, Andrei Serban, and Joseph Papp. La MaMa became a magnet for the most adventurous European and American companies, including Peter Brook's Paris group, Eugenio Barba's Odin Teatret, and the Belarus Free Theater. She brought Jerzy Grotowski, Ryszard Cieslak, and Ludwig Flaszen to America, and produced site-specific performances all over the world, including *Medea* created by Mr. Serban and Ms. Swados at the ruins in Baalbek, Lebanon in 1972. She turned a former monastery in Umbria, Italy into an international theater center. Ms. Stewart was inducted into the American Theater Hall of Fame, the first Off-Off Broadway producer to receive this honor. Among her many awards and honors included the Praemiun Imperiale and the Stanislaw Ignacy Witkiewicz Award,; she became an officer in the Ordre de Arts et des lettres of France, and received a "Distinguished Services to Art and Culture" Award in the Ukraine. Ms. Stewart died in 2011 (this interview was conducted in 1999).

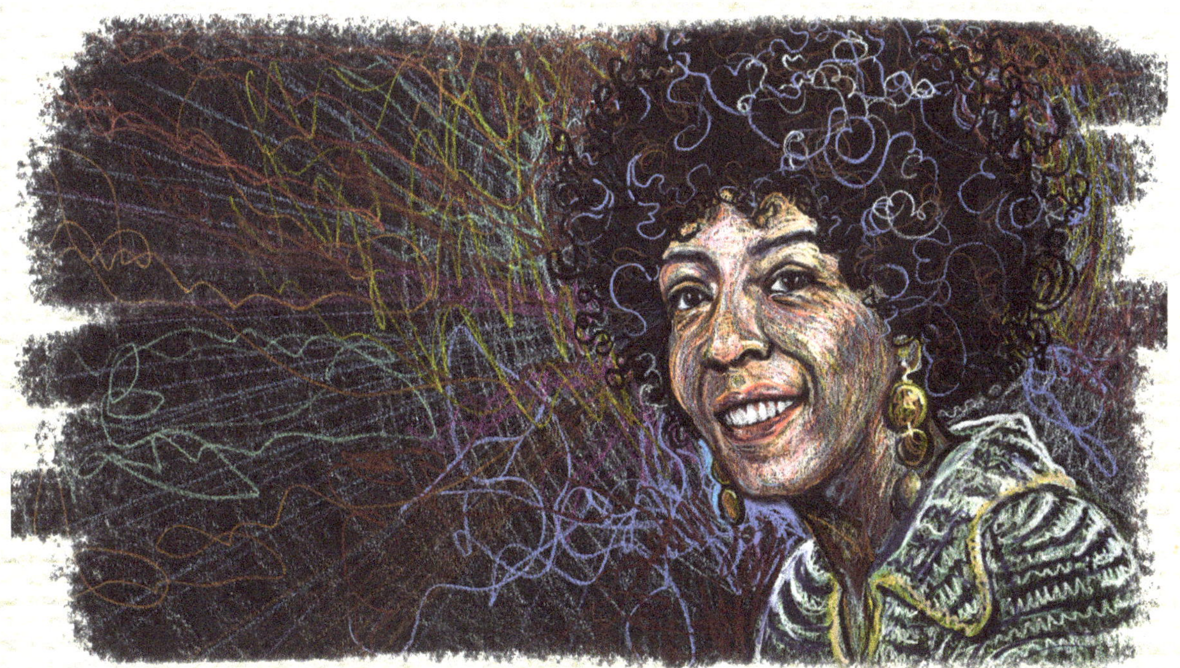

Ellen Stewart artwork: Fred Hatt for A Film by Fred Hatt for American Montage, Inc. on La MaMa, ETC

Q You helped define a new voice in the American Theater when it was desperately needed, giving a stage to a whole new generation of playwrights. Was that your aim when you began?

I didn't have any aim. I had some friends who wanted to write plays. I began in a small basement. My foster brother, who was like a brother to me, had a big disappointment on Broadway and wanted to continue writing. And I had lots of problems with the New York City Building Department, and so I ended up moving a lot. Often I was in jail for doing entertainment without a license. Each place we moved to was larger and everyone's ambition was to write a play for an hour.

My first stage was only big enough for a bed, and we'd keep moving. Sam Shepard was there and he would serve coffee and sometimes the ash from his cigarette would fall into the cups of coffee for the customers.

So finally I decided, "I'm moving to Germany." Someone said, "Why don't you call the Ford Foundation?" So I did, and when they showed up, this building had three walls, you could stand in the basement and look up into the heavens. But we finally had a home because they agreed to help.

Q Is theater for exploring the human condition?

I've never concerned myself with the "big" questions. I do what I want to do and not try to think for the public.

Q What is the artist's responsibility?

I think any artist that has been blessed by God has an obligation to society to share his art, to communicate to the entire world, not just your own special town, city, or your own country.

Society takes it for granted what you're doing. The painter, the poet, the sculptor knows this, but the playwright doesn't think enough about it and that has got to change!

Take Shakespeare. He wrote a lot of text but every word he wrote is a picture. When we fail is when we don't show those pictures. Maybe he's got pounds of text but it's a kaleidoscope and it never stops.

Q Who's been the greatest influence on you?

I tell everyone—First, there was God, and then there was Ed Koch, and he would chase me.

Q What would enable us to appreciate what theatre and our artists can do for us?

We must become a more sensitive America to the arts and Americans should be encouraged to see the best theaters where they are. Just like I'm La MaMa of the American Indian; I'm part Cherokee. Until Americans realize the value of the different areas of our country we won't be any place. We have to look beyond our noses. Having a vision has everything to do with being an artist in the theater today.

Q How would you complete this sentence. Art is—

Love. And La MaMa is a home for the Artist. ■

TADASHI SUZUKI

One of the world's foremost thinkers, directors, and teachers of acting training, Mr. Suzuki is the founder and director of the Suzuki Company of Toga, SCOT, based in Toga Village. He is the organizer of Japan's first international theatre festival, Toga Festival, and the creator of the Suzuki Method of Actor Training. Mr. Suzuki has also served as General Artistic Director of Shizuoka Performing Arts Center from 1995 to 2007. He was a member of the International Theatre Olympics Committee, a founding member of the BeSeTo Festival, and Chairman of the Board of Directors for the Japan Performing Arts Foundation from 2000 to 2010. Mr. Suzuki's works include *On the Dramatic Passions, The Trojan Women, Dionysus, King Lear, Cyrano de Bergerac, Madame de Sade*, and many others. He has directed several international collaborations including *The Tale of Lear*, co-produced and presented by four leading regional theaters in America; *King Lear*, presented with the Moscow Art Theatre; *Oedipus Rex*, co-produced by Cultural Olympiad and Dusseldorf Schauspiel Haus; and *Electra*, produced by Ansan Arts Center/Arco Arts Theatre in Korea and the Taganka Theatre in Russia. In 2001, Tadashi Suzuki and SCOT performed *Electra*, *Oedipus Rex*, and *Dionysus* for their North American tour. Mr. Suzuki has had his writings published in English in *The Way of Acting* and *Culture is the Body*," and has taught in schools and theaters around the world, including The Juilliard School in New York City and the Moscow Art Theatre. In Toga, Mr. Suzuki has established one of the largest international theater centers in the world.

Q Why did you choose the challenge of shaping an actor's mind, body, heart, and soul?

I'm fascinated by human beings, and am always surprised by how different other people can be from myself. I wonder what it is that causes these profound differences? Ultimately, it is this question that led me to become a director. This, along with my interest in texts, particularly tragedy.

I'm curious about what causes the excess energy and criminal behavior we see articulated in these texts. The individual features of the protagonists in Greek tragedy, for example, are completely different from my own, and this intrigues me. Which is to say, I believe the fundamental question we, as artists, have to pose is, "What does it mean to be human?"

Q At what point in your life did you realize this was your mission?

My fascination started when I was young. Though it wasn't until I reached thirty years of age, and despite whatever misgivings I may have felt, that I realized this path was my destiny. Before then, in my teens, and for the next ten years of my life, there was wandering, hesitation, and uncertainty.

Q Why did you feel so strongly that actors' voices and instrumental music should be delivered directly without amplification?

Even though I occasionally resort to the use of a microphone or recorded music, I believe that "animal energy," unmitigated by machines or electricity, is what makes the theater unique. If you're going to depend on non-animal energy, then you might as well make a movie.

Q Can you talk further about what you mean when you say you are striving to restore the wholeness of the human body in the theatrical context?
In modern life we rely much more heavily on sight and hearing than we do on smell, taste, and touch. This imbalance between the five senses makes our actions quite dysfunctional, especially among actors. For them, the primary, visceral sense of touch in particular must be highly developed. In short, the more we rely upon "non-animal energy" in this world, the more our senses will deteriorate. The theater can help restore the full range of sensual experience to our organism.

Q Why did you decide to collaborate with Anne Bogart and form the Saratoga International Theatre Institute-SITI?
An American friend of mine recommended me to her. She was one of several American directors who came to Toga, where I am based, as part of the Japanese-U.S. Friendship Program. As Anne Bogart and I met and began a dialogue, I learned that she had already been teaching the Suzuki Method in America, and that there were already many actors training in my method in the U.S. Later, with the help of Peter Zeisler and TCG, we created a company together made up of American actors based in Saratoga Springs, New York.

Q In your director's note for your production of *Electra*, you described the entire world as a hospital, and all men and women as inmates in that hospital, and that this belief was the driving force behind all of your theater creations. What gives you hope that we can be healed?
I use the hospital metaphor because I believe that all human beings are ill to some degree, even the "would-be doctors" who we seek to treat our illnesses. Once we understand this, it becomes clear that our only hope to heal lies within ourselves. If you find yourself in a state of despair, I say, don't look to others, but rather find your own hope. People seem to always be looking to doctors for a quick fix. However, as human beings in the modern world, we must acquire the patience to create our own hope, each one of us.

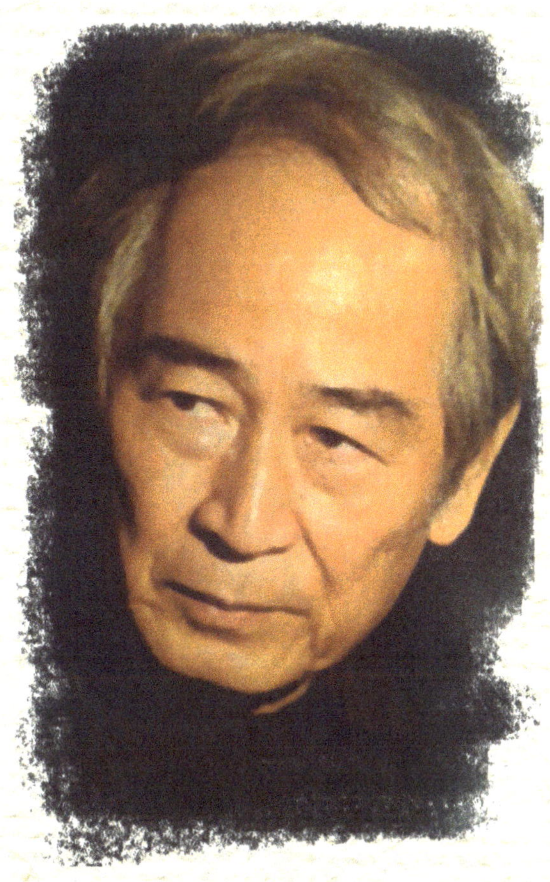

Tadashi Suzuki photo: courtesy of Suzuki Company of Toga Archive

Q How has that helped you in your exploration?
Basically, because the theater is a collective art form, with this kind of collaboration, based on a shared philosophy, the company and I can go further in the total sense...because of their understanding of me, my worldview, and the way I work. With younger actors it takes a while before they can be helpful to the company.

Over time, however, actors, in addition to improving their performance skills, also become adept with sound, lights, and are able to direct as well...in short, they become complete theater artists. Since my company is composed of such theatre artists, and not a collection of individuals, each specializing in only one area of the theatre, I'm able to take a smaller troupe when I tour.

Q The performances in *Electra* possess great intensity. What do you expect from your actors during rehearsals?
For me, it's all about concentration and focus. We're all human beings, we have our own lives, families, and must constantly deal with social conventions and conflicts, but what is important in rehearsal is that the actor does not become rattled or lose focus and concentration.

Q Do you make many notes before you begin a new piece? Do you block the scenes out?
We figure it out as we go. We're always together, training from morning until night. We're like a family, constantly talking together, coming up with ideas to make the piece better.

Q Why do you feel theater is essential for a culture's survival?
Ideally, within any given culture there is a smooth, harmonious flow of "animal energy" within and between human beings. However, when one group or "culture" becomes stronger than another, they often collide. We have come to the point where we need new rules of how to co-exist. The theater could help us discover them.

Japan has always been a homogenous society until recently. Now we're being challenged to devise new rules. And of course, all this especially relates to the acts of terrorism that have become so prevalent around the world today. ■

ROBERT WILSON

Theater visionary, internationally acclaimed director, designer and artist, he founded the New York based performance collective "The Byrd Hoffman School of Byrds" in the 1960s, and developed his first signature works, including *Deafman Glance* and *A Letter for Queen Victoria*. With Philip Glass he wrote the seminal opera, *Einstein on the Beach*, in 1976. Wilson's artistic collaborators include many writers and musicians such as Heiner Müller, Susan Sontag, Laurie Anderson, William Burroughs, and Jessye Norman. He has directed, and/or performed in Beckett's *Krapp's Last Tape*, *Threepenny Opera*, *Pelléas et Melisande*, *Faust*, *Odyssey*; Jean de la Fontaine's *Fables*, *Madama Butterfly*, and *La Traviata*. Mr. Wilson's productions include *The Black Rider: Casting of the Magic Bullets* at Los Angeles' Ahmanson Theater; *Lohengrin* at the Metropolitan Opera; *Aida* at Festspielhaus Baden-Baden; and *Der Ring des Nibelungen - Das Rheingold, Die Walküre, Siegfried*, and *Götterdämmerung* at Theatre du Chatelet. Among the other theatre pieces and performances he has created are *The Life and Times of Sigmund Freud*, *The Life and Times of Joseph Stalin*, *A Letter for Queen Victoria*, *Byrd woMAN*, *Ka Mountain and the Guardenia Terrace*, *Edison*, *The Black Rider*, *Alice* with Tom Waits, *POEtry* with Lou Reed, *I was sitting on my patio this guy appeared I thought I was hallucinating*, *The Forest*, and *the CIVIL warS*, receiving a Pulitzer Prize nomination. Mr. Wilson has directed *Peer Gynt*, *Hamlet*, *King Lear*, *Alcestes*, *Medea*, *Orlando*, *Hamletmaschine*, *Quartett*, *Dreamplay*, *The Lady from the Sea*, *Three Sisters*, and *A Winter's Tale*. His productions also include *The Magic Flute*, *Salome*, *Parsifal*, *Time Rocker*, *Woyzek*, *The Old Woman* with Willem Dafoe and Mikhail Baryshnikov, *Pushkin's Fairy Tales*, and *Faust I* and *II*. His art, including his VOOM portraits, has been shown in museums internationally, including the Guggenheim Museum, Berlin's National Gallery, the Boston Museum of Fine Arts, and the Centre Pompidou. Mr. Wilson founded The Watermill Center, an international, multi-disciplinary center for studies in the arts and humanities on Long Island.

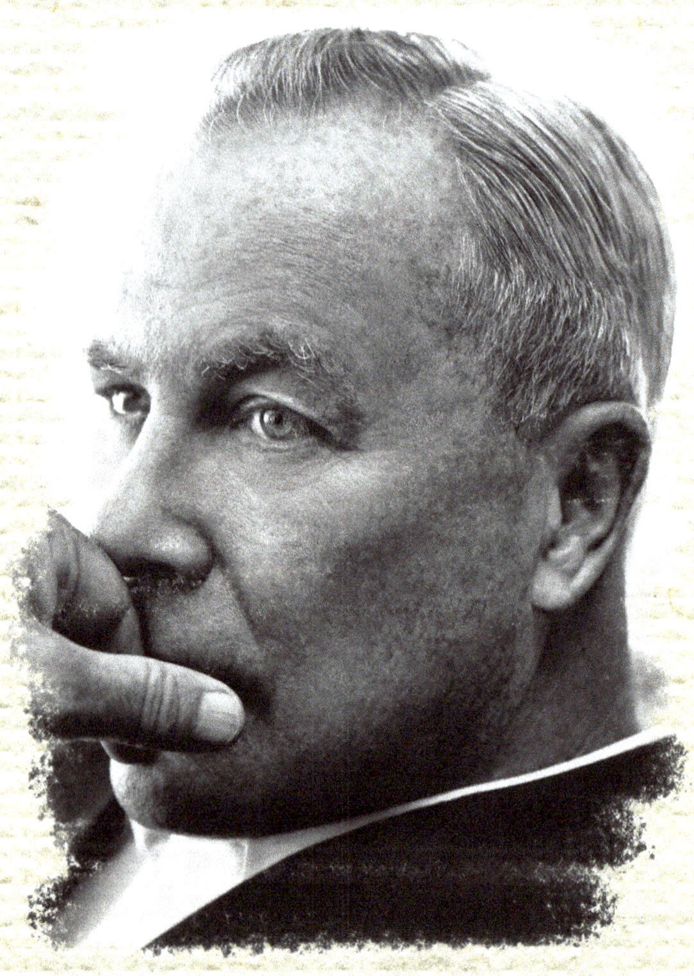

Robert Wilson photo: © Lesley Leslie-Spinks

Q Your *Peer Gynt* at BAM was a beautiful and magical production. What kind of a challenge was it working on *Peer Gynt* in Norway?

I think it was the challenge as a foreigner to design and direct a national treasure in Norway. I am from Texas and it was an adventure to go to Norway to direct this play, in Norwegian, for an audience that knows the text well. Norwegians have an approach to theater that is very different from mine. It is naturalistic and psychological. My theater is formal and not interested in psychology. I eliminated that in the acting.

Martha Graham told the story of watching Eleonora Duse perform. She was holding a letter and then she dropped it. She did not express the action outwardly, but inwardly felt it. Graham said her life was changed forever. I first staged *Peer Gynt* silently a year and a half before it premiered in Oslo. It was very strange for the actors to do Ibsen without a text. It took them a while to get used to performing with their bodies in maintaining a physical tension. I always start with stillness and the awareness of movement that is in stillness. Then, when one moves outwardly, the line of movement continues.

Ezra Pound said the fourth dimension was stillness and the

power of the wild beast. The theatre I do creates a space for actors and the audience to listen to one another. I work on each component of a play separately. While developing the movement, I also work on the lighting and the stage set. Once the visual book is in an order, I place the audio score with the movement. Often, the text is rehearsed separately from the stage action. In a sense, the stage is presented with layers of activities that may relate to one another, or may not.

Of course, this approach is very different for the actor who might be accustomed to plays that start rehearsals with the text. For me, the movement must come first. Some anthropologists believe that man was dancing and singing before speaking. I went to the zoo some years ago in Berlin, just before closing time. The gatekeeper said I could only stay for a few minutes. I went to the back of the zoo where there was a pack of gray wolves standing on rocks. I stood there for ten minutes. I never moved and the wolves never moved. I was aware of them and they were aware of me. We were a pack, one entity. In an ideal situation, it is this kind of awareness that I try to create with the actors on stage.

My first play was written with a thirteen-year-old deaf boy. I discovered he listened with his entire body; he picked up vibrations. His body listened the same way a dog listens. If you watch a dog, the way his foot touches the ground, they listen with their whole body. As Kleist said, "A good actor is like a bear; he never strikes first."

I liked what Arthur Miller said in your newspaper about Marlon Brando's performance in *Truckline Café*. The audience did not know how to react when Brando entered the stage. He simply stood there for five minutes and held the attention of the audience; they were paralyzed. They did not know whether he would kill them or caress them or whether he had forgotten his lines. It must have been like waiting for the toast to pop out of the toaster. This is pretty much where I come from.

Q You work with artists of many different countries in many different languages. How have you learned to communicate your vision to them?

I have directed works in many different languages: Japanese, Farsi, Italian, Russian, Portuguese, Spanish, French, German, Dutch, etc. I only speak English. It was a challenge to direct Strindberg's *Dreamplay* in Swedish, *Osüd* in Czech, *Les Fables of Lafontaine* at the La Comédie Française, *Leonce and Lena*, *Votzak*, and *Dantone's Tod* in German and, of course, *Peer Gynt* in Norwegian.

Truth in language can always be felt. I frequently say to the actor, "I must believe you." In a formal theater, the emotion is placed deeply. If its text is deeply felt, that will be the expression; it does not have to be outwardly portrayed. If one touches an ice cube, it is cold. That feeling is truth. It does not need to be expressed outwardly. If one touches a lit light bulb, it is hot; that will be your expression. This, too, does not need to be outwardly expressed. On the other hand, one can, in a formal theater, exaggerate emotions—as in a melodrama.

Take for example, Eisenstein's film, *Ivan the Terrible*. We see the actor acting "evil." He himself sees himself acting "evil" and it is fun. This is truth and it is believable. In either case, whether the expression is internalized or externalized, it must come from the gut; that is the center. I find, far too often, the body is blocked and the expression is generated from the mind. In my theater, I think of the mind being a muscle. The awareness is throughout the entire body. Listening and seeing are not done only with the eardrum and the eyes, but with the body. The way a dog walks to a bird; the way I was standing together with the wolves in Berlin.

Q Since you founded The Watermill Center in 1992, it has become a unique laboratory for artists and students of all backgrounds to explore the creative process. What remains your greatest hope for the Center?

I do not want to have a Robert Wilson school or to have one way of doing something. I share with others what I have learned. I develop all my work at the Center. But, at the same time, I bring in people who have very different aesthetics and very different ideas and allow them to develop their work. Not only in the arts, but in all fields: anthropology, science, math, etc. Being at the Center, one has awareness of other activities and of other viewpoints. Art and culture are at the core of the Center.

Q How different is the way audiences in America grasp your artistry from the way they do abroad?

If you look at the theater around the world, India, Africa, Latin America, China, Japan, they are all formal theaters. In Europe and in the Unites States, we have a naturalistic and psychological theater. We lack a visual theatrical language. If we look at the classical theater of India, China, Japan, or Indonesia, one begins one's training as a performer with movement: Standing, walking, movement of an eye or of a gesture. In Japan and China, the movement for classical theater can be abstract. Movement is pure and does not have to relate to text, it can stand on its own as movement for movement's sake.

Andre Malraux said that the Western theater had been bound by literature. By this, I think he meant that Westerners have not adequately developed a visual theatrical language. In my theater, what we see can be as important as what we hear. In this dualism, when we put the audio score with the visual score, ideally they can reinforce one another without having to illustrate, decorate, or second one another. This is something that is often misunderstood by the critics.

My opera *Einstein on the Beach*, which dealt with abstraction and theme and variation, and my production of *Four Saints in Three Acts* by Gertrude Stein and Virgil Thompson, are about time and space construction. A critic asked me recently if I was still directing in the same manner, and I was reminded of what Gertrude Stein said when she arrived from Paris to New York in 1932, for *Four Saints*. An interviewer asked, "Ms. Stein, are you still writing in that same way?" She took a deep breath and spoke one sentence for five minutes with a conjugation of a single thought.

I remember seeing Barnett Newman's face in the 1960s when a critic asked, "Are you still painting in the same way?" and he smiled. Proust said he was always writing the same novel. Cezanne said he was always painting the same still life. When Albert Einstein was asked by a reporter to repeat what he said, he responded, "There's no need to repeat what I just said because it's all the same thought."

From the beginning, my work has been formal. I like ballet. I was influenced by the work of Merce Cunningham and George Balanchine. I liked their work because it was abstract and I also liked the way the dancers performed for themselves, allowing the audience to come to them without insisting too much on the audience attention. A good actor will always perform for himself first. In Balanchine and Cunningham, the movements were formalized and rehearsed until they became mechanical and free.

My work is architectural. The texts, the movement, the music, the light, the stage set, are all thought about separately and then they can stand on their own independently. But, when seen together, ideally, they create an experience that one does not have when seen separately. My theater is an epic theater in the sense that Brecht talked about an epic theater. It is a non-interpretive theater.

Interpretation is not the responsibility of actor, director, or author; interpretation is the responsibility of the public. We as creators should ask questions. That is to say, what is it and not say what something is. ■

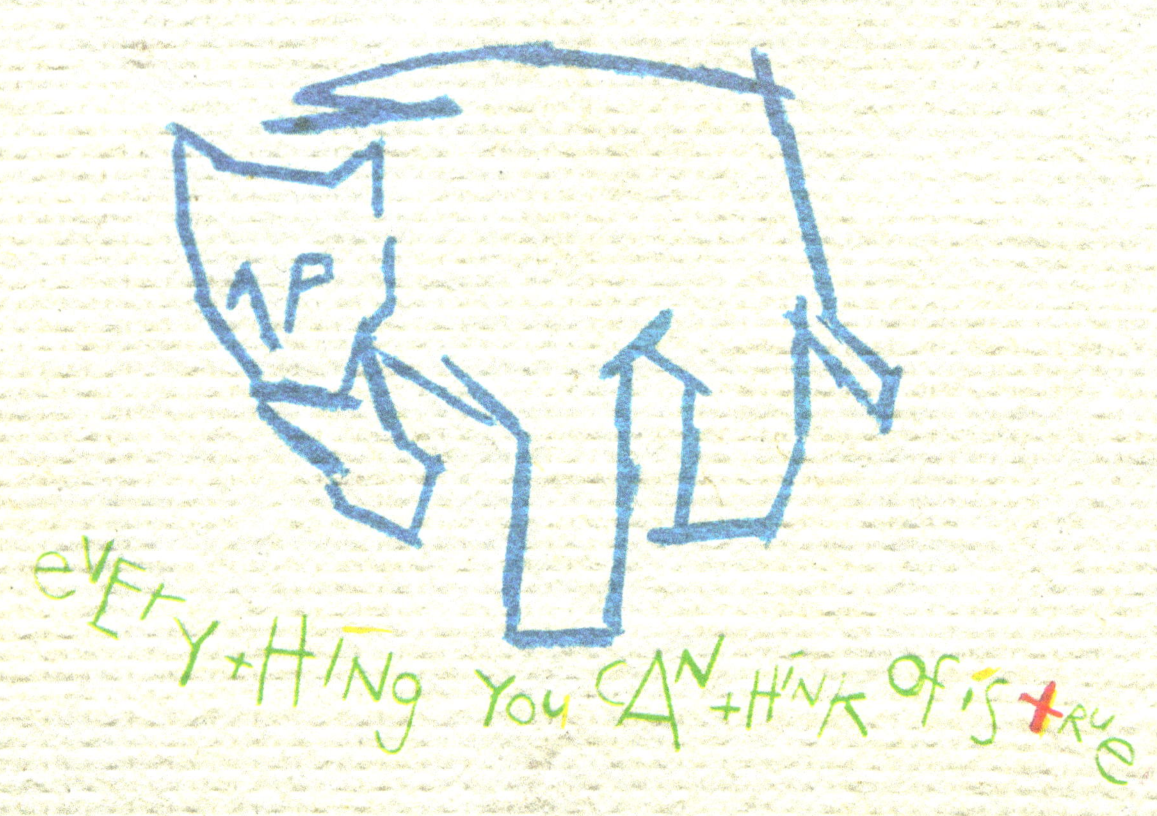

Robert Wilson artwork: "Alice Cat" by Robert Wilson, courtesy of the artist

EDUCATORS

PATCH ADAMS

An American physician, author, comedian, social activist and clown, Dr. Adams, M.D. is the founder and director of Gesundheit Institute, a free health facility in operation since 1971. His distinctiveness and universal appeal led to the films, *Patch Adams*, starring Robin Williams and Philip Seymour Hoffman, and the Bollywood film, *Munna Bhai*. As a speaker, Dr. Adams travels around the world lecturing on his work and doing theaterthe-atre shows about various aspects of health, particularly dealing with self-care and preservation. Among his talks are "The Gesundheit Institute: Medicine for Fun, not for Funds," "The Joy of Caring," "Humor and Health," "How to be Nutty," "Happiness/Joy," "Wellness," "Poetry and Medicine," "Self Esteem," and "Laughter Meditation." Mr. Adams received the Peace Abbey Courage of Conscience Award. He also teaches at Wavy Gravy's circus camp, Camp Winnarainbow.

Q What led to your decision to devote your life to the well-being of others?

I am seventy-one, and I grew up in a military academy on military bases. My mother showed me the miracle of being kind and generous as a way of life. When I grew up, my father was a military man, he died as a soldier; I became a war orphan. We then moved from Korea, back to the south. It was while I was in high school at the age of sixteen, that the great battle for civil rights took place. I was a dork in school, called a "sissy boy."

When I saw a "Whites only" sign, I realized I could not walk by the water fountain and not tear that sign down, and I did. I was beaten up almost every day when I was in high school because I took a stand for civil rights. I was present at Martin Luther King Jr.'s speech in Washington, D.C. I didn't want to live in a world of injustice, so three times in one year I was hospitalized for this desire to die. I was in three mental hospitals between the ages of seventeen and eighteen.

At the age of eighteen, I made two decisions in that mental institution: to be an instrument all the time, and to serve humanity all the time. I began a revolution for loving because my mother gave me self-esteem. I decided to be a doctor. I gave my life to a revolution for peace and justice and care. I decided I would be happy every single second of my life.

Q How did you decide to use clowning as a way of changing people?

I love clowning. When I go to a hospital, I find who is suffering the most and cover them with a huge amount of love. I'm here at Wavy Gravy's circus camp, Camp Winnarainbow; Wavy Gravy's eighty years old, and still cooking for the kids. I noticed clowning got me close to people. When I was in medical school, I saw a world that was serious. So I began clowning everywhere because the adult world is oppressed by the global idea of money and power.

Now a movie came along, and it had to sell tickets—with violence and being funny, so they turned Patch into a funny doctor, and everyone thinks Patch is a funny doctor; but I want the world to be loving.

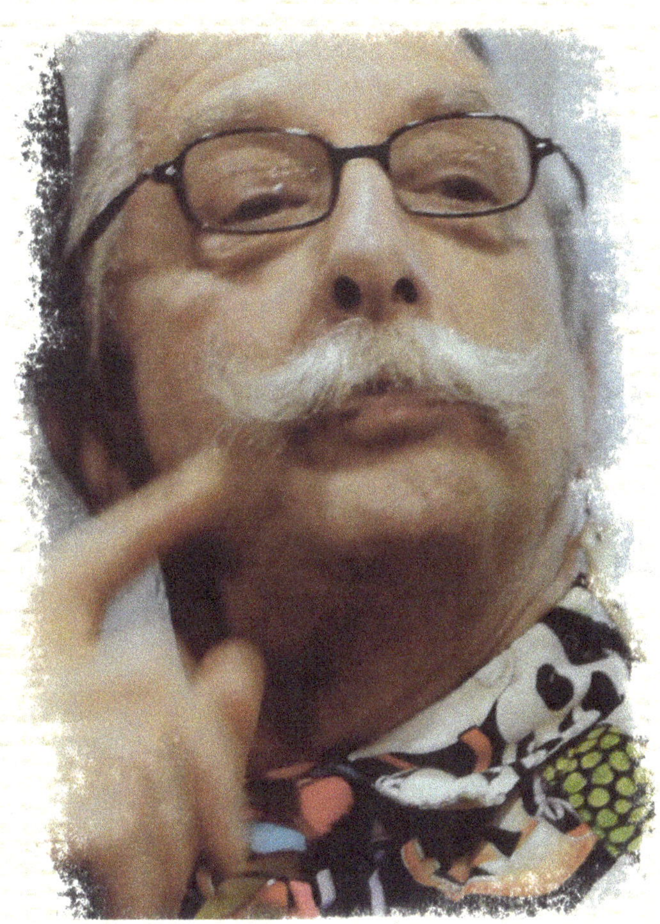

Patch Adams photo: Craig Y. Fujii

I thought organized medicine was an embarrassment, so I became a free doctor, an instrument of freedom and care, and I decided I would never have a bad day. I would live happy, funny, loving, creative, thoughtfully. I've done it for fifty-three years. The way I dress is to put joy into a public space. I try to stop violence and connect people. Loving is the most important thing in life.

Q How would you describe Gesundheit Institute?

Gesundheit Institute is about free

medicine and medicine as a joyful celebration. I decided I'd make a hospital for social change, that didn't charge money, to refuse malpractice insurance.

As a doctor I would go and visit the homes of my patients. We had a large big house where patients could come, but no one gave us donations, so after twelve years I owed a great deal of money. I realized what sells in the United States is fame so I realized I had to become famous. We had refused publicity; as soon as I could I became a public figure.

For the past thirty-two years I have traveled to eighty-one countries making speeches. I've done over a hundred and fifty clown trips; I've done them during wars, countless disasters. Over the past twenty-three years, I have visited over six hundred orphanages, going to Russia, to Nepal. I want us to live in a world of compassion and generosity. I've even done eleven speeches in a day.

Because of my speaking fees I've been able to create Gesundheit! Institute, a free, full-scale hospital and health care community on over three hundred acres in West Virginia. I'm creating a library of over fifteen thousand films and forty thousand books, every single one I've individually chosen. I read Dickens; he understood people. I loved reading about the nineteenth century, the world of Dostoevsky. I have never used a computer. I write over four hundred letters a month to friends in a hundred and thirty countries. I want those who come to read.

Q What remains to you some of our biggest challenges as a human race?
I don't see a single school teaching one of our most important things in life which is loving one another. Loving is the most important thing in life. The smartest thing is to teach love as an intelligence from first grade through the twelfth grade. We would be a different people. I would triple teachers' salaries, and make no tests.

I want us to live in a world of compassion and generosity. Today thirty thousand children will die of starvation. But I don't want us to focus on the pain of this; I want us to ask: How can it change? I've done so many interviews and no more than three percent tell me they love themselves. I say, let's go and help the people next door. The only hope for human survival is through a loving change, with values of generosity. ■

ROBERT BRUSTEIN

Founding Director of the Yale Repertory Theatre and American Repertory Theater, he has been the theatre critic for *The New Republic* since 1959. Mr. Brustein is a Senior Research Fellow at Harvard University, and formerly a Distinguished Scholar in Residence at Boston's Suffolk University. He was Dean of the Yale School of Drama from 1966 to 1979, and founded the Yale Repertory Theatre. He founded the American Repertory Theater at Harvard University, and became a Professor of English. As the Artistic Director of Yale Rep from 1966 to 1979, and of ART from 1980 to 2002, Brustein supervised over two hundred productions, acting in eight shows and directing twelve plays. He retired in 2002 from the Artistic Directorship, and now serves on the faculty of the Institute. Mr. Brustein has written eleven adaptations for A.R.T., including *Ghosts, The Father, The Wild Duck, The Cherry Orchard, Six Characters in Search of an Author*, for which he received the Boston Theatre Award, and *The Changeling*. He conceived and adapted the musical, *Shlemial the First* based on Issac Bashevis Singer's stories, which was presented across America. His klezmer musical, with composer Hankus Netsky, *The King of Second Avenue*, is an adaptation of Israel Zangwill's *The King of the Schnorrers*. Mr. Brustein's plays include *Demons, Nobody Dies on Friday, The Face Lift, Spring Forward, Fall Back*, and his Shakespeare Trilogy: *The English Channel, Mortal Terror, The Last Will*, and *Exposed*. Mr. Brustein is the author of sixteen books including *The Theatre of Revolt: An Approach to Modern Drama*, "*Making Scenes: A Personal History of the Turbulent Years at Yale, Reimagining American Theatre, Dumbocracy in America, Letters to a Young Actor: A Universal Guide to Performance*, and *Word Plays*. Included among the many awards Mr. Brustein has received are George Jean Nathan Award for Dramatic Criticism, twice; George Polk Award; Elliot Norton Award; and the National Medal of Arts. Mr. Brustein was elected to the Academy of Arts and Letters, American Academy of Arts and Sciences, and inducted into the Theater Hall of Fame.

Q How was your deep love for the theater born?
It all happened really because as a child I had a lisp, and I couldn't pronounce the letter "L." So my parents sent me to "elocution school" to learn how to articulate, I was also learning how to act, because elocution schools were actually drama schools in disguise. In those days, training programs were not allowed to use the word "theater" or "drama" with parents, for fear their children might run away and join the circus. I was put into some plays. We'd work on poetry. In one piece, I was a pirate who would "make fair maidens walk the plank."

Q I remember in the "Yale/Theatre" issue of Spring 1977, you were asked the question: "Can we identify an 'American style' of acting"? Now twenty-five years later, what would your answer be?
No question. It encompasses a passion for truth, honesty on stage, emotional eloquence, and intellectual eloquence as well. And a capacity to work as an ensemble. The ideal was set up by The Group Theatre.

Q What remains our greatest strength in fighting for the future of creative expression in this country?
That we have individuals who care enough about it. We really

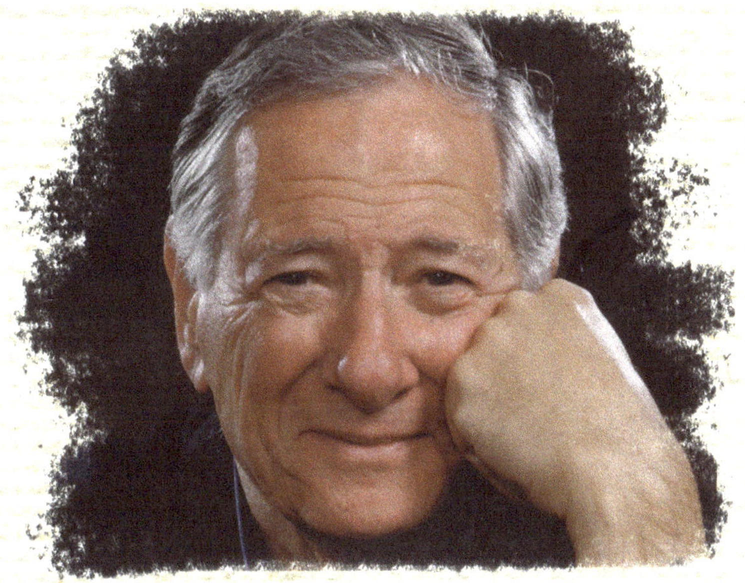

Robert Brustein photo: Bachrach Photography

need to get more people on our side that understand the value of the arts in preserving the society.

Q What was the first theater company you were involved with?
I helped found a theater, along with John Stix, Al Hurwitz, and Eldon Elder, in New York City called Studio 7. Then I became associated with another theater called Group 20, which developed from an amateur theater into a full Equity company on the Wellesley campus, called Theatre on the Green, devoted to classical summer theatre. It was one of the earliest classical repertory companies in post-war America. Artists like Fritz Weaver, Rosemary Harris, Elliott Silverstein, Max Adrian, and Benno Frank were a part of it. It ran for about seven or eight years until I was tapped to be Dean of Yale University Drama School in 1966 and I got my wish.

Q What were some of your first productions?
We did a lot of anti-war plays. We imported The Open Theater, Joe Chaikin's group, in *Viet Rock*. The first play we produced was *Dynamite Tonite*, an actor's opera, with music by William Bolcom and lyrics by Arnold Weinstein. Paul Sills directed, and in the cast we had Linda Lavin, George Gaynes, and Alvin Epstein. The second year Stacy Keach was with us, Ron Liebman, Kenneth Haigh, Kathleen Widdoes, Richard Jordan, and Harris Yulin.

Q Are you seeking something specific from an actor at a first read-through?
I'm not looking for a performance; I'm not evaluating. My intent is to explore the play. You sit around the table probing what the play means, what it means to each of us, to society.

Q Are there playwrights that continue to challenge you?
Shakespeare, of course. Pirandello—he's always finding a way to break appearances, to show us the illusion, and what's behind it. He fascinates me. It has to do with the way we think about the stage. Moliere, the Greeks. Contemporary writers—Mamet, Rapp, Letts, Vogel. What excites me is the way they look at reality; it's a different reality. They're daring, adventurous. Life is full of surprises.

Q How would you describe the current state of the American Theatre?
Well at the moment it's on its knees and wobbling. Something is struggling to be born, but it doesn't know what it is yet. And we're in a very difficult situation as far as funding is concerned.

We also continue to have a lack of understanding about the art of the actor in this country. Stella Adler always called acting "a noble profession." Uta Hagen spoke of "respect for acting." In America there's very little nobility for the actor, little sense of respect. Those old laddies of the British theatre always knew the importance of the profession—Laurence Olivier, John Gielgud, Ralph Richardson—and so did the best of our stage actors—Alfred Lunt, Luther and Stella Adler, all the Group Theatre artists. But something happened with the younger generation.

Q In what way do reviews have an impact?
At times, it seems a lot of what passes for theatrical criticism today crosses the line between constructive criticism, which might help the writer and inform the public, to empty opinionating. It's true, certain reviewers can annihilate a play. With the increased pressure on the reviewer not to disappoint their audience, they have to give a big "yes," or a big "no." They've missed on a lot of great work, failing to recognize what they were seeing at the time. Audiences should judge for themselves, but are prevented by the high price of tickets.

Q What lesson have we learned from how the creativity of theater impacts upon a country's growth?
The lesson is in the form itself. In a sense, theater is an extension of society. The one reflects the other. Movies, which are canned, are best enjoyed alone, like television. You watch them most comfortably in your own home. Theater forces you to go out and connect.

Q What would you consider your greatest contribution?
If I have had any purpose, if people remember me in future, I hope they will remember me as a facilitator, as someone who helped artists grow. Because I still believe that it is those visionaries who have the unique capacity to tell us where we are going and where we have been. That's why they command our gratitude and respect. ■

DICK CAVETT

Spanning five decades, Dick Cavett's television career as a talk show host started at ABC in 1968, and he also appeared regularly on PBS, USA, and CNBC. Some of his classic TV interviews included Groucho Marx, Katharine Hepburn, Judy Garland, Marlon Brando, David Bowie, Janis Joplin, and John Lennon. His television appearances include the PBS special *Dick Cavett's Watergate*, *Dick Cavett's Vietnam*, *The Odd Couple*, *Cheers*, *Kate & Allie*, *The Simpsons*, *What's My Line?*, *To Tell the Truth*, and *Password*. Mr. Cavett has also appeared on Broadway as the narrator in the revival of *The Rocky Horror Show*, *Otherwise Engaged*, and Stephen Sondheim's *Into the Woods*. He starred Off-Broadway in *Hellman v. McCarthy* in 2014 and in Los Angeles at Theatre 40. Clips from his TV shows (actual or enacted) have been used in the films *Annie Hall*, *Forrest Gump*, *Apollo 13*, and *Frequency*. Mr. Cavett's books include *Cavett*, and *Eye on Cavett*, co-authored with Christopher Porterfield, *Talk Show: Confrontations, Pointed Commentary, and Off-Screen Secrets*, and *Brief Encounters: Conversations, Magic Moments, and Assorted Hijinks*. He has written an online opinion column for *The New York Times*, and has also written for *The New Yorker*, *TV Guide*, and *Vanity Fair*. Mr. Cavett has been nominated for eleven Emmy awards, including for the HBO special, *Mel Brooks and Dick Cavett Together Again*, and has won three Emmy Awards.

Q You've done a surprising amount of acting, in school in Nebraska, in summer stock, at Yale, Williamstown, in Shakespeare festivals, and on and off Broadway. When did the acting bug first "bite" you?

It was in eighth grade—Miss Lula B. Moore's "Drama 2 Special" class at Irving Junior High School in Lincoln, Nebraska. I have no idea what the precise function of the word "Special" was in the title of her class. Was there a lesser version called "Drama 2 Ordinary"? Anyway, I thought it sounded fun, and it was. And it proved fateful. Because years later and because of it, it was what I came to New York, heart in mouth, to pursue.

So the day came in Miss Moore's class when I spoke my very first words before an audience as an actor. It was a one-act play, *Great Caesar*. It came from a collection of plays for schools, and was, appropriately, about young kids putting on a play. The first line of the play was mine. My first utterance as an actor before an audience. I don't think anything could drive that first line from my memory.

The play opens and we're seen sitting around on the floor busily working on stuff for the play, and I say, "Is this the way you want the sign painted, Harry?" I raise a board from the floor that I had just finished painting. It reads: "JULUS CAESAR." That's exactly what was on the board. The play's first laugh. A sight gag.

But the next line, also spoken by me, which I have forgotten now, also got a huge laugh. But I can't ever forget that feeling. Nothing comparable had ever happened before in my life. An auditorium full of people laughing at what I had said. An electric charge coursed through my body. What happened inside me was akin to what I've heard professional comedians and comic actors report many a time. While bathing in that first, rolling laugh, a little voice inside me said, "This is where I belong."

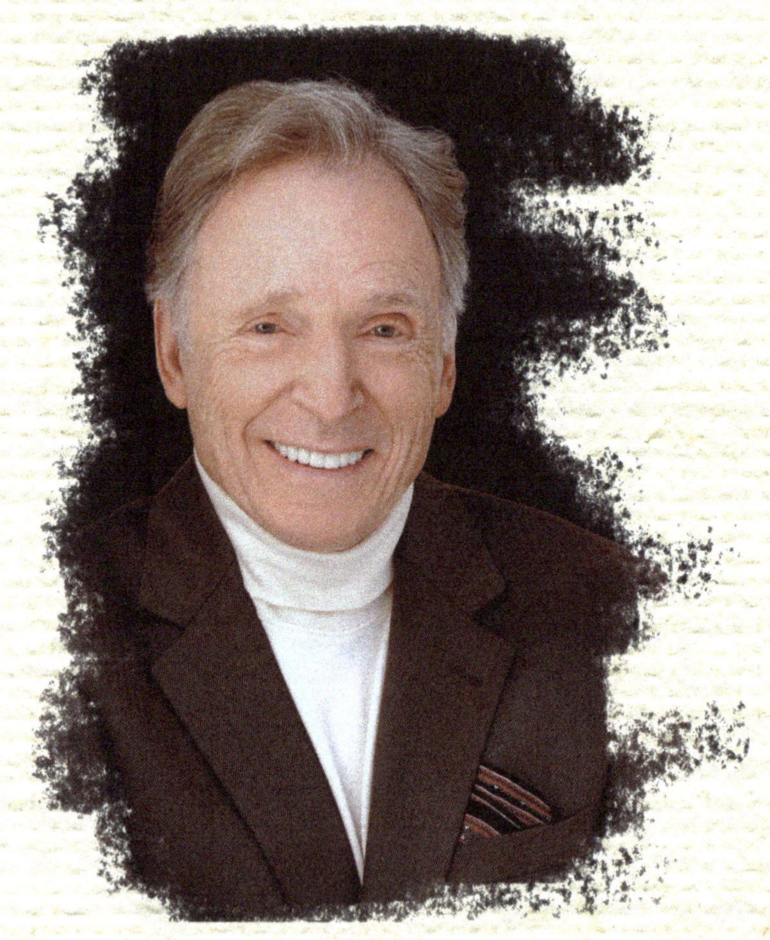

Dick Cavett photo: courtesy of the artist

Q Were you nervous stepping onto the boards?

Totally. When it came time to first tread those boards, I *was* scared. What if I should forget my lines? That was the primary fear. It didn't happen that day. But years later…it's like a bad dream. All actors know that awful moment when it's not even opening night, and the play's rolling along as usual, Suddenly dead silence strikes across the stage. It feels like years going by. Everyone's as silent as a statue. You wonder who screwed up. And then it hits: "It's me!" But you don't want to speak because then they'll know it's you. Finally, you have to. It makes me sweat now even thinking about it. Nothing comparable happens in "ordinary life." It's one of the horrors risked by the thespian.

Q Where did becoming a "thespian" land you next?

When I moved on to high school, I tried out as soon as possible for a play. I was cast in one, which you may not be as familiar with, as you are with, say, *Hamlet* or *A Streetcar Named Desire* or *Charley's Aunt* or *Death of a Salesman*.

Q What was the title?

How well do you know the play, *Soldadera*?

Q It doesn't spring readily to mind.

It was by a woman with a melodious name—Josefina Niggli. A Samuel French edition of the play described it as "…bold and gripping, a very affecting account of feminine heroism. Taut with suspense and doubt. It gives supreme characterizations of women acting under stress during the terrible Mexican Revolution."

And I was the only man among the war-trapped ladies, so I had to summon what few acting chops I possessed back then to boldly bellow the immortal words, "You're not going to blow me to hell!" They, incredibly, then changed the word "hell" to "heck," when my protests failed. Until the night when I scandalized the school, by putting the original word back in.

In one of my books, there's a picture from *Soldadera*, and you can see me, with an attractive small blonde girl in the role of "Adelita." It might have been a pretty good play, but at the time I resolved never to be in another play that has a line beginning: "Tell us, Old One…"

At the first read-through, a shy, anonymous young woman, whom no one could remember ever seeing before, either in class or in the halls, cried real tears where the script called for it. She did it again every time, in rehearsal and in performance. We were astounded. "Who is that?" we all wondered, and, "Where did she come from?" I hadn't even bothered to learn her name. Someone said they didn't know, but thought her first name might be "Sandra." It was.

In about third grade, our sour teacher, Miss Graham, asked us all to write down what we wanted to be when we grew up, suggesting, of course: dentist, lawyer, nurse etc. She ordered, "Now don't write down movie star because none of you is going to be one." How could she know that, I wondered, having no idea of course, how movie stars did get to be one. And didn't they have to come from somewhere?

According to her, they sure didn't come from Grand Island, Nebraska, or even Nebraska! Henry Fonda was one actor who proved Myrtle Graham wrong. As did Marlon Brando, who came from Omaha, and to the world's disbelief, Fred Astaire. And that shy, blonde Sandra who could cry on cue can be added to the list, with an Oscar all her own: "Sandra" became Sandy Dennis!

Q One of the shows you appeared in was Simon Gray's *Otherwise Engaged* on Broadway.

Yes, I couldn't wait to get to the theater each time. One night, while another actor was speaking, I happened to glance down at the floor and I remembered the six-inch high platform that had been our stage in Miss Moore's class, and I thought, "Those boards were in Lincoln, Nebraska." Then I quickly thought, "These fairly dirty boards under my feet are on *Broadway*!! How on earth did I span that dream of distance?"

Q Do you ever read reviews or just put them out of your mind?

I remember one—when I was at Williamstown. I felt my performance "knocked 'em dead" in *Charley's Aunt* that summer. So when *The Berkshire Eagle*" review came out, I breathlessly turned to read my rave review. I wasn't mentioned in the first few paragraphs. Or the next few. I began to perspire. But then I could see my name coming. G. Gordon Bullett, I think that was his name, reviewed my hilarious performance, by proclaiming, "Dick Cavett in no way detracted from the enjoyment of the evening." Now you can't buy a review like that! ■

VICTOR MASAYESVA, JR.

A Hopi photographer and videomaker, Mr. Masayesva, Jr. began working with video in 1980, initially teaching students to document the oral histories of elders in Hotevilla. He created his film, Itam Hakim, Hopiit, in 1984. He was selected for a Media Arts Fellowship in 1988, founded by the Rockefeller Foundation, by ITVS for creating his film, *Imagining Indians*, in 1991. Mr. Masayesva's work has been exhibited at several museums, including the Art Institute of Chicago, the Museum of Modern Art, and the Whitney Museum of Art. His book, *Husk of Time: The Photographs of Victor Masayesva* was published in 2006. He also co-edited *Hopi Photographers/Hopi Images*. In 1995, Mr. Masayesva received the American Film Institute's Maya Deren Award for Independent Film and Video Artists.

Q What was your childhood like?
I grew up in a village, which was really a spinoff from the old mother village. The way we lived was based on traditional values. We then moved to one of our ancestral Hopi sites, Kawestima, in north Arizona and south Utah, where the village was built in a huge cliff face. After we left mother village, we stopped here in Hotevilla. The soldiers were there to act as a buffer between us and the village we had left. This was the background I grew up in. We were anti-white man, anti-government, and all the villages around us called us hostiles because we wished to remain apart. Our elders were strongly against us getting a white-man's education. But my mother was equally strong. She said we needed to know more if we were to survive in this culture. We're a matriarchal society; that's our identity.

So when I was fifteen, I was able to go to high school in New York City. It was a private preparatory school named Horace Mann School. We didn't really know where New York City was. We were very insulated at Hotevilla, only speaking Hopi at the time. We were self-sufficient; we didn't need help from the outside world.

Q How curious were you as a young person?
I was curious; I didn't know a lot about the white-man's world. My father left it up to me to make the decision if I wanted to go; I did go. Three days later I ended up in New York City after traveling by bus. The Horace Mann School was not like anything I could have imagined. We had our own teaching systems. This was a White-man's way of teaching and educating. They expected me to fail but I hung in there. Yes, it was mostly curiosity that kept me going, coupled with my tenacity. They didn't think I should succeed there with my Hopi education.

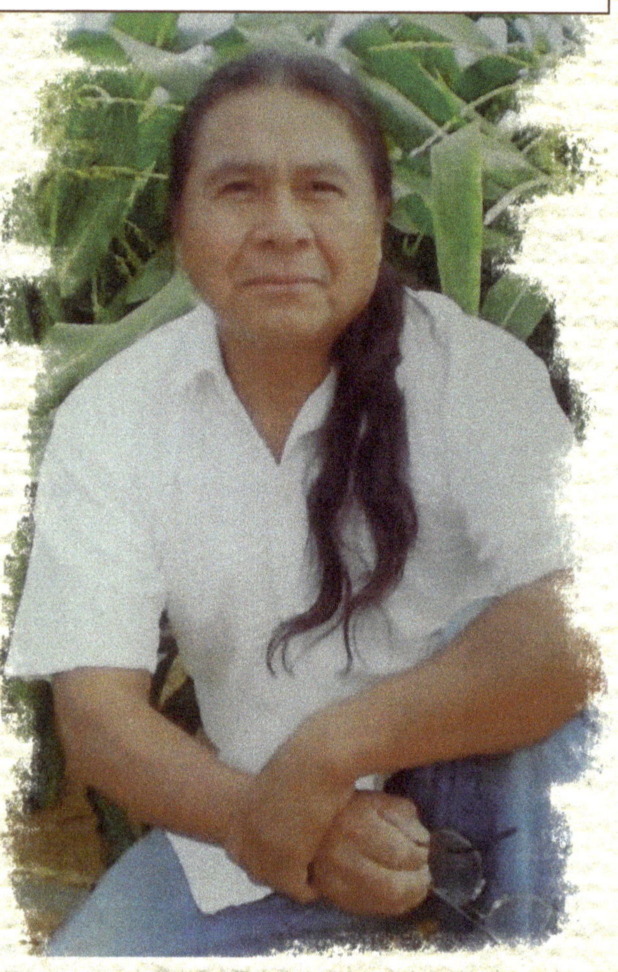
Victor Masayesva photo: courtesy of the artist

Q How would you describe the path leading you to create the art that you have?
I grew up immersed in my culture and language. Once I started to engage in the outside world, I realized my communication skills were lacking. I thought about what the word—communication—meant. It was very important to learn how to communicate. I thought I would get involved by being a lawyer or teaching, but eventually I realized my skill in the use of the English language would be sufficient enough, so I turned to taking pictures. Then eventually to the screen—to moving pictures—which is where I'm at now. I'm also a farmer.

Q What are you growing?
Corn, melons, beans, peaches, apricots, apples. My dad taught me. He raised ten of us. I grew up this way. Farming is a big part of our culture. The Hopi culture is made up of dryland farmers. We're pretty insulated out here but we have managed to hold onto many of our traditions and ceremonies. A lot of tribes regard us as a grandfather tribe.

Q Today a lot of us don't grow our own food, and we've lost our connection with the earth.
As a farmer when I'm out there I see things growing. The songs we sing are tied to the rains. Growing the corn situates me in the field. I'm connected but so many young people are not, they're in cities.

But if you're not in a field, but in the city, it's still your responsibility to look upwards and look at the sky, at the moon, the stars, the planets at night. You can be aware of the melting of the snow. I go every morning to pray to the sun, and in the evening I'm grateful that He has not given up on us.

Q Why did you want to create your very important book, *Husk of Time*?

It was a dedication to my mother and father; they were always wondering what I was doing. I didn't seem to have a "regular" job, and they didn't exactly understand what I doing—taking pictures. I rushed to get the manuscript to a publisher but my mom passed two months before it was published. That was my main focus—for her to have seen the book. My dad was moved. I did show my mom some of the pictures I had taken prior to the book.

Q I understand kachina masks and kachina dancers first appeared in rock art around 1300 A.D. What compelled you to make your documentary film, *Imagining Indians*, in 1982?

It was an interesting way to start in my work. In our culture, yes—we have our kachinas—spirits that come into the village. At the beginning I asked questions about our rituals: "Are we acting? Are we involved in make-believe? Is it still something necessary to assume that our culture will continue?" That's how it started. I also went and asked the different tribes, "Is it not make-believe what we are doing?" Some of them were offended. Because I know when the kachinas come, they are not assuming a costume or a face, they are becoming a rain-making entity along with you.

But what I was also realizing at one point, was that the young people who were pretty much involved with kachinas, were instead detaching and letting their egos take over. This didn't occur when I was growing up. Then the dances were done for religious reasons, and not for cultural reasons.

Now that we're getting more and more people to attend the dances, what's happening is that kachinas are "becoming" entertainers. We're also not dancing in a physical space that's set up for the cultural ritual but entertaining as a spectacle to show-off the dances. Once, these dances were done in intense meditation and prayer.

We're also putting on the dances when it's convenient, when an audience can come, when the young people are free from their jobs to come and participate on the weekends, not when the moon calendar requires that the dance be done. We're putting out empty prayers in the forms of the kachinas. So we're losing communication with the forces that we need to deliver our prayers to. These are some of the reasons we're having problems with the climate extremes.

Q In your film, *Itam Hakim, Hopiit*, which you created in 1984, a tribal elder recounts Hopi philosophy and prophesy in an eloquent personal and cultural history as we're immersed in the ancient landscape. You have said, "We must listen to the songs being sung, for experience is being offered in sacred terms which we must accept in the spirit of the offering."

Originally the film was done in the Hopi language at a time when nobody was working in our mother tongue. We were ignoring the fact that these stories were being told in a foreign tongue. I learned early that our altars were not "portable," that you can't just go to New York City and sing our songs there. We are caretakers of this place, and collaborators with these sacred songs. I can't just go somewhere else and have the same response that our songs have here. There are specified ties to a place.

Q Your film, *Ritual Clowns*, is part collage, part animation, and part documentary, relating the Hopi cosmology of the Hopi nation. What were your motivating reasons for creating this film?

I see young people who can mimic and speak the words addressing the forces, but until you have the years necessary to establish the relationship with what you're saying, the words don't bring up the meaning that they hold. There may be a rare person whose words can connect but I think it's a matter of time and experience. You can't mimic the significance, the import.

We had originally only allowed those who were forty-five years or older and were really dependent on age and experience to participate in the rituals. We tended to select people for these ceremonies who we felt were responsible. But now I think we need to work to involve young people earlier, to give them responsibilities early. They will make mistakes but I hope that will contribute to their maturation. So I'm working with younger people, and I believe in giving them more responsibility.

Q As you walk the spiritual road of your ancestors, what are you learning about the importance of ritual in your life?

I guess ... that you have it walk it alone. No one can walk it for you. And at the very least, to know why I am here, and with my limited ability to support others with what's going on in the village. To know I have to be aware of the times when things are supposed to happen more and more.

This is also a period when we've been getting together with international indigenous timekeepers; we're very conscious of a cycle, which began in 2013; it is necessary to be conscious of why we are on this earth, and how we go forward. In that regard, as a group of indigenous timekeepers from various countries, we made a decision in Hotevilla in 2013 to involve young people in experiencing the planets and their movements. To give them an idea of our natural world. We feel we have to be very conscious, to make a strong effort at this time, because to make a difference is up to each one of us. ■

HENRY MUTTOO

Artistic Director of the Cayman National Cultural Foundation for more than twenty years, Mr. Muttoo is one of the Caribbean's foremost cultural educators and theatre practitioners for over thirty-five years. He is an award-winning actor, director, and designer whose work has achieved acclaim throughout the region and internationally. Mr. Muttoo is a former Senior Tutor at the Edna Manley College in Jamaica, has taught Design at the University of the West Indies, and directed and designed for the University of South Florida. He has received numerous awards for his work, including a Jamaica National Drama Award, two Cacique Awards from the National Drama Association of Trinidad and Tobago, Best Actor in Guyana, Cayman National Theatre Company's Director of the Year, and Officer of the Order of Cayman. In 2013, Mr. Muttoo was honored by Queen Elizabeth with the MBE and in 2015 was made an Honorary Doctor of Arts by the University College of the Cayman Islands.

Q How would you describe what makes Caymanian art and culture so unique?

As an artist, conscious of my own indebtedness to other artists and cultures and ideas, I am reluctant to view any culture or art as unique. The word "unique" has an aura of exclusivity, a comfort level that can be stifling and counter-productive to making art. Human beings want to feel special. We crave an identity that allows us to experience comradeship with a people whose physical and social signals we readily recognize. We need to acknowledge our similarities to our greater human family. I prefer to say that Caymanian culture and art have many distinguishing features, which makes it special to the people who live on the islands and who have invested their lives in the daily act of survival towards the making of tomorrow. This allows me to remain open to the knowledge that other cultures also have their own distinguishing features.

Q What have been your most important goals as the Artistic Director leading the Cayman National Cultural Foundation?

The vision still remains to help build a country that is culturally at ease with itself. Before I joined the organization in 1989, I worked as Production Manager for the now-defunct Cayman National Theatre Company. That experience revealed the strong and fast-held traditions, which Caymanians continue to be proud of, and which sustain them. But the country has been developing rapidly. People from other cultures come to service newly-created businesses. Cayman's great playwright, Dr. Frank McField noted this in his play, *Time Longer Dan Rope*, when he wrote: "Caymanians have the same weaknesses as any people. And the more the island develops, the more those weaknesses will be exposed, will come into play..."

The mission focuses on preservation, development, and celebration of Caymanian traditions through the creative arts process; to move culture and arts from small gatherings mainly "behind the breadfruit tree," and give the people a sense of what is possible in human endeavor. To not stifle freedom of thought, creative expression, but to rekindle enthusiasm, hopefulness about the possibilities of the creative process through the pursuit of art, theater, poetry, painting, sculpture and photography. It has been a long journey, but Tennyson tells us "to strive, to seek, to find and not to yield."

Q What originally led you into a life in the theater?

When I was invited to join the Theatre Guild of Guyana. I entered the world of the theater—education, terrific and erudite friends and mentors. Every artist before me, whose work and teaching has been part of my education on this same "landscape-signifying" journey. It was only natural I would follow. Art should speak to one's personal and collective condition through the appreciation of beauty.

Art and the theater have afforded me the opportunity to understand our society, the tenement world I occupied as a boy in Guyana and this new globalized world I negotiate as an adult. My education prepared me to open minds. It is a labor of love to which I have happily shipwrecked my life.

Q You've mentioned that Harold Clurman's book, *On Directing*, had an impact upon your life.

It did. I came across the book, and because I had directed a production for the school, it immediately caught my eye. I still have the copy, and to this day, tattered as it is, I keep it close. I know of no better book to teach a young director the technical aspects of directing. And, of course, when I learned of your show, I knew we had to have you bring Harold alive in Cayman. And how you did!

Q Who have been inspirations in your life in shaping your vision?

There are so many: Peter Minshall, Ming Cho Lee, Derek Walcott, Ken Corsbie, Dennis Scott, Ralph Koltai, Michael Annals, Susan Adams, the Dadaists, the Surrealists, and a tutor at Croydon who taught me more about stage design in one session than anyone before or since.

Q In 1992, you were selected as the designer for Derek Walcott's *Dream on Monkey Mountain* for a special Nobel Celebration in honor of the poet and dramatist. What did that mean to you and how did you approach creating your designs for that particular production of Mr. Walcott's play?

I've known of Derek since 1965, a long time before he received the Nobel Prize. I was reading his poetry and directing his early plays in high school. I have tremendous respect and admiration for his genius, which I only fully appreciated after an enlightening session with my former headmaster, Edgar Wilson. The story is worth telling. Mr. Wilson taught us Literature.

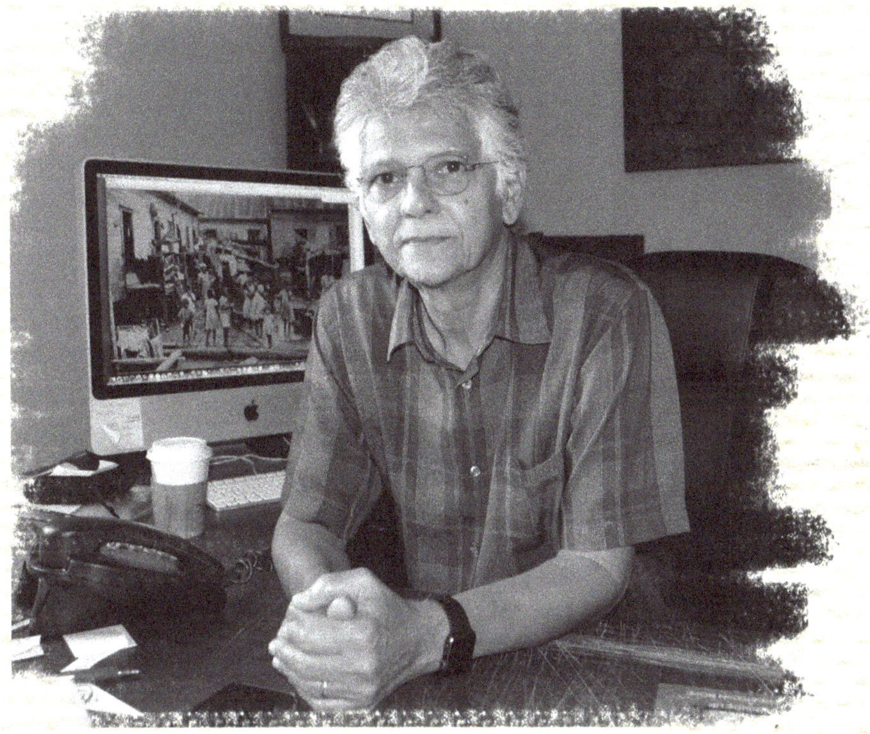
Henry Muttoo photo: courtesy of the artist

One day we arrived in class for our lesson on criticism. There were two poems, sonnets, written side by side on the chalkboard. One was by Derek Walcott and the other by Shakespeare. We were assigned to write critiques of the poems. We all knew Shakespeare was the greatest writer in the English language, but no one had ever heard of Derek Walcott. We tore Walcott's poem to shreds, exclaiming how bad a writer he was with no rhyme pattern, no alliteration, assonance, dramatic irony, using all the terms we had learned that a good poem should have.

The following day Mr. Wilson arrived in the class with a broad smile on his face. He walked calmly up to the chalkboard, erased the names and switched them. We had actually destroyed Shakespeare's poem. Mr. Wilson smiled and said that he hoped we had learned something by the exercise.

I met Derek several times when I performed on stage around the region and directed many of his plays as a professional director. I was delighted when I got the news that he had won the Nobel Prize. The Trinidad Theatre Workshop—a company Derek had founded and directed—decided to do a celebratory tour with *Dream on Monkey Mountain*. Albert LaVeau, one of Walcott's major actors and the director, hired the brilliant Trinidadian, Rawle Gibbons, to direct the production. Rawle knew my work from the time we both were tutors at the Jamaica School of Drama and invited me to be the production designer. They accepted my central concept of using stilt figures or, as they are called in Trinidad and Tobago, "Moko Jumbies."

Q You've spent a great deal of your energies educating young Caymanians in the arts.

Education is critical. For it to be useful, it has to encourage and promote freedom of thought, expression, and creative thinking—even when such thinking is in opposition to established dogma. It has been an uphill climb to convince Cayman's educators to the necessity of the arts in people's lives. One understands that in a small country like Cayman, there are few opportunities to make a decent living as a full-time artist; but art never started out as a commodity. Yet art can dignify, enlighten, and enhance our humanity, leading to changes we would like to see occur in our society.

Q How would you describe how the nature and wildlife of the Cayman Islands have fed your creativity as a gifted painter, sculptor, and photographer?

Yours are kind words. My efforts in these creative endeavors has more to do with enquiry, exploration, and notation of thought. I try and look beyond to discover what I truly feel is something greater than physical beauty—the beauty of spirit. It is ever present, mainly the folk with their simple—but not simplistic—ways of seeing their home and the world, and their wisdom.

When one lives here long enough and is unafraid to be open to the island and the call of its spirit, it comes from the flora or the fauna, and one is soon seduced into the act of being Caymanian. That act nourishes me as an artist and a person and helps me connect the dots of this journey. If my art can reflect only a small portion of that distinguishing spirit, that is a gaining a whole lot. ■

TINA RAMIREZ

Founder and Artistic Director of Ballet Hispanico from 1979 to 2009, Ms. Ramirez is recognized around the world as the foremost dance interpreter of Hispanic culture in the United States. During her tenure, Ballet Hispanico performed for over two million people across three continents. The Company's national tours included engagements at such major venues as The John F. Kennedy Center in Washington, DC, the Music Center in Los Angeles, The Wortham Center in Houston, Boston's Celebrity Series, and Jacob's Pillow. Ms. Ramirez' professional performing career included tours with the Federico Rey Dance Company, the Xavier Cugat Orchestra, and solo engagements in Spain. Ms. Ramirez' performing includes tours of the United States, Canada, and Cuba with the Federico Rey Dance Company, in Spain, at Spoleto's Festival of Two Worlds with John Butler, in the Broadway productions of *Kismet* and *Lute Song*, and the television adaptation of *Man of La Mancha*. In 1967, she conceived and directed Operation High Hopes, a professional dance training program for inner-city children. Ramirez' contribution as an educator is in many ways as important as her legacy as an artist and director. Today, the Ballet Hispanico School of Dance offers year-round professional training in ballet, Spanish dance, and modern dance for over six hundred students. Leelee Sobieski and Jennifer Lopez also took their earliest dance classes at the School. Ms. Ramirez has received the National Medal of Arts, the Honor Award from Dance/USA, Dance Magazine Award, the Hispanic Heritage Award, Governor's Arts Award, Mayor's Award of Honor for Arts and Culture, and a GEMS Woman of the Year Award.

Q Did your dancing on Broadway influence your creativity about dance?
I don't see any difference in dance. Whatever you do, it's either good or bad. I look at technique last. I look at the dancer's motivation or the images they have chosen when they dance—those are most important. Sometimes you're working on an abstract piece. Yet while it may be abstract, it has to come from an emotion. The question then becomes, how do you do it with a strong image?

Q What led you to create Ballet Hispanico in 1970?
I was greatly influenced by my teachers. I believed in them. Wherever I went as a young dancer, if I toured to Spain, I studied there. I believe our entire body is an instrument, and it shows how much love and tenacity you have for the art.

I was training students, and one day a student, she was twelve years old, asked me: "What is a professional?" I told her, "It's making your living from what you do." She said, "I want to be a professional." So I think to myself, "In a way I'm lying to these young people, because I am training them but for what?" I always told them, "Don't lie." That was when I began to think, how could I create a company for them to be a part of? That gave me the idea. I called the company: The New York City Hispanic Dance Company.

Q What are some of the challenges Ballet Hispanico continues to face?
I love my art. I'm always looking forward. In the performing arts you need to have an audience. It's not like a painter who can paint alone. Audience development is so important. How to get the word out so that people understand better what Ballet Hispanico is doing, about the excitement of our dancers, about what is being said through the work that is being created. The more we perform, the more it fuels the support we receive. I hope our fans will come out and support the work.

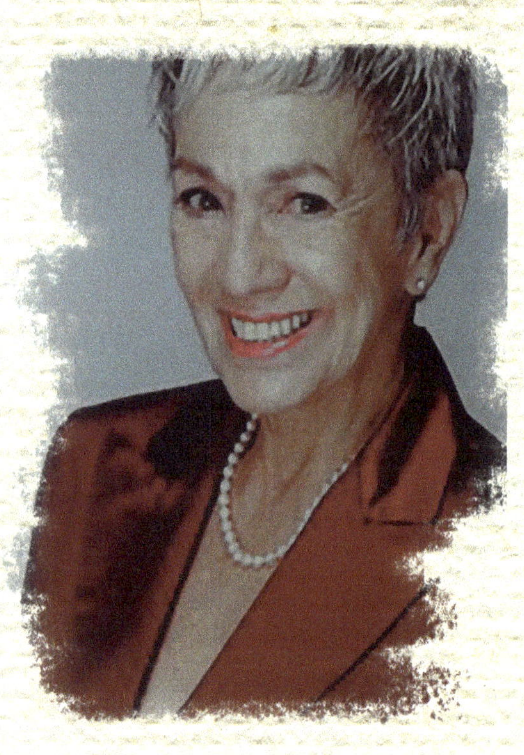

Tina Ramirez photo: courtesy of the artist

Q Could you describe the importance of the Ballet Hispanico's "First Steps"?
I believe everyone needs art in their life. Art makes you a better person. You're sensitized to the world. You learn to how to work with others, become better at solving problems. The important thing is to know how to get things done.

The earlier you're able to get a child in this kind of environment, it becomes part of his or her language. What they learn affects their minds, their bodies, in such a positive way. That is what "First Steps" is all about.

Q You were also able to commission over seventy-five new works for Ballet Hispanico's repertory from such choreographers as Alberto Alonso, Talley Beatty, Graciela Daniele, George Faison, Vicente Nebrada, Ann Reinking, and William Whitener, and young artists including Susan Marshall, Ramón Oller,

David Roussève, and Pedro Ruiz. All these artists helped Ballet Hispanico grow. It's thrilling to see how they can push the Hispanic art, the music, the storyline. When the choreographer comes to work with the company, it's always such an exciting experience. The kind of dancers we pick are kinetic dancers, creating a special relationship between the performer and the audience. This is so important in our being able to reach our audience, otherwise we won't exist. We have to bring people to the theatre.

Q What keeps you inspired to create?
I've always been inspired by challenges. Seeing young dancers inspire me. The art inspires me. Art is my life. I also like going to see shows by other artists, experiencing their work; I keep learning new things. It's all about the art itself, you have to be so committed. That's how you can tell if someone is a dancer. You can't ever slack off. If you do, it's time to get out. You cannot be safe in art. You have to take chances every day. ■

CHARLIE SOAP

Mr. Soap, a full-blood bilingual Cherokee, has dedicated his life strengthening many Cherokee communities. He served as Director of the Cherokee Nation Community Development Department and for seven years as the Oklahoma Area Director of the Christian Children's Fund. Mr. Soap is the Producer/Director of the film, *The Cherokee Word for Water*. Mr. Soap was Wilma Mankiller's husband, a community development partner for more than thirty years, and a leader in the Bell Waterline Project that inspired the film, working with the construction of eight community buildings and numerous other critical self-help initiatives. He served as the founding Director of the Boys and Girls Club of Tahlequah. Under Mr. Soap's leadership, the Club operated a comprehensive summer enrichment program, working with Tahlequah Public Schools to develop the first after-school programs in the school system. The collaboration between the Boys and Girls Club and the Tahlequah Public Schools has served as a national model. Mr. Soap is a fancy war dancer, and photographer, and has photographed his travels as a performer with Ray Charles around the world.

Q What would bring communities together with greater understanding and compassion?
One of the ways is by going out to help. As one of the elders told me, back on the Waterline, "If you know someone who needs help, don't ask, just go ahead." Leadership is about listening to the people; it makes it easier to get things done.

We have twenty-one projects going. Some volunteers worked on a house and helped a family. We've been working with churches, helping with the gardening. A friend contributed a plow and gardened as a volunteer. We purchased fences. It's all about having compassion for the community; we need to help each other.

Q How would you describe what made yours and Wilma Mankiller's partnership in serving people work so well?
We thought along the same lines with the same philosophies. Wilma was a "people-person" like myself, working with "gadugi" (working together). She listened and really believed in our People. She'd talk to the communities in English, I'd translate it into Cherokee. Wilma believed in strengthening the Indian Nations. Being a full-blooded Cherokee, while she was originally from Oklahoma, she had come from California, and even though she had health problems, it didn't slow her down.

When we met with those in the community, she would tell them, "We're here to turn the power over to you, to help you meet your goals." She believed in the people, in strengthening the Nation's "gadugi." We'd find ways to write grants for the real needs in the communities.

We've been able to create the Wilma Mankiller Foundation, which was one of the things we developed after Wilma left us.

Q Why it is important that the film you produced, *The Cherokee Word for Water*, is seen by as many of today's audiences as possible?
Wilma and I talked a lot together about this film. There is a lot of need in the Native communities across the country in telling the history of the past. There was a lack of money for the Bell Waterline Project. We had to do something innovative. Wilma and I got together to use this self-help method to help the Bell Community. She and I believed that "gadugi" would be very important. We showed that if it could work in our community, it could work everywhere. That's what the film is about.

Wilma had approved the script. Eight days before she passed, she said to me at her bedside, "I won't see the completion of the film, but it's my wish for the film to be made. You have to help Kristina make the film."

After Wilma had passed, Kristina (Kiehl) and I raised the money in a year. I was amazed that it was actually happening. It was an emotional experience for me to direct the film. I've watched it in over a hundred cities and communities and still enjoy it.

The film is a magnet, educating people, bringing them together in a very rich and emotional way. Wilma was noted around the world and had met many world leaders. Young people need to see this film. We need to create young heroes. We're doing a documentary about Wilma Mankiller. It will be shown on PBS.

Q How stories get passed on is a very important way of connecting young and old, the past and the future.

Yes, the Cherokees have their own story to tell, their traditional dances, language, their medicines. I believe it's important to talk about connective-ness, the inner with outer worlds, all of the planets, and how everything is balanced. We learn this from the elders.

Passing down the oral history goes back a long way. I appreciate your putting these words out about our people. I see you had interviewed Oren Lyons in your newspaper; he is a great friend. He is very special to all people, all Nations. We were so honored to have him participate as Grandfather in the film.

Q How can we respect our planet?

As I get older, I understand how the elders do this. They watch the environment—how if you disturb the land they see what happens. I've learned. I see what supports the land and what can cause erosion. That's because my family were farmers. Nature will take care of itself. But we face a lot of problems on this planet. Water is an important issue. A lot people don't always think about it but we need to be careful how we protect our water. We can't live without water. We really need to pay attention. We've caused the melting of the ice.

You learn a lot by listening. As you grow, watch the birds when it'll get cold. The black birds will all flock together. A rain frog will come out if it's going to rain. The squirrels, the deer, the horses—they all teach us respect. Our planet is sacred; climate change has been created by us. There's too much cutting down of trees and forests. It affects every one of us.

Q You've given so much by being who you are and the things you've done. You're a link from those elders who have come before.

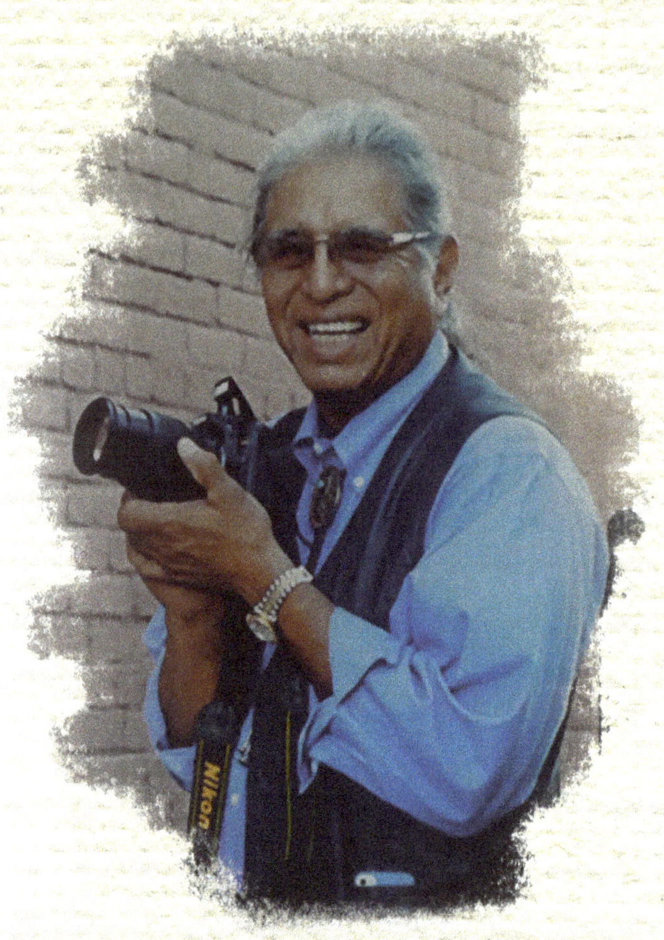

Charlie Soap photo: courtesy of The Mankiller Project, Tahlequah, Oklahoma

That's really a compliment. You lead by example. We all can inspire, impact on someone's life by how you live. When I sit down with the poor, they're someone important to me because they're human beings. It's all about how you treat people. Each of us has to be careful how we conduct ourselves.

My brother goes out and helps other people. He said to me, "I did this because I like what you do, so I go and help. It makes me feel good even if I don't get paid." It's the compassion of how you feel about other people. You do it because it comes from the kindness of your heart. I think about my mom and dad coming from a poor family. We were poor, they didn't have credit at the store to get groceries. I think about those things and try to be helpful.

Q How can we engage young people to see a brighter future for themselves?

Education is something we should all be working towards. These young people are our future. They want to be loved, to be somebody; they don't know their importance. If you talk to teenagers individually, you can make a little wedge inside their minds; I find it means a lot to them. They have so much energy. They're smart, they can figure things out. We need to cultivate that in a good way.

With the farm project we've begun, we involve them to work on a farm, growing vegetables, work with the livestock; we're able to promote leadership. They learn skills, making cheese, extracting honey from the beehive; you can see it means a lot to them.

When I was young, we had a farm, and we didn't use plastic back then. We'd walk to go places through the woods. We'd talk to each other; we weren't busy punching on things. We need "gadugi"—to be in service to our community—to pull together and help one another. There's so much more we can do to help each other. ■

DR. BARBARA ANN TEER

A visionary, producer, writer, teacher, and actress, Dr. Barbara Ann Teer founded Harlem's National Black Theatre in 1968, the first revenue-generating black theater arts complex in America. As a dancer, she toured with the Alvin Ailey Dance Company and the Pearl Bailey Las Vegas Revue; on Broadway as dance captain in *Kwamina*, choreographed by Agnes de Mille; and in the film of *Purlie Victorious*. In 1963, she co-founded The Group Theatre Workshop with Robert Hooks, which later became the Negro Ensemble Company. Five years later, Dr. Teer founded the National Black Theatre at 125th Street and Fifth Avenue. As executive director, Dr. Teer directed a theater troupe that toured to Bermuda, Guyana, Haiti, South Africa, and Trinidad, across America, appeared at Lincoln Center, and on the public television program, *Soul*. She lectured at Yale School of Drama, NYU, Brown University, and the Schomberg Center. Dr. Teer received more than fifty awards, including a Drama Desk Award, Vernon Rice Award as Best Actress, an Audelco Award, Harlem Community Builder's Award, and a Women Who Dared Award. Dr. Teer died in 2008 (this interview was conducted in 2001).

Q How did your family influence your desire to be an artist?

I was raised in East St. Louis, born into a family of community activists, politicians, and educators of the creative talent that lies deep inside each human being. My parents were always around creating, committed to helping those less fortunate members of the community. This is a quality I find extremely valuable, to "give back."

Q At the University of Illinois you majored in dance—

Yes, studying European-American art standards. The first time I experienced anything different was when the famous African dancer, Pearl Primus, came to the University. There were only two black students in our class, myself and one other young woman. When Pearl came in with her drummers and she hit that drum—a vital life force inside me was triggered, igniting a spark! I had never felt that kind of energy flooding my inner being before. It was then I realized I needed to pursue a different path. After graduating with honors, I studied in Paris with Decroux, in Berlin with Mary Wigman.

When I came back to New York City, I went down to Henry Street Settlement and studied and performed with Alwin Nikolais. He gave me an assignment to choreograph a dance from a painting. I selected a painting from the Museum of Modern Art, and the only painting I saw that inspired me was a Picasso. I also used Miles Davis's music. Nickolais thought my piece looked like a night club routine. After that I studied with Martha Graham.

Finally, I studied acting for seven years with Sandy Meisner. He said to me one day, "Get out and get a job." Great advice because I had become a "professional student." I also studied with Paul Mann and Lloyd Richards, and decided to start the Group Theatre Workshop with Robert Hooks. I developed a theatrical production using an eight-line poem by Gwendolyn Brooks, "We Real Cool." This was the beginning of the Negro Ensemble Company. I was an actress on the rise but the only roles I was offered were maids and prostitutes.

Q This was at the time of the Civil Rights Movement in this country—

At the peak of the Movement, I was married to Godfrey Cambridge, and we were invited to the White House. My sister was a co-founder of CORE. She asked me, "Why don't you get involved in the Movement? So we formed the Committee for the Employ-

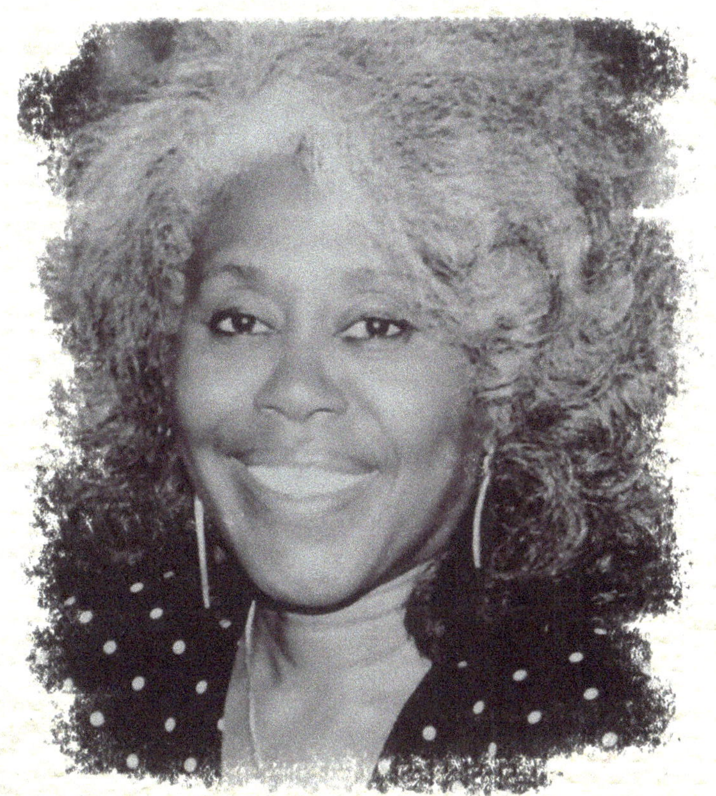

Dr. Barbara Ann Teer photo: courtesy of the artist

ment of the Negro Performer, and we picketed Broadway shows, until Actors Equity changed a few of its laws. At this time, I also saw Melina Mercouri perform. I was awed that an actor could gain such recognition for supporting the political life of a country.

I decided to leave Broadway for Harlem to create an institution designed to meet the cultural sensitivities found in the Black community, a mighty task. I'm in the business of cultural conservation, human development, and creating an alternative learning environment where the creative potential of a human being can be fully realized.

I decided to remove the psychic distance between audience and the performers. I took them off the stage and had the whole audience holding hands in my theater. I believe there's no separation, we can share the joy and oneness of humanity—transformed, uplifted.

Q Who have been some of the strongest inspirations in your life?

My sister, Fredrica L. Teer, was such a strong force. Diana Sands, I was her understudy in practically every show she did. Maya Angelou, Nina Simone, Abby Lincoln, Katherine Dunham, Guru Mayya, guru of Siddah Yoga. So many people in Nigeria; I've been there thirty times.

Q What is your creative mission today?

My mission is to build a cultural Institution, which conserves, educates, and codifies the creative contribution of people of African ancestry. The National Black Theatre offers to the entire world the opportunity to become lifetime members in the "Keep Black Theatre Alive: Your Culture Counts" campaign. We are seeking to bridge the gap between the culturally privileged and the culturally deprived.

When I teach, I move people to a higher dimension of Self. I create new possibilities for spiritual enlightenment, of knowledge, of information. Theatre is the perfect medium. I see artists rejoicing, even in heavy drama. With young people you have to use the right triggers to bring it out from them. I believe it's a holy craft, a barometer for how loving you are.

What I saw in *The Lion King* was a rare marriage—actors moving within the audience, the detailed visual work, the music, the spirit, the synergy of colors. It unfolds what it means to be human. I believe we have to retrain ourselves to love one's self—to empower the Self. ■

MUSICIANS AND SINGERS

LEON BATES

One of America's leading pianists, Leon Bates performed in Carnegie Hall with the New York Pops, Skitch Henderson conducting, and across the United States, in Canada, Italy, France, Austria, Ireland, England, as well as Africa, appearing with the Vienna Symphony, The Sinfonica dell' di Santa Cecilia in Rome, the Strasbourg Symphony in France, Czech National Symphony, Prague, and the Quebec Symphony. He has also toured South Africa, performing in Johannesburg with the National Symphony Orchestra and with the Natal Philharmonic. Mr. Bates has performed with many major U.S. symphonies including the Philadelphia Orchestra, Cleveland Symphony, New York Philharmonic, Los Angeles Philharmonic, San Francisco Symphony, Atlanta Symphony, Detroit Symphony and the Boston Symphony, at the Kennedy Center, Philadelphia's Academy of Music and Kimmel Center, and with Lorin Maazel at the Orchestra of France. He has also performed with the Bournemouth Symphony, Duke Ellington Orchestra in Rome's Olympic Stadium as a tribute to Christopher Columbus, the Detroit Symphony, U.S. Air Force Band, Napa Valley Symphony, Brooklyn Philharmonic, Czech National Symphony, and in a Gala concert with the Philadelphia Orchestra. He has composed prominent pieces of music with the accompaniment of Janet Vogt for a method book, *Piano Discoveries*. Mr. Bates received a lifetime achievement award from the National Association of Negro Musicians, and the Raoul Wallenberg Humanitarian Award for his extensive work with children.

Q I understand you began playing the piano when you were about five or six years old?

My first real exposure to the piano was in kindergarten. My teacher played classical music, and I heard the piano and became excited about the sound of all those keys, high tones, low tones. I told my parents I'd like to play the piano. Every time there was piano in a store, I'd go over to it and start playing.

My mother found me a wonderful teacher; I was with him for about six years. He had a great sense of how to work with children. Christopher Sanjani was a fiddle player, he also played the violin, the mandolin, the accordion, and when I'd go for a lesson he'd also take out his fiddle and play it as I played the piano. He had a great sense how to work with children. I didn't know at the time that I was being taught how to accompany someone. I also learned how to sight-read.

When I was about eight years old, my parents bought me a record player that played 45 rpm records. It sat inside a little red box. The first music they got me was a recording of Tchaikovsky's 6th Symphony. It has an opening in the first movement of a bassoon playing a lugubrious ominous sound; I became fascinated with the sound. I'd lie on the floor, listening to it over and over; it was very transforming. I then listened to Haydn and Mozart. After playing my first recital, the

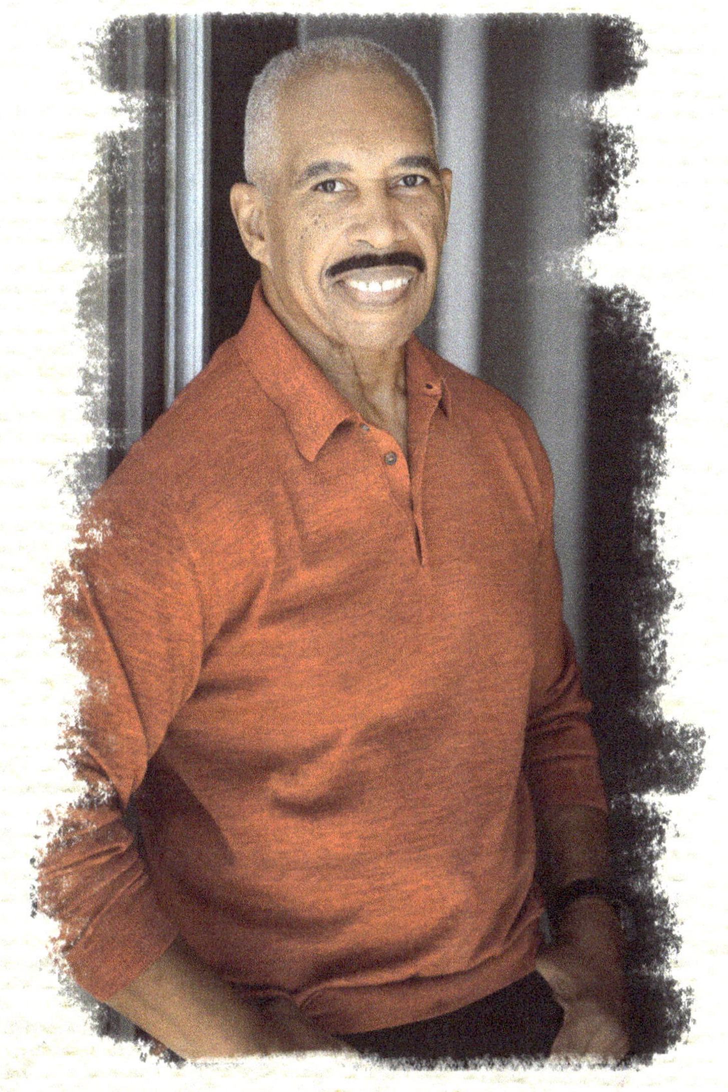

Leon Bates photo: Paul Sirochman

reaction I received spurred me on; everyone responded so positively.

Q Do you think children at an early age should be encouraged?
Yes, if they have an affinity. It's opening a person to experience aspects of their personality. They may not aspire to becoming a professional, but having this exposure basically enriches their life and education which they'll bring into adulthood. It's fascinating to watch how children respond and immediately identify with a specific music. They might dance, or want to play an instrument, or draw or paint to it. If they're talented, they may go forward in that direction.

Q You seem to have had two passions when you began your career: the pursuit of music and body building—
I got interested in body building as a teenager at a YMCA during the summer. When I was in college as a freshman at Temple University, where I studied music, I just happened to pass by the gym, and I saw all these weights in the gym. So I started experimenting, and basically I've been doing it ever since; it's another part of myself.

What I discovered was the process between the two had a lot of similarities—the work ethic involved, dealing with repetition while working with resistance. Learning to play a particular passage fast is your ultimate goal as a pianist; you have to work on it every day. They have fueled one another ever since.

Q You've been involved with writing pieces in collaboration with Janet Vogt, for a method book entitled *Piano Discoveries.*
Yes, they asked me if I would be involved, to work with another piano teacher. I thought it was a great idea. It involves taking well-established music, for example a Mozart or Beethoven theme, and putting together transcriptions of the melodies so they can be easily played by young people at an elementary level.

We also compose new melodies so they can learn five-finger excerpts on one hand and the corresponding hand—how to pivot the thumb and cross one hand underneath and cross over. They're actually able to play a movement of a Mozart sonata, making it an enjoyable process. In a sense, it was how I was trained, and it's a wonderful way to take their creativity to their ability to be comfortable reading the notes.

Q What are your expectations during a concert?
With an orchestra, with the conductor or if it's with a smaller group, I know on a certain level, the music will all fit together; whether it will be a particularly exceptional performance has to do with all us bringing something brand new. We're all playing in tempo, but what makes it exceptional is for all of us to "live the music in that moment," like it's never been heard before.

There's a sense of conversation happening, so when the other instruments come in, I acknowledge their presence. I might play a supportive role in the melody. Perhaps the melody shifts to a flute, the next instrument could be an oboe—I respond by giving a richer accompaniment. There might be three French horns, so I'll play high in the register to balance the moment. When I'm playing twenty-three concerts in twenty-three days, I notice differences and subtleties from one concert to the next.

Q How do you bring your own creativity to a particular piece, for example, a waltz by Chopin?
Of course, he wrote a particular melody that sings itself, and this is my chance to deal with this great art. Sometimes I'll hear a voice leading me how to play. At a certain point on a given day, let's say I'll hear the F minor in my head, all of a sudden; I realize I need to play that melody in a way that resonates strongly with me, so I perform it a certain way.

Q I understand you present two lectures: "Brown vs. the Board of Education," based on the May 17, 1954 Supreme Court ruling, and another, "American Originals," recognizing the achievements of America's extraordinary composers of our time.
My role model was my teacher from college at Temple University— Natalie Hinderas—a wonderful pianist and a magnificent teacher. She would collaborate with many different musicians. She was a conductor at school and would give lectures that dealt with different composers. Through these lectures, I enjoy bringing something else to an audience, showing another side of myself as a creative artist.

Q How does music help heal us?
First of all, when we hear music, we listen with our being. We might be in the house or in the car, and even without realizing it—it's therapeutic - providing us with a different atmosphere inside ourselves. For me, it's very important to my existence every day.

I definitely believe there needs to be many more music education programs in schools across this country. It's a very necessary tool for today. Because when we let music wash over us, we discover our creativity. As a performing artist, as a creative person, I need to counteract the negatives in our society in as many ways as possible, to motivate myself, to motivate everyone through music. ■

JULIE BUDD

Considered one of the most exciting singers in the world, Ms. Budd began her professional career at age twelve, appearing on *The Merv Griffin Show*. After hearing her sing, she became the "Mini Girl with the Maxi Voice." Subsequently she made more than one hundred appearances on *The Merv Griffin Show*. She also sang on *The Tonight Show*, *Entertainment Tonight*, and almost every major TV show. Ms. Budd has co-starred with such legendary performers as Frank Sinatra, Bill Cosby, Carol Burnett, and Liberace. Her concert performances have included Lincoln Center, Carnegie Hall, The Kennedy Center, The London Palladium, Tel Aviv's Israel Performing Art's Center, Las Vegas, and Atlantic City. She has also appeared with many symphony orchestras, including: Baltimore Symphony, National Symphony, Pittsburgh Symphony, Austin Symphony, Alabama Symphony, Philadelphia Symphony, Boca Pops, Milwaukee Symphony, and Dallas Symphony. As an actress, she appeared on Broadway in Neil Simon's *They're Playing Our Song*, and *On Broadway*; Off-Broadway at Circle Rep and Playwrights Horizon. Her film roles include starring in *The Devil and Max Devlin* with Bill Cosby and Elliot Gould, and in *Two Lovers* with Joaquin Phoenix and Gwyneth Paltrow. Ms. Budd has worked with Marvin Hamlisch and Carol Bayer Sager, and they penned the title song, "Roses and Rainbows" for her. Ms. Budd has taught master classes, bringing her method of "The Art of Vocal Technique" to students at universities across the country. She appears each season as one of the hosts of the Variety Children's Charity telethon, and also supports MDA and The Saint Jude Children's Hospital Organization. Her CD, *The New Classics*, was released in 2005. She is recording a new CD, and writing a book about her life.

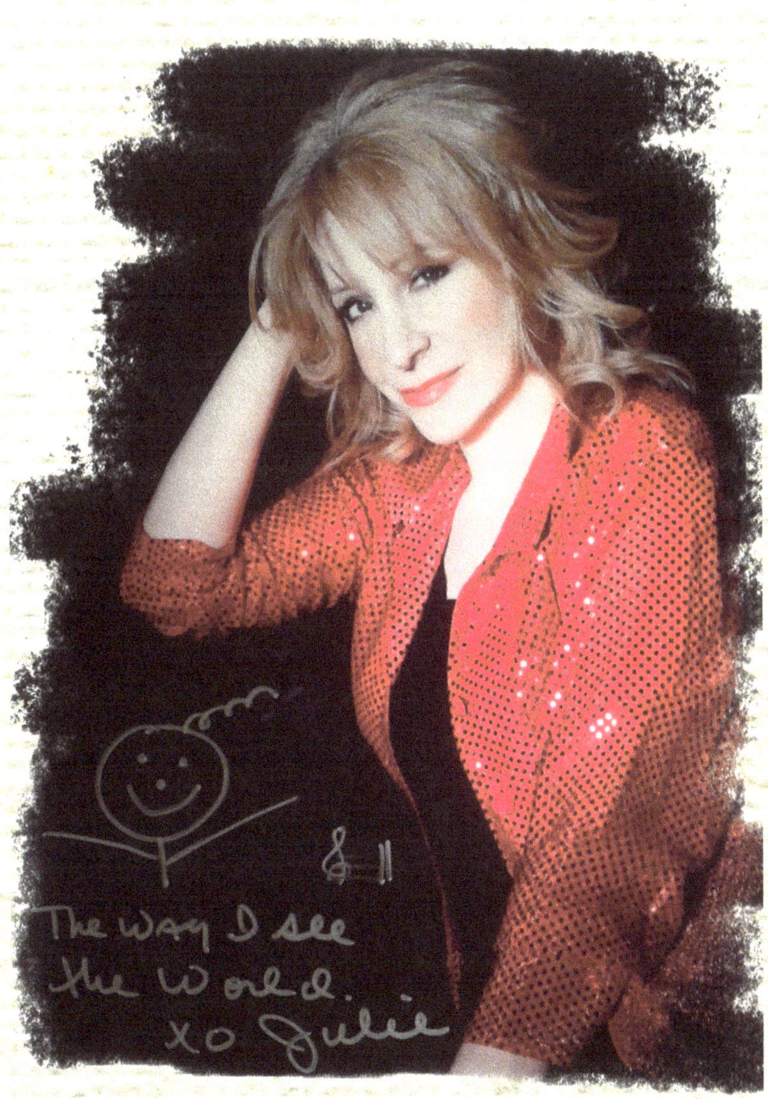

Julie Budd photo: courtesy of the artist

Q How would you describe your CD, *The New Classics*?

What makes it special is I'm tipping my heart to the traditional "American Songbook." We have a lot of new writers today who are carrying the torch into the future. I decided to do a CD filled with unforgettable songs, written prior to 1965 with songs by Anthony Newley and Leslie Bricusse, John Lennon and Paul McCartney, Ann Hampton Calloway, Paul Anka, and Steve Dorff. They're songs of our generation, the ones we grew up with; I think of the American songbook as a continuous artistic process.

Q How did you develop your particular style of performing?

For me, it's all about creating a connection. In a way, I think you need to be born to do this kind of work, to understand it instinctively. I've learned a lot since I began when I was about ten years old.

Doing a show is creating an entity, like a Broadway show. I put all the pieces together, and each moment is a moment in its own. The show has a flow—a beginning, a middle, and an end. There needs to be a sense of art, a sense of anticipation that something magical will happen.

When the audience comes to have a good time, it's up to me to create this, that they'll be happy going on a journey with me.

Those who have come to see my shows tell me they feel like they're meeting a real person, an old friend; I'm very flattered.

Q What do you keep learning about the art of performing?

I'm always evolving. I've learned from the great ones I've worked with, that I've taken my cues from, that every day there's something new to learn. I pay attention. I keep asking, how I can be a better communicator? If you're nervous, it's not such a terrible thing, because it keeps you more alive. A show grows as you grow. It takes certain things to keep going: stamina, a sound, a fearlessness.

I continually refine how I work, how I create, what my method is; I've learned to create my own way of working. Over time you create your own recipe.

Q How did you choose the songs you sing in your show?

It starts with the text—the material has to suit me; it's like putting on a suit. It has to fit—stretching me, allowing me to grow. I think when you've pick the right material in the right key for yourself, it really fits you at that right time in your life. If you gave the same song to Shirley Bassey, Maureen McGovern, and I, we'd all do it with a different take.

So it's knowing how to put the right arrangement and the right interpretation onto the text, so when you put it all together you're able to make magic. You don't always know whether it will work; it's very personal. Over forty years I grew up with my material. Now we're like "old friends traveling together."

When Yul Brynner did *The King and I* in the original production on Broadway, and then when he did it years later, I'm sure he had changed, and found new ways to bring the part alive. Hal Holbrook has been doing his *Mark Twain Tonight* for many years, or you with your show as Clurman for the years that you've been doing it, I'm sure it's changed and so have you. That's what keeps it interesting. You allow your life to color the material.

Q The songs you sing also touch people in a very deep way.

They are primal. Whether the audience is young or older, married or not, the songs are about the human condition. I'm drawn to those writers who have something to say, and I can hear myself singing it. I never do a song unless I feel that.

Q You've also had the fortune of performing with some extraordinary performers—from Frank Sinatra to Liberace to Carol Burnett. What kinds of lessons did you learn from them?

I learned from all of them. Each one of them was highly unique; each one a teacher for me. I will never forget when I worked with Sinatra. He was ultra-generous. He taught me about the technical aspects of the business. I learned from Carol Burnett to perpetually be a student. That's just who she is. She's always improving her craft. Before we went into the studio to record together, she taught a stretch class.

Then there are those times when a rare person will come into your life. For me, that was Liberace. I had an incredible close relationship with him. We would talk together, about having a real life, being a humble person. I knew him from the time I was fifteen until he passed. In my house I have a very special chair he had made for me. He gave so much to me as a friend, and as an artist, that I will never forget.

Q What have you discovered about touching audiences across America and around the world?

Today everyone is chatting on the internet, on Facebook, from Brooklyn to Zimbabwe, to everyone around the world, experiencing the same information at the same time. I see it as a positive thing, because I can take a show as sophisticated as mine to New York City or to a small town in Wyoming, and they'll appreciate the material in my show.

I like to feel "heart and soul" is the driving element of what I do. I bring material I feel is true, and if the audience feels it; that's my number one goal. To make the word come off the page, then the audience experiences it. That's what it's about—bringing something alive and real into their lives—to really connect everyone to the universe. That's what makes what you have to offer so rich. That is "gold." ■

STEPHANIE CHASE

Recognized as "one of the violin greats of our era" through solo appearances with more than one hundred seventy orchestras, including the New York Philharmonic, Chicago Symphony, and London Symphony, Ms. Chase garners continuing acclaim as a soloist, performing in twenty-five countries and offering an enterprising repertoire of over fifty concertos. Her performances at the Tchaikovsky Competition in Moscow led to concerts throughout the world and the award of the prestigious Avery Fisher Career Grant. She has collaborated with conductors including Zubin Mehta, Leonard Slatkin, Leon Barzin, Herbert Blomstedt, Frans Brüggen, Marin Alsop, Roy Goodman, Hugh Wolff, and Stanislaw Skrowaczewski. Her discography encompasses major concerti, chamber works, and collections of salon pieces by diverse composers including Beethoven, Mozart, Saint-Saëns, Ravel, Friml, Schoenberg, and Kapralova. Ms. Chase has premiered music by composers that include Earl Kim, Edward Applebaum, Eleanor Hovda, Joan Tower, Yehudi Wyner, and Taavo Virkhaus. A Professor of Violin at the Steinhardt School of Culture, Education, and Human Development at New York University, she has also given master classes at many prestigious institutions including Juilliard, San Francisco Conservatory, University of Texas at Austin, and the Milwaukee Conservatory.

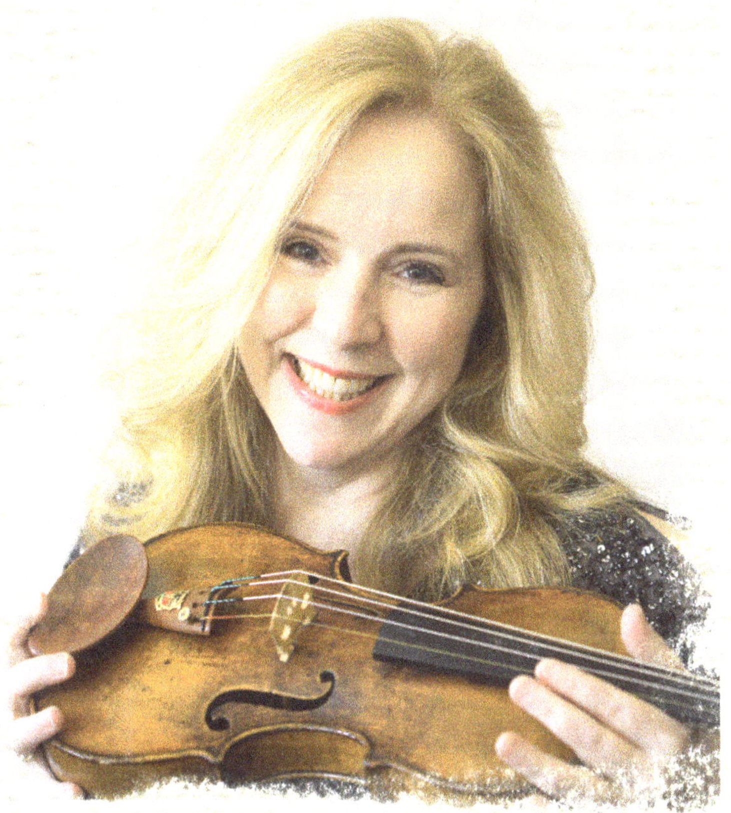

Stephanie Chase photo: courtesy of the artist

Q I understand you grew up in a family of musicians as the daughter of two musicians, the noted arranger and composer, Bruce Chase, and violinist Fannie Paschell Chase, and are the granddaughter of violinists.

I was under two years of age when I started playing. I think the fact that my older sisters were also playing made me want to. I recall being attracted to the sound and the physicality of playing. This developed into a real fascination with the violin. I played by ear for a couple of years before my mother, who was an excellent teacher of young children, gave me lessons and taught me to read music. My father also played the piano. We soon began performing concerts in the greater Chicago area, mostly for local women's and music clubs.

Q You were six years of age when you appeared on the *Ted Mack Original Amateur Hour* show. At age nine, you made your debut with the Chicago Symphony, the youngest winner of the orchestra's Youth Competition—and you even played for Jack Benny.

Yes, he was doing his show in Chicago, and had heard about me. So we went to his hotel suite in the Palmer House Hotel. I played some of the Mozart concerto I had played for the Chicago Symphony competition, then Jack Benny took out his violin and we played Bach's "Double Violin Concerto" together. He played on a Stradivarius, which was the first I had ever seen. I recall noting his rather loose bowing style.

Although he used his violin for humor, he had studied earnestly when he was young, and continued to play regularly as a comedian. It turned out that Jack Benny asked my parents if I'd be interested in playing on his shows with him in California, but my parents declined. They both recognized I was going to study seriously rather than become a novelty act. I could have had a whole different career!

Q So at an early age you embarked on a concentrated period of study and performances.

When I was seven. My parents had read about Ivan Galamian, called the greatest violin teacher of his time. So accompanied by my mother, I traveled to New York and played for him and his principal assistant, Sally Thomas. I distinctly recall being unable to decipher much of what he said.

Galamian was born in Persia, raised in Russia, and had lived in France for fifteen years before coming to America; this contributed to his thick fog of accents. He recommended I work with Sally before coming to him. I wound up studying with her for ten years.

Q You had your Carnegie Hall debut at age eighteen when you appeared as a soloist in the retirement concert of the eminent conductor Leon Barzin. You then went to Belgium to study with the legendary Belgian violinist, Arthur Grumiaux.

When I played for Leon Barzin, he recommended I study with either Jascha Heifetz, Nathan Milstein, or Arthur Grumiaux. I was very fortunate Grumiaux accepted me as a private student. I moved to Belgium to study with him for a year and half, an extremely intense period but very rewarding. As a violin professor, he emphasized the need to listen closely to the phrase and its quality of sound. At that time there were a number of violinists I admired, including Francescatti, Milstein, Stern, Ricci and Oistrakh, Itzhak Perlman, Pinchas Zukerman, and Kyung-Wha Chung.

Q You also received laurels at the Tchaikovsky Competition in Moscow during the Cold War.

In terms of preparing for the Tchaikovsky competition, it was unlike any other. Not only were the repertoire requirements demanding, but the entire competition took about a month. This was when U.S.-Soviet relations were at an all-time low; Russia was truly an "Iron Curtain" country.

My performance in the competition drew a lot of attention, which is why I was willing to endure its rigors. I recall liking the audiences. They seemed very knowledgeable about music and able to overlook politics to a surprising extent. The two students who studied with the chairman of the jury, Leonid Kogan, shared the first prize.

Q You're a noted interpreter of Beethoven's music, actually the first violinist ever to record his Violin Concerto, featuring your own cadenzas on original instruments. How did you come by the violins you play?

My "usual" concert violin was made in Venice in 1742, by Pietro Guarnerius. My mother had fallen in love with it when she was a young adult and managed to buy it. In those days you could buy instruments with a down payment and a payment plan.

When I was eleven, I was able to play on a full-sized instrument. It's a miracle that she allowed me to play it; I've always revered it. When I became a young adult, I purchased it from her.

In the mid-1980s, I was asked to play at a festival in Cape Cod by the pianist, Samuel Sanders, its artistic director. He was the top American collaborative pianist and had partnered with Itzhak Perlman. He had also invited the renowned fortepianist, Steven Lubin, to perform on his replica of a Mozart-era piano. Steven and I then played a Mozart sonata together and, for that concert, I played my Guarneri violin with lowered pitch. The character of the sound altered my way of playing Mozart.

Steven then invited me to play in his series at The Metropolitan Museum, where musicians play on instruments of the period of the composer. The violin I used was from the Met's collection, a Stradivarius that had been "baroqued," and borrowed Baroque bows. That's how I also met my husband. He was the conservator of musical instruments at the Met Museum.

When Steven and I were invited to Vienna to make a recording for a wonderful documentary series about the history of music, we played a selection from Beethoven's "Spring Sonata," filmed at the former Razumovsky Palace. Count Razumovsky had been a diplomat and one of Beethoven's major patrons. My luthier provided me with an instrument with a very nice sound for the Classical style. I've done all my period instrument recordings on it.

Q How do you prepare before a performance?

I have a rehearsal either in the morning or early afternoon, carefully going through the work I'm performing. For an evening concert, I may take a walk, and later I often take a nap. I generally arrive a half hour before I go out on stage, to warm up for about twenty minutes. I want to be in a relaxed, alert state, and avoid talking to others. When I'm on stage performing as a soloist, it can feel like I'm "disembodied." I can be playing so deeply that at times I feel like I'm not even there.

Q How do you work on a new piece for a concert?

I start by figuring out the notes and rhythms, the performance tempos of the work, because this affects the fingerings and how I'll use the bow. I consider the demeanor of the music. The technique and manner of playing Bach is very different from Brahms or contemporary music. I find it very important to consider the culture, the philosophical ideas behind the music, to know some of the composer's life story.

I work a lot with a metronome to be aware of when I'm not staying in the same tempo. I may listen to recordings to feel inspired, but I also learn how another violinist has resolved or not resolved some technical issues. One important aspect is to be self-critical, but remain objective and neutral. I don't want to introduce a feeling of tension or insecurity. Music that is particularly difficult to memorize, I'll play short phrases reading the music score, and then repeat them without it.

Q What kind of courage does it take to perform the way you do?

You have to believe in what you're doing. It's never perfect; it's genuinely a process that's always changing. It's putting yourself out there to say, "This is what I believe in." And every once in a while, everything really comes together—a sensitive conductor, responsive orchestra, and lovely hall—which is delightful.

What's wonderful is having a great work of art that's yours to interpret to bring to life, whether it is a contemporary piece of music or something written three hundred years ago by Bach. Music composed by Mozart, Schumann, Schubert, Beethoven, and Berg, and many others—remains a life-affirming inspiration. Isn't it astounding how this music came out of a human being! ■

KAREN DRUCKER

An award-winning singer/songwriter and inspirational teacher, she is the creator of nineteen CDs and the author of the book, *Let Go of the Shore*. Ms. Drucker travels throughout the United States and around the world each year with her heart-centered compositions, performing concerts, speaking at conferences, retreats, churches, and organizing her own spiritual retreats. Her songs include "I Am So Blessed," "I Lost the Right to Sing the Blues," "I've Got the Power," "Lighten Up," "We Are All Angels," and "My Religion Is Kindness." Ms. Drucker also co-presents healing and transformative workshops with other authors. She swam the English Channel, becoming the first American women relay team member to make a successful crossing. Ms. Drucker has received Grace Note Award, Spiritual Beacon Award, and the Marin County "Volunteer of the Year" award, and an Honorary Doctorate from the Centers for Spiritual Living.

Q What gives you the greatest blessings each day?

It would have to be the freedom that I have created a life for myself that has wonderful people in it. I have gotten to a point in my life where I never take anything for granted. When I come out on stage now, audiences sing with me; they know the words to my songs. And I'm in so many different places every week: I do women's keynote talks, travel to many different places, and have the freedom now to create my own work. It's really a blessing living in northern California where I'm surrounded by nature.

Q Who were some of the early influences in your life?

Well, I didn't come from a musical family. I was a competitive swimmer. I lived in Laurel Canyon at fifteen years old. I had the blessing that the singer, Carole King, moved in two doors down from where we lived and I became a baby sitter for her children. She was my biggest influence. I had no training in music, no role model, and she became the role model. She had a recording studio in her home and when she remodeled, I wound up getting her piano for a year. So I began to write songs.

Q I understand you were a big fan of Carol Burnett growing up.

I would take a bus every Friday after school to the CBS Television Studios to watch her tape her shows. At the beginning of her show, she would always ask if there was anyone in the audience who had any questions or comments. As if I was possessed, one day I raised my hand and said I'd like to challenge her to a Tarzan Calling Contest. I was ready because I had practiced it over and over. I went up on stage, took a deep breath, and let out my best Tarzan call. The crowd went wild, as did Carol Burnett. That hooked me onto performing, and I realized that I could "go for it!"

Q One of the greatest challenges we face every day is "living in the moment."

Yes—it's a daily spiritual practice for me personally. It's all about coming back to center. I do it with my music. My main thing is swimming; it completely grounds me. I swim four days a week. It's my meditation, breathing and moving my body that way, and being in nature. I live right near the ocean. It helps me get in touch with my spirit and my inner voice. Nature slows down the pace of the monkey mind.

I think one of my mottos is: "Just keep showing up to life with a 'Yes' every day." It's what I teach in my workshops. Go for your dreams! It may not necessarily be a clear path but if you keep doing the things that take you forward on your path, you'll reach your dreams. When I went for my dreams to be a professional singer, along the way I wondered if I could do it. I knew what didn't fulfill me, but once jobs came along they helped show me how to find my true passion. I just had to keep showing up and trying things.

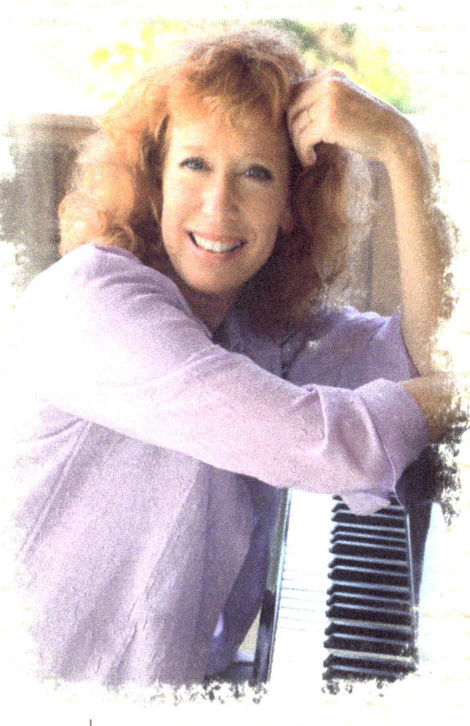

Karen Drucker photo: courtesy of the artist

Q Loving kindness for one's self can help.

Yes, to be kind to yourself allows you to live with a loving heart. You can give loving kindness to other people but it always starts with yourself first, and then to the world. I've found this to be true with myself; it's what I share at women's retreats. Why do we think it's okay to say degrading things about ourselves, or to think we have to be perfect? My mission statement, and what I say in my keynote talks is: "Be gentle to yourself." We can lighten up on ourselves, and give more joy to ourselves and to others.

Q How have you learned to deal with your "inner critic"?

I believe we all have it. It could be said it's your ego, your learned response, what you heard from your parents. You've embodied it into this voice about what you're doing wrong. I truly believe the inner critic is there to guide you, to show you where you're headed, and to protect you. Let it say what it needs to say, and choose who you give your power to. We can't allow it to run our lives, but you can let it work with you.

Q Your songs remind us, and for me personally, about bringing harmony and peace into the soul. How have you learned to deal with the realities of life while maintaining your positive energies?

I don't think I'm living a life with a blind eye to the realities of the world. With the philosophy of "New Thought," you get to choose every day how to focus your energy. I choose the positive things in life to focus on, say my affirmations, while still have a reality of the world. When people have had a hard day, I think my songs like "All is Well," "I'm So Grateful, or "I'm So Blessed" can bring you back to center. I'm a big advocate to feel what you're feeling. You don't just put a Band-Aid on and move on. We can either decide to stay in a hard place or say, "I can raise myself up and learn a lesson." ■

CHAKA KAHN

Chaka Khan is a true Renaissance Woman: a singer, songwriter, producer, visual artist, author, actor, philanthropist, entrepreneur, activist, and mother, Chaka is an international music icon who has influenced multiple generations of artists and continues to do so. She recently celebrated her 40th anniversary in music and entertainment. A ten-time Grammy Award winner, with twenty-two Grammy nominations, Chaka has the rare ability to sing in eight music genres, including R&B, jazz, pop, rock, gospel, country, classical, and dance music. Chaka has released twenty-two albums and earned ten #1 *Billboard* magazine charted songs, eight RIAA certified gold singles and eleven RIAA certified gold and platinum albums. Stevie Wonder penned her first smash hit with Rufus, "Tell Me Something Good." Chaka made her Broadway debut as Sofia in Oprah Winfrey's musical, *The Color Purple*, in London's West End; starred in *Mama, I Want to Sing*; and in Las Vegas, starred in *Signed, Sealed, Delivered*, a musical based on the music of Stevie Wonder. Her honors include a street named after her in her hometown of Chicago—"Chaka Khan Way"; induction into the Apollo Legends Hall of Fame and the Hollywood Bowl Hall of Fame; a star on the Hollywood Walk of Fame and with the United Negro College Fund's An Evening of Stars Tribute; a Soul Train Legend Award; a BET Lifetime Achievement Award; and a World Music Lifetime Achievement Award. Her autobiography, *Through the Fire*, was published in 2003, and is being adapted into a screenplay. Another book featuring the music and lyrics of many of her hit songs, *The Chaka Khan Songbook*, was released in 2015. A documentary series on her, *Being*, premiered on the Centric Channel. Chaka is currently at work on a series of mixed-media visual works with a planned gallery exhibition. In 1999, she established the Chaka Khan Foundation, which includes a variety of programs and initiatives that assist women and children at risk. Chaka currently resides in Los Angeles, and has two children, Indira Milini and Damien.

Q Reading your wonderful autobiography, *Through the Fire*, you mention that when you were growing up, your father created drawings and your mother would paint them in, and of course you grew up singing. Do you think there's something empowering, that makes so much more possible, if we are creating and singing when we're young?
Absolutely. Every child has a left brain and a right brain, and I think it's definitely important that the two sides should be equally stimulated. I grew up in a neighborhood of Chicago, and it was a terrific city to grow up in; there're universities and all these museums there, it's a place of learning. I had great parents, and in spite of some of the madness that existed, I still had something higher to have faith in.

Chaka Khan headshot photo: Kwaku Alston

Q You've said you've been "through the fire" a few times over, and it's very moving listening to you sing "I'm Still Here." How would you say music has helped heal you?
Music is definitely my balm; it's my big outlet, in the same way playing for people is. It's not just the love I feel; music is everything, it's my sanity—it's all of it.

Q Why was it important for you to record your beautiful new single, "I Love Myself"?
It spoke a truth that I think many people forget. How important it is to love yourself. It's important to accept everybody. But you've got to love yourself first.

Q Hearing you sing "A Secret Place" is unforgettable. You said before you sang it, "We all have a secret place where we hide, where we should not hide. I sing it in the spirit of having a secret place; not to hide, but to come closer to my higher power." Singing that song must hold a special significance for you.
The words appeal to me. A lot of its power goes back to making your own place of power. When you take the time to find out your own force and energies, it feeds your relationship with the Creator. You make a foundation for yourself and keep it strong, and it leads you forward.

Q What was your reaction when you first heard "Through the Fire"?
When it was first played for me, it was in instrumental form. David (Foster) had written on his CD, "Chaka"; and then perhaps a year later, he put words to the melody, and played the song for me. That's when it became "Through the Fire." It's a beautiful song.

Q You bring so many incredible and classic songs alive in each show you do across America and around the world, including "I Feel for You," "Ain't Nobody," "I'm Every Woman" "Everlasting

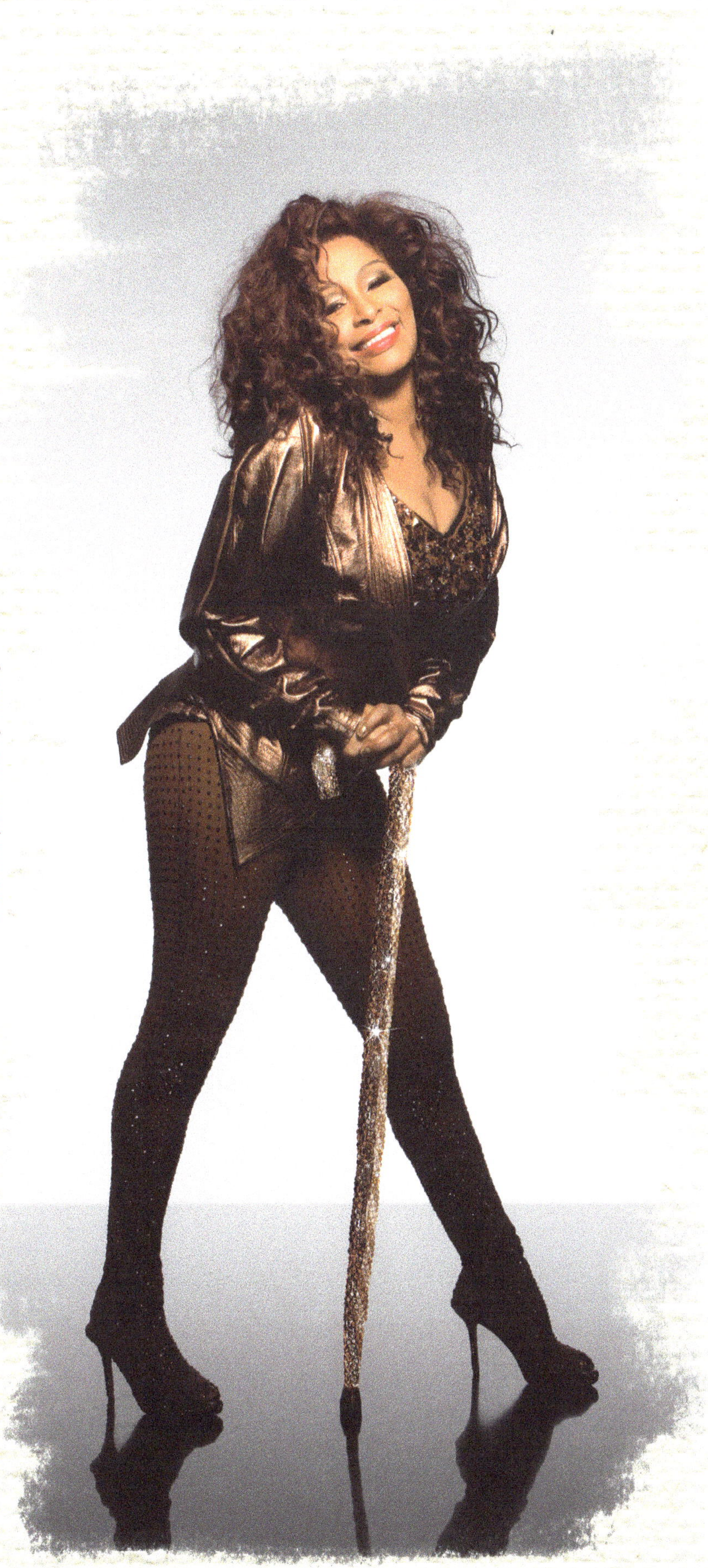

Chaka Khan photo: Timothy Fielding

Love," "Love Me Still," a medley of "Stay" and "Sweet Thang," and of course, your powerful version of your signature ballad, "Through the Fire," among others.

I tend to be in love with the ones I like; it's my own musical appreciation. Sometimes I feel that not all of them are as incredible as some of the others. And what I love is not necessarily what people like hearing. But I'm committed to doing all these songs. We find a way to make them happen, though at times, it can sometimes be a constant battle to keep it real.

Q **You've had the blessing to work with and learn from so many of the world's finest artists including Stevie Wonder, Prince, Miles Davis, Quincy Jones, to mention a very few. Were there some "lessons" you picked up along the way from collaborating with them?**

Focus. Being prompt. That's very important, and throwing yourself into it, not holding back, giving your all. There's so much to attain, to seek out your mark of excellence. Working with those people you're always fine-tuning your skills as an artist.

Collaborating is like a painting. You're painting a picture, and the more colors, shades, tones you can bring, just like in a painting, the more it comes together. You want to paint as full a picture as you can with every song.

Q **You also starred in *Mama I Want to Sing* on London's West End, in Las Vegas in *Signed, Sealed Delivered*, and on Broadway in the musical, *The Color Purple*. What did you learn about yourself from those experiences?**

That I was not "Broadway material," because I'm not willing to commit my life to performances seven days a week, every week. I really like traveling; it's part of what works for me—seeing new places, seeing new people, experiencing new things—that's what's exciting for me!

Q **I understand Atlanta named one of their days, "Chaka Khan Day," and you gave an amazing performance at**

Atlanta's Cobb Energy Centre. That must have been special for you?
Just to be acknowledged in that way was beautiful. It meant so much to me.

Q What brings you the most joy touching the hearts of those who come to hear you?
The reciprocal love I feel. I get all this love en masse; it's like a big love fest, a musical and spiritual orgy. It's beautiful!

Q Are you tired after a show or are you still powered-up when you come off-stage?
I have a lot of juice after I come offstage. It takes me hours to come down from all the energy.

Q You have a deep commitment to women and children at risk, which led you to establish the Chaka Khan Foundation in 1999. Are you seeing a large willingness in the communities to reach out and help one another even more?
More than ever. Not only that, but those who have the ability and the power to help, are stepping up to help those in trouble, those who fall through the cracks. There're so many demons present for young people and today they seem to lack the ability of eyeballing these temptations. I think the lack of the ability of communication is a problem. So many young people can't finish a sentence. They can text, but it's all an abbreviation of a conversation. They can't look across the table and have a conversation; that's to our detriment. In the last twenty years it's gotten worse; there're many more demons to fight. They're too dependent on all these electronic games; it's become a form of insanity. There needs to be a way to bring much more love to combat it in as many ways as possible.

Q I personally believe love is the greatest force in the universe.
It is—it's the impetus of everything. It's the impetus of life; the fundamental aspect of existence. Of course, there're many kinds of love. There's some good love and not-so-good love. But I have found when love is at the seat of your action, it can't be mistaken. Everyone can understand love, and I do love people. ■

MEREDITH MONK

Composer, singer, director/choreographer, and creator of new opera, music-theater works, films, and installations, Meredith Monk is considered one of the most significant creative forces in the performing arts of the past fifty years. She has been celebrated as a pioneer in what is now called "extended vocal technique" and "interdisciplinary performance." Ms. Monk's work has been presented in venues including the Brooklyn Academy of Music, Lincoln Center, Houston Grand Opera, London's Barbican Centre, and the Guggenheim and Whitney museums, including commissions from Carnegie Hall, Michael Tilson Thomas/San Francisco Symphony, New World Symphony, Kronos Quartet, Saint Louis Symphony Orchestra, and Los Angeles Master Chorale. In 1999, she performed a Vocal Offering for His Holiness the Dalai Lama as part of the World Festival of Sacred Music in Los Angeles. In 1968, Ms. Monk founded The House, a company dedicated to an interdisciplinary approach to performance. In 1978, she founded Meredith Monk and Vocal Ensemble to expand her innovative exploration of the voice as a multifaceted instrument. Ms. Monk has made more than a dozen recordings, including the Grammy Award-nominated *Impermanence.* Her music has been featured in films by Jean-Luc Godard, David Byrne, and the Coen Brothers. Her own award-winning films include *Ellis Island* in 1981, and *Book of Days* in 1988. As a pioneer in site-specific performance, she has created such works as *Juice: a Theatre Cantata in 3 Installments* in 1969; *Ascension Variations* in 2009 for the Guggenheim Museum; and *American Archeology #1: Roosevelt Island* in 1994. Monk has received numerous awards, including a MacArthur "Genius" Award, a Doris Duke Artists Award, and two Guggenheim Fellowships. She was named Carnegie Hall's 2014-15 Debs Composer's Chair, an Officer of the Order of Arts and Letters by the Republic of France, *Musical America*'s 2012 Composer of the Year, and one of NPR's 50 Great Voices. In September 2015, Ms. Monk received the National Medal of Arts from President Obama.

Q How important were your first works to your exploration as an artist?
One of my early breakthroughs was *16 Millimeter Earrings*, a thirty-minute solo integrating music, images, objects, movement, and film. It was the first time that I worked with film and I used it in a sculptural way, projecting on different surfaces in the space. For example, in one section, I placed a giant white dome over my head and projected images of my face performing four emblematic emotional states—like my hair slowly standing on end representing fear—to create a living mask. It was also the first time I composed a full score of music from beginning to end. By weaving all of these elements together into a whole, juxtaposing the different layered realities, I was able to create a multi-dimensional, multi-perceptual performance work. This form was something that I had been envisioning for a long time.

Around that same time, I had a revelation that the human voice could be like an instrument, and that it could have within it male and female, different ages; that it could delineate landscapes and characters, limitless colors, timbres and range, textures and ways of producing sound. And that it didn't need words. As a singer, I had come from a classical and folk background. From that moment on, exploring the human voice became the center of my work.

A year later I began working outside of a theater. *Blueprint* in

1967 was my first site-specific and durational piece. That eventually led to *Juice: a Theatre Cantata in 3 Installments* in 1969, and *Vessel: an Opera Epic* in 1971. Those pieces were explorations of architecture, the relationship between audience and performer, scale, memory, and time as experience.

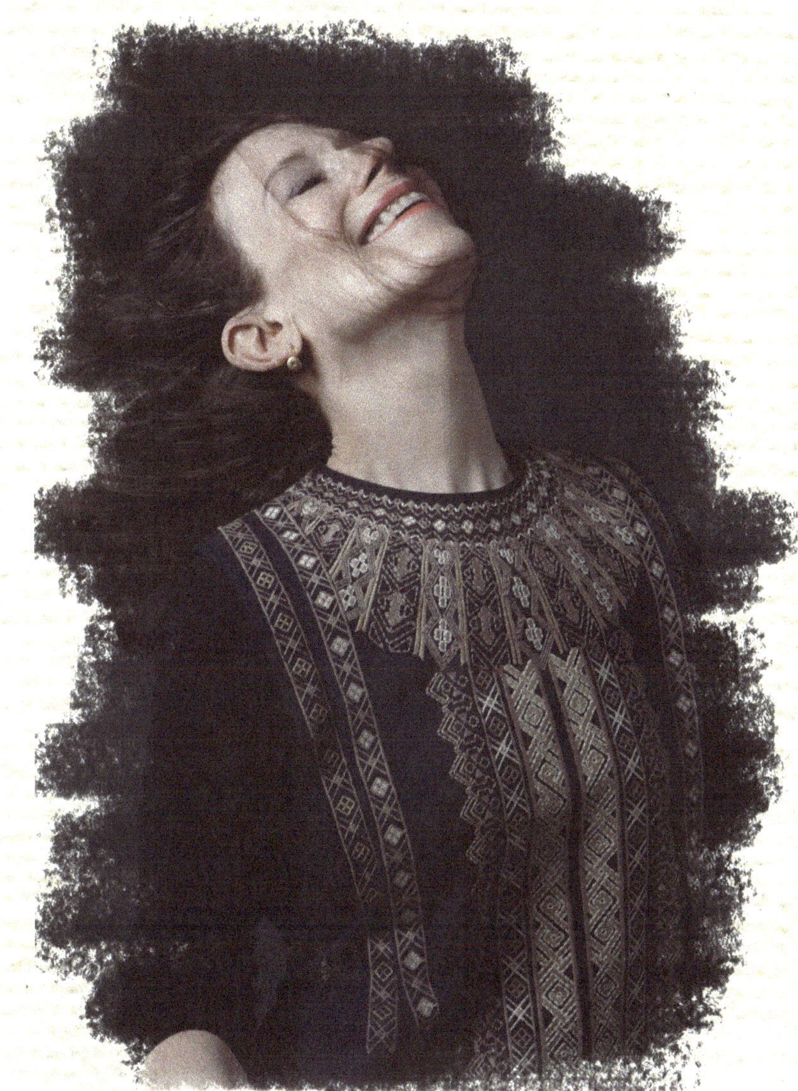

Meredith Monk photo: Julieta Cervantes

Q It was such a moving experience seeing your work, *A Celebration Service* at Danspace Project. What a soaring spirit was unleashed with the Buddhist texts, Hasidic sayings, Islamic poetry, and African, Native American, and Christian prayers. Was it your way of affirming the infinite connection to life that flows through each one of us?
Definitely. I had been thinking about how music and performance can create a space of awareness and how much we need contemplative art in this time. When the Union Theological Seminary asked me to make a service for the American Guild of Organists' conference, I jumped at the chance. I chose short texts from different spiritual traditions to convey their commonality and wove them through selections of my choral and organ works. In a time when so much violence and suffering is perpetuated in the name of religion, I wanted to get to the essential spirit in all of us. It was also a way to explore what the relationship of audience to congregation might mean.

Q I attended one of your performances of *Quarry* at Brooklyn Academy of Music, portraying images from World War II as seen through the eyes of an eight-year-old girl. The piece actually moved across this huge space and in other pieces you asked the audience to move from site to site. Why do you choose to involve the spectator this way?
I really like the tactility, presence, and fluidity of space. I want the audience to have a direct experience of the environment and to be aware that we are all in the same space at the same time. *Break* in 1964 was one of my first pieces dealing with space. I performed it in the large, open room of an art gallery, the Washington Square Galleries. At one point, I left the performing area and stood behind the audience, leaving an empty space with no figure in it. It was a way of reversing or subverting the situation. A few years later, I began moving the audience from space to space within one piece. That concept offered a more three-dimensional immersive experience than the pictorial frame of a proscenium stage. Basically, I would like people to see and hear things in a new way.

Q Your remarkable *A Celebration Service* took place inside St. Mark's Church on a site where worship has taken place for more than three hundred years, and no doubt even longer. Has spirituality always played a role in your creative process?
I've always felt that live music and performance can be an antidote to the speed and information bombardment that we live with day after day. Live performance can offer a time and space to slow down, let go of habitual patterns of thought for a short time, and be connected to the wonder and magic that is always there if we pay attention. The original idea of art was literally worshipping and negotiating with nature, and acknowledging the ineffable. When I am working on something, I try to start from zero with no assumptions or expectations. I have learned to tolerate the discomfort of hanging out in the unknown; but by doing that and taking the time to listen, the work eventually makes itself known.

Q How does art fit into people's lives?
Good art always makes us feel more alive. It also asks questions. There is a lot of fear, distraction, and confusion in our world. It seems essential to keep working, sharing insights and discoveries that are life-affirming and useful. Art affirms freedom of the imagination, curiosity, and playfulness. We really need that now. I have been very fortunate to live a life doing what I love. This privilege makes me aware of the responsibility of being an artist, of not taking anything for granted. The voice is the heart of my work and I continue to believe that it is an eloquent, universal language that can bring us closer together. ■

VINICIO QUEZADA

Mr. Quezada is a Guatemalan composer, piano soloist, music director, arranger. and pianist. At five years of age, he began his study of piano. His grandfather, father, and uncles studied at the National Conservatory of Music. He graduated from the National Conservatory of Music at sixteen years old, and later directed the piano program and became its artistic director. After he had graduated from the National Conservatory of Music in 1977, he performed in Washington D.C. in a concert with violinist, Henry Raudales. Mr. Quezada received a scholarship to study music at the Alabama School of Fine Arts in Birmingham, Alabama. For ten years, he served as musical director and arranger with DIDECA International with artists including Ricardo Arjona. Mr. Quezada's discography includes fourteen albums, two CDs in the United States, and one in Chile. He was appointed Director of the Filarmonia del Ballet Guatemala with Felipe de Jesus Ortega. Mr. Quezada is a professor at the Escuela superior de Arte de la University de San Carlos de Guatemala.

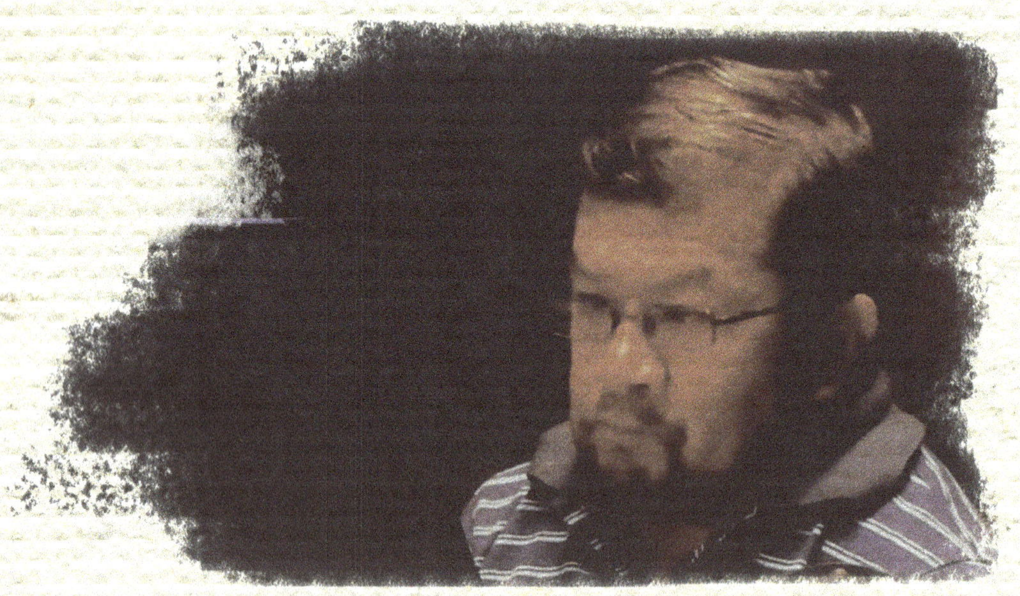

Vinicio Quezada photo: courtesy of the artist

Q What is the most beautiful gift you feel when you share music?
For the interpreter, the personal satisfaction one can have is helping to change the lives of those who hear the music. I'm most pleased when I'm able to give happiness to others through the music I play, and as a conductor.

Q What does it mean to you, especially being a conductor?
Personally, I work with very young musicians. Teaching them to work together and have a common goal. It gives me the greatest pleasure, as I introduce these young people to orchestral music.

Q When you're conducting, what are your feelings bringing great music to life by composers such as Bach, Beethoven, and Mozart?
I feel a significant connection with these great composers of music. I try to convey all of my passion of what I'm feeling to my students when I'm conducting.

Q Can you describe the passion it takes to help your students create stirring music together?
The passion for music comes from the heart. I live in a country of poor people. My students are boys from poor neighborhoods with economic difficulties to study. But when I speak to them about the passion of music coming from the heart, they get excited, and they study with an even greater desire and discipline. ■

STEVE ROSS

Steve Ross has long delighted audiences on six continents with his shows celebrating the American Songbook and saluting figures like Noël Coward, Cole Porter, Stephen Sondheim, Johnny Mercer and Alan Jay Lerner. He rose to fame as a cabaret entertainer during his lengthy sojourns at New York's Ted Hook's Backstage in the late 1970s, followed by years of residency at the celebrated Oak Room at the Hotel Algonquin. Mr. Ross was on the Concerts and Lecture roster at the Metropolitan Museum of Art for eight years, and has also hosted radio series on the BBC and NPR radio. He starred Off-Broadway in *I Won't Dance - Steve Ross Sings and Plays Fred Astaire*, and on Broadway in Noël Coward's *Present Laughter* with Frank Langella. Mr. Ross received a MAC Lifetime Achievement Award, and his excerpts were featured on Garrison Keillor's *Prairie Home Companion*, on APR radio. He has performed his shows including *Set to Music: Steve Ross Celebrates Noel Coward* at Carnegie Hall, and at the Savoy Theatre in London. His other shows include *Mischa, Marlene and Me*, *Cheek to Cheek* co-starring Karen Oberlin, *We Got Rhythm* co-starring Judy Carmichael, *Gotta Have Hart and Hammerstein!*, *Cole Porter in Paris*, *Noel Coward and his Ladies*, and *Tin Pan Alley Tune-up*, part of Lincoln Center's *Real to Reel* shows. Mr. Ross received a MAC Lifetime Achievement Award.

Q When did you begin playing the piano?

Let's go back "a few thousand years," as they say. I started playing when I was about five years of age; my mother played the piano by ear and I started doing the same thing. I never gave much thought to it—just took to it naturally, I guess. I was given classical music lessons but always played popular standards right through high school and college. When I was drafted into the army in 1961, I would play show tunes in the hospital wards for the GIs. Before that, when I was studying to be a priest, I played the organ in chapel. It's just always been there; I'm very fortunate.

Q I remember being so moved by Bobby Short performing at The Café Caryle, and I would hear Mabel Mercer sing in Greenwich Village. Did they inspire you?

Yes, I went to see them many times; how lucky we were to be around during their days. They were the pillars, they showed us the way. I moved to New York when I was thirty years old, not realizing that the saloons I was looking for work at wanted a *singing* pianist. So...I sang! I studied voice with many teachers over the years. It took a long time but I figured it out; now I can't imagine not singing.

Watching Bobby Short, I learned how he utterly owned his persona, and the audience. It was a lesson hearing him play at The Carlyle. He'd always adjust to whatever kind of audience it was with a clean confidence; always aware of everything. It's a lesson I think of often. Mabel Mercer would move me to tears; I never knew someone could have that affect. Sitting regally in her chair and holding musical court was certainly not traditional, but it was magical nonetheless.

Q What have you discovered singing the poetry and language of Noel Coward?

I love Coward! I try as much as I can to emulate his audacity. When I first heard his songs, I thought, "How can you say such outrageous things in a song!" But I realized in doing so, he was saying things people were afraid to say. In lesser hands, it would have been irritating, but his genuine wit and talent carried the day and make us laugh. And then there's his other side—his sweet, often bitter-sweet love songs. I find audiences really respond to his beautiful melodies and the truth of his lyrics.

When I was in Australia playing to audiences of all ages, they got what he was saying. I mean, there's a certain level of sophistication necessary but they were open to it, and they wanted to know more about the world of Noel Coward.

Q How did your performing at Ted Hook's Backstage Restaurant allow you to grow as a cabaret performer?

It was a chance to take center stage, right before I moved on to play at the Hotel Algonquin. I wanted the job at Backstage, and when they offered it to me, I realized it was a big break and I grabbed it. Now, I had to perform in front of many actors and performers from Broadway who came, and I had to know what I was doing. I'm so glad I had that job. In our lives we have to react to what comes along, and as it turned out, I got to accompany and sing with, among many others, Liza Minnelli and Ginger Rogers.

Q Why do the songs of Gershwin, Alan Jay Lerner, and Cole Porter continue to move us today?

I think a prerequisite is having an openness of mind and heart. These songs can be funny; you can be dazzled by their creativity, the cleverness in the lyrics, plus being aware of the craft and intelligence behind their composition. When I perform, I'll sometimes give the audience a little context to the songs, and it helps them understand their appeal. When you hear a love ballad like "Night and Day," it reaches inside you because it's talking about the obsessive and transient nature of romantic love.

Q How would you describe what happens when you're creating the special vibrations between you, the song, and those who are listening?

In a way I feel I'm a channel; it's an odd combination. I'm putting myself into the picture with my own emotions, but I'm also delivering the words and music more or less as they were written. They used to say in English pubs, "C'mon love, give us a song," and that's basically what I try to do.

When I'm singing a song like

Lorenz Hart's "Glad to be Unhappy" about unrequited love, I find I can't help but go to my emotional memory. Things come up that infuse and inform my performance, taking me into my own experience. I harvest these feelings and put them into the songs.

Nietzsche said, "Without music, life would be a mistake." We all seem to have some kind of music in our lives. When I'm playing, and the fingers and voice are working, I feel such a feeling of joy—I think it's what we all want—not only to live but to feel alive.

"Music is life's last unpunished rapture," Sidney Smith said. I think music connects us with a power like love. We all feel these feelings but sometimes they can only be expressed through art and music. I'm always hoping the audience will take that journey with me, because sometimes it will actually be a healing experience for them and myself. ■

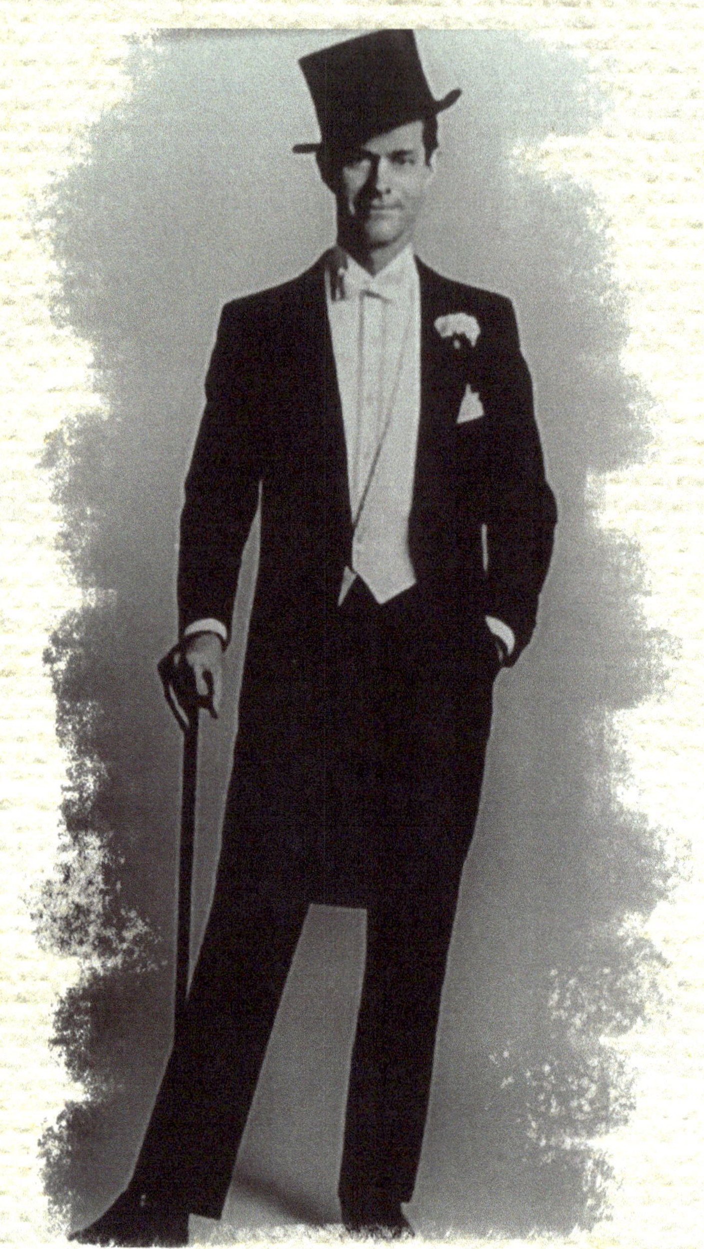

Steve Ross photo: courtesy of the artist

JIM SEALES

A guitar legend, Mr. Seales is a member of the country music band, "Three Wheel Drive" with the renowned violin player, fiddler, vocalist Donny Carpenter, and vocalist, string instrumentalist Mitchell Curtis, performing regularly at FloBama in Florence, Alabama, across the state and throughout the United States. He was lead guitarist and vocalist of "Shenandoah," an award-winning band founded in Muscle Shoals in 1984, with Marty Raybon, Ralph Ezell, Stan Thorn, Mike McGuire, and Mr. Seales on lead guitar and back-up vocals. He retired from the band in 2014. "Shenandoah" released nine Studio albums, and was the most successful band to come out of the Muscle Shoals area, with two gold albums, twenty-six singles on Billboard's Hot Country Songs chart, including nine albums. Their number one hits included "The Church on Cumberland Road," "Sunday in the South," "Two Dozen Roses," "Next to You, Next to Me," and "If Bubba Can Dance, I Can Too." They toured across America and on several international tours. Shenandoah received County Music Association award nominations, and received the Vocal Group of the Year Award in 1991 and 1992 and the Grammy Award in 1992 for Best Country Collaboration with Vocals for "Somewhere in the Vicinity of the Heart" with Alison Krauss.

Q What led you into music?
I started when I was about ten years old. My father and others in my family played country and folksy music. So I asked my father, "Can you show me how to play?" He showed me two chords. That's the same guitar hanging there (pointing towards a guitar hanging nearby). So he kept showing me and that's how I learned how to play.

I actually did very well in my studies and was thinking of being a teacher. At the same time, I was playing and singing at dances. I made the decision to pursue music while I was in college; that's why I didn't graduate. I looked at the starting pay for an English teacher—eighteen thousand a year. I was already making twenty-five thousand a year playing, so I said to myself, "I'll give playing the guitar till I'm thirty."

Q Who were inspirations in music for you growing up?
Eric Clapton had a big impact. As a kid I'd play The Beatles, The Monkees. I think it was in 1967 when I was thirteen years old that a "Cream" album came out—"Disraeli Gear," with a psychedelic cover in purple and pink. I played it, and when I heard "Sunshine of Your Love," I had no idea that that kind of music existed. I discovered there's more things you can do with your guitar; it was a wow! I thought, "There's some cool stuff you can do with music—you can express yourself."

Q How would you describe the effect music has had on your life, having played the lead guitar for "Shenandoah" all those years?
Music and the guitar have made me a good living. I've been playing for fifty-two years, and for over forty of those the guitar has supported my family, put my kids through school, given me the luxury of being able to teach, and now I play with "Three Wheel Drive."

I owe it to my father. He always told me the guitar would take care of me if I worked hard, showed up on time, didn't drink or do drugs or chase women, and always played what the client wanted to hear. If I didn't, I'd wind up with nothing. My father was right.

When I came to Muscle Shoals in 1984, I was thirty years old. I had my first record deal at thirty-two, and for many years worked seventy-five to ninety hours a week. I treated it as a business. Until one performance on the road.

One of the songs we sang—"Mama Knows," mentions a guy named Jimmy Crowder—and we had played the song in all our shows. Well, at the end of one of our shows, a couple came up to us, and they told us that their son had been killed in an accident. His name really was Jimmy Crowders, and they told us the song we sang meant everything to them. It was then I realized, at that moment, that there were real feelings attached to these "products" we were singing. That the people coming to hear us were having a real emotional attachment to our "product," and that softened me.

Q What led to the founding of the band, "Shenandoah," in 1984?
I've built bands my whole life, moving one artist together with another one. It was a steady income between doing recording sessions. I didn't think of myself as an artist; I was just trying to write songs.

Robert Burn, a gem of a guy, had a CBS record deal to find acts to produce. Well, one night he stopped in the club we were playing in. He heard us and wanted us to record an album. He kept trying to get us to record until we decided to record. We thought we'd just make some session money from it. Well, CBS needed us to have a name as a group, but we didn't have one. We finally settled on "Diamond Rio." But Rick Hall, who was producing the album with our mentor, Robert Byrne, didn't like it. He said, "Either call the band "Shenandoah" or "The Rhythm Rangers." We didn't like "The Rhythm Rangers" so we picked "Shenandoah."

After we had gained a lot of success, and right after several hit records and the release of our third album *Extra Mile*, we found out Rick Hall didn't have the trademark for the name, "Shenandoah." In fact, there were other groups called Shenandoah, including the Arlo Guthrie band. When they all threatened to sue us, we finally had to settle; it must have cost over a million dollars. But that's how it all happened. We got dragged and kicking into a record deal, and became the most successful act to come out of Muscle Shoals; it had to have been predestined.

Q How were your songs created?
We wrote some of the songs ourselves, but many came through

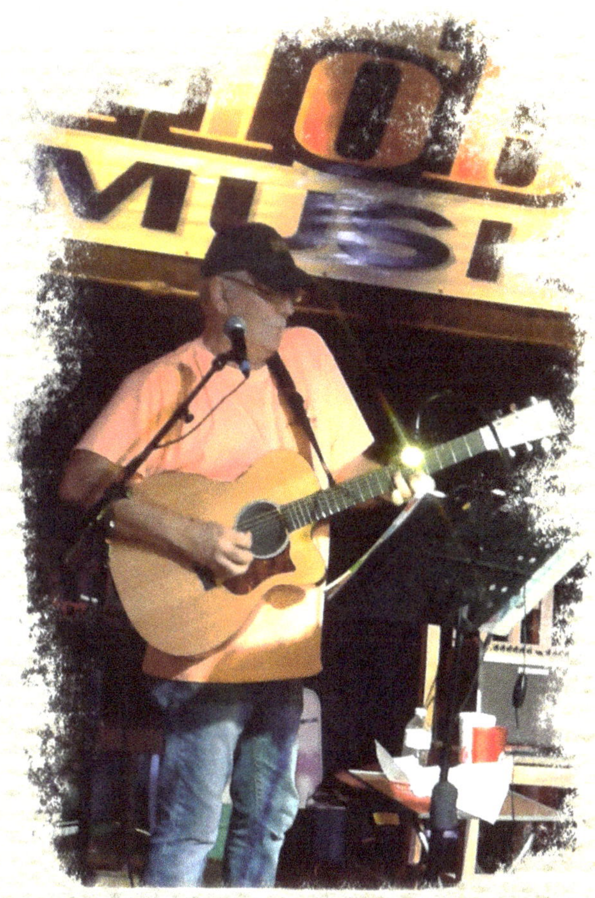

Jim Seales photo: Ronald Rand: Jim Seales performing with Three Wheel Drive at Flobama, Florence, Alabama, 2016

the traditional channels—writers going through publishers, who in turn pitched those songs to us personally, or our producers.

We recorded several songs from Muscle Shoals and many from Nashville. "The Church on Cumberland Road," was our first number one record written by Bob DiPiero, John Scott Sherrill, and Dennis Robbins. It actually happened when they were coming back from London. They flew over the Cumberland River coming into Nashville, and they were just so grateful to see home that they vowed to write a song about the river.

Q How would you describe the collaboration it takes to play as a band?
I call it the "foxhole mentality." You rely, in an improvised situation, on reading signals from the other players. You have to have some structure so that once you're in a "foxhole," you know you can depend on the other person to cover you. It's sometimes emotionally awkward for two men to hook up as artists do, but you have to let your wall down working day after day. You read body behavior; you know what they're going to play. The best musicians are good at that.

Q What was the reason you left "the road"?
I had a stroke about seven years ago; that changed everything. Once I recovered, I decided that I wanted to go ahead and hold a pic in my hand and play music. But I also wanted to teach; It made sense to me. So I taught the only thing I knew—I began to give guitar lessons. That changed my life. And it's so rewarding to see the "ah-ha" moments from my students. And a mentally-challenged young student is able to make a chord; that gives me so much satisfaction.

Q You've been performing for a couple of years now with Donny Carpenter and Mitchell Curtis in the band, "Three Wheel Drive," at FloBama in Florence, Alabama.
Three Wheel Drive has been an experiment that's changed my life. My dad was a lay preacher, but I had a .33 of "mustard-seed" faith. I confess I'm still not religious, but I've become spiritual. I knew I had to retire from Shenandoah after doing it for so many years. And the thought that I could do this new band and not do it for the money, but more for the fun, really made a transformation possible.

At FloBama it's a very intimate setting, you can almost reach out and touch the crowd, and I try to emotionally. Most of these people are here every week so we get to know them ... after four years, it's like playing to a room full of some of your best friends.

Well, when we play, we put out a small bucket to collect tips; we just agreed all our tips would go to help others, and it somehow has turned out to change so many lives. It was guided, I have to tell you, by my wife, Donna Kay, and time and again, the tips have gone on to help folks with personal health problems, breast cancer, prostate cancer; it makes a small dent but it really has changed the way I relate to people, too. I know I'm supposed to be doing this, especially because we're making people feel better, adding something to their lives.

Q Your very talented wife, Donna Kay, also performs with you. What has it meant having her a part of your life?
I waited a long time for her. We had both been in pretty loveless marriages. With my first marriage, because I was always on tour I was never home; I was never unfaithful but I just wasn't there. We had a mutual parting of the ways.

When I met Donna Kay, I wasn't in a good place. But we became friends, and we didn't even realize that we had also fallen in love with one another. She did the accounting at Counts Brothers Music, and I had my studio here. Every day she'd let me out at the end of the day before she'd locked up.

Well, one day, as I always said, I told her, "I'll see you tomorrow." But she said, "I won't be here tomorrow, I'm on vacation." Well, I said, "You're half the reason I come here." She said, "Well you're half the reason I come here, too." After we said our goodbyes, as I walked away, I thought to myself, "Why in the world did I say that?" And she told me later, she also felt the same way, and she didn't end up leaving. We went out for coffee and talked and both agreed we were both lonely, and that's what started it for us.

Q How would you say music and the songs you've created and sing help us?
If the spirit is in the river here, it's everywhere. I see it in the little bits of the music we play, how it can be transforming in ways I can't even begin to describe. Music is always a soother, especially in emotionally-trying times, high times, or low times. Sometimes it can be a smile, but other times, music can alter a person's life. I've seen how the music at FloBama can change lives. People who have gone through hell, gradually they're laughing—discovering life again. I think it's always about a few people who care and reach out; and when everyone does the same thing, miracles can happen. ■

TRAVIS WAMMACK

Mr. Wammack is known as the "fastest guitar player in the South." He began his professional music career when he wrote and recorded his first record at eleven years old. He made his mark on the music world at the age of sixteen with his 1963 number one hit, "Scratchy." He was the first to develop and use the fuzz tone for an electric guitar. Mr. Wammack has played his guitar on hit records recorded at Fame Studio in Muscle Shoals, Alabama, that have sold over 60 million copies by artists including Aretha Franklin, Liza Minnelli, Wilson Pickett, Little Richard, Mac Davis, Clarence Carter, the Osmond Brothers, Bobbie Gentry, Candi Staton, Delbert McClinton, and Narvel Felts. His solo artist career was produced by Rick Hall with the release of his albums in 1971 and 1975. He traveled the world as Little Richard's band leader from 1984 until 1995, performing on several shows on television including at President Bill Clinton's inauguration party. Mr. Wammack's CDs include *Still Rockin'*, *Snake, Rattle & Roll in Muscle Shoals*, *Rock 'n' Roll Party*, *Memphis + Muscle Shoals = Travis Wammack*, *Almost Home*, *Country in My Soul*, *Rock 'n' Roll Days*, and *Rock 'n' Roll Days Vol. II*. He is a member of the Memphis Music Hall of Fame, and received the Professional Musician Award from the Alabama Music Hall of Fame. In 2005 he was inducted into The Southern Legends Entertainment and Performing Arts Hall of Fame. In 2011 Travis was inducted into the Rockabilly Hall of Fame.

Q You began playing when you were eight years old. I understand you never had a lesson. What was it about the guitar that attracted you to it?

I was voted into the musicians' union the youngest member ever, at eleven years old. They had to vote me in up in New York City. My dad had bought us a guitar. I had two sisters and three brothers, and he said, "Here's a guitar for anyone if you want to play. I know a few chords." And he showed them to us. Well, I took it up. I used to go to sleep with that thing; I'd be in the bed and my foot would be tapping away.

Q You recorded your first record at age eleven. What led to the creating of your hit, "Scratchy"?

We were very poor. I was born in Walnut, Mississippi and then we moved when I was about four years old, and I grew up in Memphis Tennessee, went to high school there, in a suburb called Binghampton. After school, I'd get my guitar and I'd go and play in the grocery store near the juke box. When someone was going to put their music in the box, I'd ask them what they wanted to hear, and I'd tell them I could play it for them, and they'd put the dime in my guitar.

One day I was walking down the street and a DJ by the name of Eddie Bond came up to me and he said, "Do you know who I am?" I told him, "I do. My parents listen to you all the time." Well, he told me he wanted me to play in a Jamboree he was putting together. I told him, "I'd love to but I'd have to ask my parents." So I did and they agreed. That's how I started doing Jamboree Shows with Carl Perkins and Johnny Cash.

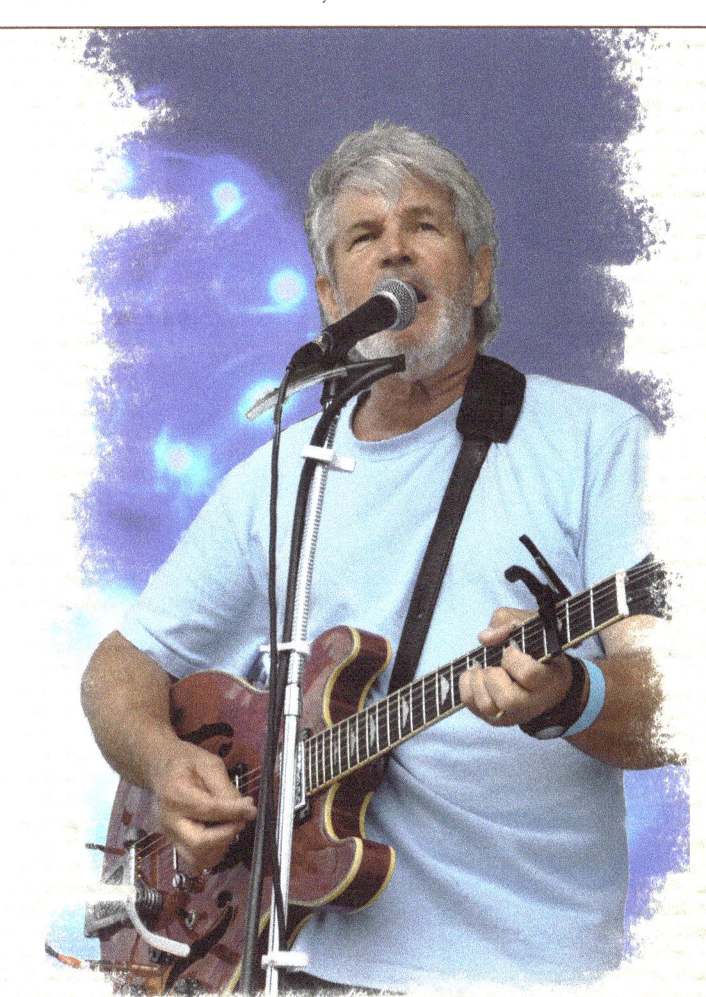

Travis Wammack photo: Local Legends

When I turned sixteen, I went to a studio of one of the famous guitar players, Roland James; he had played on many of the classic Sun records, the recording of "Great Balls of Fire," on a lot of hits, and he took me under his wing. He first produced me. I told him, "I want to be your session guitar player." Well, he told me, "I've heard you sing. Why don't you bring your guitar in?" So I played for him. He said, "All right, here's what we're going to do. We'll do a session. You got some instrumentals? That's what I want to record." So I did an instrumental on one side called "Scratchy," and I did a vocal on the other side. So we recorded the two sides.

Q How did you go about creating the "fuzz" tone on your number-one hit "Scratchy"?
I think when I began, the only guitar players I really listened to were maybe Chet Atkins and Merle Haggard. I started teaching myself, and I came up with a sound. I created my own distortion unit. I over-loaded it with my amp creating a weird distortion sound. It was the first "fuzz" tone—by over-driving the speakers gives you the sound—then we reversed the tape on the instrumentals. It was actually the first record ever made with a reverse tape, even before The Beatles.

Q I love listening to "Greenwood Mississippi." How did that song take off?
Me and another guitar player, Junior Lowe, we wrote the song in 1970. It sounded like a cross between Credence Clearwater revival and Little Richard. I did a demo and two weeks later Little Richard comes to Fame Studio and I tell him about the song and he said "Play it for me." I do and he said, "I want to record it." About two weeks later, Tom Jones came to the studio and he said to me, "I heard Little Richard recorded one of your songs." "Yeah, it was 'Greenwood, Mississippi.'" He said, "I'd like to hear that." I tell him, "Well, I've got it in a cassette in my truck." He listened to it and he said, "I want to record it." I never wrote a number-one hit I've sung but I sure had two of the best Rock 'n' Roll singers ever singing it.

Q You also have had a prolific relationship with Little Richard. How did that begin?
We cut an album some time in 1969-1970, called *The Real Thing*, that was his first chart record since "Tutti Frutti." Then I never heard from him until 1984 when I get a call. In the meantime, he had become an ordained minister, but now he was thinking of coming back to Rock 'n' Roll. But he asks me, "Do you think Rock 'n' Roll is the devil's music?" I tell him, "When I think of good times, I think of 'Tutti Frutti' and 'Good Golly, Miss Molly.' They're good southern Rock 'n' Roll songs." So we put a band together and there wasn't nothing like it, the crowds loved it. I was with him for about twelve years, but then I developed a fear of flying. He's a great artist, a fantastic entertainer.

Q What do you love about singing?
The people, the fans—that's what keeps me going. I go by what the crowds are in to. I always know what I'm going to play by watching the people.

Q A big part of what you do is helping others in need. You gave a benefit concert to raise money for Percy Sledge, and a big concert to help those in need when the tornadoes came through Alabama in 2011. Why has this become an important part of what you do?
I've had two close calls with death. I felt "the man upstairs" had other plans for me. So anytime I can help someone, I'm just that way. I give away a lot of guitars to young kids to get them off the street. I just try and help as much as I can.

Doing what I've been doing is all I ever wanted to do since I started out at age eight, and I've never looked back. I feel I'm playing better and singing better; I'll be seventy-two in November. I think it's about having longevity, and I just love playing. ■

EVE WOLF

Founder of the Ensemble for the Romantic Century in 2001, Ms. Wolf has dedicated herself to an innovative form, the "theatrical concert," which combines drama, music, and multi-media. She has written twenty-five of the Ensemble's forty-plus original productions and has performed in most of them, including *Tchaikovsky: None but the Lonely Heart, Peggy Guggenheim Stripped Bare by her Bachelors, Frankenstein: Every Woman's Nightmare, Van Gogh's Ear, Toscanini: In my Heart Too Much of the Absolute,* and *Jekyll.* Ms. Wolf has performed with the Ensemble for the Romantic Century in America and around the world. The Ensemble's two most recent productions, *Jules Verne: From the Earth to the Moon* in 2015, and *Anna Akhmatova: The Heart Is Not Made of Stone* in 2016, both written by Ms. Wolf, were presented at Brooklyn Academy of Music in Brooklyn. She has appeared in Europe and the United States as a chamber musician and soloist. Ms. Wolf is on the faculty of the Curtis Institute of Music and teaches piano at Columbia University-Teachers College, and has served as a professional mentor at The Juilliard School.

Q How young were you when you were first introduced to classical music?
There were no musicians in my family. But we had a broken-down spinet with very few of the keys working. I begged for piano lessons at age two, and started at age three. I have perfect pitch, so when I was little if I heard something, I would try to play it. My father died when I was three, and we moved in with my mother's parents, who were immigrants. My grandparents were very excited that I wanted lessons, and they chipped in with my mother and bought me a new Knabe spinet. I still have that little piano; it is a very sentimental possession. When I was fourteen I was introduced to my most important piano teacher and true mentor—Seymour Bernstein. I was very, very lucky to meet him at that age.

Q How would you describe him?
Seymour is a philosopher-teacher, a great artist. I studied with him for much of my life. He

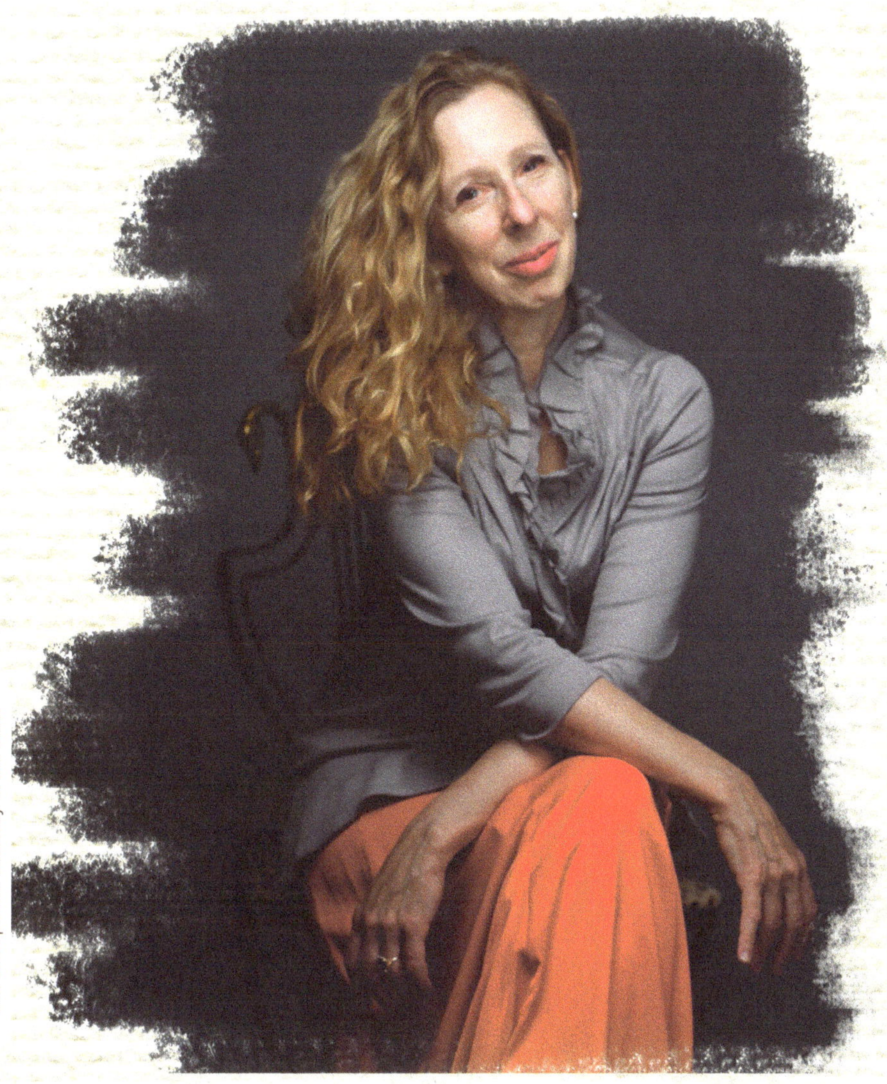

Eve Wolf photo: courtesy of the artist

recognized talent and nurtured it. He is very constructive, an incredible diagnostician. He would ask, "What do you want to say in the music?" He taught that you need to find the physical means—very detailed physical choreography—to express your musical intention. *That* was "technique"! Seymour was and still is very positive about focusing on being an artist. He taught me to think for myself, to be creative. He is the subject of an award-winning documentary by Ethan Hawke called *Seymour: An Introduction.*

Q Why did you want to create Ensemble for the Romantic Century?

I've always been interested in many subjects. I got a degree in art history, read a lot of music history, and studied languages. I'm interested in the connections among disciplines. Whenever I hear music, or read a story, I see the emotional arc; it's like language to me. Music speaks to me, like a narrative.

I think that Beethoven's music is very autobiographical. In Mozart's music, I hear characters. I originally thought, "Wouldn't it be great if the stories of the composers could be told during the concert?" I love letters, memoirs, biographies, and when I was asked to do a concert for a law presentation, I chose the famous love story about Clara and Robert Schuman.

I wrote a script called *Lawsuit for Love*. I had two people read the letters about the Schumann's lawsuit to get married. In between the readings, I played chamber music. The concert was so well received that I decided to create a group that would incorporate words and music. It has evolved since then to include complex drama, production design, staging, costumes, lighting design, and projection design.

Q What's most stimulating delving into these extraordinary artists, especially your recent show, *Anna Akhmatova*?

There's something in the stories of these lives that touches me. In the case of *Anna Akhmatova*, historically, it was the drama of the Soviet period that resonated with me. The subject of the production I created is about Akhmatova having a one-day meeting with Isaiah Berlin. I was fascinated by the fact that a one-day meeting could provoke such emotions that Akhmatova would write about it for the next twenty years, even though she and Berlin were separated for that entire time—what a love story!

The music of that period, especially Shostakovich's music, gives us a glimpse into the political and emotional reality of that time: a fascinating soundscape. I experience this almost like 'time-travel"; it's what I want audiences to feel.

Q What keeps it a growing creative experience for you?

I'm always thinking of new ideas and new scripts I want to do. I become obsessed with the subject, reading everything I can, which fascinates me. I form a script using the actual words of the protagonists. My scripts become fully realized through a creative team including Donald T. Sanders, our stage director; Vanessa James designs the sets and costumes; Beverly Emmons is our lighting designer; and David Bengali creates the projection designs. The production takes on a life of its own and is transformed through the artistry and collaboration of the entire team. I have to pinch myself when a production goes up as it seems like magic!

Q Why does teaching music mean so much to you?

I have students from age nine to age seventy-five, and I learn so much from all of them. I empathize with them as they try to do something that is very difficult—play the piano! I feel both esteem and fondness for my students, no matter what their abilities; there is always more to learn and there is no such thing as a finished product.

I'm very patient with my students. I really believe in patience and kindness when I teach because you can't tell in advance what each student's path will be, what part music will play in their lives, or ultimately what *they* will contribute to society. With younger students you cannot predict when a spark will be kindled or when a talent will blossom. The most important thing for me as a teacher is to help other people on their individual journeys.

Q What is your greatest hope your creations will bring to an audience?

I want the experience to be life-changing. With each show I try to open a door that the audience can walk through and experience history through words, music, and drama. The one theme that comes up in my scripts is the idea that art can be a kind of salvation. Art helps us to understand that there's something greater than ourselves. I wrote a script about Beethoven and his search for the perfect wife, whom he never found. In Beethoven's music, you feel his struggles, his loneliness, and ultimately hope. That is what I think the function of art is. ■

EUGENIA ZUCKERMAN

Recognized as one of the greatest flutists of our time, Ms. Zukerman has enjoyed musical collaborations with Emmanuel Ax, Yo-Yo Ma, Jean-Yves Thibaudet, the Shanghai String Quartet and fellow flutists Jean-Pierre Rampal and James Galway. She made her heralded debut at the Verbier Festival in Switzerland, partnering with violinist Dimitry Sitkovetsky, violist Nobuko Imai, cellist Frans Helmerson, and pianist Elena Bashkirova. Her numerous guest appearances have included engagements with the Tokyo Philharmonic, the Royal Philharmonic, the China Philharmonic, Montreal and Vancouver Symphonies, National Symphony Orchestra of Mexico, Scottish Chamber Orchestras, and more than eighty orchestras nationwide, including the Los Angeles Philharmonic, and the National Symphony. She was Artistic Director of the Bravo! Vail Valley Music Festival from 1998 through 2010. Ms. Zukerman is the Music Director of Clarion Concerts in Columbia County's "Leaf Peeper Series," and Music Director of Classics on Hudson in Hudson, New York. She was Arts Correspondent for *CBS Sunday Morning*, receiving an Emmy nomination; she continued her role as an arts journalist by creating video blogs for many music conservatories and organizations, and Noted Endeavors, a new video blog, launched by Ms. Zukerman, Dr. Emily Ondracek-Peterson and Dr. Erik Peterson. Her recordings include over two dozen discs. She has written two novels, two non-fiction books, screenplays, articles, and book reviews in *The New York Times*, *The Washington Post*, *Esquire*, and *Vogue*. Ms. Zukerman has received many awards including New York City's Open University of Israel's Lifetime Achievement Award, and Woman of Achievement Award from the National Hadassah Organization. She is a frequent guest teacher at conservatories nationwide.

Q How young were you when you began to play the flute?

My parents were very musical. My father was an inventor and an engineer, my mother and my father both played the piano. My mother mother was a mathematician and a dancer. I studied the piano early on, and started playing the flute when I was ten years old.

We lived in West Hartford, Connecticut, and in those days the public schools brought in members of the Hartford symphony to play. When I heard the flute, I was enchanted. I ran home and said to my mother, "I have to play the flute!" I was provided with a teacher, and an instrument. I got a scholarship and started lessons; years later I'm still learning.

Q What was it about the flute that attracted you?

It was the sound, I think. When I talk to my colleagues they say something about the sound of a particular instrument spoke to them. The flute spoke to me.

Q Why do you feel music can inspire a young person to create?

For a young person, music is a friend. It's a way to express yourself, a way to say how you feel about everything in a wonderfully cathartic way, to get in touch with your feelings and emotions.

Teenagers are often, you might say, harmonically, emotionally in turmoil, and music can be a real comfort. If they take up a flute or violin or a piano and sit and play, it becomes one of the most important ways of self- expression, a way of reaching out to something larger than yourself.

You read scientific statements that if you smile during the day or if you play music you'll be happier. It's an instant uplift, sort of like coffee with a little champagne.

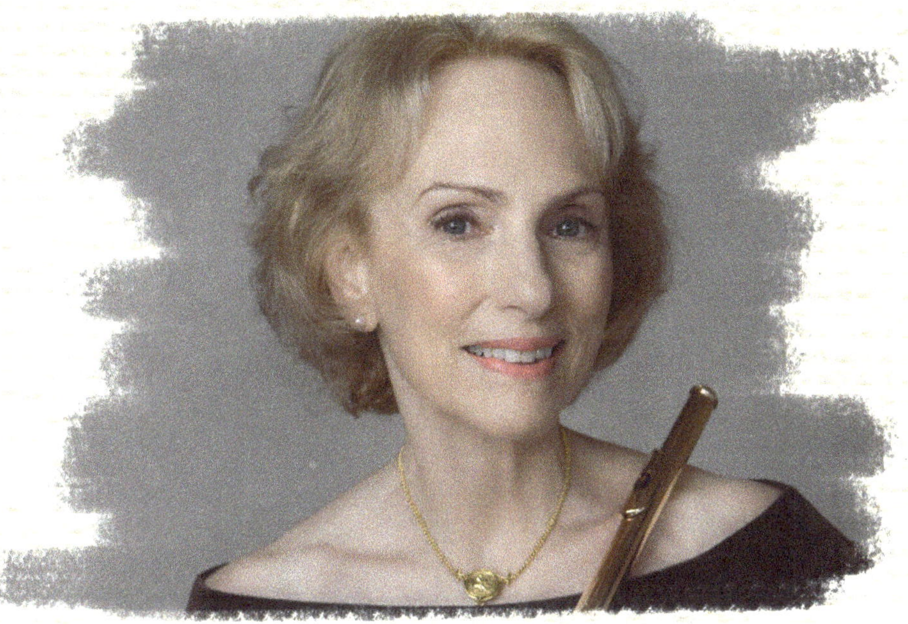

Eugenia Zuckerman photo: courtesy of the artist

Q You've also found many more ways to communicate your love for music.
Yes, I've created video blogs to bring music and musicians closer to their audiences. I have written novels which share my love for music, and I also give master classes. I feel very lucky.

Q How would you describe the experience you have when you're playing?
I think there are times what I'm feeling might be described as an out-of-body experience. In fact, I'm unaware of anything physically. Music is a path between ourselves and the infinite. It takes me out of myself, that's part of why I love it so much. We're wrapped so much in our ideas, but when you can release yourself and become a part of something larger, your experience becomes a part of the greater good.

We've lost a sense of this, and music is about our humanity. We need to spend more time chatting with others, sitting on the "town green," not glued to our iPhones and computers. It's about getting outside of our own little selves. Making music is a very giving experience. Sometimes, it can be quite draining, but it's also restorative.

Q Do you feel your playing has changed since you began?
I certainly hope so. I no longer worry about extraneous things. I lose myself in the music, and in the moment. I'm playing music at an age when I've noticed my muscles have also changed, so there's a tremendous contradiction; a paradox.

My ability to make music, my knowledge of how to phrase and how to create the quality of a sound has grown, but I can't always play the way I'd like to. Being a musician is an extremely physical activity. I can jump in the air but not as high as I used to. Nonetheless, I think I still have quite a number of years left in me.

Q What does playing do for you now?
I know music heals me. If I'm feeling agitated, concerned about something, it's the best cure. I can pick up the flute and play. I have friends in the field of healing, and they tell me music does the same thing for them.

Q Is there particular music which is your favorite to play?
It's like saying, "Which of your children do you love the best?" It's all great music. I love the contemporary music I play; it's really thrilling. I know we always look back but there are truly great pieces of the early 21st century, and new ones being created all the time. I feel we're in a rich moment of creating music, and there're many magnificent artists that need our support.

Q Is it an inspiring moment in your life?
This is the best time of my life. I've become a grandmother and my two granddaughters are the lights of my life. So is my husband. I'm in love in a way I have never been before. My husband and I have six children between us, and I adore them all. My husband has a farm in upstate New York, and I have an apartment in Greenwich Village. He's in broadcasting and he loves music and is very supportive. There's so much I feel grateful for.

I've gone to many places across the country and around the world. This is also a difficult time. Musicians have to create their own opportunities, and work hard to find a place for themselves. But I know that music can be a joy, a solace, a companion and a great source of inspiration. ■

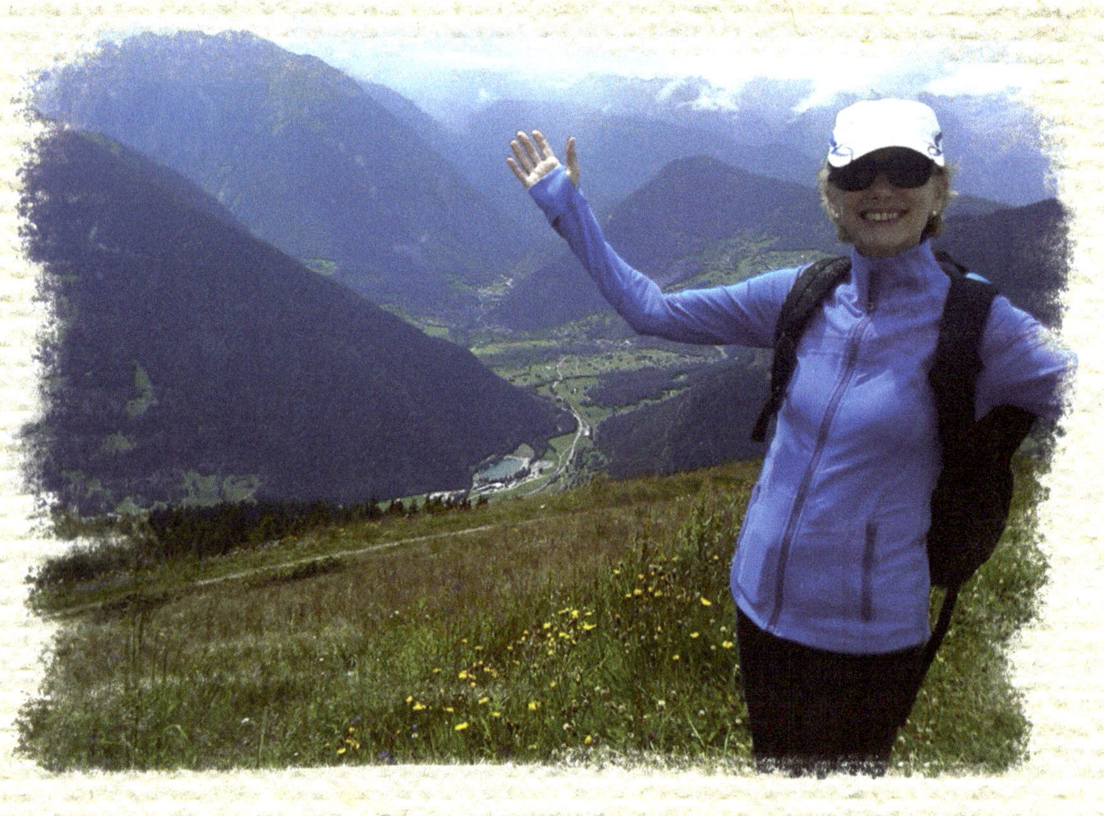

Eugenia Zuckerman's Verbier Vlog (MusicalAmerica Worldwide), courtesy of Ms. Zuckerman

PLAYWRIGHTS, POETS, AND WRITERS

EDWARD ALBEE

Edward Albee was born on March 12, 1928, and began writing plays thirty years later. His plays include *The Zoo Story*, 1958; *The Death of Bessie Smith*, 1959; *The Sandbox*, 1959; *The American Dream*, 1960; *Who's Afraid of Virginia Woolf?*, 1961-62, for which he received the Tony Award; *Tiny Alice*, 1964; *A Delicate Balance*, 1966, for which he received the Pulitzer Prize and the Tony Award; *All Over*, 1971; *Seascape*, 1974, for which he received the Pulitzer Prize; *Listening*, 1975; *Counting The Ways*, 1975; *The Lady from Dubuque*, 1977-78; *The Man Who Had Three Arms*, 1981; *Finding The Sun*, 1982; *Marriage Play*—1986-87, *Three Tall Women*—1991, receiving the Pulitzer Prize, *Fragments*—1993, *The Play About the Baby*, 1997; *The Goat or, Who Is Sylvia?*, 2000, 2002,for which he received the Tony Award; *Occupant*, 2001; *At Home at The Zoo* (*Act 1, Homelife* and *Act 2, The Zoo Story*), 2004; and *Me, Myself & I*, 2008. He is a member of the Dramatists Guild Council, and President of The Edward F. Albee Foundation. Mr. Albee was awarded the Gold Medal in Drama from the American Academy and Institute of Arts and Letters in 1980. In 1996, Mr. Albee received the Kennedy Center Honors and the National Medal of Arts. In 2005, he was awarded a special Tony Award for Lifetime Achievement.

Q *The Zoo Story* remains one of most potent one-acts ever written, and it's as vital for us today as when it was written. What can we learn from Peter and Jerry today, when we're facing an even greater erosion in our ability to make contact with others?

The play is an example of how we relate to ourselves, to others, of participating in the world. Poor Peter. When he says, "I don't understand your landlady or your dog," it's a perfect example of all the stuff we limit ourselves to. We close ourselves down. It's about how we confine ourselves to glass cages.

Q Your play, *The Goat, or Who is Sylvia?* is a profound work about tolerance. Martin, the main character, at one point, confesses that his wife didn't need to know what he did, and he could've worked it out in his own way. Though once his secret's out, it's like Humpty Dumpty's fall. Does a person have a moral responsibility to reveal a truth, full well knowing that it has the power to destroy?

He has a moral responsibility to himself. Martin couldn't live with it; he knew it would have to come out. If you have something eating away at you, you feel better when you tell someone else. You can see he's falling apart, and he felt by telling his best friend, he would be able to deal with it. He had no idea his best friend would turn around and write a letter to his wife. So there are times when you're just left with no other choice. You have to face it, in spite of what's occurred. You want help in this situation.

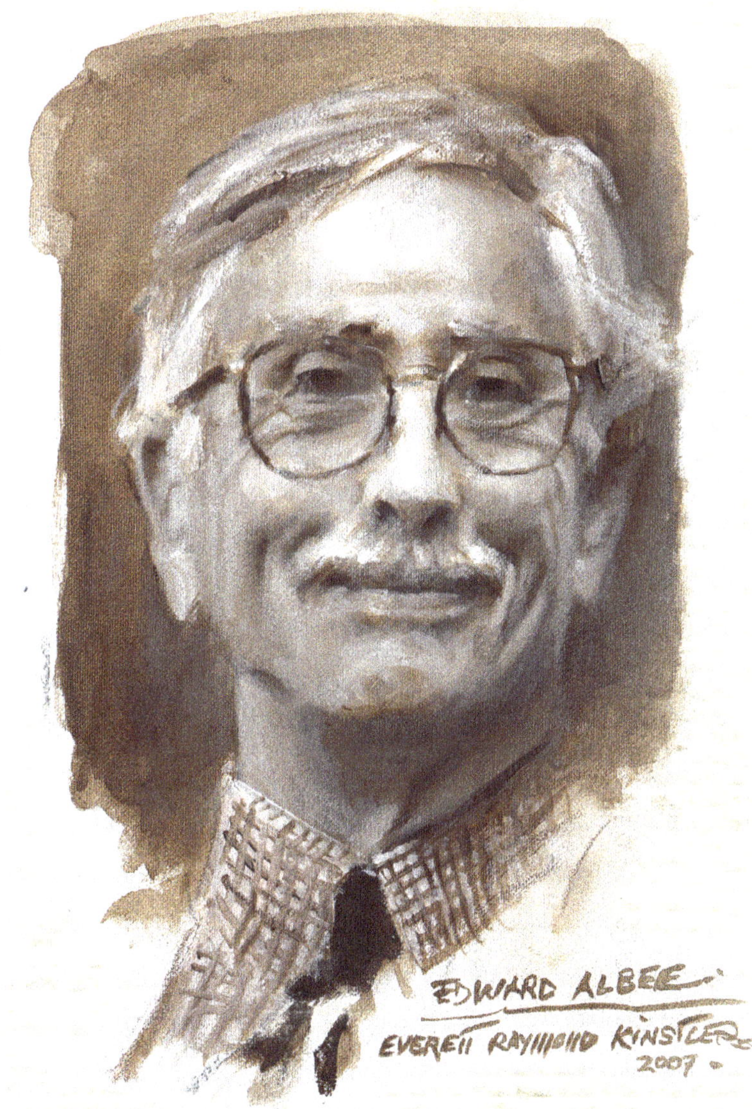

Edward Albee artwork: Everett Raymond Kinstler, courtesy of Mr. Kinstler

A psychiatrist can't do it. You have to talk to who you love.

The play is also quite shocking as well. Yes, and the critics gave me a going-over, seeming to say, "How dare he put this on Broadway?" But we do put things under the rug. Translate things into something easier we can handle. Some events that occur change life infinitely: the unleashing of the Atomic bomb, for instance, and more recently, 9/11.

Q What do you think it revealed about us?
The World Trade Center disaster revealed that we thought we were so insular and how naïve we were. It was extraordinary. We want to be loved, and we didn't realize there were so many people in the world who hate us.

Q You're also very fortunate to have very fine actors in your plays. Are there certain qualities you seek from actors?
I like actors with intelligence, passion, with an awful lot of talent, that they're capable of being the character. It's a very intuitive thing, casting actors. I was very happy with the cast I had on Broadway in *The Goat.*

Q You wrote a beautiful tribute recently in *The New York Times* for Irene Worth. She also appeared in your plays *Tiny Alice, The Lady from Dubuque*, and your radio play, *Listening*. When you worked with her, what kind of an impact did it have on you?
Her death is a tremendous loss for all of us. She was a tower for the Theater. It keeps you being an optimist, knowing that there must be other people out there who feel the same way about what we do.

Q Was there something that compelled you to write *The Goat, or Who is Sylvia?* at that point in time?
I never know. What I write comes out of my desire as I think about things. I write to test our limits of tolerance. *The Goat* is really a play about love.

Q When you saw the revival of *Tiny Alice* in New York City, how did you connect with the play since you had written it so many years ago?
I enjoyed seeing it very much. I was able to make a cut in Julian's speech at the end of the play, that John Gielgud always had a problem with in the original production. I feel I was able to bring it to its right proportions. I can't reconnect the feeling of the first performance. I look at the piece straightforward and objectively, as an informed observer.

Q There was also a revival of *All Over*.
Yes, it was lovely seeing it again. Of course, I love everything I've ever written, but I have a speech at the end of the play, that Rosemary Harris does, and I felt it slowed everything down. I ended up cutting three-quarters of a page. I didn't want to lose it, no one did; but I can adjust a play I've written if I have to.

Q What led you to want to write about Louise Nevelson in your play, *Occupant*?
I wanted to write about how she created herself. So the play is really less about the art. She presented herself as this "public" person, but I also knew the "private" person. She was a good friend of mine.

Q Sometimes we see directors decide to set a play somewhere other than what the playwright intended, or to try to change the gender of the characters.
They tried to set one of Beckett's plays in a subway. Beckett was very clear about how he wanted his work done. I've run into that problem. I hold the line. There's a difference between creativity and distortion. That's where I draw the line.

Q You also created the William Flanagan Memorial Center for writers, painters, and sculptors, through the Edward Albee Foundation. Why was that important for you to do?
I began it over forty years ago. You have to give back what you have. That's why I teach. Back in the 1950s there weren't that many places for young writers, so as soon as I was able to, I wanted to do what I could.

Q You've been involved in many public causes, especially that of dissident writers. Do you feel an artist has a responsibility to society?
An artist does have a responsibility to make an informed response, not an emotional one; to do the research so you know what you're talking about. The issue has to drive you. There have been individuals like Arthur Miller, Harold Clurman, who have been very vocal, while Tennessee Williams never really did. I spent a lot of time in Eastern Europe, in response to the totalitarian states and their policies. Here in this country, I've done the same to make sure nothing like that happens here.

Q I think you've said you think a lot about a new play, then you sit down and it comes out?
I try not to think about being too specific, to not limit myself. I get a sense of the reality of the situation. And after a long period of gestation it comes. I never know how it will turn out. ■

HAROLD BLOOM

Sterling Professor of the Humanities at Yale University and Henry W. and Albert A. Berg Professor of English at NYU's Graduate School, Mr. Bloom is the author of over twenty books and the editor of more than thirty anthologies of literary criticism, including *Hamlet: Poem Unlimited, Genius: A Mosaic of 100 Exemplary Creative Minds, Yeats, A Map of Misreading, Kabbalah and Criticism, Agon: Toward a Theory of Revisionism, The Anxiety of Influence, The Western Canon, Omens of Millennium: The Gnosis of Angels, Dreams, and Resurrection, How to Read and Why, Where Shall Wisdom Be Found, Anatomy of Influence*, and *Shakespeare: The Invention of the Human*, which was a finalist for the 1998 National Book Award. A MacArthur Foundation Award recipient, he served as the Charles Eliot Norton Professor of Poetry at Harvard, and received the American Academy of Arts and Letters Gold Medal for Criticism.

Q You're always in the midst of many different projects. Your enthusiasm is unflagging, especially in your pursuit of inspiring young minds.

If one does inspire young minds—and it's kind of you to say so—I still feel I am a pariah in my profession. But I take pride in it. I don't expect good reviews for my work, but I do seem to have thousands of readers who read my books.

Q Have there been specific writers who inspired you?

William Shakespeare, of course; Milton, Hart Crane, M.H. Abrams. There is my great hero, Dr. Samuel Johnson. My mentor, the late Kenneth Burke. Also Wallace Stevens.

Q Did you go to the theater when you were young?

The first plays I saw were in Yiddish. I remember seeing Maurice Schwartz as Shylock in *The Merchant of Venice*, I'll never forget it. As he approached Antonio, he cried out as he dropped the scalpel, "After all, I'm Jewish!" The play is really an outrage.

The greatest theatrical experience in my life was when I was sixteen, seeing all in one day: *Henry IV Part I* and *Henry IV Part II*. There was Ralph Richardson as Falstaff, and Laurence Olivier as Hotspur, and then in the evening Olivier returned as Justice Shallow! I was in awe.

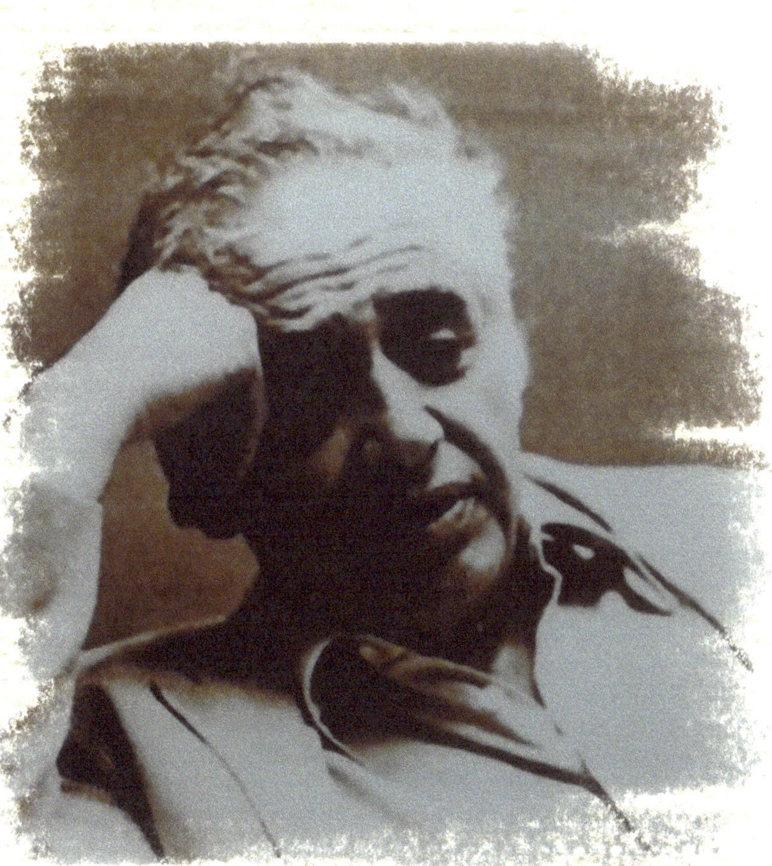

Harold Bloom photo: courtesy of the artist

Q Have you noticed a change in how we engage with a theatrical performance?

There seems to have been quite a drift in the theater in the last thirty years, with the technical aspects taking over the dramatic ability to illustrate the story, and a great loss of inspiring language. I'd call it a destruction of any aesthetic and cognitive level. That's become the norm, more than any kind of a reflective mode in the theater. It's about "high concept directors," with a political correctness directing our aims all the time. Even what I'm saying to you will probably be manipulated or misconstrued. All literary fame is based on misinformation.

Q And in the face of adversity, you push forward.

What alternative do I have? It's no sin to labor in one's vocation. I assume that imaginative values and cognitive insights, in spite of the universe, will prevail. ■

ED BULLINS

Mr. Bullins was playwright-in-residence at the New Lafayette Theatre in the 1960s and editor of *Black Theatre Magazine*. He was Distinguished Artist-in-Residence of Northeastern University, and Director of the New Federal Theatre Playwriting Workshop. As one of the best known playwrights to come from the Black Arts Movement, Mr. Bullins has delivered to us more than fifty plays, including *The Taking of Miss Janie*, which received the New York Drama Critics Circle Award; *The Fabulous Miss Marie* and *In the New England Winter*, for which he received the Black Arts Alliance Award; *Goin' a Buffalo*; *Harlem Diva*; *How do You Do*; *Clara's Ole Man*; *Dialect Determinism*; and a collection known as *Ed Bullins Plays*, for which he received a Drama Desk Award. He was an in-residence playwright for the American Place Theatre, and at the New York Shakespeare Festival's Writers Unit. During that time Bullins wrote two children's plays, *I am Lucy Terry* and *The Mystery of Phillis Wheatley*, and the books for two musicals: *Sepia Star* and *Storyville*. Mr. Bullins has also written a novel, *The Reluctant Rapist*, and several short stories over the years. His work can be found in *Ed Bullins: Twelve Plays and Selected Writings*, published by University of Michigan Press. He received the 2012 Theatre Communications Group Visionary Leadership Award.

Q Back in the 1970s, you were the playwright-in-residence at the New Lafayette Theatre in Harlem founded by Robert Macbeth, and the editor of *Black Theatre Magazine*. How did it help you express yourself at that time?
It met many needs. We were involved in creating the Black Theatre movement, a part of the Black Arts movement, which came out of a catalytic movement, an activity of Black Power. It was a time of self-awareness. We were black activists. I still have this nature.

Q Has today brought more opportunities for African-American playwrights?
It's a paradoxical time. When we began, there was a cadre of playwrights; we all knew one another. Today more and more plays are being done. In the early 1960s I did a survey; I was a young student of literature writing about Black Theater and I found out there were really four or five theaters that could call themselves "Black Theaters." Less than ten years later, there were hundreds of theatres doing Black plays. Today, a number of them are still around. And even with all this activity, people are not saying enough. We're on a cusp, waiting to see what happens.

I teach playwriting and I'm continually fighting them to get away from the clichés and tell them: if you're writing for the stage, you have to read plays. Look at the plays of the 60s, the absurdists, the Black Theater of that time. Each generation wants to ignore their forebears.

Q How do you cope with the ups and downs of being a playwright?
I write a lot and try different things, not always good choices, but my art form is writing a good play and moving the audience, dealing with the process of theater. I feel the theater is alive, not well, but they won't snuff the playwright out.

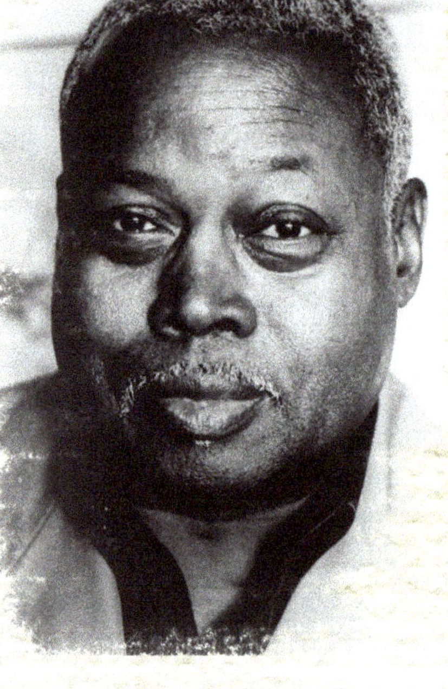
Ed Bullins photo: courtesy of the artist

Q Did writers like Langston Hughes, Lorraine Hansberry, Richard Wright, Louis Peterson, William Branch, Alice Childress, Loften Mitchell, and James Baldwin have an effect upon you when you began?
Secondarily more so perhaps. I was more influenced at the time by Amira Baraka and Adrienne Kennedy. Through study and experience I learned more. Now that I'm older I realize those writers you mentioned had some effect on me. I acquired them through reading their works or seeing their plays. I had rejected *A Raisin in the Sun* for a decade or so. I couldn't connect with it.

As I've grown older, I appreciate it much more. I teach it now as a catalyst, an historical bridge. It was political in a Pan-African way, with the African seeking his identity, the housing question, the awareness, the lack of empowerment, the seeds were there. At the time I was going into more of the Theatre of the Absurd, plays like *The Blacks*, *The Kitchen*, *The Connection*, *The Brig*, and Albee's early work.

Q Where do you find your inspiration?
From all over the place. One of my plays, *Spelta: A Numbian Coronation*, is about a Black pharaoh in 600 B.C. A museum curator commissioned me to write it as a spectacle to bring visitors into an exhibit.

Q I saw one of your plays at The New Federal Theatre—*A Son Come Home*–
I had written it in the late 1960s; it was done first at the American Place Theatre. It's a very sensitive piece about a mother and her son. I've also been writing a series of plays, *Twentieth Century Cycle*. Doing the cycle was inspired by my first play, *Goin' a Buffalo*—the stories of a group of hustlers and their women. They continued into *In the Wine Time*.

Q How do you look upon creating art?
Art is my type of religion, my calling, my spiritual vector. When I've tried to do my better work I feel I'm serving art. The situation's never been right—that's why we playwrights are trying to get it right. ■

NILO CRUZ

The first Latin playwright to receive the Pulitzer Prize for his play, *Anna in the Tropics*, starring Jimmy Smits, directed on Broadway by Emily Mann, Mr. Cruz also received the Steinberg Award for Best New Play, and a Tony Award nomination. Mr. Cruz's other plays include *Beauty of the Father*, *Lorca in a Green Dress*, *Night Train to Bolina*, *A Bicycle Country*, *Dancing on Her Knees*, *A Park in Our House*, *Two Sisters and a Piano*, *Capricho*, *The Color of Desire*, and *Hortensia and the Museum of Dreams*. He wrote adaptations of Lorca's *The House of Bernardo Alba*, *Dona Rosita the Spinster*, and *Life is a Dream*. Mr. Cruz wrote the book of the Frank Wildhorn/Jack Murphy musical, *Havana*. His plays have been performed regionally across America and around the world. Mr. Cruz is a frequent collaborator with Peruvian-American Latin Grammy composer, Gabriela Lena Frank, collaborating on a set of orchestral songs, *La Centinela y la Paloma*, for Dawn Upshaw and St. Paul Chamber Orchestra, *The Saint Maker* for Jessica Rivera, Ranchel Calloway, San Francisco Girls Chorus, and the Berkeley Symphony, and *Journey of the Shadow* for the San Francisco Chamber Orchestra. Mr. Cruz penned the libretto to Jimmy Lopez's opera *Bel Canto*. Mr. Cruz has taught at Brown University and the Yale School of Drama. Among the other awards Mr. Cruz has received are: American Theatre Critics/Steinberg New Play Award, Rockefeller Grant, Alton Jones Award, Kesselring Prize, AT&T Award, Barrie Stavis Award, and he received the PEN/Laura Pels International Foundation for Theatre Award.

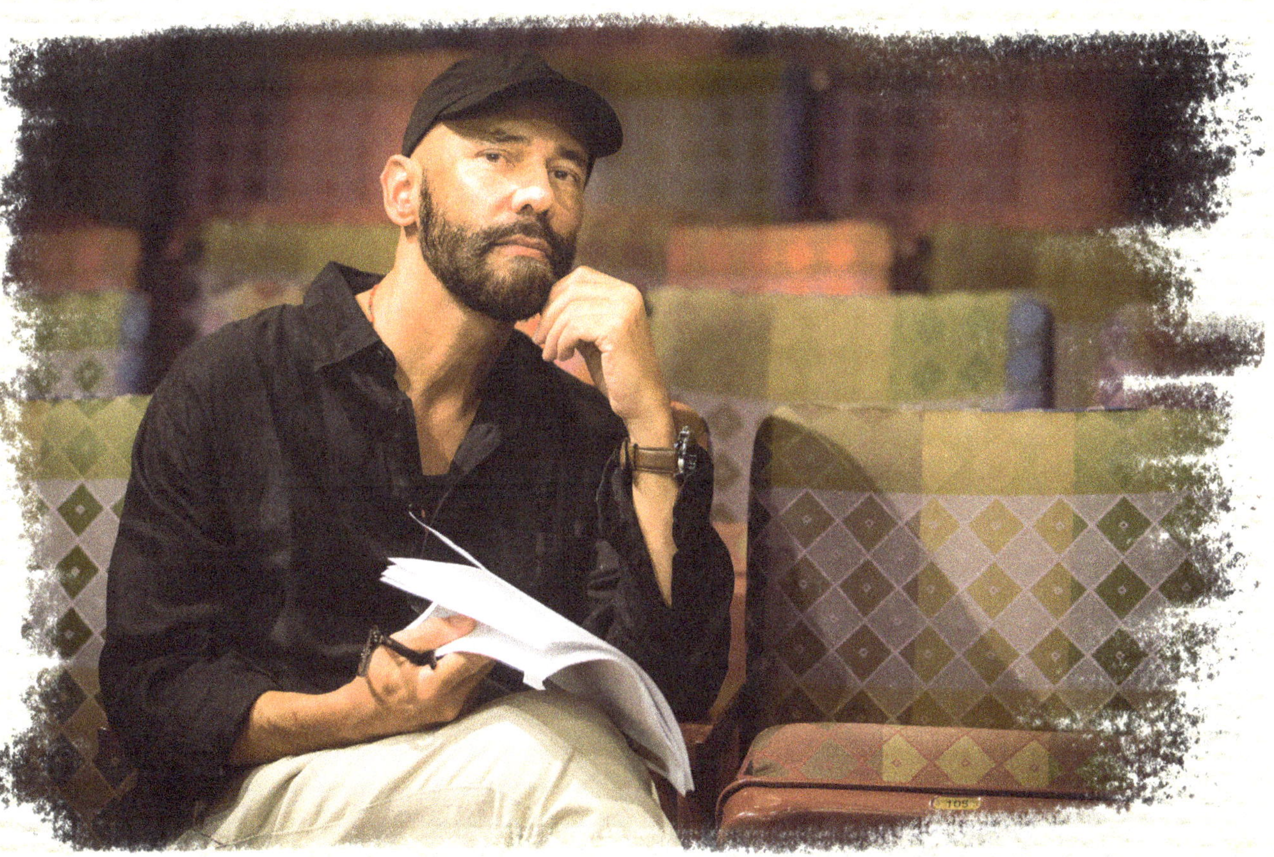

Nilo Cruz photo © Matt Pilsner

Q How important is structure for you?
Very much so, but what's more important are the characters, and then little by little, as I'm looking at what I have written from the characters' perspective, I find out the structure.

Q How do you begin to work on your characters?
I visualize them.

Q What did it mean to you receiving the Pulitzer Prize?
It was really wonderful to receive that kind of acknowledgment. It did allow more of my work to be seen in a different light. For me, it's about where I am as an artist, where I am with I'm writing, and what I'm discovering.

Q Why do you choose to write for the theater?
There's something about the theater unlike anything thing else. It's an ancient art form—so ceremonial—a meeting of minds and souls and bodies in one special space who are going to suspend their imagination for a certain amount of time and enter another landscape. I think of the theatre as a noble art form. It's so close to life because it's happening before your eyes. It's alive, constantly changing, like life, that's why it's so frail. It's why I'm in the theatre. ■

CHRISTOPHER DURANG

Mr. Durang's play on Broadway, *Vanya and Sonia and Masha and Spike*, received the Tony Award; it was directed by Nicholas Martin, and starred Sigourney Weaver, David Hyde Pierce, Kristine Nielsen, Billy Magnussen, Shalita Grant, and Genevieve Angelson. Mr. Durang's other plays include *The Nature And Purpose Of The Universe*; *A History of the American Film*, which received a Tony Award nomination; *Sister Mary Ignatius Explains It All For You* with Elizabeth Franz, for which he and Ms. Franz both received an Obie award, and the play has also been performed by Nancy Marchand, Mary Louise Wilson, Kathleen Chalfont, Cloris Leachman, Peggy Cass, and Lynn Redgrave; *Beyond Therapy* starring Sigourney Weaver and Stephen Collins, directed by Jerry Zaks, and on Broadway with Dianne Wiest and John Lithgow; *Baby with the Bathwater* at Playwrights Horizons; *The Marriage of Bette and Boo* with Joan Allen and Olympia Dukakis, for which he received an Obie award; *Laughing Wild*; *Betty's Summer Vacation*, for which he received an Obie award, *Mrs. Bob Cratchit's Wild Christmas Binge*; and *Sex and Longing* with Sigourney Weaver. As a performer, he's appeared in his own plays, in film and television, including *The Secret of My Success*, starring Michael J. Fox, *Housesitter*, *The Butcher's Wife*, *Life with Mikey*, *Simply Irresistible*, and *Kristin*. He also performed in the Stephen Sondheim revue, *Putting It Together*, at the Manhattan Theatre Club, with Julie Andrews. Mr. Durang and Sigourney Weaver performed in and co-wrote *Das Lusitania Songspiel*, and he wrote a musical, *Adrift in Macao*, with music by Peter Melnick. His film and television work includes *Trying Times* starring Swoozie Kurtz; he wrote for Carol Burnett's special *Carol and Robin and Whoopi and Carl*; and *Sister Mary Ignatius* starring Diane Keaton. Mr. Durang received the Kenyon Festival Playwriting Prize, Sidney Kingsley Playwriting Award, and Lila Wallace Readers Digest Writers Award, and is a member of the Dramatists Guild Council.

Q Who inspired you when you were growing up?

God, I wish someone had. I found Martin Luther King, Jr. inspiring. There have been many admirable people. But I just can't seem to think of any right now. I also get uncomfortable with the need to lionize people.

Q Did you see a lot of theater when you were growing up?

My mother liked musicals and we saw all the shows at the Paper Mill Playhouse. I grew up with the musicals of Rodgers and Hammerstein, *Damn Yankees*, *How to Succeed...* I loved that "cartoon style." I also liked Noel Coward, partially because my mother did. In high school my taste darkened. I found Joe Orton and saw all of Fellini's movies.

Q How much of your own life influenced your play, *Sister Mary Ignatius Explains It All*?

That's my most controversial play, at least within pretty conservative circles. The play came out of my own personal upbringing in the 1950s and 60s. There were so many rules back then; I felt the rules were highly questionable, and often messed people up psychologically. That's the point of the play. The play came from my memory. In the 1950s, you never questioned the moral authority of the Church.

Q Your plays continually challenge the audience to question their own values.

I think when I was younger, from my college days until I was thirty-five, that was probably true. With age, I've become less interested in being confrontational. Sometimes I think it's good to just be entertaining. Sometimes that's all I want to do.

When I wrote *Betty's Summer Vacation*, I thought it was going to be a "light" comedy, like my old play, *Beyond Therapy*, but then a serial killer showed up, and mutilation and incest, and suddenly the topic of us as a nation "enjoying" horrible things on television, looking at life's disasters as a weird mini-series, took over the play. So that is a challenging play for some audiences, though I think it's also entertaining.

But I think my work is not as constantly challenging as it was when I was younger. Truthfully, both *Adrift in Macao* and *Mrs. Bob Cratchit's Wild Christmas Binge* are more of me in a good mood, having fun, rather than looking at something dark and worrisome.

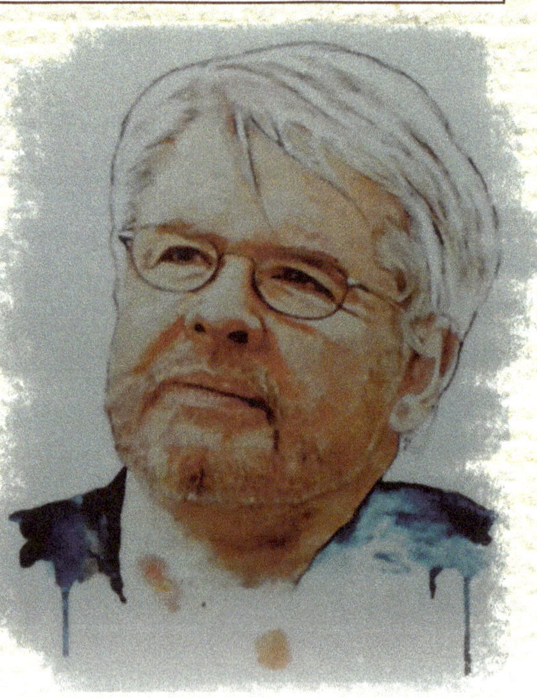

Christopher Durang artwork: © Jimmy Turrell, courtesy of Mr. Turrell

Q You had taught playwriting at Juilliard with Marsha Norman. How did that happen?

Marsha approached me. She had been hired to be one of two playwrights to teach a playwriting class, and she asked me to join her. I said "yes," then I said "no." I was a little afraid of how time consuming it might be. She said, "Just try it." And I did like it. We actually "team-taught"; we were in the class at the same time. We got to choose our students from the work they submitted.

Q Was it a rewarding experience for you?

I found I liked teaching. Most of the time I felt invigorated by being around younger writers who were still full of hope, and who were brimming with ideas.

In terms of teaching, I don't believe in rules of playwriting. I sort of don't know what they are, and I'm suspicious of generalizations. However, I eventually found I actually have a few rules when I write that I didn't know I had. That there should be a topic for the play you should feel strongly about. If not, you're just meandering. I discovered, oddly, that I often brought up exposition.

I write comedy, and even in life you have to have a set-up for a joke, and you have to get the information out to the audience in order for it to work. As a teacher I'm also interested in the psychology going on in the scene, in the interaction, which is a fairly old-fashioned, basic thing to be interested in. Even with absurdist plays, I like there to be a psychological truth underneath.

Q What do you see the purpose of art and theater?

I feel that art basically gives us a sense of what it means to be alive if we've forgotten. Other times it can reflect life back so you realize, "I never thought of that."

Q How do you maintain your sense of humor and equilibrium?

I once read that Stockard Channing said in an interview, something like, "You're hot or you're not. You just have to be realistic that your life in theatre goes up and down, and when it's down, you're patient, and you wait for it to go up again." I find that thought comforting. You can't always sustain the same level. I'm a Capricorn; I'm supposedly the goat who goes up the mountain. At times I'm depressed, but I have to be careful not to give in to it.

In my 20s I needed therapy. As I've gotten older, depression doesn't last as long; I think I'm a worrier. But I'm open to other options. I've tried affirmations. I watched Joan Hickson as Miss Marple to give myself comfort. I love how detectives find solutions. "I have always longed for a solution," a character of mine says in my crackpot play, *Titanic*. Well, I have, too. ■

EVE ENSLER

A Tony Award-winning playwright, activist, performer, Ms. Ensler wrote the theatrical phenomenon, *The Vagina Monologues*, which has been published in forty-eight languages, performed in over a hundred and forty countries, and received the Obie award for Best New Play. Ms. Ensler is founder of V-Day, a twenty-year-old global activist movement to end violence against women and girls, which has raised over a hundred million dollars to end violence, and One Billion Rising, a global mass action campaign in over two hundred countries. Her plays include:*Necessary Targets, OPC, The Good Body, Lemonade*, and *Emotional Creature*. An acclaimed author, her books include *Insecure at Last: A Political Memoir, The New York Times* best-selling book, *I am an Emotional Creature*, and her critically acclaimed memoir, *In the Body of the World* which she adapted and performed at the American Repertory Theater (A.R.T.), directed by Diane Paulus. Her play, *Fruit Trilogy*, was performed at the Women of the World Festival in London, and at The West Yorkshire Playhouse in the spring of 2016. She writes for *The Guardian, Time* magazine, and the *International Herald Tribune*. Ms. Ensler was named by *Newsweek* as one of "150 Women Who Changed the World" and by *The Guardian* as one of the "100 Most Influential Women."

Q What has given you the greatest joy in creating?

The last production I did, *In the Body of the World* at A.R.T., was a profoundly joyful experience. There was such an incredible synergy of all these different artists coming together to create this piece. It was at once—metaphysical, political, personal, ecological—and very beautiful. And the making of the work was joyful. I think everyone felt it—the producers, the director, the designers, everyone who did the outreach, all the speakers who came and spoke at the end of the show; and of course, the audience. Even though the material is difficult, there was an underlying joy. It is so rare that everyone is in sync and lifting each other higher. It had a lot to do with Diane Paulus, her energy, her care, her trust, and her direction.

Q Creating a theater piece from your book, *I am an Emotional Creature*, with Diane Paulus as your director must have been quite stimulating—

It was magnificent! One of the most favorite experiences of my career. She has an incredible ability to listen, to hear what's going on in each moment, to boldly pursue those elements. When we worked on adapting the book into a play, we'd literally go sentence by sentence.

What was exciting was trying to find out what to leave in, and what to leave out of the book. When we mapped it out, ultimately we found out the strongest story we wanted to tell, and what events and characters served that story.

Q How did you feel the first time you performed it?

I was really nervous because it's so personal, so visceral, so raw. That first night I thought I'd pass out before I got out onstage. But to see how marvelous the audience was, how generous in their emotional responses, and how willing they were to play, laugh, cry, and even dance. So many in the audience would come up every night to me to tell me afterwards what inspired them about the show, to talk about their cancer or a family member's cancer, or their love of trees. And I loved that the final set piece was a lit-

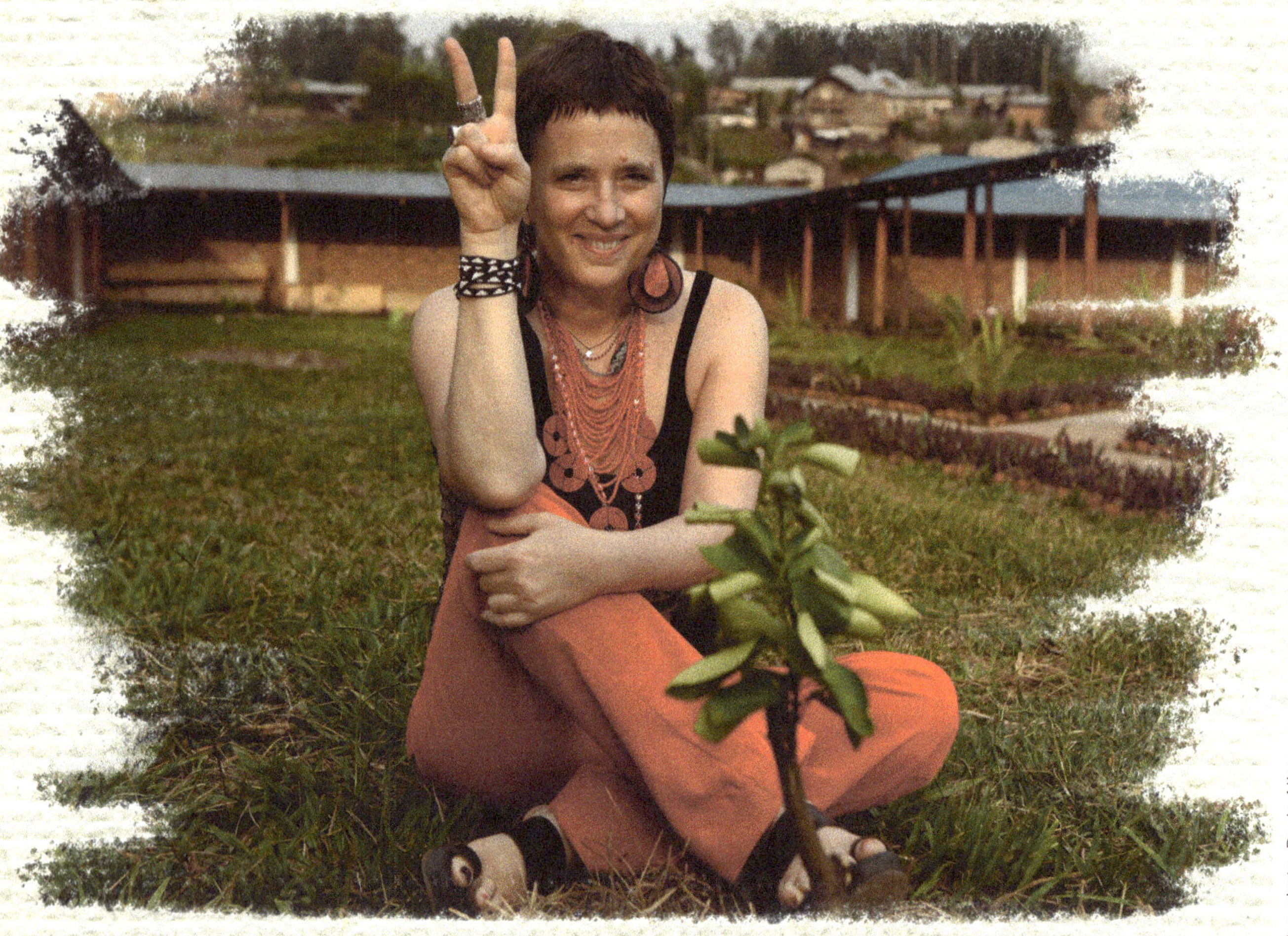

Eve Ensler photo: Paula Allen

eral place the audience could visit and rest in and where we held the talk-backks.

Q You have a wonderful photo of yourself as a young girl on your website. Were you already writing and expressing yourself creatively at that age?
It was how I survived. I grew up in such a violent dark environment, and writing helped create an alternate persona and gave me a way to make sense or at least a way to make art out of what was so terrible.

Q You had conducted over two hundred interviews with women, which led to your writing the first draft of *The Vagina Monologues* in 1996. As you were writing the play, did you see yourself performing it?
I think what happened was I did all these interviews, and out of them came a piece that was fictional—not the direct interviews, but I'd take a line or a theme or a paragraph from the transcripts, and I created the piece that way. What became clear to me was what these women had entrusted me with their deepest secrets.

When it came time for it to be performed, I knew, because of the material, it could easily be corrupted and I wanted to protect it so that it would be transmitted in the most honoring way. The first performance was utterly terrifying, but the response from the beginning was so strong. It became the play that would determine so much of my life. It was really wonderful to pass it on to such extraordinary actors. I am beyond amazed and grateful to see the range of actors and women who have performed this play over these twenty years.

Q In 1998, V-day was launched—a global non-profit movement working to end violence against women and girls through the benefit of *The Vagina Monologues*. How would you describe the effect of what that play meant to those who came, and continues to mean around the world?
When I performed the piece, everywhere I went, women would line up to talk to me, wanting to tell me their stories. The stories were mainly about being raped or abused or incested or battered. Women would have extreme emotional reactions to the play. In Oklahoma City, a woman fainted and we had to stop the show as she remembered being raped as a child by her stepfather. I knew there was violence in the world towards women. I am a survivor myself, but I had no idea of the epidemic proportions.

In 1998, I felt compelled to do

more so I got a group of activists together and we talked about how we could use this play to end violence against women.

We began with one amazing performance to raise money for grassroots groups in New York City who work to end violence. We did a performance of *The Vagina Monologues* at the Hammerstein Ballroom, filling over twenty-five hundred seats. Marisa Tomei, Glenn Close, Susan Sarandon, Whoopi Goldberg, Lily Tomlin, Rosie Perez, and many amazing others were all a part of it. Everyone was terrified and exhilarated but it turned out to be one of the most extraordinary nights. It felt like the earth moved. That evening really gave birth to the V-Day movement.

It was as if a flower had been blown open by a huge performance wind and seeds scattered in every direction. Since then the play has been performed all over the globe, in a hundred and forty countries! In 2018, it will have its twentieth anniversary. And so many women have broken the silence and stood up to end the violence against them.

Q What would it take for a greater respect for girls and women to occur on this planet?

I think it's always about changing the ground story, the cultural beliefs. We live in a patriarchal society. I think the basic archetypal myths still have to shift. Art can work to make transformation on those deeper levels. When I started, women couldn't say the word, "vagina," practically anywhere. Women have risked their lives to put on the show and perform it. In the Philippines, they've been doing the show there for twelve years, and it's helped change the laws of sexual violence against women. It was done in Pakistan where everyone thought it was impossible.

In the Congo, after the ministers of the government saw the play, it caused a huge upheaval in discourse. I was present when I saw brilliant and brave women perform it in the Haitian Congress. It was performed by the female Members of Parliament at the European Parliament. To hear such powerful women moaning in those prodigious halls was quite something. I've seen things I never dreamed would be possible.

I think women have to constantly tell their stories and put out their truths. Women have to come back into their bodies.

I think so much of ending violence has to do with men. I never understood why it became a women's issue. We actually don't rape ourselves. I think when men make this issue as important to them as it is to women, there will be real liberation. We move forward, we move back. Patriarchy is stubborn and we know power is rarely given, particularly from the privileged insecure. I do believe that when men know in their beings, in their hearts, that their liberation is tied to the liberation of women, there will be a radical shift.

Q And the theater remains a place of creation for you—

I believe in the theater. It's of the body. It's where we're present together, in the moment. It's spontaneous, physical, political, psychological, spiritual. So much of this high tech neo-liberal capitalist world takes us out of the present, isolates us, makes us lonely.

Theater is a place of revolution. We create it each night together. It's always changing, happening right now. It's of the body and it's of community. It's dangerous and it's holy. ■

HORTON FOOTE

A Pulitzer Prize-winning playwright for his play, *The Young Man from Atlanta*, starring Rip Torn, Shirley Knight and Biff McGuire, Mr. Foote is also known for his screenplays, receiving two Academy Awards for *To Kill a Mockingbird* starring Gregory Peck, *Tender Mercies* starring Robert Duvall, *The Trip to Bountiful* starring Geraldine Page, for which she received the Academy Award, and *Baby the Rain Must Fall* starring Steve McQueen and Lee Remick. During the 1950s, as one of the leading television writers writing for live television, the shows he wrote for included *The Gabby Hayes Show, Studio One, Playhouse 90*, for which he received several Emmy nominations and awards. He also adapted *The Trip to Bountiful* into a play starring Lillian Gish and Eva Marie Saint on Broadway. Mr. Foote's plays, which premiered on Broadway, Off-Broadway and Off-Off Broadway included *A Young Lady of Property, Valentine's Day, The Widow Claire, Lily Dale, The Habitation of Dragons, Dividing the Estate, The Young Man From Atlanta, The Last of the Thorntons, The Carpetbagger's Children, Dividing the Estate, and Harrison TX: Three Plays*. His nine-play biographical series, *The Orphans Home Cycle*, ran in repertory Off-Broadway during 2009–2010 at The Signature Theatre, and received a Drama Desk Award. Mr. Foote adapted John Steinbeck's *Of Mice and Men*, into a play directed by and starring Gary Sinise with John Malkovich, and William Faulkner's short story, "Tomorrow," into a film starring Robert Duvall. Mr. Foote provided the voice of Jefferson Davis in Ken Burns' documentary, *The Civil War*. Foote's final work was the screenplay for the film, *Main Street*, starring Colin Firth, Patricia Clarkson, and Orlando Bloom. Mr. Foote accepted the title as "Visiting Distinguished Dramatist" with the Baylor Department. His memoirs included *Farewell: A Memoir of a Texas Childhood*, and *Beginnings*. Mr. Foote was inducted into the American Hall of Fame. Mr. Foote died in 2009 (this interview was conducted in 2001).

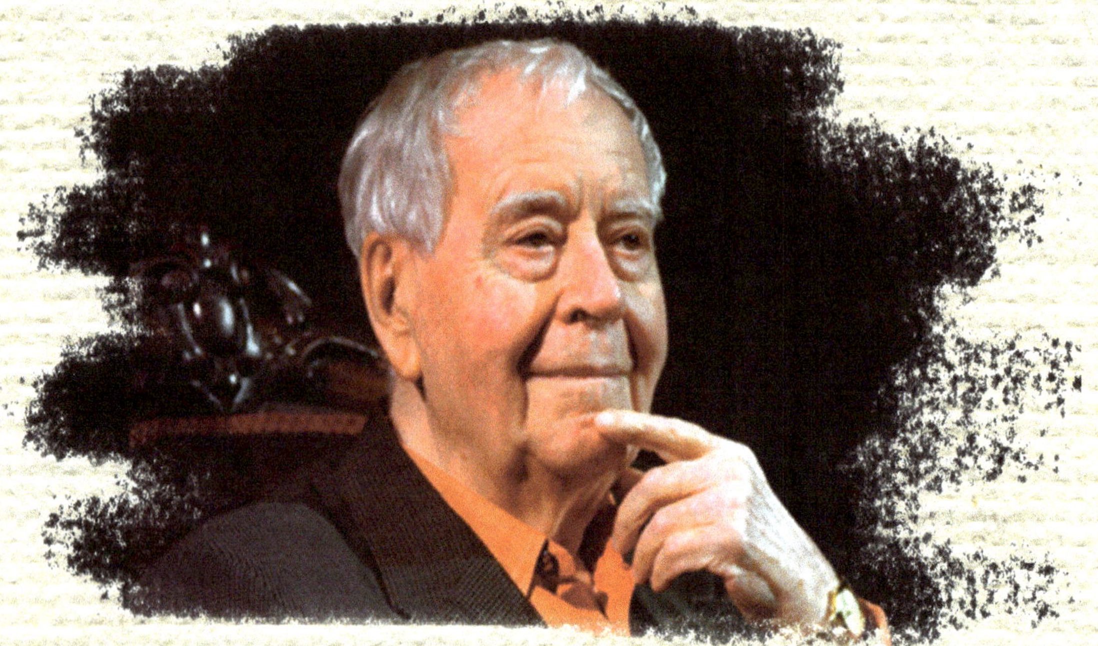

Horton Foote photo: courtesy of The Texas Collection, Baylor University

Q You've had a long collaboration with your family performing in many of your plays. How does that impact upon your creative process?
I've worked often with my family and it really doesn't hurt. Hallie, my daughter, is a wonderful actor. I've had several wonderful actors in my plays, among them Geraldine Page, Kim Stanley, Lillian Gish. I just can't write with someone specifically in mind.

Q Was there any kind of a similarity working on the screenplays of Harper Lee's *To Kill a Mockingbird* and John Steinbeck's *Of Mice and Men*?
Well, I liked doing *Mockingbird* very much; I'm very devoted to Harper Lee. When I worked on it, it was a world I knew. It was about a very special society with very rigid taboos. *Of Mice and Men* was more free-ranging, although it did have a black man who was discriminated against.

I've learned through the years that if I'm going to adapt, whether it's Faulkner or whomever, to pay attention to the structure and the intent of the author. I began as an actor, and I learned to have enormous respect for the written word, to learn what the author was going for. I have enormous respect for the theatre.

I studied acting with Vera Soloviova and Andrius Jilinsky, two former members of the First Studio of the Moscow Art Theatre, and with Tamara Daykarhonova. The theater's not a place of self-aggrandizement. It's a place to encourage group activity.

Q Did you like to act?
I liked it a lot. The transition from actor to writer came about gradually.

Q You've also directed some of your plays.
I haven't directed all of them, though I happily directed my daughter's play. I was interested in doing that. The same rules apply, whether it's your own work or someone else's. You have to have a certain affinity for the work, to be willing to explore and share it with the world.

Q Your play, *The Last of the Thorntons*, is a very revealing picture of how these individuals try to sort out their memories, coping with how they lived their lives.
I think my plays focus on mortality often. I live in a certain place in Texas, I'm the fifth generation, and the way I was raised, the past is just as important as the present. I was raised by a family of storytellers. In a sense, the past was more vivid than the present. So I think the past surfaces much more as people live longer and longer.

Q Were there certain things you specifically learned having your plays done at The Signature Theatre?
I've had four plays done there. It's been very valuable to go back to an earlier work; to see it before you, very subtle things happen. You see what's happened to you over time. The forces that shaped you.

Q Have you seen any of your plays done in other countries?
I've seen many of my plays across the country and I know many of them are done across the world. But I don't wander.

Q Do you approach actors any differently, especially if a new actress is playing the same role in a play of yours that was done in the past?
I learned about this early on, with *The Trip to Bountiful*. I saw three really great actresses, Lillian Gish, Geraldine Page, and then Ellen Burstyn. They were all different and I welcome that. You don't want to straightjacket the actor's creativity. The thrill is what they can contribute, not make it some role to be acted, to say, "This is the way to do it." I always welcome the actor's creative gifts. ■

MARIA IRENE FORNÉS

A distinguished Cuban American playwright and director, Ms. Fornés was a leading figure of the Off-Off Broadway movement in the 1960s. When she first arrived in America, Ms. Fornés worked in the Capezio shoe factory, learned English, and became a translator. Interested in painting, she studied abstract art with Hans Hofmann in New York City. When she moved to Paris to continue painting, she was greatly influenced while seeing a production of Samuel Beckett's *Waiting for Godot*, although she had never read a play and didn't understand French. Ms. Fornés' notable works included *Promenade*, for which she received her first Obie award, with music by Al Carmines; *And What of the Night?* which was chosen as a Pulitzer Prize finalist; *Fefu and Her Friends, Mud, Tango's Palace, The Successful Life of 3, Lolita in the Garden, The Danube, A Matter of Faith, Oscar and Bertha, Enter the Night, Abingdon Square*, and *Letters from Cuba*. She adapted Lorca's *Blood Wedding* and *Life is a Dream*, and Chekhov's *Uncle Vanya*. She received nine Obie awards, the New York State Governor's Arts Award, Robert Chesley Award, and the PEN/Laura Pels International Foundation for Theatre Award. She was committed to teaching and mentoring, and influenced many young playwrights, including Tony Kushner, Paula Vogel, and Nilo Cruz. (This interview was conducted in 2000).

Q You've given so much of yourself to young new writers. Why is that necessary for you?
I want to turn everybody onto something I like. I get enormous pleasure when I inspire a young writer in a manner where you feel the heartbeat of the character. I teach them not to make up your mind what the play is going to be about, by letting the characters speak from their own point of view.

Q Why do you direct most of the premieres of your work?
The first time a play is on stage for me there are always a lot of rewrites. One becomes aware of certain things. I've never been at that point to not change one word. I make changes even after a play is published, to add a line, a silence. Putting a play up is so painful. The theatre has its traditions, its rules which are stubborn, so old-fashioned. As if tradition is more important than quality.

Grotowski, Joseph Chaikin, they questioned the reversal process, from A to Z, turning everything upside down. How plays develop, the blocking, the way things work. I believe the movement of a character is completely connected with the expression of the plays in the same way a frame is connected to a picture. Directing is painting to me. In sense of form, staging, behavior, movement, all that is painting.

Q You continually take the audience to places we need to go but are afraid to. What compels you to go there?
I'm bored when I don't go there. I want to let the character lead. I want to be surprised. The character takes over and I am amazed. We have that in our dreams. In our unconscious something happens, as in a story form. We let it happen because we are sleeping. The subconscious knows the truth that we don't want to know.

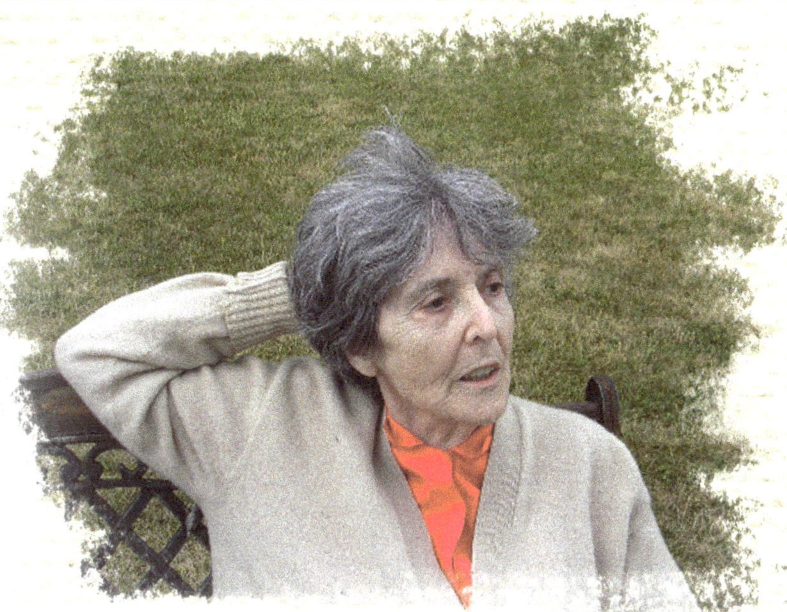

Maria Irene Fornes photo: courtesy of Bonnie Marranca, 2007

Q How do you overcome writer's block?
I try to visualize the place. Just by starting, you start to connect, by bypassing the rational part of your mind. I always think of a tape recorder when the reel goes fast, it's not catching. Don't visualize the character on stage but in real places, then it will be true.

Q You were at The Actors Studio—
Yes, I was in the Playwrights Unit and we would sit in the acting classes and watch. I was there when Lee Strasberg directed *The Three Sisters* on Broadway; there was such excitement. Finally, they were going to "do it."

In class, I couldn't understand the Method, but the exercises were magical, but I still didn't know how they were doing it. I wasn't getting it so I went to Gene Frankel and learned "sense memory"—the heavens opened. I now realized there was a way to be inspired. Through those exercises I was able to write.

Q What is the greatest challenge facing a creative artist today?
The only thing that keeps an artist down is that they have to be successful. I read something beautiful and interesting because it excites me. I love writing. And if it's going well I do it, like when I

was a kid playing with paper dolls.

When I played with dolls, I wasn't doing it to please my parents; I did it because it was fun. When the craft is developing, you feel the writing getting better and better. You can stretch, it's the only way it can be really good; when it's beyond yourself, you say, "How did I do it?" and you don't know how it happened. It's like being in love.

A source of inspiration has to come, you can't "make-believe" you're writing a play. To be inspired, the characters have to take over. You have to recognize there is a force of presence. There is a knowledge in our dreams that is a part of us. Sometimes dreams frighten us, you have to be conscious of this. If you spend the time with your eyes closed, not deciding what needs to be done, one character will take over, and things will come to you.

Q Can you describe the challenges you faced with your play, *Letters from Cuba*, your first play to deal with your roots?

It was the hardest thing I've ever done: the structure, and there were two different sets on stage. If you could see a large apartment and cut it open, the back room was three rooms, and above was the roof. The play became a dialogue between an artist in New York and my brother, who is an artist in Cuba. Another character is a ballet dancer and she lives with the two men, a poet and a painter. It was really innocent.

You have no idea how hard it was to structure the scenes. The actors were incredibly good but something wasn't working. On paper the structure worked, until I realized there was an added element—the sets, on top of each other. I began to make changes.

Finally, as we got closer to the opening, I decided to move the last scene and put it third to the last. Why did I think that? But it still wasn't right, still a problem. The last run-through, my last chance—inspiration or guess—until it works, it's a guess. I had to try something. I took the scene and moved it second to last. Inspiration? Yes. It worked. I've learned there're always changes until it works.

All this made me think and feel a lot about the well-made play. There are so many elements always evolving to recognize—time, space, rhythm; when it's working well, it excites me. Yes, I love it! ■

MICHAEL FRAYN

Mr. Frayn is most well known as the playwright of the Tony award-winning *Copenhagen*, *Noises Off*, and his critically-acclaimed novels, *Towards the End of the Morning*, *Headlong*, and *Spies*, for which he received the Whitbread Prize. Mr. Frayn's plays also include *Democracy*, performed at London's National Theatre and on Broadway; *Afterlife*, *Alphabetical Order*, *Clouds*, *Make and Break*, *Donkeys' Years*, *Benefactors*, and *Audience*. Among Frayn's other novels include *The Tin Men*, for which he received the Somerset Maugham Award; *The Russian Interpreter*, for which he received the Hawthornden Prize; *A Very Private Life*, *The Trick of It*, *Stage Directions: Writing on Theatre*, and *My Father's Fortune: A Life*. He also wrote a book about philosophy, *Constructions*, and a book about his own philosophy, *The Human Touch*. He wrote columns for the newspapers, *The Guardian* and "*The Observer*. Mr. Frayn's film screenplays include *Clockwise* starring John Cleese, *First and Last* starring Tom Wilkinson, *Jamie on a Flying Visit*, and the television series *Making Faces*, starring Eleanor Bron. Considered by many to be Britain's finest translator of Anton Chekhov's work, he has written translations of *The Seagull*, *Uncle Vanya*, *The Cherry Orchard*, *Three Sisters*, *Wild Honey*, and *The Sneeze*. He also translated Yuri Trifonov's play, *Exchange*, Tolstoy's *The Fruits of Enlightenment*, and Jean Anouilh's *Number One*. Mr. Frayn has received many awards for his plays, including the Laurence Oliver Award twice, several London Evening Standard Awards, an International Emmy Award, Golden PEN Award, and the St. Louis Literary Award.

Q What was your reaction when *Noises Off* had its revival on Broadway in 2001?

It was very curious to see a farce at that time. The cast actually had started rehearsals a day before the tragedy of 9/11. I thought, "Well, that's the end of that." I couldn't get through to the director, Jeremy Sams, to find out what was happening. When I finally did reach him the day after, he told me the cast decided they wanted to continue. Well, I saluted their courage and fortitude in the face of it all.

Q What role does theater play in people's lives today?

I must tell you I remember what Lynne Meadow had said once at an American Theatre Wing Seminar: the audience besides coming just to enjoy themselves, they want to have a communal experience and support the artists. I mean, when you get three or four hundred people or more coming together, it becomes a community.

Q You raised the question in your postscript of your play, *Copenhagen*, that if Heisenberg had made the calculations, could the Germans have built the bomb? And you answer it by saying, "The line of ifs is a long one. It remains just possible, though. The effects of real enthusiasm and real determination are incalculable. In the realm of the just possible, they are sometimes decisive." Is it always a very thin line that

separates us from such cataclysms?
There is always a large element of chance in it all. There was a long line of ifs at that time. I personally think it was very unlikely the Germans could have built the bomb. But if you look at the other way, there was also a long line of ifs separating the allies to do it as well. But, we know in fact, they did it. Just because America was prepared to put all their efforts and resources into making it a reality.

Q I had heard you say that when your adaptation of Chekhov's *Wild Honey* was going to be presented on Broadway, the producers actually wanted you to eliminate Chekhov's name from the program.
It was more that they wanted my name to appear rather than his name. They thought at the time, for whatever reason, that it was "box office poison" on Broadway. On the other hand, in London they were doing revival after revival of Chekhov. You can't quite think why these producers felt that way in America. After all, they're very, very good plays and reveal to all of us a certain working of the human heart, showing us the failures and disappointments and hopes of these people. We see the lives of these people in the countryside, with a certain amount of time on their hands. There's an amount of nostalgia, but it's also quite a bit false, since their lives weren't really like this. These are really hard-working professionals, and we just happen to see them on their break. It happens to be this moment in time and we catch them.

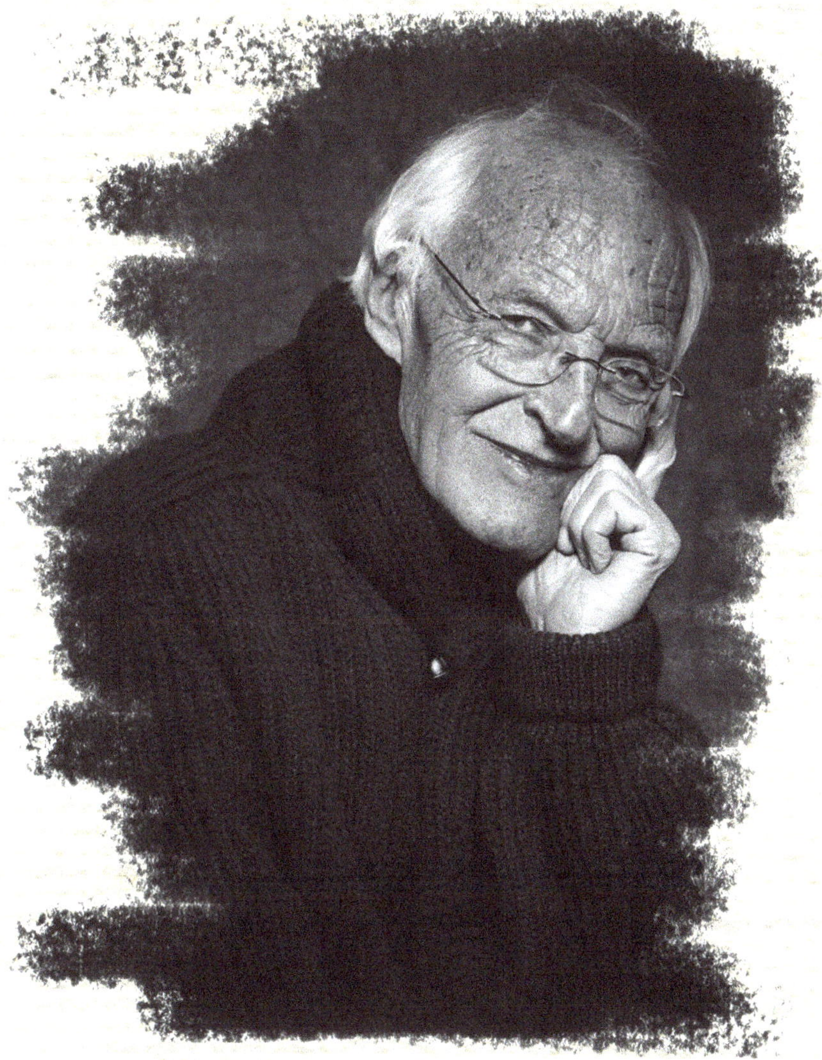

Michael Frayn photo: © Jillian Edelstein, courtesy of Ms. Edelstein

Q You have a special relationship with the director, Michael Blakemore. But how do you remain true to your vision if a director you're working with becomes adamant about their point of view?
I don't always agree. But Michael brings up things I hadn't thought of. And he's very skilled and makes suggestions that release my imagination. You can be easily pushed over if a director is very strong, but Michael's not that way at all.

Q How do you decide what you write will become a play?
I don't have much choice. They present themselves to me in such a way that the only way to do it is as a play, when the ideas happen to fall into my head. Once I've gotten the idea, the problem becomes how to do it for the theatre.

When a play works, it's a very intense experience, or an entertaining one, for those people who are involved and for those watching. Dialogue can be just extraordinary when it's written by gifted writers. When I go to see other writers' plays, they either make me run in the opposite direction, or when they really work, they magnify my reaction to life, and make me love even more what I like and what I do. ■

LARRY GELBART

Mr. Gelbart is most known as a creator and producer of the television hit show, *M*A*S*H* starring Alan Alda; *A Funny Thing Happened on the Way to the Forum*, with Burt Shevelove, for which he received a Tony Award, starring Zero Mostel on Broadway; the films, *Tootsie* with Murray Schisgal, for which they received an Academy Award nomination, starring Dustin Hoffmann; and *Oh God* with George Burns and John Denver. Mr. Gelbart wrote jokes for *The Jack Paar Show*, *Eddie Cantor Show*, and *The Bob Hope Show* on radio. As a television writer, he wrote for Sid Caesar, Bob Hope, Red Buttons, Danny Kaye, and *Duffy's Tavern*. He also wrote *Barbarians at the Gate* starring James Garner, *Weapons of Mass Distraction* with Ben Kingsley and Gabriel Bryne, and *And Starring Pancho Villa as Himself* starring Antonio Banderas. His other films included *Movie, Movie*, which he co-wrote, and which starred George C. Scott; *Blame it on Rio* with Michael Caine; *Bedazzled*; *Rough Cut* starring Burt Reynolds; and *A Funny Thing Happened on the Way to the Forum*. Mr. Gelbart's shows on Broadway included the musical *City of Angels*, for which he received a Drama Desk Award and an Edgar Award; *Mastergate*; *Sly Fox* starring George C. Scott; and a musical adaptation of the Preston Sturges film, *Hail the Conquering Hero*. He titled his memoir, *Laughing Matters: On Writing M*A*S*H*, Tootsie, Oh God! And a Few Other Funny Things*. Mr. Gelbart was inducted into the American Theater Hall of Fame and The Television Hall of Fame. Mr. Gelbart died in 2009 (this interview was conducted in 2004).

Q I understand seeing the original Broadway production of *Born Yesterday* with Judy Holliday made a great impact upon you.

Oh yes. It was the only play I had ever seen except for my high school production of *The Royal Family*, in which I starred. I was really a "movie" kid. When I saw *Born Yesterday*, I just marveled that someone was able to create dialogue like that, how the play talked about the role of the citizen, and the humor! All of it so informative, all of it so entertaining! I was literally inspired by Garson Kanin's work.

I remember when we were doing eight weeks of previews of *City of Angels* on Broadway, I was standing at the back of the "house." I literally lived there, and at one performance, Garson came up the aisle with his wife, Marian (Seldes). To have been able to write a theatre piece and for him to see it, the "cycle" felt complete. He stopped when he saw me. "Oh God," I thought, "what is he going to say?" "I just have one suggestion," he said. I held my breath. "Don't change a word." Well, you can imagine how I felt!

Q You were a writer for radio's *Duffy's Tavern*, for Bob Hope, Red Buttons, and Art Carney. On *Caesar's Hour*, you wrote alongside Neil Simon, Carl Reiner, and Mel Brooks. What did you learn about "taste" in comedy?

I think something must have "stuck to my shoe." You don't really learn "taste"; it's got to be one of your sensibilities. I did learn a

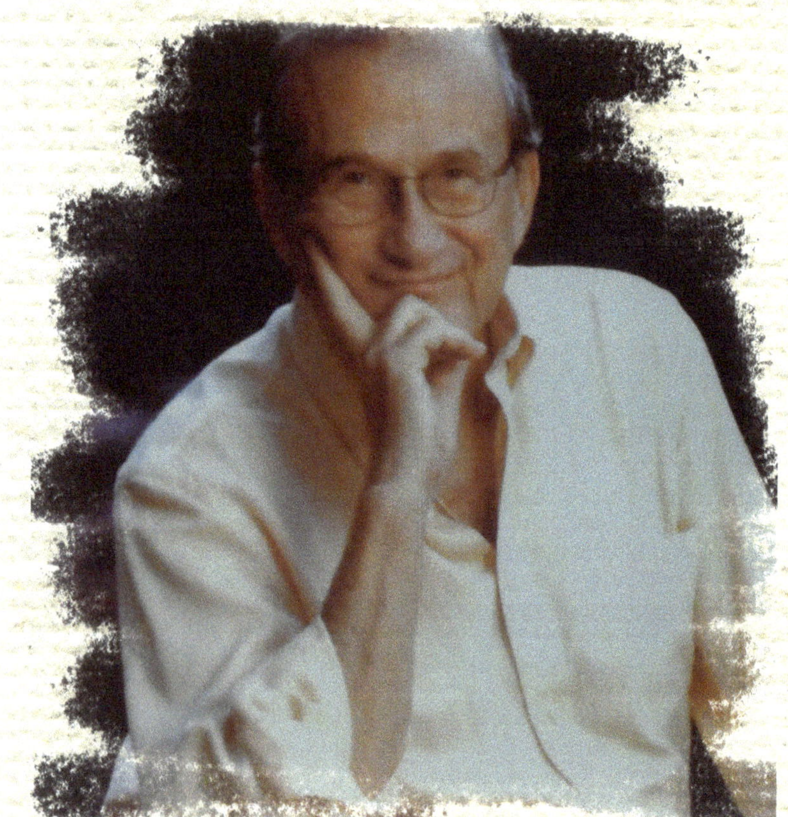

Larry Gelbart photo: courtesy of the artist

lot from Red (Buttons), because when I worked with him in *52 A.D.*, my only experience, up to that point, had been writing for radio. When I speak about writing for the people like Danny (Thomas) and Bob (Hope), it sounds like "passengers on a ghost ship."

Writing for TV was like writing for people on radio, only wearing "funny hats." I really didn't know what a constructed sketch was like. Red (Skelton) had been schooled in burlesque, performing sketches that told a story, all with a sense of structure, not just a series of jokes. It was very much like going to a "sketch school" for me.

Q When you were eighteen years old, you were drafted into the army, served for over a year, then you were part of Bob Hope's "team" writing jokes for his show, touring the country and the world, including Korea in 1951. Being at the "frontlines," you must have seen how humor can play a role in the face of the possibility of losing one's life.

I did see that in person, yes. I saw countless young men taking a break from the war, having their spirits lifted before returning to what was, for some of them, the end of their lives. There's that old saying: "Chance or luck favors the prepared." I didn't say to myself at that time when I was at the front, I wish I'll have the opportunity to work on something that can utilize the "humor" people need in times of war, but then *M*A*S*H* came along, and turned out to be all of the above.

Q Plato wrote: "The mask which an actor wears is apt to become his face." We see how your characters wear certain masks at times to get what they need, from *Tootsie* to *Sly Fox*.

I worked with Plato—both of them. The guy back then, and the stuff my grandchildren and I make funny shapes out of.

Kenneth Tynan had a wonderful description about acting. He said something like: all great acting roles require actors to pretend to be someone they're not.

With *Tootsie*, and with every role an actor does, it's a "double pretense." The actor is pretending to be someone other than himself just as the character he portrays is likewise pretending to be someone else. The same sort of thing happens with the writer, who, as he writes, is pretending to be the actor, who is pretending to be the character. It's "puppetry" in a way. Only the actor is not the writer's dummy. The actor is his partner in pretense.

In an early draft of *Tootsie*, I wrote a speech that didn't make it to the final screenplay, in which a youngster, waiting at a stage door asks the anonymous-looking Michael Dorsey, "Are you anybody?" Michael, unrecognizable, not wearing the drag which brought him a measure of fame, gives the following answer: "Am I anybody? Me? Are you kidding? I've been a Prince of Denmark! I've been Cyrano! I've been Willie Loman! I've been Romeo. Hell, I've been Juliet, too! Am I anybody! I'm everybody! I'm an actor, man!"

As writers, we "hear" our characters, write the dialogue, then it has to be read aloud again, this time by actors. It's got to be transmitted, and hopefully the audience will receive what we originally heard. I often regret there isn't a writing system for the written word that matches what the composer has, to accent a note, to indicate with italics what it is we exactly want.

When I write, I'm hearing it a specific way, and when I'm reading what I wrote, I'm also hearing it a specific way. Now, I have had actors, to name just a few, like Alan Alda and George C. Scott, with whom I shared the same "ear." They were astonishing. They didn't need a single stage direction. They got it!

Q What gives you the greatest joy in writing for the theater?

The theater offers me the only refuge, a very unique kind of environment, where an audience comes to enjoy what's in front of them, and are never less than honest. I learn so much from them. They're daring us to say something that's never been said before, that doesn't exist anywhere else.

With a movie, you can't sweeten or change a movie depending upon their reaction; same thing goes for television. But the people in the theatre—it's you and them.

I saw *Sly Fox* in New York, and I was standing in the back. I hear this "Rrrrrr, rrrrrr" and I think: "Oh no, someone must be having a heart-attack or something." But out of the corner of my eye, I spot this seeing-eye dog. One of the patrons was there with her dog. So that's what it's about—the communal experience. It's the sense of community. Make that humanity. ■

JOHN GUARE A leading American playwright, his plays on Broadway include *The House of Blue Leaves*, for which he received the New York Drama Critics' Circle Award and an Obie award, and subsequently received four Tony Awards for its 1986 revival at Lincoln Center Theater, and then was revived on Broadway in 2011 with Ben Stiller; *Six Degrees of Separation* starring Stockard Channing at Lincoln Center Theatre, revival on Broadway in 2017 starring Allison Janney; *Landscape of the Body*; *Bosoms and Neglect*; and *Four Baboons Adoring the Sun*, for which he received a Tony nomination. His other plays include *Muzeeka*, for which he received an Obie Award; *Lydie Breeze*; *Lake Hollywood*; *A Few Stout Individuals*; *Three Kinds of Exile*; and *A Free Man of Color*, directed by George C. Wolfe, with Jeffrey Wright and Mos Def, chosen as a 2011 Pulitzer Prize drama finalist. Mr. Guare wrote the libretto with Mel Shapiro for the musical, *Two Gentleman of Verona*, performed at the New York Shakespeare Festival in the Park, for which they received a Drama Desk Award. He wrote the book for the musical, *Sweet Smell of Success* on Broadway starring John Lithgow and Brian d'Arcy James, for which he received a Tony Award nomination. Mr. Guare's film screenplays include Louis Malle's *Atlantic City*, starring Burt Lancaster and Susan Sarandon, for which he received an Academy Award nomination; and *Six Degrees of Separation*, starring Stockard Channing and Will Smith. He is co-executive editor of the *Lincoln Center Theater Review*, which he founded in 1987; co-produces the New Plays Reading Room Series at the Lincoln Center Library for the Performing Arts; and teaches in the Playwriting department at the Yale School of 1986. Mr. Guare received the New York State Governor's Arts Award, Dramatists Guild Lifetime Achievement Award, was honored at the William Inge Festival, and was elected to the Theater Hall of Fame.

Q When one sees or reads your plays, one is immediately thrust into a very unique world of characters groping with the unexpected in life—very much like the artists' lives. How have you learned to cope with the different directions life has taken you?
You have to accept life; in a way, you have to be like a secret service agent. It's all coming at you so fast and you have to accept that it's going to happen, knowing that the ground is never secure and you do everything you can within your power to keep up.

Q What did it mean to you when The Signature Theatre Company chose you as their Playwright-in-Season?
It was sort of like coming out of a Oliver Sachs novel, that kind of consciousness. It was a re-experiencing of that period, and it made me glad I got through that time. It was very rewarding, just a great experience of rediscovery.

Q What's been your most satisfying experience in the theater?
The next one!

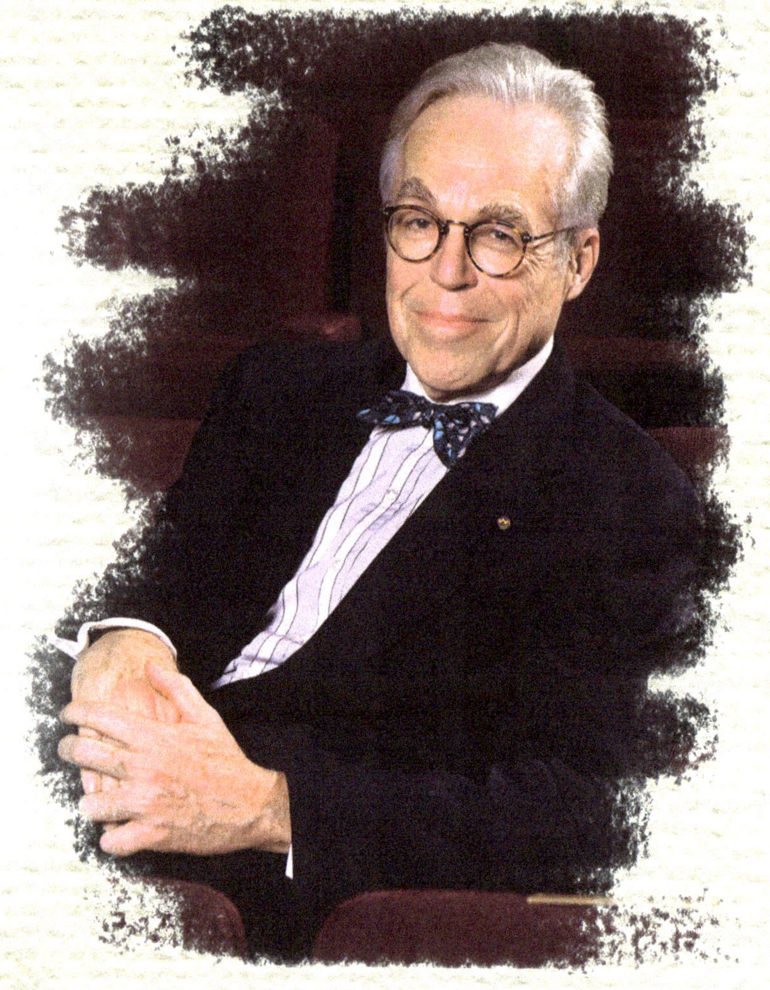

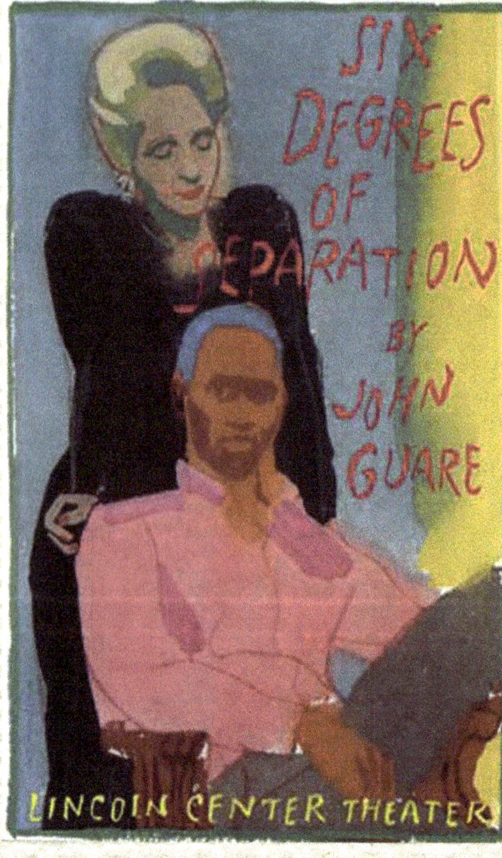

Q What makes it necessary to experience new plays in the theater today?
It's all the more necessary. It's the only place where you're told the truth, that's why we go to the theater—to be shown what it's like to be alive. A lot of these plays we see—like *Angels in America*, or plays by Shepard or Mamet—this is what "marks our time."

Q Was it challenging taking your play, *Six Degrees of Separation* to the screen?
I trusted the director, Fred Schepisi, and we just listened to the play. There were certain secrets that I'd share with the different actors, certain things I'd tell Stockard Channing. It was a wonderful experience.

Q A lot of what you write speaks of a deep-seated need we have of making contact. Does the theater make us a more humane people?
Absolutely, theater's been doing that for twenty-five hundred years. It's a communal effort. We come and share an experience—a talking-theatrical event takes place between the actors and the audience; it's what it's always been. Broadway is a marketplace, and it's extremely rare that a serious play makes it there, but you can have both escapist entertainment and serious challenging theater. The Theater is a place of celebration! ■

John Guare photo: Paul Kolnik artwork: "Six Degrees of Separation" poster © James McMullan, courtesy of Mr. McMullan

TINA HOWE

A two-time finalist for the Pulitzer prize, Ms. Howe's most produced plays include *Birth and After Birth, Museum, The Art of Dining, Painting Churches, Coastal Disturbances, Approaching Zanzibar*, and *Pride's Crossing*. Her other plays include *One Show Off, East of the Sun and West of the Moon, Rembrandt's Gift, Cheri*, and *Chasing Manet*. Ms. Howe's works have premiered at New York City's Public Theater, Kennedy Center, Second Stage, Old Globe Theatre, Lincoln Center Theater, Actors Theatre of Louisville, Atlantic Theater Company, Primary Stages and translated and produced abroad. Her works can be read in numerous anthologies including in *Coastal Disturbances: Four Plays by Tina Howe*, and *Birth and After Birth and Other Plays: A Marriage Cycle*. Ms. Howe's other publications include her translations of Ionesco's *The Bald Soprano* and *The Lesson*, and *Shrinking Violets and Towering Tiger Liles: Seven Brief Plays about Women in Distress*. She is the subject of *Howe in an Hour*, edited by Judith Barlow. Ms. Howe's many awards include an Obie award, a Tony Award nomination, an Outer Circle Critics Award, an Obie award, Sidney Kingsley Award, New York Drama Critics' Circle Award, William Inge Award, and PEN's Master American Playwright award. Ms. Howe has taught at NYU, Columbia University, and UCLA, and is a Visiting Professor at Hunter College. She created the Rita and Burton Goldberg MFA in Playwriting. Ms. Howe is proud to have served on the council of the Dramatists Guild since 1990.

Q Your father was an editor, historian, and news commentator. Your mother was a painter. Do you consider yourself essentially a product of your family?
Very much so. Growing up, most of the conversations around the dinner table were about literature, who was reading or writing what. When I was recovering from hepatitis after my year abroad, my father visited me every day in the hospital. And what did he choose to read aloud to me—James Joyce's *Ulysses*. He also took me to hear e.e. cummings, as well as hilarious vaudeville acts at the Palace Theatre.

Q Have you ever acted in a play?
I took an acting class at Sarah Lawrence, but it was a total disaster. My finest hour on a stage was inserting myself into a student production of *The Bald Soprano* at Hunter College years ago. I've always longed to be folded into that insane household. So through a series of coincidences I was able to play the maid for a few performances. It was terrifying, but a valuable wake-up call about what actors go through on stage. It was also an enormous help in terms of writing the translations I did years later.

Q You had the unique experience your senior year at Sarah Lawrence College having fellow student and actress, Jane Alexander, direct your first play, and also act in it.
It was the spring of 1959, and student work had never been produced before. Since Jane was the leading lady on campus, when she approached the theatre department about doing the play, they blindly said, "Of course, anything you want!" It was a one-act "end-of-the-world" play called *Closing Time*, mimicking Beckett whom I had never read, so you can imagine how dreadful it was—complete with actresses dressed as pigeons, chattering nonsense perched on top of rickety ladders. The leading lady got sick at the last minute, so Jane went on in her place, assuring the play's success. When the audience yelled, "Author, Author!" at the end, I ran on stage blowing kisses, until I was finally hauled off with a hook. That's how it all began.

Q How did your rich connection to Ionesco's work come about?
Shortly after graduation, my father presented me with an insane choice: "You can either go to Europe for a year, or graduate school. Which will it be?" Three months after our theatrical triumph, Jane and I set sail for Europe. She to study mathematics at Edinburgh, me to study philosophy at the Sorbonne. Within two weeks, she was acting in the Edinburgh Fringe; I was writing my first full-length play.

It was seeing Ionesco's *The Bald Soprano* at the tiny Théâtre de la Hachette that changed my life. It like a thunder bolt ripping into my head. I marveled: "So *this* is what you can do in the theatre!" Even sweeter, his play, *Rhinoceros*, opened with Genet's *The Blacks*.

I finally got to meet Ionesco in 1986 when I introduced him at the 92nd Street Y in New York City. He did a wonderful reading of his novelization of *Rhinoceros*. Being given a grant to do new translations of *The Bald Soprano* and *The Lesson* was the biggest thrill of my life. The challenge of trying to render his work into English was to capture his antic, yet desperate tone, a much crunchier French, chock full of caramels, peanuts, and exploding cigars. I was actually working on the translations during the attack on the World Trade Center. There was something comforting about being held in Ionesco's antic embrace.

Q What led you to create your play, *Rembrandt's Gift*?
The Actors Theatre of Louisville commissioned me to write a ten-minute play for their 24th annual Humana Festival. Eager to check out this legendary breeding ground for new American plays, I immediately said "yes," contributing my two-hander, *The Divine Fallacy*. When they offered me a commission to write a full-length play, I was thrilled. Louisville was clearly the place for visionaries like Charles Mee, Anne Bogart, and Sarah Ruhl.

Q Is *Rembrandt's Gift* a very personal play?
It's about the artist's struggle to keep heart and create in his old age, specifically to help a couple in their late 60s, who've been married forever and are being threatened with eviction by their

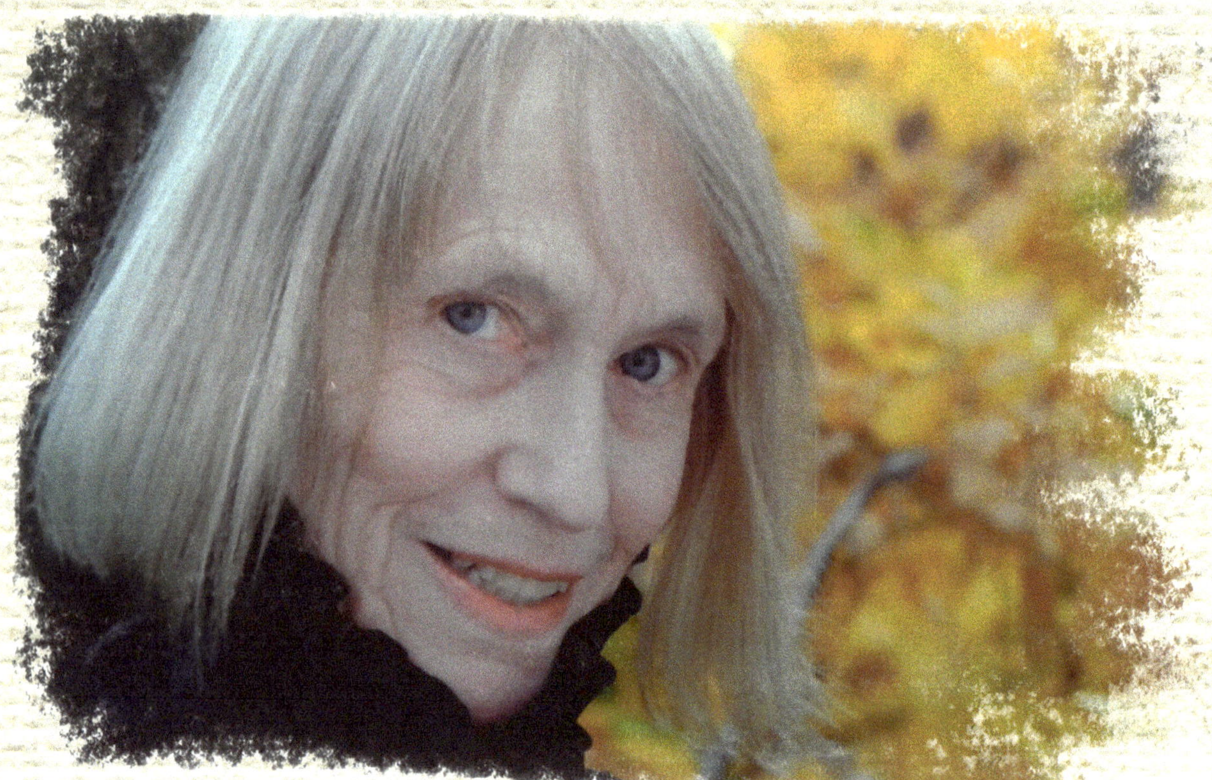

Tina Howe photo: courtesy of the artist

landlord. Just as they're about to lose hope, Rembrandt Van Rijn shows up and spends the day with them. Everything changes. The play is about an artist's need to transcend.

My plays are all personal, essentially showing me at different stages of my life, trying to keep going. I felt it was high time to write a piece about an older couple who try to maintain their dignity as the walls close in around them. The reason I chose Rembrandt as the catalyst was that like the couple he visits, he was bankrupt at the end of his life, all his worldly goods having been seized and sold at auction. He survived on bread, cheese and scraps of pickled fish.

As a dramatist, I wanted to explore how he might feel if he discovered the enormous fame that came after him. The play is a fable that explores the panic and exhilaration of the creative process.

Q How would you describe the current state of the American Theater?

What producers seems to love are stars; they're bewitched by them. Serious theater is something else. Exploring new ideas can get dicey. My first play closed in a night. The subject and tone were just too shocking. As to my second play, no one would touch it for twenty-three years, so it became clear that if I wanted a career in this fickle world I'd have to change. When treated as a money-making proposition, theater is by nature conservative. There's much more room to experiment in dance, the visual arts, or music.

Our son is a musician. He plays guitar with Obie award-winning Ethan Lipton and his orchestra. His work is ten times nervier than mine. I'm always amazed when young people want to study playwriting.

Q When you teach playwriting, what kinds of things do you learn from your students?

Over the years I've been finding them writing shorter and shorter scenes. Since I never took a playwriting class, I've never known what the rules were. I've always worked on instinct. As a teacher, I've always seen my role as being like a mirror. My duty is to stand in front of my students and show them their reflection, as if to say, "This is what I see ... this is what you've done." That way, they're responsible for their art, not me. But it can be excruciating; I'm much more relaxed when I'm by myself, doing my own work. But I do love my students. If only I didn't have to stand up in front of them, trying to sound wise.

Q Has art helped us become a more humane people?

I'm no sociologist, but I do feel we're more aware, which doesn't necessarily mean we're more humane. Self-preservation will always be a basic instinct. We're still animals, after all. But there will always be that small percentage of guardians that transcend their own interests—artists, teachers, healers, and good Samaritans who reach out to comfort us. ■

DAVID HENRY HWANG

Best known for his play, *M Butterfly*, which won a Tony Award, Drama Desk Award, John Gassner Award, and Outer Critics Circle Award, he was also a finalist for the Pulitzer Prize. Mr. Hwang's plays include *Golden Child* on Broadway, which received three Tony nominations, and an Obie Award; *Yellow Face*, which premiered at Los Angeles' Mark Taper Forum and New York's Public Theater, received the Obie Award, and was a finalist for the Pulitzer Prize; *Chinglish* on Broadway and Chicago's Goodman Theatre, which received a Jefferson Award;*FOB*, which received an Obie award; *The Dance and the Railroad*, which received a Drama Desk nomination; *Family Devotions*, which received a Drama Desk nomination; and *Kung Fu*. Mr. Hwang's operas include four works with composer Philip Glass, including *1000 Airplanes on the Roof*, he wrote the libretto for *An American Soldier* with music by Huang Ruo, and *The Silver River* and *Dream of the Red Chamber* with scores by Bright Sheng. His operas have been performed at the Metropolitan Opera, Santa Fe Opera, Bavarian State Opera, Lincoln Center, Spoleto Festival USA, and around the world. Mr. Hwang's Broadway musicals include a new book for Rodgers & Hammerstein's *Flower Drum Song* for which he received a Tony Award nomination, and Disney's *Tarzan*' and he co-wrote *Aida*, with music and lyrics by Elton John and Tim Rice, which received four Tony Awards; and *The Forgotten Arm* with Aimee Mann and Paul Bryant. Mr. Hwang's film and television work includes *M. Butterfly* directed by David Cronenberg, *The Lost Empire*, co-authored *Possession* starring Gwyneth Paltrow, and *Chinglish* directed by Justin Lin. Mr. Hwang is the writer-producer for *The Affair*, and *Shanghai*. Mr. Hwang received the William Inge Award, Asia Society Cultural Achievement Award, the PEN/Laura Pels Award for a Master American Dramatist, and Steinberg Award. He is a Resident Playwright at the New York City's Signature Theatre, and the Director of Columbia University's School of the Arts' M.F.A. program in playwriting.

Q Who have been some of your inspirations as an artist?

At the beginning Sam Shepard was a big hero. I took a playwriting workshop with him twice. Besides him, Shaw, Stoppard, Brecht, they were playwrights of ideas. You can see the Brechtian influence in *M Butterfly*. As I've gotten older, I've become more interested in playwrights of things I can't do, like Chekhov and Friel, on intimate details of closely human behavior. I was very moved by the adaptation of *The Joy Luck Club* I saw at the Pan Asian Repertory. That's a perfect example of inspiring theater.

Q How did you begin creating *Golden Child*?

The source material for *Golden Child* began when I was ten. My grandmother remembered our family history when I visited her during a summer in the Philippines. It became an oral history for me. I compiled it into a ninety-page review and didn't think about it for decades and then I returned to it.

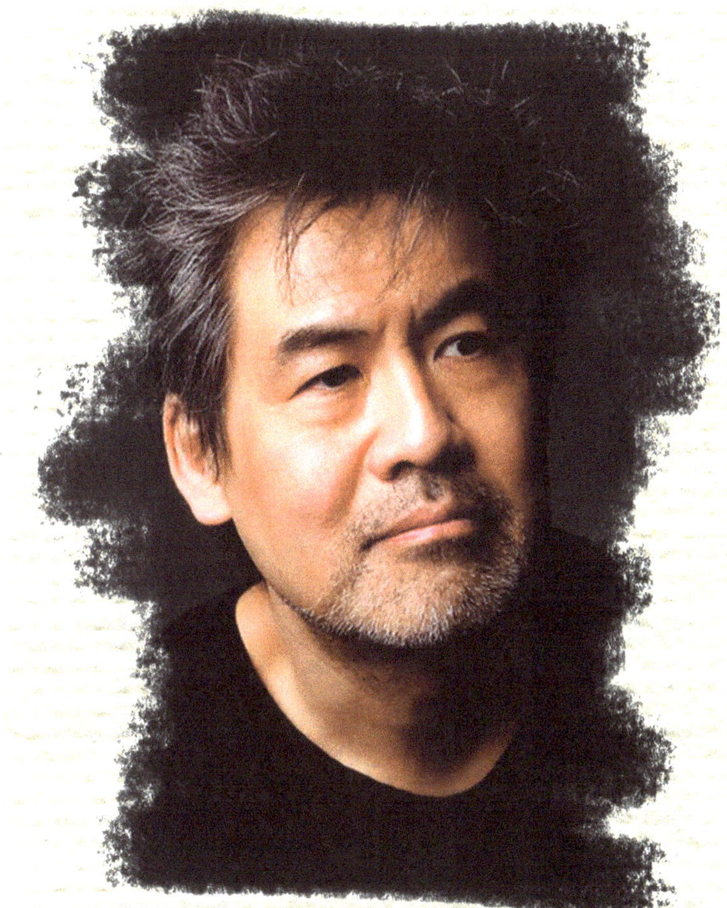

David Henry Hwang photo: Gregory Costanzo

Q You also rewrote the book of Rodgers & Hammerstein's *Flower Drum Song*. Why do you feel this story is pertinent for us today?

Flower Drum Song has always had a complicated place for my generation of Asian-Americans. We grew up thinking it was stereotypical, but it meant a lot to our parents. It was the first time we saw Asian-Americans singing and dancing on a Broadway stage. The characters are quite complicated—the love story between an Asian-American man and an Asian-American woman. And what a wonderful score.

I felt if I could make it more personal, this was my goal, then it would become a really new musical, to write the book as if Richard

Rodgers was Asian-American. I feel as if I've been given the keys to go someplace very special.

Q You've also written the libretto for four works with Philip Glass, the libretto for *An American Soldier* with music by Huang Ruo, *Dream of the Red Chamber and The Silver River* with music by Bright Sheng. What drew you to create within the operatic art form?

I guess I come from a musical background; I was a violinist in high school. Theater is metaphysical, there's such a suspension of belief. What I like about opera is the audience. Today, opera and musical theatre are the two largest theatre forms in the western world, and Philip is great, just incredibly easy to work with. Seeing shows about Asian-American families and themes are a rarity on Broadway.

Q What are some of the biggest challenges for theater to reflect the diverse face of our society?

A great deal has been done for theater in America to reflect the varied world. I still feel in nonprofit theater there's a great lack of diversity in administrative positions. Of course, we want to create universal works if we're striving to make a theater that reflects America. In terms of Broadway, it's hard to get any new American play on Broadway. I've had some of my work done there. What becomes a problem is that straight plays on Broadway are so star-driven.

Q One of the strongest currents I feel running through your plays is how the human spirit cannot be constrained by traditions of culture. Human nature will find a way. Is that what ultimately links us with those who have come before us?

There is a tension that continues to exist between individual wants and desires and societal dictates. While it is true the character represents the human spirit, we want to transcend the position we're born into. The characters in my plays find or commit themselves to their positions.

There's certainly something that links us with those who've come before us. We have the desire to change, and we achieve it with a certain ambivalence, and at a cost. ■

ODILE GAKIRE KATESE

Associate Director of the University Centre for Arts and Drama at the National University of Rwanda. Ms. Katese is a playwright, novelist, screenwriter, poet, drummer, and actress. Born in Rwanda, she fled with her family to the Congo during the genocide. She and her siblings were raised "in exile." Educated in the Congo, she was not taught the language of the country of her birth, and for a time did not even know she was Rwandan. Ms. Katese came to love her country, embraced her heritage, and undertook the job of building hope and happiness through art. Ms. Katese participated as the 2008 "Playwright in Residence" at Sundance Institute East Africa and as a director with *The Book of Life* at the 2010 East Africa Theatre Lab. Her play, *Nwgino Ubeho—Come and Be Alive*, was also featured at the 2009 Theatre Lab. She received the Gilder/Coigney International Theatre Award.

Q How did you begin to learn about your country and share yourself through art when you found out that you were born in Rwanda?

I was born in exile. When I was eighteen, someone on the road said to me, "What are you doing in Zaire when people are killing each other in your country?" I asked him, "My country? Which country?" and he said, "Rwanda." This is when I came to hear about the genocide in Rwanda. I was twenty when my family and I went back to Rwanda. My parents were longing to go *home*, and it was finally possible.

I didn't know a lot of things about Rwanda beside the melancholic music that my parents used to listen to. My biggest regret is that I didn't know my mother tongue. I can't write in Kinyarwanda. I write in French, and my work is translated into Kinyarwanda.

When I went back to Rwanda, for a long time I considered myself a "zairoise" (from Zaire), which I think I am to a certain extent. Therefore, I needed to own the history of Rwanda and the terrible legacy of the genocide. This process was only possible through artistic work.

It is through the University Centre for Arts and Drama of the National University of Rwanda that I started to offer images, symbols, and emotions to reason and to the heart, to confront the violence of the genocide by increasing poetical representation and intervention.

Q What led you to write your play, *Ngwino Ubeho*, and how was it first received?

Since 2004, I've have worked on the commemoration of the genocide every five years. For the tenth commemoration of the genocide, I co-wrote the play *Iryo Nabonye* (*What I Saw*), which toured for the next three years to villages, schools and universities, and prisons.

Ngwino Ubeho is a play in loving memory of the dead that mixes dance, music, and poetry. It tries to reconcile Rwandans with themselves, with happiness, with their history, with death, with the present and the future. It's an attempt to propose an appeased memory. It involved fifteen Rwandan artists and an international artistic team from Togo, France, Burkina Faso, and the U.S., and performances were performed in Rwanda and in France, at the Festival Arts

Azimuts.

People in Butare and in Nantes were touched by our approach to the theme of the genocide. The quest of an appeased memory led us to find delicate choreographies, songs, and words to soothe the pain and despair related to genocide and its legacy.

Q You were part of the Sundance Institute in East Africa as a "Playwright in Residence." How did it feed you as a writer, actress, and director?
Sundance East Africa started in Utah and went to Manda in 2010 and 2011. Utah is a place of unique beauty. The Theatre Lab was a life-changing experience—a unique chance to look at my work with a new and different eye!

Working with American directors such as Rebecca Taichman and Mame Hunt was a great honor. Meeting Jennie Dundas, an American actress and Co-Proprietress with Alexis Miesen of Blue Marble Ice Cream in Brooklyn prompted a very sweet journey: the launching in 2010 of Inzozi Nziza "Sweet Dreams," Rwanda's first local ice cream shop with the women drummers of Ingoma Nshya.

The work of American artists I met in Utah in 2008 and 2009 fed my imagination and my life. Roberta Levitow, Philip Himberg, Chistopher Hibma and Deborah Asiimwe make me stronger, hopeful and audacious in my work. They contributed to strengthening the faith I have in life.

Q Why is making art vital for the culture of Rwanda?
I agree with the Prince Claus Fund of the Netherlands, one of the main partners in my work, that "culture is a basic need." I also like the words of Pablo Picasso: "Art washes from the soul the dust of everyday life." For a country like Rwanda, a post-conflict society whose social tissue has been deeply destroyed, artistic tools help very much in the healing, reconciliation, and peace-building processes which require time and different approaches.

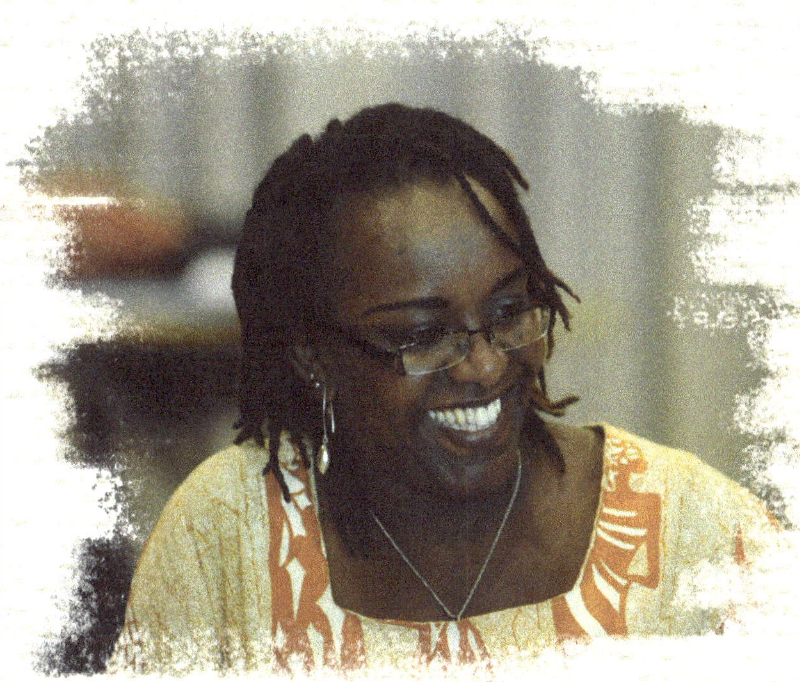

Odile Gakire Katese photo: courtesy of the artist

Q What have you learned from your students teaching at the University Centre for Arts and Drama at the National University of Rwanda?
The ingenuousness and freshness of students always amaze me. I've been learning and experiencing the possibility of pulling up life from the emptiness, from nowhere. I'm always very alert when we start a project with just an idea and an empty stage. I like to watch how a play comes to life, how a costume, a light, a sound, a laugh, a word come to help us build a story. And I use the same process in my own life.

In situations of an impasse, I know I have to be attentive and patient to pinpoint the element that will come. I feel, at times, to pretend to know what is going to work...or not—what is ready to happen or not...

Q What can we do even more to open the hearts and souls and minds of young people?
We need to increase and facilitate their access to artistic expression and experience, to be humble and honest in our work. To work hard and find the language they hear and are sensitive to. To never give up, no matter what.

Q Are you seeing a rebirth of appreciation for art and culture now?
The appreciation of arts and culture has always been there. A sound of a drum can attract hundreds of people in a second. Rwandan people are hungry for spaces of joy, freedom, and dreams. What we miss is a committed policy of culture to set up an appropriate environment for artistic and cultural activities to develop and sustain.

Q What gives you the strength each day to wake up and want to create new art?
I take my strength from the conviction that art makes miracles and transcends our lives. The lives of a hundred Rwandan women, which have changed because they have touched a drum, convince me of the necessity of bringing art into the world. And art is the only language I speak to engage in a conversation with the world. ■

ARTHUR KOPIT

Arthur Kopit is a two-time Pulitzer Prize finalist and Tony Award nominee for his plays, *Indians* and *Wings* on Broadway. His book for the musical, *Nine*, on Broadway received a Tony Award nomination in 1982 starring Raul Julia, and a revival of *Nine* on Broadway in 2003 received a Tony Award starring Antonio Banderas. In 2009, Rob Marshall directed the film, *Nine*, starring Daniel Day-Lewis, Judi Dench, Nicole Kidman, Marion Cotillard, and Penelope Cruz. Sophia Loren, Kate Hudson and Fergie. Mr. Kopit's plays include *Oh Dad, Poor Dad, Mamma's Hung You in the Closet and I'm Feelin' So Sad*; a new translation of Ibsen's *Ghosts*; *End of the World with Symposium to Follow*; the book for the musical, *Phantom*; the book for the musical, *High Society*; *Road to Nirvana*; *Because He Can*, originally entitled *Y2K*; and an original musical *Tom Swift and the Secrets of the Universe* with David Yazbek. Mr. Kopit has taught playwriting at the Rita and Burton Goldberg Graduate Department of Dramatic Writing at NYU, Yale Drama School, Yale College, Columbia University, Harvard, and Princeton. He is a member of the Dramatists Guild, the Dramatists Guild Council, and he heads The Lark Playwrights' Workshop at The Lark Play Development Center.

Q How did your becoming a playwright happen and lead to your writing *Oh Dad, Poor Dad, Mama's Hung you in the Closet and I'm Feelin' So Sad*?
It all happened at Harvard; I thought I was going to be an engineer. But within the first few days, not weeks, but days, I realized that it may not be for me. So I began to take creative writing courses because I couldn't imagine doing anything that was more fun. I thought there's got to be some kind of mistake, because I'd do it for no credit at all.

At the end of the semester, one of my professors announced that if any of us wanted to write a play during spring break, he would direct it whether he liked the play or not. Talk about opportunities! So over spring break, I wrote a short play called *The Questioning of Nick*. Up until then I had only written short stories. Somehow with the very first line, the characters took over; I was simply the person writing down what they said. It was a revelation. I thought, this is me! The next fall there was a playwriting contest, I submitted the play and it won! It was produced in a major way, wonderfully received, and very successful—I mean, for a one-act play.

What I loved most was the feeling I got from seeing it done, and, just as important, experiencing the audience's response. I thought, what a wonderful way to spend one's life! I was hooked. I started writing more plays. There was so much theater going on at Harvard in those days, it was not hard to get them produced. By the time I graduated I had had six plays produced and had directed five of them. It was right after I graduated that I wrote. *Oh Dad*, and I could never have written it if it hadn't been for those other plays.

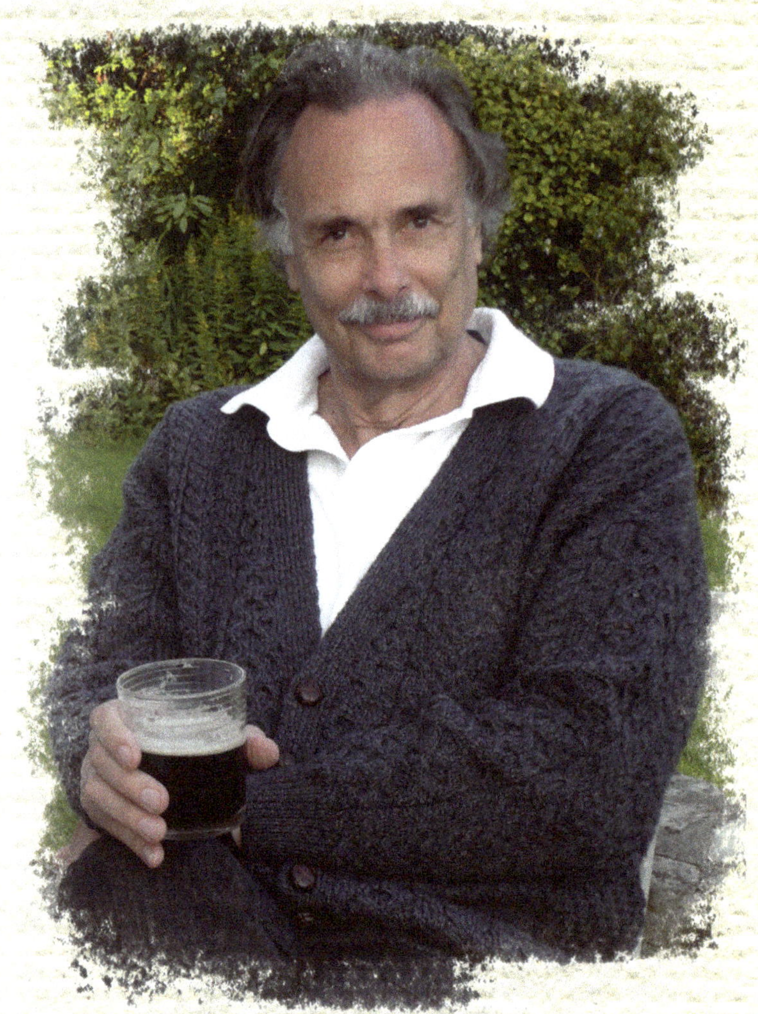

Arthur Kopit photo, courtesy of the artist

Q You received the 2006 Edward Albee Great Plains Playwright Award at the Great Plains Theatre Conference. What did it mean to you?
It was a great honor to be honored the first year of the Conference. It's always exciting to be among colleagues whose work you know and respect, as well as being among other playwrights, whose work you are seeing for the first time. It's a strange experience when playwrights get together. There's an energy that happens, and everyone feels it. In

addition, both times I've been at the Conference, I've had an opportunity to present part of a new play, and that proved very helpful.

Q You share your knowledge a great deal at workshops, universities, conferences.

The only reason I teach is to learn something. I've been fortunate to have good students. Playwriting is problem-solving. What makes it especially interesting is there is no one right answer. I know that I've been changed by great plays and great performances. Art is how we discern the truth, and when it comes to truth, every little bit counts.

Q *Nine* had a fabulous revival on Broadway with Antonio Banderas and Chita Rivera. Were you involved in the rehearsal process?

I was. The few changes I made were mostly to help with transitions. Maury (Yeston) also made some changes, mostly to help with transitions. I loved the production, the entire company, but especially Antonio (Banderas). He was remarkable. He was so much like Raul (Julia), who played Guido in the original production; both great human beings. You have to have a Guido you love in some way, and that's not something you can just "act." Antonio enabled us to love and care for Guido. It's a hard show to do well.

Q You have talked a great deal about not rushing when you write, letting each moment unfold. Are there keys you've learned in "staying in the moment?"

It's a fundamental question, and it's hard to know, because it's different from play to play. But I do know—or at least, this is true for me—that if you don't get it essentially right in the first draft, it's very possible you might not get it at all. But when you have done the proper preparation, which can take a very long time, or very little, then it's fun to write scenes. You let your characters take over. I'm fascinated by the process. Fortunately, I can sense when what's written is indulgent, and when I'm just treading water until something real happens. When you're in trouble—look to your characters for the answer—they will show you. And if they can't, then you don't know them well enough. ■

ARTHUR LAURENTS

One of the theater's most gifted librettists, a prolific stage director and screenwriter, Mr. Laurents is most well-known for writing the books for the musicals, *West Side Story*, *Gypsy*, and the screenplay for the film, *The Way We Were* starring Barbra Streisand and Robert Redford. He made his Broadway debut with *Home of the Brave*. His films included the scripts for Alfred Hitchcock's *Rope* starring James Stewart, *Anastasia* starring Ingrid Bergman, *Anna Lucasta* with Philip Yordan, *Summertime* starring Katharine Hepburn, *West Side Story* with Natalie Wood and Richard Beymer, which received ten Academy Awards, *Bonjour Tristesse* with Jean Seberg and Deborah Kerr, *Gypsy* written with Leonard Spigelgass, starring Rosalind Russell and Natalie Wood, and the Academy Award-nominated *The Turning Point* starring Shirley MacLaine and Anne Bancroft. Mr. Laurents' plays on Broadway included *The Bird Cage* with Melvyn Douglas and Maureen Stapleton, *Hallelujah, Baby!* with Leslie Uggams, which received a Tony Award, *The Time of the Cuckoo* starring Shirley Booth, and *A Clearing in the Woods* starring Kim Stanley, and *Anyone Can Whistle* written with Stephen Sondheim. On Broadway, Mr. Laurents directed *Invitation to a March*, and wrote and directed the musical, *I Can Get It for You Wholesale*, with Barbara Streisand. Mr. Laurents transformed his play *The Time of the Cuckoo* into a musical, *Do I Hear a Waltz?* set to Mr. Sondheim's lyrics and composer Richard Rodgers' music. Mr. Laurents directed and co-wrote Phyllis Newman's one-woman show, *The Madwoman of Central Park West*. He directed the Broadway musical version of *La Cage aux Folles*, winning six Tonys, a revival of *Gypsy* starring Tyne Daly. He wrote and directed the musical, *Nick and Nora*, and directed a revival of *West Side Story* in 2008 and 2009. Continuing to work well into his nineties, Laurents wrote the drama, *Come Back, Come Back, Wherever You Are*, which premiered in 2009. His memoir, *Original Story by Arthur Laurents: A Memoir of Broadway and Hollywood*, was published in 2000. Mr. Laurents died in 2011. Among his many honors, Mr. Laurents received the Sidney Howard Award, the American Academy of Arts and Letters Award, and was inducted into the Theater Hall of Fame. Mr. Laurents died in 2011 (this interview was conducted in 2001).

Q Did you always have faith in your ability to tell stories?

From the age of ten I wanted to write. A very big influential comment came early on when I was writing radio scripts. One of the editors told me I was really talented but I was too facile in words. I was using them for the transitions, and not letting the emotion happen.

Q And now, after writing as many plays as you have, has it gotten any easier?

I'm still astounded when I start a play; I still make mistakes. The way I'm writing plays today is totally different from when I began. I believe you have to learn the rules before you can break them. I'm very good at structure. I use to make outlines; I was very methodical. But this last play I started with a picture in my mind. I wrote a scene, and I never knew where exactly it would end.

Q Was that exciting for you?

It was exciting to write this play. I showed it to my friend, Stephen Sondheim, and he told me it looked like it had been spewed out. I think you need experience to be able to do that. Consciously, subconsciously, the rules are there; it's a matter of being open to them.

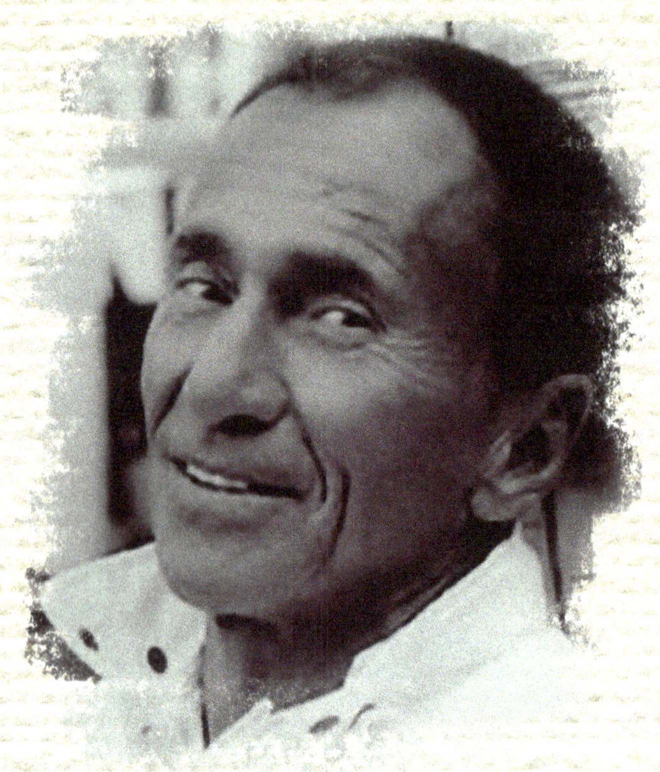

Q Especially when you're making cuts to the play you're working on.
Right, today a lot of writers don't rewrite or cut and it shows. A lot of plays are based more on a notion, not an idea. They're based on a situation, with no arc. That's why they don't end up with good second acts. Words sound like they come too easily, they're too glib, and the stage directions cover up the telling, like the writer's writing for the camera.

Q Do you trust other people's opinions about your work?
Everything I write I show to my friend, Tom Hatcher. He's very good, I trust his taste. He'll tell me what he thinks and he doesn't try to have me alter to his viewpoint. He helps me to achieve what I had set out to do.

Q How have you learned to deal with the challenge of finding the right collaborators for your work?
I don't think the challenge has ever changed. It's always been a problem. We have very few producers today. The producer used to be an objective eye; there are almost none today. On my last few plays, I've had a very good relationship with my director, David Saint.

Q How did you view the recent revival of your play, *Home of the Brave*?
Actually, very objectively. I really don't believe in going back, looking at my past work. I don't run to see them when they're done again. But when I saw *Home of the Brave*, I was startled. "How did I know that at that age? How did I have that depth in the writing?"

Q What drew you to write your newest play, *Claudia Lazlo*?
I had always been haunted by what happened to the opera star, Elizabeth Schwarzkoff. She was a great opera singer, and she was a Nazi. What struck me was the question: How much bad behavior do we allow artists? I believe everybody's an actor; we're constantly creating ourselves. I wrote this as a play within a play.

Q What makes the theater necessary for our culture today?
The theate is the only place where you're really moved by something that's alive in every sense of the word. That's what makes it so thrilling. You don't know what's going to happen. TV, film—they can't take the time to examine life in the same way.

Q How do you feel about your work being revived? Would you like to go back and change something, for example, in *West Side Story*?
Well, I don't think it's perfect the way it is, and if *West Side Story* was done again, I don't believe it should be thought of as a revival. It should be thought of as a new production—in much the same way we think when we do *The Cherry Orchard*. The whole style could be changed.

Q But wouldn't that change your vision?
Having a vision is connected to values that you acquire as a child. I'm glad they come out through one's writing, and they'll still come out even if the style's changed, because of the writing. When I think about it, I believe I have never written anything that didn't have hope, because I'm innately optimistic. I just look for joy in people. I think about Beckett, I would have liked to have asked him, "If you thought life was so terrible, why did you want to write so much?" ■

Arthur Laurents photo: courtesy of the artist

BUDD SCHULBERG

Gifted author, screenwriter, and producer, his novels included *What Makes Sammy Run, The Harder They Fall, The Disenchanted,* which he adapted into a Broadway play starring Jason Robards, *Sanctuary V, Loser and Champion: Muhammad Ali, The Four Seasons of Success,* and *Some Faces in The Crowd.* Mr. Schulberg's celebrated screenplays include *On the Waterfront,* starring Marlon Brando, Rod Steiger, Karl Malden, Lee J. Cobb and Eva Marie Saint,which received the Academy Award; *Wind Across the Everglades,* written with his brother, Stuart, and directed by Nicholas Ray; *A Face in the Crowd* starring Andy Griffith and Patricia Neal; *Government Girl;* and *Winter Carnival,* written with F. Scott Fitzgerald. In the wake of the Los Angeles riots in the mid-1960s, he helped create the Watts Writers Workshop. He co-founded in 1971 the Frederick Douglass Creative Arts Center in New York City. Mr. Schulberg is the only non-boxer honored as a Living Legend of Boxing by the World Boxing Association. He published a collection of his boxing pieces, *Sparring with Hemingway,* and a second collection, *The Hardest Games.* In 1982, Mr. Schulberg wrote his autobiography, *Moving Pictures, Memoirs of a Hollywood Prince,* weaving his personal story of his youth in Hollywood growing up in the 1920s-1930s as the son of B.P. Schulberg, head of Paramount Studios. Mr. Schulberg died in 2009 (this interview was conducted in 2005).

Q It sounds like a very busy time for you—

I've been writing pretty intensely. I'm putting out a book which combines Malcolm Johnson's original series about the "Waterfront," and my pieces I wrote about the waterfront as part of my research for *On the Waterfront.* I'm also advising Spike Lee on a film based on the Joe Louis-Max Schmeling fights.

Q I understand as a young man you read Gorky and Issac Babel, that they made a deep impression on you.

That kind of writing—"on the dark side"—didn't pull any punches. It made life painfully real; I was hooked by it.

Q You have talked about the time you spent time with Thomas Heggen, the young writer who wrote the novel, *Mr. Roberts*, which was subsequently made into the film starring Henry Fonda and Jack Lemmon. That he wasn't sure how he could go on writing after having such a huge success.

That's true. He got in touch and told me he wanted to talk. I told him, "Come out and see me." I had never met him before.

When he arrived, we talked and he told me he had $11,000 a week pouring in from *Mr. Roberts,* being a bestseller, and now it was being made into a movie, and they were going to do a play of it. But he couldn't put a piece of paper into the typewriter and write. He didn't know how to go on.

He said to me, "You had a big success with *What Makes Sammy Run,* and you've written your next novel. How do you do it?" I told him, "You should get out of New York City, and with all that money, and you don't have to worry about a thing, get on a freighter, go around the world, get off at every port where they've never heard of *Mr. Roberts.* Write about 'How you recover after writing a best seller.' That would be an interesting book."

He got all excited and said, "I'll do it." About two weeks later, I go to "21" and there was Tom surrounded by beautiful women, celebrities. I could see that when our eyes met, he looked at me in a guilty way. I knew what was happening. He was sucked into all that fame. He could never do what he had done again. He was only twenty-nine years old, and then... he killed himself in a bathtub. He was so gifted, so good looking—like a young F. Scott Fitzgerald.

Q You've said you spent two years watching and listening in the bars, meeting the people who lived there, so you knew how to write the screenplay for *On the Waterfront*?

I was so full of the subject, I felt comfortable writing about them. I felt I knew these people inside and out.

Q I understand with the famous taxi scene in the film, *On the Waterfront*, between Marlon Brando and Rod Steiger, that initially Brando wanted it to be different?

What happened was just before we started shooting, Brando kept saying he didn't like the taxi scene in the script. I asked Gadge (Elia Kazan, the director of the film), what Brando thought was wrong with it. Brando kept saying he couldn't do it, that it wasn't real. Well I tried over and over again to meet with Brando, but every time when I'd come into town (it was a two-hour drive), I'd find out the meeting had been cancelled. I then found out it was being cancelled because Sam Spiegel (our producer) was afraid that I would get into a fight with Marlon, since he had been backed into doing the movie, and Sam was afraid Marlon would walk off the film.

Once we started shooting, again Brando tells Gadge that he doesn't like the taxi scene. Well, I blew up. "Godammit!" I said, "What doesn't he like about it!" I must have spoken up too loudly.

Kazan was shooting a scene; we were up on the roof. So after the shot, Gadge comes over to me, he said, "Let's go down at lunch time and the three of us will have a talk." So we do.

I say finally, "Marlon, what is it that's bothering you about the scene?"

Marlon says, "What's wrong is this: I'm saying 'I could have been a contender, I could have been somebody,' and don't you realize I'm saying all this while Steiger (who's playing his brother), has a gun pointed at me? I don't think I can say all that, I can't play it if he's pointing a gun at me."

Gadge then said, "What if you just reach out to Charley and move the gun down and go on with the scene?" Marlon said, "That'll be fine." And Brando was actually sort of right with that.

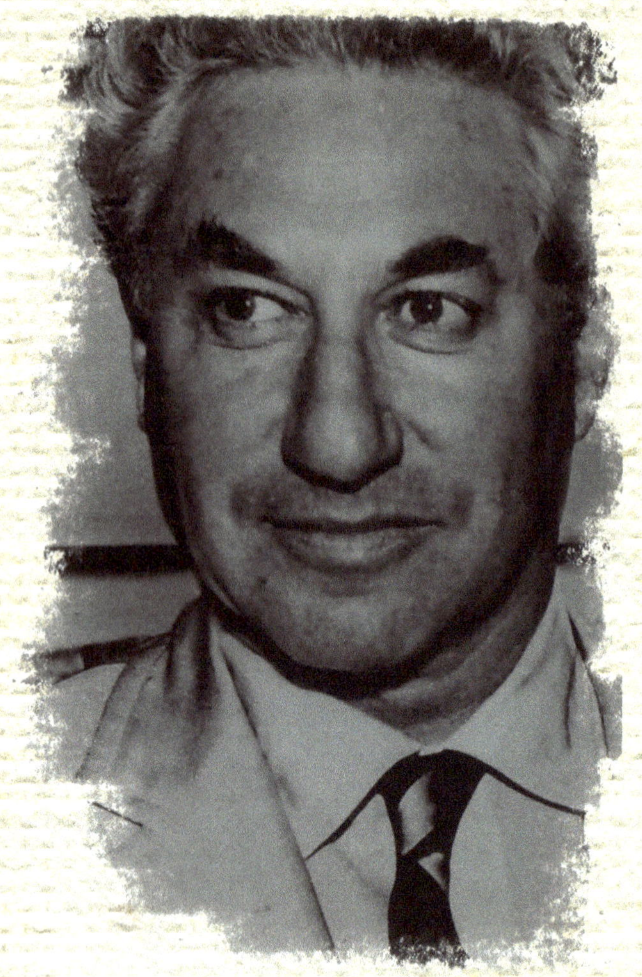

Q Did any of the dialogue change during the shooting of the scene?
Nothing changed. Even the interruption I decided to have in the script, that overlaps the dialogue. It looks like it's ad-libbed but I really wrote it. I remember at one point when Marlon and I were walking back to the hotel, he said to me, "I didn't think I could do the part."

I think he said that because the only films he had done had been *The Wild One* and *The Men*. But he was totally in character as a longshoreman. When we were walking the streets, or when we stopped and had a drink at a bar, nobody would recognize him.

Q What was it like working with Humphrey Bogart on *The Harder They Fall*?
I found Bogie kind of difficult. The way he'd learn things in the script was almost like he was attacking you. He'd say, "What the hell do you know about boxing!" That was the way he'd get information, always in a combative way. It wasn't as easy as it was with Brando.

Q It's difficult for young people of my generation today to understand what the "Blacklisting" period was like in the 1950s.
Absolutely, it's like another century; we could be talking about the 13th century. I have two children, who are now in their early twenties, and they don't know many of the names of those involved, or a lot about who they were; it's amazing how much is lost. And it's really not that long ago.

Q Which writers have made the deepest impression on you?
I think for me, the social writers influenced me the most—Jack London, Upton Sinclair, Sinclair Lewis, John Steinbeck, and James T. Ferrell.

Q Did you see some of The Group Theatre's productions in the 1930s?
Oh yes, Odets' *Waiting for Lefty* made a huge impression on me. Odets played the doctor in it, and he was very good. And so was Kazan as the cabdriver. At the end he said, "Strike! Strike! Strike!" And when the play was over, I started walking, and I kept walking. Seeing it inflamed me. At that time Odets meant a great deal to all of us. I saw a great many of his plays; I saw *Golden Boy*, and the Robert Audrey play he did.

Once in a while I do a creative workshop on writing, and I urge them to first know what their aim is, I tell them, "You have to write people who are real. But you have to entertain your public, you can't preach at them."

Writing is entertainment. Its value is bringing people to life. What you write should reflect your point of view, but at the same time, try and make it entertaining. It may sound old-fashioned but I don't believe in "art for art's sake." I believe the artist has a responsibility. He has to understand his society, and through the people he writes about, say something, but always through the storytelling. ■

Budd Schulberg photo: courtesy of the artist, Budd Schulberg in 1967

JOHN PATRICK SHANLEY

Mr. Shanley's Pulitzer Prize-winning play, *Doubt: A Parable* was first performed on Broadway directed by Doug Hughes, with Cherry Jones, Brian F. O'Byrne, Heather Goldenhersh, and Adriane Lenox, receiving a Tony Award, a Drama Desk Award, among others. The play became an award-winning film directed by Mr. Shanley, starring Meryl Streep, Philip Seymour Hoffman and Amy Adams, and receiving the Writers Guild of America Award. His films include *Moonstruck* starring Cher, Nicolas Cage, Olympia Dukakis, and Danny Aiello, which received the Academy Award and Writers Guild of America Award; *Five Corners*, which received the Barcelona Theatre Festival's Special Jury Prize; *The January Man* with Jodie Foster and Tim Robbins; *Joe Versus the Volcano*, which he directed, starring Tom Hanks; *Alive*, *Congo*, based on Michael Crichton's book, with Laura Linney; *Live from Baghdad*, which received an Emmy Award nomination, and *The Waltz of the Tulips*. Mr. Shanley wrote the libretto for an opera of *Doubt: A Parable*, with music by Douglas J. Cuomo. Mr. Shanley also wrote the songs for the films, *Marooned Without You* and *The Cowboy Song*. His play, *Outside Mullinger*, was performed on Broadway starring Debra Messing and Brian F. O'Byrne. Mr. Shanley has written more than twenty-five plays including *Pirate*, *Romantic Poetry*, *Defiance*, *Danny and the Deep Blue Sea*, *Savage in Limbo*, *the dreamer examines his pillow*, *Beggars in the House of Plenty*, *Pirate*, *Welcome to the Moon*, *Four Dogs and a Bone*, *Italian American Reconciliation*, *Missing/Kissing*, *Psychopathia Sexualis*, *Dirty Story*, *Storefront Church*, *Sailor's Song*, and *Prodigal Son*. Mr. Shanley was inducted into the Bronx Hall of Fame. *Doubt: A Parable*, is featured in *The Fourth Wall*, a book of photographs by Amy Arbus, in which he also wrote the foreword.

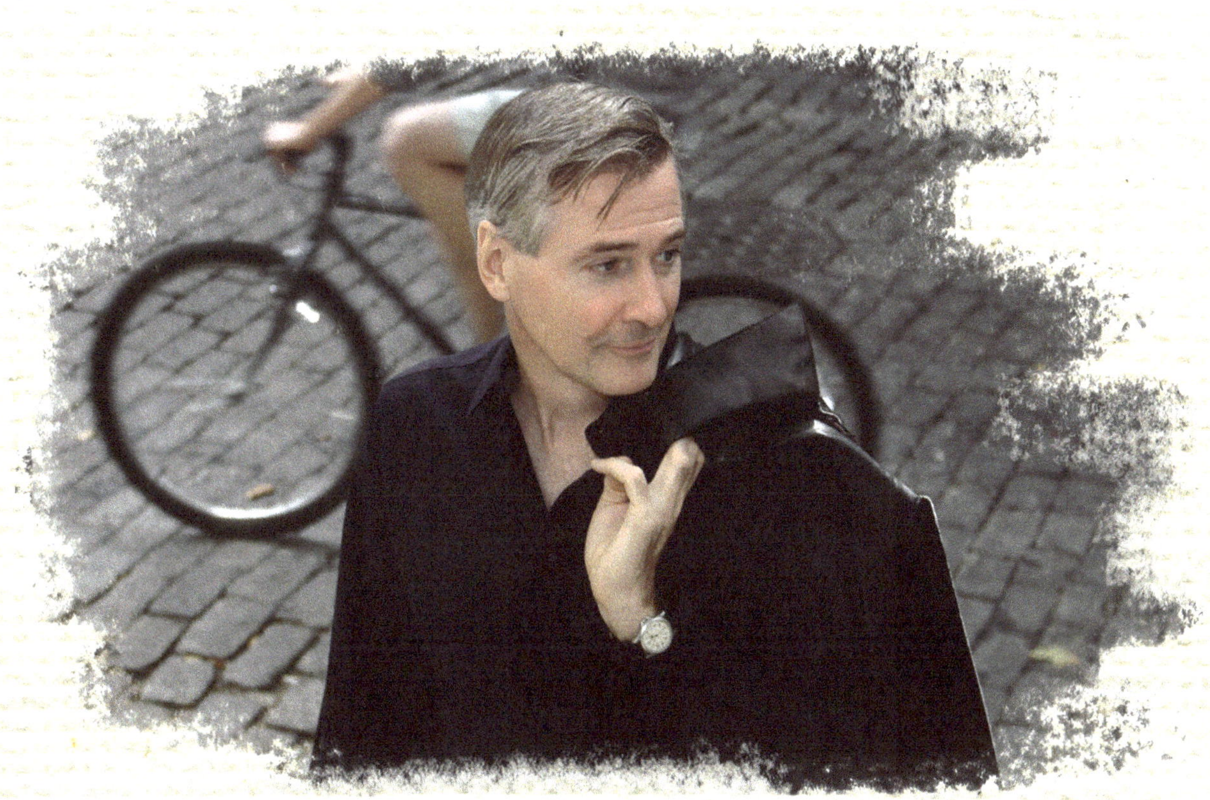

John Patrick Shanley photo: Monique Carboni

Q How young were you when you began writing plays?
I started writing around eleven-years old. When I was thirteen, I was on the stage crew for a good production of *Cyrano* at Cardinal Spellman High School in the Bronx. It's also where Justice Sonya Sotomayer went. I was thrown out of school; she graduated, I did not. It made a great impression on me. I decided to write plays after writing a lot of poetry, novels, and short stories.

When I was at New York University, I wrote a play for a playwriting course, and then another. They put them put on. My second play was moved to a new theatre and done with Vinnette Carroll at Urban Arts Theatre. She produced *Saturday Night at the War*. Then I pretty much got every play I wanted to be produced after that. I had a couple which were never produced. Many plays were done at the Open Eye Theatre, or at The Vineyard Theatre.

Q Were there playwrights at the time whose plays you were drawn to?
Certainly Edmond Rostand. John Millington Synge's *Playboy of the*

Western World. It's a terrific play in terms of structure, incredible beauty of the language. Some of the plays by John Galsworthy, including *The Silver Box*, and Shakespeare.

Q As you've kept writing, what kinds of discoveries have you made?

To be still and be able to stand outside of yourself. One day I was surprised when a new play had come to me. I was very happy, a little shocked. It came about from a real faith. I was in Paris and I had sort of a vision; a vision that seemed to make no sense. I decided to write it down, then a second character appeared. I was fascinated by it. I realized the character within. When I had a second vision, I saw the whole play—it was dynamic, thrilling, as I wrote it. When I got to the last scene I was shocked; I knew what the play was about. I was shocked just as much as the audience was hooked by what they were watching when it was performed.

Q You've said you've used playwriting to solve your life. Are you still doing that?

I resolved that. At a certain part, for the first half of my life, I used it to address my personal issues. Then I turned more outwards, to society. The universal or political has become personal to me, as I become more of a member of the adult community.

Q You shift between writing for the stage and film. Does it affect when you write again for the stage?

Oh sure. When you become more aware of the structure of storytelling, it can be very helpful returning to the stage; it can be a powerful thing in telling stories. I think my writing has certainly gotten better. I think in my latest plays, you can see a stylistic leap, in *Doubt* and in *Pirate*, from what I've done before.

Q How can a writer remain honest and truthful in their work?

How can they not? What's the point if you're going to write to please others, if you never reveal who you are? Writing is where you get to declare what you actually feel in all humility, because there's always a tendency to not see everyone else has problems, shortcomings. It's most interesting to look at yourself and suspect yourself as a culprit.

Q You've directed many gifted actors, among them Meryl Streep, Philip Seymour Hoffman, Kevin Kline, and John Turturro. Has the way in which you talk to actors changed from when you began directing?

I guess I have. When I first started directing, I had no idea what I was doing. I knew what I liked, which is not a small thing. John Turturro, the people I liked, told me I said too much at first.

Fairly quickly, I realized the big job was to see what they're doing—to be a "magic mirror" to what was really working, to build on that, to hold to the truth. I learned a lot from very fine actors, like Kevin Kline and John. I want them to be truthful; I don't want anything phony. If they happen to be big, if they're pushing, my job is to calm them down.

With *Doubt*, when Cherry Jones came in and did the first read-through as the character; who she was, was present in the first read-through. I thought it was a great characterization and I embraced it.

Q What allows the act of creativity to grow and flower?

You have to have guts. You have to be willing to recognize what worked yesterday may not work today. To be willing to experiment, to fall on your face or expect to fall on your face.

Q Do you have a specific routine to how you write each day?

I had started a schedule: I'd get up at 5 a.m., write for three hours. At 8 a.m. I was done for the day. In many ways the discovery from doing that for five to six days a week for many years stayed in my bones. Everything in my life is hard, and writing is the pleasure, my reward, my dessert, for the main course, which is my life.

Q How has mankind managed to survive and prosper?

I'm not sure. In some sense it could be in terms of our spirituality. It's been improvised a lot over time. In the West, because the spiritual measure is not being applied to material problems, what we face lacks a spiritual dimension, causing many people to long for a sense of community. There's a constant pushing for material productivity. The country of Bhutan came out with a yearly domestic gross of happiness. People could create more beauty other than thinking always in material terms.

Q What responsibility does the artist have to their community?

Service. It's not about your service in the artistic community, which is still alive, constantly gored and trampled on. It's the idea of serving others, of being help to another, which should be our number one concern. It's about making other people happy instead of making yourself happy. ■

PETER STONE

The first writer to win an Academy Award, an Emmy Award, and a Tony Award, Mr. Stone is probably most well-known for his musical, *1776*, which won the Tony Award, and his film screenplays of *Charade* with Audrey Hepburn and Cary Grant, *Father Goose* with Cary Grant, *Sweet Charity* with Shirley MacLaine, and *Mirage* with Gregory Peck. His other screenplays include *Silver Bears*, *Who is Killing the Great Chefs of Europe?*, *The Taking of Pelham One, Two, Three* with Walter Matthau, *Arabesque* starring Sophia Loren and Gregory Peck, and *The Secret War of Harry Frigg* starring Paul Newman. He made his Broadway debut with the libretto to Wright and Forrest's *Kean* starring Alfred Drake. He adapted Billy Wilder's film, *Some Like It Hot*, for Broadway, into the musical, *Sugar*, starring Robert Morse, and adapted Shaw's *Androcles and the Lion* into a musical with Richard Rodgers, *Woman of the Year* starring Lauren Bacall, receiving a Tony Award. His other shows on Broadway included *Titanic*, *The Will Rogers Follies*, *My One and Only* starring Tommy Tune and Twiggy, *Skyscraper*; and *Two by Two* starring Danny Kaye, which received a Tony Award. Mr. Stone's television work included *Adam's Rib* starring Ken Howard, *One of My Wives is Missing*, and *The Truth about Charlie*. For eighteen years, Mr. Stone was president of the Dramatists Guild of America. In 2011, *Death Takes a Holiday*, which he completed with Thomas Meehan and Maury Yeston, was produced Off-Broadway. He was posthumously inducted into the American Theater Hall of Fame. Mr. Stone died in 2003 (this interview was conducted in 2003).

Q Did you see a lot of theater growing up?
I grew up in a film family in a film town. There wasn't a lot of theater to speak of. I remember going to see a musical no one remembers today, but in it, Bobby Clark comes out, takes off his hat and he sails it across this enormous stage and it lands on the hat tree on the other side of the stage. He got it there in one toss. I've always been drawn to that kind of immediacy, the danger, the thrill of theater.

Q Did you plan early on to write musicals?
No, I didn't start thinking "musicals," I wrote plays. It just so happened my agent told me they were adapting a play by Jean-Paul Sartre into a musical, starring Alfred Drake, and they asked me if I'd be interested. Drake was an amazing performer; I had seen him in *Kiss Me Kate*. So I said "yes." And I also wanted to get on Broadway.

Q Is the opening of a new show still as exciting for you?
It's still very fulfilling, even with all the mistakes I see. Of course, after seventeen shows later, I don't enjoy going back to see one of my shows once it's been running. But I remember on *1776*, I did make some changes after I saw it again.

Q Was there someone who made a deep impression on how you learned your craft?

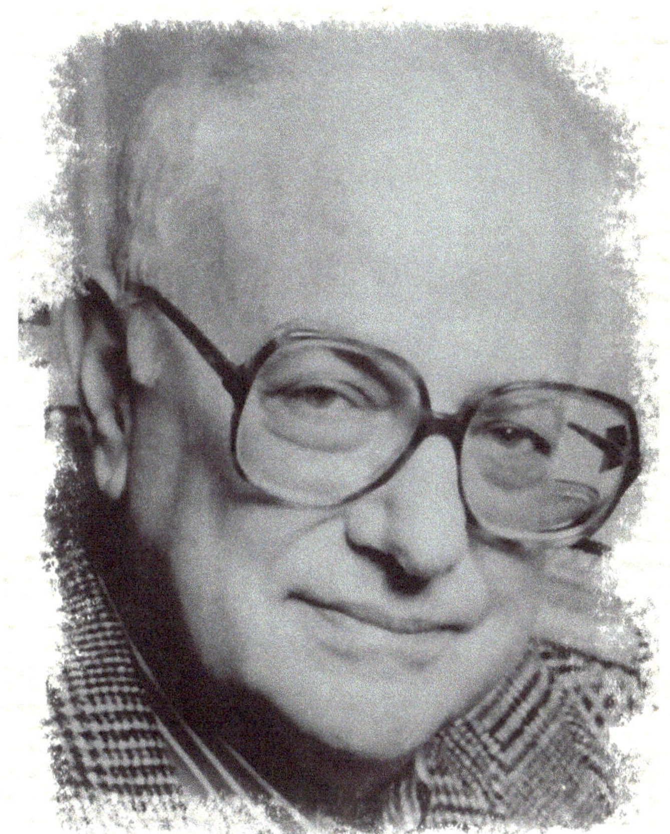

Peter Stone photo: courtesy of the artist

I had an apprenticeship with Frank Loesser and Abe Burrows. They knew everything. When I asked them, "How do you do that?" they could explain it.

Q How important is your relationship with a director?
It's very important. The director is your link between you and the actor. When you get to a certain point in this business, you're able to pick who you want to work with. You depend on him or her for staging ideas. Inspiration doesn't happen very often so you have to work with someone who can do the work. You can't depend upon a great idea hitting on you out of the blue.

Q What did you initially think of turning the story of our founding fathers and their fight for America's independence into a musical?
Initially I thought *1776* was the worst idea I had ever heard! And just think about the title—"1776!"—

it's the worst title. All those shows that have one word for a title—*Oklahoma, Hamlet*!

Before I went into this business it had been my desire to teach; I was a pretty good history student. When I saw how Sherman Edwards had found a way to tell the story of America's independence, that made all the difference. He had found *his* right level. Abe Burrows would always use that word, "level," meaning that everyone involved in the show works on different levels.

Q Did some shows come more easily to you to write than others?

In an odd way, *1776* happened very quickly. The one I enjoyed the most was *My One and Only*. Mike Nichols was called into work on it up in Boston. And he called me. I thought I had nothing to lose. So we tore apart what was there and came up with a brand new book. It was a very happy experience, one I never tired of.

Q Do you enjoy teaching?

I do; though it's tricky finding students who are up to the task. One of my happiest moments was teaching at New York University, and George Wolfe showed up. You knew immediately how talented he was.

Q You've certainly seen musical theater go through a lot of ups and downs.

It's become more exciting to take a movie and turn it into a show. And because musicals cost so much, all that those involved want, is a hit. I'm 72 years old, and you look at writers like myself: Kander and Ebb, Cy Coleman, Comden and Green, Charles Strouse, Tom Meehan, just to mention a few, who are also up there in age. We came up reared on a certain way of writing music. Today's new writers have abandoned melody. They're talented people, but it's just not on their palette. I think it was Sondheim who set them off in another direction.

Q And with it all, you have an unflagging all-embracing attitude towards what you do.

I go on because I believe in what I do. ■

APRIANA TAYLOR

An award-winning writer, a prolific poet, playwright, novelist, short story writer, storyteller, actor, painter, and musician of New Zealand, he is of Ngati Porou, Te Whanau a Apanui, and Ngati Ruanui tribes, and also Māori and Pākeha heritage. His poetry and prose have been published nationally and internationally, and translated into several languages. His stories are frequently accompanied by traditional and contemporary Māori music. Mr. Taylor's publications include: *The Breathing Tree*, *Five Strings*, *Eyes of the Ruru*, a book of poetry, *Three Shades*, a book of poetry, *He Rau Aroha*, short stories, *Ki Te Ao*, short stories, *He Tangi Aroha*, a novel, *Soft Leaf Falls of the Moon*, poetry, *Kohanga* and *Whaea Kai Rau*, two plays, and *Iti te Kopara*, short stories. Mr. Taylor has been published in many major New Zealand Anthologies including: *Doors: Poetry for Secondary Schools*, *Jewels in the Water: Poetry for Secondary Schools*, *Where's Waari: A History of the Maori through the Short Story*, *Growing up Maori*, *The Puffin New Zealand Story Book*, *An Anthology of New Zealand Poetry*, *The Penguin Book of Contemporary New Zealand Short Stories*, and *Parihaka*. His first play, *Kohanga*, was voted play of the year by the *Dominion and Evening Post*. He was a prominent member of the Māori theatre cooperative, Te Ohu Whakaari, which he helped form, at a time when no such theatre existed. He has acted in and written many plays, and received a New Zealand Television award nomination as Billy in *Tiger Country*. His film appearances include *Moby Dick* and *The Swiss Family Robinson*. Mr. Taylor has been Writer-in-Residence at Massey and Canterbury Universities, Rangi Ruru, St. Andrews College, New Zealand Drama School, Whitireia Polytechnic, and Hagley High School. Mr. Taylor won the 1994 Te Ha Award for Poetry, the I.B.M Young Writers award, and was runner-up in the Pegasus Book Awards.

Q I understand your father was a storyteller and you began writing at an early age. Do you think writing that early stimulated your imagination, and began to help you find out who you were?

My father was a journalist. He had a truly magical way with words and a love of playing with the language. I believe I inherited my love of playing with words from him. As a child, I wanted to be a writer like Dad. I had dyslexia, but once I overcame this difficulty I began to indulge my love of writing.

Writing at an early age stimulated my mind, but more than that, it gave me an opening into which I could channel my active imagination and brought me a sense of relief. Writing has certainly helped me on my voyage of self-discovery.

Q Can you describe the effect that the poet, Alistair Campbell, had on you, and how that led to your writing *The Life of Te Kooti*.

In my first year at University, I happened to see and hear Alistair Campbell reading his poetry on television. I loved this poet's beautiful imagery, and his poetry re-awakened a forgotten dream of mine to write.

The next day I decided to write an epic poem about Te Kooti. The poem was to be about five hundred pages long and would, I believed, earn me millions of dollars. About a week or so later, I emerged from my student's room with a poem called, "Te Kooti." It was fourteen lines long.

Once I had the last word in place, I felt such a huge surge of

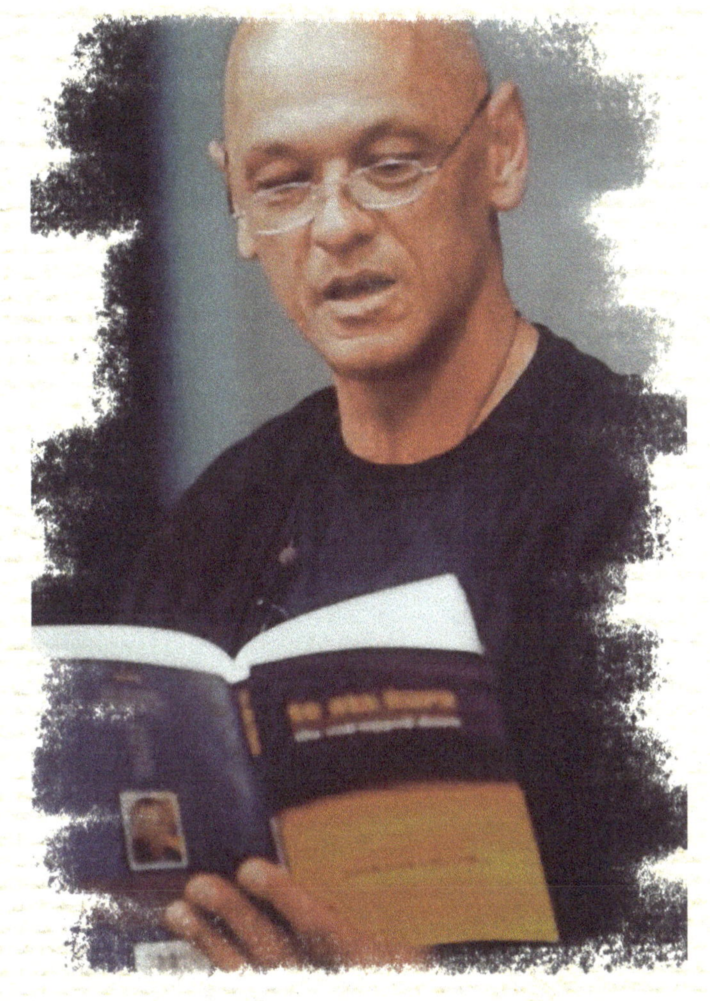

Apriana Taylor photo: courtesy of the artist

satisfaction and fulfillment that I realized that writing poetry was what I wanted to do. I walked out of University shortly after that, I put a pack on my back, and armed with little more than a notebook and a pen, I went for a walk several hundred miles up the spine of the North Island. My aim was to write poetry as I went and that's what I did.

Q What drew you to the theater?

When I was about six or seven I appeared in the musical, *The King and I*, at the St James Theatre. The cast was basically an international one but that meant little to me. About the time I was ten years old, I appeared in another musical, *Porgy and Bess*. The cast was made up of Maori people and black actors from the United States. Porgy was played by the famous Māori singer, Inia Te Wiata. I remember falling in love with the beauty of the lights, and a feeling of exhilaration and fulfillment as I looked out into the audience. I felt at home on the stage.

I had nothing more to do with theater after that until I was in my mid-to-late twenties. I was writing but had trouble writing dialogue. I asked my brother, Rangimoana, if I could get a job working on set design for the Maori Theatre Co-Op called Te Ohu Whakaari. My brother was the director and he said yes.

On my first day on the stage, he said words to the effect: "Forget about your set designs. We do minimalist theater. Start writing scripts. Learn your lines because you're on in a couple of weeks." Working at the theater reawakened my love for the stage. I keep going back to acting for the same reason I keep going back to writing poetry, I have to breathe.

Q Your first play, *Kohanga*, produced in the mid 1980s was a huge success, and ran in Wellington for three weeks. It was probably the first full-length Maori production, written by a Maori, directed by a Maori, and with a Maori cast. What did that experience mean to you and to those in the audience who came to see it?

On some nights the audience would be mainly Pakeha, and they would laugh at certain parts in the play. On other nights, the audience would be mainly Māori, and they laughed in parts that were different from the Pakeha. I realized the two different cultures tended to laugh in the places where they recognized themselves. I thought that was a wonderful thing; it made me feel good being a playwright.

Q You begin one of your programs with a song, "The First Breath of Life." Why did you choose that particular song and by singing, playing musical instruments and telling the stories you tell—can you describe what it means to you to carry on this oral tradition?

I often begin my reading with a poem about the first breath of life because I've realized that is, to a large degree, the underlying spirit of all my poetry. No matter who we are, if we don't take the first breath, we pass very quickly from life into death.

Also in Māori culture, if you speak we expect you to accompany your speech with a song. It's a very beautiful and powerful aspect of Māori culture. This is why I present my work the way I do.

Q What gives you your greatest joy being a storyteller and poet?

I feel it's using whatever talents I may have to communicate with people to the best of my abilities. ■

VIJAY TENDULKAR

Mr. Tendulkar was the most influential dramatist and theater personality in Marathi, the principal language of the state of Maharashtra in India, which has had a continuous literary history since the end of the classical period in India, with nearly seventy-five million speakers today. He was best known for his plays, *Shantata! Court Chalu Aahe* (*Silence! The Court is in Session*), *Ghashiram Kotwal* (*Officer Ghashiram*; with over six thousand performances, it remains one of the longest-running plays in the history of Indian theatre), and *Sakharam Binder* (*Sakharam, the Bookbinder*). He wrote twenty-seven full-length plays including *Gidhade* (*The Vultures*), *Safar*, *The Masseur*, and *His Fifth Woman* in English. Mr. Tendulkar wrote eleven movies in Hindi and eight movies in Marathi, including *Nishant*, *Akrosh* (*The City*), and *Ardh Satya* (*The Half-Truth*). Others were *Manthan*, which received the National Film Award, *Samama* (*Confrontation*), *Simh asan* (*Throne*), and *Umbartha* (*The Threshold*), which was a groundbreaking feature film on women's activism in India, directed by Jabbar Patel, starring Smita Patil and Girish Karnad. His last screenplay, *Mukhabhinoy*, was directed by Shyamanand Jalan, starred Ashish Vidyarti and Pawan Malhotra. Mr. Tendulkar translated nine novels, two biographies, and five plays by other authors into Marathi, including Mohan Rakesh's *Adhe Adhure*, Girish Karnad's *Tughlaq*, and Tennessee Williams' *A Streetcar Named Desire*. He wrote an acclaimed television series, *SwayamSiddha*, with his daughter, Priya Tendulkar, in the lead role. Mr. Tendulkar received two Maharashtra State government awards, Mahārōshtra Gaurav Puraskār, the Sangeet Natak Akademi Award, and their Lifetime Award, the Padma Bhushan Award from the Government of India for his literary accomplishments. Mr. Tendulkar died in 2007 (this interview was conducted in 2004).

Q When you came to New York City in 2004, there was a month-long celebration of your work at several theaters, and I was also able to present *An Evening with Vijay Tendulkar* at The Players with excerpts from your works. You also received a special award from Aroon Shivdasani, Executive Director of the Indo-American Arts Council. What did the celebration of your work mean to you?

I was pleased by everything I had seen, what everyone had done, most thankful. It was good to be there with everyone.

Q How do you see the theater's role today?

The theater is like a mirror in front of the audience. People like to escape the search of themselves—the real you, which you may never understand. They spend a lot of their time in pleasantries, fantasizing. Theater gives us meaning by asking questions about who we are.

Q What is the artist's responsibility to the world today, especially for the younger generation?

We carry our responsibility like a burden. The young today live in a world of insecurity, major disturbances, upheaval, a faster pace of life. In India, the commercialism is shaping the younger generation, the language. They have their own way of expressing things. Everything is losing its relevance today very quickly. We have a tradition that seems to feel like a burden to them. Certain values consciously and unconsciously bother them, yet it still has gone into their genes. Sometimes the past can be a hindrance.

I hope our new artists in India will stick to the theater, and make a difference. In American theatre, things go according to a plan. In my country that is rare.

Q What has it meant for India to have a National School of Drama in New Delhi?

Before it came into existence there was no place where you could get the basic training of theater. The practice in the past was to learn through experience. Working this way there are limitations to learning. You keep doing what you know. NSD is a place where a young person can learn for years from good masters. Students come from every part of India. In some areas professional theatre didn't exist before. Now there are many other schools, too.

Q What are your feelings about Mahatma Gandhi and his impact?

I considered him a fantastic person, when it came to his views. A number of his views are dated; there has been a huge change in the world. Certain of his ideas are still valued. There's a tremendous curiosity about the man. He was a very complex man.

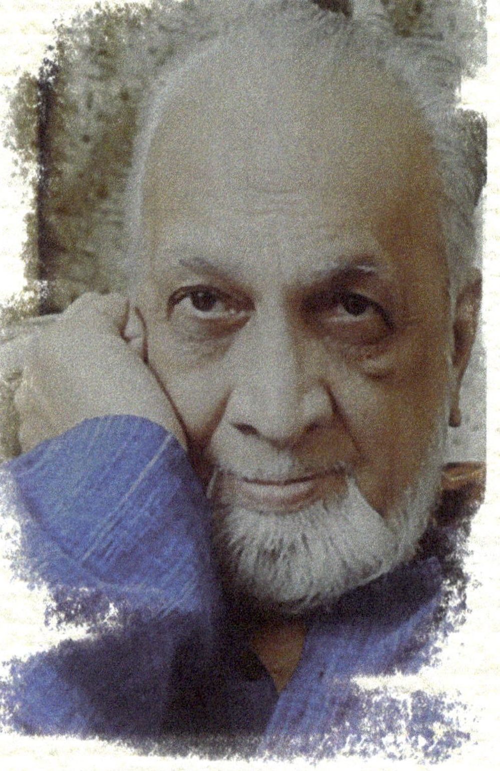

Vijay Tendulkar photo: Satyen K. Bordoloi, courtesy of the artist

Q How can a writer know if what he's created and intends is getting through to the audience?

A writer always wonders if it is being communicated. There is a gap in the understanding, but something does reach the audience. I've spent many years in the theater, and what I write comes to me and I have a duty of telling others what I have realized. It needs to be shared. The first priority is always the audience. ■

ELISE THORON

Playwright/director, translator and educator, her plays include *Green Violin*, music by Frank London, performed across America and at St. Petersburg's Teatr na Mokhvaya; *Charlotte: Life? or Theater?*, music by Gary Fagin, performed in America, London and Amsterdam; *Prozak and the Platypus*, music by Jill Sobule performed across America, and a Cuban nightclub opera; *Hatuey: A Memory of Fire*, music by Frank London. Ms. Thoron created *Recycling: washi tales*, a collaboration with Japanese paper artist, Kyoko Ibe, performed in Japan and across America; *Country of Kings*, a solo show with Tony award-winning poet, Lemon Andersen. She developed and directed Lemon Anderson's play, *ToasT*, and *Eleni the Shining One*, with classical Indian dancer, Rajika Puri, performed at the Puri Chennai Dance Festival. Ms. Thoron adapted and directed in Russian, *The Great Gatsby*, continuing in repertory for over a decade at the Pushkin Theater in Moscow. As Associate Artistic Director at American Place Theater, she developed and directed new plays and solo shows, and co-founded with Artistic Director, Wynn Handman, "Literature to Life," a performance-based literacy program in 1994. For the program, Ms. Thoron adapted and directed several books including Sandra Cisneros' *House on Mango Street*, Junot Diaz's *The Brief and Wondrous Life of Oscar Wao*, and Zora Neale Hurston's *Their Eyes Were Watching God*. Since 1986, she has worked on cross-cultural collaborations with Russian and American theater artists through the Eugene O'Neill Theater Center, and was one of the co-founders of A.S.T.I.- American Soviet Theater Initiative. She directed a bilingual production of Oleg Antonov's *Egorushka* in America. Ms. Thoron has translated the work of the Russian playwrights:Liudmila Petrushevskaya and Alexander Galin, and translated *3 Sisters* with Sarah Ruhl, commissioned by Cincinnati Playhouse, Berkley and Yale Repertory Theaters.

Q In 1989, you co-founded the American Soviet Theatre Initiative—

I had the good fortune to meet George C. White, the founder of the O'Neill Center, and we organized the first group of Russian students to come for a month to the O'Neill to study musical theater with twenty American students.

We started the American Soviet Theater Initiative with George and Gregory Nersesyan in Moscow, to be a conduit for exchanges in all disciplines of theater. George is a kindred spirit for me. He's allowed a channel to develop between our two countries and deepen over time. I was part of the first Russian playwrights' conference modeled on the O'Neill, and the first music theater conference in St. Petersburg, which continues to this day.

Q How did you go about creating your memorable play, *Green Violin*?

Working on that play had been a real challenge; during the collaboration a true synthetic style developed. It's the story of the legendary Soviet actor Solomon Mikhoels, the leader of the first Soviet Yiddish Theatre (Goset), and the painter Marc Chagall, who painted sets and murals for the company in Moscow in 1920. The play follows Chagall and Mikhoels' relationship: how they met and collaborated in Moscow, and their different life choices. Frank London of The Klezmatics wrote the music, David Dorfman incorporated Chagall's paintings into his own unique movement idiom.

During one visit to Russia to do research for *Green Violin*, I actually found an actress who had come from the Ukraine in the 1930s during the famine. She had a beautiful singing voice. She had been in Mikhoels' company, and survived the purge in the 1940s, when he and most of the members of the company were killed. I interviewed her in her small kitchen in Moscow, and she showed me the original dance steps she had learned and then performed them, and told me all about Mikhoels. She told me, "How he did so much for us. He'd spread his big arms, protecting his artists."

Q When did you first come in contact with Chagall's paintings?

As a child, I remember looking at Chagall's murals at the Metropolitan Opera. I didn't know he was a Russian artist, I thought he was French. Through my working on *Green Violin*, I became fascinated by his early period. His work is so powerful and energetic in that period.

Q What did the experience mean to you having *Green Violin* performed in Russia?

We worked with twenty students from the Theatre Academy in their fourth year of training. They really threw themselves into a period of Soviet history that they were not that familiar with, to become Mikhoels' Yiddish company in movement and song.

As each number was staged, we learned more about the play, with Chagall's paintings influencing the movement profoundly. We had an amazing violinist, a classically trained virtuoso, and he carried the soul of the piece in his playing. From the process, I realized there was a whole layer of depth in the piece I didn't know was there when I began. It showed me I didn't need to have so much exposition, or rely on the words as much. It gave me the desire to reach deeper into the characters.

The staging of Mikhoels' death at the end of the play was very powerful. It was accomplished simply with syncopated clapping in rhythm of a company song that ran through the whole piece. As the clapping got louder and louder, to a deafening point, it was then silenced. Chagall had his hands on Mikhoels' face, and then Mikhoels removed his face leaving the empty hands, and you could just feel the audience connect with it. I think the audiences were astounded by the creativity of the company functioning in two languages. Being able to trust the actors and the expression of

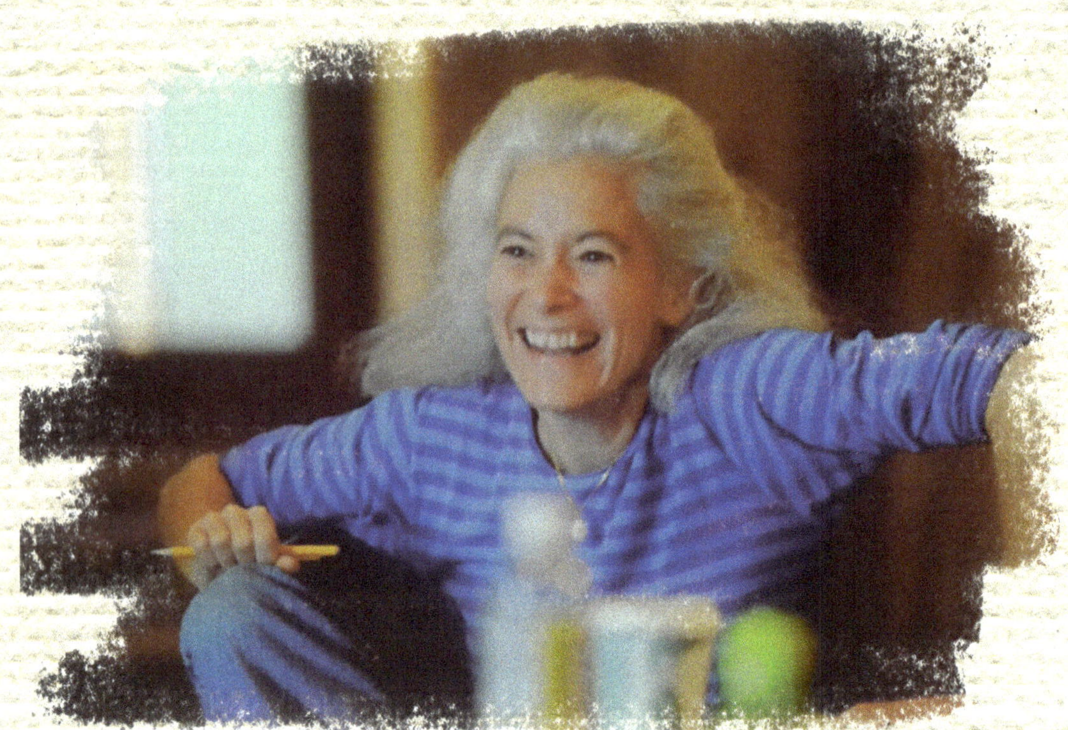

Elise Thoron photo: courtesy of the artist

theater is really about "beyond the words."

Q Was it challenging adapting *The Great Gatsby* and directing it in Russian?

It was the first piece of writing I did in Russian. I incorporated elements from "The Last Tycoon" and Fitzgerald's essay, "The Crackup." The trick in adapting *Gatsby* was finding a way to dramatize the narrative voice, which is the engine of the novel. I gave the central conflict of the play to Nick, the narrator, a washed-up screenwriter: whether to tell the truth about the Gatsby story, or sell out and give the story a happy ending as the film studio demanded. It took a good solid six to eight months to rehearse.

One of the reasons I wanted to work in Russia was to work with a large cast and a long rehearsal period, but it was a real challenge. At one point the actors went on strike because they didn't like the minimalist set, which ended up being terrific. Still, when we arrived at opening night, all the misery was forgotten and the show ran for seven years in repertory. Working with Yuri Yeremin, the artistic director of the Pushkin Theater, was a very good collaboration. I remember him saying after *Gatsby*, "Nothing you do will ever be this difficult."

Q Can you describe the personal effect creating *Recycling: washi tales*, in collaboration with the Japanese paper artist, Kyoko Ibe, has had on your growth as an artist?

Kyoko's deep connection to nature through the paper-making craft and the rhythms that are a part of her world, have become a part of my life. I have always loved being in nature, trekking in the wilderness, but the Japanese sense of nature is quite different. It focuses on the relationship with humans: the harmony of that dialogue, whether it be haiku, a tree tended for hundreds of years, temple stones gardens, or the tea ceremony, the relationship with nature is highly conscious, articulated, and aesthetically framed, while not diminishing nature's power. The mountain itself is a god, and a part of daily life.

Our typical work day in Kyoto involved an early morning walk and climb to the local shrine, set amid the densely populated Kyoto suburb. The shrine is an island of woods, stones, and pine trees tied with rope and paper. Working in the quiet rhythms of papermaking, and the everyday physical rituals that a craft entails, I learned a kind of discipline more like a river, less bound in your personal pride or ego, to do with the immediate work at hand, and the way others who have gone before you have made things. I discovered this from my collaborator, Kyoko, a visual artist, and the traditional Japanese performers I worked with. There could be intense creativity and subtle innovation working within a tradition that has continued generation to generation for hundreds, even thousands, of years. I was very struck by a different sense of time and individual responsibility to a larger collective.

In many ways working on *Washi Tales* felt like coming home. It is the sparsest theater text that I have written, and perhaps my favorite—each word is essential, poetic, and distilled from my experience observing papermakers and talking to Kyoko. Two languages: English and Japanese move through the piece, as the sound of water is what the papermaker listens to as she works.

After performances, audiences are invited to come on stage to touch and view the washi that Kyoko has made, to examine the little paper-making vat that Karen Kandel, our papermaker and story teller, has been working at. They pick up the tools, finger the pulp. *Washi* is created by human hands in harmony with the natural world. It brings us into the present moment and carries the ghosts of the past. As the paper-maker says: "Hands, many hands have made paper before me."

Finding one's place in a continuum of craft and history, is a different notion of being an artist than what I was taught in America—where everything pivots around individual self-expression—even in the collective act of making theater.

Q How does a theater piece like your play, *Charlotte Salomon, in Life? Or Theater?* touch the audiences who experience it?

Through the power of creative expression to heal—the power of art to transform people. People who commit themselves to art as their life are willing to sacrifice.

The inspiring character of Charlotte, a young German-Jewish painter in *Charlotte Salomon, in Life? Or Theater?* is alone in a room in the South of France during the Second World War, far from her family in Berlin, and decides to paint the play of her life rather than commit suicide. Charlotte is really the character who taught me how to write. Music was integral to her painting; she hummed and sang as she painted her characters into being from her memories, and through that, she discovers their truth. Charlotte's actual work exists in over a thousand gouaches.

I feel this piece is a profound affirmation of life in face of annihilation. She died in Auschwitz right after completing the work at age twenty-six. I'm grateful to be able to write plays infused with music, to work through an organic process with these strong voices telling their stories in sound and color—twisting sorrow into joy. ■

JEAN-CLAUDE van ITALLIE

One of America's most gifted playwrights, translator, painter, and teacher, his trilogy of one-act plays, *America Hurrah*, was hailed as the watershed Off-Broadway play of the 1960s. Mr. van Itallie was one of Ellen Stewart's original "La MaMa playwrights." As principal playwright of Joseph Chaikin's Open Theater, he wrote *The Serpent*. His other plays include his often-produced versions of Chekhov's four major plays; *Tibetan Book of the Dead; The Doris Plays: Almost Like Being* and *I'm Really Here; King of the United States; The Traveler; Secrets of the White House; Struck Dumb* written with/for Joseph Chaikin; *Bag Lady; Ancient Boys;* and *Light*. His translations include Jean Genet's *The Balcony*, Bulgakhov's *Master and Margarita*. He has performed his one-person autobiographical shows: *Confessions and Conversation* directed by Rosemary Quinn, and *War, Sex and Dreams* at La MaMa in New York City, and at Highways in Santa Monica. He co-wrote the libretto with Lois Walden for a new opera: *Mila, Great Sorcerer*, with music by Andrea Clearfield. A painter of large black-on-white calligraphies, Mr. van Itallie's exhibit, "Characters" was at the Open Center Gallery in New York City in May, 1993. Mr. van Itallie has taught playwriting and performance at Princeton, NYU, Harvard, Yale School of Drama, Amherst, Middlebury, Columbia, University of Colorado, Boulder, Naropa University and many other colleges. He teaches workshops in acting, writing, and creativity in Los Angeles, New York City; and at Shantigar Foundation, for theater, meditation, and healing, which he directs on the old farm where he lives in Western Massachusetts. Mr. van Itallie's books include *The Playwright's Workbook* and *Tea with Demons, games of transformation*.

Q You were part of one of the most innovative theaters in America—The Open Theatre. What was it like for you working with The Open Theatre, culminating in creating the Obie-winning ensemble play, *The Serpent*?

Being young in Greenwich Village, working in theater in the mid-1960s, was thrilling. We were at the right place at the right time and sensed it. In lofts like the Open Theater's and newly opened small experimental theaters like the Cafe La MaMa, we would-be actors, directors, and writers collaborated in giving birth to revolutionary theatrical forms that reflected our challenges to conventional values and reality.

We were outlaws questioning everything political, sexual, and social within and around us. Writing in these new forms, I wanted to honestly express our new hard-found emotional truths in striking poetry, using words as pistol shots.

Q Why did you create your two solo shows, War, Sex and Dreams, an amazing experience of honesty and intimacy from your childhood escape from the Nazis, to your life as a gay man, to your sudden fame, and *Confessions and Conversation*?

I felt as if the many streams of my life were increasingly running into a single river. I wanted to express that river not only on paper but with movement and voice. I have always kept journals and have written down my dreams. Now I wanted to physically vibrate some of those secrets and dreams to an audience. I wanted to bodily release secrets. Keeping secrets inside is denying them.

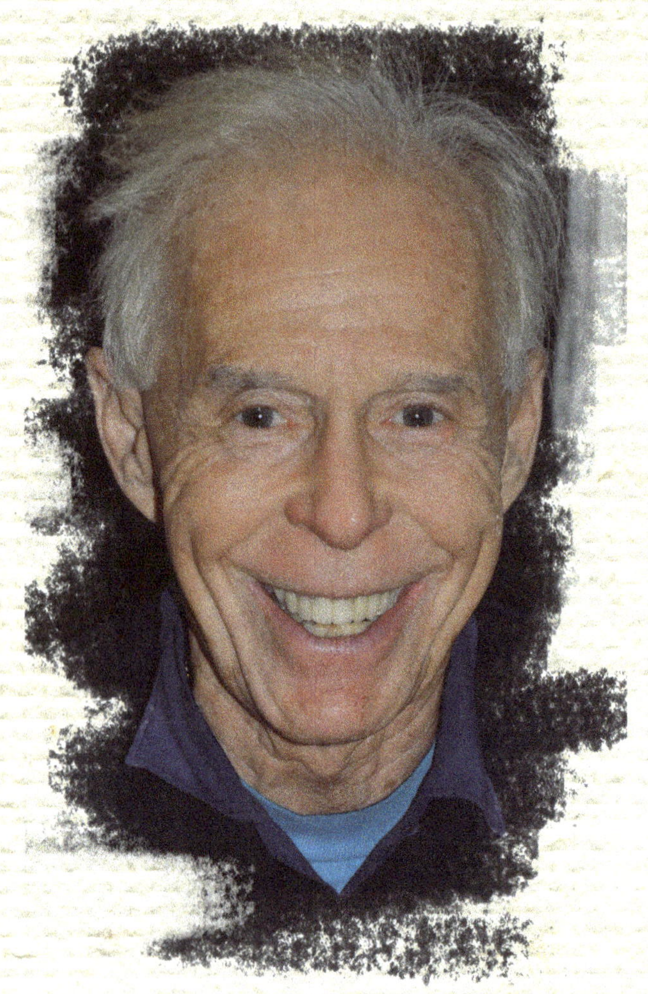

Jean-Claude van Itallie photo: Barbara Beaussacq, New York City, 2011

Merely writing secrets down isn't enough. I wanted to perform them, exorcise them by embodying them.

Q You've written some of the most accessible and lyrical translations of Chekhov's major plays. A memorable production of your translation of *The Cherry Orchard* was at Lincoln Center Theatre in 1977, directed by Andrei Şerban, with Irene Worth and Meryl Streep. What led you to create your translations of Chekhov's plays?

When the actor Dan Seltzer, head of the Princeton Program of Theater and the McCarter Theatre, unexpectedly asked me to make a translation of *The Seagull*, I was startled. I asked him, "Why me? I don't even speak Russian and there are many translations around." Dan replied, "Take a good look at those translations. They may be accurate literally but they're dated. They're either too British or too colloquial. You don't speak Russian so we'll get you a trans-literation. But you know how to make English flow rhythmically and movingly from an actor's mouth."

I began by reading Chekhov's letters. I had to demystify Chekhov, take him "off his pedestal," so I could identify with him. I discovered Chekhov's work is centered on family and home. While translating, I had, in a sense, to let Chekhov flow through me. I worked aloud with a French translation, and with an assistant who was a performer. Words begin to leap alive when spoken aloud, especially words in plays.

Q You often teach a workshop entitled "The Healing Power of Theater." Why did you choose that title?

Western Theater began with the ancient Mysteries. The Mysteries were not something you merely watched as audience as we watch our modern theater. In ancient Greece, you participated in the Mysteries in order to transform yourself into a healthier more clear-sighted person. You prepared by fasting and ingesting a sacred substance. Priests led you down into a dark cave and scared you out of your usual wits. After three days you returned to the light of the earth, bathed in the sea, and returned home with a saner sense of reality.

Today, when movies, television, and the internet monopolize popular entertainment—live theater has the opportunity to return to its sacred origins. In the Workshop, performance exercises, in conjunction with meditation and movement ,offers a unique way for workshop participants to creatively effect positive change in themselves. This I call: "The Healing Power of Theater."

Q What led to your creating the Shantigar Foundation, for theater, meditation, and healing on the old farm, where you live in the remote mountains of Western Massachusetts?

The forest and fields of this beautiful land have nourished me for decades. My father bought the farm in the late 1940s. As a teenager, I found it too remote. But in the 1960s, I started to come here with Open Theater friends. Joe Chaikin would direct an improvisation in the morning, at lunchtime I would write it into a play, and that afternoon the actors would have it on its feet. It was glorious! I learned to love the farm and bought it from my father in 1968 after the success of *America Hurrah*.

In the 1970s, my spiritual teacher Chogyam Trungpa, Rinpoche, the pioneering Tibetan lama, retreated here for a year while writing his Shambhala teachings. So for me, this place unites the potential of family, nature, theater and spirituality. I offer it as a haven to grow and create.

Q Another of your plays, *Light*, premiered at the Boston Court Theatre in Pasadena in 2004. How did you go about creating this engrossing play about the love triangle of Voltaire, Frederick the Great, and the mathematician Marquise Emilie du Chatelet?
I researched and visited the stately homes of these elegant Enlightenment superstars. I identified with all three: smart and aristocratic Emilie, gay obsessive King Frederick, and the great Voltaire, who I think was bisexual, and whom I so admire for his many incandescent insights and his social activism, which ultimately led to the French revolution.

Q You co-wrote the libretto with Lois Walden for a new opera: *Mila, Great Sorcerer*, with music by Andrea Clearfield. What led you to Milarepa?
Writing about Milarepa, Tibet's beloved teacher, singer, and folk hero who lived a thousand years ago, felt inevitable. I have been thinking about Milarepa since Trungpa, Rinpoche first asked me in 1973 to write a narrative for a short film about him.

Mila's life is indeed operatic. His father, a rich trader, died when Mila was seven, leaving Mila and his mother in the care of Mila's uncle and aunt who enslaved them. Demanding revenge, Mila's mother sent Mila to sorcery school to learn to conjure devices that could kill at long distance. At his mother's urging, Mila killed thirty-five people. Later he was sorry and needed to redeem his soul. Mila is able to climb back up the emotional slippery slope to sanity, and ultimately became Tibet's greatest teacher.

Q You also created a new book, *Tea with Demons: games of transformation* with forty-nine ways of discovering yourself through imaginative games—
Tea with Demons, in which I have put a lot of my pictures and calligraphies, is part-memoir, part about theater, part a set of games for contemplation and change. I fancy the book is my attempt to bring together different streams of what I know and dream about, and to offer that.

Q What inspired you to transform *The Tibetan Book of the Dead* into a play, which premiered in 1983 at La MaMa ETC, in what is now The Ellen Stewart Theatre, and then into a book, The *Tibetan Book of the Dead for Reading Aloud*?
Over a thousand years old, *The Tibetan Book of the Dead* is traditionally read aloud to the dying by a friend or priest, telling the dying person in essence: "Do not be afraid. Everything that is happening is natural, as you are yourself. Any demons you might imagine are only emanations of your own mind." These friendly admonitions apply to living as well as dying. In life, too, often our greatest demons are those we imagine but deny being ours.

As we worked on the production—Ellen Stewart, La MaMa's astute founder—reminded us that *The Tibetan Book of the Dead* is a celebration of life. I think the production shone brilliantly because we kept that in mind. Turning *The Tibetan Book of the Dead* into a play confirmed for me that meditative and acting techniques are complementary and similar in intent.

I made the play into a spare illustrated book, *Tibetan Book of the Dead for Reading Aloud* so that anyone who wants it would have a concise poetic text of Tibetan Book to read aloud in times of crisis. Actors, meditators, and all of us are striving to live as fully as possible on stage and off—to use practices to hone presence and awareness. ■

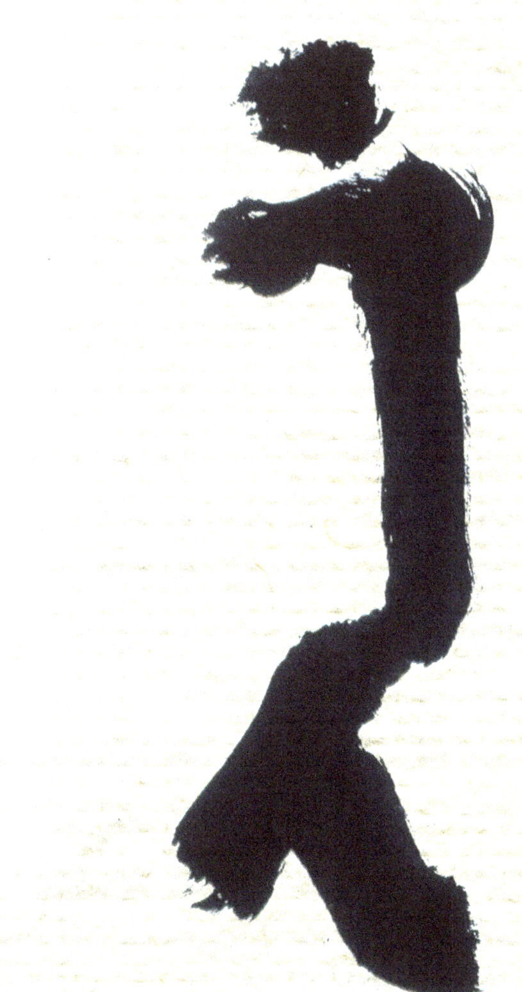

"Dancing Man" by Jean Claude van Itallie, courtesy of Mr. van Itallie

SIR DEREK WALCOTT

Distinguished poet, playwright and essayist, and the winner of the 1992 Nobel Prize in Literature, Sir Walcott was born in Castries, the capital of St. Lucia, in the West Indies. In 1957, he was awarded a fellowship by the Rockefeller Foundation to study the American theater. In 1959, he founded the Trinidad Theater Workshop, and his plays have been produced by the New York Shakespeare Festival, the Mark Taper Forum in Los Angeles, and the Negro Ensemble Company. He has published eleven books of poetry, including "*Selected Poems, The Arkansas Testament, Tiepolo's Hound*, and *Collected Poems: 1948-1984*, which won the 1986 Los Angeles Times Book Prize for Poetry. His poems have appeared in *The New Yorker, The New York Review of Books, The Nation*, and other periodicals. He has written over twenty-five plays including *Henri Christophe: A Chronicle in Seven Scenes, Wine of the Country, Tri-Jean and His Brothers, Dream on Monkey Mountain, The Joker of Seville, The Isle Is Full of Noises, Odyssey, Walker and The Ghost Dance, O Starry Starry Night*, and *The Capeman* (with book and lyrics in collaboration with Paul Simon). He co-authored *Homage to Robert Frost*, with Joseph Brodsky and Seamus Heaney. Mr. Walcott teaches at Boston University. He has been painting oil and watercolor paintings for more than five decades. His first one-person show in New York City was shown at the June Kelly Gallery. Mr. Walcott's awards include the Guinness Award for Poetry, a Royal Society of Literature Award, the Cholmondeley Prize, and the Welsh Arts Council International Writers Prize. In 1988, he was awarded the Queen's Medal for Poetry. He is an Honorary Member of the American Academy and Institute of Arts and Letters. Sir Derek Walcott died in 2017. (This interview was conducted in 2002).

Q What leads you to keep creating?
Destiny, fate. I've always wanted to write since I was a child.

Q Your adaptation from Homer's epic, *The Odyssey*, had its premiere in New York performed by the Willow Cabin Theatre Company, and had first been done by the Royal Shakespeare Company. The dialogue is mysteriously lyrical, and it's rare to hear a play done in verse.
In fact, there is no dialogue in *The Odyssey*. I had to make a complete play in the sequence, in the way *The Odyssey* was written, giving a line to each character, within a symmetrical design, and make it all rhyme.

Q How can we encourage more writers to deepen our theater in this direction?
Educate our critics. Only a few notice any of this at all. You feel the trend—"stick to reality," which is basically banality. Another critic had no idea who Ulysses' son was. If I come from the "colonies," the "outer reaches," and come to the cultural capital of the world, this level of illiteracy shocks me, in terms of responsibility. In terms of poetry in the theater, it really doesn't exist, and I'm not talking about "poetic affects."

Q So why write plays in verse?
Not many writers try. Maxwell Anderson was one of the few.

Q What led you to incorporate rituals from the Caribbean, like Shango, into this story from ancient Greece?
They are parallel. The actual sacrifice was a common occurrence in ancient Greece, whether it was a goat, or a ram, or a bull. And when we of today think about it, we think it's neat, when it was actually a bloody mess. In Haiti, when it's done, it's called barbaric, although colorful. These similar Gods also exist in Haitian culture. It's still a ritualistic reality today.

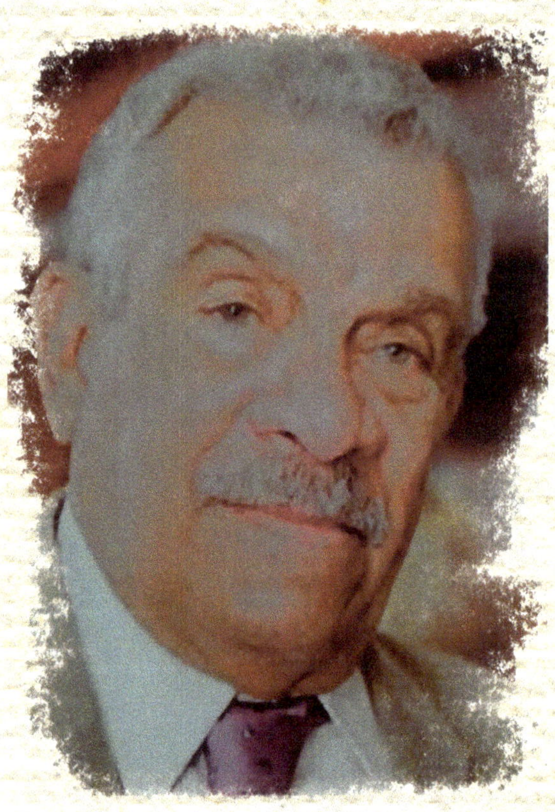

Sir Derek Walcott photo: Bert Nienhuis, courtesy of the artist

Q Was creating your own theater something you had thought of doing when you were growing up? Did you attend the theatre growing up?
No, we didn't have a theatre to go to. Though my mother recited, and my father produced. So I think it was hereditary for me to form the Arts Guild of St. Lucia, and then the Trinidad Theatre Workshop.

Q Does theater and poetry civilize man?
If I thought so, we wouldn't need to be worried about a nuclear disaster. I do believe the achievement of the truly great American poetry that has been created is equivalent to the poetry that was created during the Elizabethan period, in terms of grandeur, size.

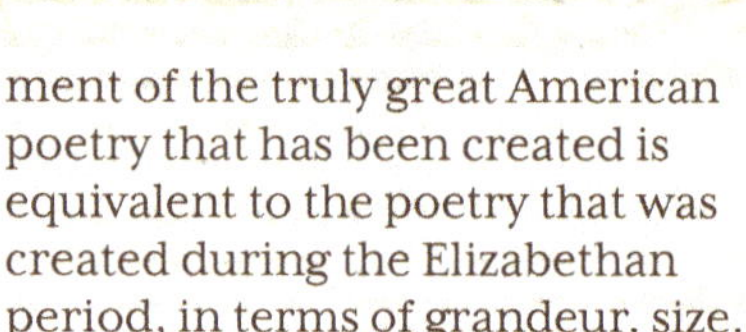

Writers like Lowell, Stevens, Frost, Whitman; they introduced a colloquial of theater into poetry. They gave the human voice over the meter.

Q Your play, *Dream on Monkey Mountain*, was produced at The New York Shakespeare Festival, the Mark Taper

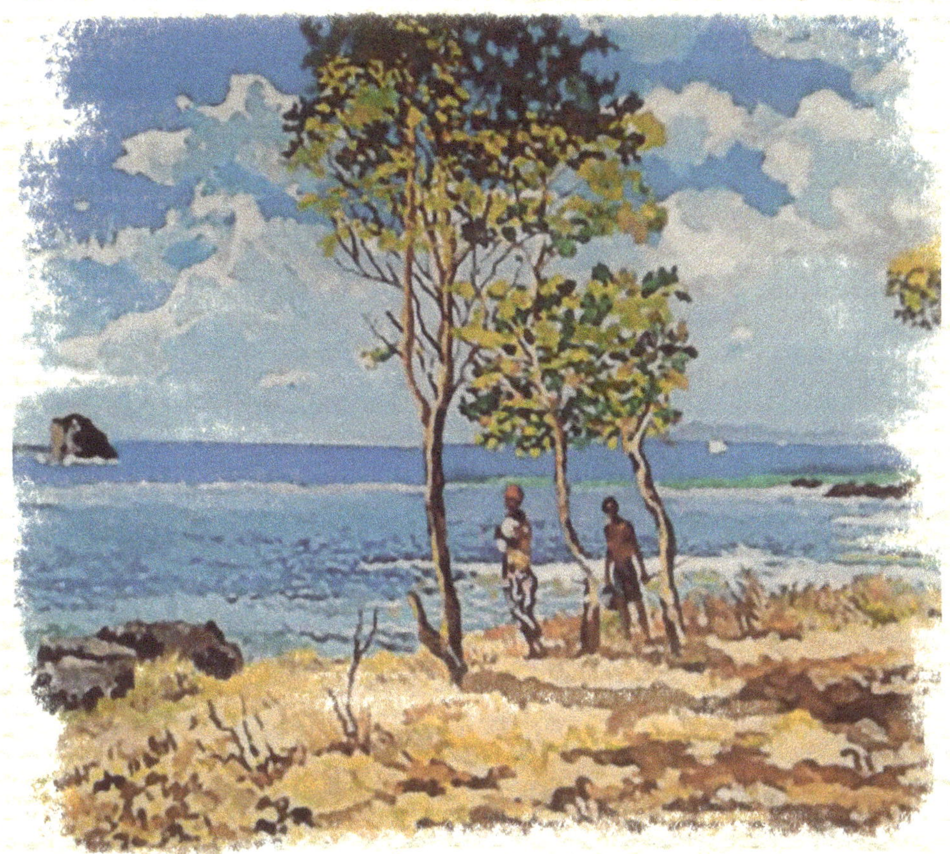

"Seascapes with Figures" by Sir Derek Walcott, courtesy of the artist and The June Kelly Gallery, New York City

Forum, and the Negro Ensemble Theatre. Were you involved in the different productions? How was that play created?
I really wasn't involved in them. The play was actually first performed at the Trinidad Theatre Workshop, that was its premiere. Then it was done at the O'Neill Theatre Center, because Gordon Davidson wanted to do it. When it was performed, Roscoe Lee Browne was magnificent. There was also a wonderful RSC production.

What I arrived at, I arrived at painfully. You have to ask in watching a production of mine: what is valid and what is authentic? They're not quite the same thing.

Q Who are you writing for?
If I write a book of poems, I have an immediate audience: the Caribbean people, and I must satisfy them. They have to be moved. The greatest theaters in ancient Greece never had a literate audience, but those great tragedies had to please thousands who sat in the sun. I don't think of the applause of London or New York; that kind of success doesn't matter to me. A play I wrote with Galt McDermott, *The Joker of Seville*, was done in the Caribbean; it was satisfactorily accepted. My heart was released by that production. That to me is enough.

Q Do you have a usual time when you write?
I used to write very early in the morning because I wanted to smoke and have coffee. Now I write usually during the morning.

Q Do you ever encounter writer's block?
No, I have too many things to work on. If you give yourself enough to do, you never have to worry about it. The Japanese Noh master Zeami said: "Every phenomenon in the universe develops itself through a certain progression."

Q What can we say to this generation to keep the flame of hope burning brightly?
Perhaps the opposite of having hope and having a lot of belief—to teach pessimism, instead of a loosely defined optimism. That man is capable of the "enormity," capable of elaborate means of self-destruction. To not be surprised by the conduct of the human animal.

We see with Ulysses' journey, his progression. When one examines man's progression, we see a deep-seated need to survive, of self-expression, but always rearing its ugly head, a desire for power, and yes, destruction. We see the destruction of Atlantis, the Towers of Troy. They were also symbols of authority, power, wealth—temptations to those who hated and wished to destroy.

How we look at man is getting narrower. The hubris of man will bring its own destruction. In a sense, the self-destruction is fated, when we act in defiance of nature. These destructors are basically idiots, and you have to teach the young not to be idiots. I believe poetry saves by its reality of the truth. ■

ELIE WIESEL

Writer, educator, scholar, and humanitarian, Mr. Wiesel was the recipient of the Nobel Peace Prize. Mr. Wiesel was born in Sighet, Transylvania, which is now part of Romania. He was fifteen years old when he and his family were deported by the Nazis to Auschwitz. His mother and younger sister perished, his two older sisters survived. Mr. Wiesel and his father were later transported to Buchenwald, where his father died shortly before the camp was liberated in April 1945. After the war, Mr. Wiesel studied in Paris, and later became a journalist. The distinguished French writer, Francois Mauriac, persuaded Mr. Wiesel to write about his experiences. Mr. Wiesel was the author of more than sixty books of fiction and nonfiction, among them *Night*, which has been translated into more than thirty languages; *Dawn*; *The Accident*; *A Beggar in Jerusalem*, which received the Prix Medicis Award; *The Fifth Son*, winner of the Grand Prize in Literature from the City of Paris; *From the Kingdom of Memory*; *The Forgotten*; *The Testament*, which received the Prix du Livre Inter Award; The Jews of Silence; and *All Rivers Run to the Sea and the Sea is Never Full*. He wrote two plays: *The Trial of God* and *Zalmen: or The Madness of God*. In 1977, President Carter appointed Mr. Wiesel as Chairman of the President's Commission on the Holocaust. He was the President of The Elie Wiesel Foundation for Humanity. He had been the Andrew W. Mellon Professor in the Humanities at Boston University. Among the many honors Mr. Wiesel received include the Nobel Peace Prize, Presidential Medal of Freedom, National Humanities Medal, the Medal of Liberty, Ellis Island Medal of Honor, the rank of Grand-Croix in the French Legion of Honor, the first David Ben Gurion Award, and the U.S. Congressional Gold Medal. Mr. Wiesel died in 2016 (this interview was conducted in 2002).

Q Realizing one has a gift as an artist, the decision to express one's self this way can be a difficult choice. How did you decide how your stories would be told?

I did not decide. The subjects decided themselves that they could only be expressed as tales, whether in prose, or in fiction. I also wrote two plays. They could not be written any other way except in the way they were. Each topic demanded its own formality.

Q One of the greatest challenges an actor may face is portraying an evil person. I sometimes wonder if the portrayal of an immensely evil character helps our fellow human beings see evil when it's done in such graphic detail? Is it helping us gain a deeper understanding of our own good and evil? And what if those watching become seduced to want to become as evil as the character? Where is our responsibility in all this?

This is a very complex question. We see what the characters imply by their behavior. If the character is evil, it can affect the actor, especially if the actor decides to succumb to evil. I believe the actor needs to create a distance between himself and the character. What to do and how to do it remains the challenge.

I don't think the acting-out of evil situations seduces those watching them. Why should a spectator be seduced if he or she realizes, if they understand, it takes place only in a character, in a play or in a movie, not in real life. Only those who want to be seduced will be. On the other hand, there are instances when fictional characters can have a negative effect.

Q What would you say to those who aspire to write?

I don't teach creative writing. I teach philosophy, literature, ethics—in other words: creative reading. My advice is: If you can go on living and doing whatever

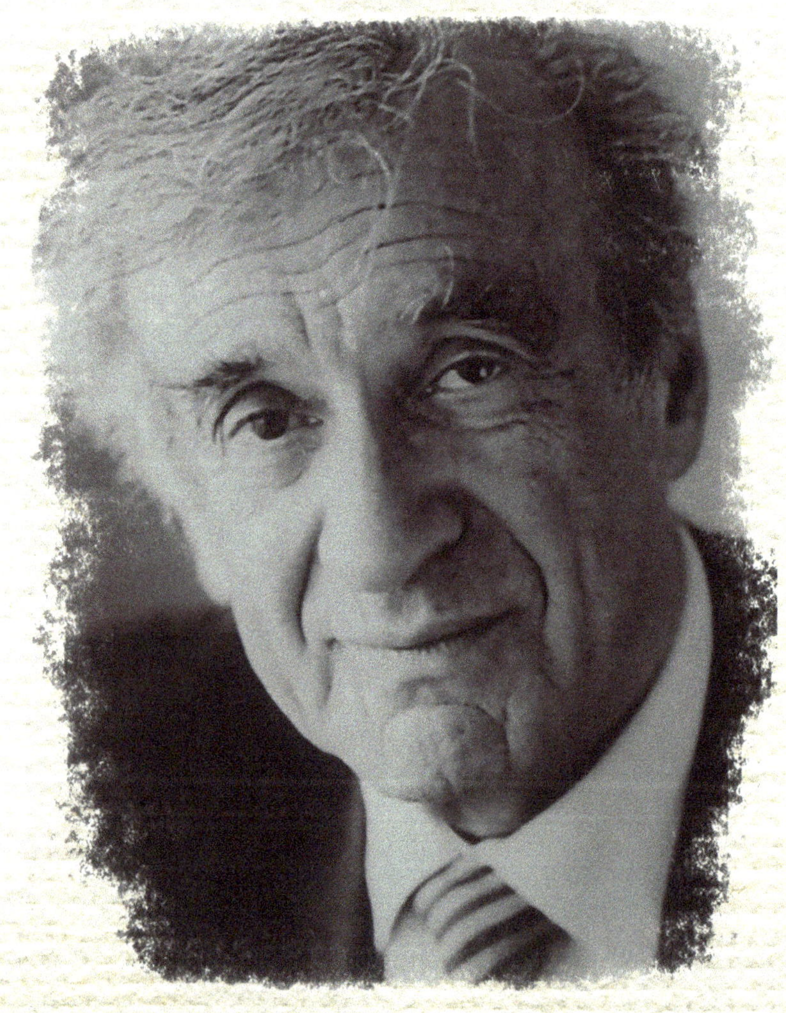

Elie Wiesel photo: courtesy of the artist

you do without writing, do it. But if you can't, write. It can be an agonizing pleasure, or a pleasurable agony.

Q What led you to write for the stage?
I found it impossible to say the things I had to say, in any other way.

Q Did you see theater when you were a child?
I came from a small town. There was no theater to speak of. Yiddish companies would occasionally come to perform but I was too involved with my studies to see them. I only saw theater when I got to Paris.

Q What was the first play you remember seeing?
Peer Gynt.

Q What books do you feel are your most important?
I don't think in terms of important or most important. I have published over sixty volumes. I believe everything I have done is based on my first book, *Night*. Another one, *The Jews of Silence*, created an awareness of Soviet Jewry. I stand by everything I've written. There is a special communal experience created, a bond, between actor and spectator, as there is between a reader and the person who sits down to read a book.

Today though, with all the technological advances, less and less time is being spent in direct physical contact, and young people aren't reading as much.

Q Can art keep us human?
Art does have the ability to humanize life, to present a meaning you didn't think about before. In the theater, an actor faces an audience with the responsibility of making every spectator feel as if he alone is being addressed. For me, literature is the dialogue of solitude, containing the mystery of life.

In the act of reading a book, the author is in the hands of the reader. It is the reader's obligation to say: take me a certain way. That's a bond. I personally prefer the literal word to the spoken word. ■

WILLIAM YELLOW ROBE, JR.

A member of the Assiniboine people, Mr. Yellow Robe, Jr. is from the Fort Peck Indian reservation in northeastern Montana. Author of over fifty plays, many having been produced by companies including Trinity Repertory, Penumbra Theatre, and The Public Theatre in New York City. A member of the St. Paul's Penumbra Theater Company in Minnesota, and New York's Ensemble Studio Theater, his plays include *Grandchildren of the Buffalo Soldiers, A Stray Dog, Better-n-Indins, Pieces of Us: How the Lost Find Home, Sneaky Blood of the Rez. Paper Wars, The Council, The Star Quilter, A Broken Bottle-A Broken Family, The Independence of Eddie Rose, Wood Bones, and The Pendleton Blanket*. He is a Professor of Multi-Culturalism at the University of Maine, and has written two books, *Grandchildren of the Buffalo Soldiers: and Other Untold Stories*, with Dr. Margo Lukens of the University of Maine, and *Where the Pavement Ends*. He has garnered several honors including a Princess Grace Foundation Theater fellowship, the Playwright's Center Jerome Fellowship, and a Native Writers' Circle of the Americas First Nations Book Award for Prose.

Q For the first eighteen years of your life you grew up on a reservation. During those years, how did you become aware of your abilities, your identity, your culture?
I learned my identity in fourth grade. I had a white teacher who grabbed me by my hair. We were spelling the fifty states and I had misspelled Tennessee. She grabbed me and faced me and said, "Is that all you Indians do is sit in your teepees and make beads!" It's what I had heard growing up; I wasn't a good student. I couldn't stay in school because basically, as a Native kid, it was hard for me to feel engaged in school. Everything being taught didn't really offer me anything about my culture, even though the school was established on Native land.

In second grade my teacher caught me skipping school. She brought me back to school and asked if I wanted to do something different. That's when I wrote my first play as a school assignment. I wanted to act at that time, and they were doing plays in school. But we weren't allowed to have speaking roles; I was always a tree. Ironically, I directed some of the shows but never had a chance to act.

The first play I wrote was a play about Cleopatra. Ironically, the night before, *Cleopatra* with Elizabeth Taylor had been on TV. Years later, when I had my first professional reading with the Native American Theatre Ensemble in L.A. with Hanay Geiogamah in 1985, I got an envelope in the mail. It contained the two plays I had written for Ms. Dorothy Grose's sixth-grade elementary class. They were basically rip-offs—a play based on *Cleopatra*, the second about Hercules. I had been an Indian child on a reservation studying Roman and Greek culture.

Q Who were inspirations for you as you learned your craft?

August Wilson the most. I think his work is an over-all inspiration to me, because the one play that really gets to me is *The Piano Lesson*. I understand and identify with it because it reminds me of my family members. It's a great play. In fact, one of my plays, *A Stray Dog*, is sort of influenced by August Wilson's play.

Hanay Geiogamah was a big influence, Phillip Gan Kotanda, Jose Rivera, David Henry Hwang, Suzan-Lori Parks, Luis Valdez, David Henry Hwang. I have to say Eugene O'Neill's work made a big impact, and Shakespeare. I also read the Greeks—Euripides, Aristophanes.

The play that pushed me into theater was a state touring production of Eugene O'Neill's *Long Day's Journey into Night*. That production made my heart decide I wanted to be a part of this art form.

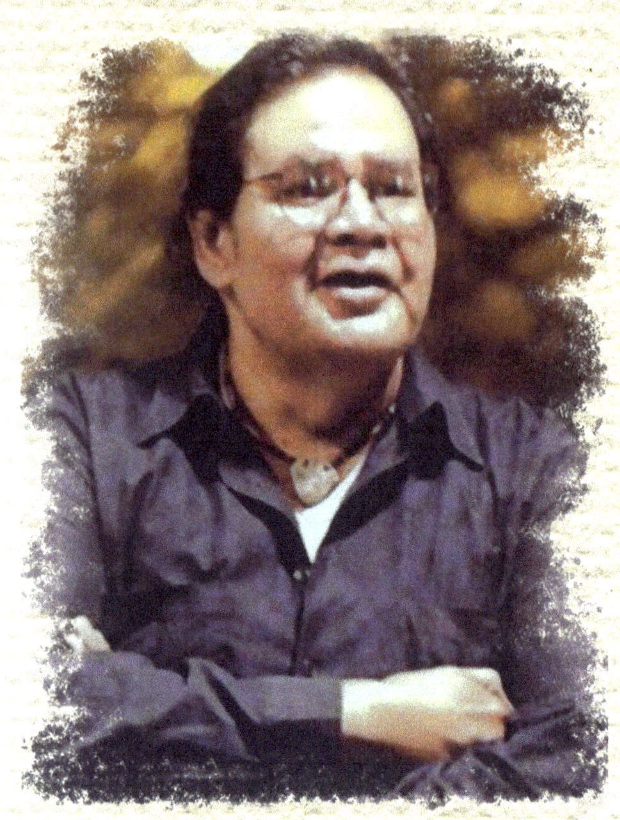

William Yellow Robe, Jr. photo: courtesy of the artist

Q You began with a non-Indian professor, Dr. Rolland Meinholz, who had been among the first instructors at New Mexico's Institute of American Indian Arts, learning playwriting, acting, and directing. You also worked with John Kauffman, Jr., and Hanay Geiogamah of the Native American Ensemble Theatre. Is that when you were first introduced to what we refer to as "Western Theater"?
Dr. Meinholtz taught me to respect the art form. He gave me an understanding of Euro-American history; I acknowledged it and respected it. He taught Native-American Theatre as a very valid form of expression. Ironically, I entered theater as an actor at the University of Montana. I'd audition for every role that came up, every project, whatever it was. One time a student director said, "Bill, you're a good actor, but we don't have any Indian roles."

John Kauffman, who had started out as an actor with the Red Earth Theatre Company in Seattle, became the Artistic Director of the Honolulu Theatre for Youth. It was phenomenal when he commissioned me to write a play called *The Council*. He did a play of mine. He moved with such grace and beauty on stage; he represented to me the humanity of theater. Tragically, we lost John to AIDS.

Hanay showed me the complexity of theate. He developed the ensemble there and Will Sampson established the Native American Indian Registry for Arts Organization to help Native Americans to have workshops. The person who taught playwriting and was a major influence early in my writing was Dr. Bill Kershner. He taught Theatre History and Dramatic Literature at the University of Montana. He had opened a door for his student; a very graceful man.

Q How did it happen that you collaborated with Dr. Margo Lukens of the University of Maine to complete the book, Grandchildren of the *Buffalo Soldiers: And Other Untold Stories*, a collection of your full-length plays?
It happened during 2003-4. She brought her students to see my play, and asked me if I'd come up to Maine and see her. I learned they didn't offer a course in Native American literature until she came there to teach at the University of Maine, even though there's a large Native Tribal reservation and community nearby, the Penobscot Nation. When she first came there, she read Native American plays and encouraged the students to do readings from my play, *Grandchildren of the Buffalo Soldiers*. They formed a Native American theater company that was able to sustain itself, and it encouraged other people to form their own companies.

Q I attended a presentation of your play, *Thieves: in the Red Way* at The Public Theatre in New York City. When did you begin writing it?
When I was a student at University of Montana. I've also been able to present other works at The Public, first when George Wolfe had been there, and then with Oskar Eustis. They were in-

terested in doing my work, bringing it to the community. Oskar continued the legacy of Native Theatre started by the late and great Joseph Papp. I feel these plays are an important legacy for young Native actors. I also feel the work of those before us who have come and made their sacrifices; they gave us the freedom of choice.

I hope I can provide some clarity, perhaps a possible solution to the conflict we face in our daily lives as Native Tribal people and all our relations. Theater has an incredible capacity to do tremendous healing—in healing an individual, a community—and I think it comes from trust and respect. With my plays, I look upon it as part of my responsibility.

Q What do you continually learn about yourself and the process of writing?

My weaknesses and frailties, my arrogance; it takes boldness to write. I actually think I'm privileged—lucky to get my plays done, it's humbling. It's been good when I'm able to get a reading or a production a year. When I go to conferences, I recognize the privilege of being a part of a beautiful community and having the honor of being listened to.

When I've written a play, I've given it a skeleton; I put flesh on it. Basically I'm building a house with a frame. It's like wood stripped to the bones. The best thing I can do is to remind myself to examine what I'm doing. I try to be more careful. I talk to the director to see where their head and heart is. When I talk about the play itself, I talk in a way so everyone can understand.

I have diabetes and had a heart procedure so it's all a blessing. I know I'm writing for a lot of audiences who are not Native American. They may not understand what I'm saying, so I try and be as clear as I can to make it accessible. I write because communication is one of the most peaceful art forms we have to bring forth change.

Q How would you describe the oral tradition that's carried forth?

In acting, you learn from hearing stories from those who have come before. When I worked with Hanay Geiogamah, I would ask him questions about the exchange of information. He had great information about acting and Native American actors. How they comforted themselves when faced with frustrations, what they had to overcome. It's necessary we share that kind of information.

Q What are your aspirations for what's possible for young Native American artists?

When I work with Native communities I work with very raw talent; they have no inhibitions, no fear. They want to train but the question is where do they go? I push for a national indigenous center; I'd love to see it in New York City. All kinds of young people would benefit from it. I'd also like to see a school for performing arts for indigenous artists.

I've also worked on another project, addressing gender roles, developing a piece about the difference between being tough and being able to survive, and being vicious and spiteful, and how people confuse the two. The title is *Indian Men Are Mean, Indian Woman Are Tough*. For instance, I admire how strong women are to give birth; we men have never endured that kind of pain.

Q How does art sustain the human spirit?

I really think art breathes; it can tell us what it means to be Native. It shows us is how to go on, and embrace the other world. Art can communicate within global communities everywhere, to share our life experiences, our thoughts—so we can all develop our consciousness as human beings.

Art feeds the soul. It feeds the heart and consciousness of a community, representing the humanity of a common thread, allowing every community to develop to its fullest potentiality.

I tell young people to learn to tell stories the best way you know how, but be honest. Tell the truth when you share these stories because they are no longer just yours. It's how we can all nurture one another. So do it through your heart, your soul, your humanity—because it's how we create our humanity. ■

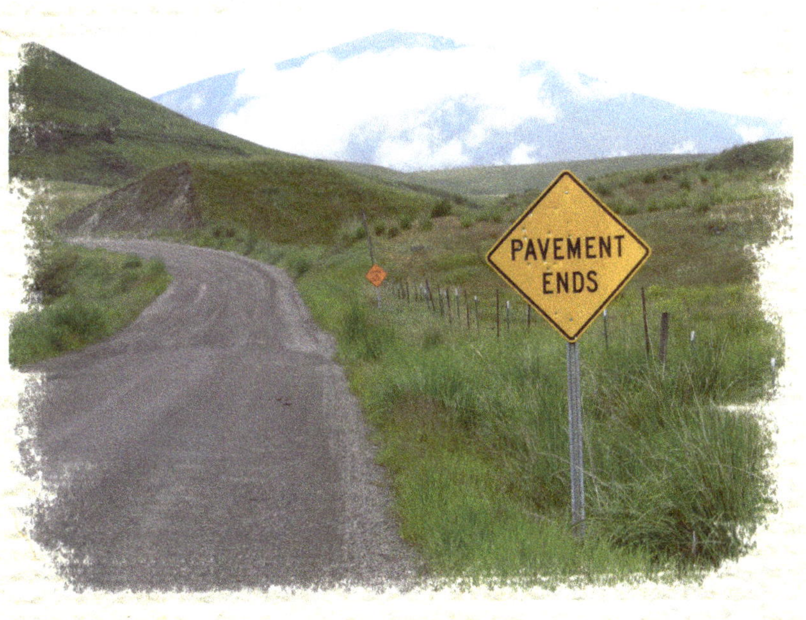

photo: by William Yellow Robe, Jr., courtesy of Mr. William Yellow Robe, Jr.

INDEX

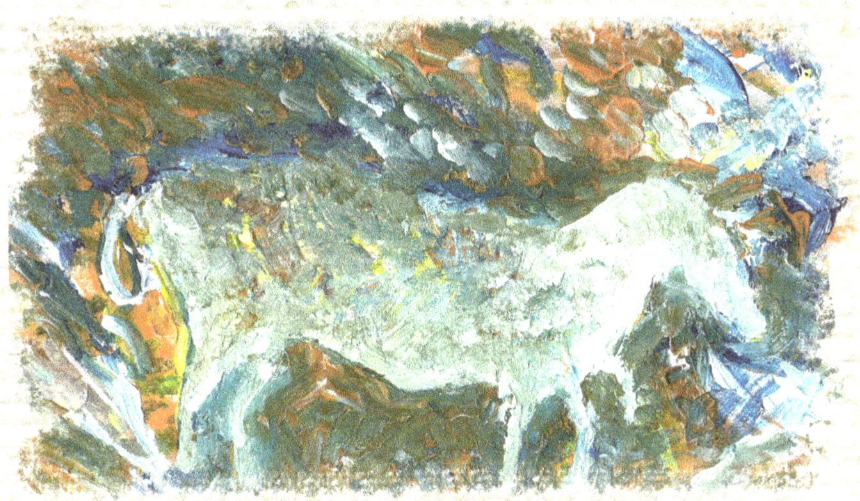

"Across the Ages" by Ronald Rand, courtesy of the artist

www.ingramcontent.com/pod-product-compliance
Lightning Source LLC
LaVergne TN
LVHW060617110826
845147LV00019B/1039

* 9 7 8 1 9 4 2 5 4 5 4 2 2 *